SLAVE CULTURE

SLAVE CULTURE

Nationalist Theory and the
Foundations of Black America

———————————————

Sterling Stuckey

OXFORD UNIVERSITY PRESS
New York   Oxford

Oxford University Press

Oxford   New York   Toronto
Delhi   Bombay   Calcutta   Madras   Karachi
Petaling Jaya   Singapore   Hong Kong   Tokyo
Nairobi   Dar es Salaam   Cape Town
Melbourne   Auckland

and associated companies in
Berlin   Ibadan

First published in 1987 by Oxford University Press, Inc.,
200 Madison Avenue, New York, New York 10016

First issued as an Oxford University Press paperback, 1988

Oxford is a registered trademark of Oxford University Press

Library of Congress Cataloging-in-Publications Data
Stuckey, Sterling.
Slave culture: nationalist theory and the foundation of Black America
Includes index.
1. Slavery—United States. 2. Afro-Americans—Race identity—
History—19th century. 3. Pan Africanism—History—19th century.
I. Title.
E441.S97 1987   305.8'96073   86-18136
ISBN 0-19-504265-4
ISBN 0-19-505664-7 (PBK)

4   6   8   10   9   7   5   3

Printed in the United States of America

For my mother
who first spoke to me of slavery
and
for Sterling A. Brown
mentor

Preface

Though the subject of slave culture has occupied my thought for the past twenty years, it was not until six years ago that I began to reflect on it in entirely new ways, or so it first seemed. Actually, however, the theoretical grounding for a wholly new way of viewing the subject was set forth in my "Through the Prism of Folklore: The Black Ethos in Slavery," an essay done in a graduate seminar at Northwestern that later benefited from the criticism of Sterling A. Brown and Guy B. Johnson. That essay's argument that slave culture flowed forth from an essentially autonomous value system in some ways anticipated the view of Africa's impact on slave consciousness that one finds in this book. Moreover, a year or so after the appearance of that essay, I was startled into considering, for the first time, the possibility of great African cultural influence on blacks in America in this century. If this is indeed the case, I then reflected, African influence on slave culture was vastly more important than we have been led to believe.

The thesis that black Americans today are basically African in culture was almost routinely presented—though hardly received that way—by a friend in the spring of 1969. In New York for a brief stay, I decided to go over to Princeton, New Jersey, where he was in residence at the Institute for Advanced Study, Mathematics Section. It was on that occasion that Joshua Leslie, a Jamaican who grew up in Chicago and had by then lived nearly ten years in West Africa, stated that the American Negro is basically African in culture—an observation that evoked in me a certain incredulity, although I knew no one with a better grasp of African culture than he.

It was not until years later that the implications for slave culture of Leslie's observation found increasing support as I read anthropological studies of a number of West African peoples while continuing to explore the folklore of the American slave. Indeed, the use of various disciplines, singly and in clusters, to interpret slave folklore revealed a whole new world of slave culture that enabled one to venture an answer to the most perplexing of all questions concerning slave culture: How was a single people formed out of many African ethnic groups on the plantations of the South? Moreover, the identification of ethnic African cultural forms enables one to assert the presence of particular peoples—or those affected by them—in the regions of the country in which the forms find expression.

Relevant evidence concerning the fusion of African peoples in America, as it turned out, was available practically everywhere black people were found, once the organizing principle of the study—the centrality of the ancestral past tó the African in America—was determined. And while the ancestral past was revered through the most important African ritual in antebellum America—the ring shout—there is reason to believe that the ring shout figured prominently in the formation of slave culture, whatever the demographic realities, from the earliest periods of slavery on the continent. The emphasis on the nineteenth century in this study, despite some attention to slave culture in the eighteenth century, has resulted from the availability of an abundance of sources that enable one to put together an answer to the question: how was a single culture formed out of the interaction of African ethnic groups in North American slavery?

Whether black culture since slavery has remained largely African is addressed in these pages, as black nationalists since slavery have reflected on slave culture in environments in which the impact of Africa is too evident to go unremarked. More precisely, however, even with a theorist who argues a continuing Africanity or its absence, the emphasis here has been on relating such arguments to the governing principles of black culture in slavery rather than to their manifestations since that time. In a word, while there is in this book more than a suggestion of the degree to which African culture continued to inform black thought and behavior following slavery, the continuing African influence in America since slavery is a subject, more appropriately, for future study.

Here an effort is made both to describe and to interpret slave rituals. The descriptions suggest an African aesthetic, since manifestations of slave art are not compartmentalized. That is, the object of the interdisciplinary approach in this work is to abandon disciplinary barriers, so that lived reality is reflected in its wholeness. The act of description, impelled by what the sources reveal, is itself, therefore, not infrequently the act of interpretation. Moreover, when slave ceremony is rooted in traditional African cultures, much that was heretofore unknown regarding its origins and meaning is revealed and the comparative approach to scholarship on the subject is established as indispensable.

The main argument, set forth in chapter 1, is drawn from a consideration of how slaves themselves responded to cultural challenges before them. That consideration led to the inescapable conclusion that the nationalism of the slave community was essentially African nationalism, consisting of values that bound slaves together and sustained them under brutal conditions of oppression. Their very effort to bridge ethnic differences and to form themselves into a single people to meet the challenge of a common foe proceeded from an impulse that was Pan-African—that grew out of a concern for all Africans—as what was useful was appropriated from a multiplicity of African groups even as an effort was made to eliminate distinctions among them.

Ntabaningi Sithole is right in arguing that most Africans had to be detribalized to aspire nationally—a process set in motion more fully in antebellum America than on the African continent. And just as modern nationalism on the continent of Africa "is the product of European stimuli," so has nationalism in North America resulted from European stimuli. Hans Kohn's contention that the "prime ingredient of nationalism" is "the *will to be a nation*" applies to the aspirations of the leadership and of large segments of both slave and free black communities of antebellum America and of significant numbers of blacks since then.[1]

It is therefore ironic that free blacks during and since slavery, even those who wanted to see their people shaped into a nation or thought they largely were already, were unaware, in varying degrees, of the sophistication of the slave community. Much of this book is a study in irony because the depths of African culture in America have been greatly underestimated by most nationalist theorists in America. Moreover, most were exposed to main currents of African culture without understanding how those currents might contribute to the surge toward liberation they wanted to initiate. Yet the work of nationalist theorists on problems of slave culture, as we shall see, ultimately went far toward reconciling the theory and practice of black culture in America.

Several people read chapters of the manuscript that concern nationalist theorists. Eugene Genovese sent back detailed and penetrating criticism, all of which was seriously considered and most of which was useful. Otey Scruggs reacted with perceptiveness and offered encouragement that meant more than I, as I look back on that time, can repay. And David Roediger provided critical analyses that were helpful. My colleague David Joravsky read a very large portion of the manuscript and offered warm support. Though he did not read a word of the manuscript, Joshua Leslie closely followed its development to its completion and would not hear of my not finishing it. His judgments regarding certain of its features were

---

1. See Hans Kohn, *African Nationalism in the Twentieth Century* (New York: Van Nostrand, 1965), 9, 10.

crucial to my determination to complete what at times seemed an interminable project.

While former students, except for Roediger, did not read any portion of the manuscript, some of them, without knowing it, contributed to its unfolding both indirectly and directly. Todd Jacobs, Robert Neustadt, Rebecca Purnell, and Chantal Sanchez, in the "Arts and History" seminar, through their discussions of and papers on Herman Melville and the folklorist William John Faulkner, provided such intellectual excitement that it affected my own work in very positive ways indeed. Anne Spurgeon and Greg Burns in the "Slavery in Cross-Cultural Perspective" seminar were directly involved in considering aspects of the subject treated in this book, which refers to their work. Special appreciation is also due Jean Brown for her valuable contributions to discussions in that seminar. And the work of Laurie Abraham, in "Survey of Afro-American History," was of such value that it is referred to in this volume.

I must express appreciation to George H. Daniels, whose support meant more to me than he could possibly have known, and to George M. Fredrickson for his example of devotion to scholarship, and for encouraging, in his seminars, the free play of ideas.

Henry McGee, Jr., Professor of Law and Acting Director of the Center for Afro-American Studies at UCLA, and Ewart Guinier, Chairman of the Afro-American Studies Department at Harvard, provided research acommodations at their respective institutions in the 1970s—and ideal housing arrangements as well—that greatly facilitated my work on this project.

I wish to thank the Andrew Mellon Foundation for a grant that made possible my presence at the Center for Advanced Study in the Behavioral Sciences, Stanford, California, in the academic year 1980–81. It was during that time that my perspective on slave culture began undergoing a major tranformation, and I could not have been better situated for sustained intellectual inquiry with the resources of several outstanding libraries available to me without my having to visit them. One has to experience being a Fellow at the Center to appreciate its wonders.

Finally, Harriette not only offered helpful criticisms of the manuscript but for six years lived through my involvement with it without jealousy.

Evanston   S.S.
August 1986

Contents

SLAVE CULTURE

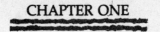

CHAPTER ONE

Introduction:
Slavery and the Circle of Culture

> He recalled the Spaniard's manner while telling his
> story. There was a gloomy hestitancy and subterfuge
> about it. . . . If Don Benito's story was, throughout, an
> invention, then every soul on board, down to the
> youngest negress, was his carefully drilled recruit in
> the plot: an incredible inference.
> —HERMAN MELVILLE, *Benito Cereno,* 1855

The final gift of African "tribalism" in the nineteenth century was its life
as a lingering memory in the minds of American slaves. That memory
enabled them to go back to the sense of community in the traditional
African setting and to include all Africans in their common experience of
oppression in North America.[1] It is greatly ironic, therefore, that African
ethnicity, an obstacle to African nationalism in the twentieth century, was
in this way the principal avenue to black unity in antebellum America.
Whether free black or slave, whether in the North or in the South, the
ultimate impact of that development was profound.

During the process of their becoming a single people, Yorubas, Akans,
Ibos, Angolans, and others were present on slave ships to America and
experienced a common horror—unearthly moans and piercing shrieks,
the smell of filth and the stench of death, all during the violent rhythms
and quiet coursings of ships at sea. As such, slave ships were the first real
incubators of slave unity across cultural lines, cruelly revealing irreducible links from one ethnic group to the other, fostering resistance thousands of miles before the shores of the new land appeared on the
horizon—before there was mention of natural rights in North America.

I

Perhaps because the South Carolina slave trade was so intense and lasted
until the outbreak of the Civil War, tales of the traumatizing experience of

the middle passage—as the voyage of a slave ship was called—have been retained in the folk memory of South Carolina blacks. Among the oldest and most important of these is "The King Buzzard," a tale that has two parts, the first symbolic, the second an artistic working out of its meaning. Told by Thadeus Goodson—Tad, in the collections of folktales of E. C. L. Adams—"The King Buzzard" contains the interplay of storytellers whose voices, impossible to capture adequately on paper, add dramatic tension to the tale. "The dialect is of course English shot through and influenced by the traditions and sentiments of the African slaves." In that dialect, "there is a marked influence of the African sense of melody and rhythm. . . . Sometimes a word that is pronounced correctly has several dialect meanings, and several sounds of the same word may be found in a single sentence."[2]

It is this language, the language of English-speaking Africans, that is heard around a campfire at night, as storytellers, encircled by their people, await Tad's return from a swamp in which eerie noises are heard and animals roam. As flames command shadows to dance, a dramatic dialogue about where Tad is takes place, setting the stage for his return "wet and covered with yellow mud." Though it should have been obvious that he had not been enjoying himself, he exhorts those present, "Look at me, do it look like I been enjoyin' myself?" He recounts having seen and struggled against a huge buzzard that "spread he whing out an' say, 'Uuh!' He eye been red an' he de nastiest lookin' thing I ever see. He stink in my nostrils. He so stink, he stink to my eye an' my year." In terror, he dodges as the buzzard flies around him in the moonlight and "spewed he vomick every which er way, an' I see de leaf an' de grass wuh it fall on [an'] dry up. All de air seem like it were pizen." As the buzzard got nearer to him, Tad somehow crawled in a canebrake and was there "for God knows how long." "An' when I find myself," he notes with irony, "I been lost."[3]

The buzzard represented something more dreadful than he realized. A buzzard was not encountered; rather, the spirit of a traitor took the form of a buzzard. Tom joined in the telling of the tale and said he "hear 'bout dat ole thing 'fore 'dis," that his "pa" told him "dat way back in slavery time—'way back in Africa"—there was "a nigger," "a big nigger" who as chief of his tribe tricked his people into slavery, betraying thousands. The chief had to entice them onto the boat "into trap" so that "dem white folks could ketch 'em an' chain 'em." On the slave traders' last trip to that section of the coast, they "knocked dat nigger down an' put chain on him an' bring him to dis country."

An' when he dead, dere were no place in heaven for him an' he were not desired in hell. An' de Great Master decide dat he were lower dan all other mens or beasts; he punishment were to wander for eternal time over de face

> er de earth. Dat as he had kilt de sperrits of mens an' womens as well as dere bodies, he must wander on an' on. Dat his sperrit should always travel in de form of a great buzzard, an' dat carrion must be he food. . . . An' dey say he are known to all de sperit world as de King Buzzard, an' dat forever he must travel alone.[4]

Those hearing this tale, if born in Africa, knew a life superior to anything encountered in slavery, a life symbolized by the repudiation of the traitor, who then must enter upon an endless journey of spiritual unrest, a punishment markedly African. Moreover, the tale is replete with suggestions of the Africans' resistance to being robbed of their way of life: they must be tricked into manacles; even the chief who betrayed his own into bondage resisted being enslaved and had to be knocked down and subdued. There is no question of the self-generative nature of their impulse toward freedom.

The importance of spirituality to African slaves—"Dat as he had kilt de sperrits of mens an' womens as well as dere bodies"—should not be undervalued. The notion that the spirit was killed and that there was no life of any kind suggests the heinous nature of the chief's crime against his people. Thus, the traitor must suffer spiritual unrest through time, which is a form of hell. But the categories of heaven and hell do not suggest, as it first appears, the distance of the storyteller from the original African chroniclers of the event, and they reflect not New World religious concepts but rather African ones. Indeed, endless wandering and restlessness are at the heart of a tale told in almost every particular from an African point of view, yet a tale that stands as a metaphor for treachery performed anywhere and at any time in history. So universal in Africa is concern for the fate of the spirit that the restlessness of "The King Buzzard" would have been understood by Africans on the plantations of the South, in the North, and elsewhere in the Americas[5] especially in the case of a chief who turns on his own, for the socially prominent in West Africa generally receive a lavish funeral to ensure harmony between them and those to whom they were responsible on earth. The chief's betrayal of his people removed the obligation of any funeral observance, and therefore his spirit was condemned to be restless.

Features of "The King Buzzard" appear to be especially of Ibo influence, and this suggests that the experience recounted occurred in eastern Nigeria during the slave trade:

> All Ibo place great faith in the due and proper observance of the funeral ceremony, for they are of the opinion that it enables the soul to go to God, and to its final destination, and without the sacred rite the soul is prevented by other spirits from eating, or in any way associating with them, and, in this manner, from entering into the Creator's presence. So in this way it becomes an outcast and a wanderer on the face of the earth. . . .[6]

According to the Ibos, the spirit of the deceased returns to this world in the form of an animal if, before death, the deceased "murdered" one or more human beings. Though the return of the spirit in the form of an animal may be widespread in West African religions, its return as a "buzzard" as a consequence of crimes committed does not appear to be. Moreover, the principle that spirits are not able to enter the presence of the Creator is the Ibo equivalent to the Christian hell. When one adds the denial of food to the spirit (the King Buzzard ate carrion) and the Ibo reference to God as "the great Spirit" (the reference in the tale is to the "Great Master"), it seems evident that the "The King Buzzard" is an Ibo tale in which other Africans, especially the Yorubas, found enough features of their faith to all but claim it as their own. It was also understood by many West Africans that the eternal wandering of the soul meant that it could not return to its native town in Africa or communicate there with the souls of relatives and others it had known in its lifetime. Such elements of the tale probably discouraged members of the slave community from collaborating with their slave masters.[7] Indeed, the purgatory described in "The King Buzzard" evoked sovereign precepts of West African religious life that almost certainly helped enhance spiritual and political unity in slave communities in which the tale was told.

The King Buzzard experience occurred prior to the nineteenth century, for one of the storytellers says his father made reference to "dat ole thing" occurring "'way back in slavery time—'way back in Africa." Since the tale was alive over generations in South Carolina, the character of black life there, with its movement away from ethnic allegiance, perhaps explains why no explicit mention was made of a specific tribe, for the condemnation of the traitor related to all Africans suffering the humiliation and degradation of the slave trade and slavery. The Ibo elements in the tale were used to interpret the concrete experiences of those who created it. Important at the time of its creation, African ethnic qualities at some point lost much of their relevance, beyond revealing what was commonly understood across ethnic lines, all else serving to divide rather than unite Africans in the slave community.[8]

When the old men sat around the fire and recalled the past, they measured themselves by the most rigorous standards of the black community as they faced each other. Such an ensemble provided particular roles to be played by each person in the dialogue on the illness, infirmity, or death of a participant: Tad had heard Joe's response, and Joe Tad's question, on innumerable occasions. Following the same pattern, Tad asked him once more, "Joe 'fore you come here wey did you originate—wey was you' home?"

And Joe answered, "I come from Af'ca."

An old man, Joe had been tricked into slavery as a youth:

> When I been a boy, a big vessel come nigh to my home. An' it had white folks
> on it an' dey hab all kind er bead an' calico an' red flannel, an' all kind er
> fancy thing. An' dem white folks gee a heap er thing to de people er my tribe
> an' entice 'em on de boat. An' dey treat 'em so good for two or three days, till
> atter while de people ain't been scared. . . . An' one day dey hab de boat
> crowd wid mens an' womens an' chillun, an' when dey find dey self, de boat
> was 'way out to sea.[9]

The Africans understood, in a flash, that they were being carried out of
the land of their birth to an unknown destination. Even though they were,
from what Joe tells us, in this instance ethnically homogeneous, the conditions described help explain why less homogeneous African populations
often lacked a strong sense of ethnic bonds during their forced movement
from one world to another.

"Gullah Joe" covers the fate of Africans from capture on the west
coast to enslavement in the New World and provides additional evidence
that Africans had a previous way of life that they preferred to slavery on
North American plantations. Through the group designation he assigns to
blacks, Joe betrays a considerable degree of acculturation or adaptation
to his environment in the United States, for the old African refers to
"some er dem niggers" jumping off the boat and being drowned. Then
comes the passage that even more effectively symbolizes the Africans'
desire to maintain freedom from captivity: the European "overpowered
dem what was on de boat, an' th'owed 'em down in de bottom er de ship.
An' dey put chain on 'em. . . ."[10]

Almost from the start, Joe noted the new (for him) factor of color:

> Dey been pack in dere wuss dan hog in a car when dey shippin' 'em. An'
> every day dem white folks would come in dere an' ef a nigger jest twist his
> self or move, dey'd cut de hide off him wid a rawhide whip. An' niggers died
> in de bottom er dat ship wuss dan hogs wid cholera. Dem white folks ain' hab
> no mercy. Look like dey ain' known wha' mercy mean. Dey drag dem dead
> niggers out an' throw 'em overboard. An' dat ain' all. Dey th'owed a heap er
> live ones wha' dey thought ain' guh live into de sea.[11]

The tension between loyalty to the tribe and loyalty to the community
of blacks in South Carolina is revealed in Tad's question to Joe "Is you
satisfy?" and Joe's reply:

> It seems to me I would be satisfied if I jes could see my tribe one more time.
> Den I would be willin' to come back here. . . . I is a old man now but I has a
> longin' to walk in de feenda. I wants to see it one more time. I has a wife an'
> children here, but when I thinks er my tribe an' my friend an' my daddy an'
> my mammy an' de great feenda, a feelin' rises up in my th'oat an' my eye well
> up wid tear.[12]

The longing to see his tribe "one more time" is strongly linked in Joe's
mind with the idea of freedom. The spiritual pain of enslavement becomes

strongly personalized in the conflict between longing for one's tribe and attachment to new relations in the American environment. The word *feenda*—Kikongo for "forest" and spelled "mfinda" in the Congo—suggests the old man's place of origin and represents an instance, linguistically, in which the folktale reflects a precise geographic reality: the presence in South Carolina of Africans from Congo-Angola. Moreover, to the Bakongo that word reflects a spiritual reality of great import—later to be explored at length—evoking the symbolism of the circle and the presence of God in the Bakongo faith.[13]

Though it contains no apparent trace of ethnicity, the poem "The Slave Barn" is characterized by a sense of African autonomy. And though it is possible the Africans described in the poem were recent arrivals, it is not likely. The evidence suggests that the poem is based on experiences long observed, that it is deeply ethnic yet universal in meaning and speaks of collective survival and hope for eventual liberation. All who experienced or might experience the barn, irrespective of ethnicity, would find meaning in it. The opening stanza, through stark imagery, conveys the cold harshness of life in the New World,

> See dis barn here
> Wid its iron window,
> Its walls er brick?

The second stanza, though life in Africa at its worst was superior to domination by the white man, implies a sense of nationhood in slavery:

> Here wey de wail an' moan
> Of Af'ica sound
> Wuss dan de cry
> Of Af'ica chillun
> When dey bone been crack
> By de lion' jaw.

The pain of "niggers" was the pain of Africa, their religion utterly ignored in the process of slave trading:

> Here wey de last
> Er de slave-trader
> Sing a song of misery
> To a nigger in pain.

> Here wey man an' he woman
> Is parted forever,
> An' a prayer was answered
> Wid de song of a whip.[14]

At times resistance was fierce and roused feelings of unity in blacks, especially when they were fighting to hold on to their children. When the separation of parent and child did occur, Africans who witnessed or heard of it could empathize with them, and this in turn helped preserve their own humanity. But resisting such separation could mean death:

> Here wey de brains
> Of a baby wid fever
> Stain de walls,
>
> Kaze a ooman for sale
> Shed tears an' fought
> For de chile dat she love.[15]

The indictment of slavery is so severe that one can conclude that this poem was not meant for the ear of the master. It not only rejects slavery but also depicts the means by which slavery was perpetuated and questions the society in which it was flourishing:

> An' de trader live
> To die in honor
> Forgiven by de church,
> Prayed for, held up,
> He sins forgotten,
> He name guin to a school—
> To de young as a sample
> Of virtue an' trute.
>
> . . . .
>
> A dollar to a school
> An' a dollar to a church
> Would hang de poor nigger
> Dat told dat tale.
>
> But God's my witness,
> An' de tale's no tale
> But de trute.[16]

The poem appears to be more recent than "The King Buzzard," from roughly the same time period as "Gullah Joe," which would probably make it a nineteenth-century work, although the African spiritual values are perhaps thousands of years old. The peculiar mixture of Africanity and assimilationism, the latter symbolized by the word *nigger*, does not hide the fact that the values are African throughout. There is indeed an ethnic component in the poem, the clue to which is found in "Ole Man Rogan," which pronounces judgment on crimes of precisely the sort committed in "The Slave Barn." But the application of the tale to slaves of different ethnic groups is confirmed by the language of the storyteller, which speaks to all Africans brought into South Carolina via the domestic slave trade.

A slaver, who "brings 'em here in drove . . . have 'em chained together," Ole Man Rogan "always buy ooman wid chillun, and ooman wid husband, and ain't nobody can buy from Ole Man Rogan mother and chile or man and ooman." Ole Man Rogan "love to part a man and he ooman, sell de man one place and sell de ooman another, and dat look like all Ole Man Rogan live for, and when he ain't 'casin stress dat er way, he been on restless." Rogan's deeds leave men with their heads "bowed down in 'stress" and "chillun holdin' out dey arms cryin' for dey mother" and "tear runnin' down de face of er ooman when she weepin' for her chile." Tears evoke laughter in Rogan and so does stress: "You see him look at de womens and mens and chillun, and you see him laugh—laugh at de 'stress and de tears on Boggy Gut."[17]

The tale was also told in this century, the storyteller returning to scenes of slavery, like a blues singer to his tragic song: "And you kin set on de edge of Boggy Gut and you'll see mens in chains bent over wid dey head in dey hands,—de signs of 'stress." After dark, one can hear a baby crying "every which er way" and "a mother callin' for her chile in de dark night on Boggy Gut." After Ole Man Rogan's death, "he sperrit wander and wander from Boggy Gut to de river and wander 'cross de big swamps to Congaree. Whether it be God or whether it be devil, de sperrit of Ole Man Rogan ain't got no res'." The rejection of Ole Man Rogan by God and by the devil recalls the King Buzzard and Rogan's purgatory that of the Buzzard wandering restlessly through time.[18]

The South Carolina storytellers, like those elsewhere, told tales in which the dominant spiritual configuration provided the means by which Africans, whatever their ethnic differences, found values proper to them when the slave trade and slavery divorced them from their homeland. Consequently, listeners in the slave community who had previously been unexposed to those tales immediately understood what was being related, irrespective of the section of Africa from which their parents came. Moreover, those who told or listened to one set of tales also listened to and told others, all the common property of the community. A number of storytellers, therefore, held in their heads, as did those who listened with rapt attention, African cultural patterns that were dominant not simply in North America but in the African diaspora as a whole. When one bears in mind that slave folklore was not created to be transcribed or even to be heard by whites, one must conclude that what was eventually transcribed is probably just a small portion of that which died on the night air or continues to live, undetected by scholars, in the folk memory.[19]

I I

The majority of Africans brought to North America to be enslaved were from the central and western areas of Africa—from Congo-Angola,

Nigeria, Dahomey, Togo, the Gold Coast, and Sierra Leone.[20] In these areas, an integral part of religion and culture was movement in a ring during ceremonies honoring the ancestors. There is, in fact, substantial evidence for the importance of the ancestral function of the circle in West Africa, but the circle ritual imported by Africans from the Congo region was so powerful in its elaboration of a religious vision that it contributed disproportionately to the centrality of the circle in slavery. The use of the circle for religious purposes in slavery was so consistent and profound that one could argue that it was what gave form and meaning to black religion and art. It is understandable that the circle became the chief symbol of heathenism for missionaries, black and white, leading them to seek either to alter it or to eradicate it altogether. That they failed to do so owes a great deal to Bakongo influence in particular, but values similar to those in Congo-Angola are found among Africans a thousand or more miles away, in lands in which the circle also is of great importance. Thus scholarship is likely to reveal more than we now know about the circle in Africa, drawing West and Central Africa closer together culturally than they were previously thought to be.

The circle is linked to the most important of all African ceremonies, the burial ceremony. As Talbot shows, in discussing dance in Southern Nigeria, "The Ekoi also in some of their dances imitate the actions of birds, but the most solemn of them all is perhaps the Ejame, given at the funeral of great chiefs, when seven men dance in the centre of an immense circle made by the other performers." In that ceremony, the men keep their eyes to the ground and the songs they sing are said to be "so old that their meaning has long since been forgotten," which suggests the ancient quality of dance within the circle, the immemorial regard for the ancestral spirits in a country in which dance exists mainly as a form of worship and appears to have developed as a means of achieving union with God, of "exerting an influence *with his help* on the fertility of men and of crops."[21] Talbot notes the prime importance of rhythm to dance, and his description of "one variety" of dance parallels descriptions of dance in the ancestral circle in the Congo and in America since "the main object appears to be never to lift the feet off the ground and to leave a clear, even, continuous track." The ordinary method of dancing among the people of Southern Nigeria—among them Ibos, Yorubas, Ibibios, and Efiks—appears monotonous and unattractive

since it consists of slowly moving round in a circle—always in the opposite direction to the hands of a clock, widdershins—with apparently little variation in the few steps employed. It takes time to appreciate the variety and detail in the different movements and the unceasing, wave-like ripple which runs down the muscles of the back and along the arms to the finger-tips. Every part of the body dances, not only the limbs.[22]

In Bakongo burial ceremonies, according to art historian Robert F. Thompson, bodies were sometimes laid out in state in an open yard "on a textile-decorated bier," as bare-chested mourners danced to the rhythms of drums "in a broken counter-clockwise circle," their feet imprinting a circle on the earth, cloth attached to and trailing on the ground from their waists deepening the circle. Following the direction of the sun in the Southern Hemisphere, the mourners moved around the body of the deceased in a counterclockwise direction. If the deceased lived a good life, death, a mere crossing over the threshold into another world, was a precondition for being "carried back into the mainstream of the living, in the name and body of grandchildren of succeeding generations." From the movement of the sun, Kongo people derive the circle and its counterclockwise direction in a variety of ways. "Coded as a cross, a quartered circle or diamond, a seashell's spiral, or a special cross with solar emblems at each ending—the sign of the four moments of the sun is the Kongo emblem of spiritual continuity and renaissance. . . . In certain rites it is written on the earth, and a person stands upon it to take an oath, or to signify that he or she understands the meaning of life as a process shared with the dead below the river or the sea—the real sources of earthly power and prestige."[23]

Wherever in Africa the counterclockwise dance ceremony was performed—it is called the ring shout in North America—the dancing and singing were directed to the ancestors and gods, the tempo and revolution of the circle quickening during the course of movement. The ring in which Africans danced and sang is the key to understanding the means by which they achieved oneness in America. Knowledge of the ancestral dance in Dahomey contributes to that understanding and helps explain aspects of the shout in North America that are otherwise difficult to account for. For instance, the solo ring shouts noted by Lydia Parrish in Virginia and North Carolina are in the ring dances of Dahomey done in group *and* solo forms, the two being combined at times. Thus, as the drums sounded, a woman held a sacrifice under her left arm, slowly dancing in a "cleared space three times in a counter-clockwise direction, ending with a series of shuffling steps in front of the drums, while the young women who followed her cried out a shrill greeting to the spirits." Solo dance combined with other patterns of dance:

With the drums sounding they formed a line of twos, and one couple behind the other they danced in the customary counter-clockwise direction about the edges of the cleared space, finally forming a single line in front of the drums, which they faced as they danced vigorously. Retreating in line to their place on the South side, before the ancestral temple they remained standing there, while one after another of their number danced singly, moving toward the drums and then retreating before circling the dance-space.[24]

An impressive degree of interethnic contact, representing large areas of black Africa, at times took place at such ceremonies in Dahomey. F. E. Forbes, who spent two years in Dahomey and kept a journal of his observations, reports that one such instance of ethnic cross-play involved "groups of females from various parts of Africa, each performing the peculiar dance of her country." When not dancing a dance with elements unique to a given country, they performed dances common to many different countries of Africa: "the ladies would now seize their shields and dance a shield-dance; then a musket, a sword, a bow and arrow dance, in turns." Finally, "they called upon the king to come out and dance with them, and they did not call in vain." The king's response had its own unifying influence and was understood by the women from the various countries of Africa, just as the response of Daha, the chief observed by Herskovits almost a century later, would have been understood by them as he "twice circled the space enclosed by the 'bamboos' in a counterclockwise direction before he retired to the portico, where several of his wives solicitously wiped the perspiration from his face and otherwise attended him."[25]

A Kongo ancestral ritual that is profoundly related to counterclockwise dance among the Kongo people occurs, according to Thompson, when they place a cross in a circle to derive the four moments of the sun. While counterclockwise dance in itself achieved as much, the graphic representation does so in more explicit terms, marking off in precise ways the important stages or moments along the way: "In each rendering the right hand sphere or corner stands for dawn which, in turn, is the sign of life beginning. Noon, the uppermost disk or corner, indicates the flourishing of life, the point of most ascendant power. Next, by the inevitable organic process as we know it, come change and flux, the setting of the sun, and death, marked by the left-hand mediam point or disk."[26]

The horizontal line of the cross, referred to as the Kalunga line, deserves attention, for we shall later encounter it in American slavery—associated, as in the Congo, with those who lived long and were generous, wise and strong "on a heroic scale." Such people, in the imagination of the Kongo people, "die twice . . . once 'here,' and once 'there,' beneath the watery barrier, the line Bakongo call *Kalunga.*" According to Thompson, "This is a line marked by the river, the sea, or even dense forestation, a line which divides this world from the next."[27] When that line, which extends from dawn to sunset, is evoked by the Kongo staff-cross, it symbolizes the surface of a body of water beneath which the world of the ancestors is found, and this casts additional light on why water immersion has had such a hold on blacks in America and why counterclockwise dance is often associated with such water rites.

The art historian Suzzane Blier has written that the circle is the most frequently employed linear mode of movement in Togo: "In the funeral, circular lines are formed as clockwise movements when linked to women, but are counter-clockwise motion sequences when employed for men." In the funeral, circular movement is used to represent themes of together-ness and containment. For example, when the deceased is carried around the house before being taken to the cemetery, the act "is said to call together the house ancestors so that they will come to the cemetery for the ceremonies to be performed there." The clockwise movement of women in Togo is a significant departure from the counterclockwise movement indigenous to much of Central and West Africa and does not appear to have an analogue in North America. The most likely explana-tion for its failure to survive in North America is that Africans from Togo who might have continued the clockwise movement in slavery yielded to the overwhelming preference of other Africans for counterclockwise movement.[28]

An indication of the complex rites to which people other than the Bakongo put the circle is found in ethnic groups from Sierra Leone. The connection of the circle to the ancestors and to the young is so various in that country, from which Africans were imported to American markets, that one better understands the strength and varying patterns of the circle in North America by understanding its antecedents in Sierra Leone. The Sierra Leonian Earl Conteh-Morgan's scholarship illuminates the rela-tionship of the circle to the storyteller as dancing in a counterclockwise direction occurs: "Instances of dancing in a circle occur during storytell-ing time in the villages as the storyteller sits in the middle while the lis-teners sit around him and listen attentively." Since storytellers, or griots, focus mainly on the history of their people, ancestors are usually the prin-cipal subject of a particular chronicle of the past—the ceremony framed, as it were, by the listeners gathered around the storyteller. Depending on the demands of the narration, they either listen or, on signal from the storyteller, become active participants.

> Clapping and dancing usually occur in stories with a song that takes the form of a refrain. The refrain is repeated by the listeners at a signal from the story-teller. Although it may not involve physical touching of the storyteller, it nonetheless gives the whole exercise an air of celebration. It also adds an air of vivid drama in the whole process of storytelling.[29]

Such singing of refrains and clapping of hands as dance occurs in a counterclockwise direction are similar to those of the dance described by Thompson in the Kongo funeral scene. Conteh-Morgan observed coun-terclockwise dance among the Bundu in Sierra Leone during a burial cere-mony, and such dancing around the deceased, given the prominence of sacred dance in traditional societies, would seem to be widespread in Si-erra Leone.[30]

The Sierra Leoneans reveal much about the circle in relation to the life process; indeed, the circle may well be the principal African metaphor for it. Among Mende and Temne secret societies, dancing in a circle with people in the center is a common practice on sacred occasions, for example, during rites of passage for young girls. When they are eligible to be selected for marriage by young men, they go through rites in "the secret house, usually in the bush, or in huts specifically built for that. A couple of days are set aside, or one big day, when they are brought out into the open for all to see as they participate in final ceremonies." At this time, the women stand around the girls, who are generally teenagers, clapping and singing as the girls sit in the middle of the circle. "From time to time, dancing in a circle takes place either by the girls themselves or by the women surrounding them. Touching of the heads or shoulders of those in the center and many types and styles of dancing take place as the music varies in rhythm and tempo."[31]

The circle, among Mende and Temne, is the chief symbol of a ceremony that leads to marriage and the renewal of the life process with the birth of children. Although counterclockwise dance of the Mende and Temne continued in North America as a function primarily of religious activity, it is highly unlikely, considering the mockery that was made of slave marriage in America, that the associated institution of preparation for marriage in the secret house survived even in secrecy in slavery.

Nevertheless, other African institutions and African priests were brought to America in large numbers and, unrecognized by whites, found their places in the circle and elsewhere. Some were among the first and last slave preachers. Herskovits tells us that a variety of them came to the New World, which greatly encouraged the preservation of African values in slavery:

> . . . the river spirits are among the most powerful of those inhabiting the supernatural world, and . . . priests of this cult are among the most powerful members of tribal priestly groups. It will be . . . recalled how, in the process of conquest which accompanied the spread of the Dahomean kingdom, at least (there being no data on this particular point from any other folk of West Africa), the intransigeance of the priests of the river cult was so marked that, more than any other group of holy men, they were sold into slavery to rid the conquerors of troublesome leaders. In all those parts of the New World where African religious beliefs have persisted, moreover, the river cult or, in broader terms, the cult of water spirits, holds an important place. All this testifies to the vitality of this element in African religion, and supports the conclusion, to be drawn from the hint in the Dahomean data, as to the possible influence such priests wielded even as slaves.[32]

Priests were present on the plantations of the South, but whether they were, in specific instances, African-born or products of African influence in America is usually difficult to determine. This distinction is mainly theoretical, since at times one finds their practices, irrespective of the period of slavery, to be of nearly pristine purity and highly esoteric, as when they surface in the folktale. There, as in life, they gathered on the principal occasions of worship, above all at ancestral ceremonies, the most important of which in North America was the ring shout, which often was but one aspect, however important, of multifaceted African religious observance. The ring shout was the main context in which Africans recognized values common to them. Those values were remarkable because, while of ancient African provenance, they were fertile seed for the bloom of new forms. Moreover, understanding the function of ancestral ring ceremonies elsewhere in the Americas makes it possible to determine the function of the ring ceremony in its most arcane form in North America.

The argument that *shout* is used as one of the two words in the phrase *ring shout* because dancing was regarded as "so sinful that it was wise to avoid even the name" is less interesting than the contribution of Lorenzo Turner, whose work on Afro-American culture is of primary importance: "Dr. L. D. Turner has discovered that the Arabic word *saut* (pronounced like our word 'shout'), in use among Mohammedans of West Africa meant to run and walk around the Kaaba." Turner's remark concerning the term is particularly interesting owing to his association of the ring shout with the ritual in which hundreds, tightly assembled, move around the Kaaba in a counterclockwise direction. There is, however, reason to question the view that *saut* refers to "shout." One authority on the Arabic language argues that the word is not pronounced like *shout*, which calls into question Turner's tantalizing view. What is certain is that Moslems move about the Kaaba in a counterclockwise fashion. But it is just as certain that their movement is more of a trot than a dance and that spirit possession apparently has no place in the ceremony around the Kaaba.[33]

Melville and Frances Herskovits, the distinguished anthropological team, note the persistence of the circle ceremony among the descendants of Africans in Suriname who are centuries removed from their ancestral home in the Gold Coast. Indeed, the Suriname bush Negro retained some features of his heritage, including priestly functions, in almost pristine form.[34] With drums speaking to and interpreting the messages of the dead, they dramatized spiritual attitudes through the language of dance, at times moving in a counterclockwise direction. Ashanti dance style was common to the bush Negro and to black Africans generally. R. S. Rattray writes of dance in the Gold Coast at 4 A.M. in a yard "packed with people sitting all around the circle of singers and in the open Verandah Rooms." The head priestess rushed into the yard before disappearing. She returned and "jumped into the ring," clapping her hands, and "began to dance that curious shuffling, stooping, mincing dance alternated with wild gyrations, so peculiar to West Africa." It was that dance, essentially, that was encountered in Suriname. But the Herskovitses found African dance in that country precisely related to elements of ancestral ring dance in North

America: the feet executed "figures in place without leaving the ground, the arms hanging loosely at the side." And in generic African style—"the arms flexed and held rigid at the elbow and knees bent but rigid"—as the feet continued to execute intricate steps, "the movement of the feet, angular and precise, was reiterated by the outstretched palms, while all the muscles of the hips took up the rhythm."[35]

Associated with the ancestral ceremonies in Suriname is the Anansi trickster tale told to amuse the deceased during burial ceremonies. The Herskovitses report that in honoring the dead, the bush Negroes of Suriname appreciated the role of humor, not uncommonly turning to the dead to share amusing stories of tricksters. "Some Trickster proverbs were spoken to bear upon the shortcomings of the white man." One or two of the bush Negroes then turned "to repeat to the dead what had been said, and there was great laughter." The father of the dead man assured the anthropologists that "the dead man liked it very much. For the dead, it appears, were especially susceptible to humor and to exceptional occasions." This explains the prominence of trickster tales of Anansi, the spider, being used "to amuse the spirit" of the dead in Suriname.[36] But since tricksters, most notably the hare, pervade much of black Africa, as does the ring ceremony honoring the ancestors, and since the trickster and the circle are associated not only in South America where Africans were enslaved but in North American slavery as well, the evidence implies a wide association of the two in black Africa and, consequently, among numerous African ethnic groups in North America. That may have been the case, for what is more ironic than the continuing interplay of the living and the dead, and where a more appropriate setting for the trickster than in that Spiritual context? Besides, the trickster's character, certainly that of Anansi and Brer Rabbit, is not known to differ significantly from one region to another.

Marshall Stearns offers a description of ring shouts in South Carolina in the 1950s, some years after John and Alan Lomax saw shouts in various parts of the South. Stearns's description is, in most respects, a characteristic one but also helps us understand an abstruse problem, to be considered later, relating to a particular manifestation of the shout:

> The dancers form a circle in the center of the floor, one in back of another. Then they begin to shuffle in a counter-clockwise direction around and around, arms out and shoulders hunched. A fantastic rhythm is built up by the rest of the group standing back to the walls, who clap their hands and stomp on the floor. . . . Suddenly sisters and brothers scream and spin, possessed by religious hysteria, like corn starting to pop over a hot fire. . . . This is actually a West African circle dance . . . a complicated and sacred ritual.[37]

I I I

The most stunning illustration of the trickster's involvement in ancestral ceremonies is contained in the tale "Bur Rabbit in Red Hill Churchyard,"

collected in South Carolina by Adams. In this tale, Rabbit is trickster in
ways never before associated with him (except in the work of the great
collector and storyteller William John Faulkner): he is keeper of the faith
of the ancestors, mediator of their claims on the living, and supreme master of the forms of creativity. As presented in "Red Hill Churchyard,"
Brer Rabbit is shown as a man of God, and new possibilities are opened
for understanding him as a figure in Afro-American folklore heretofore
unappreciated for religious functions. In the Adams tale, ancient qualities
of African culture, some of the most obscure kind, appear to yield new
and original artistic forms within the circle of culture and are directly
related to Anansi and Akan priests in the Suriname bush. More precisely,
the tale reveals African tradition and the future flowing from it, the ground
of spiritual being and the product of its flowering.

But the Red Hill ceremony seems, on its face, just one of the many in
which Brer Rabbit uses his fiddle as a kind of magic wand—for example,
to realize his will against predators or in competition for the hand of a
maiden. What seems equally obvious, though inexplicable, is the strong
convergence of the world of the living and that of the dead as a function, it
seems, of nothing more than Brer Rabbit's genius with his instrument.
That a deeper meaning lies beneath the surface of the tale is suggested,
even to one without a command of the African background, by slave
folklore, which holds that all sorts of things, under the right conditions,
are possible in the graveyard. Headless horsemen race about, a rabbit is
seen walking "on he hind legs wid a fiddle in he hands," and the sacred
and the secular are one in moments of masterly iconography as the "buck
and wing" is danced "on a tombstone." "It look lik in de Christmas ef de
moon is shinin' an' dere's snow on de ground, dat is de time when you
sees all kind er sights." At such times, day appears to light up the night,
but the glow is from the moon and "every star in de element . . . geeing
light." The "diff'ence been it ain' look as natu'al."[38] The real seems unreal, the unreal real as the story unfolds in the depths of winter in the
South.

> De ground was kiver all over wid snow, an' de palin's on de graveyard fence
> was cracklin; it been so cold. . . . An' I look an' listen . . . an' I seen a rabbit
> settin' on top of a grave playin' a fiddle, for God's sake.[39]

The dance of the community of animals occurred:

> All kind 'er little beasts been runnin' round, dancin'. . . . An' dere was wood
> rats an' squirels cuttin' capers wid dey fancy self, and diff'ent kind er birds
> an' owl. Even dem ole Owl was sachayin' 'round look like dey was enjoying'
> dey self.[40]

Brer Rabbit got up from his seat on the tombstone, stopped playing and
"put he fiddle under he arm an' step off de grave." Then he gave "some
sort er sign to de little birds and beasts, an' dey form dey self into a circle
'round de grave." Within that setting, several forms of music were heard:

> Well, I watch an' I see Br'er Rabbit take he fiddle from under he arm an' start to fiddlin' some more, and he were doin' some fiddlin' out dere in dat snow. An' Br'er Mockin' Bird jine him an' whistle a chune dat would er made de angels weep. . . .[41]

Probably a spiritual, the song whistled by Brer Mockingbird is made sadder as Brer Rabbit accompanies him on the violin, the ultimate instrument for the conveying of pathos. But sadness gives way to a certain joy as Brer Rabbit, with all the subtlety of his imagination, leads Brer Mockingbird as they prefigure a new form of music:

> Dat mockin' bird an' dat rabbit—Lord, dey had chunes floatin' all 'round on de night air. Dey could stand a chune on end, grab it up an' throw it away an' ketch it an' bring it back an' hold it; an' make dem chunes sound like dey was strugglin' to get away one minute, an' de next dey sound like sump'n gittin' up close an' whisperin'.[42]

The music of Brer Rabbit and Brer Mockingbird resembles the improvisational and ironic flights of sound that characterize jazz, especially on Fifty-second Street in New York in the mid-twentieth century. The close relationship between the music in Red Hill Churchyard and jazz finds further support in the behavior of Brer Rabbit, whose style calls to mind Louis Armstrong's:

> An' as I watch, I see Bur Rabbit lower he fiddle, wipe he face an' stick he han'k'ch'ef in he pocket, an' tak off he hat an' bow mighty nigh to de ground.[43]

That scene and the others recall the broader context of Louis Armstrong's musical environment in New Orleans, where jazz was sacred in funeral ceremonies and where African secret societies were important to its sustenance and definition. A further consideration of the tale reveals its irreducible foundation in Africa.

The Herskovitses' discussion in *Suriname Folklore* of the drum harks back to the Akans of the Gold Coast and enables us, by transferring the power of the drum to the fiddle, to understand the central mystery of the ritual, which at first glance seems inexplicable. The drums have a threefold power in the mythology of the bush Negro. Of the first power, the Herskovitses write, "Tradition assigns to them the . . . power of summoning the gods and the spirits of the ancestors to appear." After Brer Rabbit stopped fiddling, wiped his face, and with the other animals bowed in a circle before the grave, the storyteller tells us,

> de snow on de grave crack an' rise up, an' de grave open an' I see Simon rise up out er dat grave. I see him an' he look jest as natu'al as he don 'fore dey bury him.[44]

The second power of the drums of the Akans is that of "articulating the message of these supernatural beings when they arrive." A flesh-and-blood character capable of speech, rather than a disembodied spirit, appears as the ancestor in the tale. Consequently, the other characters are able to communicate directly with him, and he is greatly interested in them:

> An' he [Simon] look satisfy, an' he look like he taken a great interest in Bur Rabbit an' de little beasts an' birds. An' he set down on de top of he own grave and carry on a long compersation wid all dem animals.[45]

The third power of the drum is to send the spirits of the gods or ancestors "back to their habitats at the end of each ceremony."

> But dat ain't all. Atter dey wored dey self out wid compersation, I see Bur Rabbit take he fiddle an' put it under he chin an' start to playin'. An' while I watch, I see Bur Rabbit step back on de grave an' Simon were gone.[46]

The intensity of the dancing in the circle, to the music of Brer Rabbit and Brer Mockingbird, was great, as indicated by the pace of the music and the perspiration of the performers, though snow covered the ground. From internal evidence alone—and a large body of external data also suggest as much—we know the dancers fairly whirled in counterclockwise movement. To them dance was sacred, as in Suriname, where "one of the most important expressions of worship is dancing." There the dancers "face the drums and dance toward them, in recognition of the voice of the god within the instruments."[47] The Gold Coast myth, it appears, was elegantly applied in Red Hill Churchyard, but descriptions of the ceremony there and elsewhere in North America make no mention of dancers facing percussionists as a necessary aspect of ritual. This is not surprising, for drums were rarely available to slaves.

Since the functions of the drum in Suriname and of the violin in South Carolina slavery are the same, on the evidence of the tale and the work of the Herskovitses, it is very tempting to conclude that South Carolina slaves, not having access to the drum, simply switched to the violin to express the threefold power. But a case can be made for another explanation of why slaves in South Carolina, and almost certainly elsewhere, used the violin on so sacred an occasion. In this context, David Dalby's assertion that some understanding of "the history and culture of the great medieval empire of Mali" is crucial to an understanding of slave culture is particularly relevant.

> The civilization of Mali included a rich musical culture, based on an elaborate range of string, wind and percussion instruments and on a long professional training for its musicians. This musical culture has survived in West Africa for at least a thousand years and, by its influence on American music, has enabled the United States to achieve an independence from European musical traditions and to pioneer new forms. A bitter aspect of the American slave trade is the fact that highly trained musicians and poets from West Africa

must frequently have found themselves in the power of slaveowners less cultured and well educated than themselves.[48]

Dalby's thesis takes on added significance when one looks at slave culture and discovers the extraordinary degree to which slaves, at gathering after gathering, relied on the fiddle. When one takes into account that the one-string violin was used in the Mali Empire, and is used today among the Songhai of Upper Volta, which is within the boundaries of the old empire, to summon the ancestral spirits, new light is cast on "Bur Rabbit in Red Hill Churchyard," revealing a vital Songhai component in the tale and among South Carolina slaves.[49] The presence of the old Mali Empire, then, is felt in a way that could scarcely be more important—in the ancestral ceremony directed by Brer Rabbit with his fiddle.

Among the ethnic groups of the empire, the violin was widespread, in contrast to the banjo, which was used to accompany the griot's declamation or recitation of stories. Where one had to be apprenticed to griots to learn to master the banjo—in Upper Volta and, possibly, elsewhere in West Africa—a nonprofessional could pick up and, after long practice, achieve mastery of the violin without being apprenticed. The violin was a democratic rather than an aristocratic instrument for the Songhai; this helps explain, together with its use elsewhere in West Africa before and through the centuries of the slave trade, its widespread use by American slaves. In fact, the violin was the most important instrument of slave musicians and important among Northern slaves as well. It is small wonder that in "Bur Jonah's Goat" the storyteller says, "Ef you was to take dat fiddle 'way from him [Brer Rabbit], he would perish 'way and die."[50]

Missionaries in Georgia attempted to eradicate the widespread use of the fiddle on the Hopeton plantation, where five hundred slaves, very large numbers of whom were children and some "old and superannuated," formed a slave community. Sir Charles Lyell, who visited the plantation in the 1840s, wrote about efforts of Methodists to rid slave culture of that instrument even though nothing raucous was associated with ceremonies in which it was played. So pervasive was the use of the fiddle at Hopeton that the Malian tradition of string instruments to which Dalby makes reference is the background against which Lyell's remarks should be placed.

Of dancing and music negroes are passionately fond. On the Hopeton plantation above twenty violins have been silenced by the Methodist missionaries, yet it is notorious that the slaves were not given to drink or intemperance in their merry-makings.[51]

Even when we include the large numbers of children and the very old, we find the astonishing average, on Hopeton, of approximately one fiddler for every twenty slaves in a population of five hundred. When we exclude the young and old, our calculations show that about one in every ten slaves played the fiddle, which makes it difficult to conceive of any ceremony, especially burial rites, in which not even one fiddle was present. And since slaves from Upper Volta were represented on so large a plantation, there was probably a Songhai presence, with ancestral spirits and gods being called forth with the fiddle, as in Red Hill Churchyard, at least until the campaign against its use was launched. It is a study in contrasting cultures that missionaries thought the fiddle profane in religious ceremonies and the African thought it divine in that context.[52]

The ceremony Brer Rabbit directed in Red Hill Churchyard was one with which great numbers of Africans in North America could identify because it involved a burial rite common in enough particulars to West African ethnic groups as a whole. Whatever their differences in language, slaves from many different ethnic groups might easily, at such a ceremony, assume their places in the circle, dancing and singing around the deceased, whether in Virginia, South Carolina, North Carolina, Georgia, Louisiana, Pennsylvania, Maryland, the District of Columbia, or elsewhere. What is certain is that African customs in a more openly expressed form in the North were more likely to occur secretly and in the inscrutable language of the tale in the South. Since the fear of slave insurrections was much less there than in the South, slaves in Philadelphia, for example, were permitted to come together in large numbers for ceremonies.

> Many [in 1850] can still remember when the slaves were allowed the last days of the fairs for their jubilee, which they employed ("light hearted wretch!") in dancing the whole afternoon in the present Washington Square, then a general burying ground—the blacks joyful above, while the sleeping dead reposed below![53]

The burial ground provided an ideal setting, under the conditions of enslavement, for Africans from different ethnic groups to relate to one another, to find shared religious values that must have been an enormous source of satisfaction as they struggled to prevent their numbers from being smaller still as a result of ethnic allegiances. When customs vital to West Africa as a cultural complex were indulged, such as the relationship and obligations of the living to the ancestors, bonds among Africans of different ethnic groups, if before unknown to them, were recognized and strengthened in America despite differences in language and despite certain differences in burial ceremonies. Occasions for such discoveries were not infrequent, since slaves, permitted to participate in the last days of the fairs, decided that a collective ancestral rite would become an annual event. That meant scores of first-generation members of a particular ethnic group chose to participate in a ceremony practiced in Central Africa and all over West Africa as well. The choice of the graveyard for the setting did not prevent white onlookers from concluding that the slaves were carefree, because they did not understand that African dance was a form of worship essential to sacred ceremony or how painful it was for Africans to practice such a ceremony in an alien land, and as slaves.

> In that field could be seen at once more than one thousand of both sexes, divided into numerous little squads, dancing, and singing, "each in their own tongue," after the customs of their several nations in Africa.[54]

If they had been preserved, the lyrics of what was sung would tell us much about the impact of slavery on the consciousness of first-generation Africans and much about African religious ceremonies generally. But given the context of the songs, the overall meaning is clear enough: they were songs concerning the ancestors, songs some notes of which, like those of Brer Mockingbird in Red Hill Churchyard, conveyed the pain of being on the ground of the dead in an alien land far from the ancestral home. Under those conditions, the degree of musical improvisation must have been exceptional, even for a people noted for improvisational brilliance. Their annual movement to the burial ground in Philadelphia meant a continuing affirmation of their values, so they sang and danced in a circle "the whole afternoon," the ground beneath them being common ground.[55]

But when African languages were sung, the requirements of ethnicity at times made random scatterings of singers unrealistic, which guaranteed the ethnic patterns of behavior in the Philadelphia graveyard. As the English language became more their property, it was easier for the mixture of ethnic peoples to occur in myriad circles in that graveyard and in others. There was, inevitably, some unevenness of movement toward cultural oneness because of the language factor alone; some years in the New World were required before those from different ethnic backgrounds achieved cultural oneness by being able to use the same language. Ironically, it was a degree of harmony that could not be reached through African languages. But from the start of the ceremonies in the graveyard, complementary characteristics of religion, expressed through song, dance, and priestly communication with the ancestors, were organic to Africans in America and their movement in a counterclockwise direction in ancestral ceremonies was a recognizable and vital point of cultural convergence.

Though the number of Africans brought into Pennsylvania in the eighteenth century was small—they accounted for just 2 percent of the state's 333,000 people in 1790—their influence on their descendants for generations determined the nature of most of black religion in the state, and with it sacred song and dance style. This raises a question regarding the relationship of slave culture to demography that deserves an answer different from the one offered until now.[56] From what we know of black religion in Pennsylvania, small numbers of Africans were sufficient to constitute the "critical mass" for the retention of essentials of African religion in slavery. Moreover, what is true of black African culture is true of any culture rich in artistic and spiritual content: initiation into it in youth guarantees its presence in consciousness, and to a considerable extent in behavior, for a lifetime.

Fortunately for the slave, the retention of important features of the African cultural heritage provided a means by which the new reality could be interpreted and spiritual needs at least partially met, needs often regarded as secular by whites but as often considered sacred to blacks. The division between the sacred and the secular, so prominent a feature of modern Western culture, did not exist in black Africa in the years of the slave trade, before Christianity made real inroads on the continent. Consequently, religion was more encompassing to the African in slavery than before, the ring shout being a principal means by which physical and spiritual, emotional and rational, needs were fulfilled. This quality of African religion, its uniting of seeming opposites, was perhaps the principal reason it was considered savage by whites. It was the source of creative genius in the slave community and a main reason that whites and free blacks thought the slaves lacked a meaningful spiritual life.[57] Opposition to African religion, therefore, was limited in effectiveness because the African was thought to have a religion unworthy of the name, when, in fact, his religious vision was subtle and complex, responsible for the creation of major—and sacred—artistic forms.

For decades before and generations following the American Revolution, Africans engaged in religious ceremonies in their quarters and in the woods unobserved by whites. From the time of the earliest importations of slaves to the outbreak of the Civil War, millions of slaves did the ring shout, unobserved, with no concern for white approval. But the possibility that whites might discover the guiding principles of African culture kept blacks on guard and led them, to an astonishing degree, to keep the essentials of their culture from view, thereby making it possible for them to continue to practice values proper to them. Such secretiveness was dictated by the realities of oppression and worked against whites acquiring knowledge of slave culture that might have been used to attempt to eradicate that culture. While Lydia Parrish fails to appreciate that political consideration, she effectively draws on African tradition to explain her difficulty in securing certain types of cooperation:

> It took me three winters on St. Simon's to hear a single slave song, three times as many winters to see the religious dance called the ring-shout, still more winters to unearth the Buzzard Lope and similar solo dances, and the game songs known as ring-play. . . . The secretiveness of the Negro is, I believe, the fundamental reason for our ignorance of the race and its background, and this trait is in itself probably an African survival. Melville J. Herskovits . . . quotes a Dutch Guiana Bush Negro as saying: "Long ago our ancestors taught us that it is unwise for a man to tell anyone more than half of

what he knows about anything." It is amusing to question Southerners as to the number of times they remember hearing Negroes volunteer information. Not one so far has recalled an instance in which something has been told that was not common knowledge.[58]

For the African, dance was primarily devotional, like a prayer, "the chief method of portraying and giving vent to the emotions, the dramatic instinct and religious fervour of the race."[59] That whites considered dance sinful resulted in cultural polarization of the sharpest kind since dance was to the African a means of establishing contact with the ancestors and with the gods. Because the emotions of slaves were so much a part of dance expression, the whole body moving to complex rhythms, what was often linked to the continuing cycle of life, to the divine, was thought to be debased. But a proper burial, not what whites thought, was what mattered, unless they were present on so sacred an occasion. A proper burial, for the great majority of slaves throughout slavery, was one in accordance with African tradition. "Wen one uh doze Africans die, it wuz bery sad," an old man recalled of slave days in Georgia. "Wen a man's countryman die, he sit right wid um all night . . . . You know . . . doze Africans ain got no Christianity. Dey, ain hab no regluh religion." After praying, before leaving the "settin' up," the countrymen "put deah han on duh frien and say good-bye."[60] The placing of hands on the dead was an African custom practiced in West Africa and elsewhere in the Americas, including Dutch Guiana, just as drumming was practiced in Africa and, when permitted, in slave America. But the drummer's tempo apparently varied from place to place in Africa, ranging from the rapidity of some tribes in the Congo area to the slow beat of the Africans who influenced some of the drumming in Georgia graveyards: "We beat duh drum agen at duh fewnal. We call it duh dead mahch. Jis a long slow beat. Boom-boom-boom. Beat duh drum. Den stop. Den beat it agen."[61] On such occasions, there was at times the singing of African lyrics but more often the new lyrics of the spirituals.

Spirituals were born as the religious vision of the larger society was caught, as by centripetal force, drawn to the innermost regions of black spiritual consciousness and applied to what blacks were experiencing in slavery. In an African ritual setting on one such occasion, a black man got on his knees, his head against the floor, and pivoted as members of the group around him moved in a circle, holding his head "down to the mire," singing "Jesus been down to de mire." The arms of those circling "reached out to give a push" and from overhead looked somewhat like spokes in a wheel—a continuation of a tradition centuries old in Sierra Leone and one maintained well over a century in America, which argues a significant Mende and Temne presence in slavery in Georgia. As descendants of Temnes and Mendes in America sang in this century, inspiration was drawn from awareness that Jesus knew despair. This confronting of tragedy was somehow strangely comforting, the throwing of one's whole being into the performance a possible source of the blues in the song sang—the sacred side of the blues, what they owe to the spirituals:

> You must bow low
> Jesus been down
> to de mire
> Jesus been down
> to de mire
> Jesus been down
> to de mire
> You must bow low
> to de mire
> Honor Jesus
> to de mire
> Lowrah lowrah
> to de mire
> Lowrah lowrah
> to de mire
> Lowrah lowrah
> to de mire
> Jesus been down
> to de mire
> You must bow low
> to de mire
> low
> to de mire

"The refrain—repeated relentlessly—corresponds in its character and rhythmic beat to that of drums," the words so filled with emotion that, after a while, they dissolve into moans and cries.[62]

For all her merits as a student of folklore, Parrish, who observed that particular shout, never understood the depths of its spirituality. She considered the shout "a kind of religious dance," and this has been the going thesis for well over a century. Nevertheless, she concluded that "Sperrichels were most often sung at night on the plantations when the 'shout'" was held, a context that should have deepened the meaning of the shout for her, as the relationship between the shout and the spirituals deepens the meaning of the latter for us: "The people, young and old would gather in the praise house, or, if there was none, in one of the larger cabins, where the ceremonies were usually prolonged till after midnight, sometimes till 'day clean'." Thus, slave youths were introduced to the circle and to the singing of spirituals within it—all the while dancing in ways scholars acknowledge to be little different from black "secular" dance of today.[63]

I V

Too often the spirituals are studied apart from their natural, ceremonial context. The tendency has been to treat them as a musical form unrelated to dance and certainly unrelated to particular configurations of dance and dance rhythm. Abstracted from slave ritual performance, including burial ceremonies, they appear to be under Christian influence to a disproportionate extent. Though the impact of Christianity on them is obvious and considerable, the spirituals take on an altogether new coloration when one looks at slave religion on the plantations where most slaves were found and where African religion, contrary to the accepted scholarly wisdom, was practiced. Because that was true, principles guiding African culture were found there, none in greater force than the practice of one determination or form leading to and containing vital elements of another. This is seen when one adds to the words of the spirituals the African rhythms that regulate all movement as the worshipers circle counterclockwise in the shout.

The relative simplicity of spirituals sung in the circle was noted by Higginson and others, among them James Weldon Johnson. But the possibility that those who sang them in a circle also sang them outside the circle appears not to have been considered. Given the complexity and irony of Negro-African culture and the reciprocity of forms that characterizes black music in this country, it would follow that, as the contexts in which Higginson observed and discusses the spirituals changed, many of the slaves who sang them in the circle sang them in other contexts as well. Certainly Higginson gives us no reason to doubt it. It is not sufficient, then, to ascribe the simplicity of the spirituals when sung in the circle merely to their stage of development. Rather, it is more likely that the songs in the circle are simple because dance is so pronounced and indispensable a component of the ceremony. As a result, the lyrics are driven by complex percussive rhythms, and often give way to chants, whose repetition can have a hypnotic effect and contribute to the high religious purpose of possession.

That the spirituals were sung in the circle guaranteed the continuing focus on the ancestors and elders as the Christian faith answered to African religious imperatives. In that context and in that way, they were sung by the majority of the slaves who sang them as Higginson, a colonel in the Union Army, observed the shout on South Carolina plantations:

> Often in the starlit evening, I have returned from some lonely ride by the swift river . . . and, entering the camp, have silently approached some glimmering fire, round which the dusky figures moved in the rhythmical barbaric dance the negroes call a "shout," chanting, often harshly, but always in the most perfect time some monstrous refrain. Writing down in the darkness, as I best could,—perhaps with my hand in the safe covert of my pocket,—the

words of the song, I have afterwards carried it to my tent, like some captured bird or insect, and then, after examination, put it by.[64]

Unlike most students of the spirituals, who treat them as a musical form unrelated to dance, Higginson understood that the rhythms of dance regulated all movement and affected the singing of the lyrics. As the names of those participating in the ceremony were called out, the line between the living and the dead was blurred when the celebrants focused on the ancestors, all to "the measured clapping of hands" and "the clatter of many feet." "Hold Your Light," a favorite of the children as well, was sung:

> Hold your light, Brudder, Robert,—
>   Hold your light,
> Hold your light on Canaan's shore.
> What make ole Satan, for follow me so?
> Satan ain't got notin' for do wid me.
>   Hold your light
>   Hold your light
> Hold your light on Canaan's shore.[65]

A more resounding but plaintive spiritual was sung, and the participants added names, in turn, as the dust rose about them, the tempo quickening. The song conveyed a sense of the inevitability of death but no longing for it:

> Jordan River, I'm bound to go,
>   Bound to go, bound to go,—
> Jordan River, I'm bound to go,
>   And bid 'em fare ye well.
> My Brudder Robert, I'm bound to go,
>   Bound to go . . .
> My Sister Lucy, I'm bound to go,
>   Bound to go . . .[66]

At times hand clapping and foot stomping took on a more sorrowful meaning, underscoring pain, urgency, and a longing not even the ring shout could satisfy:

> O, my mudder is gone! my mudder is gone!
> My mudder is gone into Heaven, my Lord!
>   I can't stay behind!
> Dere's room in dar, room in dar,
> Room in dar, in de heaven, my Lord!
>   I can't stay behind!
> Can't stay behind, my dear,
>   I can't stay behind!
>
> O, my fader is gone! my fader is gone
> My fader is gone into Heaven, my Lord!
>   I can't stay behind!

> Dere's room in dar, room in dar,
> Room in dar, in de heaven, my Lord!
> I can't stay behind!
> Can't stay behind, my dear,
> I can't stay behind![67]

The repetition of stanzas as the dancers circled around and around with ever greater acceleration reinforced and deepened the spirit of familial attachment, drawing within the ancestral orbit slaves who may not have known either a father or a mother, their involvement being an extension of that of others, the circle symbolizing the unbroken unity of the community. Familial feeling in the broad sense of clan and in the personal sense of one's own parents was a dominant, irresistible theme of slave consciousness when "Room in There" was sung. When it was, "every man within hearing, from oldest to youngest, would be wriggling and shuffling as if through some magic piper's bewitchment; for even those who at first affected contemptuous indifference would be drawn into the vortex." Such a response, from the oldest to the youngest, could not easily have been evoked by an appropriation from another culture; rather, the magical pull was an expression of traditional values of a people, those that moved the oldest to engage in sacred dance and the young to join them in the circle. All within hearing of the shout joined in the last chorus of the song:

> I'se been on de road into heaven, my Lord!
> I can't stay behind!
> O, room in dar, room in dar,
> Room in dar, in de heaven, my Lord!
> I can't stay behind![68]

While the clapping of hands and dance were clear manifestations of the ancestral context of the songs, the monotonous refrains, characteristic of ring shout spirituals, had the effect of reinforcing in the consciousness of the participants the concerns of the song and the ceremony generally, thereby building emotional and physical tension. The wider African context, not the words alone, should be kept in mind when interpreting, as slaves moved in a circle, their meaning when singing:

> Nobody knows de trubble I sees,
> Nobody knows de trubble I sees,
> Nobody knows de trubble I sees,
> Nobody knows but Jesus.[69]

And

> I know moon-rise, I know star-rise,
> Lay dis body down.

> I walk in de moonlight, I walk in de starlight,
>   To lay dis body down,
> I'll walk in de graveyard, I'll walk through de graveyard,
>   To lay dis body down.
> I'll lie in de grave and stretch out my arms;
>   Lay dis body down.
> I go to de judgement in de evenin' of de day,
>   When I lay dis body down;
> And my soul and your soul will meet in de day
>   When I lay dis body down.

Though Higginson read the song brilliantly in noting that in "I'll lie in de grave and stretch out my arms" man's desire for peace had never been "uttered more plaintively," death and reunion with the ancestors—"And my soul and your soul will meet in de day"—a process endlessly renewed, was an aspect of that peace for most Africans in American slavery.[70] The achieving of spiritual peace involved a complex ritual essential for harmony between the living and the dead, command of a symbolic world in which the circle steadily appears.

Although spirituals with poetry of a superior cast, such as "I Know Moonrise," were in fact better suited for being sung outside the ring, to the swaying of bodies, slaves who sang spirituals in the ring shout apparently were the ones who, in the main, sang them outside the ring, for Higginson makes no distinction between them and other blacks. Marshall Stearns writes, "If we start with a more-or-less African example such as the ring-shout, we can see that as the rhythm dwindled, the melody lengthened and harmony developed." In other words, the ring shout itself may well have provided the creative breakthrough that led to spirituals being sung outside the ring:

> This process is enormously complicated by the West African tradition of improvisation, augmented by the free style of the folk hymn—no one melody is sacred; it can always be changed by spontaneous embellishments. Thus, although many Spirituals are written down and ring-shouts generally are not, it is conceivable that the former's sustained melody could have emerged momentarily from a ring-shout. The evolution is fluid, proceeding at different speeds in different mixtures, with much depending upon the performer.[71]

While one differs with Eugene Genovese regarding the extent to which slaves were influenced by Christianity, his discussion of slave religion contains a profound insight: "The black variant of Christianity laid the foundations of protonationalist consciousness and at the same time stretched a universalist offer of forgiveness and ultimate reconciliation to white America."[72] In arguing that protonationalist consciousness was achieved, Genovese sensed a greater degree of autonomy in the slave community than scholars before him had found. Still, he underestimated the degree of nationalist consciousness, for slave consciousness was grounded in a continuing awareness of the fundamentals of African faith.

But there is no question of the force of his argument that Christianity enabled the slave to stretch "a universalist offer of forgiveness and ultimate reconciliation" to whites—an achievement that began, if Stearns is right, in the ring shout during moments of sustained melody. Considering their rich experiences with multiple ethnic groups, it is fitting that Africans attempted to make Christianity real in the lives of others—in effect, to give it universal appeal.

Like South Carolina, Virginia offers a rich field for the study of the spiritual in relation to African values. Though the slave trade came to an end in Virginia by 1808, the impact of African culture on slaves there was not that much greater in 1800 than in the 1850s, a consideration, as we shall see, vital to understanding the context in which the spiritual evolved in the South. In this regard, it is essential to study the spiritual within the context of the folktale, especially since African religious culture is expressed more faithfully and with greater power in the tale than in other sources. Nowhere was that culture richer than in Virginia.

By 1800, Virginia contained large numbers of African-born slaves. Between 1727 and 1769, nearly 40,000 slaves were brought into the state, and "Africa overwhelmingly was the source, more than four-fifths of the slaves coming from that continent." With the slave population of Virginia at 187,000 in 1770, slaves formed 40 percent of the inhabitants; by 1790, nearly 60 percent of slaves in the United States resided there and in Maryland.[73] Since the overwhelming majority of the slaves brought into Virginia until the end of the trade were African born, they provided the foundation of values from which slave culture was erected, New World experience being interpreted largely from the African point of view. "At the beginning of the nineteenth century," an authority writes, "Virginia had something over 300,000 Negroes, of whom 285,369 were slaves and 20,124 free Negroes. By 1860, the slaves had increased to 490,865 and the free Negroes to 58,042."[74] One of the blacks born in Virginia near the close of slavery was Simon Brown.

Born into slavery in 1843, Simon participated in the most sacred of rituals in the 1850s by the age of thirteen—a common practice in slave communities in both the North and the South, as children, within a year or two after they were able to walk, joined in some ceremonies, especially in the ring shout. In fact, slave culture was, despite its centeredness upon the elders and ancestors, a culture in which the very young played a more vital role than scholars have assigned them. The preference of slaveholders for African males aged sixteen or under helped determine that role, as did the importance of family to Africans. Consequently, slave culture was preeminently a youth culture in which there was great respect for the aged and for the ancestors. Indeed, in 1750 over half the slave population over much of Virginia was under sixteen.[75]

Simon Brown's relationship to that tradition was unusual, since he helped to extend slave customs as a practioner in youth and as a storyteller later on. Much of what he recounted had shaped his life in lasting ways and helps explain his precise revelations of slave experiences. His keen intellect and his extraordinary artistic sense enabled Brown to assimilate much of what he witnessed in slavery, to shape it into the folktale, and to do so with a faithfulness as exacting as that of the most gifted historian, working in conventional sources, in recording the past. More than that, his gifts as an artist gave him a dimension of talent rare among historians, the ability to give expression to human feeling as a factor in shaping past and present, the ability to link the subjective to the communal. Those qualities made him a great teacher, able to convey values of slave culture to children at the turn of the century, as other storytellers conveyed them on plantations more than three decades earlier.

One finds in Brown's tales references to the means by which slaves prevented their true feelings from being detected in the presence of the master, and references to what is distinctive about slave culture and why. But many of the tales, certainly the greatest, have a dimension that is so esoteric, so African in meaning, that the master class missed their meaning altogether. On that level, that of Africanity, as we see repeatedly in the tales of Tad, the tale was the greatest device, next to the actual ceremony it recounts, for imparting the values of the culture to the young and for reinforcing them in adults, for preparing slaves to cope with the world of slavery and for revealing the process by which that world unfolded. Like the ring shout that helped give it birth, the spiritual was, for slaves, integral to that process.

How slave experience, including ceremonies in which the spiritual was sung, was communicated to succeeding generations and cultural continuity maintained is demonstrated through the contact between Simon and William John Faulkner, his prize student, who met the ex-slave in Society Hill, South Carolina, in 1900 at the age of nine. Brown became the model storyteller for the young Faulkner, and the latter attempted to tell the tales like Brown, whom he so greatly admired that even now, at the age of ninety-five, he remains inspired by Brown. That inspiration helps explain why Faulkner has held the most precise details of the tales in mind for more than three-quarters of a century. His intelligence, his powers of retention, and an artistry reminiscent of that of Simon Brown are factors in the remarkable correspondence of the tales, like those of Tad, to the *processes* of African culture revealed by art historians, anthropologists, and students in related fields like linguistics and musicology. Transcribed over thirty years after Faulkner first heard them from Brown, but recounted on hundreds of occasions, Faulkner's tales enlarge our knowledge of African religion in America on its own terms and in relation to Christianity in new and striking ways. This is even more remarkable because Brown, no doubt following a practice learned in slavery, refused to respond to inquiries from Faulkner regarding African culture except to say, "We used to have great times." But in "How the Slaves Worshipped" Brown put his finger on important differences between slave religion and that of the master class, suggesting that slaves brought intuitive, aesthetic, and other values to black Christianity, distinguishing it from white Christianity:

> I use' to drive my Massa's family in town to church, in the "two-horse surey," on a Sunday. I had to sit upstairs with the other slaves. We act like we enjoy' the services, but we didn't. . . . But the slave' had they Christian religion too, an' it wasn't cole and "Proper," like in the white folk' church. The fact is, the black folk in my day didn't even have a church. They meet in a cabin in the cole weather an' outdoors, under a tree or a "brush arbor" in the summer time. Sometimes the Massa's preacher would "talk" at the meetins 'bout bein' obedient to our massas an' good servants, an' 'bout goin' to heaven when we die.'. . . But, oh, my, when my people got together to "Wishop" (Worship) God, the Spirit would "move in the meetin!"[76]

Religion was for many slaves, by the mid-nineteenth century in Virginia, an African version of Christianity marked by an awareness of the limits of the religion of whites.

> The folk' would sing an' pray an' "testify," an' clap they han's, jus' as if God was right there in the midst with them. He wasn't way off, up in the sky: He was a-seein' everybody an' a-listen' to ever' word an' a-promisin' to "let His love come down." My people would be so burden' down with they trials an' tribulations, an' broken hearts, that I seen them break down an' cry like babies. . . . Yes sir, there was no pretendin' in those prayer-meetin's. There was a livin' faith in a jus' God who would one day answer the cries of his poor black chillen an' deliver them from they enemies. But they never say a word to they white folks 'bout this kine of faith.[77]

At laying-by time on some plantations, revival meetings were held over several nights in the heat of summer. With "sisters and brothers" clapping their hands and singing and mourners coming to their bench, the slaves sang songs created within the ancestral circle of dancers:

> Sister (or brother), you better get ready;
> You got to die, you got to die.
> It may not be today or t'morrow
> You never know the minute or the hour
> But you better get ready, you got to die.

It was important to be at peace with oneself. For those sinners who had trouble "comin' through," the slaves sang another spiritual:

> Go down to the River of Jordan, go down,
> Singing Hallelujah
> Singing Hallelujah
> Sing Halle-, Sing Halle-,
> Sing Hallelujah.[78]

A deacon assisted the preacher with his flock of white-gowned men and women in a ceremony common to West African religions and to Christianity—water immersion, or baptism. As a rule "the converts was made ready to be baptize' the next-comin' Firs' Sunday, soon in the mornin', down by the Mill Pond." The new converts and friends as well as members of their families would make a pilgrimage, Simon Brown tells us, down to the Mill Pond. Herskovits writes, "In ceremony after ceremony witnessed among the Yoruba, the Ashanti, and in Dahomey, one invariable element was a visit to the river or some other body of 'living' water . . . for the purpose of obtaining the liquid indispensable for the rites." Thus, Yorubas, Ashantis, and Dahomeans would easily have identified with the pilgrimage to the Mill Pond for a ceremony that was heavily influenced by Bakongo religious ritual.

Simon Brown relates that slaves would secure passes and "come from all 'roun'—in buggies an' carts an' on mule-back"—to attend revival meetings. "But mos' of them walk' on foot. The candidates for baptism would gather 'roun' an' march down the Big Road all dress' in white to the edge of the pond." As they waited for the ceremony to begin and as the congregation began singing a "baptism' song," "one of the Deacons would hole in his han' a long staff built like a cross . . . would wade out into the water, usin' his staff as a soundin' stick in fron' of him. When the staff reach' the proper depth, he would drive it down hard into the bottom." With the cross visible above the water, the preacher was "fetched" by the deacon and stood near it as the congregation sang:

> Wade in the water, Chillen
> Oh wade in the water, chillen,
> Wade in the water, chillen,
> Wade in the water to be baptize'.[79]

The staff made like a cross was, for the Bakongo, "a tree across the water's path, a bridge that mystically put the dead and the living in perpetual communication."[80] In America, therefore, its retention was an illustration, as described by Simon Brown, of how a particular feature of the African religious vision, whatever the fate of its other features, might radiate the fullness of that vision without outsiders having the slightest awareness of its significance. So it was that the deacon in the ceremony was not simply a "deacon" but "the good leader" or priest who was capable of introducing the living to their ancestors through the ritual of water immersion. Moreover, to the Kongo people the staff-cross represented authority that was also legislative, judicial, and executive.[81] On the slave plantation, therefore, the authority of the religious leader might have been enhanced because Africans recalled the enormous authority their religious leaders once held. But given the restraints of slavery, the radically different context in which the staff was revealed, legislative and judicial authority ceased to exist, and political authority, to the extent that it persisted, was so greatly reduced as to be all but unidentifiable in the African sense of leadership. But the remaining substance, the African religious role of the deacon, had political overtones because its meaning was vital to the slave's sense of autonomy, was kept from slaveowners. The white gowns of the slaves as well as the staff-cross recall Bakongo religious mythology:

> In the world below, called *mpemba,* land of kaolin, land of all things white, the lordly dead, through powers commensurate with the relative goodness of their life once lived on earth above, lose the impurities acquired in life, acquire a new freshness of existence, and reenter the world.[82]

The cross portion of the staff symbolizes the four moments of the sun and represents, to the Bakongo, the four corners of the earth and the four winds of heaven. The horizontal axis of the cross signifies the sea or river that divides the world of the living and dead, the heavens above and the earth below, this world and the next. The staff-cross enabled the deacon, as it did the Bakongo king, to traverse the watery barrier—the horizontal portion of the cross—and, like Brer Rabbit in Red Hill Churchyard, to mediate between the world of the living and that of the dead. When the deacon brandished his staff, it was as if the sun in its orbit was suddenly mirrored, revealing the fullness of Bakongo religion. And since those who lived a good life might experience rebirth in generations of grandchildren, the cycle of death and rebirth could hardly have been more suggestive than through the staff-cross—a symbol of communal renewal.[83]

What appears in "How the Slaves Worshipped," despite the African context of the creation of the spirituals, as primarily a Christian ceremony is actually a conversion within the circle of the cross, a movement from one state of being in the Kongo religious system to a higher one. Substantial numbers of Bakongo, Angolans, and west coast Africans were enslaved in Virginia, and even if first-generation Africans were not much in evidence at the ceremony witnessed by Simon Brown, their descendants across a number of ethnic lines were doubtless among those who had come from all around, in buggies and on foot, to participate.

In the ceremony before and at the pond, as in most "Christian" ceremonies on slave plantations, Christianity provided a protective exterior beneath which more complex, less familiar (to outsiders) religious principles and practices were operative. The very features of Christianity peculiar to slaves were often outward manifestations of deeper African religious concerns, products of a religious outlook toward which the master class might otherwise be hostile. By operating under cover of Christianity, vital aspects of Africanity, which some considered eccentric in movement, sound, and symbolism, could more easily be practiced openly. Slaves therefore had readily available the prospect of practicing, without being scorned, essential features of African faith together with those of the new faith.

When the convert in "How the Slaves Worshipped" is held underwater—under the Kalunga line—he "dies a small death, and then is reborn, emerging from a short commune with the ancestors." It is small wonder that Simon Brown tells us that a candidate, after immersion, would "come up from the water so happy he would begin to shout right out in the pond, an' it would take both deacons to bring him safe to shore." More than one song, sung at the Mill Pond, takes on a new meaning now: "Sister, you better get ready / You got to die / You got to die." One can hardly doubt that the meaning was double, as it certainly was for Bakongo in the baptismal ceremony. The convert was wiped with a towel, and then his family or friends would cover him with a quilt as the singing of the congregation evoked the Kalunga line—since it was also imagined as a dense forest or, in Gullah Joe's language, feenda:

> Oh, my soul got happy when I come out the wilderness,
> Come out the wilderness,
> Oh my soul got happy
> When I come out the wilderness,
> I'm leanin' on the Lawd—
>
> CHORUS
> I'm a-leaning' on the Lawd,
> I'm a-leaning' on the Lawd,
> I'm a-leaning on the Lawd,
> Who die' on Cal-va-ree.[84]

That last image was also enriched by the staff-cross, by the African concern for the relationship between the world of the living and that of the dead, because reciprocity was crucial in ceremonies of the Bakongo and of Africans generally. Thompson believes, because of the "wheel" effect, the Kongo cross "should make clear the rhetorical point of its existence, as forever distinguished from the standing emblem of Jesus Christ." The complex uses to which the Kongo peoples put the symbolism of the cross and circle as a cosmogram help explain the power of the two as means of extending the basis of commonality among Virginia slaves and of linking them in cultural unity with Africans practicing the ring shout in the South and the North. Something of the complexity of the circle in the Congo is discussed by Thompson:

> Fu-Kiau's diagrams illustrate the fundamental circularity of the Kongo sign of cosmos, a circularity which bursts into full view where a snail shell spirals at the center of one cruciform or, in another instance, where a circle spins around the endings of the cross. . . . Dots or small circles added to the intersecting arms of the Kongo cross indicate man or woman as second suns, moving through time and space, following the circle of the sun.[85]

The cross represented an intricate field of circularity to the Bakongo and Angolan in Virginia, and against that radiating field they placed Christ when converting others to Christianity.[86] Thus, priests through the symbolism of the "long staff built like a cross" maintained an African defining power in the slave community that lent a peculiar irony to the crucifixion, deepening the pain of spirit of those who sang the song under Kongo influence, calling to mind a whole complex ancestral heritage as Christ is imagined on the cross: "I'm a-leanin' on the Lord (3) / Who die' on Calva-ree."[87]

In all of the ceremonies we have described, black artists occupied a place beside black religious leaders at the center of slave communities. Both artist and preacher—the two were often the same—thrived among the masses. The preacher was as much a part of the masses as the artist and related to followers in much the same way, the one reaching out to the other as in Africa. At times African art and religion in slavery were sustained by supporters who rivaled the priests and priestesses who stood before them at the ceremonial sites. That process won ultimate sanction in the folk art of the tale and bears a profound relationship to the melding of various African ethnic groups in slavery. In this regard, the evidence drawn on to see the process unfold may at first glance appear to be primarily Christian, as in "How the Slaves Worshipped," but it seldom is. In fact, the great bulk of the slaves were scarcely touched by Christianity, their religious practices being vastly more African than Christian. The slave preacher on the plantation was able to relate to slave communities touched by Christianity and to those with little or no Christian characteristics, the latter because otherwise he could have had no credence whatsoever among the majority of his people.[88]

No less an authority on slave conversion to Christianity than the Reverend Charles C. Jones, writing in 1834, had this to say regarding slaves and Christianity: "It is true they have access to the house of God on the Sabbath; but it is also true that even where the privilege is within their reach, a minority, (and frequently a very small one) embraces it." Moreover, Jones noted the inability of churches in the South and the Southwest to accommodate "one-tenth of the Negro population; besides others (areas of the South) in which there are no churches at all." To compound the problem, Jones concluded, "great numbers of masters have very few or no religious privileges at all." That being the case, William W. Freehling's finding that, as the year 1833 ended, "only twelve white men in the whole South devoted themselves exclusively to ministering to the slaves" underscores the inability of Christianity to Christianize the slaves. "Only one slave in twenty," according to Freehling, "was a communicant in white churches," and those who were in attendance were unprepared to comprehend the erudite sermons addressed to educated citizens." Freehling notes, "As evangelical Christianity swept over the Old South, another burden was added to the uneasy consciences of many slave-holders.'' The attempt to Christianize slaves was at best "an abortive affair. . . . Protestant sects believed that the Savior had enjoined all Christians to read His words, and planters kept slaves from reading the Scripture.''[89]

Not surprisingly, the old Negro preacher and other religious leaders in the slave community were the ones who spoke for their people whatever their ethnic origins. The authority of major religious leaders on the plantations owed much to the divine-kingship systems of West Africa and for that reason was the least likely to be questioned. Whereas the warrior-king was typical of Europe, much of black Africa was characterized by the priest-king, which gave the religious leader a high status in slave communities. In Africa the priest was at times king, reaching his highest rung of authority, performing religious roles that determined the vital functions—presiding over harvests and mediating with ancestral spirits. The life forces were regulated by and passed through the king-priest, whose importance was paramount; this helps explain the authority of the black preacher through slavery and later. Except for that authority the "scattered and often clandestine" praise houses may not have surfaced, without which the Negro spirituals may well not have come into being. It is small wonder that Johnson observed, "The Negro today [1927] is the most priest-governed group in the country.''[90] Thus, the powers of priests, and those of artists, especially storytellers and musicians, on the plantations of the South caused African-born slaves to recognize central features of life in the various ethnic homelands as they moved toward a single ethnicity in their new environment, which was precisely the nature of the process Brer Rabbit did so much to further in Red Hill Churchyard.

One errs in assuming that the slave preacher was primarily Christian and did not play a variety of religious roles, especially that of African priest. Indeed, the categories of religious leadership on plantations were so fluid that the functions of class leader, deacon, and "preacher" were often indistinguishable, as they were in cities. The preacher's priestly or African function, and that of deacon and class leader, was guarded from whites, who thought anything African of a religious nature was pagan or heathen, an insult to Christianity. Therefore, if the African religious leader was to operate in the open, the safest cloak to hide behind was that of Christianity. African religious leaders predominated in slavery and in that oppressive environment orchestrated their people's transformation into a single people culturally. James Weldon Johnson makes the penetrating observation that it was through the old Negro preacher that "people of diverse languages and customs who were brought here from diverse parts of Africa and thrown into slavery were given their first sense of unity and solidarity.''[91]

Simon Brown was a supreme articulator of that process. His grounding as a storyteller, as we have seen, was lived experience, which must be taken into account in the attempt to understand his tales' remarkable faithfulness to the past. A mulatto house slave, he found the only culture he knew and respected in the quarters. It was there that he witnessed and participated in an African burial ceremony at thirteen. Other youths joined him in becoming inheritors of the culture of their ancestors, directly responsible for the sacred act of digging and filling up the grave, apparently as soon as they were strong enough. In the 1850s, these youths participated in burial customs common to Central and West Africa, customs known to vast numbers of slaves, although by then second- and third-generation Africans greatly outnumbered those born in Africa. Even slaves to whom aspects of a particular African custom, such as the constructing of the burial mound, were unknown, and therefore not at first understood, got a sense of solidarity with those who knew the custom through the genius of the preacher and that of singers responding to him. Rapport was established through song style, which powerfully affected preaching style, both peculiarly African and widespread, both regulated by the rhythm of dance at the burial site.

Brown tells us that slaves helped each other in illness as in death. If a woman fell ill, "other women came over to help her with the chillen, or to cook the meals, wash the clothes or to do other necessary chores." He recalled medical and other practices that were African:

> It wasn't like it is today, when ever'body seem like they tryin' only to git the dollar. Women would come over jus' to sit a spell an' sing an' pray 'roun' the sickbed. Nobody was lef' to suffer alone. Sometimes a man or woman with a healin' touch would brew a herb tea, mix a poultice, or apply peach tree leaves to the fevered brow, to help the sick git well. All of this lovin' care cheer' up the trouble' soul, whether he got well or died.[92]

When Sister Dicey died, the women washed and dressed her and laid her out in a homemade coffin, resting it on chairs. Slaves from all over came to sit, sing, and pray. "The singin' was mostly sad songs with happy endin's, 'cause the folks felt that now Aunt Dicey was freed from all the trials an' tribulations of slavery an' was safe in Heaben, at res' an' in peace forever more. She wouldn't be a bare-foot slave dress' in rags anymore." And so they sang,

> I got shoes
> You got shoes
> All God's chillen got shoes
> When I git to Heaben
> I'm a-goin' to put on my shoes an'
> Walk all over God's heaben
> I got a robe
> You got a robe
> All God's chillen got a robe.

> When I git to Heaben
> I'm a-goin' to put my robe an'
> Shout all over God' Heaben.[93]

Some of the people "git so happy with this picture of Heaben that they burs' out cryin' an' shoutin' for joy. An' so the 'sittin' up' went on all night—some folks comin' an' goin' all the time." The African custom of "sittin' up" was accompanied by the singing of spirituals, the sadness-joy of the songs in Virginia resembling the feelings at the burial ceremony conducted by Brer Rabbit in Red Hill Churchyard in South Carolina, and by New Orleans blacks in the nineteenth and twentieth centuries.[94]

The next morning, at the grave, the preacher offered Christian words of comfort in an African style that finally led, as the tension mounted, to dance growing out of rejoicing, and to resolution. According to Simon Brown, the preacher's voice carried softly, then with rising emphasis as he sang the sermon:

> "Sister Dicey, since God in His mercy has taken your soul from earth to Heaben, an' out of your misery, I commit your body to the groun', earth to earth, ashes to ashes, dus' to dus', where it will res' in peace. But on that Great Gettin' Up Mornin', when the trumpet of God shall soun' to wake up all the dead, we will meet you in the sky an' join the host' of saints who will go marchin' in. Yes, we'll be in that number, Sister Dicey, when the saints go marchin' in." Before the preacher could finish his benediction, some of the women git so happy that they jus' drown' him out with they singin' an' han' clappin' an' shoutin'.[95]

The variety and depth of African customs in the Virginia slave community of Simon Brown form the background against which "they singin' an' han' clappin' an' shoutin'" should be viewed: the "sittin' up," the African medical practices, the Kongo cross at the baptismal ceremony, the rhythms of song, sermon, and dance—all these elements marked the Virginia slave community as African in important ways. The shouting and hand clapping, in context, then, was the ring shout, the circular movement around the old lady's grave being a key symbol while a sermon was delivered that was as Christian in message as its mode of delivery and the response it evoked were African, its call and response pattern common to blacks the world over. The counterclockwise movement of those at the graveside opposed the movement of the sun. For first-generation Africans from Congo-Angola and for those in their tradition, each rising and setting of the sun was a painful reminder that they were indeed in a new world, but their counterclockwise movement was a form of spiritual and physical resistance to this reality, as it was for some that day at Sister Dicey's grave. What followed, however, was a ceremony practiced by millions in Africa above and below the equator:

> Then the men an' boys begin to fill up the grave. When it was full they roun' it up real purty-like, an' put a wood shingle at the head an' another at the foot of

the grave. The women-folk lay some flowers an' "ribbon-grass" on the top, an' put different color' bottles, broken glass an' sea-shells all 'roun' the grave of Aunt Dicey. In that way they show they love for her. It was the bes' that slaves could do in them days, when ever'body was poor an' own' by they massas. But no man could own they souls or keep them from lovin' one another. Them gifts come only from God.[96]

The "sittin' up" and the burial mound are bridges to the hereafter, making communication with God and the ancestors less abstract, because being in proper relation to Sister Dicey eased one's own passage in turn. While the preacher spoke of meeting her on that great getting-up morning, the preparation of the burial mound by relatives meant an awareness that continuing contact with Sister Dicey's spirit was unavoidable. Hence, by being certain that her spirit was at rest, contact with her thereafter was more likely to be of a harmonious kind. The two visions of religion in the tale, the traditional African and the Christian, were complementary and explainable in relation to the African view of religious experience, which does not function from a single set of principles but deals with life at different levels of being. The African spiritual vision of the universe is synthetic, does not claim everything can be deduced from a single principle—that is to say, the center of the African's morality is the life process and the sacredness of those who brought him into existence. The African's relationship to the future is determined by his relationship to the young, his relationship to the past determined by his relationship to his parents. The maintenance of this continuity from generation to generation is justification for his being and the basis on which he determines proper behavior. The needs, physical and spiritual, of the actual, concrete human being are recognized as important, and an attempt is made to satisfy them in African societies: those needs were multiple before Christianity became a part of the African's faith. The absorption of aspects of Christianity—such as a belief in Christ—did not mean they ceased being multiple, as can be seen in burial and other ceremonies in slavery.

Just as slave music reflects the unity of West African culture through syncopation, antiphony, group singing, improvisation, and instruments used, and through its organic tie to dance, the essential unity of large sections of Central and West African religion was reflected in the burial mound of slaves in antebellum America and later. The African character of slave burial ceremony was unmistakable: "Them dishes and bottles what put on the grave is for the spirit and ain't for nobody to touch them. That's for the spirit to feel at home." "You put dishes and bottles and all the pretty pieces what they like on the grave. You always break these things before you put 'em down. You break them so that the chain will be broken. You see, the one person is dead and if you don't break the things, then the others in the family will die, too."[97] Robert Farris Thompson observes,

Two early twentiety-century graves in Mississippi . . . glitter with surface china, suggesting the rumpled vitality of a vanished life. The use of the fragments seems deliberate: pieces are aligned to show the length of the grave in a simple axial statement. . . . An intimate act characteristic of the deceased is [sometimes] recalled forever on the surface of the grave by means of a particular object selected. What appears to be a random accumulation is in fact the distillation of a life. . . . The deposit of chinaware and other objects on the Afro-American grave is in contrast with the stark plots of grass which cover the graves of Americans of European descent.[98]

The preacher presiding over the deceased, overseeing the ritual, assumes major responsibility for the fate of the deceased's spirit. The obligation of the occasion suggests a power beyond the grave for him, leads him to assume the role of the African priest over the burial mound. Thus, the divine-kingship function of mediating with the ancestors was reborn on the plantations of the South, as Africa was recalled on a level of precise symbolism. Slaves found objects in North America similar to the shells and close enough to the earthenware of West Africa to decorate the grave in an African manner—and in the African manner to celebrate the lives of those who, like Sister Dicey, lived long and won the admiration of their fellows. Africans from different points of the continent shared this vision, which could have *strengthened* an African trait under the conditions of North American slavery: "The fusion of slaves from the Gold Coast, the Congo-Angola area, and other parts of the Guinea Coast in Southern slavery could mean the reinforcement of the African notion that the funeral is the climax of life and that the dead should be honored by having their possessions placed upon the top of their graves."[99]

In *Black Thunder,* a superb treatment of a conspiracy led by Gabriel Prosser in Virginia in 1800, Arna Bontemps portrays a ceremony like the one described by Faulkner, capturing an aspect of the ethos of contempories of Gabriel:

They were burying old Bundy in the low field by the swamp. They were throwing themselves on the ground and wailing savagely. (The Negroes remembered Africa in 1800.) . . . Down, down, down: old Bundy's long gone now. Put a jug of rum at his feet. Old Bundy with his legs like notty canes. Roast a hog and put it on his grave. Down, down. How them victuals suit you, Bundy? How you like what we brung you?

Faith in the continuing influence of the dead on the living was as great as faith that the living influenced the dead:

Anybody knows that dying ain't nothing. You got one eye open and one eye shut old man. We going to miss you just the same, though, we going to miss you bad, but we'll meet you on t'other side, Bundy. We'll do that sure's you born.

There was African song—a moaning cry—and dance:

They had raised a song without words. They were kneeling with their faces to the sun. Their hands were in the air, the fingers apart, and they bowed and rose together as they sang. Up came the song like a wave, and down went their faces in the dirt . . . at the place where the two worlds met.[100]

V

Being on good terms with the ancestral spirits was an overarching conceptual concern for Africans everywhere in slavery. But nowhere was there greater consciousness of African values than in South Carolina in the early 1820s, where blacks were in the majority and constituted an African population. Blacks in that state, especially those in the countryside, where they were largely isolated from whites, could scarcely have been more distinct culturally from other Americans had they been born in Africa, which was indeed true of the thousands entering the state in unprecedented numbers for a quarter of a century before the suppression of the slave trade in 1808. That the trade continued illegally in South Carolina until the Civil War meant African cultural values were steadily being replenished.

It was this climate that produced the Denmark Vesey conspiracy in Charleston in 1822. There an essentially African religion was being practiced, with blacks, slave and free, gathering to worship. Since the majority of blacks in South Carolina came from regions of Africa, like Congo-Angola and the western slave coast, in which the ring ceremony was prominent, the shout could hardly have been practiced less fervently there in the 1820s than in the 1860s, the decade in which New Englanders entered the state to find it performed on innumerable occasions, day and night.[101]

To assume that American-born blacks were the only acculturated blacks and that being acculturated meant not being African is to oversimplify African culture and to overestimate the culture of the master. No one has yet demonstrated that skilled slaves sought to cut themselves off from their spiritual base in the slave community. If skilled slaves did not remove themselves from that base they remained connected to the African heritage on the profoundest possible level. Robert Starobin's argument that native-born Africans in the Vesey conspiracy, because of a continued commitment to the values of their national heritage, were more likely to favor rebellion than acculturated blacks is intriguing and cogent. But, like Gerald Mullins, he assumes that for them to be acculturated was to be more American than African. Freehling, however, strikes a convincing balance:

The secret of Vesey's charismatic power was his skillful fusion of the high ideals of the Age of Reason with the ruthless savagery of a barbaric chief. His most important lieutenant, Gullah Jack, made the amalgam more weird and potent by supplying a pipeline to the African gods. . . . A brilliant man, well traveled and well read, Vesey found abundant evidence in the Bible, in American political theory, and in the congressional debates on slavery during the Missouri Controversy to prove the immorality of slavery and the legitimacy of revolt.[102]

Vesey effected another, essential fusion—that of relating to Africans from various parts of Africa and the New World. Purchased by Captain Vesey on one of the captain's voyages between St. Thomas and San Domingo, he was about fourteen at the time and was placed on board the captain's ship with 390 slaves, a scene that must have left an indelible imprint on his consciousness. He was "for 20 years a most faithful slave," during which time he accompanied his master, as a cabin boy, to the West Indies, which once again provided him with the opportunity to observe Africans from many parts of Africa and to relate to the variegated sweep of their ethnicity. Whether or not he had made the Atlantic voyage—some say he did—he knew something of its nature from the West Indian passage. As he grew older, he practiced a form of polygamy, producing with his wives numerous slave children and in "1800, he drew a prize in the East-Bay-Street Lottery, with which he purchased his freedom from his master, at six hundred dollars, much less than his real value."[103]

A teenager and young adult when hundreds of thousands of Africans were imported into the West Indies and North America—nearly forty thousand were brought into South Carolina alone between 1800 and 1807—Vesey lived in a Pan-African environment in both locations; he was a slave when Pan-African consciousness was being formed. Indeed, he lived among men and women in South Carolina and in the West Indies who had experienced the middle passage and retained memories of the complexities of African culture. His formative values came from contact with Africans and, to a lesser extent, with whites, the latter process accelerated by his facility in several European languages, an achievement not uncommon for talented Africans in the New World.[104] He was, consequently, able to draw on both sets of experiences, to bring them together to enrich his political vision and inform his religious outlook, which left him ideally suited to lead a movement against slavery.

His grievances were many. As a slave who gained his freedom in his early thirties, "all his children were slaves," and "he wished to see what could be done for them." A man of conviction, he held a certain peace with slavery for more than two decades, then actively dedicated himself to its overthrow: "Denmark Vesey frequently came into our shop which is near his house, and always complained of the hardships of the blacks— he said the laws were very rigid and strict and that the blacks had not their rights—that everyone had his time, and that his would come round too."

The once "faithful slave" was known to be courageous, in the white-owned shop speaking "of the creation of the world, in which he would say all men had equal rights, blacks as well as whites . . . *all his religious remarks were mingled with slavery.*"[105]

Well off, thanks to a successful trade, he had no patience with privileged slaves who thought their condition different from that of the most oppressed of their people, as Mrs. Ferguson's slave Frank confirmed:

> I know Denmark Vesey and have been to his house—I have heard him say that the negroe's situation was so bad he did not know how they could endure it, and was astonished they did not rise and fend for themselves, and he advised me to join and rise. . . . Vesey said the negroes were living such an abominable life, they ought to rise. I said I was living well—he said though I was, others were not and that was such fools as I, that were in the way and would not help them, and that after all things were well he would mark me.[106]

The lack of concern for material possessions, and the willingness to risk all in attempting to better the lot of one's people, through revolution or reform, was a powerful strain in nationalist thought, in Vesey's time and later, and contained the seeds of socialism that flowered in the programs of Afro-American theorists in the twentieth century. In Vesey's time, slavery encouraged in blacks a powerful opposition to wealth acquired at the expense of others. Exploited in more ways and more fundamentally than any proletarian, the American slave provided in his folklore the rationale for Vesey's hatred of oppressors and of the privileged Negro who lacked a commitment to the liberation of his people. Vesey might have provided the critique of class society and its interlocking institutions found in "The Slave Barn," the South Carolina revolutionary folk poem. But neither he nor anyone else could have improved on the poem's portrayal of class conflict, as the oppressor and oppressed faced each other in deadly opposition. Yet he had that fundamental antagonism in view, and in the context of his conspiracy the Ibo ethic of the poem—accessible to all Africans—takes on its sharpest possible focus and relevance. He framed his argument with a series of questions when querying a slave named Bacchus Hammett, who reported

> how he was carried to Veseys by Perault, How Vesey sat him along side of him, and . . . asked him . . . queries such as—"*Did His master use him Well—Yes he believed so,* Did he eat *the same* as his master, Yes sometimes not as well as his master—*Did his master not sleep on a soft bed,* Yes. Did he Bacchus sleep on as soft a bed as his master—No—who made his master—God—Who made you—God—And *then ar'nt you as good as your master if God made him and you, ar'nt you as free,* Yes, *Then why don't you join and fight your master.* . . . Does he whip you when you do wrong, Yes sometimes,Then why don't you . . . turn about and fight for yourself.*[107]

There was "a fat black fellow" at one meeting at Vesey's who was thought, according to Bacchus, to be "Denmark's son, as he looked very much like Denmark." Vesey took Bacchus aside and told him, "We shan't be slaves to these damn rascals any longer. We must kill every one that we can get hold of, and drive the rest out of the city." All the men rose, raised their right hand, and vowed, "We will not tell if we are found out, and if they kill us we will not tell on any one." Monday Gell and Perault told Bacchus that Vesey "said that if they caught him, he would tell no body's name, and that I must not tell his, Perault's name, nor Monday's and they would not mention mine." However, Bacchus admitted, "The night they carried me to Denmark, I was so frightened that I was obliged to say yes; for they threatened to kill every one that did not wish to join."[108]

There was concern that "those waiting men who receive presents of old coats . . . from their masters" might, if recruited, carry the intelligence to their masters. But with so many native-born Africans in South Carolina, a horrible punishment for treachery would be recalled on hearing "The King Buzzard," a tale available to South Carolina blacks of Vesey's time. But there are limits to what the culture of a people can accomplish when they are faced with odds so overwhelming that life itself is threatened. Under such circumstances, those not determined to be free commit acts of treachery for the same reason they are slaves—out of fear of death—and so it was in the Vesey conspiracy. And since the genius of African culture could not save them from entrapment in the homeland, it could not after so short a period of time be expected to save them in American slavery. As essential as spiritual and artistic values were, more than that kind of culture was needed. A shattering of the structures of oppression was vital to freedom, and all available resources were drawn on by Vesey to that end.

Owing to his political genius, Africans were at the center of the conspiracy and at its far-flung reaches. An assignment took two of them to an African, "marked on both sides of his face" and called "old daddy," who would be joined at the appropriate time, at the farm he worked, by Negroes from the country. Vesey attempted to involve the high and the low among his people, those from the city and those from the countryside, the native born and those born elsewhere, believing they suffered a common fate. Within that diverse grouping were revealing networks of relationships, as when the Africans Perault and Caesar, close friends, conferred with each other and at times with Vesey:

Denmark told me that he gave the sword to Perault, and Perault gave it to a man named Caesar—I know no other Caesar but a Drayman named Caesar—Smith a tall Negro, an African, who is an intimate acquaintance of Perault's, and who is often at the stable where Perault keeps his horses—Perault told me that French Negroes were amongst them—Denmark said country born, African and all kinds joined—Monday and Perault appeared to be intimate friends of Denmark, he thought a heap of them—Denmark took the pistol for himself, it was given to him in his own hand—those meetings were held at Denmark's house, where he had a black wife—two or three women were at the house ironing.[109]

Vesey gave all his energies and thought to effecting the liberation of slaves within a wide radius of Charleston. It was a plan that counted on the involvement of several thousand slaves, those from the countryside figuring prominently in the enterprise. But it also counted greatly on the participation of urban slaves, who constituted over 60 percent of the Charleston population. That percentage and a slave-to-white ratio of nine to one in the countryside were distinctly advantageous to the conspirators and help account for the fear of South Carolinans that their slaves might one day rise against them. "Ultimate success," writes Freehling, "depended on a complete initial victory."

> If the . . . attacking bands captured the arsenal and roads, the impoverished, poorly armed insurgents would control almost all the weapons in Charleston and could hope to hold their own against the tidewater aristocracy. Plans were geared for winning the battle of Charleston: ultimate intentions were vague.[110]

A certain vagueness was in the nature of plans for slave revolts in North America, a product of the depressing knowledge that the overthrow of whites in the region of the revolt would not mean final freedom; rather, that victory was a prelude to more, seemingly endless battles if the revolutionaries hoped to remain on American soil. To carry out a plan to sail away, which might have been Vesey's intention since the Atlantic was nearby, would almost certainly have invited the predicament faced by Joseph Cinqué, who led a revolt on the Cuban slaver Amistad in 1839, and, more than three decades earlier, by Babo of the Trial: reliance on whites to navigate the ship. In both revolts at sea varying ethnicity was a factor, and in both the Africans displayed a capacity to work in concert, which again linked them to the Vesey conspiracy.[111]

In the Vesey conspiracy the very process by which Africans were being transformed into a single people is revealed. Vesey surrounded himself with lieutenants from several African ethnic groups: Monday Gell, an Ibo; Mingo Harth, a Mandingo; and Gullah Jack, an Angolan. His choice of leaders from different African peoples was designed to maximize cooperation among elements further down. Apparently, the involvement of such elements was considerable, Since Gell, Harth, and Jack led ethnic companies, which suggests that the bulk of slaves of fighting age may well have been a combination of African-born and first-generation American blacks. The conspiracy gave direct political expression to the values found in the folklore of South Carolina blacks, one in which Ibo and Congo-Angolan influences were considerable.[112]

As study of the conspiracy indicates, the cultural outlook of the slave with the greatest exposure to whites was not always, perhaps not usually, unidimensional or even primarily American. On the contrary, the most acculturated slaves, like slaves generally, appropriated values from the larger environment and relied on African values that pointed the way to creative solutions to a variety of problems, cultural and political. To find, for example, some aspects of Christianity extremely useful and satisfying did not mean—certainly not for most slaves or for most slave preachers— that they ceased to be African anymore than those blacks who embraced aspects of Christianity in Africa ceased to be African. That is the argument that one must make for slave culture, for at that time solutions to cultural problems were affirmed or rejected by Africans of different ethnic groups with aspects of African cultures in mind. But when African values were drawn on, there was no necessary opposition between being African and having command of or responding to the values of another people.

In the conspiracy, African nationalism provided the thrust toward autonomy, for diverse African peoples were represented and bent their efforts in pursuit of independence from their oppressors. Starobin notes, "The memory of their previous cultural identity and national independence was still strong, and they could appeal to other blacks on this basis." A "profound consciousness of the African homeland was certainly revealed when Prince Graham, after his conviction, at his own request, was transported to Africa on board a vessel which sailed from Charleston." That independence was their goal and national fulfillment the object of their quest was recognized by Starobin as essential to the conspiracy and represents a lasting contribution to black nationalist scholarship and to scholarship on American slavery. In fact, Starobin's conclusions parallel the ones of this book, that the profoundest critiques of black oppression in America came from native-born Africans and those close to them rather than from acculturated blacks.[113]

The spirit of disaffected black South Carolina Methodists—ministers, class leaders, and up to five thousand others, free and slave—was nationalistic, demonstrating that their former membership in the white Methodist church in Charleston was probably indicative of their lack of racism, and of the expectations of their masters. As developments following their break from white Methodism illustrated, African nationalism was strong in their consciousness. When slaves erected their own house of worship, the African Church, in the suburbs of Charleston in December of 1821, it was labor that made them more conscious of their dignity as human beings and represented an effort to institutionalize their spiritual autonomy. But there was certainly room for Vesey's brand of Christianity: "At the church and in his home, Vesey preached on the Bible, likening the Negroes to the children of Israel, and quoting passages which authorized slaves to massacre their masters. Joshua, chapter 4, verse 21, was a favorite citation: 'And they utterly destroyed all that was in the city, both man and woman, young and old, and ox, and sheep, and ass, with the edge of the sword.'"[114]

Off the coast of Charleston in 1816, African and European political ideals were united in a manner that anticipated Vesey's uses of the Bible. Indeed, the principles of the Age of Reason and those of African nationalism were joined, illustrating their compatibility for disaffected blacks who sang,

> Hail! all hail! ye Afric clan,
> Hail! ye oppressed, ye Afric band,
> Who toil and sweat in slavery bound
> And when your health and strength are gone
> Are left to hunger and to mourn,
> *Let independence be your aim,*
> Ever mindful what 'tis worth.
> Pledge your bodies for the prize,
> Pile them even to the skies![115]

A sense of African identity characterized the thought of these singers, who just as certainly felt the spirit of the Declaration of Independence, whether or not they had heard of it. In short, African and European political as well as religious ideals at times mingled and were united, the one preparing the ground for the other. Some who sang the song were said to have been involved in the Vesey conspiracy and probably attended the African Church, and there is no reason to doubt that more than one ethnic group was represented among the groups that sang of revolt and independence.

Since the transformation of Africans, under Vesey's leadership, was occurring on the highest levels, it follows that on the lower ones, with the example of the most gifted leaders before them, the mass of blacks were finding it easier to move toward oneness. The promotion of such ethnic harmony as one means of achieving independence from America was Vesey's achievement, his recognition of necessity: an ethnic conspiracy in which different ethnic leaders act in concert was a reflection of what was happening among ethnic groups in every area vital to the life of the slave in America. But such clearly orchestrated activity is what is particularly illuminating, for it affirmed the interests of the slaves as a whole. A sophisticated ideologue, Vesey promoted the use of radical Christianity and encouraged, through one of his lieutenants, its melding with African religious practices. "Beyond a general antiwhite attitude," Starobin writes, "Vesey combined the Old Testament's harsh morality and the story of the Israelites with African religious customs." Indeed, Vesey used Christian radicalism to reinforce and rationalize his call to arms:

Though Vesey's room was full I did not know one individual there. At this meeting Vesey said we were to take the Guard—House and Magazine to get arms; that we ought to rise up and fight against the whites for our liberties; he was the first to rise up and speak, and he *read to us from the Bible, how the children of Israel were delivered out of Egypt from bondage.*[116]

Vesey's brand of Christianity complemented the African religion of Gullah Jack. Jack drew on African cultural practices widespread in black Africa to encourage insurrection, preaching the conjuror's doctrine of invincibility. His personality, from all accounts, was African and as intact, despite the horror of the Atlantic voyage, as one could expect of one grounded in the heritage of his people. Purchased in Angola, he "had his conjuring implements with him in a bag which he brought on board the ship, and always retained them"—tangible evidence of his belief that his God lived. Described as a small man, "a Gullah Negro, with small hands and feet and large whiskers," Jack "kept alive African religious traditions," offering recruits African religious symbols "to guarantee victory." At a meeting at Vesey's, "Vesey supported Jack, referring to him as "*a little man named Jack, who could not be killed, and who . . . had a charm and he would lead them.*"

> Jack Pritchard also called on me about this business—he is sometimes called Gullah Jack, sometimes Cooter Jack; he gave me some dry food, consisting of parched corn and ground nuts, and said eat that and nothing else on the morning it breaks out . . . and you can't be wounded, and said he, I give the same to the rest of my troops.[117]

An Angolan said, as he looked in Jack's direction,

> Gullah Jack is an enemy of the white people. I attended a meeting of several at his house, and he was the head man there—all present agreed to join and come against the whites—Jack was my leader—he is the head of the Gullah Company—I heard that amongst them they had charms—Jack said if any man betrayed them, they would injure him, and I was afraid to inform—the little man standing before me is Gullah Jack, who had large black whiskers which he has cut since I last saw him. . . . I must beg the court to send me away from this place, *as I consider my life in great danger for having given testimony.* I have heard it said all about the streets, generally, I can't name any one in particular, that whoever is the white man's friend, God help them; from which I understood they would be killed—I was afraid of Gullah Jack as a conjuror. . . .[118]

William, "a Negro man belonging to Mr. John Paul," testified against Gullah Jack, saying that "all those belonging to the African Church are involved in the insurrection, from the country to the town—that there is a little man amongst them who can't be shot, killed or caught." And he reported that there was a "Gullah Society [a society of Angolans] going on which met once a month."[119] He did not directly link Gullah Jack to the African Church, nor did he link him to the African Association, which had two churches, but he did testify that both the African Association and the African Church were involved in the conspiracy. Secrecy shrouded the services of the African Church and the religion of the two churches of the African Association, secrecy born of the exigencies of planned revolt, secrecy natural to slaves worshiping in a town like Charleston. The churches of the association appear, because so little is known of them, to have been comfortable settings for a man like Jack, and almost certainly were centers of intense African religious worship. But it hardly matters which "church" Jack attended, since he moved with ease in the Charleston setting, persuading with his mystic powers:

> Until Jack was taken up and condemned to death, I felt as if I was bound up, and had not the power to speak one word about it—Jack charmed Julius and myself at last, and we then consented to join—Tom Russell the Blacksmith and Jack are partners, (in conjuring) Jack learnt him to be a Doctor. . . . Jack said Tom was his second and when you don't see me, and see Tom, you see me. Jack said Tom was making arms for the black people—Jack said he could not be killed, nor could a white man take him.[120]

The hats worn by Tom Russell as blacksmith and conjuror, as a skilled slave affirming African religious values, were not uncommon. It is proper to recall that Monday Gell, an Ibo, was "a harness maker who hired out his own labor and kept a workshop in the center of the city," and that Mingo Harth was a Mandingo and a mechanic. Though it is unclear whether Peter Poyas, a "first-rate" ship carpenter, was African born, there is no evidence that he objected, or was in a position to object, to the prominence of Africans and African values in preparing the conspiracy. Starobin writes that Vesey's "lieutenants were all slave craftsmen and preachers."

> Undoubtedly these slaves had through their work gained a greater sense of independence and more education than most common laborers. And artisans and preachers could articulate shared grievances more easily than most common laborers whose rage at oppression revealed itself mainly through action.[121]

The conspiracy was betrayed. This led one of the betrayers, Monday Gell, to testify against his fellow blacks in exchange for leniency, the court believing it "to be politic that the Negroes should know that even their principal advisers and ring leaders cannot be confided in, and that under the temptation of exemption from capital punishment they will betray the common cause." But Mingo Harth, Gullah Jack, Peter Poyas, Vesey, and other leaders held fast, Poyas "responding to the court's interrogation with only a 'cryptic smile,' and from the gallows stated to other blacks: 'Do not open your lips; die silent, as you shall see me do!'"[122] Vesey was unwavering, it appears, from the moment the plot was conceived until he silently met his end, defending himself, in the words of the court, "with great art and plausibility, to impress a belief of your innocence," before the "Sentence on Denmark Vesey, a free black man":

> Your "lamp of life" is nearly extinguished; your race is run; and you must shortly pass "from time to eternity." Let me then conjure you to devote the remnant of your existence in solemn preparation for the awful doom, that awaits you. Your situation is deplorable but not destitute of spiritual consolation. To that Almighty Being above, whose Holy Ordinances, you have trampled in the dust, can you now look for mercy, and although "your sins be as scarlet," the tears of sincere penitence may obtain forgiveness at the "Throne of Grace."[123]

Thirty-five blacks were hanged, over half one morning in a mass execution, their bodies dangling on a series of gallows. Fifty-three were released, either found innocent and discharged or not brought to trial and discharged. One found guilty was sentenced to be transported outside the state of South Carolina. Thirty-one were sentenced to death but pardoned on condition they be sent out of the United States, while eleven were found not guilty but their owners were required to send them outside the boundaries of the United States. More than forty blacks, therefore, were sent to Africa or to the West Indies.[124]

Freehling fully grasped the African dimension of the Vesey conspiracy, and the role of ethnicity in the 1820s: "Plantation owners who believed African immigrants were savages and had a large number of them trembled when they remembered Gullah Jack's witchery and the potency of old tribal loyalties," which was the root concern of an eminent South Carolina jurist, William Henry Desaussure, who had had no illusions about the African personality of slaves. Writing in the South Carolina *Gazette* in 1822, Desaussure put forth the thesis that, because of the outlawing of the slave trade, "that leaven of barbarism which was heretofore continually infused into the mass is thus withheld," which could mean "that the descendants, born and bred in the country, may gradually become a docile, and in some degree a civilized people." Desaussure thereby shed light on the cultural indebtedness of American-born blacks to their African parents. To be sure, he seemed none too hopeful that the acculturation process would take hold any time soon, although the trade had been outlawed. Moreover, he understood the connection between the religion of the African and the Africans' "barbarous" qualities, wisely if cruelly recommending that the slaves "should have no separate place of worship."[125]

Many slaves, as a direct consequence of the Vesey conspiracy, could no longer worship in Carolina churches, for the conspiracy "demonstrated that churches could be centers of intrigue and that slaves could acquire what seemed to Carolinians the most erroneous religious visions." Consequently class meetings and Negro churches were disbanded. A long debate ensued over the matter of reading the Bible. . . . Teaching slaves to read, although not legally barred for over a decade, had largely ended by 1822. Even oral religious training was frowned on. Some slaves attended services with their masters, but in the lowcountry no missionaries sought out the vast majority of bondsmen who lived miles from a white church. Slave preachers supplied coastal Negroes with the only available religious instruction. Soon these meetings were discouraged. . . . Most tidewater slaves were "left without any religious instruction."[126]

VI

Fredrika Bremer witnessed, in a "separate place of worship," an expression of Africanity that in some ways seems almost as obscure as the most inaccessible aspect of the ceremony in South Carolina's Red Hill Churchyard or the one in Virginia in which the staff-cross was used as the slaves worshiped. But unlike most African ceremonies in America under review here, the one described by Bremer, which occurred in the 1850s in New Orleans, appears not to have a precise analogue in Africa. Indeed, an incontestably African outlook, such as reverence for the ancestors, is not apparent from Bremer's description despite her belief that what she witnessed, for all the genuineness of its Christianity, was African. Her account of what took place is particularly useful because it is one of the few on record in which the religious ceremonies of slaves in separate churches are described in detail. What Bremer saw occurred under circumstances that the South Carolina jurist thought most likely to encourage the continuation of "African barbarism." She visited what was, despite the passage of thirty years, in some respects—not the least of which was that the New Orleans slaves were "Methodists" with class leaders—the New Orleans counterpart to the Charleston African Church attended by the Vesey conspirators.

The Christian and African aspects of the ceremony witnessed in New Orleans so complemented each other, were in such reciprocal relation, that the two faiths appear altogether harmonious though each stands out vividly, the one a catalyst for the other. Yet, as Bremer notes, the defining faith is ultimately African, an "African Tornado," though the setting was one in which "Sunday schools for Negro children" provided "instruction about the Savior." Though she had seen black Methodists in Washington, D.C., where the ring shout was a powerful influence in the lives of blacks, her expectations "were quite exceeded" in New Orleans: "Here we were nearer the tropical sun than at Washington."[127]

Christian elements in the ceremony were unmistakable, as African religious leaders calmly preached the Christian Gospel in an atmosphere otherwise hardly Christian. The tempo of activity at the start of the ceremony was relaxed and slow but quickened as exhorters moved along the benches and stopped to talk to individual worshipers during the "so-called class meeting." "These exhorters," Bremer observes, "go around at the class-meeting to such of the members of their class as they deem to stand in need of consolation or encouragement, talk to them, aloud or in an under voice, receive their confession, impart advice to them, and so on." The exhorters' words quickly served to establish an antiphonal rela-tionship, the action accelerating, the exhorters' calls answered by the consoled, who experienced exaltation and began "to speak and to per-orate more loudly and more vehemently than the exhorter himself, and so to overpower him"—a scene not unlike the ceremony around Sister Di-cey's grave when the preacher's voice was drowned out by responsive singing and shouting and hand clapping.

> There was one exhorter in particular, whose black, good-natured counte-nance was illumined by so great a degree of inward light, by so much good-humor and joy, that it was a pleasure to see him and to hear him, too; for although his phrases were pretty much the same, and the same over again, yet they were words full of Christian pith and marrow, and they were uttered with so much cordiality, that they could not do other than go straight to the heart with enlivening power. . . . And it was only as the messenger of the joy in Christ that he preached.[128]

That the preaching of the exhorter—the regular sermon had ended be-fore Bremer and her associates arrived at the church—was Christian un-derscored the defining power of African religious faith as registered in the response it evoked. Messages such as

> Hold fast by Christ! He is the mighty One! He will help! He will do everything well! Trust in him my sister, my brother. Call upon Him. Yes. Yes. Hold fast by Christ! He is the Lord!

before long evoked a leaping response from the worshipers like "corn starting to pop over a hot fire." It represented the Africanization of Chris-tianity not only in emotive and intuitive force but in a larger religious sense:

> By degrees the noise increased in the church and became a storm of voices and cries. The words were heard, "Yes, come, Lord, Jesus! come oh come, oh glory!" and they who thus cried aloud began to leap—leaped aloft with a motion as of a cork flying out of a bottle, while in the air, as if they were endeavoring to bring something down, and all the while crying aloud, "Come, oh come!" And as they leaped, they twisted their bodies round in a sort of corkscrew fashion, and were evidently in a state of convulsion; some-times they fell down and rolled in the aisle, amid loud, lamenting cries and groans. . . . Whichever way we looked in the church, we saw somebody leaping up and fanning the air; the whole church seemed transformed into a regular bedlam, and the noise and tumult was horrible.[129]

In that atmosphere, the "tropical exhorter, the man with the sunbright countenance," together with the other exhorters, made his rounds, perfectly at home, "as if everything were going on as if it ought to do." Just a few words from an exhorter to a tall, handsome mulatto woman drew words from her that took the shape of art. Like musical instruments at play, the woman and the exhorter preached to each other, conveying a Christian message through an African form. They preached with pleasure until "she sprang aloft with such vehemence that three other women took hold of her by the skirts, as if to hold her on the earth." Still she leaped and twisted and threw her arms about before falling and rolling about "amid convulsive groans." Her rising and walking from one part of the church to another exclaiming "Hallelujah!" meant that Christianity was being used to affirm and spur on the African faith and the African religion Christianity as the ceremony built to a climax:

> Amid all the wild tumult of crying and leaping, on the right hand and the left, she continued to walk up and down the church in all directions, with outspread arms, eyes cast upward, exclaiming in a low voice, "Hallelujah! Hallelujah!" At length she sank down upon her knees on the platform by the altar, and there she became still. . . . What has happened to her? we inquired from a young negro girl whom she knew. "Converted!" said she laconically, and joined those who were softly rubbing the palms of the converted.[130]

This scene calls to mind the relationship of the preacher to his congregation in the sanctified churches of Chicago and Harlem, where the congregation is on its feet responding to the preacher, dancing and shouting. Moreover, Melville and Frances Herskovits, in *Rebel Destiny*, note similarities between Suriname blacks, those of the Gold Coast of West Africa, and blacks in sanctified churches in the United States, where the "saints" dance and shout. A marvelous description of the process that occurs when blacks in America in our time are most African when worshiping is found in James Baldwin's *The Fire Next Time*. What is described is of the twentieth century and of the nineteenth, and in a number of respects is remarkably similar to what Bremer found in the New Orleans ceremony. Baldwin writes,

> There is no music like that music, no drama like the drama of the saints rejoicing, the sinners moaning, the tambourines racing, and all those voices coming together and crying holy unto the Lord. There is still, for me, no pathos quite like the pathos of those multi-colored, worn, somehow triumphant and transfigured faces, speaking from the depths of a visible, tangible, continuing despair of the goodness of the Lord. I have never seen anything to equal the fire and excitement that sometimes, without warning, fill a church, causing the church, as Leadbelly and so many others have testified, to "rock." Nothing that has happened to me since equals the power and the glory that I sometimes felt when, in the middle of a sermon, I knew that I was somehow, by some miracle, really carrying, as they said, "the Word"—

when the church and I were one. Their pain and their joy were mine, and mine were theirs—they surrendered their pain and their joy to me, I surrendered mine to them—and their cries of "Amen!" and "Hallelujah!" and "Yes, Lord!" and "Praise His Name!" and "Preach it, brother!" sustained and whipped on my solos until we all became equal, wringing wet, singing and dancing in anguish and rejoicing, at the foot of the altar.[131]

As W. E. B. Du Bois recognized, possession during religious ceremonies is not new to the world, not the exclusive experience of a particular people, but is ancient and transcultural.[132] The context and content of its occurrence, however, may differ markedly, as we see, in contrast to European tradition, in ring ceremonies designed for ancestors to take possession of the celebrant at the highest point of exaltation. And even when black Christians experienced possession, it was mainly in that same circular context where the degree of emotional fervor and the intensity of convulsions—and the particulars of dance that finally give way to them—were also African. Especially in the tradition of Africans in America, passions are unleashed that are to some extent called forth and polarized by oppression.

The ultimate expression of the passion witnessed by Bremer and Baldwin indicates that the community in which the celebrant attains such a state basically rejects the authority of those who exercise control over it, since outbursts of general fervor, followed by the incapacitation of some worshipers through possession and convulsions, challenged the master's sense of discipline (unlike drunkenness, in that its sources were not understood and its particular flowering remained, therefore, a mystery). The anthropologist Mary Douglas comments, "I don't ask why people are doing it [having convulsions], but why they are not doing it."[133] That perception enables us to grasp what was powerfully felt by the slave master—that what was not understood and seemed not to lend itself to discipline was threatening and consequently should be discouraged—and this was a principal reason for Africans continuing to practice their religion. But there was a more important reason for the persistence of certain features of the Africans' faith. In slavery, African religion, while losing its character in some respects, was intensified in others because of the need to gain relief, however temporary, from oppression by throwing one's whole being into the ceremony and giving oneself up totally to a more transcendent state, in which the ancestors—and possibly the gods—enter approvingly upon the communal ground of being.[134] In the process, indescribable suffering and grief are given ritualistic expression and briefly overcome, and slaves were aware of how such an experience differed in content and form from white worship, as Simon Brown notes in "How the Slaves Worshipped."

Where slaves had Christianity largely under their control, what usually occurred was what occurred in New Orleans—conversion within the circle of culture. But that conversion in New Orleans, in the case of the slaves observed by Bremer, was under conditions as calculated to protect them from censure as those in the Virginia conversion ceremony described by Simon Brown. In New Orleans and Virginia the exhorter, while consciously Christian, was as African in faith as Brer Rabbit in Red Hill Churchyard. Bremer tells us, "The tornado gradually subsided in the church, shrieking and leaping, admonishing and preaching, all became hushed." The key to the precise nature of African religion in the ceremony is in that sentence. It unlocks mysteries of the relationship of the exhorter and worshiper in the New Orleans church, for in *Elements of Weather* we read, "Tornadoes are revolving storms, turning counterclockwise in the Northern hemisphere."[135]

The ring shout comes vividly to mind, the force of the ceremony witnessed by Bremer suggesting tremendous African religiosity a few years before the end of slavery. Within the circle new life was breathed into Christianity, as the African felt the need for a salvation from slavery that, it must have seemed, only a miracle could effect. Hence the appeal of Christianity: "He is the mighty One! He will help!" But Christ did not replace the God of the Africans, for the African God was more an Absentee Landlord than a personal God on intimate terms with His followers; this helps explain, together with the brutality to which the slaves were subjected, the prominent strain of fatalism in the fabric of so much of black folk life and lore. The circle of culture had plenty of room for Jesus, and there he was received as he could not have been through racist pastoring. In the African Church, there was no segregation, and no one was told he was born to serve. What Bremer witnessed was Christianity shot through with African values, and she said as much. In that church, the Africans did not end their conversion ceremony because whites were present, as they were known to do at camp meeting conversions, for their leaping movement in the church had no apparent connection with the ring shout. It is possible, moreover, that the constricted architecture of the church ruled out the conventional shout except in front of the altar unless the benches were movable (in the New Orleans ceremony in question, there is no indication that they were). What is crucial here is that leaping was at times a variant of the ring ceremony in Africa, which made such a maneuver useful as a force for affirming the African religious vision in America, without being easily associated with the outlawed ring shout. Though not devised to conceal the ring shout, leaping served, like the staff-cross, to give powerful expression to its meaning.

The long and narrow aisles became the place for many to gather and leap as others leaped from where they sat. In this regard, it should be noted that leaping or jumping was associated with the shout by Bishop Payne, who saw the shout performed in and out of churches before all-black groups. Unlike others, he had no illusions about the relationship between the shout and jumping, having seen both in churches in which he was defied, and on one occasion, in Maryland, physically attacked, by his people. Perhaps herein lies part of the answer we are seeking concerning the dance movement employed in New Orleans: since blacks in churches pastored by Payne did not hesitate to do the ring shout collectively, there was no reason for them to jump about to disguise anything, which indicates that the leaping movement referred to by Payne and Bremer—and later by Stearns—may be associated with some versions of the ring ceremony in Africa as in America.[136]

The constricted quarters of the church, the proselytizing manner of the exhorters, and the confessional aspects of Christianity all encouraged a subjective experience of great intensity, which was heightened by the accelerating rhythms of the "preachers" as they faced each other. There was much to confess about oppression, so it is small wonder that slaves in the New Orleans church, like those observed by Simon Brown in "How the Slaves Worshipped," broke down and cried in a tumult of lamentation. The possibility should be seriously entertained that the spirit possession of the ring shout, and as slaves leaped in the air, is a principal source of "shouting" in most black churches today. In that and other respects, the ring ceremony and the art associated with it, such as the spirituals, often underwent change when introduced into the church. But since it was common practice for the ring shout to be seen in front of altars of black churches, the ceremony reaching its high point when spirit possession ensued, the shouting in the ring and that of the leapers probably constitute the antecedents of shouting as we know it in black churches today.

As African dance movement underwent change in the church—except for dance in the area of the altar, in which only so many could participate—the singing of the spirituals was altered, especially when not accompanied by the counterclockwise movements of groups of dancing worshipers. Though the swaying of the body and the clapping of hands could be done from the benches and elsewhere, on the whole it was not nearly as easy to engage the many parts of the body in the performance; this affected the rendering of the spirituals, especially as efforts to rid black churches of the shout and the singing of spirituals while not dancing were mounted before and after emancipation. The deemphasis on dance meant more stress on the words, a development associated with the introduction of choirs and "audiences." Even so, those audiences of slaves and ex-slaves were not like white audiences, which did not sway with the music and erupt, individually and collectively, in responsive song. Meanwhile, the line between the spirituals and Gospel music in the church, as on the plantation, was frequently obliterated in response to the propulsive clapping of hands, stomping of feet, and swaying of bodies. And we should remember that urban slaves were not divorced from the larger black community, in which the shout touched the lives of almost everyone. This could hardly have been otherwise, especially since slaves from the countryside were at times in attendance at slave churches in cities.[137]

Following the lead of whites, some black ministers inveighed against dance in religious ceremonies. But in and out of church blacks found ways of getting around Christian strictures when not ignoring them altogether, as they often did. "I have since heard it said," writes Bremer, "that the Methodist missionaries, who are the most effective teachers of and preachers among the Negroes, are very angry with them for their love of dancing and music, and declare them to be sinful." Though she is correct in noting such hatred of African music and dance—the missionaries would hardly have opposed one without the other, since music and dance were to the African all but inseparable—she is in error when she goes on to state, "And whenever the Negroes become Christian, they give up dancing, having preaching meetings instead, and employ their musical talents merely on psalms and hymns." In fairness to her, it must be said that she made that observation before she attended the camp meetings in which slaves were converted and before she visited the all-black New Orleans church in which slaves worshiped. Still, she would "let them have sacred dances, and let them sing to them joyful songs of praise in the beautiful air beneath the flowering trees," a position opposed by white practioners of Christianity and by free Negro Christians.[138]

Rather "thoroughly amused by the frolic," Bremer revealed a limited understanding of the precise nature of what she experienced in the African Church. Yet she perceived that it was indeed a religious ceremony and not, because of the vigor of bodily movement or the joy and pain, "semi-religious." In a passage that recalls a Thomas Wentworth Higginson description of a ring shout, Bremer writes, "Of the whole raging, exciting scene there remained merely a feeling of satisfaction and pleasure, as if they had been together at some joyful feast."[139] In her account, we find Africans at home with Christianity because they did not permit the essence of their faith to be violated by their adoption of tenets of the new religion. Indeed, hers is perhaps the best portrayal in print of "Christian" exhorters, amid the most extraordinary African religious passion, serenely going about their work. Despite her belief that blacks were not generally equal to whites, she sensed the potential importance of African religion to America and to the West:

In spite of all the irrationality and want of good taste which may be felt in such scenes, I am certain that there is in them, although as yet in a chaotic state, the element of true African worship. Give only intelligence, order, system to this outbreak of the warm emotions, longings, and presentiments of life, and then that which now appears hideous will become beautiful, that which is discordant will become harmonious. The children of Africa may yet give us a form of divine worship in which invocation, supplication, and songs of praise may respond to the inner life of the fervent soul!

How many there are, even in our cold North, who in their youthful years have felt an Africa of religious life, and who might have produced glorious flowers and fruits if it only could have existed—if it had not been smothered by the snow and the gray coldness of conventionality—had not been imprisoned in the stone church of custom.[140]

That was slave religion in New Orleans in the fifties, a city noted for Congo Square and public expressions of Africanity, the very name of the square an indication of the place of origin and style of ceremony of many of the slaves in the Louisiana area. More precisely, Congo-Angola blacks, and certainly descendants of Africans from those areas, were found there in abundance during slavery, as were numerous signs of their presence in dance and musical expression, and in the sign of the cross with the circle touching its four points, forming the four corners of the earth. In addition to Congo-Angola blacks, there were many from other African civilizations in Louisiana who interacted musically with each other and, through the relative freedom city life provided, with Europeans.

The tremendous creative energies released, when Kongo-derived traditions combined in New Orleans with those from the equally sophisticated Malian, Nigerian, and Cameroonian traditional civilizations, must have been amazing. This does not even take into account the final fillip, the blending of all that with the equally complex mix of musics—French, Spanish, and English—in that culturally strategic city.[141]

Frederick Law Olmsted observed that three-fourths of the slaves on Louisiana plantations in the 1850s were "thorough-bred Africans," and he found the same proportion of Africans on Mississippi plantations.[142] He meant thorough-bred in culture, which suggests the continuing power of African culture when passed from one generation to another. His attribution of Africanity to the great bulk of slaves in those states is supported by his observations regarding their religious practices. While walking in "a rather mean neighborhood" in New Orleans one morning, he was drawn to an open door of a church, entered, and was given "the uppermost seat facing the pulpit where there were three other white persons," one of whom "was probably a member of the police force in undress—what we call spy when we detect it in Europe." Scenes of tumult followed that recall those in the African Church visited by Bremer. While many in the congregation had "light hair and hardly any perceptible indications of having African blood," their behavior was generally indistinguishable from that of the darkest of blacks.[143] There was something infectious about the ritual, an "indescribable" ecstasy of "stamping, jumping and clapping of hands":

The tumult often resembled that of an excited political meeting; and I was once surprised to find my own muscles all stretched, as if ready for a struggle—my face glowing, and my feet stamping—having been affected unconsciously, as men often are, with instinctive bodily sympathy with the excitement of the crowd . . . and I have no doubt that it was [the preacher's] "action" rather than his sentiments, that had given rise to the excitement of the congregation.[144]

With that, Olmsted demonstrated his understanding of a feature of Negro-African culture that is as important to the preacher as to the singer of sacred or secular song. Though the preacher's message was ostensibly Christian, his performance style, as at the church attended by Bremer, was African, the rhythms of his delivery stirring some to jump and clap their hands and others to shriek in a voice "impossible to be expressed in letters." As the first preacher drew his sermon to an end,

a small old woman, perfectly black, among those in the gallery, suddenly rose, and began dancing and clapping her hands; at first, with a slow and measured movement, and then with increasing rapidity, at the same time beginning to shout "ha! Ha!" The women about her arose also, and tried to hold her as there appeared great danger that she might fall out of the gallery, and those below left their pews that she might not fall on them.[145]

Then "a tall, full-blooded negro" with "a disgusting expression of sensuality, cunning and vanity in his countenance" rose to preach. At times "breaking out into a yell with all the strength of extraordinarily powerful lungs," his striking attitude and extraordinary gestures created an excitement in the congregation that led to "the loudest and most terrific shouts," which could be compared to "nothing else human" one might hear. In language generally unintelligible, the preacher engaged irreligious forces in combat, shadowboxing, countering imaginary blows with "knock-down" replies. As he strode before the congregation and engaged evil, four people went into hysterics, but none so violently as the woman in the gallery.[146] In time, the seeming chaos of ecstasy was ordered by song. The preacher had picked up the sole hymnal in the church and repeated "the number and page and the first two lines" of a song. "These were sung, and he repeated the next, and so on, as in the South Presbyterian Service." As the congregation sang, its movements were those of sacred and secular singing groups in the mid-twentieth century:

I think every one joined, even the children, and the collective sound was wonderful. The voices of one or two women rose above the rest, and one of these soon began to introduce variations, which consisted mainly of shouts of oh! oh! at a piercing height. Many of the singers kept time with their feet, balancing themselves on each alternately, and swinging their bodies accordingly.

It is evident, from Olmsted's description of the ceremony, that, while a hymn was being sung, rhythms of the ring shout, which were the rhythms of the spirituals, were being applied as the Africans took possession of the hymn. And there was little apparent concern that whites were present as the preacher raised his voice above all others, clapped his hands, laughed aloud, then danced "first with his back, and then with his face to the audience."[147]

Indeed, Olmsted refers to him as "the dancer," and there is no doubt that he, the other preachers, and the congregation brought dance into the church, as Africans in another part of the city had done when Bremer attended their church. Here, as in the earlier case, the dance was distinctly African, involving a leaping about and a flailing of arms. As the singing ended, the preacher "continued his movements, leaping with increasing agility, from one side of the pulpit to the other," his movements threatening the security of the preachers "shut into the pulpit" as he threw himself back and jammed one, "who was trying to restrain him, against the wall."[148] The architecture of the church not only limited the freedom of the shouters but also, under the circumstances, threatened the physical well-being of those near the shouters. What would otherwise have been a concerted shout involving up to fifteen people was in that setting fragmented by the fear of injury in such constricting surroundings.

The thought that those who danced in the gallery might lose their footing and fall to the main floor caused those below to leave their pews so that the dancer or dancers would not fall upon them. As the tall preacher demonstrated, those in the pulpit were in great enough danger, especially since, as with individual dancers elsewhere, the order of group performance, with its rhythms regulating the movements of all, was in this case absent, the violent jerks of arms and legs "like a supple-jack, in every direction," increasing the danger of injury. It is little wonder that the preacher who leaped about like those who formed the tornado ended up with another preacher "sitting on the stair holding his head on his shoulder, and grasping one of his hands, while his feet were extended up into the pulpit." The prostrate man rose and released the young preacher, who pronounced, ironically enough, "the Apostle's blessing."[149] The poor spy, who had more than enough to report concerning "dance," must have left more than a little confused.

William Wells Brown observed ceremonies in which Negro spirituals were sung and the shout was done with great vigor. His description of African religion in a Nashville church recalls both Bremer and Olmsted, which deepens our understanding of the ring shout and the contexts of its expression after slavery. It was in 1880 that he encountered the shout and thought that it contributed to "moral and social degradation," failing to note the irony of his observation that its practitioners were "generous to a fault." At St. Paul's in Nashville—he does not give its denomination— the minister used a Christian theme to excite those in his congregation to dance. Women first moved their heads, then began "a shout," with five or six "fairly at it, which threw the house into a buzz. Seats were soon vacated near the shouters, to give them more room, because the women did not wish to have their hats smashed by the frenzied sisters."[150] Here was an instance of shouting in coordinated form with little or no leaping, the area of or near the pulpit being the place of ceremony. In that Nashville church, the small ring was enlarged as others joined in, the tempo at intervals challenging some to enter with vigor.

> The shouting now became general; a dozen or more entering into it most heartily. These demonstrations increased or abated, according to movements of the leaders, who were in and about the pulpit; for the minister had closed his discourse and first one, and then another would engage in prayer. The meeting was kept up till a late hour, during which, four or five sisters becoming exhausted, had fallen upon the floor and lay there or had been removed by their friends.[151]

The constraining church architecture, with its benches and chairs, was the setting, undoubtedly, of individual, as opposed to collective, shouting in the black church; indeed, it was the setting in which the shout was practically divorced from dance for those who could not get to an aisle or to the area of the pulpit; overcome nonetheless, one had little choice but to get to one's feet and cry out, struggling for room in which to move.

In the 1880s in Tennessee, there were no signs that the ring and associated forms of religious expression were disappearing. There was "the wildest excitement" at "one of the most refined congregations" in Nashville. Brown concluded that it would not be easy "to erase from the mind of the Negro of the South the prevailing idea that outward demonstrations, such as shouting, the loud 'amen,' and the most boisterous noise in prayer are not necessary of piety."[152] The scene was not dissimilar to what Bremer witnessed—"not less than ten or fifteen were shouting in various parts of the house," and "four or five were going from seat to seat shaking hands with the occupants of the pews"—as call and response punctuated dance and song. Shouting was the ultimate test of religiosity in that Nashville church. One young lady of "good education and refinement" said that "not until she had one shouting spell did most of her Sisters believe she had the witness.'" She was told by one of her sisters, "Sister Smith, I hope to live to see you show that you've got the witness for where the grace of God is, there will be shouting, and the sooner you comes to that point the better it will be for you in the world to come."[153]

Institutions other than the church existed to help blacks prepare for "the world to come." Indeed, as William Wells Brown understood it, a powerful current of African faith swept the black South: "To get religion, join a benevolent society that will pay them 'sick dues' when they are ill, and to bury them when they die, appears to be the beginning, the aim, and the end of the desires of the colored people of the South." In Petersburg, Virginia, he was told that there were "thirty-two different secret-- societies," and he "met persons who held membership in four at the same time."[154] Brown correctly reasoned that much of the stimulus for the securing of homes and the providing for other expenses is taken away by multiple attachments to secret societies for protection during illness and for burial at death. What he did not know was that without a proper burial it was thought the spirit would be restless and the relatives of the deceased might fall on hard times.

V I I

Coming from cultures in which work and art were united so completely that any notion of art for art's sake lacked meaning, Africans in North America created while working, as they had done before. For all the comparative leisure available to whites, the African used his imagination to reflect on life in the new land with an originality sufficient to bring indigenous artistic forms into being. The objective reality that Africans combined, under the humiliating circumstances of slavery, the hardest and most prolonged work with a creativity the Helots never knew, illustrates that their influence on the development of the country, culturally and economically, was greatly disproportionate to their numbers. And slave creativity helped ease the pain of labor that might otherwise have been intolerable. Above all, strength was drawn from the ancestral spirits, and from the Creator of the fruits of labor.

At harvest time in Virginia and elsewhere, dances were held outdoors to climax the planting season, an expression of the slaves' gratefulness to forces bigger than man, to the ancestral spirits for the fertility of the soil and the renewal of the life process. Such celebrations were frequent on the plantations of the South. One survivor of slavery recalled, "Everybody bring some uh duh fus crops. We all gib tanks fuh duh crop an we dance and sing." An elderly Georgia woman, a youth when emancipated from slavery, recalled in the 1930s, "We pray and gib tanks fuh duh crop and pray fuh duh nex yeah. We all eat and sing an dance. One uh duh dances call duh Buzzard Lope. We still dance dat today." Henry Williams, when almost ninety years of age, recalled slave festivals in Georgia in the late 1840s and during the 1850s with an accuracy and vividness that support the sources on the subject. Again there is the same dominating, organizing symbol:

> Remembuh the big times we use tuh have wen I wuz young. We does plenty uh dances in those days. Dance roun in a ring. We has a big time long bout wen crops come in an evrybody bring sumpin tuh eat wut they makes an we all give praise fuh the good crop and then we shouts an sings all night. An wen the sun rise, we stahts tuh dance.[155]

"Hahves time wuz time fuh drums," the ex-slave Katie Brown remembered. It was also time for rattling "dry goad wid seed in um" and for beating flat tin plates. "Dey shout an moob roun in succle an look lak mahch goin tuh heabm."[156]

Harvest festivals were excellent occasions for passing on African cultural traits from one generation to the next. Some of the best dancing and music took place then, because of the high purpose of the occasion. Aware that few if any whites understood the deeper purpose of the festival, blacks found it an ideal situation, within the context of oppression, for them to give full expression to their Africanity:

> We use tuh hab big times duh fus hahves, and duh fus ting wut growed we take tuh duh chuch so as ebrybody could hab a piece ub it. We pray obuh it and shout. Wen we hab a dance, we use tuh shout in a ring. We ain't have wut yuh call a propuh dance tuhday. . . . One uh duh dances wuz called duh Buzzard Lope.[157]

Slave celebrations were regarded by whites, who allowed them to take place, as "innocent pleasures," though harvest festivals had existed for centuries in Africa before blacks had arrived in North America. "The festival dance was commonly a 'cake-walk,'" writes Roscoe Lewis in *The Negro in Virginia*. The slaves assembled in large numbers in "their Sunday best and with glowing tallow dips or pine knots forming a ring of light. . . . The cake-walk has been ascribed to African tribal celebrations." And like dance in African celebrations, the cake-walk and other dances at festival time on Virginia plantations usually represented vital aspects of religious expression. In that context, festivities and work were combined at corn-shucking time, with specific kinds of work an inspiration to slave creativity. While some slaves formed their glowing circle with pine knots, others, in the center, danced "the motions of labor,—swinging a scythe, tossing a pitchfork of hay into a wagon, hoisting a cotton-bale, rolling a hogshead of tobacco, sawing wood, hoeing corn—without the restriction and effort imposed by the load."[158] In that dance the slave reviewed much of the labor performed on the plantation that made it possible for the master to exist and to prosper. In the New World, that kind of festival dance was a means of distancing slaves from the purely exploitative reality of work, of extracting from the experience spiritual and artistic rewards, which helped slaves affirm their dignity through labor.

Important here are the specific forms of work and the uses to which work is put in a ceremony analogous to the martial dances of the various African women in Dahomey. In both cases we have responses to the environment that transcend ethnic considerations but reflect an unmistakable African response to problems common to all. Dances like "pitchin' hay," "corn-shuckin'," "cuttin' wheat," and "spottin'" (dancing with the hands and other parts of the body without moving the feet) are as African as the buzzard lope. So are the "pony's prance," "the Swan's bend," the "kangaroo," and "shooting the chute"—all of which could be a part of dance competitions during festivals and helped establish the precedent for later "cutting" sessions in which jazz artists exchange ideas. Those watching the festival dances usually acclaimed the winners, demanding that the couple continue to dance: "When the judges had made their decisions (it was a brave judge who went against the decision of the crowd), the other couples were called to the sidelines."[159]

In general, Saturday nights were spent as slaves pleased, as long as they remained in the quarters. But when they had the opportunity, they left the quarters for greater privacy in the woods. At times, dances conceived for religious purposes were performed in a setting that to Westerners might appear to serve mainly for entertainment but that to the African was suffused with religious spirit. The use of sacred dance for entertainment was natural to the ancestors of those whose dances today derive mainly from slave sacred dance. Moreover, there is no convincing evidence that the rhythms of sacred dance or music required much change when used outside the circle in which they were most often felt and heard. The scene on one such occasion in Virginia in the late 1840s or 1850s was clearly African; what at first appears secular was from the African vantage point sacred, the influence of Christianity coloring the retrospective view:

> But Sadday nights we'd slip out de quarters an' go to de woods. Was a ole cabin 'bout five miles 'way from de house, an' us would raise all de ruckus dere we wanted. . . . Ev'y gal wid her beau, an' sech music! Had two fiddles, two tangerines, two banjos, an' two sets of bones. Was a boy named Joe dat used to whistle too. Dem devilish boys would git out in de middle of de flo' an' me, Jenny, and de devil right wid 'em.[160]

The African presence was evident in musical instruments, in the formal dance expression, and in the placing of an object on the woman's head as she danced:

> Set a glass of water on my haid, an' de boys would bet on it. I had a great big wreaf roun' my haid an' a big ribbon bow on each side, an' didn't waste a drop of water on none of 'em. Dem was de days when me, Jenny, and de devil was runnin' in de depths of hell.

Apparently that last sentiment was not so firmly held when she was young: "Wouldn't do it now fo' nothin'. Lord Christ in heaven, God knows I didn't know no better."[161] And she was young, considering her testimony in the 1930s, in the last years of slavery, perhaps only in her teens. From the references to her youth, this ex-slave found nothing "sinful" about dancing while in slavery, nor did her peers or most of the older people around them. Sometime following slavery, perhaps much later in life, judging from the strength of African religious values for most ex-slaves decades following slavery, she came to regard such practices of her youth with some regret. Still, there is no reason to believe she lacked the ability or, for that matter, the inclination to do the dances in old age.

Slaves preferred to be as far away from the big house as possible: "We used to git back in de end cabin an' sing an' dance by de fiddle till day break. Sho' had one time, swingin' dem one piece dresses back an' fourth, an' de boys crackin' dey coattails in de wind." In that description by the eighty-two-year-old Charles Hancock, one can imagine the movements of the jitterbug, prominent in the North in the 1940s, but the sacred sources of which predated the arrival of the first African in North America: the left hand of the man clasping the woman's right hand, his right arm around her waist guiding her as they release each other's hand, their attire swinging in the wind. Again, from Hancock's description, emblems of Africanity: "Den dey would set a glass of water on dey haid an' see how many kinds of steps dey could make widout spillin' de water."[162] Improvisational dance under difficult circumstances was a successful test of continuing Africanity, when the water was balanced and a variety of dance figures were executed.

In North Carolina towns, especially on Christmas Day, slaves in groups of ten to twenty played instruments and sang songs "not remarkable for their melody but of pronounced rhythm":

SOLO: Young gal go ROUND de corner!
CHORUS IN HARMONY: My true love gone Down de lane!
SOLO: Wet on de grass where de djew been poured.
CHORUS: Hey, me lady, go Down de road;
Go DOWN de road; go Down de road!
My true love gone Down de lane.

As whites and a few blacks crowded before them, one of their number danced up to the crowd for a few coins as others rattled bones, danced, and shouted

Hah! Low! Here we go!
Hah! Low! Here we go!
Hah! Low! Kuners comin'[163]

before disappearing to collect more contributions. This ceremony, which outlasted slavery, was African. Initial performances, dating from the eighteenth century, were very likely conducted for slaves, the singing in African languages. By the nineteenth century, the words of the songs heard by whites were English, but the overall effect of the ceremony could scarcely have been more African to the slaves, nor could the means of achieving it in musical instruments, dance and mode of singing, and attire. Whether in North Carolina cities or in the countryside, the general effect and purpose were African:

They were dressed in "tatters," strips of cloth of gay colors sewn to their usual garments and producing an effect of exotic grotesquerie. All were men, but a few wore the clothes and acted the parts of women actors . . . frequently wore masks known as kunerfaces. . . . The leader carried a raw-hide whip with which he prevented interference from urchins in the streets.[164]

Thought by Europeans to be mainly for children, the ceremony, called John Kunering, had a deeper significance. The literature of West African secret societies seems to indicate that it was only because the original Kuners and their descendants in America were slaves that children and women were able to congregate before them to be entertained. Of a Nigerian ritual that closely resembles John Kunering, Talbot writes, "In many cases the headdress consists of human masks which appear to have originally represented the ancestors who had returned to life for the occasion; while the dances are expressions of prayer to the forefathers for the granting of fertility in crops and children." Talbot adds, concerning the people of Southern Nigeria, that the mysteries of the ceremony "are kept from women." The principal festival takes place

in June, when the crops are ripening in the farms, the first fruits begin to come in and the help of the dead is most needed. The eve of the festival is called Ikunle, kneeling, since the principal members spend the whole night in the sacred grove on their knees while they hold communion with, and pray to, the ancestors. . . . The Images, dressed in their long robes with a net or wooden mask over the face, parade the streets, jumping about [dancing] . . . accompanied by friends who keep the bystanders at a distance with their long wands.[165]

The critical point here is that the ceremony was performed to honor the ancestors, especially those who founded towns: "The next morning, following the night in the sacred grove, they form a procession to visit the ruler of the town, who salutes them and receives their blessing, after which a dance is held and the tunes peculiar to them are played." As in Kunering, women were not permitted to participate in the ceremony, and, again as in Kunering, an instrument similar to the whip was used to prevent interference with the ceremony.[166]

Over a period of eight years, during the 1950s and 1960s, Joshua Leslie observed the Egun masquerade on numerous occasions among the Yorubas, for whom the circle was an important, recurring symbol. His description of the Egun secret society recalls Talbot's findings and reinforces the view that Egun rites are an analogue to, perhaps one of the sources of, the Kuners dance in North Carolina, a state in which Yorubas and other Nigerian peoples, including Ibos, were represented:

In traditional Yoruba Society there are masquerades in which the founding fathers of the village or town are worshipped and the wearing of the mask is meant to embody the ancestral figure. Sometimes you get men wearing masks representing all the ancestors of the town. The Egun masquerade is also a way of establishing certain rights and authorities of age and sex. The whip is carried so that certain people can't see the masqueraders—the embodiment of the spirit—carrying the God. Certain families have the right to carry the gods and certain people can't witness them doing so—women and children.[167]

Owing to the impact of Nigerian culture on Dahomey, Africans from Dahomey were familiar with Egun ceremonies, and the presence of Dahomeans in North Carolina, together with Nigerians, could well account for the visibility and strength of Kunering there. Because of that presence, Kunering took at least two forms, with or without the suggestion of female involvement. When some men masqueraded as women, it was apparently because Dahomeans made up the bulk of their ranks—first-generation Yorubas or Ibos would hardly have participated—and Dahomean women were not present to play female roles.

It is obvious . . . that the Egu cult in Abomey has been strikingly assimilated to the Dahomean patterns of ritual observance. . . . One of the outstanding characteristics of the Egungun in Nigeria is the fact that women are strictly prohibited from having any contact with the masked figure; indeed, since for a woman to see any part of the body of a masked dancer meant death for her as well as for the dancer, the contrast of the Abomey Egu ceremony with the Nigerian Egungun customs is apparent at once.[168]

Africans were so given to secret societies, and their purposes and characteristics were generally so similar, that a great many ceremonies across Central and West Africa involving the use of masks and costumes—signs that ancestral figures are being represented—might resemble and be related to John Kunering, and might have enabled Africans from various parts of Africa to identify with and join in Kunering in North Carolina, since masks are used universally to represent ancestral figures. Moreover, a number of African secret societies excluded women and children, keeping them at a distance during their ceremonies, as in the case of the Egun. Yet one Egun ceremony bears, it appears, directly on Kunering. Referring to that ceremony, Talbot remarks, "In several ways it resembles the European Christmas, as it is an occasion for the reunion of the family and of friends, and is treated as a general holiday. . . . Presents are given and the 'play' is repeated in the various 'quarters' of the town."[169] Such practices are not that dissimilar from Kunering in North Carolina, where Africans found reinforcement for Egun-type practices in the Christmas season. Knowing that in North America Christmas was the main religious period for the dominant group when families gathered, exchanged gifts, worshiped, and enjoyed the festivities of the occasion, the slaves took advantage of that time to revive African cultural expression along somewhat similar lines, since in Africa exchanges of gifts at reunions of family and friends on holidays were not uncommon, especially on important religious occasions. Exchanges of gifts, such as they were, among slaves were often accompanied by the receipt of gifts from the master and, in the context of John Kunering, "presents" in the form of donations after performances.

At the elaborate Collins estate, Somerset Place, on Lake Scuppernong, in Washington County, North Carolina, influential whites frequently gathered and witnessed African rituals, especially John Kunering, which were in full flower in the 1840s and 1850s. The approximately three hundred slaves working "several thousand acres of arable land," which yielded "a princely income" annually, could scarcely have been more African; this was understood by Dr. Edward Warren, who visited the plantation over many years and was an intimate associate of its rich ruler. There he saw Africans and their descendants "John Kunering," decided that the ceremony had some tie to religion as other white observers found the ring shout "semi-religious," and shrewdly but not altogether accurately offered as evidence of the "connection" that the slaves only participated in it on the most sacred Christian holiday.[170]

As African as the Kunering performances in North Carolina towns were, they were more rarefied in the countryside at the Collins estate, where the majority of blacks, "never having been brought into relations with other representatives of their race . . . had retained many of the ideas and traditions of their native land." Warren heard some speak a language that probably was typical of that spoken by Africans in places where they outnumbered or had little contact with whites: that is, like Gullah--speaking blacks who lived on the Sea Islands, off the coast of South Carolina and Georgia, they could shift from intelligible English to an incomprehensible mixture, except to the trained ear, of African and English words regulated by African grammar and syntax, the African words increasing in proportion to the desired degree of unintelligibility. Warren thought the mysterious language confined to "'Guinea negroes . . . remnants of the cargoes of African slaves . . . brought into those waters and sold at handsome prices to the neighboring planters."

> These antiquated darkeys spoke a sort of gibberish, which was a medley of their original dialect and the English language, and to me was perfectly unintelligible. They retained all of their original fetich superstitions and were as uncivilized, even in their old age, as when they roamed in youthful freedom among the jungles of the dark continent.[171]

The influence of Africa was present in most if not all aspects of "kunering," especially in the "ragman," the "leading character"

> whose "get-up" consists in a costume of rags, so arranged that one end of each hangs loose and dangles; two great ox horns, attached to the skin of a raccoon, which is drawn over the head and face, leaving apertures only for

the eyes and mouth; sandals of the skin of some wild "varmint"; several cow or sheep bells or strings of dried goats' horns hanging about their shoulders, and so arranged as to jingle at every movement; and a short stick of seasoned wood, carried in his hands.[172]

Another "character" in the ceremony, Number Two, was played by "the best looking darkey of the place, who wears no disguise." He wore his "Sunday-go-to-the-meeting suit" and carried a small cup or bowl to collect the "presents." His attire appears to have been perfectly accept-able to the other slaves, even welcome, perhaps an acceptable aspect of improvisation, in that context. In any case, another half a dozen impor-tant performers wer_____ "each arrayed fantastically in ribbons, rags, and feather_____ _een them several so-called musical instru-ment_____ consist of wooden frames covered over wit_____ _an-made instruments in North America. The_____ _followed by a motley crowd of all ages, dress_____ clothes, which seemingly comes as a guard_____ [173]

Thei_____ ted to a procession or parade, first to the grea_____ _hed the front door, the musicians "beat th_____ and the "ragman" and character Number _____ a dance of the most extraordinary char-acter," str_____ _llowing for freedom of invention, "a combination of bodily co_____ _ions, flings, kicks, gyrations, and antics of every imag-inable description, seemingly acting as partners, and yet each trying to excel the other in the variety and grotesqueness of his movements."[174] However assimilated Number Two may have appeared, his performance in the dance was wholly African, the forms of dance and their substance sacred. It thus seems that, despite the Sunday-go-to-meeting attire he wore, he was an African religious figure of some stature on the Collins estate.

In Kunering there was not only the usual improvisation in dance paral-leling the endless variations on themes in music but also the extempo-raneous creation of song, or so it seemed to Warren, with character Number Two leading with lines full of irony:

> My massa am a white man juba!
> Old missus am a lady, juba!
> De children am de honey-pods, juba! juba!
> Krismas come but once a year, juba!
> Juba! juba! O, ye juba!
> De darkeys lubs de hoe-cake, juba!
> Take de "quarter" for to buy it, juba!
> Fetch him long, you white folks, juba! juba!
> Krismas come but once a year, juba.
> Juba! juba! O, ye juba!

Building on the irony of the performance, "the whole crowd joined in the chorus, shouting and clapping their hands in the wildest glee." After singing his song, Number Two danced toward the master "with his hat in one hand and a tin cup in the other, to receive the expected 'quarter,' and while making the lowest obeisance," with great irony shouted, "May de good Lord bless old massa and missus and all de young massas, juba!" All the while the "ragman" was singing "at the top of his voice,"

> My massa am a white man juba!
> Old missus am a lady, juba!
> De children am de honey-pods, juba! juba!
> Krismas come but once a year, juba!
> Juba! juba! O, ye juba![175]

In that context, the opinion of a great authority on slavery is relevant: "The real feelings and opinions of the slaves were not much known or respected by their masters. The distance between the two was too great to admit of such knowledge." So it was when slaves sang,

> I am going away to the Great House farm,
>   O, yea! O, yea! O, yea!
> My old master is a good old master,
>   O, yea! O, yea! O, yea![176]

Warren was convinced that Kunering "was based on some festive ceremony which the Negroes had inherited from their African ancestors." While in Egypt, he met "the exact counterpart of the old 'Guinea negroes' of the Lake," who evoked memories of his days among slaves in North Carolina. Except for the lyrics of the Kuner song heard at the Collins estate, he had witnessed a ceremony by blacks "absolutely identical" with the one he had seen in Carolina. In Egypt they "amused themselves," he thought, with Kunering "at Byram—the principal feast of the Koran."[177] The finding by Warren is intriguing and deserves investigation because it raises the important question of whether Kunering originated in Egypt and because it strongly suggests that the phenomenon, thought to be widespread in West Africa, was indeed even more pervasive. A critical point is that Warren's reference to the religiosity of Kunering at the Byram feast is further evidence of its religious nature in North American slavery.

The importance of the African religious component was recognized by him more generally. This was a key consideration because the Collins family had a resident pastor to impart Christianity to the hundreds of slaves on the plantation. Consequently, the slaves on the Collins estate received more than the usual amount of attention from whites interested in Africans becoming Christians. Though they were "rampant Christians, with 'the service' on the tips of their tongues," slaves at Somerset Place retained "faith in evil genii, charms, philters, metempsychosis, etc., and they habitually indulged in an infinitude of cabalistic rites and ceremonies." It is small wonder, therefore, that Warren found it "a constant source of interest to see the negroes flocking to church on Sundays, participating in the services—for they knew every word of the 'prayer book'—and partaking of holy communion at the same table with their master and members of his family."[178]

The composition of the crowd of Kuners in the North Carolina countryside, with slaves of all ages represented, guaranteed the persistence of the tradition, the old Africans forming the principal links to the past and being succeeded in that role, in graduated stages, by younger Africans—the whole process sustained by all of the participants, for they came from cultures in which immemorial custom was valued. If, then, the old in slave communities commanded respect on most matters, on those of greatest import to their people cultural transmission was all but guaranteed, especially in religion, with its attendant dances and songs to the ancestors. The scores of young blacks participating in the Kunering ceremony were, therefore, as vital to its perpetuation as the children who participated in the ring shout were to its transmission to succeeding generations.

VIII

The earliest memories of many slave children were of the ceremonies of their parents, relatives, and other blacks in the slave community. It was not, in fact, uncommon for special arrangements to be made for the attendance of infants on such occasions. When one considers that the most important ceremonies occurred in the slave quarters, where the children lived, and in the secrecy of the forests, where the children were found as well, the transmission of culture from the old to the young seems inevitable, a development that could not be prevented, short of the destruction of black people. The preservation of their culture in the North is a measure of the extent to which, year after year, they successfully congregated, then dispersed, retaining values fundamental to their culture though greatly outnumbered.

No doubt the scattering of slaves in tiny numbers in the households of Northern slaveholders contributed to the view, widely entertained by historians, that African culture never took hold in the Northern colonies, let alone lasted throughout and beyond the slave era—not an astonishing view, since African culture is not thought to have taken hold substantially in the South. What was once noted in the nineteenth century but has since been ignored by almost all scholars is that African cultural influence in the North was widespread and continuous during the slave era.[179] The power of that influence was due in part to slaves and free blacks seeking out each other for cultural reinforcement, their relative scarcity contributing to their determination to be in each other's company and to the vitality with which they expressed themselves culturally, dominating the festivals in which they participated.

What the African offered in music and dance to most whites appeared so peculiar in expression and so light of heart, some whites must have thought, as to constitute the soul of holiday cheer. Besides, there were practical reasons for allowing blacks to "amuse" themselves. The calculus of control often required their overindulgence in drink, particularly in the South, where revolt was most feared and measures taken to prevent it exceeded all reasonable lengths. Though the matter of control, for obvious reasons, was not of equal weight in the North, it nonetheless was one reason that whites permitted such ceremonies as New England's election day or parade of governors. The New Englander's disinclination to suppress the African to anything like the degree to which he was suppressed in the South was illustrated by the size of the election day ceremonies in several New England colonies, the masters permitting slaves to travel considerable distances to participate.

New England slaves gathered on holidays in large numbers for public recreation and amusement and, though whites usually did not know it, for religious observance. Hubert H. S. Aimes, an early student of African culture in America, notes that "one of these days was election day when the whole community took a holiday and gathered in towns to vote." It was "the occasion for a pompous and ceremonious parade by the Negroes," a practice apparently begun around 1750 and continued for a century.[180] Though the parades of blacks were African in inspiration and style, their elections were modeled after those of whites. In fact, blacks staged mock elections of their own as a result of encouragement from whites, elections that replicated the form of those of whites.

Between 1730 and 1750, African imports to New England increased substantially, and "at the latter date, numbered as slaves . . . about 3,500." Before that time, blacks were not sufficiently numerous to have introduced and sustained a parade, at least not one impressive in size. By 1780, in Connecticut, however, they numbered 6,000, and the parade was enthusiastically supported in several towns, as it was in Rhode Island towns, where they numbered 4,000 in 1780. Africans seasoned in the West Indies and those directly from Africa constituted the bulk of the slaves brought into New England, that is, most of them were African in sensibility and outlook. Advertisements indicate Gold Coast Negroes, considered "of highest quality," were most sought after, as "in South Carolina and the West Indies." In 1762, for example, a New England merchant offered "a few prime men and boy slaves from the Gold Coast," which meant that there, as in other sections of New England to which Gold Coast blacks were brought, a ring dance in some form was practiced as in the South and in sections of the North other than New England. According to

Lorenzo Greene, Africans were "conspicuously 'played up' in advertising columns of the newspapers, including very likely, agreeable and healthy Negro boys and girls lately imported from Guinea."[181]

Thousands of young Africans, with the permission of their masters, joined older ones in parades in Massachusetts, Rhode Island, and Connecticut:

> They decked themselves out in striking or fantastic costumes, and on horseback or on foot accompanied their "governor" through the streets. The parade included an accompaniment of hideous music, and was followed by a dinner and dance in some commodious hall hired for the purpose. Sometimes, however, the dinner and dance were not preceded by the parade.[182]

Since first-generation Africans constituted the bulk of adult blacks in New England in 1780, whatever the significance of the parade in the minds of the most acculturated among them, the majority paraded, danced, and made music as Africans. This should not surprise us, considering what we know of the functions of dance and music in Africa and their strength in the American South. Moreover, the literature reveals no attempts on the part of white New Englanders to place severe restrictions on the manner in which the slaves carried out either the festivities of the parade or the dinner, which took place in several New England towns, and the dance that followed. The accretions of Africans that made possible New England parades by 1750 guaranteed, since music and dance were at the heart of the parades, a sacred dimension to the ceremonies that allowed ample room for joyous expression and entertainment—as on ceremonial occasions in Africa.

In Rhode Island, election day gave "great delight to the young and animated sons of Africa," who found the time to entertain and instruct by telling tales in their native languages. In fact, the announcement of the election of a new governor of the blacks was known to occasion "a general shout . . . every voice upon its highest key, in all the various languages of Africa," which meant a sense of community, of underlying cultural unity, was felt despite linguistic and other differences among them.[183]. Within the language groups represented, on the occasion of the parades and at other times, there were Africans who found it safer and more resonant spiritually to express their deepest concerns and fondest hopes in their native tongues, an aspect of slavery no less real for being largely and forever lost to history. But we do know that Africans were speaking in various languages in New England, as they were in Philadelphia in 1800, and found their native languages an important means of communicating all sorts of sentiments they would not have dared utter in English. The clearest indictments of slavery and the deepest expressions of sorrow must have been spoken in the native tongues and sung as well, but they are unrecorded. We are left, at best, with expressions of joy

shouted in many languages upon the announcement of the Negro governor, their essential oneness affirmed through the consensus reached.

A wide range of activity excited Africans on election days. They played
games, played on the instruments of their native countries and fiddled,
danced and drank. They were the center of attraction for all: when they
cudgeled, jumped, and wrestled, whites stood observing, as they did
when they paraded before the election ball, which was a favorite. Jane De
Forest Shelton notes that it was common for entire families of blacks to
participate in the events of the day in Connecticut—"a babe in arms being
no drawback, as the tavern keeper set apart a room and provided a care-
taker for them" during the dinner and dance. The dancing characteristically lasted into the next day.

> Sometimes more than a dozen little wooly-heads would be under surveil-
> lance, while the light-hearted mothers shuffled and tripped to the sound of the
> fiddle. New Haven and Hartford, as well as intervening towns, were repre-
> sented. Supper was served for fifty cents each, and they danced and feasted
> with a delight the more sedate white man can hardly appreciate, spinning out
> the night and often into the next day.[184]

Platt writes that "the old negroes aided in the plan" of the Negro governor, a plan that, according to Issac W. Stuart, included "ceremonies."
Given the role of elders in Africa in helping to determine the spiritual
direction of their people, it follows that old Africans in New England
played a similar role, helping to determine what would take place, and
how, on election day, the most important public ceremony for New England blacks.

Historians who argue that African dance was "subdued" among slaves
in America are contradicted by the vigorous rhythmic motion, and the
words of New England Negroes. "A newspaper notice of more than fifty
years ago," Shelton wrote in 1894, "strikes the key note of the great
day":

> ATTENTION . . .
>
> There will be a general election of the colored gentlemen of Connecticut,
> October first, twelve o'clock noon. The day will be celebrated in the evening
> by a dance at Warner's tavern, when it will be shown that there is some
> power left in muscle, catgut, and rosin.
>
> By order of the Governor
> From Headquarters.[185]

Slave dance in New England was not substantially different from black
dance in the South, on the continent of Africa, or wherever black men and
women gathered, for New England slaves had come from many different
sections of black Africa, as had slaves in the South and elsewhere in the

Americas. The same is largely true of the music made by New England and Southern slaves in the eighteenth century and later. Since African music was described as "hideous" by some whites, the fact that Africans did not regard it that way suggests the presence in New England and the South of an African aesthetic or standard of beauty radically different from that of whites. The rhythms and the means by which they were conveyed formed, across ethnic lines, cultural bonds for slaves on ceremonial occasions generally, helping to determine performance style in dance and song and group interplay, including walking and talking. Such was the case in New England, where the drum was among the instruments "played on." The pronounced rhythms, pervasive both in black Africa and in black America, despite differences in language, were especially unifying when blacks danced, sang, played instruments, or paraded.

Blacks selected "their best and ablest men" as governors. Though the Negro governor had no legal power, he exercised, together with the lieutenant governor, justices of the peace, and sheriffs he sometimes appointed, "considerable control over the Negroes throughout the state" of Connecticut. The parade, led by a prominent black leader, and the election were used by slaveowners as a means of indirectly ruling blacks. The irony was sharp as the Puritan gentry promoted a certain democracy among blacks the more effectively to enslave them. Respect for Connecticut's Negro governor was substantial enough to reinforce values drawn on for the parade, and other aspects of ceremonies of the blacks, and more:

> The person they selected for the office in question was usually one of much note among themselves, of imposing presence, strength, firmness and volubility, who was quick to decide, ready to command, and able to flog. . . . He settled all grave disputes in the last resort, questioned conduct, and imposed penalties and punishments sometimes for vice. . . . He was respected as "Gubernor" . . . by the Negroes throughout the state, and obeyed almost implicitly.[186]

Platt refers to elderly Negroes aiding the governor in his effort to assure the morality and honesty of their people, a process carried out less obviously to outsiders but apparently with some degree of rigor in slavery and later. Whatever the ultimate intent of New England slaveowners in fostering limited Negro rule, a great deal that was African in morality, especially respect for elders and ancestors and the immemorial uses of art to those ends, was conveyed to younger blacks, extending Africanity over time. We can establish the existence of storytelling in New England by elders, and art there, like the telling of tales in the South, was a primary means of pointing to a terribly complex reality, and the lessons arrived at from dealing with it. A special freedom was afforded slave storytellers in the last half of the eighteenth century, when the number of first-generation Africans was considerable, in the North and the South, because whites did not understand their native tongues (or even acknowledge them as legitimate languages). The stories told in New England, like those collected later by Adams and Faulkner in the South, must have been based mainly on actual experiences at a time when large numbers of New England slaves had experienced the Atlantic voyage. There is little question that, considering the rich variety of African languages heard in New England, tales at least as ethnic as those later rendered in English and collected in the South were routinely told, especially since African cultural resources were then accessible to storytellers who were themselves born in Africa.

If Africans chose their election day leader out of concern for ethnic background, the available documents do not record it. For two, possibly three, generations, those engaged in the selection process were from various ethnic groups, as were those selected to represent them. Yet a common perception of their predicament led first-generation Africans in the North as well as the South to subordinate ethnic prejudices to the demands of the New World, to their interest in rising above their status as an enslaved people, and there is no indication that their masters played off one ethnic group against another. Nevertheless, the influence of the master class was a factor to be reckoned with in the election process and ceremonies. There is some evidence that the prospective governor's financial backing was important to his chances for election, just as the support of their masters made it possible for blacks generally to participate in the events of the day and the night. Nevertheless, the background of oppression led slaves, when the votes were counted and announced, to become more united than before as the "defeated candidate was . . . introduced by the chief marshal and drank the first toast after the inauguration, and all animosities were forgotten." The governor, at dinner, "was seated at the head of the long table, under trees or an arbor, with the unsuccessful candidate at his right and his lady at his left." [187]

Ethnic allegiances were greater in Brazil and in islands like Cuba, where parades paralleling those of the Negro governor occurred. While the concentration of Africans of specific ethnic groups in Cuba and elsewhere in the Americas was greater, African cultural features were not that much greater there than in North America. For instance, Africanity in the parade of kings in Cuba was certainly not in every particular more pronounced than in the parade of governors in New England. Perhaps an important factor regulating perceptions of culture in the West Indies and Brazil is that the white observer, because of the larger numbers of Africans in proportion to whites and the consequent impact of African culture generally, more readily conceded what was African in the cultures of the blacks. In America, by contrast, much of African culture was hidden from whites, and when not hidden, as in the parade of governors, was less likely to be considered influential. But understanding what is African in cultural expression outside America is, as we have seen, an important means of more easily identifying African culture in America. In a passage that bears directly on New England governors, Aimes notes regarding Brazil and Cuba,

> There is an abundance of contemporary evidence showing the condition of the Negroes in these colonies, and the government, in Cuba at least, legally recognized and made use of their African customs as a part of the local police as a means of controlling the Negro population.[188]

A critical passage, from *Letters from Havana, during the Year 1820,* is quoted by Aimes:

> Each tribe or people has a king elected out of their number, whom they rag out with much savage grandeur on the holidays on which they are permitted to meet. . . . Almost unlimited liberty was given to the Negroes. Each tribe, having elected its king and queen, paraded the streets with a flag, having its name and the words *Viva Isabella,* with the arms of Spain, painted on it. Their majesties were dressed in the extreme of the fashion, and were ceremoniously waited on by the ladies and gentlemen of the court. . . . They bore their honors with that dignity which the Negroes love so much to assume.[189]

The behavior of blacks in New England on election day was not dissimilar. Caulkins, an authority on election day, describes Governor Samuel Huntington following an election:

> Riding through the town on one of his master's horses, adorned with painted gear, his aides on each side, *a la militaire,* himself sitting bolt upright and moving with a slow majestic pace, as if the universe was looking on. When he mounted or dismounted, his aides flew to his assistance, holding his bridle, putting his feet into the stirrup, and bowing to the ground before him. The Great Mogul in a triumphant procession never assumed an air of more perfect self-importance than the Negro Governor.[190]

In each case, the governor or king carried himself as ruler and treated his followers like subjects; in each, African cultural forms were similar enough for the followers to act in concert; in each, the black "ruler" controlled on behalf of others; in each, there was also more latitude for African autonomy than slaveowners imagined, thanks to the impenetrability of numerous African cultural forms, including linguistic ones, to almost all whites. The parallels are strong enough to suggest the existence of elements of a Pan-African culture in New World slavery in the parades of governors and kings and more, especially since substantial numbers of slaves in Cuba and North America came from essentially the same areas of Africa, from the undulating stretch of land along the Guinea Coast that, curving through Angola, helped give the world the ring shout. Related to the question of origins is the fact that, in the New World, Africans evolved along parallel lines in their cultural forms—in Cuba "screeching out the songs of their nations to the music of rattles, tin pans, and tambourines,"[191] in New England shouting approval of election results in "all the various languages of Africa," in Philadelphia singing the various languages of Africa while dancing the ring shout in squads.

The evidence suggests that the parades of kings and governors were parts of a larger cultural configuration, and this reinforces our claim that a Pan-African culture existed in the Americas. For example, in Albany, New York, on Pinkster Hill, there was "this great festival of the negroes," whose similarity to the New England parade of governors and to the Cuban parade of kings is striking. Pinkster festivals occurred at a time "when every family of wealth or distinction possessed one or more slaves." Usually beginning in May and lasting for a whole week, the ceremony was also known as "the carnival of the African race," and it was thought the Africans "indulged in unrestrained merriment and revelry," a judgment made of African rituals generally. The surroundings were at times not unlovely, nature being generous with her beauty despite human oppression. Spring lilacs "were everywhere," and azaleas "saturated the bright morning air with their ever-delicious fragrance," so there were grounds for merriment, especially for the young, white and black, who wore their best clothes for the festival on Albany's Pinkster Hill.[192]

While whites participated in the celebration in a variety of capacities and attended the events of the week in large numbers, apparently mingling freely with the blacks, the center of attention was the black Pinkster king and his throng of followers. And though it is not certain how the idea of a Pinkster king was born or whether he exercised an authority among his own comparable to that of the New England governor or the African king in Cuba, he was treated like a sovereign by his people. It is likely that regard for the Pinkster king extended beyond the days of celebration since, in addition to being a man of impressive manner and carriage, he was nearly seventy, a distinguished elder to the slave population by the time of the last Pinkster celebration, in 1811, and presumably the king of all New York blacks. On that occasion, the crowd wound its way up avenues toward Pinkster Hill over the seven days of the festival. On the second day—the day when the king made his appearance—important whites, carefully guided by trusted slaves through the densely populated streets, could hear before them "sounds of many voices, harmoniously intermingled with the occasional shouts of boisterous mirth," and, on arrival, found the field "darkened" by the gathering crowd,

> consisting chiefly of individuals of almost every description of feature, form and color, from the sable sons of Africa, neatly attired and scrupulously clean in all their holiday habiliments, to the half clad and blanketed children of the forest, accompanied by their squaws, these latter being heavily burdened with all their different wares, such as baskets, moccasins . . . and many other

things . . . and boys and girls of every age and condition were everywhere seen gliding to and fro amid this motley group.[193]

Everyone was out to witness the performance of black "royalty," which had stayed in seclusion on the first day, as if to heighten the interest it inevitably provoked among whites and blacks and Indians. A portent of what was to come was the body servant to one of the wealthiest of New Yorkers—a servant acting as master of ceremonies whose "grace and elegance of manner . . . characterized his progress through life until his dying day" and to whom "was unanimously entrusted the arduous duty of reducing to some kind of order this vast mass of incongruent material, which his superior ability soon enabled him to accomplish with complete success."[194] This sense of Negro aristocracy was not uncommon among blacks in the colonial and early national periods or, for that matter, in antebellum America and later, and owes a great deal to African tradition. One need only recall that thousands of members of royal families were removed from Africa and taken to North America, where they often became the slaves of far less cultivated men and women. But some recognition of those traits was accorded at Pinkster ceremonies, as in New England at the governor's parade, and the parallels were also noticeable in other respects:

> The hour of ten having now arrived, and the assembled multitude being considered most complete, a deputation was then selected to wait upon their venerable sovereign king, "Charley of the Pinkster Hill," with the intelligence that his respectful subjects were congregated, and were anxiously desirous to pay all proper homage to his majesty their king. Charles originally came from Africa, having . . . been brought from Angola. . . . He was tall, thin and athletic; and although the frost of nearly seventy winters had settled on his brow, its chilling influence had not yet extended to his bosom, and he still retained all the vigor and agility of his younger years. Such were his manly attributes at this present time. . . . Never, if our memory serve us, shall we forget the mingled sensations of awe and grandeur that were impressed on our youthful minds, when first we beheld his stately form and dignified aspect, slowly moving before us and approaching the centre of the ring.[195]

Arrangements were completed for the dancing to commence, the king having already been greeted by many in the crowd. Assisted by his aides, the master of ceremonies had "partially restored" peace and tranquility as the audience awaited the next, decidedly African stage of the ceremony. The dancers on the green were prepared to dance until exhaustion and joined in the dance at various times with "utmost energy until extreme fatigue or weariness compelled them to retire and give space to a less exhausted set." The intensity of the performance matched that of dancers in Virginia, South Carolina, North Carolina, and other areas in the South, the rhythms danced to being no less complex since the drum was the principal instrument, and so "the dance went on with all its accustomed energy and might . . . until the shades of night began to fall slowly over the land, and at length deepen into the silent gloom of midnight." Still the performance continued, and the keen observer's eye, "weary in gazing on this wild and intricate maze," sought in the general throng the king, "and there, enclosed within their midst, was his stately form beheld, moving along with all the simple grace and elastic action of his youthful days, and sometimes displaying some of his many amusing antics, to the delight and wonderment of the surrounding crowd. . . . And thus the scene continued until the shades of night and morning almost mingled." [196]

The physical exertion evident here matched the energy expended in dance on the continent. The infrequent opportunity to congregate contributed to the explosions of energy before the flame of movement died in the dusk of morning. Such opportunity to celebrate—the Pinkster festival began "on the Monday following the Whitsunday or Pentecost of the Catholic and Episcopal churches"—assured a focusing on religious thought and feeling. Despite white participation, the festival was acknowledged to be African. What Dr. James Eights said of Pinkster also applies to John Kunering and to the parade of governors: "The dance had its pecularities as well as everything else connected with this . . . celebration." [197]

Apart from sharing religious values with them, the Pinkster ceremonies were similar to the parade of governors and kings in dance movement and rhythm, in honor guard and character of the processional. It is clear that Pinkster celebrations and the parade of governors were similar phenomena, variations or replications of roughly equivalent processional and political traditions of certain African regions, as were the counterclockwise dance of Central and West Africa. Moreover, both Pinkster and the parade of governors featured athletic events and "leaders" of similar demeanor inspiring similar respect from blacks and support and attention from whites. The parade of governors and the parade of kings were remarkably similar phenomena, and the Pinkster celebration was sufficiently like each, with the king and his attendants as pivotal figures, to suggest the possibility of similar or related sources. More knowledge of processions in Africa, especially since New York and New England were populated by blacks from essentially the same areas of Africa, will cast more light on patterns of Africanity in both regions and on their relation to those elsewhere in the Americas.

What we know of slave culture in the South, and of that of blacks in the North during and following slavery, indicates that black culture was national in scope, the principal forms of cultural expression being essentially the same. This is attributable mainly to the similarity of the African regions from which blacks were taken and enslaved in North America, and to the patterns of culture shared more generally in Central and West Africa. It should also be taken into account, in examining the national dimensions of black culture, that the scores of thousands of slaves who escaped to the North in the antebellum period served to assist in the sharing of cultural values, which was enhanced also by the relative absence of opportunities for blacks to secure an education in the North.

Evidence of the oneness of black culture in the twentieth century abounds. For example, the spread of Southern black music to the North with the creation of each new form, together with the migration of black musicians and blacks generally, placed Southern values within reach of all strata of Northern black communities. But because much that was Southern was African, Northern and Southern blacks from the start shared an essentially common culture.

In blinding whites to the value of African culture, racism helped the slave, as segregation helped his descendants, preserve essentials of African culture. But the preservation of that culture during slavery owed more to its affirmation by blacks than to the negative thrust of American life. Slave trading to America from 1750 to the end of 1807, a phenomenon largely neglected in its cultural dimension, greatly strengthened African values in America. Still, the preservation of those values in various forms was not an automatic process. On the contrary, slave ingenuity was indispensable to the survival of African culture in America.

I X

Thomas Wentworth Higginson and other Northerners who entered the Sea Islands during the Civil War agreed that the Christianity of blacks was different from that of whites. They knew that Christianity, as practiced by many whites, had no deep roots in slave communities, the ring shout appearing to be as ineradicable as it was pervasive. Moreover, few were the blacks who participated in Christian services who did not infuse them with their own spirituality, thereby transforming Christianity. Some notion of the place of Christianity in the ring shout, a phenomenon that fascinated Higginson, is found in his description of that ritual.

All over the camp the lights glimmer in the tents, and as I sit at my desk in the open doorway, there come mingled sounds of stir and glee. Boys laugh and shout,—a feeble flute stirs somewhere in some tent, not an officer's,—drums throb far away in another . . . and from a neighboring cook-fire comes the monotonous sound of that strange festival, half pow-wow, half prayer--meeting, which they know only as "shout." These huts are usually enclosed in a little booth, made neatly of palm-leaves and covered in at top, a regular native African hut. . . . This hut is now crammed with men, singing at the top of their voices, in one of their quaint, monotonous, endless, negro-Methodist chants, with obscure syllables recurring constantly, and slight variations interwoven, all accompanied with a regular drumming of the feet and clapping of the hands, like castanets.[198]

The language is Gullah, the rhythms of feet and hands African, the chant
African in performance style, the excitement building inside and outside
the hut. Men begin to "quiver and dance," a circle forms and winds mo-
notonously "round someone in the center," and excitement grows:

> Some "heel and toe" tumultuously, others merely tremble and stagger on,
> others stoop and rise, others whirl, others caper sideways, all keep steadily
> circling like dervishes; spectators applaud special strokes of skill; my ap-
> proach only enlivens the scene; the circle enlarges, louder grows the singing,
> rousing shouts of encouragement come in; half bacchanalian, half devout . . .
> and still the ceaseless drumming and clapping in perfect cadence, goes stead-
> ily on. Suddenly there comes a sort of *snap*, and the spell breaks, amid gen-
> eral sighing and laughter. . . . And this not rarely and occasionally, but night
> after night.[199]

It should not surprise us that the same people constructed African huts in
which they shouted and, as Higginson demonstrates in a passage that recalls Herman Melville's *Redburn*, brought African sensibility to bear on
Christianity: "Elsewhere, it is some solitary old cook, some aged Uncle
Tiff, with enormous spectacles, who is perusing a hymn-book by the light
of a pine splinter, in his deserted cooking booth of Palmetto leaves."[200]

The scenes could scarcely have been very different at the introduction
of Christianity into African communities earlier in the century. There was
a mixture of Western and African cultural qualities, but the African ones
dominated. If there were dances of "red-legged soldiers doing right, and
left and 'now-lead-delady-ober,'" and if psalms were "deaconed out"
from memory, the "everlasting shout" was "always within hearing" and
elsewhere there were "*conversazioni* around fires, with a woman for
queen of the circle,—her Nubian face, gay headdress, gilt necklace, and
white teeth, all resplendent in the glowing light." And at times, subtle
mocking of Christian prayer:

> And yonder is a stump-orator, perched on his barrel, pouring out his exhorta-
> tions to fidelity in war and in religion. To-night for the first time I have heard
> in a different strain, quite saucy, sceptical, and defiant, appealing to them in a
> sort of French materialistic style, and claiming some personal experience of
> warfare. . . he hit hard at the religionists: When a man's got de sperrit ob de
> Lord in him, it weakens him all out, can't hoe de corn. . . I mean to fight de
> war through, an' die a good sojer wid de last kick,—dat's *my* prayer![201]

The Christmas season was "the great festival of the year for this people." There were "prayer-meetings as late as they desired; and all night,
as I waked at intervals, I could hear them praying and 'shouting' and
clattering with hands and heels." The shout "seemed to make them very
happy, and appeared to be at least an innocent Christmas dissipation, as
compared with some of the convivialities of the 'superior race' here-
abouts." Praying was endemic to gatherings around camp fires, and that
was natural enough since the ring shout, the most sacred slave rite, was

itself a form of prayer often engaged in around a fire. So strong was the devotional side of the slave personality that "the greatest scamps kneel and groan in their prayer-meetings with such entire zest."[202]

Incantations were heard everywhere, together with chanting. Especially at dusk the air was full of song and clapping of hands. A song encountered before, one "full of plaintive cadences," a chant of beauty, was recorded as sung by soldiers recruited for service in the Union army:

> I can't stay behind, my Lord, I can't stay behind!
> O, my father is gone, my father is gone,
> My father is gone into heaven, my Lord!
> I can't stay behind!
> Dare's room enough, room enough,
> Room enough in de heaven for de sojer:
> Can't stay behind!

It was sung at all seasons, and Higginson heard it one night "and, tracing it into the recesses of a cookhouse . . . found an old fellow coiled away among the pots and provisions," again like some character from a Melville novel, "chanting away with this 'Can't stay behind, sinner,' till I made him leave his song behind."[203]

Edward Channing Gannett's writing on the ring shout echoes Higginson:

> The "shout" is a peculiar service in which a dozen or twenty jog slowly round a circle behind each other with a peculiar shuffle of the feet and shake of arms, keeping time to a droning chant and hand-clapping maintained by by-standers. As the exercise continues, the excitement increases, occasionally becomes hysterical. Some religious meaning is attributed to it. . . .[204]

The hand clappers standing aside serve the role of drummers in Africa or in Suriname, of the violinist in Red Hill Churchyard, but Gannett had no way of seeing such connections. Without a grasp of the African background, there was simply no way for him or any other outsider to understand such phenomena. Yet it is to his credit that he reveals key aspects of slave culture, enabling us to see the confluence of cultural forces from new angles. He tells us, for example, that at least one group of black Baptists in the Sea Islands had "nearly the whole church management" in their hands, and the evidence he presents makes it clear that they grafted African institutions onto the church they attended:

> Subsidiary to the church are local "societies," to which "raw souls" are admitted after they have proved the reality of their "striving." This "striving" is a long process of self-examination and solitary prayer "in the bush," and so unremitting must be the devotion during this stage that even attendance at school is thought to interfere with the action of the Spirit.[205]

The level of self-discipline and meditation here calls to mind Eastern rather than Western religions; the references are to rites of passage through institutionalized societies the practices of which were secret, societies existing prior to the flight of slave masters as the Union forces entered the islands. The intensely religious atmosphere was encouraged by "the plantation leader," a figure whose precise religious role was not defined, but who called slaves to praise meetings three evenings a week and "thrice again on Sundays." Those among them who moved furthest into Christianity—or led whites to think they had—the ones who seemed "to distrust the institution [of the ring shout] a little," found license for it in the Bible, "which records, they say, that 'the angels *shout* in heaven.'" The immediacy of their faith was nearly palpable: "With religious ideas decidedly material, their religious feeling seems to be a real laying hold of spiritual truths." Religion encompassed more for them than for whites, rendering irrelevant the distinction between the sacred and the secular—a false dichotomy to a people for whom emotional fervor and dance were integral to religious expression.

> Religion contributes a large part of life's interest to the inhabitants of Port Royal; perhaps because, as the plant grows toward light that is natural to it, they moved in the direction where alone they had free action. Not only their souls but their mind finds here its principal exercise, and in great measure it takes the place of social entertainment and amusements.[206]

Black youngsters were eager to "shout," forming themselves into a circle, singing and dancing on the slightest suggestion, assuring the perpetuation of important religious and artistic values of their people. Of all the literature on the shout, Charlotte Forten's writings are the most instructive on the mode of perpetuation. Again and again, she describes the young's unconscious contribution to cultural continuity in black South Carolina. "After school the children went into a little cabin near, where they kindled a fire, and had a grand 'shout.'" In a word, they expressed their regard for the Lord in African form and feeling, putting their stamp on the faith in their time as their parents had before them. "All the children had the shouting spirit. . . . They had several grand shouts in the entry. 'Look Upon the Lord,' which they sang to-night seems to me the most beautiful of all their shouting tunes. There is something within it that goes to the depths of one's soul." On another occasion, children traveled considerable distances to shout together: "This eve our boys and girls with others from across the creek came in and sang . . . several shouting tunes that we had not heard before; they are very wild and strange." One little child exclaimed, "All I want to do is sing and shout."[207] The shout was vigorously pursued in the last few years of slavery, the young regarding the practice as essential to their lives.

> In the evenings, the children frequently came in to sing and shout for us. These "shouts" are very strange,—in truth, almost indescribable. It is neces-

sary to hear and see in order to have any clear idea of them. The children form a ring, and move around in a kind of shuffling dance, singing all the time. Four or five stand apart, and sing very energetically, clapping their hands, stomping their feet, and rocking their bodies to and fro. These are the musicians, to whose performance the shouters keep perfect time.[208]

For all her recognition of the paramount importance of the ring shout to the slave, Forten never suspected a connection between it and their value system—never realized, indeed, that the ceremony was, above all, devoted to the ancestral spirits, to reciprocity between the living and the dead. Had she understood that, she might have seen the relationship between the ring shout and the place of the elders in the life of the slave, for certainly there was no absence of respect among the slaves for old people. Still, her references to the shout convey a sense of abiding commitment to the ceremony on the part of the children. Not only did they emulate their elders by kindling a fire and dancing around it at night, but they rocked to and fro in usual ring shout form. A child named Prince, a large boy from one of the plantations, "was the principal shouter among the children," and he found it impossible "to keep still. . . . His performances were amusing specimens of Ethiopian gymnastics." A child of six named Amaretta was no less dedicated, at times singing a shouting song, also referred to earlier, that was a favorite of the adults, "Hold Your Light on Canaan's Shore," singing the parts to herself as she walked along:

> What make ole Satan follow me so?
> Satan got nuttin' 't all for to do wid me.

> CHORUS
> Tiddy [Sister] Rosa, hold your light!
> Brudder Tony, hold your light!
> All de member, hold bright your light
>   On Canaan's shore![209]

A partial explanation of why the young ones threw themselves into the shout with such energy and so often, at the urging of others or on their own initiative, is contained in one of Forten's observations: "The children, too, are taught to be very polite to their elders, and it is the rarest thing to hear a disrespectful word from a child to his parent, or to any grown person." Forten's findings regarding the elders are supported by Gannett. A passage from his "The Freedmen of Port Royal" reveals much of African culture in addition to the respect the young have for the elders:

Orphans are at once adopted by connections, and the sick are well nursed by their friends. The old are treated with great reverence, and often exercise a kind of patriarchal authority. Children are carefully taught "manners," and the common address to each other, as well as to the "buckra people," is marked by extreme courtesy.[210]

It followed that the children would emulate adults in matters of importance, children of "not more than three and four years old" entering the
ring "with all their might." Since respect for the ancestors gave birth to
the shout, it was natural that there would be respect for the elders, who
were "closest to being ancestors."[211] Entering the ring was a means of
renewing the most hallowed values of their people, of expressing them
through song and dance that would later figure powerfully in the black
American's "secular" repertoire.

It was no accident that students of the shout, lacking knowledge of its
meaning in the African context, failed to grasp more than a fragment of its
significance in the slave community and among free blacks. This was so
mainly because blacks, determined to protect their culture, sent forth
conflicting, confusing signals to those asking about the shout:

> But the shouting of the grown people is rather solemn and impressive. . . . We
> cannot determine whether it has a religious character or not. Some of the
> people tell us that it has, others that it has not. But as the shouts of the grown
> people are always in connection with their religious meetings, it is probable
> that they are the barbarous expression of religion, handed down to them from
> their African ancestors, and destined to pass away under the influence of
> Christian teachings.[212]

Much of the religious behavior of the elders, from whom children
learned the shout, was in slavery concealed from whites in the way blacks
generations later concealed African religious values from whites. Though
whatever children do seems less threatening to their oppressors, those
shouting with all their being found models for that as for other activity in
their elders, the line of transmission extending in descending chronolog-
ical order with the young learning much from each other. Culturally, one
can almost see slave society whole by studying the role of slave youth in
relation to themselves, their elders, and members of the larger society. In
the culture of slave youths, a greatly neglected area, one finds the means
by which values of immemorial vintage are preserved and extended into
the future, passed on to youth by their elders.

The skill with which slave children mastered an African practice in one
area reflects the degree of their command of others and tells us much
about how culture is transmitted and received almost as an unconscious
ornament of the child's inheritance. It was natural to find in their environment the gift of improvisation in dance, oratory, song, marching step, and
the balancing of objects on their heads when marching. In their parades,
"the 'route step'" was a challenge to military strictness as "the depths of
theological gloom" were contrasted with jubilant chorus—a mixture of
joy-pain that characteristically informs black music. The blacks were
more at home culturally with themselves: "For all the songs, but especially for their own wild hymns, they constantly improvised" as they

marched along. "The little drum corps kept in advance, a jolly crew, their drums slung over their backs, and the drum-sticks perhaps balanced on their heads," like emblems of Africanity. The leader of the parade—the supreme majorette—found in that occasion an opportunity to express qualities of Africanity:

> At the head of the whole force there walked, by some self-imposed pre-- eminence, a respectable elderly female, one of the company laundresses, whose vigorous stride we never could quite overtake, and who had an enormous bundle balanced on her head, while she waved in her hand, like a sword, a long-handled tin dipper.[213]

That the ring shout flourished subterraneously at camp meetings in the state of Georgia and elsewhere—with children present at the ceremony and usually participating—is the surest evidence of its presence among slaves over wide areas of the South when they worshiped alone. If the shout was in fact a prominent, if mostly undetected, aspect of slave worship at camp meetings, then the extent to which Christianity penetrated the slave community without being Africanized must again be considered. The subterranean form taken by the shout at camp meetings was described by Fredrika Bremer, who visited a meeting in Macon, Georgia, in 1850, in which blacks were in the majority, numbering more than three thousand in a setting favorable to African values. The worshipers were separated before a platform on which stood preachers of both races, whites preaching to whites and blacks to blacks.

> The night was dark with thunder-clouds as well as natural darkness; but the rain had ceased, except for a few heavy drops, and the whole wood stood in flames. Upon eight fire-altars, or fire hills as they are called—a sort of lofty table raised on posts around the tabernacle—burned, with a flickering brilliance of flame, large billets of firewood containing a large amount of resin, while on every side in the woods, far away in its most remote recesses, large or smaller fires burned before tents or other places, illuminating the fir-tree stems, which appeared like columns of an immense temple consecrated to fire.[214]

Given the far-flung tents and fires, it is not surprising that Bremer found in each tent of the blacks some new phase of religious exaltation. In one she found "a whole crowd of blacks on their knees, all dressed in white, striking themselves on the breast, and crying out and talking with the greatest pathos." This could easily have been a scene in Dahomey, for there Africans were observed in similar ceremonies beating their breasts, a form of keeping time during musical performances on sacred occasions:

> Their songs are accompanied by gongs and rattles, and by a sound made by beating the chest with the open hand or clinched fist. . . . As the singing of and striking of gongs and chests and the playing of rattles continued, two of the men in the orchestra appeared to be possessed; it seemed that one of these

might begin at any instant to dance. After a time, an old woman took up the sacrificial goat. . . . As she did this, the drums began to sound, and holding the sacrifice under her left arm, she slowly danced about the cleared space three times in a counter-clockwise direction, ending with a series of shuffling steps in front of the drums.[215]

The beating of breasts that was a common phenomenon of ritualistic expression and associated with counterclockwise dance in Dahomey was not the only African practice witnessed. On entering another tent, Bremer saw women

dancing the "holy dance" for one of the newly converted. This dancing, however, being forbidden by the preachers, ceased immediately on our entering the tent. I saw merely a rocking movement of women who held each other by the hand in a circle, singing the while.[216]

Sir Charles Lyell in the 1840s witnessed a similar phenomenon, a modified version of the ring shout resulting from white objections to dance on religious occasions. On the Hopeton plantation, there was a rocking movement in the ring:

At Methodist prayer-meetings, they are permitted to move round rapidly in a ring, joining hands in token of brotherly love, presenting first the right hand and then the left, in which maneuver, I am told, they sometimes contrive to take enough exercise to serve as a substitute for the dance. . . .[217]

Yet Lyell seemed unaware of the resentment felt by Africans at having to alter religious preferences because of whites. Bremer understood, as Lyell did not, that once whites were gone, Africans were likely to return to the ring ceremony without restraining themselves. Both observed the ceremony in Georgia conversion activity, so there is little reason to expect different responses to similar religious stimuli from people of essentially the same cultural background, especially considering interaction that had been occurring among them up to that time, transforming them into a single people. As a part of that process, thousands of Africans drawn from scores of plantations had occasion to meet at camp meetings in Georgia and to share religious practices and attitudes both formally and informally.

Whatever Lyell's naîveté regarding the effectiveness of Christian strictures against African religion, he thought Christianity had by no means been absorbed by blacks, which should have led him to suspect that, when they were alone, a different religion might appear. A rather low-level, though commendable, encounter between African and Christian values, he thought, was taking place, and not a creative melding largely under African control, as the presence of the circle indicates:

However much we may feel inclined to smile at some of these outward tokens of conversion, and however crude may be the notions of the Deity which the poor African at first exchanges for his belief in the evil eye and other super-stitious fears, it is nevertheless an immense step in his progress toward civi-lization that he should join some Christian sect.[218]

Missionaries failed to halt African religion in Georgia because it took forms they did not understand or even recognize. Dahomean influence was even greater there than one would have suspected by combining the insights of Bremer and Herskovits; it also appeared in a form and a place in which whites would least expect African religious expression of any kind—in the quilts of slave women. Fashioned from throwaway cloth, slave quilts were used to clothe mysteries, to enfold those baptized with reinforcing symbols of their faith. Such quilts in Georgia bore a remark-able resemblance to Dahomean appliqué cloth. Harriet Powers's Bible quilt is a brilliant example both of that tradition and of Bakongo tradition, combining the two so naturally as to reflect the coming together of Daho-mean and Bankongo people in American slavery.[219]

Born in Georgia in 1837, Harriet Powers may have been of Dahomean descent, but her command of Bakongo religious symbols was so pro-found, their intricacies in her hands so complete, that it is possible she was of Bakongo parentage. Of course, she might have been of both Bakongo and Dahomean heritage. But given the prevalence of ethnic forms in slave communities of the South, she perhaps absorbed the values of an ethnic group she was not born into as easily as she might have taken in those native to one or more parents.[220] The values of both peoples were represented in the Georgia of her youth, and she must have known them in a general religious sense before thinking of them in relation to quilts. We should not forget that Simon Brown, one of the greatest of storytellers and a keeper of Bakongo tradition of the most obscure kind, was born in the big house yet when barely in his teens had command of symbols of African religious faith though he was neither a Christian nor, apparently, a devotee of African religion. If he was able to do so at so early an age from the big house, it is not unlikely that Powers in youth could also have absorbed African values either from there or from the quarters.

Her date of birth was approximately that of Brown, which means she was in her teens, as he was, in the 1850s and in her twenties at emancipa-tion. Almost certainly she learned to do quilts before emancipation, since it was not uncommon for adolescent slave girls, or their adolescent de-scendants in our time, to take to making quilts. Through that process, she transmitted materially what Brown transmitted orally. So faithful is her rendering of the core of Bakongo religious thought that, were it not for the Dahomean features of her work, one might conclude her quilt was done in Congo-Angola. And yet the squared patterns of the fabric and depictions of characters are so close to those of Dahomey that one might, except for the four moments and other Bakongo symbols incorporated into the quilt, conclude it was fashioned there. Thus, her quilt is a symbol of the fusion of African ethnic traditions in slavery and later.

The depiction of crosses in the upper left corner of the quilt, in which four suns are represented, calls to mind the four moments of the sun, especially since the suns are patterned exactly as they are by Bakongo, which suggests that the same religious vision informed the crosses and suns—a vision of circularity.[221] It is also possible, though unlikely, that the particular cross depicted is Dahomean with a meaning different from that of the Bakongo cross. Even if that is so, it seems inconceivable that Bakongo slaves did not, when viewing a cross in such a context, derive four moments and the circle by moving in the accustomed way from one point of the cross to another. Given the Bakongo presence in North America and the influence of that group in the ring shout, in baptismal ceremonies, and in the construction of burial mounds, such an association was almost certainly made by slaves under their influence. That association was logical for slaves who affirmed the circularity of the cross, as in Virginia at baptismal ceremonies in which they sang of Christ dying on Calvary. But the crucifixion or superimposition of Christ is explicitly realized in the lower right-hand corner of the Bible quilt and helps to form an arc around a tiny manger in an extremely subtle melding of Christian and African values.[222]

Since Dahomeans were in Virginia in the time of Simon Brown, as they had been before his birth, and since specific reference was made in "How the Slaves Worshipped" to the use of quilts in baptismal ceremonies, one could hardly imagine a more subtle affirmation of African values than that which occurred when a quilt with crosses and suns was used to warm the shivering convert. And though the Ashanti cross, like the Dahomean, may not represent circularity and four moments, such representations might have been associated with it on a plantation on which the staff-cross was brandished and Gold Coast burial mounds constructed. The presence of customs grounded in ancestral concerns, such as the decoration of the burial mound, made it easier to invest another African cross, whether Ashanti or Dahomean, with the values of the Bakongo when the staff-cross was a focal point of ritual. Although these possibilities were real enough, there is no doubt that the Powers quilt, in its exacting reproduction of African symbols and processes, illustrates the persistence of African values in her consciousness at least as late as the 1890s, the decade in which the quilt was made. When asked about the meaning of her quilt, Harriet Powers responded at considerable length and in much detail, asserting that the quilt in every particular is Christian.[223]

Perhaps no one was better qualified to judge the impact of Christianity on free blacks and slaves than Bishop Daniel Alexander Payne, of the African Methodist Episcopal Church (A.M.E.). In 1878, in Philadelphia, Payne attended a "bush meeting" of black Christians and was so disturbed at seeing them do the ring shout that he "requested the pastor to go and stop their dancing." At the pastor's request, "they stopped their dancing and clapping of hands, but remained singing and rocking their bodies to and fro." The momentum of the performance continued through singing and rocking until Payne approached the leader of the shouters and "requested him to desist and to sit down and sing in a rational manner." Payne told him that such worship was "heathenish . . . disgraceful to themselves, the race, and the Christian name," at which point they broke up the ring and "walked sullenly away." But that was not enough for Payne, who had encountered the ring shout over a period of decades and still looked upon it as a powerful, dominating presence among the black masses, in the North and the South.

> After the sermon in the afternoon, having another opportunity of speaking alone to this young leader of the singing and clapping ring, he said: "Sinners won't get converted unless there is a ring." Said I: "You might sing till you fell down dead, and you would fail to convert a single sinner, because nothing but the Spirit of God and the word of God can convert sinners." He replied: "The Spirit of God works upon people in different ways. At camp meeting there must be a ring here, a ring there, a ring over yonder, or sinners will not get converted."[224]

The resistance to the jettisoning of African spiritual values in the conversion to Christianity was widespread among blacks, and no one was more aware of that than Payne, who had a dreadful time and dismal results in the effort, never understanding that the shout was a primary means of contact with and respect for the ancestral spirits and the source of artistic expression to that end. It is small wonder that Payne, in believing there could be no Christian conversion for his people without abandonment of the shout, encountered severe and wide opposition, for they believed there could be no conversion except through the ring. In a word, he was asking them to give up the products of ancestral genius as well as the means by which spiritual autonomy was preserved, and with it a certain unity of being. And because the shout, prevalent in the folktale, associated with the burial mound, and the primary means of encouraging that unity, was the single most important cause of the formation of a common consciousness and ethos, Payne drew almost uniformly hostile reactions in attempting to extirpate it from black Christianity.

Nowhere was that hostility more actively expressed than in Baltimore, Maryland, though Payne also had problems in Washington, D.C. Having opposed the singing of spirituals in Bethel Church in Baltimore, he was rejected by a congregation led by two women who, rising from a front row and approaching the pulpit with clubs, attacked him and an assistant pastor. "The trouble grew out of my endeavor to modify the extravagances in worship," including "their spiritual songs," he admitted. His assistant was left in a puddle of blood, but Payne was not seriously injured, the blow directed at him glancing off his shoulder. Though he contended he was able "to correct some bad customs of worship, and especially to moderate the singing and praying bands, which then [1850] existed in the most extravagant form" one wonders whether his successes, if they occurred, lasted, considering a later assertion:

> As to the "songs," as already stated, I had attempted to modify some of the extravagances in worship in Bethel Church. These songs were known as "Corn-field Ditties." I left them, considering myself unjustly rejected; nor would I return upon being urged by Bishop Quinn to go to take possession of the charge, supported by civil and ecclesiastical law. I declined on the ground that the people had deliberately rejected me, and as I had always exhibited a disinterested friendship for them, and had voluntarily rendered them signal service, if they did not want me, I did not want them.[225]

In fact, that is his tone in summing up the movement to end the ring shout of black Christians. If anything, it is despairing, and Payne favored expulsion of the vast majority of black Christians from the church as late as the 1870s, if the ring shout could not be curbed. He admitted success only among the "intelligent," presumably the tiny minority of "educated" blacks, among whom he succeeded in making the ring shout appear "disgusting"; the ignorant masses regarded "the ceremony as the essence of religion," and that applied to the masses in the District of Columbia, Pennsylvania, Maryland, and other places to which he had traveled. "So much so was this the case that," like the young man with whom he debated in Philadelphia, "they believed no conversion could occur without their agency, nor outside of their own ring could any be a genuine one." Though he remonstrated with numerous pastors for allowing such practices, he met with the invariable response "that they could not succeed in restraining them, and an attempt to compel them to cease would simply drive them away from our church."[226]

Payne thought a critical juncture was at hand, that the time had come when the A.M.E. Church "must drive out this heathenish mode of worship or drive out all the intelligence, refinement, and practical Christians who may be in her bosom."[227] One can almost sympathize with Payne, despite his ignorance of African religion and its impact on the spiritual, political, and artistic life of blacks and the nation. As slavery ended and the membership of black Baptists and Methodists increased and black churches proliferated, there was simply no easy way for the regular black Christian ministry—those ministers not grounded in the religion of the plantation slave—to affirm the religious vision of the new converts, which was alien to their sense of what was proper. Payne's predicament in 1878 and later was that the majority of black Christians in Pennsylvania and elsewhere seemed actually to be more African in religious practice than European.

> These "Bands" I have had to encounter in many places, and, as I have stated with regard to my early labors in Baltimore, I have been strongly censured because of my efforts to change the mode of worship or modify the extravagances indulged in by the people.[228]

The A.M.E. Church, headquartered in Philadelphia, the home of its founder, Richard Allen, with branches in many states, found its masses infected as by an "incurable religious disease," so much so that it was with Payne "a question whether it would not be better to let such people go out of the Church than remain in it to perpetuate their evil practice and thus do two things: disgrace the Christian name and corrupt others." What was all too frequently observed, that Christianity made little impact on the slave spiritually, was so revolting to Payne that it led him to oppose any semblance of African influence in the black religion of his era. He found the force of African spirituality almost superhuman, calling for a "cure" proportionate to the affliction, one that ruled out any compromise of visions, any synthesis of faiths. A powerful counterforce was needed because some of the most influential and popular preachers labored "systematically to perpetuate this fanaticism."

> How needful it is to have an intelligent ministry to teach these people who hold to this ignorant mode of worship the true method of serving God. . . . My observations lead me to the conclusion that we need more than an intelligent ministry to cure this religious fanaticism. We need a host of Christian reformers like St. Paul.[229]

But it was too late for African religion—and therefore for African culture—to be contained or reversed, because its advocates were practically the whole black population in America: the essential features of the ring shout were present in one form or another, and hardly a state in the Union was without its practitioners during and following slavery. Moreover, the shout continued to form the principal context in which black creativity occurred. Marshall Stearns had this in mind when writing that the "continued existence of the ring-shout is of critical importance to jazz, because it means that an assortment of West African musical characteristics are preserved, more or less intact, in the United States—from rhythms and blue tonality, through the falsetto break and the call-and-response pattern, to the songs of allusion and even the motions of African dance."[230]

The ring shout, prominent in Louisiana well before Bremer and Olmsted observed it in the 1850s, helped form the context in which jazz music was created. With scores of secret societies flourishing in New Orleans, financial as well as spiritual support was available to jazzmen performing on behalf of the societies, including performances at funerals, in which circularity was noted: In church, before reaching the cemetery,

those who belonged to the various benevolent societies "circled the cas-
ket. Some . . . would shout and scream hysterically." After marching
solemnly to the grave, they returned in a different mood, dancing "individual and various dances" as the band "burst into 'Just Stay A Little
While,'" with relatives of the deceased "soon trucking with the rest of
them."[231]

Of the shout and the life that accompanies it, Stearns offers the important insight that a large number of jazzmen "even among the ultra--
moderns are familiar with all or part of it because they lived near one of
the sanctified churches during childhood."[232] So it was with Milt Jackson, and so it was with perhaps the most original of jazz composers,
Thelonious Monk, who frequently rose from his piano, cigarette in
mouth, and proceeded to dance in a counterclockwise direction, his feet
beating out intricate figures before he returned to the piano and joined his
combo in playing music as advanced as any of his era.[233]

But jazz musicians merely formed the apex of the pyramid. Farther
below, down among the masses that produced the jazzman and responded
to his art, the ring shout continued to be expressed in even its most complex forms, at times in ways that recalled the Bakongo religious vision
with almost startling clarity. Even among a people who practiced the
shout vigorously and ubiquitously in the closing decades of the nineteenth
century, the discovery of the ritual in the fullness of its Bakongo expression in the 1920s is but additional evidence of their ability to respond to
oppression in ways that affirm values proper to them—in the teeth of that
oppression. The classic case of such values melded with and transforming
Christian values is that of Maum Hester of South Carolina.

> She was possessed with the idea that every day that passed carried with it a
> record of the deeds and thoughts which had been performed by each person.
> The sun carried the record somewhere to the center of the earth, where the
> moon and stars, the signs and seasons, all rested until their appointed time to
> appear. The "Lawd Jedus" presided over the entrance to this region, and
> observed the record which each day bore of the doings of mortal men which
> were to be stored up against the Judgment Day. Maum Hester's chief concern
> was that the record which the sun bore to her Lawd Jedus each night might
> prove acceptable to him.[234]

"Only the figure of Jesus Christ identifies Maum Hester's beliefs as Christian; the rest is saturated with Bakongo imagery," writes Anne Spurgeon
in a brilliant paper on African spiritual influences in black American culture. Spurgeon's analysis is persuasive, for we have seen that "concepts
of heaven and judgment" were not foreign to large numbers of Africans,
especially Ibos and Bakongo, entering America.[235] The place of the cosmogram in the shout, however, was inspired in North America by the
Bakongo, its presence within a ritual being the source of definitive power
to all familiar with the four moments:

She first opened her shutter wide toward the west, and then told how, as soon as the sun looked in at the window and told her he [the sun] was going to see the "Lawd Jedus," she stood there, "jus' lak-a-dat" . . . and repeated three times this formula: "Do, Lawd Jedus, is I please you dis day?" Each time that she repeated this form of invocation, after walking around the room in a circle with the peculiar posture, step, and rapt expression which is characteristic of the Negro "shout." . . . After the third question, her emotional state bordered on hysteria. . . . "But de t'ird time, de sun he 'gin move, I see he shoutin'. Den I happy, by I know den I done please de Lawd Jedus dat day!"[236]

The anthropologist and folklorist Zora Neale Hurston makes the pioneering comment that

the Negro has not been christianized as extensively as is generally believed. The great masses are still standing before their pagan altars and calling old gods by a new name . . . so the congregation is restored to its primitive altars under the new name of Christ. Then there is the expression known as "shouting" which is nothing more than a continuation of the African "Possession" by the gods. The gods possess the body of a worshipper and he or she is supposed to know nothing of their actions until the god decamps. This is still prevalent in most Negro protestant churches and is universal in Sanctified churches.[237]

The basis for the shout's flourishing in the North was laid by the great migrations of blacks from the South from the close of the nineteenth century to the 1940s and later. The implications of this movement were enormous not only for black religion but for American culture—a subject of great importance that awaits full exploration. But already we know that the ring shout exists in America today with all the power of its expression more than a century ago. Stearns's and Hurston's suggestion regarding the sanctified church as a harborer of the shout is borne out by Baldwin's *Go Tell It on the Mountain* when, during Sunday morning services in the slums of Harlem in the 1940s—"the sisters in white, the brothers in blue, heads back; the white caps of the women seeming to glow in the charged air like crowns"—the piano player "hit the keys, beginning at once to sing, and everybody joined him, clapping their hands, and rising, and beating the tambourines."

While John watched, the Power struck someone, a man or woman; they cried out, a long wordless crying, and, arms outstretched like wings, they began the Shout. Someone moved a chair a little to give them room, the rhythm paused, the singing stopped, only the pounding feet and the clapping hands were heard; then another cry, another dancer; then the tambourines began again, and the cries rose again, and the music swept on again, like fire, or flood, or judgment. Then . . . like a planet rocking in space, the temple rocked with the Power of God. John watched, watched the faces, and the weightless bodies, and listened to the timeless cries.[238]

CHAPTER TWO

David Walker:
In Defense of African Rights
and Liberty

> [Y]our full glory and happiness, as well as all other coloured people under Heaven, shall never be fully consummated, but with the entire emancipation of your enslaved brethren all over the world.
>
> —DAVID WALKER, 1829

In 1785, the General Assembly of North Carolina, seeking greater control of slaves and free Negroes, passed legislation aimed at Wilmington, where David Walker and his mother lived, and three other towns.

> And in order to discriminate between free Negroes, mulattoes, and other persons of mixed blood and slaves:
>
> X. Be it enacted . . . that all persons of the above mentioned description who are or shall be free on or before the said first day of May next, apply to the commissioners, trustees or directors of the respective towns aforesaid, in order to have their names registered; and every such person coming into said towne . . . to reside, shall within three days . . . make like application; and the commissioners, trustees, or directors are hereby authorized to give every such free person a badge of cloth . . . to be fixed on the left shoulder, and to have thereon wrought in legible capital letters the word FREE.[1]

Had Walker's father not died a few months before his son's birth in that year, he might have walked the streets a slave beside a wife and son wearing the word *FREE* upon their shoulders, for Walker's mother had to register herself and David as free Negroes and to obtain the badges of cloth. Since David, after growing up, was "indignant at the wrongs which his father and kindred bore," the badge must have burned like a brand upon his shoulder.[2] His involvement with his family is also indicated by his remark that "we feel for our fathers, mothers, wives and children, as well as the whites do for theirs."[3] His father's death in slavery and his mother's oppression as a free Negro must have been painful sources of strength for Walker when he reflected on the tragedy of their lives.

Racial oppression in North Carolina dictated a recognition of common interest among slaves and free Negroes, and no one was more aware of that than whites. Whatever the predilections of individual slaves or free Negroes, the laws of the state and the will of whites to enforce them reduced free Negroes, by the turn of the century, almost to the level of slaves. Johnson summed up the plight of the free Negro at the beginning of the century:

> The nineteenth century opened with only three important laws in force restricting the freedom of the free Negro. These curtailed his relations with the dominant race, his mobility, and his association with slaves. In 1746 all Negroes and Mulattoes, both bond and free, to the third generation were declared incapable of appearing as a witness against a white person. In 1777 the legislature extended the disqualification to Negroes to the fourth generation. Such a restriction upon the free man's civil rights made him little better than a slave. It meant that the free Negro was at the mercy of the dominant race.[4]

In that repressive atmosphere, news of slave revolts elsewhere sent currents of fear through white communities, and this applied even to resistance on the small scale that characterized revolts in North America. Thus, events in Haiti that led to French withdrawal and the defeat of Bonaparte's army were fearfully regarded by many North Carolinians, and this mainly accounts for a law in 1795—Walker was then ten years old—calling for the suppression by force of any gathering of free Negroes and slaves aimed at challenging the servile positions assigned to each. That the 1795 law was passed in response to Haitian developments is almost certain, since slaves in North Carolina had not been showing signs of overt disaffection.[5]

"Sensitive and delicate as the peculiar institution was," writes John Hope Franklin, "the least disturbance was the occasion for further circumscription of the free Negroes."[6] The slave systems of the Americas were interconnected and mutually dependent in a number of ways, especially Caribbean and North American slavery. Whether in retrospect or at the time the law was passed, Walker saw the connection and, at the time he set down his reflections on the slave uprising against France, found unity of interest between the slaves in America and those in Haiti.[7]

No doubt owing to events in Haiti, more legislation was directed against free Negroes, discouraging them from entering the state. The legislators reasoned that such a period of tension was no time for the introduction of more irritants in the form of free Negroes. The law "required all free Negroes to enter bond to the amount of £200 for their good behavior upon coming into the state and subjected all failing to do so to arrest, trial by jury, and sale at public auction.''[8] A related law was later passed that

> declared it to be unlawful for a free Negro or mulatto to migrate to North
> Carolina and required such Negroes entering the State to leave within twenty
> days after receiving notice upon pain of a $500 fine. Negroes suspected of
> entering the State illegally were to be arrested, bound over to the next county
> court, tried by jury, and upon conviction were to be sold into servitude for
> not more than ten years if unable to pay the fine. The bill also contained a
> general provision against vagabond free Negroes so that anyone able to labor,
> found spending his time "in idleness and dissipation, or having no regular or
> honest employment," might be arrested by any citizen upon warrant issued
> by a justice of the peace, bound over to the next county court, and, upon
> conviction, sold into servitude for not more than three years.[9]

Even though blacks attempted risings in North Carolina shortly after the new century opened, just as they had in Virginia under Gabriel, a possible indication in both cases of a response to the Haitian example, their efforts at the time in retrospect impressed Walker far less than they impressed white Carolinians and Virginians. It appears he very early decided that only massive slave challenges were worthy of serious attention because only they, short of divine intervention, would bring down the system of slavery. Yet it is doubtful anyone in the state, outside the slave population, was as interested in successful slave revolt on any scale as he, because the need for slave emancipation, by the time his *Appeal* appeared, was the organizing principle of his life.

The abortive insurrection that took place in more than four counties of northeastern North Carolina in 1802 served to impress upon radicals sympathizing with the rebels the need for greater resistance in spite of the price to be paid. Those insurrections were followed by the usual executions and the usual tightening of the laws:

> Be it . . . enacted, that if any free person shall join in any conspiracy, re-
> bellion or insurrection of the slaves, or shall procure or persuade others to
> join or enlist for that purpose or shall assist any slave or slaves in a state of
> rebelling . . . by furnishing, or agreeing to promise to furnish such slaves with
> arms, ammunition or any other articles for their aid and support, every free
> person so offending and being thereof legally convicted, shall be adjudged
> guilty of felony, and shall suffer death without benefit of clergy.[10]

The brand *FREE* did not protect blacks from being kidnapped and enslaved or, in some cases, reenslaved. It is likely the word *FREE* on the shoulders of blacks greatly simplified the problem of identification and served as a magnet for kidnappers, since their depredations could hardly hurt those already enslaved. There was, all the while, no lessening of tension, in view of the existence of legislation making it possible for free Negroes who transgressed the laws of North Carolina to be enslaved.

That legislation helped provide the atmosphere in which kidnappers plied their trade.[11] Walker and his mother lived in that atmosphere, as did all free Negroes in the state throughout slavery. Though measures were passed to help protect them from enslavement, the possibility of such disaster striking heightened tension and contributed to caution on the part of free Negroes. Their lack of money meant that most did not enjoy the luxury of being able to move to the North, though some did.[12]

Whites were at times sympathetic to the efforts of free Negroes to purchase and seek the manumission of children or other relatives. Scores of Negroes were purchased by relatives who wanted to see them free. But even when there were sufficient funds to make the purchase there was no guarantee a sale would be made. When sales were made, it was a measure of the power of whites to determine the future of blacks. But the freedom of Southern Negroes was generally predicated on the goodwill of whites, especially on the efforts of manumission societies to foster an atmosphere in which some slaves might become free. The Quakers were particularly active in this regard. In 1816 they formed

> manumission societies to create sentiment in behalf of emancipation, and in July of that year organized the General Association of the Manumission Society of North Carolina. . . . Occasionally the General Association assisted manumitted Negroes to remove to free soil and intervened in cases of kidnapping. It circulated anti-slavery tracts among its members, petitioned the State Legislature and Congress on the subject of emancipation. By 1825 the North Carolina Manumission Society had twenty-eight branches and a membership of more than a thousand. From 1828 the Society began to decline and in July, 1834, held its last meeting.[13]

There is no reason to doubt that Walker was aware of such efforts to promote the manumission of slaves, for the news traveled by word of mouth. In addition, the North Carolina press covered the activities of the societies, and Walker could read.

There had been challenging opportunities for him to learn to read, of which he availed himself, for he could not have become as educated as he was after leaving the South for Boston. One possibility was an apprenticeship system for Negro youth that brought them into contact with white pupils and their fathers. Under that system, masters in the state were required by law to teach their wards to read and write, and in general did so. But Walker was such a free man in spirit and thought that it is rather unlikely he learned to read and write under such an arrangement.[14] Franklin points to an even more interesting method of learning for the small number of Negroes exposed to it:

> Perhaps the Quakers accomplished more than any other sect in the task of educating the Negroes of ante-bellum North Carolina. . . . In 1816, a school for Negroes was opened to run two days a week for three months. The boys

were to attend until they were able to read, write and cipher as far as the rule of three, and the girls were to attend until they were able to read and write.[15]

Clandestine teaching of free Negroes was also taking place and available to Negroes in various parts of the state. Through one or a combination of such means, Walker learned to read and write.[16] It is possible the process took place intermittently and over a considerable length of time before he was at ease with written and spoken English. Since he was among the most knowledgeable of Americans on the history of slavery from ancient times to the nineteenth century, he must have begun reading widely on the subject, almost certainly, before he moved to the North.

The authorities found a way to inform free Negroes and slaves of laws passed to control them; otherwise, the enforcement of such laws would have been much more difficult. Being a free Negro meant being informed from time to time of what was expected of one and of the penalties to be paid for going against the law. Not a little of the free Negro's thought, therefore, was given to restrictions before him, to reflecting on how they might be relaxed or tightened or circumvented, depending on the circumstances. When Walker joined the tiny number of free Negroes able to read and write, he became even more exposed to legislation affecting the lives of free Negroes and slaves in North Carolina and elsewhere.

Regarded as "pests of society," free Negroes found themselves increasingly under attack. In 1809 the adjutant general of the North Carolina militia claimed that it lessened "the respectability of a military company to have men of colour in the ranks, and prevent[ed] many persons from mustering, who would otherwise do so." In 1812, the legislature responded by barring free Negroes from the militia "except as musicians."[17] Not until 1825 were there further efforts to restrict their freedom in North Carolina. In that year the legislature of Vermont served notice of its opposition to slavery and its interest in helping any state rid itself of this evil; this policy was interpreted by the governor of North Carolina as interference not to be tolerated. Moreover, the governor asserted that such misguided urgings from elsewhere required "sleepless vigilance" with respect to race relations in North Carolina—and more legislation.[18]

Though there was great opposition to contact between slaves and free Negroes and though their movements were circumscribed by opinion and law, they had opportunities to get to know each other. The main street in Wilmington was a place of contact on bustling Saturdays as slaves mingled with whites and free Negroes. Throughout the week, the slave population of Wilmington, numbering in the hundreds at the time of Walker's birth and increasing to four thousand by the 1850s, walked the sandy, unpaved streets of the town, and so did Walker as he grew older. On his walks, he saw the wretched living quarters of Wilmington slaves, perhaps once inhabited by his father. Robert Russell visited the town and found "mean Negro huts . . . by no means a pleasing feature of the place." By contrast, whenever he walked along the main street, he saw the palatial homes of the slaveholders rowed off a few yards back amid trees on either side, extending the length of the street.[19]

Slaves were usually first on the scene at North Carolina town markets, making purchases for their masters, most of whom lived in splendid contrast to the Negroes occupying the huts of the town. The immense wealth of the Collins family, owners of three hundred slaves, was not easily matched elsewhere in the state and was not seen in Wilmington. Knowing the uses to which slave labor was put and the "avarice" of slaveholders, Walker was not unmindful of even the riches described by Warren at the isolated Collins estate:

> I scarcely ever visited the "Lake" without finding a large company assembled there, having as good a time as it is possible to conceive of. Such a host of servants, horses, carriages, games, boats, guns, accouterments, musical instruments, and appliances generally for interesting and entertaining people, I never saw collected together. His table . . . groaned in fact beneath the load of every delicacy that taste could suggest, and such triumphs of the culinary art as were only possible to the well-trained darkey cooks with which his kitchen was crowded, while wines of the most ancient vintage and liquors of the choicest brands flowed around it like water from some exhaustless spring.[20]

All Walker had to do to expose himself to more slaves was to cross over the Cape Fear River at Wilmington and walk a mile along a road by the swamp to a field where rice was cultivated. Since the secret of rice cultivation was not known to the colonists until Africans revealed it in South Carolina, rice cultivation in North Carolina almost certainly was the handiwork of some African men and women. Russell visited the rice field outside Wilmington and described what he saw, a process of cultivation distinctly West African:

> A number of negroes, men and women, were cleaning out the ditches, and digging over the land, which consisted of a rich vegetable mould. An intelligent Negro told me that one man was able to manage five acres of rice—to dig the ground, sow the seed, water, hoe, reap, and thrash the crop.[21]

Not just on holidays like Christmas and the Fourth of July, when slaves came into Wilmington, but also of a Saturday afternoon or Sunday throughout the year Walker could move among slaves from the countryside, as free Negroes often did. It was easier for free Negroes to have contact with slaves in towns on weekends because the number of slaves was greater then than at any other time. Moreover, as in Southern cities generally, a kind of underground existed in Wilmington, where liquor was sold—for three cents—and where white proprietors grew wealthy while slaves and free Negroes had contact under circumstances of camaraderie that promoted a lowering of barriers.[22]

A North Carolina free Negro had only to walk the streets of his town in order to see slaves. As they moved about the towns, negative responses came from whites in town after town, and constables were directed to flog Negroes who were too loud on the Sabbath. Mostly field hands came to town on weekends, because skilled slaves and house servants constituted a small minority of the slave population, which meant that slaves with the least amount of contact with whites and the greatest sense of identification with their own people were the ones visiting Wilmington.[23] Since there were never more than a few hundred free Negroes in North Carolina towns during slavery, and since none of the towns were thriving port areas like Memphis, Charleston, or Atlanta with large white populations, a certain rural character prevailed in North Carolina towns that in some ways seemed slightly more interesting extensions of the countryside.

I

From Walker's childhood to the time of his departure later for Boston, slaves in Wilmington on Christmas Day, after arising and shouting "Christmas gif'," danced through the streets and chanted rhythmically:

> Hah! Low! Here we go!
> Hah! Low! Here we go!
> Hah! Low! Here we go!
> Kuners come from Denby![24]

Christmas Day in Wilmington has been described in detail, from the weather to Kunering:

> Christmas in Wilmington is frequently a balmy day with more of the atmosphere of early spring or late fall than of the so-called seasonable Christmas of some northerly points. On any Christmas morning . . . one could hear . . . the song of the Kuners as they came down the sandy streets of Wilmington. . . The leader stood out in front of his group and sang the verses of his song, the others joining in the refrain while they rattled their bones, made of beef ribs, and made noises upon the cows' horns, triangles, and jew's-harps. . . . The solo voice sang the first and third lines, the effect being much like that of the familiar negro working or camp meeting songs.

The performance ended with shouts from behind masks of "enormous noses, widely grinning mouths, horns and beards . . . terrifying to behold":

> Hah! Low! Here we go!
> Hah! Low! Here we go!
> Hah! Low! Here we go!
> Kuners come from Denby![25]

What appeared grotesque was the outward expression of a more complex and, at times, playful inner reality, a contrasting of visions characteristic of African irony. Africans in America constructed not only drums in the fashion known to them in Africa but also rattles and horns. Similarly, other aspects of the costumes were African, especially the bright strips of cloth and the horns and masks. When a performer, extending his hat, approached the spectators "cutting the pigeonwing," the ceremony ended in African dance.[26]

The wearing of masks, a reflection of the place of ancestors in the ceremony, had the effect of reinforcing the stereotype that Africans were frolicking, especially since Kunering was the occasion for slaves enjoying themselves. Certain aspects of the ceremony were indeed decidedly secular. One song tells the story of the arrest of a black manager of a dance hall, Beau Bill, and reveals a degree of acculturation in song lyric that could hardly be distinguished from the singing of whites but for rhythms voiced in darkly colored tones:

> Old Beau Bill was a fine old man,
> A riggin' and a roggin' in the world so long:
> But now his days have come to pass,
> And we're bound to break up Beau Bill's class

> REFRAIN
> So sit still ladies and don't take a chill
> While the captain of the guardhouse ties Beau Bill.[27]

The resolution was sufficiently edifying to please a religious man as strict as Walker, and it is a certainty that he heard Kuner songs from youth, since he came from the Wilmington black community, a stronghold of John Kunering. In fact, of the North Carolina towns,

Wilmington was the place where the festivity was celebrated most vigorously. Whether or not it spread from this . . . city to the other localities has not been determined, but it is in Wilmington that we find vestigal remains of the tradition most strongly entrenched.[28]

It was hardly possible for free Negroes to be ignorant of the presence of Kuners on holidays in Edenton, New Bern, Hilton, Hillsboro, Wilmington, Fayetteville, and Southport, where they were heard for blocks away making music, the ceremony at times ending as one of them extended his hat and approached the crowd dancing "Chicken in the breadtray." After "large copper pennies" were collected, the Kuners retreated up one street and down another in search of new fields of remuneration.[29]

One can only speculate as to whether Walker saw John Kunering—referred to as "John Canoeing" in some parts of North Carolina, the Bahamas, and Jamaica—in its most African expression at some plantations in the state. At the Collins's extravagant holding, which we referred to earlier, there were expressions of Kunering in which the lead performers, at times profiled against the sheet of water in the background, danced dances as African as could be observed in the New World. And now and then on such occasions songs were sung that resembled some heard in the ring shout—"of a strange, monotonous cadence."[30]

> My massa am a white man, juba!
> Old missus am a lady, juba!
> De children am de honey-pods, juba! juba!
> Krismas come but once a year, juba!
> Juba! juba! O, ye juba![31]

Shortly after the "present" was received from the master of the plantation, the most vigorous dancing of all occurred in an accustomed place:

> And then the expected "quarter" having been jingled for sometime in the tin cup, the performers moved on to visit in turn the young gentlemen's colony, the tutor's rooms, the parson's study, the overseer's house, and finally, the quarters, to wind up with a grand jollification, in which all took part until they broke down and gave it up from sheer exhaustion.[32]

Considering the place of religion in West Africa, where dance and song are means of relating to ancestral spirits and to God, the Christmas season was conducive to Africans in America continuing to attach sacred value to John Kunering. Warren sensed the religious impulse that led to Kunering on grounds other than the ceremony's link to the Moslem faith, arguing that Kunering in North Carolina "was more a fantasia than a religious demonstration . . . that it had, however, some connection with their religion is evident from the fact that they only indulged in it on Christian festivals, notably on Christmas day." But Ira Reid argues that Kunering was also practiced on holidays other than Christmas. Referring to "John Canoe," interestingly, as the "Negro 'king' of many a nineteenth century Easter, Christmas and New Year festival in the New World," he states that Kunering also took place on the Fourth of July and on Halloween in North Carolina.[33]

The slaves' pent-up emotion and sorrow and the encouragement from slave masters helped account for the indulgence of many North Carolina slaves in revelry and drink on Christmas and other holidays. "It is to be regretted," wrote Dr. James Norcom, "that drunkeness is too common on these occasions; but this also is habitually overlooked and never punished, unless it became outrageous or grossly offensive."[34] Perhaps the recognition of the need for some release for slaves—a recognition born of fear and guilt—caused North Carolina whites to encourage John Kunering and a festive air among slaves on the streets of their towns. But it was guilt outweighed by selfishness:

> At such a season, instead of driving these wretched creatures, with cold and unfeeling sensibility, from our doors, the heart of charity dilates towards

them, and the angel of humanity whispers in our ears that they are entitled to a part of those blessings which their labour has procured us.[35]

Slave entertainment and dances on plantations were seldom witnessed by free Negroes, yet those festivities were part of the North Carolina environment. There, on the plantations, slaves entertained themselves with much less concern for the aesthetic tastes of others than slaves and free Negroes in cities. The more undiluted those tastes, the more freely expressed, the greater the mystery they posed for those outside the culture, black or white. The fiddle and the banjo were the principal instruments on such occasions and dancing and singing a collective preoccupation into the morning. That dancing and singing into the morning occurred in North Carolina follows, since most of the slave population there came from Virginia and South Carolina, where slaves, in folklore and in life, danced and sang at length, often all night.[36]

Despite an act of 1794 that made it illegal for persons to allow slaves to dance and drink on their premises without the written consent of their owners, dancing and drinking under such circumstances were not unknown thereafter. The law was not invariably observed, and slaves and free Negroes at times danced "to the music of a banjo until a late hour," as they did when the opportunity presented itself elsewhere in America. The *Raleigh Register,* for example, recorded that slaves frolicked and danced without restriction in the house of a free Negro. Such contact between slaves and free Negroes occurred in Wilmington, but, since Walker opposed drinking and there was much on these occasions, it is hard to imagine him in attendance except rarely.[37]

Walker's later failure even to note the existence of slave art probably owed much to the seeming excesses of slaves while dancing and singing. Besides, slave art would not very likely have been a preoccupation for one for whom slavery was extremely repugnant from early in life and resistance to it emblematic of his character. And since dance and song were for slaves the chief means of artistic expression while worshiping, one who took his Christianity seriously was likely to be even less respectful of slave art in a context in which drinking took place. The performance of black art under such conditions helps explain Walker's apparent failure to perceive the legitimacy of that art on black or any other terms. Not surprisingly, the secular conditions under which he was apt to witness or hear about slave art were often those he was most inclined, given his temperament and commitments, to find objectionable. It is, in fact, hard to imagine Walker at a gathering to which blacks had come after a hard day's work and miles of walking to "pleasure" themselves with a "drop of drink" and "the privilege of flinging head, hands, and legs about in a manner which threatened dislocation." In such a setting "laughing, jumping, dancing, and singing of favorite ditties, such as Vir-

ginia Nigger Berry Good and, I Lost My Shoe in an Old Canoe, might
continue far into the night."[38]

At times, slaves gave such powerful expression to their culture that
whites were angered, and violence ensued. On the plantation of Jacob
Boyce of Perquimans County, slaves danced on holidays, at quiltings, and
at logrollings, sometimes making so much noise that they were heard almost a mile away. On one occasion when Boyce invited slaves in to dance
for visitors and family, the patrol angrily burst through the door, began
tying up slaves, and whipped fourteen. The patrol sued Boyce for keeping
a disorderly house but did not win. Chief Justice Ruffin recognized fundamental differences between black and white music and dance, and ruled
the gathering essentially harmless:

> If slaves would do nothing tending more to the corruption of their morals or
> to the annoyance of the whites than seeking the exhilaration of their simple
> music and romping dances, they might be set down as an innocent and happy
> class. We may let them make the most of their idle hours, and may well make
> allowances for the noisy outpourings of glad hearts, which Providence be-
> stows as a blessing on corporeal vigor united to a vacant mind.[39]

The judge would have regarded slave burial ceremonies as meaningless,
since most were as different from white burial practices as black music
and dance from that of whites. A Methodist circuit rider, the Reverend
James Jenkins, wrote of a feast at the time of a funeral in North Carolina—in the decade of Walker's birth—that was African and related to
practices elsewhere in the South during slavery and later. After supper
and an all-night vigil, at dawn the slaves "went to the grave of the deceased, making great lamentation over it, and broke a bottle of spirits on
the head board, or if they could not be had, meal and water were substituted in its place."[40] Africanity was demonstrated in mourning song
and dance, in the transcendence of the spirit for which nourishment was
provided on the burial mound, the broken glass left as religious art, the
contents of the bottle absorbed by the deceased while disappearing upon
the earth. Through the use of the bottle of spirits, a more generalized
West African burial rite was in essential harmony with the burial rites of
African groups in Virginia, South Carolina and elsewhere more noted for
decorating the burial mound with broken glass and other objects without
necessarily pouring libations and offering food.[41]

A ritual prominent in West Africa was also observed by the Reverend
Jenkins—the "play for the dead."[42] The return of the ancestors, represented through the living, occurred as surreptitiously as possible at the
grave in North Carolina because of hostility to African religion. That the
slave population of that state was being replenished by means of the domestic slave trade when the "play" was observed by the white minister
rather than directly from Africa provides some indication of the continu-

ing strength and complexity of African religion in the states from which slaves were brought to North Carolina. The Reverend Jenkins observed the living playing the roles of ancestors at the graveside referred to earlier but did not understand the significance of the event.

What he thought "nothing but a frolic" involved sacred dance and, despite great lamentation at the graveside, religious joy beyond his comprehension, the continuing interplay between the living and the dead—a reciprocity of spirit enhanced through an observance of a whole range of African burial practices. The slave dinner of respectable proportions met a critical African requirement for due observance of the death of a family member, strengthening bonds of family under circumstances of enslavement that were calculated to weaken them. Such ceremonies were but evidence of "heathenism" for white and black Christians observing black culture from the outside, as was the case with whites and almost all blacks except those who came to Christianity through conversion within the larger, African slave community—conversion most often symbolized by the circle.

There is no evidence that free Negroes had the preparation to understand the nature of slave religion even if they observed it in its fullness of expression. Consequently, those aspects of the slave experience that reveal commonly practiced rituals across ethnic lines, those that would have been of special interest to Walker, were incomprehensible to him. This was understandable since he was never a slave, and knowledge of African religious practices was nonexistent for nearly all nonslaves in nineteenth-century America. Those practices eased the fusion of African peoples in North America and, in the case of burial ceremonies, reflected a base so broad that slaves from almost any section of West Africa could rest their religious beliefs on it, however different those beliefs in other respects.

Similar evidence is found in slave fishing and hunting practices in North Carolina. So skillful were they at both that, despite severe restrictions on equipment and weapons, they bested whites around them. "They angled lazily with hook and worm on a Saturday afternoon in early Spring and autumn or they set fish traps and collected about them on Saturday nights to shoot craps and sing."[43] Whites claimed that slaves dominated fishing holes, robbing competitors of cash. Such concerns reached the newspaper, as complaints mounted against the highly skilled slave fishermen, precisely the sort of denial of elementary decencies to its captives for which Walker bitterly assailed American slavery above all other systems of slavery in history. If he did not find out about such disputes through the newspapers, the opportunity was available to him to see the slaves facing hostility when in town selling their catches.[44]

Until 1831, slaves could "pleasure" themselves in North Carolina by hunting with one of their number carrying a weapon. That is, during

Walker's life there the law permitted the master to secure a license for that purpose "to provide the plantation with game or to kill the crows and other birds which harmed the growing crops." It was said the Negro made up for his lack of weapons with the number of dogs he carried with him when hunting.[45] And so some combined mastery of European weapons with African hunting practices that, restrictions notwithstanding, gave them the edge. Jane De Forest Shelton, using data from the hunting practices of slaves in New England, has supplied an interesting and persuasive explanation for the hunting skill of the African. She concludes,

> Perhaps it is because the Negro is not as far removed from primitive life as the white man that he seems to have more comprehension of animal creation. He has by instinct what the white man has by training—the power to secure whatever game he seeks. And he can give to the effort a peculiarly patient, cautious, cunning, long-sustaining watchfulness, intensely animate as to his senses, and as entirely inanimate as to his physique, that seem never to fail; be it fox or partridge, possum up a gumtree or domesticated Brahma, the right second is seized, the aim is unerring.

This explains in part why a slave, holding aloft a lighted pine torch, was usually at the head of hunting parties of whites at night in North Carolina.[46]

While for free Negroes who had intimate social contact with slaves there was perhaps some sharing in a common culture, the majority of free Negroes were mulattoes with little or no contact with their brothers and sisters on the plantations.[47] Not only were efforts made to keep slaves and free Negroes apart, for fear of the political consequences of contact between the two groups, but the limitations of distance and the resulting modes of cultural expression available to free Negroes, considering their ignorance of African culture, appear to have greatly limited their cultural horizons in North Carolina. For them, however acute their sense of political realities, the cultural consequences of slavery, when not enriched by exposure to slaves in all-Negro churches or elsewhere, were disastrous. The oppression of blacks cast a shadow across the free Negroes' social relations with slaves, making ever more remote the possibility of their understanding the values in terms of which slaves organized their lives.[48]

It appears certain that the repression of free Negroes was such that, near the bottom of the economic ladder, just above slaves, unprotected by law and custom and generally scorned because of African ancestry, they found cultural concerns necessarily secondary, the struggle for survival pressing. Given their small numbers in Wilmington—no more than a few hundred at a given time in slavery—their sense of vulnerability must have been great and, therefore, unity among them more to be hoped for than realized. Besides, mulattoes constituted the great proportion of free Negroes and were less likely to identify with slaves, whether in Wilmington or on plantations, than were free Negroes with dark skins.

If Walker's grasp of the cultural dimension of slave life was far from certain, we now know that his exposure to that culture was nevertheless greater than was heretofore imagined. He was exposed not only to "John Kunering" in Wilmington for approximately forty years—to Kunering ceremonies of music, dance, and the uses of African masks and dress— but also to African linguistic influences, the latter no doubt evident in his speech.[49] His being born in 1785 means that his mother was probably born as early as 1765 and his father perhaps as early as the 1750s—that his parents were as likely to have been influenced by African as by European speech. Moreover, the probability that one or both of Walker's parents were born in Africa would explain all the more the son's interest in Africans throughout the world. But birth in Africa, given the strength of African culture in North America in colonial and antebellum times, was not a prerequisite for the African personality, which means Walker's father could have been, and probably was, African, irrespective of his place of birth.

That such a possibility was real in North Carolina is reflected in slave burial ceremony and in John Kunering, both of which were African in performance style and content, both of which were important to Africans across ethnic lines. In fact, it can be advanced as axiomatic that, when one finds a seminal African influence in one area, an influence in yet another is likely to be found, with those most powerful in Africa remaining so in the new setting to which a significant number of Africans went; this helps explain the successful movement of African religious and artistic influences from one section of the South to another, from South Carolina and Virginia into North Carolina.[50]

I I

The humdrum nature of rural life acted as a stimulus for blacks and whites to seek out and participate in activities of large numbers of people. So it was that the Great Revival meetings, which reached their peak in North Carolina in 1804, when Walker was nineteen, attracted slaves as well as whites. Just as the political consciousness of slaves was affected but hardly dominated by white thought—their oppression was a main concern of their art—the religiosity of whites left its mark on many slaves but appears never to have threatened the religion of the quarters.[51]

What was evident to slaves at revival meetings—or in the balconies of churches—was the religious hypocrisy and, at times, the cruelty of whites. Indeed, revival meetings, not entirely safe for slaves to attend, were surely not always gatherings to which a free Negro or slave might repair in peace to worship God; this had to affect, in conscious and unconscious ways, many aspects of the slave's perception of the religion of the dominant group, from the sermon of the preacher to the singing of those in attendance. Such double standards in the treatment of black and white Christians must also be considered, together with opposition to extending Christianity to blacks, in accounting for the apparent lack of interest in Christianity on the part of the great bulk of slaves, a subject occasionally alluded to statistically but not discussed by scholars in the field.[52]

The most docile or browbeaten slave was forced, at some level of consciousness, to question the faith of whites when witnessing or hearing about hot coals being poured on the feet of slaves kneeling in prayer at revival meetings. If slaves did not witness incidents of that kind, they might have seen—or heard the screams of—slaves being flogged by white Christians seeking a good time.[53] Though many slaves were attracted to such meetings, others avoided them. The young Walker lived in that atmosphere of religious brutality: "But Christian Americans, not only hinder . . . the Africans, but thousands of them *will absolutely beat a coloured person nearly to death, if they catch him on his knees, supplicating the throne of grace.*" Actual organized terror was used, and Walker's intimate knowledge of the lengths to which whites would go to prevent blacks from being Christians may well have been his principal objection to their Christianity.

Walker knew of instances of small groups of blacks gathering

> for no other purpose than to worship God Almighty, in spirit and in truth, to the best of their knowledge; when tyrants, calling themselves *patrols*, would also convene and wait almost in breathless silence for the poor coloured people to commence singing and praying to the Lord our God, as soon as they had commenced, the wretches would burst in upon them and drag them out and commence beating them as they would rattle-snakes—many of whom, they would beat so unmercifully, that they would hardly be able to crawl for weeks and sometimes for months.[54]

Ejected from their places of worship and beaten in full view of the townspeople, night and day, many blacks, whether slave or free, found the practice of Christianity not safe in either the countryside or the city. Walker's ability to measure the length of time of recovery for those beaten probably means that the religious terror against blacks occurred in Wilmington and was observed by him. The persistence of some blacks, despite the beatings, in practicing Christianity invested that tiny minority with qualities of martyrdom that eventually led Walker to believe that blacks in America would form the vanguard of Christianity in the West.

Since he once traveled half a day to be among slaves worshiping at a camp meeting, it is likely he worshiped among some slaves in the Wilmington area. In another of his rare references to his life in the South, he recounts having "embarked in a Steam Boat at Charleston, and having been five or six hours on the water, we at last arrived at the place of hearing, where was a very great concourse of people.'' His reaction to the preacher's sermon to the slaves—slaves, it is safe to conclude, judging from its message to the blacks—consisted of a certain mock innocence:

> Myself and boat companions, having been there a little while, we were all called up to hear; I among the rest went up and took my seat—being seated, I fixed myself in a complete position to hear the word of my Saviour and to receive such as I thought was authenticated by the Holy Scriptures; but to my no ordinary astonishment, our Reverend gentleman got up and told us (coloured people) that slaves must be obedient to their masters . . . or be whipped—the whip was made for the backs of fools. . . . Here I pause for a moment, to give the world time to consider what was my surprise, to hear such preaching from a minister of my Master, whose very gospel is that of peace and not of blood and whips, as this pretended preacher tried to make us believe.[55]

On that occasion Walker almost certainly heard slaves sing, as they commonly did at camp meetings, but he made no reference to singing. If they sang, alone or with whites, their song invariably and subtly rejected the view they were born to serve whites. They were clear enough about their faith to create an art form that, through emotional tone alone, spoke of their unhappiness with the very notion of slavery. While the hypocrisy of white religion was evident to Walker at an early age, the sincerity of the Negro Christian faith, slave or free, got through to him, if the value of its expression through art did not.

He was already a deeply religious man when we first encounter him in Boston, so it is difficult to avoid the conclusion, though seemingly impossible to prove, that his mother exerted a powerful influence on the development of his religious outlook. Perhaps through her he gained access to black Christian values that moved him greatly and figure prominently in his later life, for the evidence available does not point in other directions, unless one concludes that Walker felt that only blacks could provide moral leadership, since whites had for so long failed. But even there his concern for morality was rooted in religion, so a combination of the two positions might explain his attitude toward religion.

Slave coffles moved regularly through North Carolina to markets in the lower South. One such coffle, described by an English visitor to the United States, provides a partial clue to the origins of Walker's oft-repeated assertion in his *Appeal* that his people were dragged all over the world to work for and to enrich others:

> Just as we reached New River, in the early grey of the morning, we came up with a singular spectacle, the most striking one of the kind I have ever witnessed. It was a camp of Negro slave drivers just packing up to start; they had about three hundred slaves with them, which had bivouacked the preceeding night in chains in the woods; thus they were conducting to Natchez

upon the Mississippi River, to work upon the sugar plantations of Louisiana.
. . . The female slaves were, some of them, sitting on logs of wood . . . and a
great many little black children were warming themselves at the fires of the
bivouac. In front of them all, and prepared for the march, stood, in double
files, about two hundred male slaves, *manacled and chained to each other*. . . .
To make this spectacle still more disgusting and hideous, some of the principle [sic] white slavedrivers, who were tolerably well dressed, and had broad-
brimmed white hats on, *with black crape round them,* were standing near,
laughing and smoking cigars.[56]

The cultural consequences of the domestic slave trade, of which
Walker seemed unaware, were crucial to the transformation taking place
in the slave population. Slaves born in Africa were in most coffles passing
through North Carolina from Virginia up to and following 1808, but either
seeing them at a distance or hearing of the coffles was scarcely enough to
impress upon Walker distinctions of origins that, at least by the 1820s, had
lost much of their meaning even to some African-born slaves, since in
America there was so much common to Africa as a whole around them, so
much shared, enabling one to feel at home when relating across lines of
ethnicity.[57]

Since the great majority of free Negroes in North Carolina were mulattoes and thus easily distinguishable from most slaves, it was possible for Walker, who was dark-skinned, to move among slaves in
Wilmington and elsewhere without being as readily suspected of being
free. Knowing that his father was a slave and of the slave community,
he had reason to feel solidarity with his brothers in bondage, to share
their pain and joy, and to be one with them over some of the contradictions afflicting the white community. For example, it was not uncommon for slaves and free Negroes to have access to the political thought
and culture of whites. The attractions were at times substantial, for
politicians of national stature passed through Wilmington and other
towns of the state, and public celebrations, such as political barbecues
and political parades, drew on members of the black population.
Slaves as well as free Negroes had the opportunity to hear speeches
delivered on important issues of the period and thereby to inform
themselves.[58]

On holidays like the Fourth of July, the city cannon announced the day
of celebration, and it is difficult to believe that either slave or free
Negro—or, for that matter, most whites—failed to appreciate the peculiar irony of its sounding, especially so soon after the American Revolution.[59] One as sensitive and intelligent as Walker surely found nothing to
applaud in North Carolina on that occasion. But whatever the ironies of
the cannon heard at dawn, the ringing of bells at curfew time was particularly disturbing. Even when no patrol was in force, patrolmen stopped
Negroes on the street after ten at night and asked for proof of status: "If

the Negro were free, he might show his badge; if slave, his pass and thus escape punishment. Otherwise he was subject to ten stripes well laid on."[60]

It was difficult for Walker to live for so long among so many holding him in contempt, when he knew there were no grounds for that hostility. It appears his later expressions of regard for a handful of white friends were based on more than abstractions, for he could not have acquired his degree of knowledge without access to books, and it is unlikely he could have secured Plutarch's *Lives* and other classics without white assistance. He was a self-educated man with an immense store of information under control before reaching the North. And by then he had concluded that the oppression of his people was due to economic factors and hatred born of guilt. Within a year after reaching Boston, he wrote,

> I have been for years troubling the pages of historians, to find out what our fathers have done to the *white Christians of America,* to merit such . . . punishment as they have inflicted on them, and do continue to inflict on us their children. . . . I have . . . come to the immoveable [sic] conclusion, that they (Americans) have, and do continue to punish us for nothing else, but for enriching them and their country, for I cannot conceive of anything else. Nor will I ever believe otherwise, until the Lord shall convince me.[61]

Before moving to the North, Walker traveled in the South, observing the degree to which slavery and racism had deformed institutions and personalities. While it is generally believed he investigated the treatment of Southern blacks as a youth, there is no documentary evidence to sustain such a view. It seems likely he traveled in the South later in life, perhaps after he accumulated funds to manage such a costly undertaking, unless earlier employment—assisting some white person—took him through the South. What is clear is that the trip was made, for there was nothing provincial about this man from provincial Wilmington who seemed to know the world and to be at ease in it intellectually. It is doubtful that he spent years traveling in the South—especially on his own—for the danger of being kidnapped into slavery was real.[62]

While traveling in the South, Walker saw slaves working in the fields as the primary cultivators of the land. His journey by steamboat from Charleston offered constantly shifting points of vantage from which to see his people on the shore, no doubt working in the fields, since it is not likely he would have traveled extensively in the winter. Another means of getting to Charleston and other distant places from Wilmington was the "four-horse wagon system of transportation over a distance of from fifty to four hundred miles." On his extensive journey south and westward, he saw what other travelers reported seeing at the few and distant stations along the route of travel at night: Negroes with lighted splinters of pine held aloft, the light blazing with an intensity that "would have dimmed

many gas burners."[63] At such times, the presence of his people must
have seemed more prevalent than ever. Considering the modes of transportation in the prerailroad era, his travels in the South were carried out
over a period of many weeks, the dangers of the journey being outweighed by his determination to know.

One must ask why Walker, knowing what he knew, lived in the South
for over forty years. Since his mother did not arrive in Boston with him, it
is likely she had died by the time of his departure. There is the possibility
that she lived well into the new century, that her presence kept him from
leaving. To this another consideration must be added: it is likely that
Walker was strongly attached to a North Carolina slave who may well
have escaped to the North with him, since his wife revealed only part of
her name, even after Walker's death.

Considering the apathy of North Carolina Negroes—from Walker's
point of view—only ties of family and/or love of Eliza make his remaining
there understandable. And since he has been placed in Wilmington as late
as 1827, it seems logical to infer that the growing opposition to blacks in
the state may have prompted him to leave when he did and to seek a new
home in the North. If that assumption is correct, then his instincts were
sound, for hostility to free Negroes in North Carolina grew with such
strength that before the antebellum period had run its course some seeking a modicum of protection asked to be reenslaved. But of greater interest, not long after Walker's departure, is the law passed, after some
discussion and at the urging of the governor, that made it unlawful for a
slave to marry a free Negro.[64]

I I I

Before reaching Boston, Walker probably stopped in New York and may
have traveled to Philadelphia, since he gives us reason to believe he had
firsthand contact with black people in both locales—with Samuel Cornish,
an editor of *Freedom's Journal*, in New York; with Richard Allen,
founder of African Methodism, in Philadelphia; and with young blacks in
both places. He would have wanted to see something of the North and to
meet black men who were dedicated to the liberation of his people, rather
than to go straight to Boston after finally leaving the South.[65]

His first official connection with the black struggle on the national level
was through his role as "agent" for *Freedom's Journal*, on behalf of
which a meeting of the people of color was held at his home in Boston in
1828. Devoted to promoting the paper, the meeting provided no intima-
tion, as reported, of the host's smoldering resentment at slavery and
racism, of his attachment to Africans throughout the world.[66]

In fact, Walker lived in a community in which a number of blacks referred to themselves as Africans, an effort being required for some to

think of themselves as Americans. The group of men and women among whom he moved included some who were born in Africa and others, born in America, who identified with the ancestral home and with blacks everywhere. Long interested in Africa and her transplanted children, he was at the quiet center of swirling African concerns, and with others resolved to support *Freedom's Journal*—a sign of awareness of the problems facing their people, for this paper opposed all forces blocking the advance of Africans in the ancestral home and in the diaspora.[67]

An examination of the principles of *Freedom's Journal* reveals something of Walker's new intellectual environment, one charged with concern for people of African ancestry, and it discloses the editors' expectation that black people would be interested in reading reports on Africans wherever found. Although white contributors were not barred from the paper, the editors Cornish and John Russwurm recognized the need for black people to speak for themselves on matters crucial to their people. "We wish to plead our own cause," declared the first editorial of that paper. "Too long have others spoken for us"—a nationalist sentiment from editors responsible for the existence of an important black institution they expected black people to make financially viable.[68]

In the small group that promoted the paper, there was interaction between the West Indian editor Russwurm and blacks born in America, a pattern of alliance repeated, at that moment in the slave South, on numerous occasions before and following the advent of *Freedom's Journal*. The presence of a forceful, articulate Afro–West Indian like Russwurm reinforced the feeling that they shared a common destiny, especially since American slavery and racism were not respectors of geographical differences among blacks. In North America, blacks simply had nothing to gain by affirming their differences. While the headquarters of the newspaper was in New York, Walker's involvement with the paper caused him to feel a part of its destiny.

Walker quickly discovered he had risen only slightly on the ladder of freedom. The difference between freedom in Boston and North Carolina was about the same as that between slavery and freedom in Wilmington— in some ways slight but in no sense inconsequential. In any case, he thought free Negroes in the North free enough that, with unity in their ranks, great good could be accomplished, especially since one could protest and organize there, whereas in the South no protest by blacks was sanctioned by law or custom.[69]

Walker set up a used-clothes business on Brattle Street and did well enough that "had it not been for his great liberality and hospitality, he would have become wealthy." After he married "Eliza ———," his hatred of slavery increased, causing him to realize there could be no halfway measures for his people, in the North or the South, that they must be prepared to go to any lengths to win their freedom. That position became associated with him in the minds of a number of people: "He had many enemies, and not a few were his brethren whose cause he espoused. They said that he went too far, and was making trouble."[70]

Massachusetts blacks had been free for less than half a century when Walker arrived in Boston. The attitudes of most whites toward them continued to be racist. Following slavery, whites debated whether they were citizens, and there was opposition to their exercising the franchise. In those early years and later, Massachusetts, like many other states of the North and the South, wanted as few free Negroes as possible. In fact, some blacks were deported from the state for being unable to prove their citizenship.

Though conditions for blacks had not changed dramatically by the time Walker entered Massachusetts, they were better there than elsewhere in the North. Blacks were at least permitted to vote without being mobbed at the polls or on their way there, and voices were heard opposing slavery and racism. But pervasive segregation—in schools, churches, hospitals, housing, restaurants, and hotels—and menial jobs were the lot of blacks there as elsewhere in the North. There, too, blacks were considered a breed apart, inferior. This view of blacks, like their condition, enforced by law and custom, did not significantly change in the slave era. Between 1800 and 1861 there were slight shifts on the scale of oppression, signaled ominously by legal and extralegal activity; and throughout the period most Northern blacks were poor or on the verge of poverty. The combination of economic hardship and racist oppression—the two were inextricably bound—kept blacks on the lower rungs of society.[71]

Despite such conditions of oppression, Walker had vastly greater access to books than he had had in the South, and he took advantage of this opportunity. "He was emphatically a self-made man," wrote Henry Highland Garnet, "and he spent all his leisure moments in the cultivation of his mind . . . in order that he might contribute something to humanity." He must have read late into the night, because it was said he spent a great deal of time assisting those less fortunate than himself, for example, using his home as a shelter for the needy and as a meeting place for supporters of *Freedom's Journal*.[72] His reputation as a champion of his people was established as he worked at what must have been a feverish pace, for not long after his arrival he began to publish his thoughts.

From a description provided by his wife to Henry Highland Garnet, a rather complete picture of his physical attributes is available: in appearance, he was "prepossessing, being six feet in height, slender and well-proportioned. His hair was loose, and his complexion was dark." His sense of the tragedy of his people fueled the fire of asceticism within him. Garnet added, "It was in his private walks, and by his unceasing labors in the cause of freedom, that he made his memory sacred."[73]

If any event reflected the attitude of free Negro leadership toward Africans, it was the dinner in the autumn of 1828 for Prince Abduhl Rahaman of Footah Jallo, who had been enslaved in the South. Assembling at Boston's African School House, members of the dinner party formed a "colorful" procession, marching to musical accompaniment to the African Masonic Hall. The opening toast reflected a strong sentiment, "May the happy era be not far distant when Africa universally shall stretch forth her hands unto God." It was proposed that "the time soon arrive when the sons of Africa, in all parts of the world, shall be emancipated and happy, and the word slave never more be heard." And "distinguished applause" was won—"*Liberty* and *Equality*—The most inestimable gift of God conferred on man. May the time be not far distant when all the sons and daughters of Africa, who are now in bondage shall be enabled to exclaim, 'We are free!'"[74]

Walker said the guest of honor had been torn from his country, religion, and friends and "doomed to perpetual though unlawful bondage." One of the last toasts offered a belief about Africa as strongly held by blacks as any: "May the sons and daughters of Africa soon become a civilized and christian-like [sic] people, and shine forth to the world as conspicuous as their more highly favored neighbors."[75] The toasts reveal allegiance to African people while asserting their lack of civilization—the latter sentiment uttered with as much ease as the former to an audience as receptive to one as to the other.

Characteristically, those offering the toasts treated Africa as a single country with one people. That the prince was of the Moslem faith made no difference; that such a distinction was not made supports the thesis that African religious and ethnic differences were considered a handicap in America and steadily lost ground before the need for unity against overwhelming odds. By the 1820s, even when confronted with a person of a particular African ethnicity, blacks failed to highlight the ethnic factor, no doubt for that reason. But the last toast contains the neglected but profound truth that blacks in America were Africans culturally as late as 1828. There was the hope they would "become . . . Christian-like."[76]

The cast of language was not that of blacks, though what was said was theirs in spirit—an example of the uses of the language of the oppressor to further the unity of African people in the Americas. Those toasting spent time deciding how they would frame their remarks, and Walker may have provided instruction, for in North Carolina on July 4, 1823, a politician offered a toast Walker could have endorsed: "The Constitution of North Carolina—There is no state constitution so perfect, but that time may discover in it defects, and wisdom and justice suggest amendments."[77]

In a speech reprinted in 1828 in *Freedom's Journal,* Walker urged his people to make every effort to liberate themselves, provided they did not violate the Constitution. The "Address Delivered before the General Colored Association at Boston" bears the imprint of a spirit that, though turbulent, had not yet flared forth to attract attention. Perhaps political considerations at the time dictated limits to social resistance. But more was involved, for concern that the formation of the association was strongly opposed by some blacks was, for the time being, balanced by Walker's respect for the Constitution. A radical prescription for social change seemed unwise in view of opposition that, "on the opposite side, would have done great honor to themselves." Only "undeviating and truly patriotic exertions" made possible the assemblage hearing him.[78]

The meeting had come under fire from people of color, who felt it worked against their best interests to organize along racial lines. Walker considered it strange for men of reasonably good judgment to behave in a way so completely at odds with their interests. He thought the objectives of the association in the best interests of people of color, and his account of its purposes—he called it "this *institution*"-in some ways prefigured the Negro convention movement as a national organization. His conception of the association's objectives—to unite the black population of the United States in ways practicable, to establish "societies, opening, extending, and keeping up correspondences, and not withholding anything which may have a tendency to meliorate *our* miserable condition"—anticipated the form of things to come. A few years later, blacks from a number of states sent delegates to Philadelphia to attend what became the first national Negro convention.[79]

The General Colored Association was a model of what was to come in another sense as well: the forces of nationalism and integrationism clashed over it, as they would over the uses to which the Negro convention movement should be put. Walker's support of the association sparked opposition to him from some of his own people: his was a nationalist stance at a time of growing integrationist sentiment. For one who witnessed the fragmentation and powerlessness of slaves and free blacks in the South, where they were forbidden even to gather in sizable numbers, it seemed absurd for Northern blacks to reject unity and an opportunity to make themselves whole. Not long thereafter, having been written with an "overflowing heart," the *Appeal to the Coloured Citizens of the World, But in Particular, and Very Expressly, to Those of the United States of America* was published. It was at once a necessary catharsis and an actualization of will as Walker, in Otey Scruggs's elegant phrase, "lifted the floodgates and allowed the river to flow."[80]

Opposition to oppression received ultimate expression in the *Appeal*, a small volume on which Walker's reputation as the harbinger of militant abolitionism rests, and it appears that the very ardor with which he advocated slave resistance obscured a related dimension of the man: he is the precursor of a long line of advocates of African freedom, extending all the way to Paul Robeson and Malcolm X in our time. He is the father of black nationalist theory in America because much of the substance of that ideology is found in his writings, despite the sometimes disjointed way in which he presented his views.[81]

Walker described his people as the most oppressed, wretched, and degraded set of human beings seen since the world began, and he prayed that no such humiliated and oppressed "ever may live again until time shall be no more." Their condition resulted from disobedience to God and cruelty at the hands of whites, whom he thought the "natural enemies" of blacks and of people of color generally. All the people of the earth—the Greeks, the Irish, the Indians of North and South America, and the Jews—"are called men" except "the sons of Africa." America's treatment of black people had been "*more cruel* (they being an enlightened and Christian people,) than any heathen nation did any people whom it had reduced to our condition."[82] He telescoped the history of peoples of European descent:

> The whites have always been an unjust, jealous, unmerciful, avaricious and blood-thirsty set of beings, always seeking after power and authority.—We view them all over the confederacy of Greece, where they were first known to be anything, (in consequence of education) we see them there, cutting each other's throats. . . . We view them next in Rome, where the spirit of tyranny and deceit raged still higher. We view them in Gaul, Spain, and in Britain.— In fine, we view them all over Europe, together with what were scattered about in Asia and Africa, as heathens, and we see them acting more like devils than accountable men.[83]

The essence of European character was for Walker a desire for power linked to an insatiable love of gain. His criticism, stated with contempt, is a sustained attack on those using others for financial gain to purchase comfort for themselves and their families. He hated avarice as much as he loved freedom—and he said he was willing to die for freedom. References to lovers of avarice—to "avaricious creatures" who view blacks as "beasts of burden to them and their children"; to "avaricious usurpers" to whom the labor of slaves is cheap; to "that avaricious and cruel people, the Portuguese"; to "those [the Spanish] avaricious wretches"; to "degraded and wretched sons of Africa, rendered so by the avaricious and unmerciful among the whites"; to "avaricious whites . . . too busily engaged in laying up money"—accumulate and are a distinguishing feature of the *Appeal,* in which Walker identifies greed as the motive force of human oppression. In that context, he noted that some of his people were seekers "more after self aggrandisement, than the glory of God." In a tribute to Samuel Cornish, minister and editor of *The Rights of All,* Walker wrote, "I believe he is not seeking to fill his pockets with money, but has the welfare of his brethren truly at heart. Such men, brethren, ought to be supported by us."[84] Walker's cry was at bottom one of hatred of the spirit of capitalism as well as of slavery and racism.

There is evidence that he met Cornish on a visit to New York, perhaps on the same trip that took him—on his way north from Wilmington?—to other Northern cities as well, for it was not like him to arrive at conclusions that were not empirically grounded. This aspect of his personality should be kept in mind when considering his relationship to Philadelphia's Richard Allen and when considering a reference from him to Philadelphia when he discusses educational opportunities for black children there and in other cities:

> I have examined school-boys and young men of colour in different parts of the country, in the most simple parts of Murray's English Grammar, and not more than one in thirty was able to give a correct answer to my interrogations. If any one contradicts me, let him step out of his door into the streets of Boston, New-York, Philadelphia, or Baltimore, (no use to mention any other, for the Christians are too charitable further south or west!)—I say, let him who disputes me, step out of his door into the streets of either of those four cities, and promiscuously collect one hundred school-boys, or young men of colour, *who have been to school,* and who are considered by the coloured people to have received an excellent education. . . .[85]

Despite those shortcomings and more, Walker believed people of color, owing to circumstances of history, if not to providential design, superior to whites in matters of character. In his opinion, black people of Africa and "the mulattoes of Asia" did not behave like people of European ancestry, were not half as unmerciful and driven by lust for gain. Indeed, he deepened his indictment, stating that Europeans, having moved beyond heathenism to Christianity, were more cruel than ever, dumping overboard, during the slave trade, whole cargoes of men, women, and children.[86] The *Appeal* carries an expression, later developed to a high degree by nationalists in Walker's tradition, of Third World sentiment—a conception of the reciprocity of interests of Afro-Asians and people of color in the Americas suffering from oppression at the hands of whites.

The Jews fared better under the heathen Egyptians, whom Walker considered African and colored, than blacks under Christian whites. He offered as an example of more humane slave overlords the liberties granted by Pharaoh to Joseph, for he pointed out that they were not available to blacks in America. Using the illustration of the Egyptians encouraging Joseph to marry one of their own, he raised an issue considered important to most black nationalists since his time: the relationship between the black man and the white woman. Walker held strong views on the subject. In North Carolina he had witnessed, in the free Negro population of mulattoes, the hypocrisy of whites on this question, and in Boston he found laws against miscegenation as well. His position on miscegenation was clear—"I would not give a *pinch of snuff* to be married to any white person I ever saw in all the days of my life." He thought the black man who would leave his own "colour (provided he can get one, who is good for any thing) and marry a white woman, to be a double slave to her, just because she is *white*, ought to be treated by her as he surely will be, viz: as a NIGGER!'' The day would come when whites would be glad to be in the company of blacks, though whites were treating them "worse than they do the brutes that perish.''[87]

In one of his few references to the need for land, Walker quoted the Bible, again mentioning the treatment of the Jews, to point out the relative generosity of the Egyptians on the land question: "The land of Egypt is before thee: in the best of the land make thy father and brethren to dwell; in the land of Goshen let them dwell: and if thou knowest any men of activity among them, then make them rulers over my cattle." With full sarcasm, he commented, "I ask those people who treat us so *well*, Oh! I ask them, where is the most barren spot of land which they have given unto us?''[88]

Of all the assaults on his people, the one that seems to have disturbed Walker most was the charge that they were inferior to whites—were not even members of the human race. He challenged racists to show him a page of history, sacred or profane, that contends Egyptians visited the "insupportable insult upon the children of Israel" of "telling them that they were not of the human family.'' After denouncing the view that blacks, unlike whites, had "descended originally from the tribes of *Monkeys* or *Orangutangs*,'' he took exception to Jefferson's somewhat tentative assertion, in *Notes on Virginia,* that blacks are inferior to whites in body and mind, stating that Jefferson had compared "our miserable fathers" with "philosophers of Greece.'' But to Jefferson's charge that Roman slaves of white ancestry were often great artists Walker, seeing great degradation among African slaves in America, offered no direct rejoinder.[89]

Walker helped establish a pattern repeated down to the close of the century and beyond—the almost total failure of most nationalists to recognize the artistic and spiritual genius of their people, a recognition essential to building on the positive and the distinctive in black culture, to blacks' estimating their cultural worth and that of the world around them. Failing even to acknowledge the existence of slave culture, though he had been exposed to it, he had little alternative to denouncing most of what he saw in Afro-American life as the tragic by-product of slavery and African backwardness. This was ironic since he had opportunities in Wilmington and, the evidence suggests, in Baltimore and Philadelphia, to witness important African ceremonies; yet it was an understandable failure, given the state of knowledge of African culture and, consequently, of slave culture.[90]

A central theme in the *Appeal* is the indispensability of unified struggle by blacks for them to be free and to defend their freedom. It was a lack of unity that led to victims of slavery being dragged "around the world in chains and handcuffs" in order to work for white people. In fact, in his speech before the General Colored Association he had predicted that, if free blacks, who were "two-thirds of the way free," were determined to support each other to the extent of their power, they could effect great deeds for their people. They would either become unified or confront each other as enemies—a position brilliantly argued a decade later by Sidney.[91]

Walker confronted black participation in the slave trade as directly as he faced white crimes against his people. He was not exceptional in this regard, merely one of many black leaders who did not close their eyes to black participation in the trade—a position more than affirmed in slave folklore. The fact that Africans, under duress, usually rounded up Africans for the slave trade served no more to mitigate their treachery to their people in Walker's view than African treachery was mitigated in "The King Buzzard." An observer in the North might see blacks working in collusion with slaveholders "by selling their own brothers into hell upon earth," not unlike "the exhibitions in Africa, but in a more secret, servile and abject manner." Such behavior was perhaps the most painful of all reminders that his people suffered from deep degradation, for he knew something of the slavery to which his brothers were to be subjected. The mere thought of it was difficult to bear:

> O Heaven! I am full! ! ! I can hardly move my pen! ! ! There have been and are at this day in Boston, New-York, Philadelphia, and Baltimore, coloured men, who are in league with tyrants, and who receive a great portion of their daily bread, of the moneys which they acquire from the blood and tears of their more miserable brethren, whom they scandalously deliver into the hands of our *natural enemies! ! !*[92]

Those who worked with slaveholding interests were a "gang of villains." Not only were such traitors active among blacks in the United States, but treachery by people of color was being perpetrated "against the government of our brethren, the Haytians," forming "powerful auxiliaries" that work toward the destruction of people of African ancestry. Walker recalled how Africans had paid dearly in the past for disunity. "O my suffering brethren!" he exclaimed, "remember the divisions and consequent sufferings of Carthage and of Hayti." He conjured blacks to know the history of Haiti and draw the appropriate conclusions. Judging from the attention devoted to that country in the pages of *Freedom's Journal,* and from the inspiration Haiti was providing black people during the first quarter of the century, he did not exaggerate in describing Haiti as "the glory of the blacks."[93]

The extent to which self-hatred was prevalent among blacks, in the North and the South, was understood by Walker, who gave it attention appropriate to its seriousness. His description of the debased behavior of Northern "free" blacks, of the fighting and treachery that took place within the group, is unsparing. That description contains, by inference, suggestive insights into the character of sizable numbers of people of African ancestry in the South, slave and free. He wrote that certain blacks in the North were known to tell "news and lies, making mischief one upon the other." If this was true in the North, as it doubtless was, then Walker provided strong indications of the nature of the behavior of not a few oppressed Southern blacks, and revealed the arduous task ahead for black leaders in seeking to unite their people.[94]

The defects in his people were not inherent, Walker thought; rather, they probably arose from "our father's" disobedience to God. Whatever the source of their horrid plight, Africans everywhere would soon be aware of the need for unity, and only those who delighted in the degradation of blacks would deny this. Because of the long absence of this awareness, blacks were made to undergo "intolerable sufferings" and had been plunged into a slumbering state from which they only occasionally cried out against their miseries. They seemed unable to change their condition, or the shape of their future.[95]

Ignorance and treachery were so strong among African peoples in the Americas and on the continent of Africa that Walker thought they threatened to destroy all of worth that remained. While deceit and ignorance did indeed exist, he underestimated the spiritual strength, even wisdom, that inhered in slave communities. Moreover, he might have made more explicit what is implied in much of this *Appeal,* that violence was used to smooth the path to opportunism and treachery for the less stable in mind and spirit. In justice to him, it can scarcely be ignored that in the *Appeal* he vividly portrays the violence on which the system of oppression was based, a violence that he believed reduced large numbers of slaves to loving those who oppressed them.[96]

I V

So devastating were the effects of the slave trade and slavery on black people that they were prepared, in the words of the *Appeal* to endure tyrannies to which Asians and American Indians would offer the most violent resistance. He thought that Africans were trapped in a profound state of apathy, that all, except for the Haitians, everywhere possessed "a mean, servile spirit." They were reduced to such a state that servility of spirit and love of masters prevented them from resisting the institution of slavery. In fact, Walker considered all Africans, except for the Haitians, traumatized. What was worse, they were cowering before, in almost all instances, a vastly outnumbered white people. To "pass in review" before the world the sorry state of African people, he said that he would "only hold up to view" Jamaica "as a specimen of our meanness."[97]

In that Island, there are three hundred and fifty thousand souls—of whom fifteen thousand are whites, the remainder, three hundred and thirty-five thousand are coloured people! and this Island is ruled by the white people . . . (15,000) ruling and tyranizing over 335,000 persons! . . . O! how long my colour shall we be dupes and dogs to the cruel whites? . . . (15,000) whites keeping in wretchedness and degradation (335,000) viz. 22 coloured persons for one white . . . when at the same time, an equal number (15,000) blacks, would almost take the whole of South America, because where they go as soldiers to fight death follows in their train.[98]

Walker's belief in the reserves of physical power and courage of blacks—a belief shared by numerous black leaders and one that courses through Afro-American folklore—was so strong that he claimed 450,000 armed blacks in the United States could take on all of the white people on the continent, because "the blacks, once they get involved in a war, had rather die than to live, they either kill or be killed."[99] Thus, he juxtaposed in the personalities of blacks the most terrible ferocity and the most abject submissiveness, contending that if blacks were not in awe of murdering others their relation to whites would be different. How much this awe was credited to natural inclinations and how much to fear born of oppression he does not make clear. In fact, he offered an excellent illustration of this ambiguity when he alluded to the "*groveling submissions and treachery*" of blacks, to their "ignorant deceptions and consequent wretchedness," and exclaimed,

But when I reflect that God is just, and that millions of my wretched brethren would meet death with glory—yea, more, would plunge into the very mouths of cannons and be torn into particles as minute as the atoms which compose the elements of the earth, in preference to a mean submission to the lash of tyrants, I am with streaming eyes, compelled to shrink back into nothingness before my Maker, and exclaim again, thy will be done, O Lord God Almighty.[100]

Just as Walker overestimated the physical power and the potency of numbers among African peoples, he underestimated the power that was in the hands of whites as a result of technological changes. If science originated with his ancestors, as he argued, and was passed on to white people, whites had erected a structure, through brilliant application of scientific principles, so imposing that it cast a lengthening shadow over peoples of color everywhere, marking the place of imperialism's advance. Even though Walker placed great value on learning, the lack of a certain kind did not disturb the impeccability of his logic, for what was technological power before the determination of blacks and, more especially, the fury of a just God?[101]

For all his desire to see his people free, it was to him unthinkable that they should leave America to satisfy those interested in colonizing them in Africa or elsewhere. For at least a decade he had heard of the American

Colonization Society, for its friends were in North Carolina, as else-where, and active in support of that organization. Their appeal was made to free Negroes and to manumitted slaves to settle beyond the state's boundaries—in Haiti, Liberia, "and to the free soil north of the Ohio River." In 1821 the synod of North Carolina reported that several of its congregations had founded societies auxiliary to the American Coloniza-tion Society.[102] Thus, the plan of Henry Clay and other defenders of the American Colonization Society to colonize free blacks in Africa or else-where met in Walker a fierce antagonist. He questioned Clay's motivation for stating that Christianity, together with "the arts and civilization," should be introduced into Africa:

> Here I ask Mr. Clay, what kind of Christianity? Did he mean such as they have among the Americans—distinction, whip, blood and oppression? I pray the Lord Jesus Christ to forbid it. . . . Does he care a pinch of snuff about Africa—whether it remains a land of Pagans and of blood . . . so long as he gets enough of her sons and daughters to dig up gold and silver for him?[103]

Walker moved to the heart of the Clay position when he dealt with the latter's refusal to deliberate upon the question of the emancipation of the slave. His analysis was one that became classic among blacks: that slaveholders wanted free blacks removed to rivet the chains of slavery more securely on their brothers in the South, "and consequently they would have more obedient slaves" by removing the explosive example of free blacks. His charge against the American Colonization Society was summed up in a word, hypocrisy, and it was that quality on the part of white America in general that drew from him one sarcastic denunciation after another—"this happy republic, or land of *liberty! ! !*"[104]

Unlike his greatest admirer, Garnet, who on balance extolled the quali-ties of American institutions, Walker was unflinching in his judgment: a land of contradictions, America was for him above all a system of oppres-sion. As such, it lacked genius in its institutions, which he took up one by one. He thought whites had fought their way to triumph here as through-out their past; they felt free to deny freedom and life itself. The vital institutions of the Republic—in areas of law, politics, religion, education, and political economy—were being used to exploit others so that whites might know ease.[105]

In spite of his opposition to the "plots" of the American Colonization Society, he did not rule out emigration for all of his people, urging those who would leave to go to their "greatest earthly friends and benefac-tors—the English." Though he did not explain why the English would be willing to receive sizable numbers of blacks as permanent residents, his respect for the English stemmed from their role in opposing the slave trade. Walker admitted that the English were unjust to his people, pos-sessing colonies in the Caribbean "which oppress us sorely," but he thought they had done more to mitigate the plight of blacks "than all the other nations of the earth put together."[106] Those not interested in going to England or in forming "the residue of coloured people" remaining in America until the final disposition of the issue of slavery were urged to "go to our brethren, the Haytians," for protection and comfort—a position within the context of limited emigration that is easily explained. The Haitians, in his opinion, served as the best model of how black people should behave: they had risen to strike their oppressors, and that was sufficient reason for emigration to that island. Besides, the Haitians had shown substantial interest in receiving black emigrants from the United States, including scores of North Carolina blacks.[107] But Walker says little of the difficulties that confronted the Haitians after their revolution, perhaps because he deemed those difficulties of relatively small moment, considering the problems of Haiti's past.

Apart from emigration to Haiti or to England, Walker opposed the movement of his people from America, lashing out at the American Colonization Society with the anger characteristic of free blacks relative to that organization. Like the other black leaders of his time, he held that America was more the black man's home than the white man's. The failure of whites to recognize and protect the humanity of black people, from his point of view, in no way diminished the degree to which the country belonged to those whose blood and tears enriched the land. Thus, Walker developed a theme expounded at least as early as the establishment of the American Colonization Society (1816): that blacks had more than earned their citizenship, that their labor and their suffering had settled for all time the question of whether they had a right to be in America. He repeatedly drew attention to the extent to which white wealth resulted from black blood and sweat, and he called attention throughout the *Appeal* to the contributions of blacks to the building of the country, linking that gift to their right to remain in the land of their enslavement:

> Let no man of us budge one step, and let slave-holders come to beat us from our country. America is more our country, than it is the whites. . . . The greatest riches in all America have arisen from our blood and tears:—and will they drive us from our property and homes, which we have earned with our *blood?*[108]

Since he did not consider all whites devils, Walker believed cooperation possible with those who opposed the oppression of blacks. But his version of cooperation with whites—very similar to that of Malcolm X more than a century later—was rooted mainly in recognition of the need for blacks to combat those forces within their ranks that contributed to self-hatred and disunity, which was something of an original formulation. "That we should cooperate with them [whites], as far as we are able by *uniting and cultivating a spirit of friendship and of love among us,* is obvious, from the very exhibition of our miseries, under which we groan."[109] Walker's interest in friendship and love among blacks, a central theme in nationalist thought, was related to his recognition of their need of self-confidence, which would help them, among other things, refute white assertions of black inferiority on the deepest possible level:

> For let no one of us suppose that the refutations which have been written by our white friends are enough—they are *whites*—we are *blacks*. We, and the world wish to see the charges of Mr. Jefferson [that blacks are inferior] refuted by the blacks *themselves,* according to their chance; for we must remember that what the whites have written respecting this subject, is other men's labours, and did not emanate from the blacks.[110]

Though Walker did not object to white people writing history, such enterprise had led many among them to deny the humanity of blacks. But other whites defended the humanity of blacks against Jefferson's charges, and, while he welcomed such support from white friends, he, like nationalists following him, thought it essential that blacks take responsibility for themselves in this as in other areas. Toward this end, he urged blacks to purchase, study, and refute Jefferson's *Notes on Virginia,* a volume with which he was familiar before moving to Boston. Without a defense against that work, a nagging sense of self-doubt, no matter how earnest the defenses of whites, would remain to torment and to cripple.

Walker wrote that the "Lord shall raise up coloured historians in succeeding generations" to "present the crimes of this nation to the then gazing world."[111] Not to desire such an eventuality would be tantamount to acceptance of a largely racist version of reality—an abdication of responsibility as a man. In this connection, he renewed a quarrel between blacks and Jefferson that went as far back as Benjamin Banneker's letter to Jefferson in 1791. Just as Banneker had assured Jefferson that he was proud to number himself among those Africans "of the deepest dye," Walker called attention to millions of misguided whites who

> are this day, so ignorant and avaricious, that they cannot conceive how God can have an attribute of justice, and show mercy to us because it pleased Him to make us black—which colour, Mr. Jefferson calls unfortunate! . . . As though we are not as thankful to our God, for having made us as it pleased himself, as they, (the whites,) are for having made them white.[112]

Whites who think their victims wish "to be white" are dreadfully deceived," since blacks prefer to remain as their Creator made them. Identifying with the most oppressed of his people, Walker stated that anyone wishing to know who he was should know that he was "one of the oppressed, degraded and wretched sons of Africa, rendered so by the avaricious and unmerciful, among the whites."[113] His view that his people should not want to be white—the initial premise upon which a system of freedom for blacks in a racist society must be constructed—was a precondition for blacks entering a new and freer relationship with whites that would contain, for blacks, an irreducible measure of self-worth.

V

Walker asked "the candid and unprejudiced of the whole world, to search the pages of historians diligently" and see if anyone "ever treated a set of beings as the white Christians of America do us, the blacks, or Africans." He believed blacks had more reason to rebel against white America than whites had against England. Introduced so that the black man's cause might more readily be understood—or even supported by whites—and regarded by Walker as a serious revolutionary document, the Declaration of Independence was not the ultimate basis, as established in the *Appeal*, for revolution on the part of blacks. In fact, he argued that the suffering of his people would one day come to an end, "in spite of all the Americans this side of *eternity*." On that day blacks would need "all the learning and talents among ourselves, and perhaps more, *in order to govern ourselves*."[114]

In a moment of stern prophecy, Walker added, "'Every dog must have its day,' the American's is coming to an end." Furthermore, he predicted that the "enslaved children of Africa will have, in spite of all their enemies, to take their stand among the *nations* of the earth."[115] It is possible that, in this formulation, Walker envisioned the destruction of whites, leaving blacks in the position of governance in America. If so, his faith in a God favoring the oppressed accounts for that apocalyptic vision. There is no indication that he thought a separate nation desirable along or within the boundaries of white America.

To the question of whether irreducible essentials of nationalism in freedom among whites would be sufficient, he was willing to answer in the affirmative, for unlike some later nationalists, and despite his argument that white people are the natural enemies of blacks, he did not contend that his people could never secure freedom and justice in America. There was the possibility of reconciliation, provided certain terms were met:

> [We] ask them for nothing but the rights of man, viz. for them to set us free, and treat us like men, and . . . we will love and respect them, and protect our country—but cannot conscientiously do these things until they treat us like men. . . . Treat us like men, and there is no danger but we will all live in peace and happiness together. For we are not like you . . . unforgiving. . . . Treat us like men, and we will be your friends. And there is no doubt in my mind, but that the whole of the past will be sunk into oblivion, and we yet, under God, will become a united and happy people. The whites may say it is impossible, but remember that nothing is impossible with God.[116]

With that statement Walker laid down cardinal precepts for most nationalists following him: there should be no effective defense of the country until the country is willing to recognize the manhood of blacks; no real love of country until respect is extended to those who suffer at the hands of white Americans. And yet he pressed beyond that point, insisting on the necessity of atonement or repentance before "peace and happiness among whites and blacks can be established"; the Americans must "make a national acknowledgement to us for the wrongs they have inflicted on us."[117]

What did Walker mean by a "united and happy people"? Like later nationalists, he was willing to see Americans, black and white, as "one people," provided that blacks had significant influence in determining the direction of the country, provided America ceased being a "white" country. To be sure, though treated in brief compass, the possibility of whites and blacks living in harmony is an important subtheme in the *Appeal*. While he thought such harmony possible with God's intercession, he considered the virtual destruction of white America more likely, which explains his not dwelling on a relationship of mutual respect between whites and blacks. The burden of the *Appeal* is essentially one of doom for whites. Yet the fact that Walker gave attention to the possibility of harmonious relations between whites and blacks must be taken seriously because the search for freedom and the readiness to consider changing realities in the interest of that search were both important to him.

Despite his charge that whites are the natural enemies of blacks and his assertion that blacks hate whites—"you are not astonished at my saying we hate you, for if we are men, we cannot but hate you, while you are treating us like dogs"—Walker apparently did not mean literally that whites were the natural enemies of his people. Toward the end of the *Appeal*, he denied that whites have always been enemies of blacks, referring his readers to the Scriptures:

> Shem, Ham and Japheth, together with their father Noah and wives, I believe were not natural enemies to each other. . . . But where or of whom those ignorant and avaricious wretches could have got their information, I am unable to declare. . . . I say, from the beginning, I do not think we were natural enemies to each other.[118]

If the majority of whites became "our natural enemies by treating us so cruel," a tiny minority had resisted racism and were the friends of blacks. These friends were mostly English, but some apparently American, and Walker "would not for the world injure their feelings." Though oppression of blacks was an enormous crime, the possibility that blacks would be shipped out of the country provided whites with a last opportunity, before they were colonized, to affirm their humanity and to redeem their own: "Do the colonizationists think to send us off without first being reconciled to us?"[119] This he asked out of concern for the fate of people who could reject the humanity of those who gave them no cause to do so. And

that concern is poignantly moving evidence in the *Appeal* of Walker's
own humanity. In a passage that reflects, on the deepest level, his belief in
an irreducible unity of man, he wrote,

> Man, in all ages and all nations of the earth, is the same. Man is a peculiar
> creature—he is the image of his God, though he may be subjected to the most
> wretched condition upon earth, yet the spirit and feeling which constitute the
> creature, man, can never be entirely erased from his breast, because the god
> who made him after his own image, planted it in his heart; he cannot get rid of
> it.[120]

For Walker the humanity of the Europeans was a reality, though they
had fought each other so continually and with such conviction, he believed, that the level of that humanity was lowered from what it had been
before. And he found confirmation of his own conclusion in the Book of
Common Prayer:

> The wicked, swell'd with lawless pride,
> Have made the poor their prey;
> O, let them fall by those designs
> Which they for others lay
>
> . . . .
>
> To own a pow'r above themselves
> Their haughty pride disdains;
> And, therefore, in their stubborn mind
> No thought of God remains.[121]

People of color had never been so ruthless and, on coming to America,
had brought a sense of morality superior to that of whites, one that enabled those exposed to Christianity to take its form, to which whites were
devoted, and fill it with genuine Christian feeling. Thus, respect for the
moral capacity of Africans who embraced Christianity led Walker to propound a messianic role for them. Having been exposed to Christianity,
they were best suited to spread the faith.

> It is my solemn belief, that if ever the world becomes Christianized (which
> must certainly take place before long) it will be through the means, under God
> of the *Blacks*, who are now held in wretchedness, and degradation, by the
> white *Christians* of the world, who before they learn to do justice to us before
> our Maker . . . send out Missionaries to convert the Heathens, many of whom
> after they cease to worship gods, which neither see nor hear, become ten
> times more the children of Hell, then [sic] ever they were. . . .[122]

The transformation of Christianity in America probably occurred on a
scale beyond anything Walker imagined, since, on the plantations, African emotional fervor and artistic genius touched the faith and ultimately
led the nation to alter its perception of the place of blacks in American
life. It is ironic that the most compelling evidence Walker might have

offered of his people's inspired commitment to Christianity was in the realm of art, where the most exalted expression of the faith was occurring with the singing of the spirituals, within the circle of culture or as a result of initial inspiration there. But the *Appeal* does not mention the contribution of the spirituals to Christian faith, let alone the African context of its creation. Having rejected the value of African religion in the motherland, Walker arrived at that position logically.

Richard Allen was for him an example of the heights of Christianity that the African could command. Walker was so impressed by Allen that he called him "among the greatest divines who have lived since the apostolic age." In addition to his belief that blacks were the first tillers in America who made riches for a whole people, Allen had struggled against powers and principalities so that the Gospel might be diffused among his people. In a statement that makes indisputable his determination that blacks, even if free among whites, depend on themselves for moral authority, Walker said, in a manner that recalls William Hamilton, who will be discussed later, that Allen had "planted a Church among us which will be as durable as the foundation of the earth on which it stands," [123] so there was no reason for blacks, any more than for whites, to abandon all the institutions of their building with the coming of racial harmony in America.

Walker offered a conclusion regarding black religion that is of great interest to students of black culture in the slavery era and since—that blacks during slavery were on the whole hardly Christian.

> Yet the American ministers send out missionaries to convert the heathen, while they keep us and our children sunk at their feet in the most abject ignorance and wretchedness that ever a people was afflicted with since the world began. Will the Lord suffer this people to proceed much longer? Will he not stop them in their career? Does he regard the heathens abroad, more than the heathens among the Americans? [124]

No nonslave knew the state of Christian influence in the South better than Walker, and no one had a better sense of Christian influence nationally than Allen, whose church had affiliates in the South and who was at the hub of Christian activity among free blacks in the North. With warm approval, Walker quoted Allen:

> We are an unlettered people, brought up in ignorance, not one in a hundred can read or write, not one in a thousand has a liberal education; is there any fitness for such to be sent into a far country, among heathens, to convert or civilize them, when they themselves are neither civilized or Christianized? See the great bulk of the poor, ignorant Africans in this country, exposed to every temptation before them: all for the want of their morals being refined by education and proper attendance paid unto them by their owners, or those who had the charge of them. [125]

Though Walker, Payne, and Allen had no understanding of African culture, their conclusion that few of their people were Christian provides a perspective on African religion among their people that should be taken seriously by scholars of slave religion and culture.

Had Walker's African Methodism been that of slaves who used the ring shout to convert—and with it sacred song and dance and regard for the ancestors—had that been his choice of religion, then his contribution to the ideological development of black nationalism would have been inestimable, for he could have identified the primary source of African culture in America, the source from which most Afro-American art springs, and in so doing adjusted nationalist theory to reality. Instead, his not inconsiderable achievement was his recognition of the distinctiveness of black Christianity, even in its less creative form of expression, and his recognition of distinctive qualities in the Afro-American character.

Walker spoke at length of how black Christianity differed from religion practiced by white Christians—"can anything be a greater mockery of religion than the way in which it is conducted by the Americans?" In view of the imperatives of the future, responsibility for a significant degree of political and moral leadership should naturally fall to black people. Walker's general orientation and his belief in the potential of his people lead to the conclusion that he considered it at least as likely that blacks, under conditions of freedom and equality, would influence whites as that whites would influence blacks. Since he expected his people to play a transforming role in the world, he could hardly have expected less from them in the United States.

America and the world could not be more deeply transformed than by a determined fight for the liberation of Africans everywhere. Walker was as concerned about African liberation in one country as in another, which for him presupposed that conditions of relative freedom for blacks in a particular country would make them obliged to lead the struggle for the liberation of their people everywhere. People of African ancestry in the United States, no longer subjected to gross forms of racism, would have an even greater responsibility to further the liberation of Africans elsewhere, for their resources for achieving that goal would be greater. This explained the continuing need to promote African liberation when freedom was substantially attained by blacks in America.

Since the most oppressed and humiliated of people, the Africans, provided the foundation, in his view, upon which the wealth of whites was erected, effective struggle for their liberation would mean challenging the leaders of world economic exploitation. Though there is nothing in Walker's thought precluding black cooperation with whites in a new America in the quest for African liberation, it is the duty of blacks, above all others, to take responsibility for the liberation of their people:

> I advanced it therefore to you, not as a *problematical*, but as an unshaken and for ever immovable *fact*, that your full glory and happiness, as well as all

other coloured people under Heaven, shall never be fully consummated, but with the *entire emancipation of your enslaved brethren all over the world.* . . . Our greatest happiness shall consist in working for the salvation of our whole body. When this is accomplished a burst of glory will shine upon you, which will indeed astonish you and the world.[126]

With that, Walker helped establish the rationale for Pan-Africanism, a position eventually held with such conviction and at such length that total African liberation has achieved enduring value as an ideology. Walker's disregard for geographical barriers was the perfect ideological reflection of the process that was continuing to turn multifarious groups of Africans into one people in North America—a process the African engaged in with such mastery and with such an apparent sense of inevitability that it appears to have gone unnoticed by those outside the slave community. The perspective born of that process, especially among Africans in North America, was that of a single African people on the continent of Africa rather than that of a multitude of ethnic groups.

In the end, Walker did not place the desire for a separate state over that for freedom for his people in America. To reject the latter option, if available, would be to succumb to the virus of racism that infected the American nation. He gave primacy to values, to the quality of human character, over considerations of color. His instinct was right, though he sensed little beyond an inner spirituality that was distinctive and positive in the religious culture of his people, a spirituality on which they were likely to act. In fact, religion for him was of no value unless it was a living one, a religion of action in which the deed and word were one. Perhaps revolutionary culture flows from that perspective because it renders engagement against oppression logically inevitable.

If Walker perceived the African sources of much of black American thought and action, he believed them no more enriching than in the ancestral home—the "land of pagans and of blood."[127] Despite his profound identification with the slaves, he did not understand the value system that enriched their spiritual life, the art that functioned in terms of spiritual imperatives. But nothing in his thought precludes a joining of politics and an enlightened view of Afro-American culture. Indeed, the important role he gives to his people in a new political system leaves them better prepared to protect and build on vital aspects, once recognized, of their culture.

Walker's pride in blackness, his respect for the achievements of blacks in the ancient world, and his belief in African moral character and the need for African autonomy provided elements of cultural nationalism. As important as these views were, they did not go far enough, for people must be nourished by values in the present as well as by those in the past. This was ironic, for even as the larger society's impact on black people was a continuing oppressive reality, black culture was, for all the horrors of oppression, flourishing in several forms and destined to have a major impact on world culture in the twentieth century.

Though falling short of a theory of culture, Walker began a theory of class, the inspiration coming partly from Christianity and partly from a reading of history. Rejecting self-aggrandizement, he opposed the accumulation of wealth, inveighing against leaders and followers preoccupied with money and comfort. He found in slave labor the real productive force in the South and a major source of American wealth. And there could be no more fundamental opposition to human exploitation than his invocation of God as an enemy of slaveholders despite the efforts of the avaricious to appease Him, as in "The Slave Barn":

> A little gold to de church,
> A prayer in he name;
> An' a dog wid out honor
> Die wid a name
> Equal to a follower of Christ.[128]

The concepts of African autonomy and Pan-African revolt, so much a part of Walker's thought, did not have roots or currency among Europeans. Though Walker was deeply influenced by Western thought, especially by Christianity, it is a mistake to conclude that his revolt was grounded in European political and theological sources. Because Africans had not rebelled on the shores of their homeland, in passage to the Americas, and on arrival there at the instigation of whites, they knew that their resistance to slavery came from within. Walker was one of the foremost spokesmen of that disaffection, which he expressed in his *Appeal,* calling on his people throughout the world to resist oppression.

V I

Franklin does not exaggerate in claiming that "Walker's Appeal stands preeminent among the antislavery writings of the militant period." That it was "unwelcome in the slaveholding states" goes without saying; it was precisely the reception Walker wanted. The governor of Georgia urged the legislature to pass stringent laws against such publications, and "the legislature responded by passing several severe laws in regard to the colored population." North Carolina, aware of Georgia's new laws—and reporting them in its papers—was not long in confronting the problem posed by the *Appeal.* Governor Owens, having secured a copy of the *Appeal* from a "well-disposed" free Negro, thought Walker had exaggerated the sufferings of slaves, magnified their strength and underestimated the strength of whites while "containing an open appeal to the natural love of liberty." The governor also said,

As it has been satisfactorily ascertained that some of the free persons of colour in this State have permitted themselves to be used as agents, for the distribution of seditious publications, it is respectfully recommended that all this class of persons residing within the State be required to give security for the faithful discharge of those duties which they owe, in return for the protection they receive, from the laws of the State.[129]

Like Georgia, North Carolina passed a law to prevent "the circulation of seditious publications," moved to circumscribe further the movement of free people of color, and declared it illegal for slaves to be taught to read and write. A free Negro caught teaching a slave to read was "fined, imprisoned, or whipped, at the discretion of the court, not exceeding thirty-nine lashes, nor less than twenty lashes."[130] Georgia and North Carolina did not act alone. The *Appeal* created a storm elsewhere as well, with Mississippi, Virginia, and Louisiana also calling special legislative sessions. Such reactions to the *Appeal* were indications of the essential soundness of Walker's assessment of racial attitudes and practices in the slave South. It was with no small irony, then, that a reporter for *Freedom's Journal* in 1827 referred to a meeting of "respectable" men of color at the home of David Walker.

Urged by friends to flee to Canada, Walker refused. A company of Georgia men, offering one thousand dollars for him dead and ten times as much for him alive, took an oath to fast until Walker was captured or murdered. "It was the opinion of many," Garnet wrote, following Walker's death in 1830, "that he was hurried out of life by means of poison, but whether this was the case or not, the writer is not prepared to affirm." Walker noted before his death, "If any wish to plunge me into the wretched incapacity of a slave, or murder me for the truth, know ye, that I am in the hand of God, and at your disposal."[131] Though he counted his life precious, he was ready to offer it, for what was the purpose of living, he wrote, "when in fact I am dead." This was at the time, it is said, that Andrew Jackson was cultivating a new flowering of freedom for the common man.

Walker's *Appeal* is a cry of outrage for wrongs suffered by Africans at the hand of whites since the first transaction of oppression between the two peoples. His critique is original in character, providing a point of departure and arrival for proponents of African liberation. In his belief in African autonomy, in his grasp of the history of African oppression, and in his avowal of revolt, David Walker was one of the greatest ideologists of African liberation of the nineteenth century. It is likely that the educator Maria W. Stewart of Boston had him in mind when she remarked,

They would drive us to a strange land. But before I go, the bayonet shall pierce me through. African rights and liberty is a subject that ought to fire the breast of every free man of color in these United States. . . . [W]here is the man that has distinguished himself in these modern days by acting wholly in defense of African rights and liberty? There was one; although he sleeps, his memory lives.[132]

CHAPTER THREE

Henry Highland Garnet: Nationalism, Class Analysis, and Revolution

> When the history of the emancipation of the bondsmen of America shall be written, whatever name shall be placed first on the list of heroes, that of the author of the *Appeal* will not be second.
> —HENRY HIGHLAND GARNET, 1848

Henry Highland Garnet's family lived more than two generations in slavery, beginning with his grandfather, an African chieftain and warrior of the Mandingo people who was enslaved in America after being taken prisoner in war. The former chieftain needed no instruction in the principles of freedom in order to resent his status as a chattel slave. Indeed, "the fires of liberty were never quenched in the blood of this family; and they burst forth into an ardent flame in the bosom of George Garnet, the son of the native African warrior."[1] Even so, the Mandingo heritage was itself no source of special pride to the Garnets; it was for them an important element in the family's background but not one given preference over any other African ethnicity. No doubt the manner in which Garnet's grandfather was handed over to slavers—by those of a different ethnic group—pointed up to the Garnets, as little else might have, the limitations of the very notion of ethnicity vis-à-vis Europeans, indeed, in relation to Africans themselves.

There is no way to know if Henry, like slave children generally, participated in or observed the ring shout. The tenacity with which Africans and their offspring clung to that ceremony, however, would lead to the conclusion that the Garnets did not behave differently. We know, moreover, that the ring shout was such a potent force in Baltimore as late as 1845—a generation after Garnet's birth and two decades following his escape from slavery—that efforts to stamp it out met a resistance that left proselytizers in despair.[2] There is no mention of that or any other African ceremony in any of Henry's writings. But the fact is that there was less talk about African religion among ex-slaves, at least among those who were literate, than any other topic because African spirituality was, in the American view, at best a problematic, if not a barbarous, presence.

In Maryland in particular, black culture had long been a youth culture. Since slave youths were known to participate in the rituals of their elders with vigor, in the process extending them over time, and since up to 92 percent of Maryland slaves were coming directly from Africa in the last quarter of the eighteenth century, an African cultural substratum, a generation before Henry's birth, was laid for future development. In fact, at one time in Maryland youth "predominated with over half the black population being under the age of sixteen."[3] But the main concern of Maryland slaveholders, including Colonel Spencer, who owned the Garnets, was not their spiritual state but their physical state as property. Such emphasis was always sadly ironic but especially so when African religious leaders were enslaved, as in the case of Henry's grandfather.

James McCune Smith, Garnet's friend in youth and later a distinguished New York physician, writes that the grandfather "was as noble an ancestor as humankind could desire," one who brought "moral and religious power . . . to New Market." The religious authority he held in his homeland carried through the Atlantic voyage, eventually winning for him the "name of Joseph Trusty,—Joseph from his gifts in exhorting, praying, and praising the Lord and Trusty from his unbending integrity of character."[4] Though he melded his African faith with Christianity, it is unlikely that, through Christianity, he grafted integrity and moral authority onto Africanity, since such qualities are rarely possible without an appropriate grounding in the formative years. Disciplined examples before him in Africa were the more likely source.

When Colonel Spencer died in 1824, his descendants decided to make the offspring of Joseph Trusty "bear the veriest yoke and degradation of slavery," openly proclaiming their intent, which reached the ears of the Trustys, "a portion of whom, headed by Henry's father, held a family council, wherein they opened a new volume in which . . . they made sundry entries treating of their own rights to their own persons, and to the fruits of their own labor: in a word of their Liberty!"[5] No doubt the Trustys' resolve was reinforced by word that the Spencers were planning to separate them and take individual members beyond the family circle; this led to a planned exodus of eleven Trustys under the leadership of Henry's father, one of several sons born to Joseph Trusty.

Following Colonel Spencer's death, George Garnet quickly devised a plan for winning freedom for family members: he asked and received permission for them to attend the funeral of a slave on another plantation. Seizing that opportunity to escape, the band of fugitives traveled nights under cover of darkness, with Henry, after his legs gave out, being carried for miles on the backs of the men, and during the day sleeping in the woods and swamps before eventually reaching "Wilmington, Delaware, and that ever to be remembered half-way house for pilgrims on the road to Freedom, the barn of Thomas Garrett, the good Quaker . . . to whom so many thousands of our brethren, on the way to Liberty, are indebted for shelter, aid, and sustenance." There they separated. Seven of the company went to New Jersey, to Salem and Greenwich. Henry's family went to Bucks County, Pennsylvania, to settle for several months in New Hope, where Henry first attended school, and then, sometime early in 1825, its members moved on to New York City, where they assumed the names by which they are known today.[6]

The sources do not say how many of Henry's uncles joined his father in escaping, but it is likely that two of his father's brothers were a part of the escape party, which included three men and women and children (Henry had a sister) numbering eight. Since the group did not form itself into smaller units, to increase the chances that some would escape, no mistake could be made, it is probable, without everyone suffering the terror of a return to slavery and severe punishment. The decision to remain together meant that Henry was profoundly affected not only by George Garnet's strength, demonstrated in the course of the escape, but also by that of his uncles, so that his later reflections on how people might meet the challenge of slavery were based significantly on the actions of these three men.

The factors that led to the decision to flee were more important than any others in the development of Garnet's sense of why slavery had to be overcome. Beyond that, the way they escaped deeply influenced his views regarding whose responsibility it was to overcome slavery. It was a complex operation, one that George Garnet's being a skilled slave greatly facilitated, for it would have been virtually impossible for him to plan and carry out the escape if he had not had the relative mobility that being skilled afforded, and that helped him tap clandestine sources so that the family might negotiate the dangerous passage to Thomas Garrett in Delaware. The success of the plan required nerve and discipline, in addition to intelligence, far more than was required of a runaway with only a single life to protect. Responsibility touched all, but the greatest responsibility was that of the men, especially that of George Garnet, whose command of the details and direction of the overall plan was superb. Few blacks of the antebellum era found such an example of decisiveness and resourcefulness in their fathers and uncles, and this example strongly influenced Henry's later views about how the younger generation must not abandon the self-reliant course of those of their people who had gone before.[7]

Alexander Crummell thought the father free in spirit, a man who gave no evidence of having been a slave. He was, Crummell wrote, "a perfect Apollo, in form and figure; with beautifully moulded limbs and fine and delicate features; just like hundreds of grand Mandingoes I have seen in Africa; whose full blood he carried in his veins."[8] The qualities of spirit derived from his father's life and death in slavery, together with the family's new status as fugitives, help explain George Garnet's reticence on slavery when he was in Crummell's presence. Nevertheless, apart from what Henry later reveals, what we know of the Garnet family and slavery comes largely from McCune Smith and from Crummell, who tells us that the elder Garnet was not easily approached. Crummell recalled that he did not ask Henry's father many questions, because Mr. Garnet's appearance evoked "self-restraint" in him.[9]

In New York, Henry entered a community in which blacks were in varying stages of oppression. Such gradations and stages in acquiring freedom were related to their status elsewhere in the North and had a greater impact on their interior lives than is usually imagined. Owing to legislative action, slaves in New York were in the process of becoming free, as Emancipation Day, which would free those still in bondage, loomed before them. A small number of free blacks who had never known slavery lived in New York together with runaways like the Garnets, who in one sense, following Emancipation Day, were among the least free of all blacks in the state. This was so because, thanks to the Fugitive Slave Law, if runaways were captured by slaveholders or their agents, they could be returned to slavery. Slave runaways entering New York were greatly concerned about such matters, but they had the consolation of knowing that they could at least become members of the black community and there achieve the security of a certain invisibility.

Such realities were related to cultural interaction among New York blacks in ways too complex for us to fully understand on the basis of our current knowledge. What is certain is that the black cultural environment, both spiritual and artistic, was richer by far than has been acknowledged. In fact, as late as the 1820s there were still thousands of African-born blacks in the state, which guaranteed the presence of African values there, as elsewhere in the North. That the Garnets arrived in the North from the plantation South, like thousands of Southern blacks before them, points to an additional means by which African culture was reinforced in the North, since there were few sections of the rural South in which that culture had not taken root.

There were expressions of Africanity in New York State, especially in music and dance, so vivid that one doubts that they could have been blurred, let alone banished, by decree. Perhaps the very force of African values caused educated blacks, almost all of whom were Christians, to recoil from them on grounds of their being "wild," which was the view of their white mentors and of whites generally. The scene at Albany, New York, in 1811 is a case in point, as whites most sympathetic to what they saw used the term in describing an African ceremony:

> The music made use of on this occasion, was likewise singular in the extreme. The principal instrument selected to furnish this important portion of the cer-

emony was a symmetrically formed wooden article usually denominated an
eel-pot, with a cleanly dressed sheep skin drawn tightly over its wide and
open extremity. . . . Astride this rude utensil sat Jackey Quackenboss, then in
his prime of life and well known energy, beating lustily with his naked hands
upon its loudly sounding head, successively repeating the ever wild, though
euphonic cry of Hi-a-bomba, bomba, bomba, in full harmony with the thump-
ing sounds. These vocal sounds were readily taken up and as oft repeated by
the female portion of the spectators not otherwise engaged in the exercises of
the scene, accompanied by the beating of time with their ungloved hands, in
strict accordance with the eel-pot melody.[10]

That was Albany, but the African presence was also pronounced in
New York City, where Pinkster dance and music were of sufficient interest to observers to enter accounts of the period well into the century. As
the century opened, slaves from Long Island went to New York City for
ceremonies in the markets. New Jersey slaves and some from the city
joined them in the Catharine Market place on holidays, "among which
Pinkster was the principal one . . . and those who could and would dance
raised a collection." Each slave brought a "shingle," a wide board five to
six feet in length, "with its particular spring in it," on which dancing was
done.[11] That ceremony—the shingle dance—lasted many years following
the end of Pinkster celebrations in Albany, and appeared to have had
European as well as African attributes. Its African rhythms, much heard,
recall those of the ring shout, as part of the object of the performance
recalls Kunering:

Their music or time was usually given by one of their party, which was done
by beating their hands on the sides of their legs and from the noise of the heel.
The favorite dancing place was a cleared spot on the east side of the fish
market. . . . The large amount collected in this way after a time raised a sort
of strife for the highest honors, i.e., the most cheering and the most collected
in the "hat."[12]

Garnet had more than a little contact with native-born Africans, for the
black population in the state, thanks to a 70 percent increase over a period
of twenty years, was close to 20,000 by 1770, a large percentage of which
consisted of young Africans, since a decided preference was shown in
African slave raids for those just above "the level of children." Black
culture in New York, like that in the South, was therefore in some ways
very much a youth culture, characteristically devoted, if the logic of evidence and inference holds, to ancestral values.[13] Henry entered a Northern environment similar, with respect to black culture, to those known to
Allen and Walker in Philadelphia and Boston, one in which the relatively
small number of Africans, compared with that of New York residents
generally, was no handicap in perpetuating African forms, which is what
occurred elsewhere in the North, where African numbers were also small.
Just as the Garnets escaped to the North and freedom, former slaves by

the hundreds—"the best blood in the South"—had been entering New York for some time—seeking freedom after running away or, occasionally, after "escaping from attempts at insurrection." [14] If the best blood of the black South was indeed gradually being added to the population of New York blacks years before the arrival of the Garnets, it was carried mostly in the veins of ex-slaves who had been near the heart of slave culture, where the genius of the culture was being forced outward in many directions. African religion thereby found an outlet to the North via escaping slaves:

> Hence, in church meetings, as well as in schoolrooms, men, women and children, embracing the best energies of all the Southern States collided with the sturdy New Yorkers, to glory in giving praise for their escape from the house of bondage, to pray for the downfall of slavery, to rejoice and press forward the young in the priceless advantages of free schools. The children also took up the burdens of their fathers, and their dreams and their plays were of freedom. [15]

That was more than a decade before the arrival of the Garnets, but it applied to them after their arrival. George Garnet had followed in his father's footsteps as a spiritual leader, exercising his "gifts with so much acceptance, that he rapidly rose in the estimation of his Christian brethren, and became a class leader and exhorter in the African Methodist Episcopal Church, Bethel, then worshipping in Mott Street." [16] He had, in all probability, been a student of his father's faith. To be sure, almost all we know of the practices of slave Christianity argues that for most slaves Christianity was deeply African beneath the surface. Considering the influence of his mentor, and the African environment of the time and later, there is no basis for believing that Henry's father had not been substantially influenced by African values before arriving in New York, where such values often found expression.

As with David Walker in Wilmington, all Henry had to do in New York to meet Africans was to walk the streets. They were among the men and women who in 1827 paraded through the city with the word *African* emblazoned on banners, affirming their humanity. McCune Smith, who knew the New York black community, described the men as possessing a "feeling of independence." The occasion was the celebration of New York's Emancipation Act, at which time blacks engaged in a colorful parade led by "the New York African Society for Mutual Relief." [17] About eleven at the time, Garnet was a participant, but it is very unlikely that he and his young associates were concerned that most of those in the parade were, through their interaction on that and other occasions, in the process of being transformed into a single people in ethos.

Smith's description of certain aspects of the parade remind one of both the Pinkster festival and the parade of governors. Samuel Hardenburgh

might well have been a Pinkster king or a New England governor at the
Emancipation Day celebration. Instead, he was grand marshal, "a splen-
did-looking black man, in cocked hat and drawn sword, mounted on a
milk-white steed." And like a governor or Pinkster king, Hardenburgh
had "his aides on horseback dashing up and down the line."[18] As the
New York African Society for Mutual Relief, the Wilberforce Benevolent
Society, and the Clarkson Benevolent Society followed each other down
Broadway to the music of their bands, "splendidly dressed in scarfs of
silk with gold-edgings"—the men and boys five abreast beneath painted
and lettered banners—there was "full-souled, full-voiced shouting for
joy" from the sidewalks. These

> were crowded with the wives, daughters, sisters, and mothers of the cele-
> brants, representing every state in the Union, and not a few with gay ban-
> danna handkerchiefs, betraying their West Indian birth: neither was Africa
> itself unrepresented, hundreds who had survived the middle passage . . .
> joined in the joyful procession. The people of those days rejoiced in their
> nationality and hesitated not to call each other Africans or descendants of
> Africa.[19]

It is not surprising that Garnet probably was not aware of how African
ethnicity was shaping the culture of his people, even though hundreds of
first-generation Africans were represented at the parade and even larger
numbers were living in New York City at the time. By that time what the
participants shared was more important than any differences among
them; that was what impressed McCune Smith and caught the attention of
Henry, for Africans on that occasion were not in ethnic clusters, like
those in the Philadelphia graveyard in 1800; rather, they were mingling in
much the same fashion as those who gathered in New England to give
approval, in the various voices of Africa, to the election of their "governor." Given the presence of hundreds of Africans in the parade, there is
no reason to doubt that African languages were heard in speech and in
song, as they were in Philadelphia and in New England. The variegated
representation of African people behind the lead banner of the New York
African Society for Mutual Relief may well have been Garnet's formal
introduction to the larger Pan-African environment, and all the participants appear to have been impressed:

> It was a proud day for Samuel Hardenburgh, Grand Marshal, splendidly
> mounted, as he passed through the west gate of the Park, saluted the Mayor
> on the City Hall steps, and then took his way down Broadway to the Battery.
> . . . It was a proud day for his Aides, in their dress and trappings; it was a
> proud day for the Societies and their officers; it was a proud day, never to be
> forgotten by the young lads, who, like Henry Garnet, first felt themselves
> impelled along that grand procession. . . . [20]

For all the strength of the Pan-African environment of that day, so effective was anti-African propaganda—so convinced were educated

blacks that there was nothing of value in the ceremonies and customs of the mass of slaves in America—that consciousness of African cultural formation was no advantage to one seeking a leadership role outside the slave community. An effort to propound African values on any level of seriousness would have met with the deepest skepticism among most of the followers of black leaders of Garnet's era, and not just among those of leaders of integrationist persuasion. Considering that reality, it is not surprising that Garnet never understood the extent to which African values were, in a positive sense, a continuing and decisive force in the life of his people. In the long view, that lack of awareness severely limited his understanding of the spiritual needs of his people and, as a consequence, contributed to his expenditure of an enormous amount of energy in pursuing cultural objectives at variance with values proper to them. Yet there is no doubt that he and other black youths participating in the parade were greatly inspired by what they saw about them.

Henry had as companions at the New York African Free School several youths who were present at the parade and who later achieved recognition as defenders of the rights of blacks. They constituted an extraordinary assemblage of young scholars—Patrick and Charles L. Reason, George T. Downing, Thomas S. Sidney, Isaiah De Grasse, Alexander Crummell, Ira Aldridge (who became one of the great Shakespearean actors of the century), James McCune Smith, and a second cousin, Samuel Ringgold Ward.[21] Each of the youths lived in the shadow of oppression, spiritually and physically, as they advanced toward maturity in slaveholding New York State. Their friendship did not imply a unanimity of opinion, and several of them, especially Downing, later differed sharply and publicly with Garnet. Though Garnet early established himself as the intellectual leader of the group, these youths learned from one another that there was no shortage of talent among blacks in America, and some, Crummell and Garnet among them, came to believe that their talent should be devoted to the uplift of their people everywhere, especially of Africans in their ancestral home.

Garnet's contacts with such friends, together with his outstanding personal qualities, all but assured him a leadership role in black America. His associations in New York could hardly have served him better, but, given his talents, he would probably have become a leader of black America without assistance from influential friends. The reality is that he did enjoy advantages of environment in New York, including the spiritual guidance of Theodore S. Wright, a Presbyterian minister and Princeton graduate who was a leader in the black community. Wright, impressed by his brightness, regarded him a "son in the gospel" and warmly supported him as patron and friend. When the Reverend Wright baptized him, the ceremony took on more than usual significance, for Garnet had come to Christianity with values no doubt in some ways more African than he realized, while Wright's considerable reputation rested on a resolve to minister to

the Christian needs of his people. In that regard, his taking Garnet under
his wing and providing him with some instruction in the Christian faith
was a development with fateful consequences.[22]

Garnet thus came out of slavery to participate in a ceremony marking
an important period in his life, over which a noted black leader officiated,
just as Frederick Douglass had escaped from slavery and met the distinguished J. W. Pennington, who presided over his wedding.[23] Such personal contacts helped form critical alignments within the national black
leadership network. There was, then, an ironic level on which a charmed
life of sorts seemed to be held out, like some improbable scepter, for
Garnet's taking. The deeper irony is that his life held trials that for ordinary mortals would have outweighed any glory they brought. His apprenticeship in New York was superb preparation for his entering a league
where the leaders were highly intelligent, mostly self-made types for
whom freedom for their people was the governing passion.

I

One day Alexander Crummell, who lived next door to the Garnets in New
York, witnessed a frightening event while playing after sunset before his
father's door. Maryland slave hunters had invaded the Garnet retreat and
caused the father, in escaping, to leap from the roof of their two-story
home into the Crummell yard below. Though Garnet's mother barely elu-
ded the hunters, his sister was arrested, tried as a "fugitive from labor,"
and released when her alibi—that she was free in New York at the time
she was accused of being a slave in Maryland—proved persuasive. The
slave hunters stole or destroyed all the Garnets' furnishings, forcing the
family to start life anew, empty-handed. When Henry, who had been at
sea working as a cabin boy, returned and heard of the latest outrage, the
news fell upon him like a "clap of thunder" and brought forth flashes of
the courage that he later demanded of those in bondage. He prepared
himself for possible violence by purchasing a clasp knife with which to
attack the "men-hunters." He had returned to find his family, for security
purposes, no longer living together but scattered to various hiding
places.[24]

The possibility that one or more members of his family would be enslaved once more—that he would be hunted down himself—brought to
Garnet's consciousness, as nothing had since, the circumstances that had
led the family to escape to freedom some years earlier and the vulnerability of the status of blacks in the North. Having resisted slavery to
gain freedom, Garnet was determined never to be enslaved again. And
now that he was older, the effect on him of marauding slave catchers
seared his conscience and gave him new strength. Indeed, Crummell
thought that for Garnet it was a transforming experience, one that deter-

mined the purpose of his life—opposition to forces that oppress—and caused him to affirm the new vocation as sacred:

> So the anguish of his family calamity gave birth to a giant soul! From this terrible ordeal Henry Garnet came forth like gold thoroughly refined from the fire! The soberness which comes from trial, the seriousness which is the fruit of affliction, the melancholy and the reflection which spring from pain and suffering, for he was now a cripple [having contracted white-swelling in his right leg], soon brought Garnet to the foot of the Cross.[25]

Garnet's impulse to resist slave catchers was not dictated by abstract principles of freedom proclaimed in the founding documents of the nation. Amid threats to his own and his family's security, he again found that his opposition to oppression was a product of traditions kept alive for him and his sister largely by their parents. The raid on his family dwelling only intensified that opposition. As a friend put it, the raid "seared his soul with an undying hatred of slavery, and touched his lips with that anti-slavery fervor and eloquence which has never gone out."[26] Although abolitionist ideas helped shape his attitude toward slavery from youth on, an even more powerful factor was his having been a slave and a fugitive from slavery. In fact, Garnet's primary views on slavery took form and substance from the circumstances of his enslavement—from the perspective that his family and blacks around them brought to that institution. They opposed slavery with whatever strengths, individually and collectively, they were able to summon, and they knew the institution in ways foreign to the most sympathetic white ally.

But enslavement was not the only experience that distinguished Garnet's development of antislavery thought and feeling from that of white abolitionists, for dire circumstances forced him to take one step backward toward slavery, to become indentured to one Captain Epectus on Long Island. While we do not know how long his indenture was to have lasted, we do know that he was bound for more than the two years he served and that his years of servitude clouded his vision of freedom but strengthened his hatred of oppression, providing a level of experience even beyond that of slavery for identifying with working people. Thus, he experienced the whole range of psychological oppression attending slavery and indenture before, owing to an injury to his leg, "his indentures were cancelled, and he returned to New York, where he rejoined his family."[27]

Such was the real foundation of his antislavery thought, yet from the start of his formal education he felt the influence of abolitionists. The process began with the founding of the African Free School by the New York Manumission Society, which included among its members John Jay and Alexander Hamilton.[28] Henry could scarcely have been better suited for upholding the antislavery tradition in that school and in others he attended. Having opposed slavery on moral and other grounds, and having traveled the Underground Railroad, he did not have to be convinced that slavery had to be opposed and Africans liberated. His matriculation at the African Free School therefore reflected a convergence of values, favorably disposing him to formal abolitionism—and to its founders—in ways more personal than those experienced by most of his black contemporaries.

His instructors at the free school allowed their students to speak boldly on the subject of oppression.[29] Consequently, Pan-Africanist prescriptions for change were not uncommon in Garnet's circle. But as we have seen, the autonomy at the core of nationalism was a part of his being before he arrived in New York. The nationalist tradition in New York City, however, helped nuture that impulse into the richness of Pan-Africanism, which held that only a greatly flowering field of self-assertive blacks could free the people of African ancestry, an understanding Garnet arrived at within a few years of his escape from slavery. In some degree, such an awareness underlay the resolve of leading black men in New York City to establish "a High School for classical studies," which was attended by Garnet, Sidney, Crummell, and Downing, among others. After they had gone to the Canal Street High School for several years, their parents searched for a college or academy they might attend, but "not a ray of hope was discoverable on the intellectual horizon of the country."[30] The year was 1835.

About that time, at an invitation from New Hampshire abolitionists, Garnet, Crummell, and Sidney set out to attend New Hampshire's Canaan Academy. Crummell recalled the difficulties of the journey for Garnet, whose affliction was greatly aggravated by the circumstances in which he had to travel:

> On the steamboat from New York to Providence no cabin passage was allowed colored people, and so, poor fellow, he was exposed all night, bedless and foodless, to the cold and storm. Coaches then were in use, and there were no railroads; and all the way from Providence to Boston, from Boston to Concord to Hanover, and from Hanover to Canaan, the poor invalid had to ride night and day on the top of the coach. It was a long and wearisome journey, of some four hundred and more miles; and rarely would an inn or a hotel give us food, and nowhere could we get shelter.[31]

Crummell does not say where they slept nights when traveling by coach, but he does refer to the thirst and hunger they suffered and to the insults and taunts "at every village and town, and ofttimes at every farmhouse, as we rode, mounted upon the top of the coach, through all this long journey." He thought it hard to conceive that Christians "could thus treat human beings traveling through a land of ministers and churches!" The presence of three blacks in gentlemanly clothes, "traveling through

New England, in *those days, a most unusual sight;* started not only surprise, but brought out universal sneers and ridicule."[32]

Intolerance toward blacks in New England prevailed in an atmosphere conducive to such practices nationally. The hatred of abolitionists that was rampant in the 1830s placed them and their supporters, white and black, in jeopardy. That in part explains the contempt by proslavery forces for the lives and property of those opposing slavery. The decade of the thirties was one in which whites intolerant of abolitionists affirmed racism and proslavery violence in increasing degree. The pursuit of abolitionism in such an atmosphere was particularly dangerous.

A classic illustration of how hostility and rage followed abolitionists in that decade is the case of Elijah P. Lovejoy, a martyr to the cause. An editor of the *St. Louis Observer,* the Reverend Lovejoy criticized those responsible for burning at the stake a black man accused of homicide. It was a lynching, for a St. Louis mob had burst into a jail and removed the man. Lovejoy's criticism touched one Judge Lawless, who instructed the grand jury, after the murder of the black, "to act against the participants only if preliminary investigation revealed a 'few' men rather than 'many' men were involved." When Lovejoy offered his criticism, his establishment was destroyed, and he was threatened with death if he did not leave St. Louis. Continuing his opposition to slavery after moving to Alton, Illinois, Lovejoy helped found the Illinois Anti-Slavery Society in 1837. "The organization meeting was invaded by opponents of free inquiry" and "Colonizationists hurled bitter invectives at everyone connected with the movement. Three times the presses were destroyed, and, in defense of the fourth, Lovejoy was killed."[33] Not until the 1840s was there a significant swing in Northern public opinion in the direction of anti-slavery.

Meanwhile, Garnet and his friends were at Canaan for no more than a couple of weeks before a mob, fulfilling an earlier Fourth of July pledge, used oxen to pull the academy, at which Garnet, Sidney, and Crummell were matriculating with other youths, black and white, into a swamp. Immediately the black youths, who numbered a dozen, prepared to protect themselves from being attacked, molding bullets under Garnet's direction. He was said to have been in excellent spirits—or appeared to be—as they prepared for the worst, which was a measure of his control under pressure and sensitivity to the feelings of those around him. As expected, a mob gathered on horseback after dark, then one of their number, firing the while, broke toward the house in which the youths were staying. But when Garnet's shotgun "blazed through the window," the assailant led the mob in retreat, and the hostilities ended that night. The next day, a mob gathered "on the outskirts of the village and fired a field piece" as the black students, in the distance, were making their departure in a wagon.[34]

Garnet was described by the abolitionist Nathaniel Peabody, who heard him speak at Canaan, as "an enlightened and refined scholar, a writer and speaker of touching beauty." The foundation of his training even then had been largely laid, principally by reading and thinking on his own, for his systematic training up to his nineteenth year had been largely interrupted, as it would be in the future, by illness. Still, his training at Oneida Institute, following his departure from Canaan—under Beriah Green, "that master-thinker and teacher," as Crummell called him—was very helpful to him.[35] It was at least as helpful to Sidney and Crummell, who accompanied Garnet to Whitesboro, New York, to attend the school and were there with him over a period of several years. It was a rare opportunity for the three to study seriously and to get to know one of the leading abolitionists of the decade, Green, who was the first president of the American Anti-Slavery Society. The Oneida curriculum, which contained a significant liberal arts component, was all Garnet needed, for, despite "long spells of sickness," he assimilated the material:

> How, under these circumstances, he did study; how he took the place he did among his school-mates is a marvel. Indeed the man was more than scholar. . . . But this superiority and refinement was more the result of instinct and genius than it was of scholarship. His early, long continued illness broke up the systematic training of the schools; and so he was never the deep-plodding, laborious student.[36]

The decisiveness that marked Garnet's defense of his rights found expression in his mode of intellectual activity, helping him to affirm ideas and methods most others embraced, if at all, only after the lapse of years. Indeed his success in opposing oppression may well have contributed in some measure to his willingness to rely on himself intellectually. "His originality was astonishing," writes Crummell. "Other eminent men of our acquaintance were, of necessity, readers, investigators, students; Garnet, beyond all other men, drew from the deep wells of his own nature the massy stores of his thought and speech." Crummell argues that from an early age Garnet was largely self-willed and strong in character: shortly after graduating from Oneida, he was at ease as an active participant at a meeting addressed by William Lloyd Garrison, whom he admired. There was, in fact, little that was passive about him, intellectually or physically. From one's earliest encounters with him in the literature, he is himself a source of action.[37]

A man of culture, he was the gentleman in the presence of women, and it was not uncommon, after one of his speeches, for them to "shower him with flowers." "In his relations to them he was beyond comparison the most accomplished, most Chesterfieldian person that I ever met with," recalled one who knew him well. After his marriage to Julia Williams, who was a student at Canaan Academy when Garnet was there, those around them were "struck and charmed with the same gallantry displayed to the *wife after* marriage that he had shown her before."[38] But his refinement was not long taken for weakness by those who dared go up against him. While he was delivering an oration on one occasion, a ruffian threw "a large squash upon the stage. Garnet turned in a moment upon his crutch, and pointing at it, exclaimed: *'That's* the man's head who threw it!' The whole audience at once burst into the loudest cheers; and the fellow ever afterward was called 'Squash-head Cills!'" Of Garnet, Crummell wrote,

He was a man of great power, both mental and physical. No one could look at Henry Garnet without seeing at a glance that he was a strong man. After the amputation of his leg he developed into a new life of vigor and mightiness. Tall and majestic in stature, over six feet in height, with a large and noble head, its front both broad and expansive, his chest deep and strong, his limbs straight and perfectly moulded, his very presence impressed one with the idea of might and manliness.[39]

In contrast to the discipline blacks seemed so willing to submit themselves to under Garrison's leadership, Garnet displayed a noteworthy initiative and independence as his public career began. Whereas Frederick Douglass's apprenticeship began when he joined the Garrisonians in opposing slavery, Garnet's apprenticeship to Wright and Beriah Green had ended by 1840. A year before that, he had appeared on the same platform with Green and his own father, the elder Garnet. On the eve of his entry into public life, he was again being encouraged by his father to believe that leadership was natural for black men. Most of his contemporaries took a long time in arriving at that state of consciousness, which helps explain why Garnet was so often in the vanguard of thought for blacks. His character undoubtedly contributed to one's sense that his lame leg hardly detracted from his power, at least failed to win more than occasional notice in the sources, as when before an assemblage of abolitionits in 1840 he was seen awaiting his turn to speak, tall and black, "leaning on a crutch."[40]

His tone and his analysis in that first major speech, before the American Anti-Slavery Society, are distinguished by self-assurance. Despite his passionate commitment to principle, calm reason prevails on the printed page, suggesting that his control was not simply one of delivery as he faced his audience. Such qualities of mind and feeling were not accidental, because, in the circles in which he moved, it was traditional that speakers made such statements on slavery to their audiences. Nor could it have been by chance that Garnet was selected for so important an occasion—a meeting that commemorated the seventh anniversary of the American Anti-Slavery Society. Green had undoubtedly arranged his appearance. Garnet said,

Resolved, that all the rights and immunities of American citizens are justly due to the people of color. . . . In rising, Mr. President, to bespeak the passage of the resolution which I have just read, I cannot hope to express all the feelings of my heart. . . . I would remind you, sir, of dear-bought privileges said to be held out to all but which are, not withstanding, denied to immortal millions. . . .[41]

Beriah Green had not taught him that, for Green thought character and ability should be taken into account when considering who should participate in the democratic process. And while he believed that many blacks were qualified—and, in any case, should be judged by the same criteria as whites—he was not prepared to see unimpeded access to the ballot by any people. There is nothing in Garnet's life and writings that indicates he favored elitism of that sort. To have done so would have eroded the bedrock of his appeal to whites: the "all men are created equal" principle of the Declaration of Independence. Like blacks generally, he opposed the notion of limiting the ballot to a select few, and he sensed a danger to all in such an attitude. Beyond that difference, he and Green shared a point of view on the American Revolution to which the founders themselves had contributed strongly: that the compromises on the question of slavery at the Constitutional Convention were, with respect to the South, merely temporary, that the descendants of the founders would quickly complete the unfinished business of their fathers.[42]

His discussion of the Founding Fathers is one of the most fascinating features of Garnet's thought, one evident throughout the 1840s and as late as the mid-1860s. His position on them, though colored by personal ties that harked back to the New York Manumission Society, was complicated by the burgeoning state of slavery since the Revolution. In varying degrees, he was respectful of them but sternly critical of their descendants. While criticism of the offspring of the founders was characteristic of abolitionists of his day, Garnet arrived at a position on the question via a more specific path than most, and at an earlier stage in his development. Their descendants at New Hampshire, by wrecking Canaan Academy and threatening his life and those of others, affected his consciousness and physical being in a very direct way. The meanness with which he and his friends were greeted as they traveled to Canaan, to say nothing of the slave-hunting episode in New York and his having been a slave as late as 1824, helped establish his relationship to the sons of the Founding Fathers in ways not possible for a white colleague. He and his family knew and were owned by whites in Maryland who were determined to maintain oppression into the indefinite future, and that was more than a generation following the drafting of the Constitution. He did not say that, but it—and more—was in his consciousness when, before the American Anti-Slavery Society, he remarked that, if the revolutionists could "possibly be pardoned for neglecting our brethren's rights," if every aspect of their duty was not clear to them "in the first dawning of the day of liberty . . . now that there are ten thousand suns flashing upon our pathway, this nation is guilty of the basest hypocrisy in withholding the rights due to millions of American citizens."[43]

His respect for those who made the Revolution was stated with considerable care: "We would not question the sincerity of purpose, and devotion to freedom, which seemed to wield the swords of most of the fathers of the revolution." Yet he complained "in the most unqualified terms, of the base conduct of their degenerate sons." In drawing that distinction, in applying it over time, he carved out an ideological position that, on balance, enabled him to appropriate the best and to reject the worst of white America—consequently, to keep pressure on the descendants of the founders to live up to the best in their heritage: "Of the principles laid down in the Declaration of Independence, we find no fault . . . 'all men are created free and equal.'" That principle was the object, he tells us, of textbook consideration, possibly as early as his African Free School days.[44]

An early belief that slavery might be eliminated through the legislative process was the ultimate indication of Garnet's resolve to use political action in the struggle against that institution, a strategy triggered as much by the negative effects of the political process as by abstract considerations of rights. Restrictions on the franchise for New York blacks were so blatantly racist that the impulse of blacks to take political action was irresistible. Indeed, the texture of that oppression had a feel different from that of the disenfranchised deprived whites, who were not excluded from the franchise on grounds of race, nor had they ever been. What appeared on the surface to be a species of class discrimination was in fact so deeply racial that it impugned everything about blacks, and this was why nationalists fought against attempts to bar their people from the polls. In that fundamental sense, the fight for the ballot was for Garnet related to his opposition to slavery.

Why he thought that the political process would yield such large results—"something is doing to hasten the day when the slaves shall sit under their own vine and their own fig tree, and their claims to liberty and happiness be asserted and *established by Law*"—is not entirely clear. Blacks' participation in the political process seems logically to point, in some measure, toward freedom; that men no less radical than he, even David Walker, once had such faith suggests the power of the argument, especially when considering "the commands of God" and the higher interests of the country: "No, the time for a last stern struggle has not yet come (may it never be necessary). The finger of the Almighty will hold back the trigger, and his all powerful arm will sheathe the sword till the oppressor's cup is full."[45]

In these remarks in 1842 before the Liberty party, of which he was a member, his belief that something short of violence could rid the nation of slavery represented an unusual faith in the efficacy of political action. In fact, Garnet could not "harbor the thought for a moment" that the slaves' deliverance would be "brought about by violence." God was on their side because they counted upon "*truth,* and it is powerful and will prevail." And because abolitionists were the purveyors of *truth* regarding slavery, and slaves in the South knew of the abolitionist movement, "the heaving fires that formerly burst forth like the lava of a burning volcano, upon the inhabitants of Southampton and elsewhere, when the colored man rose and asserted *his rights to humanity and liberty,* are kept in check." He thought that the assurances of abolitionists working on their behalf prevented "a general insurrection of the slaves from spreading carnage and devastation throughout the entire South." But his very caution raised another option to view. Moreover, the results at Southampton seemed not to displease him, despite his affirmation of political action as a means of countering slavery.[46]

I I

Something occurred within a year of his appearance at the Liberty party convention that caused him to change his mind about the means by which slavery could be brought to an end. It is possible that Garnet changed his mind as a result of a logical progression of thought, as did Walker, who in less than a year moved from advocating only constitutional means in the opposition to slavery to issuing his *Appeal.* This line of reasoning has a certain plausibility, because the seeds of revolution had been flowering on the ground of Garnet's spirit for some time. Moreover, there was enough suffering in his background, and a consciousness of the suffering of his people, to explain his continuing impulse to revolt that, as far as the larger public was concerned, appeared to have surfaced only recently. It is possible, also, that Garnet was more inclined to affirm the systematic uses of violence after reading or rereading Walker—or after rethinking what he wrote. Indeed, he might have visited Boston and talked to Walker's widow about 1842 or 1843. In any case, his advocacy of violence was but a small step from his position in 1842, when he described what he would do personally if confronted by slavery in New Orleans: "Do you ask, were I there, trampled under foot by those traders in the souls of men, what I would do? I can't say precisely what I should do but, sir, in the language of Shakespeare I will say, All that man dares do, I would do."[47]

By 1843, further reflection on the suffering wrought by slavery had achieved in Garnet the purpose that he hoped for in the enslaved: a consciousness of their plight so acute that the need for revolt sprang logically to mind. His focusing on the consequences of the failure to revolt led him, in his *Address to the Slaves of the United States,* to one of the most original formulations of his time, one that established the need for revolt by calling attention to the continuum of black suffering, from the living to the dead, in seemingly endless cycles of births and deaths:

> Years have rolled on, and tens of thousnds have been borne on streams of blood and tears, to the shores of eternity. . . . Nor did the evil of their bondage end at their emancipation by death. Succeeding generations inherited their chains, and millions have come from eternity into time, and have returned again to the world of spirits, cursed and ruined by American slavery.

To such degradation, he told his listeners, "IT IS SINFUL IN THE EXTREME FOR YOU TO MAKE VOLUNTARY SUBMISSION."[48] Neither God nor angels nor just men commanded slaves to suffer an additional moment. Just as the knowledge of abolitionist activity on their behalf had in the past acted as a safety valve for slave discontent, he hoped his call for resistance, made at Buffalo in 1843, would filter through to them and make them unwilling to suffer another day of slavery. God had unsheathed His sword, and the moment of the last, stern struggle was at hand: they should use every means that promises success, whether intellectual, moral, or physical, for slaveholders were committing "the highest crime against God and man." No doubt recalling his family's escape from slavery, and especially the example of his father, he told slaves that they could "plead their own cause, and do the work of emancipation better than any others." That position, however, was balanced by severe criticism:

> But you are a patient people. You act as though, you were made for the special use of these devils. You act as though your daughters were born to pamper the lusts of your masters and overseers. And worse than all, you tamely submit while your lords tear your wives from your embraces and defile them before your eyes. In the name of God, we ask, are you men? Where is the blood of your fathers? Has it all run out of your veins?[49]

The chief inspiration for action was the manliness of the fathers, who came to North America "with broken hearts," whose love of freedom, therefore, was native to them. In stressing the self-generative nature of freedom in the slave community, Garnet was essentially advancing an African conception of freedom, one that recalled and reinforced William Hamilton's position on African resistance to European oppression:[50] "The nice discerning political economist does not regard the sacred right more than the untutored African . . . nor has the one more right to the full enjoyment of his freedom than the other." He wondered, considering the submissiveness of the slave, if the spirit of the ancestors continued to actuate them and exhorted, "Awake, awake; millions of voices are calling you! Your dead fathers speak to you from their graves."[51]

His formulation of reciprocity between the living and the dead, of the return of the dead from the afterworld to resume life among the living, is so remarkably akin to the African religious vision that he might have been aware of it. As late as the 1840s, there were enough old Africans in New York State and elsewhere in the North for him to have come by such knowledge. Then, too, by 1843 Garnet had had contact with slave runaways passing through or remaining in Troy. Opportunities for discussing slave religion were actually abundant to him through association with runaways. Even more intriguing is the possibility that he may have learned something of African ancestral concerns from his father, who may have learned them from *his* father.[52] What is beyond doubt is that by arguing from ancestral ground he offered a powerful appeal for winning slaves to his militant strategy. Since the principal religious ceremonies of the slaves were devoted to the renewal of contact with the ancestors, the ancestors at times entering their very being at the highest point of communion in the ring shout, his references to the continuing responsibility of the slave to them is a brilliant illustration of cultural thought being put to revolutionary purposes. Whether by accident or design, the confluence of cultural and political theory in his thought, the level at which the two meet, marks a rare instance of such creative union in nineteenth-century nationalist thought.

To contend that slaves should lead themselves—indeed, to suggest to them that actions taken should depend on "the circumstances that surround" them and the dictates "of expediency"—presumed in them a degree of resourcefulness of intellect virtually unheard of in Northern abolitionist circles up to that time.[53] Owing to the experience of his family, Garnet knew certain aspects of slave society from the inside, and this knowledge gave special weight to his urging slaves to act according to their circumstances in seeking liberty. That action might range from conspiracies to revolts and work stoppages; it might also include, as Garnet knew as well as anyone, escaping from slavery. Like his conception of the spiritual effects of continued oppression, the flexibility of judgment he thought slaves capable of was consonant with the complex ethos that guided them, an ethos that served brilliantly to mask the political face of the slave. But despite his view regarding spiritual reciprocity and interchange between the living and the dead and his awareness that disaffection among slaves was self-generative, Garnet revealed little knowledge of the mysteries of the slave's spiritual life.

In his *Address,* he remarked that Christians disclosed to "the first of our injured race brought to the shores of America . . . the worse features of corrupt and sordid hearts," and convinced them that no robbery and no villainy were too abhorrent, no cruelty too great, for men driven by avarice and lust. According to that analysis, his fathers began at a high level of consciousness. Brought "from their beloved native land," they were plunged into forced labor and "deep degradation." There was "gross inconsistency" in a people's enslaving others after having come to America seeking freedom, in the colonists' having won independence only to add "new links to our chains."[54] With that passage Garnet came about as close to assailing the Founding Fathers as a whole as at any other time of his life.

In urging the slaves to destroy slavery, he cited Joseph Cinqué's heroics on the *Amistad* in emancipating a shipload of Africans—an event that captured the admiration of large numbers of white and black Americans. Cinqué, he said, "now sings of liberty on the sunny hills of Africa where he hears the lion roar and feels himself free as that king of the forest."[55] In a rare attribution of positive qualities to Africans, Garnet affirmed an African love of liberty that was illuminated by flashes of resistance on board the *Amistad*. Yet he had little grasp of the value system by which the men of the *Amistad*, beyond their desire for freedom, ordered their lives, except perhaps for his conception of spiritual reciprocity between the living and the dead, which may have prepared him for understanding something of the funeral observances of Cinqué and his countrymen, but it is difficult to tell.

What we do know is that Garnet and other black leaders, almost all of whom were Christian, had a rare opportunity to acquaint themselves with important aspects of the African background, including African attitudes toward death, when interviews of the Mende and Temne men of the *Amistad*, conducted during their trial, were published within a year of their revolt. Commenting astutely on their customs, a writer in *The Amistad Captives* noted that "their funeral customs resemble much those prevalent among other tribes in Africa," indicating underlying unities that helped explain the fusion of Africans under way in North America:

> The funeral is attended with weeping and mourning, so loud that the stillness attending exercises of this kind among us seems to them surprising, and to be accounted for only on the grounds of insensibility. . . . Going to the grave in great numbers, they remove the earth at the head of the corpse and deposit a vessel filled with food.[56]

Mention of Cinqué, Nat Turner, Denmark Vesey, Toussaint L'Ouverture near the end of Garnet's *Address* points to various possibilities, in his view, for slave resistance, and argues against the notion that he was calling exclusively for a massive insurrection across the whole South. Though there is little doubt that he would have approved, there is also no evidence that such an insurrection was all he had in mind. A series of revolts like Turner's, simultaneously or one following the other, would have realized a minimum aim of his, one achieved by the Vesey conspiracy when a blast was blown on the "trumphet of freedom" before it was laid aside: "It is a matter of fact, that at that time, and in consequence of the threatened revolution, the slave states talked strongly of emancipation." But as disaffected slaves became quiet, "the slaveholders ceased to talk about emancipation; and now behold your condition today! Angels sigh over it, and humanity has long since exhausted her tears in weeping on your account!''[57]

There was a place for moral appeal by the slave to the slave master, one befitting an oppressed people. The slave masters should be told, ''in language which they cannot misunderstand,'' of a future judgment for the sin of slavery, of the retribution ''of an indignant God.''[58] But such urgings were not likely to lead to understanding in slaveowners. In fact, the greatest moral appeals that slavery be ended were continually conveyed in the songs of slaves, as Frederick Douglass, above all others, demonstrated. But blind to their meanings, untouched by even their pathos, the white South was impervious to moral appeals from its own by the time of Garnet's *Address*, to say nothing of appeals from slaves, who placed God at the center of their sacred songs. Yet it would be an error to think that Garnet was naive enough to believe moral suasion sufficient in dealing with slave masters. He knew, as every slave did, that a direct appeal from the slave to the master to do justice was tantamount to a declaration of war: ''If they then commence the work of death, they, and not you, will be responsible for the consequences. You had better all die—*die immediately*, than live slaves and entail your wretchedness upon your posterity. If you would be free in this generation, here is your only hope.''[59]

The call for slaves to resist, even to revolt, was the most serious ideological challenge to the strategy of moral suasion that had been heard up to that point. It was a curious but reasonable challenge, given the realities of the system of slavery and considering the past progress of moral suasion. In that regard, perhaps the single most powerful appeal for justice for black people in America—certainly the most moral one—had come from David Walker, whose appeal to morality in the struggle against slavery was in no way diluted by his urging his people to commit violence, if necessary. One might date the high water mark of moral suasion outside the slave community with the appearance of the *Appeal*, whose tenets deeply affected Garnet,[60] who in turn believed in moral suasion as he believed in the uses of violence, and so he harmonized the two in 1843 as Walker had done earlier.

Frederick Douglass's opposition to Garnet's emphasis on the uses of violence was decisive in the defeat of the resolution calling on the Buffalo convention to endorse Garnet's views as its own. Douglass found in Garnet's speech too much stress on physical force.[61] Of signal import in his rejoinder is his conviction that, if slaves got word of Garnet's exhortations to them, an insurrection would indeed occur, for it suggests that the two men were not that far apart on the state of consciousness of the slave. The critical difference is that Garnet thought his people had a chance of gaining from revolt, whereas Douglass apparently felt that resistance would ultimately be crushed. Both were probably right, Douglass in the short view and Garnet in the long. Unfortunately, we do not have a record of most of Douglass's remarks, but his being under the influence of the abolitionist William Lloyd Garrison meant that he was hardly in a position to endorse Garnet's position. It is likely, however, that Douglass was genuinely of the opinion that there should be no call for slave violence. Still, he was to assert two years later what he knew then: that a safety valve devised by the master class prevented slave resistance from doing significant damage to the system. His formulation in that regard was remarkably similar to Garnet's reference to safety valves and slavery: "But for these [holidays] the slave would be forced to the wildest desperation; and woe betide the slaveholder, the day he ventures to remove or hinder the operation of those conductors! I warn him that in such an event, a spirit will go forth in their midst, more to be dreaded than the most appalling earthquake." Despite that belief, Douglass called for moral suasion "a little longer."[62]

Garnet's debate on moral suasion and the uses of violence was not only with Douglass but also with other supporters of Garrison, who had made moral suasion a major strategy for opposing slavery. Consequently, Maria Weston Chapman's response to the *Address* was designed to head off additional support for Garnet's prescription of physical resistance. A Garrisonian and editor pro tem of the *Liberator*, she expressed pleasure that Douglass and Charles Lenox Remond, supporters of Garrison, were present in Buffalo to do the good they did in opposing Garnet. Though she did not accuse them of taking counsel from others, she found that Garnet had received "Bad counsels" from "the religious and the political bodies of which he is a member"—a slap at both the Liberty party and the Presbyterian church. But her question "Does he find his Divine Master counseling 'war to the knife, and the knife to the hilt,' when he addressed the heavy-laden of the earth?" had in a larger sense been answered in the *Address*, which he accused her of not having seen. He considered the heart of the matter to be the fact that he thought on his own and so did not need counsel on the subject of human rights "either from the men of the West, or the women of the East."[63]

Garnet brought slavery to the forefront of black abolitionist concerns and indicated, as he would on subsequent occasions, that no sacrifice was too great to remove slavery from the land. It was appropriate that his was the guiding hand in determining the agenda of Northern blacks, since he ordered priorities without the approval of anyone outside the black community. For years there had been no such focusing on slaves, certainly not in the context of such a remedy. Garnet remarked, "Your brethren of the North, East, and West have been accustomed to meet together in National Conventions, to sympathize with each other, and to weep over your unhappy condition." Until his *Address*, there had been no direct "word of consolation and advice" offered to slaves.[64] For his part, he had spoken to slaves with uncommon directness, giving their plight a prominence it had not enjoyed in black leadership circles since Walker's *Appeal*.

I I I

Since 1840 Garnet had been pastoring the Liberty Street Presbyterian Church of Troy, New York, which had a small black congregation. We know little of the nature of the services in his church but, considering his formal training and the relative paucity of blacks in the town, the atmosphere that prevailed there must have been different from that in most African Methodist Episcopal churches, where African religious values received powerful expression. That those values were nevertheless part of his environment is certain. Not only were ex-slaves found there, but Troy was just six miles from Albany, where Africans exploded in dance in Pinkster festivities as late as 1811, a mere blink in time before his arrival in Troy.

Though Garnet, as an adult, understood little of the cultural transformation of blacks in New York State, he doubtless observed aspects of African culture under one guise or another: even after Pinkster, for example, came to an end, the values to which it gave expression were not altogether suppressed—to say nothing of the religious practices that McCune Smith describes—as we have seen in the New York Emancipation Day parade and celebration. Being part of the historical process, those values found new outlets and contexts for expression and, because components of Pinkster rather than the ritual as a whole continued to be performed, safer disguises behind which to hide. Even the general opinion that African practices were barbaric was to some extent a source of protection for such values, because African culture was not considered, by free blacks or whites, the complex phenomenon it actually was.[65]

Because many Troy blacks, together with their descendants, generally carried African values with them, they did not have to constitute a large community in order to preserve them for future generations. So it was among the "uneducated" in and about Troy when Garnet pastored there. Nevertheless, the political uses of their numbers were more limited than the uses to which they put their spiritual values. Their potential for effecting change in political structures had to be measured against the enormous strength of the opposition as a whole—a strength without ethical restraints as the nation sought to destroy Indian nations, to quarantine others, and to perpetuate the enslavement of people of African descent. Because every segment of the society, including the federal government and the Christian churches, opposed black liberation in the 1840s, there was no possibility of a successful mass movement among blacks outside the slave states. That was a reality to be reckoned with by Garnet and by black leaders, irrespective of their place on the political spectrum.

Organizing the masses of blacks in the North was not a part of the plan of black leaders, Garnet included, because, with more than nine-tenths of the black population in the South, there were hardly masses to organize. This helps us understand how crucial Garnet's attitude toward the slave was and casts some light on how he might have related to large numbers of "free" blacks, had they been present in the North. As it was, as will be shown, he envisioned himself, quite early in life, linking up with slave masses to effect a change in their condition. In other words, for some time he contemplated pursuing the only possible path to mass involvement with his people that might have some slight chance of success despite retaliatory blows. Even then, in anticipating how he might help free his people through revolt, he gave no evidence of condescension. Not surprisingly, with little or no opportunity to organize for substantial social change beyond the state and local levels, except for efforts to place black voters in the Liberty party column, he began relations with his people on which he would build over more than two decades of pastoring at Troy and in other locales.

Though the record is not entirely clear on the subject, Julia Garnet apparently began her work with him. She was well suited to support her husband's various projects, because they tended naturally enough to have been hers. Mrs. Garnet helped her husband teach colored youth in Troy, as their daughter Mary later helped educate freedmen during the Civil War.[66] Almost of necessity, considering the composition of Garnet's congregation, education was encouraged and so was the refinement of spirit that he possessed, possibly inherited from his father. In view of the intellectual level at which his public pronouncements were pitched, it may seem remarkable that there was a sizable percentage of ex-slaves, even fugitives, in his congregation. But it should be remembered that he himself was a fugitive and, after the Buffalo speech, was among the boldest of Americans, the sort of man whom some fugitives undoubtedly found very appealing.[67]

But there were limits to what Garnet could do culturally when working with a congregation of ninety, which represented "a 200 per cent increase over the initial number. After he left Liberty Street in 1848, a series of disasters, most notably the Fugitive Slave Law of 1850, resulted in a diminution of the congregation, causing many to flee to Canada."[68] Nevertheless, there was the potential for southern black cultural expression in his church and, consequently, ready means by which he might have renewed cultural contact with the slave South, but there is no indication that he did so in any broadly meaningful sense. Still, such constant contact with ex-slaves was immeasurably important in the development of his political consciousness, sensing as he did both their courage and the precariousness of their lives, with which he could easily empathize. That a substantial portion of his congregation fled to Canada in 1850 strongly indicates that it was the force of his character and personality, years earlier for most, as they negotiated their way along the Underground Railroad, that had led them to remain in Troy and become members of his church. The money the Garnets had beyond what was required for personal necessities was mainly used to aid ex-slaves after their arrival and before the departure of those who went on to Canada. There is no evidence of Garnet's aloofness from his people, of his inability to relate to them even intellectually. Crummell observes,

> I use the word *intuition* here to indicate that special faculty of my friend, by which, without any labored processes of reasoning, and free from all metaphysical verbiage, he invariably reached, as by a straight and sudden dash, the clearest conception of his argument. With equal facility he was always able to bring that conception, the main and master idea of his topic, to the mind of the simplest of his hearers. No matter what might be the theme, he grasped it in a moment. As by an instinctive process he went, at once, to the very heart of it, and then, in a most luminous manner, set it before his hearers, so that no one, listening to his speech, could go away mystified or in doubt as to the cause which had been advocated by the orator. . . .[69]

It is hard to accept the view that Garnet began his public career with "exclusive devotion to the ministerial cause," hoping only to labor in Troy without directing his attention and energy to the national scene, as so many of the men he had known well had done. In any case, obscurity in Troy was brief, as the lure of a larger field of activity was compelling for him. In addition to his work with ex-slaves, he answered "to the call of the anti-slavery leaders" with such skill and won such favor in the opening years of the forties that the demand to hear him "came from every quarter; in city, town and village, in all New York and Pennsylvania," and in the West as well.[70] Besides devoting himself to teaching black youth in Troy, he helped foster the intellectual and political development of black women in the city, edited a number of newspapers, participated in meetings of the Negro convention movement on the state and national levels, and, as a lecturer on temperance and emancipation, furthered the cause of the American Missionary Association at a salary supplement of about one hundred dollars a year.[71]

Despite the dedication with which Garnet and other black leaders were taking up abolitionist activity, little in the black world appeared to most of them to be changing in the decade of the forties. This seems somewhat ironic when one considers the changes occurring in the interior lives of the slaves. Nevertheless, a trend of growing numbers of Northern whites toward a rejection of slavery as morally wrong was increasingly difficult to ignore. This change took place in almost direct proportion to the growing hostility of Southern whites to anyone or anything that seemed to threaten the institution of slavery.

In the period following the 1830s, harsher aspects of the black codes were dropped, violent attacks on abolitionists and free blacks occurred less frequently, and state and local governments were influenced by the antislavery movement. Thus, local magistrates were less likely to issue certificates "for the removal of a Negro without strong evidence that he was a fugitive. . . . Men seeking public office could no longer ignore the votes of antislavery constituents, the power of antislavery newspapers, the direct challenge of pre-election antislavery questionnaires."[72]

The changing mood in the white North was a factor in Garnet's relative optimism in the opening years of the 1840s as he kept a close watch on the political and social reality. Though the status of blacks was not altered in any meaningful sense, the close of each year spelled progress for the age even as it punctuated the accumulating suffering of blacks in particular.[73] There was tension between the poles, but slave oppression remained a greater balance wheel in his thought than did the "chariot of progress."[74] The very progress of the age accented the barbarity of slavery in his view and in that of enlightened men and women generally. Though the elimination of slavery was his chief preoccupation, proscriptions against Northern blacks remained a constant concern; indeed, they sprang directly from the condition of his people as a whole, the enslavement of the overwhelming majority being linked to the weakness of the free black. Garnet saw the struggle to eliminate proscriptions against free blacks, including restrictions on the franchise, as a means of strengthening their hand for the struggle against slavery.[75]

In September 1845, Garnet expressed his view on the relationship of the franchise to the obligations of his people as citizens of the United States. His support of a resolution, at a convention in Syracuse, maintaining that people of color should be "willing to perform every reasonable service in defense of our country, and in every righteous way contribute to the support of the government," was opposed by a fellow New Yorker, Thomas Van Rensselaer, who objected because "it was a slaveholding Government, and he could not support it."[76] Garnet's support of the Liberty party, his belief that the U.S. Constitution was essentially antislavery, in part accounted for his position. Relying on oratorical skill and a celebrated gift for repartee, he outmaneuvered Van Rensselaer. By provoking objections to his construction of Van Rensselaer's position, he cleverly proceeded to represent Van Rensselaer's protests as a form of contrition:

> Mr. Garnet said he believed Mr. Van Rensselaer was one among the very few who were opposed to this government and to all human government ["No Sir!" from Mr. Van Rensselaer.] Then, said Mr. Garnet, I am happy to hear that the gentleman is coming to his right mind. For himself, he could not see a single objection to the resolution. He would support his government, as he lived within its limits. When he did not think and feel so, he would take up his line of march.[77]

The Reverend Theodore Wright took the position that the Constitution was an antislavery document, making essentially the same point as abolitionists who thought political activity efficacious in opposing slavery. Another delegate, however, said that Afro-Americans should be prepared "to take the musket, if necessary, to defend our churches, our family associations, and the rights of their neighbors." His position was in line with black radical thought before him, and Garnet did not take exception to it. Indeed, few participants in the Syracuse meeting could have questioned Garnet's favoring resistance to attacks on any black person or institution. His genuine respect for American institutions never diluted his radicalism. He accepted a clarification of what constituted "reasonable" service to the country when he asked rhetorically, "If we were called upon to go to Kentucky to put down an insurrection of the slaves, would it be 'reasonable' to perform that service?"[78]

Despite his admiration for American institutions, Garnet viewed American claims of freedom from a critical standpoint. He reported out of meetings resolutions reflecting concern over the disparity between American principles and deeds, charging that it is the responsibility of a wise government to be ever mindful "of the rights of the minority," that those who object to suffrage for blacks "have no confidence in the principles they profess," and

> that the property qualification required of [New York] colored voters, is unreasonable, unjustifiable, and unnecessary: Draws one line of caste between blacks and whites, and another between colored men: and virtually says to the freeholder, property, not intelligence, integrity and patriotism, is the measure of the man.[79]

His concern over the government's obligation to safeguard rights was essential to his belief in freedom; but the resolution opposing preferential treatment on grounds of caste (he surely was using the word in the sense of "class"), opposing a distinction between blacks with property and blacks without it, was at least as significant and represents the kind of economic orientation shown by Walker. Garnet's stand against property as the primary measure of the man was therefore not made simply within the context of an appeal for the restoration of an unsullied franchise to blacks in New York: he had in mind the relationship between the franchise question and economic considerations about which he would have much to say later in the 1840s and which, together with his nationalism, would form the most original strategy of liberation to come out of antebellum black America.

The growing strength of the abolitionist cause among Americans in the 1840s helped Garnet reach a wider audience, but the very strength of that cause in the North was in the South a source of fiercely focused attention on the defense of slavery. For his part, Garnet had no inclination to ease the tension between the sections, urging in 1847, as earlier, slave resistance on a wide scale. In fact, his "address to the slaves" was repeated because he sensed a growing need for violence to rid the nation of slavery. A stream of fugitives passing through Troy in the forties provided him with a direct and continuing line to the South, and we may be certain that, through them, he sought to measure the degree of disaffection and anguish among slaves.[80] Moreover, there could hardly have been an environment in which fugitives felt more at home with themselves than that in Troy, with its little ex-slave community centered in his church. In a word, few people outside the slave South had as close and as systematic contact with ex-slaves as Garnet. Though there is no apparent mention of it in the sources, some of the fugitives must have been in attendance at the convention when their pastor, once more, addressed the slaves. What is certain, whether they were or not, is that he felt their presence on that day in particular.

Once again, there was opposition from Douglass. Apparently, their first encounter had not been mean-spirited, for Douglass was mindful of it when, while abroad in 1845, he referred to Garnet as "the most intellectual and moral colored man now in our country."[81] But at Troy he used harsh and insulting language in responding to Garnet. Chairman of the report of the committee on abolition, his influence is unmistakable in the report, though Thomas Van Rensselaer, an old antagonist of Garnet, and Crummell were also members of the committee. It is not clear what Crummell's position was, but he could hardly have approved language labeling calls from Garnet for slave insurrection "the perfection of folly, suicidal in the extreme and abominably wicked." Nor could he have approved characterizations of Garnet's exhortations to the slaves as "absurd, unavailing, dangerous and mischievous ravings."[82] It is unlikely that Crummell could have concurred, not only because of his respect for Garnet but because he himself in youth had joined Garnet in vowing to foment slave insurrection—to go to the South after being educated to achieve that purpose—which suggests that one means by which Garnet thought a plan for insurrection might best be achieved involved free blacks working in league with slaves. His resolve indicated, Crummell thought, "the early set and bias of his soul to that quality of magnanimity which Aristotle says 'exposes one to great dangers and makes a man unsparing of his life'; 'thinking that life is not worth having on some terms,'"which Crummell judged to be "rash but noble."[83]

While Douglass possessed, in his own words, "slavish adoration" of the Garrisonians, he had not hesitated to enter the company of some black men who were no less talented and no less committed to abolition and challenge their leadership from the start. After a while, Garnet must have reflected on this incongruity and wondered about Douglass. In addition, after the Troy encounter, he knew, as did all who were present when Douglass reported his committee's findings, that an attack was being made not simply on his prescription for dealing with slavery but on his integrity and intellectual stature as well. It seems more than coincidental that Douglass, not long thereafter, moved his base of operations from New England to New York, into what was essentially Garnet territory. He had radically changed his opinion of Garnet, but hardly on the basis of Garnet's militancy, since Garnet delivered precisely the address heard at the Buffalo meeting four years earlier. But there was something even more disturbing about Garnet's delivering that address again: the suggestion that somehow the historical moment was lost at Buffalo and not to be recaptured.

Within a month or so of the Garnet address at Troy, Douglass, on a lecture trip through New England, met the great John Brown, of whom Garnet, lowering his voice to a whisper, had spoken to him some months earlier. It was from the meeting with Brown that Douglass dated the beginning of the end of his faith in moral suasion. Brown, he said, was "in sympathy a black man, and as deeply interested in our cause, as though his own soul had been pierced with the iron of slavery." Less than two years later, Douglass announced that he would welcome the intelligence tomorrow, should it come, that the slaves had risen in the South, and that "the sable arms which had been engaged in beautifying and adorning the South, were engaged in spreading death and devastation."[84]

I V

In 1848, before the Female Benevolent Society of Troy, of which Julia Garnet was almost certainly a member, Garnet gave an address entitled "The Past and Present Condition, and the Destiny of the Colored Race," which suggests something of the quality of leadership he had been providing in that town, and something of the regard he had for his audience, for it was an elevated consideration of numerous important matters, a statement that might have been given before an audience of scholars, in that respect foreshadowing speeches that W. E. B. Du Bois would give to black audiences in the South in the opening years of the twentieth century.[85] It was, as it turned out, Garnet's valedictory at Troy, a summation of his views on a whole panoply of issues.

Focusing on blacks in the North, Garnet found them greatly crippled by disunity and so presented a list of problems awaiting correctives: party feuds and dissensions, disputes over names for the group, the drawing of the color line within, the expenditure of money on empty display, and idolatry and religious sectarianism. The reference to idolatry is an indication of his recognition of its force among his people, and it is a pity that he did not elaborate on the subject, for elaboration would almost certainly have led him to express views with considerable bearing on manifestations of African culture in the North. Engaging in the nationalist practice of self-criticism, he warned that, if his people did not radically alter the practices he referred to, "then much of our own blood will be found on us."[86] In that regard, he thought expressions of Africanity, presumably in the form of idolatry, a negative factor in the lives of his people. That he was conscious of such practices—though he did not mention the specific form or forms they took—is not at all surprising, considering what we know of African cultural expression in the North.

Of immense importance was his having noted the Africanness of most blacks in America. Though he did not say so before the Female Benevolent Society, it was a major reason he opposed the departure for Africa of large numbers of his people. He thought the task of missionaries there would be compounded if American blacks went to Africa in large numbers, since, in his view, they were about as heathen as Africans on the continent. As late as the 1840s, he thought that Africans in America, like those in the motherland, needed salvation, and he echoed the views of Richard Allen and Walker that the slave population had not really been converted to Christianity. Their conversion was desirable, since he saw little of value—save perhaps for the connection with the ancestors—in their heathenism. Indeed, there is hardly a suggestion of Christian influence in his measuring of slave religious "progress." He could hardly have been more categorical in noting the success of whites in keeping Africans from becoming Christians, a development he incorporated into his effort, in his address to the slaves, to urge his people to resist:

> If a band of heathen men should attempt to enslave a race of Christians, and to place their children under the influence of some false religion, surely Heaven would frown upon the men who would not resist such aggression, even to death. If, on the other hand, a band of Christians should attempt to enslave a race of heathen men, and to entail slavery upon them, and to keep them in heathenism in the midst of Christianity, the God of heaven would smile upon every effort which the injured might make to disenthral themselves.[87]

Here was another crime to lay at the door of the sons of the Founding Fathers. But at Troy in 1848 he seemed not to exempt the founders themselves from the failure to meet their responsibilities to freedom, for he charged them with having authored a "base born democracy" that was casting a deepening shadow over American institutions, as "sworn senators and perjured demagogues" officiated "around the altar of Moloch in the national capitol," hearing the cries of their victims "in their unexampled hypocrisy." Whites were slaying blacks all day long, displaying no mercy. But there were signs of a better life: "The old doctrine of the natural inferiority of the colored race, propagated in America by Mr. Thomas Jefferson, has long since been refuted," and in time blacks would "come forth and re-occupy their station of renown." To hasten that day, his people were encouraged to observe temperance, to respect peace, frugality, and industry, to love God and all men, and to resist tyranny. "We must also become acquainted with the arts and sciences, and agricultural pursuits. These will elevate any people and sever any chain."[88]

He shared Walker's conviction—indeed, derived his own mainly from a reading of Walker—that people of color were less inclined toward "the besetting sins of the Anglo-Saxon race . . . the love of gain and the love of power." He thought there were among them "some arrant cheats, but it is to be presumed that but a few will doubt that our white brothers bear off the palm in this department of human depravity." Their greed led them to launch the Atlantic slave trade, to scatter millions of Africans over the earth, and to work them as slaves. Through that process, "the great nations have been enriched." Conscious of the tremendous profits reaped by whites from the slave trade and slave labor, he thought his people were enslaved not because they were black but because Europeans wanted to exploit their labor. Hatred of blacks, then, was not a consequence of color; prejudice was "against their condition alone," a position to which "Sidney" gave expression earlier in the decade, and one that nicely complemented Garnet's class orientation on economic as well as political and legislative questions.[89]

Garnet was not alone in decrying materialism or in pointing to the obsession of large numbers of whites with the grossest form of it. Antimaterialism was a vital part of the reform movement of antebellum America and was expressed in the program of the transcendentalists especially. Still, nowhere was the theme of the exploitation of slave labor sounded more consistently and nowhere was it as often linked to the wealth of whites than among blacks. In slave folklore, in song and tale and poem, white wealth acquired at the expense of blacks is seen as a major feature of the process of history and as such is subjected to withering analysis. At its best, folklore relates the economic to the political and the cultural as the proper mode of analysis, as in "The Slave Barn." But the ultimate response, in spiritual terms, to the effects of materialism is in Negro spirituals, which rise above all sordidness, and Garnet, though he seldom referred to it, was not unaware of that quality in slave song, if not in folklore generally.[90] Moreover, his argument that whites were particularly given to the pursuit of power and gain owes more to what he had experienced than to sophisticated theories to which he was exposed in the North. The slaves' abhorrence of economic exploitation was ultimately based on their being "property," "things" to be manipulated by others.

Since early manhood, Garnet had been developing an economic interpretation of oppression, building upon the anticapitalist ethic of Walker and, in the process, laying a foundation expansive enough to let the socialist and nationalist elements of his thought rest side by side and in easy harmony. That was so although he did not refer to himself as a socialist or indict capitalism by name. It was enough for him to attack the love of gain and to attempt to live the life he preached. Put differently, many of the values one associates with socialism informed his thought and behavior, and some were not unique to European socialism. The ethos at the heart of Simon Brown's "How the Slaves Helped Each Other" was there for many slaves, and not merely for those in Virginia, to have drawn on, and it was expressed, as we now know, in a context at least as African as American. It is thus not surprising that Garnet took up a religion of service, bringing to it values in part derived from the community of his slave youth. Over half a century later, Paul Robeson would be exposed to similar values in a New Jersey black community that was led by ex-slaves.[91]

The economic perspective that Garnet brought to Christianity was the fundamental one of opposition to the use of other human beings as slaves for profit and related purposes. Not all slaves built, as he did, from such opposition to a theory of social change, but many did, as one discovers from Brer Rabbit tales in particular. Considering such aspects of Garnet's cultural background, it was no great leap for him not to consider private property sacred, in fact, for him to do everything he could to undermine property in humans. Believing "practical Christianity" to be ever at odds with monopolists—"From the beginning to end it is [in] opposition to their ways"—he claimed they feared nothing as much as "extended gospel." God, he thought, had approved the principle that a people must exert themselves to secure His help. To work to transform the world in His name, to raise an arm or to speak on such a mission, was, through God, to be reinforced so that neither one's arm nor one's word could "fall short of its destiny."[92]

Having achieved fame by calling on slaves, if necessary, to kill their masters, Garnet advanced the cause he thought central to the age—revolution. In the pages of Douglass's *North Star* in 1848, he began a discussion of oppression by warning that the greatest good in a community is to be found in educating rich and poor, the white and colored, in the same seminary. He then spoke in radical terms:

> This age is a revolutionary age, the time has been when we did not expect to see revolutions; but now they are daily passing before our eyes and change after change, and revolution after revolution will undoubtedly take place until all men are placed upon equality. Then, and only . . . then, will all enjoy that liberty and equality that God has destined us to participate in.[93]

No revolution was occurring in America, but Garnet hoped for one. Aware of developments in Germany and France in 1848, he was in no sense repelled by them and, in this regard, was not alone among black leaders. The revolution he sought for America was one in property relations, beginning with a shattering of the system of slavery and the substitution of a system of wage labor. Beyond that, he favored a transformation of economic conditions so that a handful of powerful monopolists in land would no longer hold sway. Had there been a more fully developed industrial complex in America at the time, the instinct that led him to oppose monopolists in land might have led him to oppose industrial capitalism, especially since his people would have had no more chance of reaping its real benefits than they would a century later. Though he did not specifically address that question in his writings, on balance his views leave little doubt as to where he stood on monopolies of wealth. He thought it intolerable, for example, as long as slavery existed, for those dedicated to its overthrow to live a life of comfort. That he was by no means living such a life is an indication of actual selflessness of an order that socialist theory at its best would require. His views on economics were largely an extension of his attitude toward slavery, which ordered his personal life:

> It was said by a friend, who has often taken me by the hand and sat by the same fire-side, and walked with me in the streets, and mused with me in sacred places: "I knew Garnet when he was poor and had not a cent in his pocket." I would say to him that . . . he knows me today as the same poor man. And I expect to be a poor man till slavery is abolished. If slavery is not abolished before I die, I shall die a poor man.[94]

Garnet had been developing a position on economic justice, one that was revealed in some degree as a result of an attack on Gerrit Smith, a distinguished abolitionist and benefactor of people of color whose economic views, particularly on monopolists, had an influence on Garnet. After he had inveighed against land monopolists, Smith was accused of being one himself by the editor of the *National Anti-Slavery Standard*, Sidney Howard Gay, who added that the wealthy philanthropist regarded the cause of antislavery as secondary, that "the overthrow of the monopoly of which he is so distinguished a representative is the first and real road to the destruction of the monopoly of laborers."[95] But Smith, according to Garnet, had never placed the destruction of slavery second to other oppressions; rather, he had labored "to break every yoke":

> His language is, "I regard Land Monopoly, *take the world together*, as a far more abundant source of suffering and debasement, than is slavery." Take the world together, and you will find this remark to be true. In many parts of the world, where there is no chattel slavery, there do the iron heels of Land Monopolists grind out the life of the suffering poor. Behold Ireland! Her mournful history records volumes. There is no slavery there, but the oppressions of Land Monopolists have engendered a lank and haggard famine, and the famine has swept away its thousands.[96]

Even emancipation would not mean freedom for blacks or for "free men" if the emancipated were under the control—as they would be within decades—of land monopolists. Thus, Garnet made the sort of connection between blacks and whites that he had made between slave and free blacks in his *Address to the Slaves,* observing that, as long as the emancipated black was under the yoke of the monopolists, "the free man will be heavy laden, with an up-hill course before them." There could be no freedom for white labor as long as black labor was oppressed, and his people could never be free as long as whites were under the control of monopolists in land. His position therefore anticipated that of Marx, who in *Capital* was to write nearly two decades later, "Labor in the white skin can never be free as long as labor in a black skin is branded."[97]

It is evident that Garnet regarded Gerrit Smith—and for good reason—a man of wealth different from most, for Smith had appointed him his chief aide in the distribution of thousands of acres of free land to black people in New York State. With a certain irony, he addressed the charge that Smith was a distinguished representative of land monopoly—"Long, long before Mr. Gay became the salaried editor of the *Standard,*" he began—concluding that Mr. Smith had acted in conformity with his ideals and should not be accused of being inconsistent: "There are three or four thousand poor men in this state who have received the gift of homes from Mr. Smith. . . . He has but *one table* in his mansion, and that is spread as well for the black man as for the white—for the rich and the poor."[98] A worthy tribute to a man who had shown great generosity toward the downtrodden, but not an entirely convincing one when Smith's remaining riches are recalled. Nevertheless, Garnet was correct if he was saying that Smith was by no means a typical representative of land monopoly.

There is in Garnet that same rejection of the spirit of capitalism and a similar concern for the whole of mankind that one finds in Walker. His was a statement of the right of all to economic democracy: "The chains of the last slave on earth may be broken in twain and still, while the unholy system of landlordism prevails, nations and people will mourn. But the moment that this widespread and monstrous evil is destroyed the dawn of the gospel day will break forth, and the world will have rest."[99] A widespread and monstrous evil, an unholy order from which whole nations suffer—it was a world system to be destroyed. For him, the exploitation of laborers constitutes the pivotal source of humanity's ills. Otherwise, why should, with the cessation of such exploitation, the world "have rest"? Here, then, is an economic interpretation of history with a spiritual as well as a material objective, for the destruction of the forces of oppression will effect such change that humanity will know "the dawn of the gospel day." A religious radical as well as a nationalist, he could easily have been talking of himself when he said of Gerrit Smith, "He takes a Christian view of civil government, and he withholds his suffrage from those who will not do the same."[100]

Garnet's religious radicalism was rooted in a blend of African and Christian elements. His exposure to Christianity and to the social currents of his day certainly brought him to the Sermon on the Mount and Christian communalism, and who would doubt that he took to heart those teachings of Christ? In that regard, he was hardly alone, for the North had a history of thought and practice aimed at transforming the world along Christian, communal lines long before Garnet escaped from slavery. There was, in addition, a current of thought in abolitionism that antedated Smith in opposing monopoly. Given nascent and powerful expression by Walker, it found brilliant and eloquent expression in the writings of Garrison. An avid student in youth of Garrison, as a member of the Garrison Literary Society, Garnet was not unfamiliar with Garrison's position on revolution, which was set forth nearly two decades before his own:

> Henceforth there is to be no peace on the earth—no cessation of revolutionary movements—no exhausted imbecility—until unjust rule be at an end; until personal thraldom be broken; until thrones be scattered in ashes to the winds; until hereditary titles and distinctions be effaced; until knowledge be diffused as freely as sun-light, and be as readily inhaled by all classes of people as the vital atmosphere; until landed monopolies be distributed in equitable shares, until all labor . . . be a crown of honor and not a mark of servitude. . . .[101]

All aspects of that position find expression in some form in Garnet's own work. That is why nationalism for him, and for all in his tradition, was not an end in itself. He saw nationalism as a means of achieving freedom in the United States, and a means by which Africans might be liberated in a world prejudiced against them. Since nationalism was at least in part a response to racial prejudice, he argued that, under appropriate circumstances, he would be prepared to accept a new order in which blacks would have less than complete autonomy. In this context, he declared, much like Walker, that when slavery and prejudice were uprooted and color no longer important to white people, black people "should lay aside all distinctive labors and come together as men and women, members of the great American family." But since it would take a long time after slavery for many whites to give up their belief in African inferiority, the struggle for the liberation of Africans everywhere would require, for him as for Walker, distinctive labor from blacks after emancipation.[102] Besides, the absence of racial prejudice would not immediately—or even over generations—fundamentally change the condition of the freed masses without a revolution in landownership. The thrust of his position, on that question as on others, the premise on which he rested his case for revolt among the oppressed, was that it was their responsibility to liberate themselves. Since almost all blacks following slavery would be sorely oppressed unless there was a distribution of land among them, action by this exploited class would be required for a change of significance to occur. No real hope for freedom was otherwise possible.

There is some truth to the charge that, in later heading the African Civilization Society, which favored the cultivation of cotton elsewhere in order to strike at the slave economy, he was of necessity an affirmer of capitalism. But not being a citizen of a sovereign nation with socialist foundations—since no such entity existed at the time—he chose to deal with the world as he found it, to sculpt it in places where it could not be shattered. And one should recall that compromises with capitalism mark the history of labor radicalism in the West; even Communist-led unions fight for better wages and working conditions within the capitalist order, at least until the opportunity to institute a new order is at hand. Such recognition of the limits of the possible informed Garnet's willingness to use some capitalistic means to achieve an objective that would benefit his people: had the undermining of the cotton economy succeeded, billions of dollars in "property" would have been lost by Southern landlords and thus a blow dealt to the very idea of one man's exploiting another.

Even as he called attention to the need for world revolution, Garnet did not reduce his concern for the liberation of black people, which was his point of departure on most matters. He moved from a concern over the liberation of his people, if need be through slave revolts, to an interest in ending oppression everywhere, if need be through continuing revolution. A believer in universal revolt, he was nonetheless no advocate of universalisms. In "Self-help: The Wants of Western New York," a speech reported in the *North Star,* he bared the nationalist postulate "God helps those who help themselves; and hence, if we are true to this principle, we shall have the best help that the universe can afford." The best help, then, comes from remedies based on one's particular, concrete situation, not from the blanket application of models from abroad. With his gift for keeping abreast if not ahead of his time, he pointed to a quality that augured well for his people—their growing regard for that approach, which is to an oppressed people "what Toussaint L'Ouverture was to his golden island of the ocean." The efforts of New York blacks to depart from paths of dependence, their laying aside of such an old garment, caused his heart to "leap with joy." As they entered upon their enterprises, he cheered them on and offered assurances that by helping themselves they were winning God's favor and that if He is with them "who of all the sons of men need we fear?"[103]

He thought Christianity the foundation of elevation and hope that makes tyrants quake at the thought of its spread. His was a religion purified in the fires of radicalism, and it caused him to blame blacks as well as whites for their debasement and to call on blacks to gather themselves into a people: "Much of the blame attached to this state of things [corruption among blacks] lies at the door of what is called the church, and more rests upon our own heads. This church that has torn us, must help to heal; he who has scattered, must help to gather; and both of these things we must do ourselves."[104] One should not rely primarily on God to regroup the atomized family. Responsibility carried beyond the circumstances of a particular group of Africans: black people were responsible for themselves and for one another.

Garnet was at the height of his powers near the close of the 1840s, and his influence was perhaps greater then than at any other time. But as hopeful as he was of change, burgeoning slavery with its rabid defenders and the conservatism of Americans generally were real concerns; anything short of freedom meant suffering and death and continued deprivation for all but a handful of Northern blacks. Such considerations kept him alive to new crevices to be exploited, one of which was the changing status of Liberia, which became independent in 1847. Perhaps because of that new status, he began bringing his position on emigration into line with that of selective emigrationists of his time. His prior rejection of emigration to Liberia stemmed from the association in his mind of Liberia, to which blacks had gone in some numbers to establish a state, and the American Colonization Society. Given Liberia's new status, he thought it possible the infant nation, however suspect its founding, might at least in time strike out on a course of its own.

Nevertheless, he restated with admirable clarity his long-standing belief in the citizenship rights of his people in America, at the same time defending the right of blacks of talent to leave America to build a state that would elevate the image of their people in the world. The dedicated emigrationist would fight on two fronts and not abandon his brothers and sisters in America. He differed from other emigrationists in insisting that freedom could be won in America by the overwhelming majority of blacks electing to remain while favoring the colonization of some of his people in Mexico, Africa, the West Indies, some sections of the United States—"wherever it promises freedom and enfranchisement."[105] But the "colonization" in America would be a distinctly different enterprise from the formation of a black state outside the country. With Garnet's conversion to emigration, that movement won over a man as highly regarded as Douglass by some within the national black community.

V

In 1849 Garnet was invited to England by members of the antislavery movement there. More convinced than ever of Garnet's influence, and by then going his own way from Garrison, Douglass was critical from the start. "This individual, we understand, is to leave the United States for England during the approaching autumn," he wrote in a "portrait" of Garnet. He charged hypocrisy, accusing Garnet of calling for violence at home and of asking for the "moral aid of England for the abolition of slavery." Knowing he would be read in England, and intending his remarks more for consumption there than at home, Douglass was harshly judgmental:

> The man whose convictions do not go with his words, is not fit to plead this cause—and his eloquence will merely be sound and fury signifying nothing. . . . His feelings towards us so far as we have been able to learn them, are those of bitter hostility. His cause here has been that of an enemy. . . . We prefer an open enemy, to one in disguise.[106]

Since Douglass was an "open enemy" at Troy in responding to Garnet's call to slave resistance, the wonder is that Garnet had not made an issue of his conduct.

Though the wounds suffered in their clash at Buffalo and those resulting from Douglass's reaction to Garnet's call for resistance at Troy had not healed, Douglass threw salt on them. Perhaps concerned that Garnet might make too big an impression on friends of abolition in England and detract from his own growing stature as an abolitionist, he seemed to prefer an open break. In response, Garnet said he was analyzing "poison" from a lofty source as far as influence and ability were concerned. He said that Douglass was guilty of not believing America to be the home of people of color—a peculiar accusation from a nationalist favoring emigration but understandable in light of Douglass's charge of hypocrisy. When Douglass rejoined, "We have no country," Garnet knew what he meant: the colored man did not have the rights and privileges of a citizen of the country, and as such was an "outlaw of the land." There is little reason for thinking that Garnet did not agree with that sentiment. Nevertheless, his argument that America was the home of blacks was always somewhat unwieldy, coming from as strong a nationalist as he, and Douglass made the most of it, inviting him to go to Charleston, South Carolina, protected by the U.S. Constitution, "and his country will be limited to a prison." If Douglass's was an attack more to be expected from a nationalist than from a believer in "integration," it was because nationalism was not foreign to him, just as integrationist sentiment was not foreign to Garnet.[107] Whether America was the home of blacks was not an issue of great moment between the two men; it was certainly not important enough to warrant such a vitriolic exchange. Rather, the contest for leadership, and the means by which it might express itself most effectively, possibly through the advocacy of violence or of some other means of liberation, was the basis of their differences.

Douglass thought Garnet's trip more significant than the visits of most black abolitionists who preceeded him. In Garnet's case, the English would be afforded an opportunity to observe and evaluate the talents of a man of incontestable African heritage. As relatively free of racial prejudice as the English appeared to be, the talents of light-skinned men were usually dismissed in that country by friend and foe alike, because it was thought their white ancestors were responsible for that talent. But as Mc-Cune Smith explained regarding Garnet in England,

Here was a gentleman of splendid physique, polished manners, extensive learning, well up, especially in English poetry, ably filling the pulpits of their best divines, and bearing all the laurels in eloquence, wit, sarcasm, interlarded with soul-subduing pathos . . . and this gentleman an African of pure lineage, with no admixture of Saxon blood as the source of his unquestionable talent and genius.[108]

In England, Garnet labored on behalf of an injured race "on the continents of America and Africa, and of countless numbers on the islands of the ocean." Enthusiastically received, he criticized England for supporting American slavery and for purchasing fabrics woven by slaves, in the process helping forge the slave's chains even tighter. Holding up cottons and cotton fabrics—products of nonslave labor on sale in Gateshead, Newcastle, and elsewhere—he urged free over slave products, argued that British colonies could grow cotton more advantageously than the South, and hoped that "every encouragement would be given by the Britons to this branch of industry."[109] Before the British and foreign Anti-Slavery Society, he repeated his concern that Britain was patronizing the South and declared that England could give the deathblow to slavery if she would not use products of slave labor. He urged that England produce articles of free labor in Africa and Australia, causing America to suffer such economic disabilities from holding blacks in slavery that, "instead of hearing of slaves running from their masters, they should hear of masters running from their slaves."[110]

In the tradition of Walker, he scored the American Colonization Society and its leaders, whom he considered the black man's worst enemies, because they showed several faces in the interest of a single objective: "This society had encouraged outrage and oppression towards the coloured people, and deceitfully smiled while querying, 'now had you not better go to Africa?'" When black people indicated a desire to remain in their native land, the colonizationists pressed still harder, "But don't you see that the laws are against you, and therefore you had better go?" The ones who made the laws were "the very men who would be first to transport them! The Daniel Websters, and Henry Clays, and such-like men, slave-owners, with their hundreds of slaves—these were the men who made the laws, and would then transport the black man that he might be freed from their operation!"[111]

While critical of the Colonization Society, Garnet explained that Africa was the land in which his fathers lived and died, that he loved Africa and felt "grateful to anyone and everyone who labours to promote its welfare." He was as sincere in praising friends of Africa as Walker was in expressing his appreciation for those who helped black people in their struggle for liberation. Though he retained his interest in Liberia, he thought no good could come of any relationship between that country and the Colonization Society, which had so little support among intelligent Afro-Americans that its agents "would not attempt to appear at a meeting of coloured people in any city of the free States." He spoke "in the name of the mass of the free American blacks," he said, and "whoever asserts that the coloured people or their true friends entertain any other sentiments towards the Society than the deepest contempt and abhorrence, asserts that which is entirely false."[112] He had not gone to England to denounce his ideological opponents or to alter his long-held position on the Colonization Society.

One of Garnet's infrequent references to slave music occurred in England, where he sang a plaintive slave song, a song carrying its own strength of moral suasion. Though he did not pretend to be a singer, the lyrics were suited to call forth a depth of inner feeling, especially from persons who had lived the experience. The opening refrain underscored the African presence in America:

> See these poor souls from Africa
> Transported to America.
> We are stolen and sold to Georgia;
> Will you go along with me?
> We are stolen, and sold to Georgia;
> Come sound the jubilee!

The second stanza must have called to mind, especially for Ibos and Yorubas in slavery, the punishment meted out to Old Man Rogan and the King Buzzard:

> See the wives and husbands sold apart;
> Their children's screams will break any heart.
> There's a better day a-coming;
> Will you go along with me?
> Go sound the jubilee!

He concluded,

> O, gracious Lord, when shall it be
> That poor souls shall all be free?
> Lord, break them slavery powers;
> Will you go along with me?
> Lord, break them slavery powers;
> Go sound the jubilee!
>
> Dear Lord! dear Lord! when slavery'll cease,
> Then we poor souls will have our peace.
> There's a better day a-coming;
> Will you go along with me?
> There's a better day a-coming;
> Go sound the jubilee![113]

The degree to which his delivery—the rhythms, inflections, and emotional tone of his voice—was rooted in black folk culture is not known. Such information would tell us much about black leadership in the antebellum North. But the growing evidence of African influence in the defining of black culture in the North and South, before the Civil War and later, could mean that black leaders, who in numerous ways thought themselves strongly assimilated to white values, were themselves, perhaps unconsciously, under African cultural influence in some respects at least as strong. Born to slave parents and remaining in their company throughout his formative years and later, befriended by blacks and traveling primarily in black circles, exposed to first-generation Africans in youth and to their offspring, through his church, Liberty Presbyterian, for years in touch with recent arrivals from the black South, Garnet was probably closer to Africa than he realized. It is hard to conclude otherwise for him and for numerous other black leaders in the North. We do know that, as rendered, the song "produced a marked impression on the meeting."[114]

For a while, as would be true nearly a century later of Paul Robeson during a stay in England, Garnet did not want to return to America. In traveling through England and Wales, Ireland, Scotland, France, and Germany, he experienced a degree of freedom scarcely imaginable in America. He and his family were so pleased with life abroad, especially in England, that he decided never to live in America again, unless directed by divine providence. But his love of England was not strong enough to prevent his wanting to minister directly to the needs of African peoples. Hence, he went to Jamaica on a visit made possible by the United Presbyterian Church of Scotland, which meant that on leaving England he must have known that he would in time be returning to the United States. In the intervening years, he did missionary work among his people, encouraging others from the United States to emigrate to Jamaica to begin a new life and work land there, a proposal that was roundly criticized by Douglass. Thus, contention between the two was kept alive despite their separation by sea, as Douglass continued to stand at the forefront of blacks who opposed Garnet.[115]

Following an attack of fever Garnet returned to America and accepted a unanimous call, in 1856, to pastor at Shiloh Presbyterian Church in New York City, where Theodore Wright had pastored. He soon discovered that certain positions he had once held almost alone were being affirmed: more and more blacks, Douglass among them, were rejecting moral suasion as a way of attacking slavery, and Douglass and numerous other former Garrisonians had ceased to regard the Constitution as proslavery. In addition, Garnet returned to an America in which he was no longer the only nationalist with real stature in the national black community. In his absence, Martin Delany had emerged as a theorist and political personality to be reckoned with in black leadership circles. In fact, with the promotion of emigration to Yorubaland by Delany and Robert Campbell, and of Haiti as a place to which blacks might emigrate, the fifties was a decade of growing interest among blacks in emigration. Not surprisingly, criticism of emigration, though less widespread than before, continued to be spirited.[116]

Black people lost ground before the Fugitive Slave Law of 1850, the Kansas-Nebraska Act of 1854, and the Dred Scott decision of 1857, and Garnet, after his return, was promoting emigration with greater vigor than ever. Douglass, among others, opposed him on the issue of emigration to Africa, and Garnet had to deal with him, as he had on the question of slave insurrections, if he was to mount an effective emigration movement. Garnet was partly responsible for new conflict on the question, accusing Douglass of not giving the African Civilization Society a fair hearing in *Frederick Douglass's Monthly*. Challenged to reveal his objections to the program of the Civilization Society, whose main goals were the destruction of slavery and the slave trade, Douglass accused Garnet of believing there could be no equality between whites and blacks in America—a view Garnet had denounced for twenty years. In addition, Garnet and his followers were accused of encouraging the belief, through their solicitations of funds to send black men to Africa, that America was not the Negro's true home—precisely the charge that Garnet had directed at Douglass ten years earlier.[117]

Garnet asked Douglass if he objected to the Christianization and civilization of Africa; Douglass responded that those goals were being achieved "through the instrumentality of commerce, and the labors of faithful missionaries"—an indication that both men considered Africans uncivilized. On the other hand, Douglass's belief that the way to destroy the slave trade was to uproot slavery was weighty, but he failed to take into account the role Negro emigrants to Liberia, together with the navies of the British, French, and Americans, were playing in stamping out the slave trade along the coast of Liberia. So his argument that there was "no reason to believe that any one man in Africa can do more for the abolition of that trade, while living in Africa, than while living in America" is not convincing. Yet he objected not to anyone's leaving America on his own but to the formation of organizations to encourage and support such efforts, for then the matter ceased to be private and became public, and therefore subject to legitimate opposition.[118] That was the essential background of controversy to Garnet's emigration plans. Ironically, within months of his criticism of Garnet on the emigration issue, Douglass would offer brilliant affirmation of selective emigration to Haiti. But once more, he had used his enormous prestige to counter a Garnet strategy he would later embrace in broad outline.

It was at the New England convention in 1859 that Garnet's views on

emigration were subjected to a brutal assault. Opposition from delegates
there provided the occasion for Garnet, following the convention, to elaborate on what his people had to do to win freedom. Still, he was opposed
at the New England convention by some of black America's most distinguished abolitionists, among them Wells Brown, William C. Nell, and
George Downing, who placed the African Civilization Society in the most
unfavorable possible light, a resolution being introduced equating it with
the American Colonization Society,[119] a charge reiterated in subsequent
years. To be sure, there seemed some substance to the charge, since a
founder of the African Civilization Society was Benjamin Coates, whom
some considered sympathetic to the American Colonization Society. Sus-
picion of Coates was, in fact, well founded, for it was he who wrote,
"Many consider the African Civilization Society only African colonization under another name which it really is, except that it professes to be
anti-slavery."[120]

That was essentially the position on the African Civilization Society
that blacks took at the New England convention, all the more since, as
integrationists in most cases, they recoiled from emigration to Africa, to
say nothing of colonization. And that was the position of Wells Brown,
who attacked the society on the grounds that "he could not countenance
any movement" favoring emigration. He told the convention that despite
the "very good plan" of the African Civilization Society, its tactic of
"begging" distressed him because it served to "degrade" the movement.
In resolutions of condemnation, Nell juxtaposed the American Colonization Society and the organization headed by Garnet, and charged that the
African Civilization Society was a money-making operation, that it
looked "rather *dark* [laughter]," and that no one active in the civilization
movement was interested in going to Africa. When a person on the platform said he would be, Downing countered, "The sooner you go the better [great sensation and laughter]."[121]

J. Sella Martin, presiding at the Boston meeting at which Garnet answered his critics, indicated the seriousness of the occasion in his introduction of Garnet. Of Garnet, Martin said that he had been unchanging
and unchanged in his fidelity. He continued,

[He] advocates the movement . . . has given his time and talent to it without
reward, and . . . now comes to remove the aspersions cast upon him in the
late New England Convention, and to vindicate, by his own statements, the
position he occupies with regard to this movement. Allow me, then, to introduce to you the Rev. Henry Highland Garnet. [Prolonged applause].

Garnet began by brushing aside an objection shouted from the audience
that he should have mentioned, when referring to the New England Convention, that whites were also present; he noted that he had "emphasized
'colored men' *to show that we are in an age of progression.*"[122] Opposi-

tion of the kind encountered at the outset set the agenda for much of the debate to follow, it being clear to Garnet that his nationalism was every bit as much at issue as any worry that he might be a colonizationist. He decided first, therefore, to address the respective claims of nationalists and of those who favored dependence on whites; he treated this as the real issue before the assemblage, as it had been before black leaders at other times in the past. In fact, he observed that, when there was a feeling throughout the North among black leaders that their people "need not make any effort in the cause of liberty . . . as people of color," he had told them that they were in error, but they, despising the name of color, had talked "only about universal rights and universal liberty."

> I knew that the day would come when you would think that we, as colored people, had peculiar interests—feelings and interests that no other people had—and that we understood the cause better than any others, and that if we wanted the work done at all we must do it ourselves.[123]

Years had passed, and they were still looking to abolitionists, when only they themselves could do the work of liberation. The task of the white abolitionist was to prepare the public for a full discussion of the emancipation of the slave and the enfranchisement of "free" blacks. In a word, they were to create a climate that would help drive home the blacks' thrust for freedom.[124] It was for blacks to take the vanguard action, and that involved making up one's mind about matters like emigration—even if it led one to take a position that was, in some respects, shared by white men about whom one might otherwise have all sorts of doubts. His discussion of emigration occurred in that context and aimed to counter his association with whites in the African Civilization Society. Without referring to those associates, he was both accusatory and sharply cutting. He argued that those who would not give serious consideration to leaving America for Africa because white men said they should go would not leave if Africa were strewn with gold and silver. He thought "some people wouldn't go to Heaven if a white man should say they must go," that blacks waited until whites enriched themselves in Africa before finally, if they went at all, trailing along. Already as many as eight thousand whites were engaged in economic activity along the coast of Africa, earning great sums of money. Yet some were eager to tell blacks they should not seek economic advancement in Africa, because they would interrupt trade already existing between England and Africa.[125]

Garnet rebuked his people for standing with arms folded while capital was made of the discoveries of Heinrich Barth, Livingston, and others, though "God, and science and unconquerable human energy had turned the tide of fortune in our favor." White men were laughing as black men, quarreling among themselves, failed to take advantage of opportunities presented to them. He pointed to developments in the western part of the

United States to illustrate the slowness of blacks to act, stating that after whites have mined gold "you will see my poor brother coming, all covered with dust, with his tongue lolling out [great laughter] to take what is left." Only after the Anglo-Saxon had gotten rich in Africa would blacks "begin to talk about putting our funds together and buying vessels." If blacks put a dozen ships to sail out of Boston harbor in order to trade with Africa, more would be done to overthrow slavery, to create respect for them, and to break down prejudice *"than fifty thousand lectures of the most eloquent men of this land."* [126]

The views he held as head of the African Civilization Society were those he had held all along, and no one ever made a case that he had not. Perhaps he decided he would speak his mind and lead the organization in the direction he thought desirable, and there is no indication that he failed to make the most of the opportunities it provided him to assert his people's right to total freedom in America. More than that, he posited their right to decide the means by which that freedom might be gained, and showed an independence of mind equal to that of any black leader of the 1850s and later. But whether he could move the African Civilization Society as a whole along the desired lines was another matter. One doubts the efficacy of his actions in that regard, but considering the outbreak of the Civil War in 1861 no definite conclusion should be drawn. [127]

Though on balance no integrationist or nationalist had been a more effective critic of the American Colonization Society than Garnet, he was accused of being proslavery at the New England meeting because of his alleged cooperation with that organization. In rejoining at Boston, he said anyone making the charge behind his back was an assassin and a coward and anyone making it to his face was a liar—"and I stamp the infamous charge upon his forehead!" He added that he had despised the Colonization Society since his childhood, continued to detest the sentiments advocated by its leaders, and expected to do so until that organization renounced its program of colonization before the world. The Colonization Society's statements notwithstanding, America was the home of the colored man, Garnet said, and it was his home. As to the American Colonization Society's belief that black people "cannot be elevated in this country," he believed "nothing of the kind." [128]

The accusation that he was a colonizationist dogged his path into the next decade. Integrationists finally had an instrument to use against him and, at the expense of much redundancy, and with little or no regard for his life's work, did so at every opportunity. Considering their tactics, his equanimity of mind was extraordinary, but such apparent disrespect became increasingly annoying. As usual, however, he kept the larger objective in mind no matter how personal the attacks: though he might not live to see it, he thought the day not distant when, as the sky brightened from Maine to California, "shouts of redeemed millions shall be heard" and "truth and peace shall fill the land, and songs of rejoicing shall go up to Heaven."[129]

He had suggested such a development for over a decade, except that in previous statements he had predicted final peace with the gospel day and the overthrow of monopolists. He was partly right in that deeper sense, since the country was on the threshold of a revolution in property relations through the emancipation of millions. His gift for prophecy is reflected in his vision of the emancipation of his people in America at a time when conditions seemed to be worsening for them. It was another instance of his being among the first accurately to read the signs of the future. But for all his expectations regarding the future of blacks in America, he did not want whites to escape responsibility for Africa's degradation and redemption:

> I believe that black men in general are bound by the laws of love and humanity, and the principles of the Gospel to do all they can for the land of our forefathers, and that white people are bound in particular to do it, since they have robbed us of our lives, and become rich by our blood, and it is therefore for them to make sacrifices that Africa may be redeemed, and that they may bless it as they have so long cursed it.[130]

But Garnet's formulation regarding the freedom his people might have in America was ambiguous enough to allow for several possible flowerings. In language reminiscent of Crummell's, he wanted to see established, in Africa or the United States, "a grand centre of negro nationality, from which shall flow the streams of commercial, intellectual, and political power which shall make colored people respected everywhere." If necessary to effect this end, he said, he favored the reopening of the African slave trade: "Let them bring in a hundred thousand a year! We do not say it is not a great crime, but we know that from the wickedness of man God brings forth good; and if they do it, before half a century shall pass over us we shall have a Negro nationality in the United States." He was as aware as anyone that, like the call of colonizationists for settling blacks in Africa, the call of Southern whites for reopening the slave trade was for the purpose of strengthening slavery.[131] Yet he called for reopening the trade as he urged emigration to Africa, convinced that in each instance his people would gain more than they would lose.

Though there existed in the South an interplay of religion and art as pregnant with possibilities for cultural development as any to be found elsewhere, Garnet, unaware of that reality, sensed the power of additional numbers primarily in political terms. Still, there was something positive about Southern blacks that caused him to consider them prone to self-generative activity—something about their character, as backward as he thought them in some ways, that made the South seem to him the area in which a black nation might be developed. Besides the concentration of his people there, he saw the advantage that few of them would speak of or act in terms of universal rights. Of that he was keenly aware, that approach safeguarding in some degree the distinctiveness of values among them, ironically, unknown to Garnet. There was another irony here, for of all American art, as would later be demonstrated, only theirs had potential for universal application. What is crucial is that he recognized that the great mass of Southern blacks were bound together by history and oppression, and he thought them especially receptive to a Negro nationality—unless, he added, "I am mistaken in the spirit of my people."[132] Resting on as comparatively little evidence as it did, his reference to the spirit of his people and nationalism, in light of developments then taking place in slave culture, was profoundly accurate. Yet, once again, owing to his problems with slave culture, his conclusion was a product more of a certain "feeling" he had about his people than of real knowledge of their interior world. Nevertheless, it is important that he took what appears to have been a cultural leap and landed on ground more solid than he could have imagined at the time.

But he did not explain, and must have had difficulty imagining, political and commercial power under black control in a specific geographical setting in the United States. Organized but dispersed political and economic power in the South, not a separate state, might have been what he had in mind as a nationalist objective, but his reference to reopening the African slave trade to the United States suggests he had both land and other features of a modern state in mind, including a political apparatus. In the America of the 1850s, as in that of the 1980s, such a conception seems visionary in the extreme, but no more visionary than an America free of racial oppression: that blacks were colonized in America was a powerful factor in his willingness to consider some form of separate development in this country. That formulation, however, does not seem compatible with the lifelong trend of his thought. Given his commitment to nationalism, it follows that he would champion his people's having a hand in determining their destiny, but setting them geographically apart from whites on American soil does not comport with the conception of freedom for them that he had espoused all along. But, then, no one was more aware of that than he, which probably means a black nation in America, depending on conditions, would have been a last resort for him.

Somehow he seemed on safer ground when looking beyond America for an actual black nation to help rescue his people. With an eye for population figures in the West Indies reminiscent of Walker's, he estimated that in Jamaica there were forty colored men to every white man and asserted, "Hayti is *ours*," "Cuba will be *ours* soon, and *we* shall have every island in the Caribbean sea."[133] These islands with predominantly black populations, he argued, belonged to all black people. Thus he underscored Walker's position that Africans everywhere had to be free before those in the United States could enjoy real freedom when he added that wherever land was occupied by black people it belonged to all people of African ancestry. Garnet, then, advocated a sort of communal landownership across geographical boundaries. What other position, given his hatred of land monopoly, could have suited him? The very landlessness of the Afro-American, despite centuries of toil, no doubt was a factor in his promoting a sense of African oneness on the land question, and it complemented the socialist direction of his thought on the use of land in general.

Here again the main thrust of the freedom movement for him would come out of the Americas. Given that, there could scarcely have been a more optimistic view of the future of his people in this hemisphere, one not incompatible with his stand on emigration and consonant with his prophecy, a decade earlier, that people of color would play a major role in determining the future of the West. And again his position was as ambiguous in some ways as the reality over which he sought control, and that was a strength to the extent that he took into consideration the contradictions and dominant patterns of that reality. Though he foresaw the growing influence of people of color in the hemisphere, there is no indication that he wanted them to effect racial divisions in reverse, in part because he never considered race a major force in the lives of Americans.

V I

During the Civil War years, Garnet steadied himself and held fast as a cyclone of racism, in the form of "draft riots," struck the black communities of New York. He had stuck to his post at Shiloh Presbyterian as spokesman for New York blacks and had narrowly averted death. So terrible was the violence against his people—over a hundred were murdered and hundreds more were injured—that some sought the security of jail. Neither woman nor child was spared as Irish mobs showed their outrage that some were being drafted to fight a war connected with blacks in slavery. Possibly the worst race riot in American history, it left blacks vulnerable to further depredations because for too long the fury was largely allowed to spend itself. Shortly thereafter a delegation of white merchants of the city met with Garnet. He recognized a genuine interest on their part and thanked them warmly. Though blacks had been beaten to death, hanged to lampposts, and their orphans left homeless, the head of the delegation informed Garnet that the condition and future of colored people was a problem of momentous importance—one that engaged their thought much more than it possibly could Garnet's.

Garnet responded,

If, in your temporary labors of Christian philanthropy, you have been induced to look forward to our future destiny in this our native land, and to ask what is the best that we can do for the colored people, this is our answer:

protect us in our endeavors to obtain an honest living—suffer no one to
hinder us in any department of well directed industry, give us a fair and open
field and let us work out our own destiny, and we ask no more.[134]

With that, he offered a sense of what he meant by freedom for black
people. There was no indication of a desire to be absorbed, no willingness
to let others lead that one might follow—only interest in having a controlling hand in working out one's own destiny, which is the meaning of freedom. That much Garnet asked when some would have settled for mercy.
He kept the ultimate objective in mind: that his people, in shaping their
future, would help determine the direction of the country. And he recognized what Walker knew before him: that freedom for blacks is harmony
with one's ancestry, or it is nothing at all. In that respect, he was in tune
with his African cultural heritage, and so was Walker, in a vital way. The
spiritual armor he wanted his people to put on was needed, as his white
benefactors indicated. Their words, while grating in spots, were valuable:

The path before you is full of difficulty and dangers; when you come into the
full possession of liberty, remember that true liberty is not licentiousness. . . .
You will go forth without any claims upon society beyond those conceded to
every man—you will meet at the outset a haughty, powerful and energetic
race—a race which today rules and controls all others. Can you stand before
the Anglo-Saxon and Celtic tribes? The ordeal before you is a fearful one.
Your only hope can be in fearing and obeying God's law, in industry, virtue
and education, these things only can save your people; otherwise, you will
melt away when cast upon your own resources, faster than the snow in
summer.[135]

Intellectual and moral strength were needed by blacks, the strength to
keep Africans everywhere near the center of their vision at a time when a
continuing effort was being made, in theory and practice, to discredit
them as a whole. In defending a principle as broad as African humanity,
antebellum nationalists, with Garnet in the lead, avoided the parochialism
and opportunism of the integrationists. In teaching their people that their
plight required a solution linked to the fate of Africans outside the United
States, they laid claim to a larger destiny and encouraged the possibility
that their struggles would in time help make even the majority of educated
Negroes aware of the spiritual debt their people owed to Africa. It was
that sense of obligation to African people that Garnet affirmed in asking
that his people be permitted to work out their destiny. He insisted on their
doing so when the gold of a new morn had hardly dissipated the mist of
racism that enveloped them. Nationalism, then, was for him, as for
Walker, not simply a means to secure freedom but a permanent ideal
toward which the spirit strove.

Though he continued to build on nationalist theory, the essential structure of his thought was already determined as the war years unfolded. As

much as any thinker of his time, he had anticipated the grim economic picture that would take shape following the war and had warned of the baneful effects of monopolies in land and labor for whites and blacks alike. His implicitly socialist prescription and his coupling of theory with practice strengthened the tradition begun by Walker and helped prepare the way for the radicalism of Du Bois, and especially that of Robeson, in the new century.

Garnet's advocacy of violence by the oppressed—individually and collectively—was a contribution to nationalist theory, because it was anchored in a concept of ancestry that somehow seems to derive directly from African values. Despite Douglass's criticism of his advocacy of violence, Garnet's views on the subject, though largely neglected, are relevant to the continuing debate on the subject not only in black America but wherever people suffer from oppression that is extended from one generation to another. His awareness of the consequences of oppression for succeeding generations is developed to such an extent that it constitutes an original contribution to nationalist thought and illuminates revolutionary thought in general. His consideration of generational oppression provides a sense of the necessity of revolt on spiritual and psychological grounds.

Coursing through Garnet's spirit was the force of a self-generative impulse to freedom that was communicated by his grandfather to his sons, including George Garnet, and acted out on numerous occasions by Henry. It was an impulse to freedom that first inspired a recoil from American slavery as slaveholders refused even to recognize the humanity of the slave. Conversion to Christianity was, therefore, not the *source* of moral outrage over slavery of the African; rather, conversion gave slaves a language in which to communicate that outrage in a way that would have been understood by the master class if slaves had dared to speak it, so no one had to lecture Garnet on the need to oppose slavery on moral grounds. For all his learning and exposure to abolitionists, he understood that his ancestors found their enslavement deeply immoral. In fact, his references to ancestral authority in the context of slave resistance in his Buffalo speech of 1843 could hardly have been more African in spirit.

Inspired by his parents as well as by Walker, Garnet launched the tradition of nationalist as man of learning, studying Latin and Greek. In this sense, too, he prepared the ground, within the nationalist tradition, for scholars like Du Bois and Robeson, as he refused to allow considerations of color to limit the scope of his quest for knowledge. He anticipated Du Bois and Robeson in seeing that it was the function of the educated black to help raise the masses of their people to higher levels rather than to focus on self-aggrandizement. A man of broad learning, Garnet was the living embodiment of Du Bois's conception of the Negro man of genius dedicating his life to the liberation of his people everywhere. He played that role throughout the Civil War years and later.

Predictably, the Civil War did not disturb his sense of connectedness with Africa. Since early manhood he had advocated perfect equality for his people, seeing not the slightest contradiction between that goal and love of Africa, and that was his position as the war began. On the contrary, continuing concern for the advancement of Africa and her scattered children could, in his calculation, enrich the quality of freedom in the United States and strengthen the chances for total African liberation. It was in that sense that he proclaimed, over the years, the doctrine of "Negro nationality" for all Africa's children in America. Garnet was too humane a man, too aware and committed a person, to urge upon others or tolerate in himself the selfishness at the heart of capitalism: freedom for his people would be one revolution working its course in a world in need of more.

Actively aiding in the war effort, serving on Riker's Island as chaplain to the Twentieth, Twenty-sixth, and Thirty-first regiments of the United States Colored Troops, he found the outbreak of hostilities anything but tragic. During the war, at Syracuse in 1864, his credentials as a leader were challenged on two separate occasions at a meeting of the Negro convention movement. The first challenge occurred when he was asked to define his position in relation to his people. He found the demand "exceedingly humiliating" at so late a stage in his career and detected a disposition by some to put him "on the shelf," because of his continuing association with the African Civilization Society. Though he clearly supported the Union, he reaffirmed his belief, the minutes read, "in a 'Negro Nationality,' and referred to the brave deeds of the colored soldiers, and the effect their . . . conduct had produced upon the public mind. The convention had a right to do as it pleased; but, if taken to the stake, he would utter his honest convictions."[136] He was hardly less convinced during the Civil War than he had been all along that the struggle to liberate Africans everywhere should be pressed: his unfurling of the colors of a black regiment on the stage of the convention was emblematic of his faith in the cause of Africans everywhere.

Garnet's childhood classmate and longtime antagonist George Downing was not satisfied that Garnet's integrity had already been challenged at Syracuse. He revived the insistence of others that Garnet explain his relationship to the movement. It had been nearly five years since the New England convention and the Boston meeting at which Garnet had responded to his critics. His work on behalf of the black community following the Boston meeting, like his two decades of devotion to his people before that meeting, meant nothing to Downing, who charged that he was a tool of colonizationists, that the African Civilization Society was "in perfect harmony with our old enemy, the Colonization Society." He charged that on one occasion Garnet, though present, had offered no words of censure when whites in the Civilization Society argued that there was no place in America for blacks.[137]

Garnet did not bother to respond directly to Downing, nor did he defend his integrity in any direct way. Rather, he asked

all present whether they believed, that now, so late in his public life, he had begun to falsify himself by putting himself under the direction, and being made the tool of white men. He had during all that life been unpopular, for the very reason that he was too independent to be used as a tool.

He added, "As regards the other personal remarks of Mr. Downing, I pass them by. Those who know me, know well that I could retort if I chose. But I will not retort."[138]

The attack from Downing hurt Garnet politically, for he was up for consideration, together with John Mercer Langston, for the leadership of the projected National Equal-Rights League, a post he wanted, though he was not in the habit of seeking office as such. In his effort to prevent Garnet from securing the office, it does not appear to have crossed Downing's mind that a colonizationist would not find it in his interest to speak on behalf of equal rights for blacks in America. Had it crossed his mind, he probably would not have altered his position, for it was well known—in fact, it was discussed at the Syracuse meetings—that the African Civilization Society was at the time educating black youth in Washington, D.C., where Garnet was then pastoring and, as Richard Cain noted, "doing a noble part" in looking to the needs of the freedmen and their children in that city. There was, indeed, not the slightest indication that Garnet had abandoned his belief that blacks could be free in America, or that he was not working to that end. Yet the African Civilization Society issue caused him problems with a certain class of blacks—with integrationist, well-heeled types like Downing in particular.[139]

On February 12, 1865, at the request of the Reverend William Channing, Garnet preached "to an overflow audience in the House of Representatives, Washington, D.C."[140] By then more than four million of his people were hoping as never before that they would find a place for themselves in America. With a full-length portrait of George Washington on his right, Garnet spoke feelingly about Africa and proceeded to deliver a statement that summarized, and in some instances clarified, themes he had been voicing for a quarter of a century. After talking about a slavery "worse than Egyptian bondage," he discussed the freedom he envisioned for his people and for Americans as a whole. It was evident, as on previous occasions when he addressed questions of social change, that he was speaking of radicalism even when using the term *reform:* "It is often asked when and where will the demands of the reformers of this and coming ages end?"

When all unjust and heavy burdens shall be removed from every man in the land. . . . When there shall be no more class-legislation, and no more trouble concerning the black man and his rights, than there is in regard to other

American citizens. When, in every respect, he shall be equal before the law, and shall be left to make his own way in the social walks of life.[141]

He was insistent on certain matters: "While we scorn unmanly dependence; in the name of God, the Universal Father, we demand the right to live, and labor, and to enjoy the fruits of our toil." Much like Robeson a century later, he argued that the writer, painter, sculptor, and musician must refuse "to scoff at the afflictions of the poor"; in so doing, he advanced an aesthetic postulate consistent with his opposition to economic oppression. He urged that "every class be enfranchised," suggesting that not even then could the Constitution and the statesmen of the land be revered: In traditional nationalist style—as old as Walker, as recent as Malcolm X—he spoke of the need for whites to atone. To be sure, justice held "heavy mortgages" against America and would "require the payment of the last farthing."[142]

Garnet's position on American principles and institutions may have seemed puzzling at times in 1840 and later, but it was clarified in his sermon to Congress. There he reminded his listeners of aspects of the thought of Washington and Jefferson, that, whatever their actual behavior, showed their opposition to slavery. It was the Jefferson who remarked "when his judgment was matured, and his experience was ripe, 'There is preparing, I hope, under the auspices of heaven, a way for total emancipation,'" to whom he had long been referring; it was the Washington who said, "near the close of his mortal career, and when the light of eternity was beaming upon him, 'It is among my first wishes to see some plan adopted by which slavery shall be abolished,'"[143] whom he had in mind in earlier statements. Yet, on that day in the nation's capitol, Garnet moved a little closer to Walker's position on Jefferson and even closer to Walker's assessment of American institutions, whose racist nature he now criticized, warning that there would be no peace until "all invidious and proscriptive distinctions shall be blotted out from our laws, whether they be constitutional, statute, or municipal laws," arguing that the perpetuation of slavery had weakened America spiritually, having "shorn the nation of its locks of strength that was rising as a young lion in the Western world."[144]

VII

Garnet was among the first to realize that the freedmen might not secure a substantial measure of freedom unless they, as well as poor whites, received land through a land redistribution program. They needed not merely the franchise but also an economic foothold that would enable them to achieve some degree of self-sufficiency in the South. This perception was deepened by his movement among them during a four-month tour of the South as a correspondent for the weekly *Anglo-African* maga-

zine, the staff of which he joined as an editor in July 1865. In a letter to
Gerrit Smith he remarked that, because of the federal government's failure to move decisively to aid the freedmen, developments there might
"be disastrous to the cause of freedom." Moreover, he correctly thought
that President Andrew Johnson was retreating from the government's
previous promises to the freedmen.[145]

Meanwhile, he had been laboring on behalf of the freedmen through a
number of freedmen's aid societies in the North—a natural extension of
his work on behalf of them through the African Civilization Society.
Throughout the latter half of the 1860s, he called for land for the freedmen and insisted that they did "not intend to be crushed out . . . did not
intend to die beneath the oppressor's heel." He added, "We feel that we
have God and all good men on our side. We have in us the Phoenix's spirit
which though buried in ashes cries from those ashes, 'I will arise,' and
springs up to new and vigorous life." Until the nation provided the freedmen with land and with schools and churches, their light would not
"break forth as the morning."[146]

Garnet attended a meeting of the convention movement at Washington,
D.C., in 1869, serving as chairman. In 1870, he joined Douglass and other
leaders at the last meeting of the American Anti-Slavery Society, thus
being present at its birth and death. Moreover, he organized the Cuban
Anti-Slavery Committee in 1873 and began lobbying the Grant administration to work for the emancipation of slaves in Cuba, but to no avail.[147]
What was happening to his people in America by this time was some
indication that blacks in Cuba, when finally free, might not fare better by
comparison, considering the general indifference of Europeans, whether
the Spanish in Cuba or the Anglo-Saxons in America, to black liberation.
The power of reaction in those years was a factor in reinforcing his conviction that certain black institutions, especially the church, had to be
maintained.[148]

He was active in Republican politics as the fortunes of blacks seemed
greatly to improve before being dashed on the ground of Redemption's
triumph. By the mid-1870s, his stamina began to ebb, his voice to lose its
power, his ranks of admirers to thin. Despair claimed whatever hope he
may have had for living out his life in peace in America. By the close of
the seventies, his church was paying him just enough to keep him from
falling into hopeless poverty. "It is useless to attempt concealment,"
wrote Alexander Crummell. "Sorrow and discouragement fell upon his
soul, and at times the wounded spirit sighed for release; and the strong
desire arose to escape to some foreign land. . . ."[149]

Garnet spoke in confidence to Crummell. Crummell pressed Garnet not
to accept a position as minister resident to the republic of Liberia. Garnet,
who knew the losses of sorrow, replied,

What, would you have me linger here in an old age of neglect and want? Would you have me tarry among men who have forgotten what I have done, and what I have suffered for them! To stay here and die among these un- grateful people? No, I go gladly to Africa! Please the Lord I can only safely cross the ocean, land on the coast of Africa, look around upon its green fields, tread the soil of my ancestors, live if but a few weeks; then I shall be glad to lie down and be buried beneath its sod![150]

On November 6, 1882, he preached his farewell sermon to the con- gregation of New York's Shiloh Presbyterian Church, where he had pas- tored for twenty-six years. Within a week, he sailed for Africa, never to return. The next two decades were especially dark, as winds of violence seemed at times to leave his people's spirit barely flickering.

CHAPTER FOUR

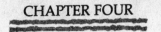

Identity and Ideology: The Names Controversy

> Ye dark-skinned peoples, are you listening?
> Those who gave birth to us, before they start to speak,
>   they ponder profound matters.
> They say: One must first consider one's tradition and
>   history, before deciding on a name for the child.
> They say: One's name is one's bridle.
> Ye dark-skinned peoples, listen to me:
> Our fathers did not play about with names.
> To hear their names is to know their origin,
> Every name a veritable testament!
>
> TOBOSUN SOWANDE

"I know the very spot where they laid him. . . . There he lies; the deep Atlantic but a few steps beyond; its perpetual surges beating at his feet." So spoke Alexander Crummell, who called Henry Highland Garnet a princely man and reports that he was buried like a prince. The president of Liberia and his cabinet, students and professors of the college, the military of the capital of the republic, various religious leaders, and citizenry from the interior as well as townspeople were in attendance at the funeral. Edward Wilmot Blyden, the black scholar, gave the eulogy.[1] It was appropriate that Garnet "returned home" just before his death to find a measure of peace, for he had been among the most loyal of African patriots. Especially because he had been in Africa for so brief a period, the presence of Africans from the interior at his funeral was eloquent proof of his having truly returned home, not to dwell among expatriates but to get to know, and make himself known to, indigenous inhabitants of the continent from whom he had been separated by forces utterly beyond his control. That he went to Africa bearing the name Henry Highland Garnet indicates the disruptive impact of the slave trade and slavery on African values and peoples. His name was a metaphor for the cultural pain inflicted on the African, pain attended in the North by considerable controversy among educated blacks.

The controversy over names in nineteenth- and early-twentieth-century America reveals important ideological and organizational developments in Afro-American life. At the heart of the controversy is the issue of identity, individual and collective, important to Afro-American nationalists and integrationists alike. Both recognize that larger issues and values are involved in the controversy, even as some have eschewed debate over a particular name as such. Moreover, the controversy has provided the occasion for the emergence of important figures in the contest between nationalists and integrationists, and it enables one to test not only the commitment of nationalists to Pan-Africanism but also the consciousness of African ethnicity among theorists of black liberation. Since they were relatively free and not a part of the slave community, questions of African ethnicity became largely abstract for them, especially for those who never knew the particular ethnic group or groups from which they sprang. Of course, that was quite different from what a great many slaves who knew the ethnic group from which they came might have thought about the use of African names. Though ex-slaves gave each other African names only rarely, their participation in naming ceremonies was one means of furthering individual and group consciousness indispensable to the upward movement of their people.[2] From what we know of it, it is not surprising that slave culture is related to the debate as background, but not as inert or static background.

I

Shortly after the Garnets escaped from Maryland slavery and entered the city of New York, Henry's father led the family in a "baptism to liberty," a ceremony solemn and simple, one enacted by thousands of ex-slaves long before the Emancipation Proclamation. In this instance—the year was 1825—Garnet's father said, "Wife, they used to call you Hennie. . . . But in future your name is Elizabeth." Then, placing his hand on his daughter, he said, "Your name is not Mary any longer, but Eliza." Turning to his son, and taking him on his knee, he said, "And my dear little boy . . . your name is Henry. My name is George Garnet."[3] Though his lineage was royal, the father conferred European names on members of his family, even though African names were available to him, for, as important as names were, apparently the grand object for Garnet's father, as for the son, was liberation. The realities of the New World, of ethnic necessity, made it so.

At roughly the same time the Garnets were taking new names, Sojourner Truth, who emerged from Northern slavery, was engaged in a similar ceremony, she believed, in the presence of the Lord. Emancipated under the New York Emancipation Act, Sojourner, formerly Isabella, cast aside her slave name because when she left the house of bondage she wanted to leave everything behind. She had not wanted to keep "nothin' of Egypt on me," she said, "an' so I went to the Lord an' asked him to give me a new name. And the Lord gave me Sojourner, because I was to travel up an' down the land, showin' the people their sins, an' bein' a sign unto them." She later asked for another name, she said, and "the Lord gave me Truth, because I was to declare the truth to the people."[4]

These re-baptisms probably owed as much to Holy Scripture as to direct African influences. Yet individual efforts at naming, whatever the immediate impetus, were related to collective quests, continuous during and following the nineteenth century, to find a name for the entire group. Just as individual naming ceremonies were an attempt to dissociate blacks from some of the degradation of slavery, the attempts to find an acceptable group name, impelled by similar historical forces, had a similar purpose. Whether most blacks were aware of it or not, naming ceremonies, however attenuated, were linked to Africa, since blacks taken from there had African names that, together with numerous other African qualities, were systematically removed. The ceremonies grew out of a sense of loss rooted in the oppression of the African.

In West Africa the names of many of the people constitute their "essence," producing deep and permanent psychological effects. In some regions of West Africa, notably Yorubaland, child naming has been a ritual for centuries. The Yoruba language, for example, at one time spoken by thousands of American slaves, consists largely of monosyllabic words, each syllable of which has its own meaning. Thus, a Yoruba name can telescope a whole sentence or phrase, and often represents much reflection on the part of the child's parents. In other sections of West Africa, from which scores of thousands of Africans were brought to North America, names are also greatly valued and respected, and have histories just as those in Yorubaland do,[5] which makes it especially ironic that the African was the victim of American slavery. The slave overlord in America attached a special negative value to the naming of slaves, so that the effect on an African of being shorn of his name with its firm personal moorings must have been traumatic.

Among Negro peoples a man's name is often identified with his very soul, and often with the souls of ancestors. Parents name children after relatives, heightening the spiritual significance of their names, all the more after the death of a relative. The efforts of some West Africans, the Ashanti and Yorubas among them, to bring the living and dead closer, thereby lessening the pain of death, is illustrated by their rituals on the death of an elder and the birth of a new member of the family. The placing of food on the burial mound or at the crossroads and the naming of infants after the deceased are related means of seeking renewal and approbation from the spirit of the dead, and were no doubt carried out by many for that dual purpose in slavery even when non-African names were given to infants. As for black people not born in Africa, resentment at not having a surname and at having a Christian name of another's choosing were causes for distress. Nevertheless, these sorrows were obviously less devastating than the pain experienced by slaves who remembered the importance of names in the African homeland and were robbed of theirs in America.

Since Ashanti in Virginia, South Carolina, and North Carolina joined Kongo peoples and numerous other groups in the same locations in practicing West African burial ceremonies during slavery, it is logical to conclude that naming ceremonies were conducted quite often, secretly on many occasions. Indeed, it is likely that African names were employed as second—but *real*—names in America, for the burden of learning languages, in the master-slave relationship, was placed on the African, and so Africans in America had to find ways to perpetuate and elaborate upon cultural practices important to them in the ancestral homeland. Since in the presence of blacks whites understood even less of African languages than of African folklore, both of which were employed for the benefit of Africans, much that was communicated from one slave to another remained a mystery to whites. English might have been used as a cover for African words or names quickly inserted between phrases spoken in the presence of whites, who were likely to regard slave speech as "baby talk," or as barbarous outpouring.[6]

Under such circumstances, the use of African names was probably common when slaves were with each other. If blacks in the twentieth century in the Sea Islands use African names when not in the presence of whites—"pet names," Turner calls them—then Africans brought into the United States during slavery almost certainly were responsible for the practice, having given their offspring "pet names" and having done so effectively enough that the practice persists in our time. Since as late as the 1930s whites studied the language of descendants of slaves on the Sea Islands without discovering their use of African names, there is even less reason to suppose that slave masters were more successful at detecting such practices, especially considering the price to be paid for transgressions.[7]

Turner's evidence is supported by that of the linguist David Dalby, who also argues that the African used language deceptively in the presence of whites and concealed information from them. That Africans and their descendants had much success in that regard was a logical development, since their systems of naming were varied and complex, allowing for subtlety by their very nature. For example, among a number of West African ethnic groups, the child received two names, one temporary, another permanent; one for good times, another when life is shadowed; one from the mother, another from the father.[8] Consequently, the forcing together of dozens of African ethnic groups on America's soil no doubt called forth a great many subtle responses in language similar to those in music and folk art generally.

A name is held at birth to be sacred by some peoples of Southern Nigeria, an area hard hit by the slave traffic:

> Names among the southern tribes are commonly chosen by the divinatory method. Thus . . . the seer decides whether the child is some re-incarnated relative. Should it appear that he is the father's father re-embodied, he will be given the name of his paternal grandfather, and treated with the utmost respect by his father.

Other peoples are pleased to see a name discarded and another taken up—for example, when "a child who cries excessively is taken to the seer, who declares that he is some dead relative, and that if he is given the relative's name the crying will cease." Among the Hausa, who were brought by the thousands to North America, "a child is often . . . given two names—the first a secret name whispered into his ear by his mother, and the second name for daily use, which is a designation rather than a real name."9

Whatever the differences of West Africans in naming ceremonies, their similarities were greater, so much so that one might argue they brought essentially the same optic to the question: that they had fundamentally the same attitude toward names and their importance. Consequently, levels of resentment were similar and resources for deflecting—or attempting to deflect—the pain of losing one's name roughly equivalent. But no matter how determinedly they named themselves, after a name was forced on slaves by the master, the imperatives of the slave system won out. In the slave's mind the new name was associated with enforced obedience and powerlessness, and this is what rendered "pet names," even African ones, of little consequence, because the language slaves increasingly heard was English. The most poignant evidence of the loss of authority of African names is the deceptive use of them in the new environment. The slave name would become the bridle. Still, for the slave the spiritual damage was not lessened by the knowledge that the question of his name had been decided through the use of whip and gun. The sharp reduction in the public use of African names reinforced a tendency not to employ them privately, especially since new names tended in time to take on their own appeal.

While the African was enslaved by people who attached no positive importance to the names of their captives, and while Americans did not attach as much importance to names as Africans did, it would be a mistake to discount their significance in the West. Freud has written that the "twisting round of a name when it is intentional amounts to an insult; and it might well have the same significance in a whole number of cases where it appears in the form of an unintentional slip of the tongue." Moreover, to distort another's name can in certain circumstances mean that the distorter inwardly despises the person whose name is being abused.[10] If in Freudian terms even simple distortions of names, conscious and unconscious (slips of the tongue), constitute acts of aggression, then the act of denying a whole people their names and giving them new ones in a new language—and only partial names at that—must be regarded as a serious act of aggression, as a reflection of their subordinate state.

Having observed the ritualization and celebration of names in his homeland, and the use of names as a weapon against his sense of humanity in an alien country, the African experienced the tension generated by the larger cultural problem confronting his people in America. In a curious way, however, the blow of losing one's native name was somewhat softened in the course of the painful but indispensable process of reaching beyond the narrowness of ethnicity to embrace a larger Africanity. Nevertheless, the crisis over names—like that larger identity crisis—was symbolized by the mark branded into thousands of Africans at the start of slavery. That branding iron proved two-edged, searing into the slave's consciousness an awareness that his identity was under attack and triggering a recoil from the attempt to depersonalize that lasted, for large numbers of slaves, throughout slavery.[11] The importance of names to the slave, however, is not our primary interest, nor is the importance of names to Africans.[12] We must understand the African background to appreciate the emotional force behind the names controversy, the cultural loss and confusion it reflects, and the spiritual pain of those engaged in the controversy. We are here concerned to measure the cultural awareness of free blacks and of blacks who were once slaves.

I I

In North America, as in the Americas generally, the word *Negro* was closely associated with *slave* and slavery. Although the two words were virtually synonymous in parts of the Americas, they were not in North America, at least not for a great many people, which in part accounts for a tendency among slaveholders to refer to slaves as Africans. In debates among blacks over what they should call themselves, one finds few complaints that *Negro* was a synonym for *slave*. This can only be because in many contexts the two words were not synonymous. In the slave states, where the overwhelming majority of Negroes were slaves, the tendency to equate the two was no doubt much greater. But if *Negro* was closely associated with slavery in the South and therefore an objectionable word to some people of African descent, *nigger* was far more demeaning. This epithet rang in the ears of slaves and frequently appears in their oral literature, sometimes as a positive term.[13] The use of the term *nigger* was so frequent as to be a reflex action, and, long before the end of slavery, many

Southern whites had practically lost the ability to pronounce the word *Negro*, sounding a word which fell between *Negro* and *nigger*—*Nigra*.[14]

The use of the terms *colored* and *brown*—more perhaps than that of any other appellations prior to the nineteenth century—reflected a certain disdain on the part of some people of mixed ancestry for the majority of their people, a tendency to look askance at them on grounds of color and class. These terms were initially used by offspring of Negro women (some of whom worked in the great houses of the South) and slaveholders. The light-skinned children of such relationships formed much of the free Negro population of the South, and it was within their ranks that early advocates of the terms *brown* and *colored* were found. So it was that in Charleston, South Carolina, the Brown Fellowship Society was established in 1790, admitting "only brown men of good character who paid an admission fee of fifty dollars."[15] Clearly the great majority of people of African ancestry would have been ruled out by their darker hue, and at least as many by the fee. Exclusive, too, were class and caste distinctions drawn by "*gens de couleur*" and "people of color" of African, French, and Spanish extraction who affected the ways of the white oligarchy of New Orleans years before the founding of the Brown Fellowship Society.[16] In affirming white values, they tried to shed their African roots.

While *brown* and *colored* enjoyed popularity among certain "free" Southerners of African descent in the late eighteenth century, the word *African* found significant expression among blacks, slave and free, in the South. Unlike the terms *brown* and *colored* as used by a minority of people of color in the South, the term *African* more often than not reflected a pride in blackness and racial inclusiveness rather than color and class distinctions. *African* was generally a far more radical term, one that blacks in the South, ironically, continued to use in organizational titles even after that practice was discontinued in the North. In Richmond, Virginia, for example, the First African Baptist Church was founded in 1841.[17] But those who put the word *African* in the titles of churches and other organizations, unless from slave communities, were not likely to understand the meaning the term conveyed when informed by a knowledge of African culture on the continent and in America.

For two centuries blacks in the North tended to call themselves African or Free African, and used the word *African* in the titles of their organizations.[18] Because of the richness of African culture reflected in the parade of governors, the Pinkster celebrations, and the ring shout in the North, blacks who participated in such ceremonies might have spoken with authority on vital aspects of African culture but apparently were not a part of the debates. Had those who knew the deeper meaning of being African been present to defend the use of the term, the controversy over names might have been less turbulent and certainly been an educative tool of great import. Instead, only rarely was light cast on African values, as an almost bewildering number of names were put forth as the legitimate name for black people in the nineteenth century, including African, Ethiopian, Free African, Colored, Negro, Children of Africa, Sons of Africa, Colored American, people of color, free people of color, blacks, Anglo-African, Afric, African-American, Afro-American, Afmerican, Aframerican, Africo-American, and Afro-Saxon.[19]

The term *African* was used in the earliest black organizational titles by persons under some direct African cultural influence. Indeed, the establishment and maintenance of mutual-aid societies in the North in the late eighteenth and early nineteenth centuries was in part due to those influences. Burial arrangements were their most vital feature, with the elders in the societies having a major role. These factors and the concerns such groups had for the well-being of first-generation Africans and their offspring indicate a strong influence of African values in an era when African cultural expression was prevalent in the North. Apparently the presence of first-generation Africans was rather common in the North in the nineteenth century. The activities of New York's African Marine Fund, founded in 1810, suggest as much. The fund not only provided education for some black children and "such clothes as the Elders, President and Trustees may think in council necessary" but also directed special attention to those born in Africa and to their descendants. Article 7 of its constitution reads,

> There shall be also a Committee appointed to visit our African brethren, and the descendants of our mother country, to give information of their several distresses and wants; and on the report of the same to the Elders, with sufficient satisfaction, the Elders may, without the consent of the Trustees, send an order to the Treasurer for such amount as in their judgment may seem sufficient to their relief.[20]

Article 8 reads,

> It is agreed, that if any of the members of this fund should die, the Committee must immediately give notice to the Elders, who shall call a meeting and see the situation of the fund; and should the fund be not altogether sufficient to inter him or her, the members shall make a collection sufficient to bury him or her decent, and defray all the burial expenses.[21]

From the last quarter of the eighteenth century until the formation of the American Colonization Society in 1816, the term *African* held pride of place among black leaders in the North, to say nothing of the preferences of the black masses, of which we are just beginning to be aware. In the period before the founding of the Colonization Society, and for a while thereafter, the term appeared in the titles of numerous mutual-aid societies in the North. On the first anniversary of the abolition of the slave trade, the New York African Society for Mutual Relief, with which Garnet had contact, was addressed by William Hamilton, the foremost black intellectual of the first quarter of the nineteenth century. Black people then, nearly two decades before Emancipation Day, "carried themselves with a free air which showed that they thought themselves free," and on that occasion caused concern among their white friends "by their bold action." Before Hamilton spoke, silk banners inscribed "AM I NOT A MAN AND A BROTHER" were unfurled as New York blacks paraded the public streets in large numbers, "easily thrusting aside by their own force the small impediments [whites] which blocked their way." The procession moved from New York's "African School Room," according to the records of the New York African Society for Mutual Relief, to the "Universalist Church" to hear the principal speaker.[22]

Hamilton offered the going thesis regarding what constituted being of the African family: that "it makes no difference whether the man is born in Africa, Asia, Europe or America, so long as he is progenized from African parents."[23] Moreover, he affirmed African qualities against charges of African darkness, and he noted a phenomenon rarely mentioned by blacks of the period—the existence of diverse African groups or nations:

> The country of our forefathers might truly be called paradise, or the seat of ease and pleasure, until the foul fiends entered. . . . Until the man-stealing crew entered, peace may be said to be within her borders, and contentment in her dwelling, but the dealers in human flesh, not contented with setting the nations on to fierce, bloody, and incessant contests. . . . They sever them from all their enjoyments![24]

Though Hamilton's was a somewhat romanticized view of black Africa, it captured much truth and, by inference, supported the worth of African values in America. In asserting that an autonomous African spirituality underwent a wrenching process with the advent of slavery and the slave trade, he advanced a thesis that was enlightened for his time and that later established an important basis for African resistance to slavery and the slave trade. That spiritual wrenching created a need for mutual-aid societies "to reciprocate joy and happiness as extensively as their mutual endeavors of relief will admit." There were "many and repeated attempts" to establish such societies, but they "soon perished or dwindled away to a number so small as scarcely to deserve the name of society."[25] Fortunately, the New York African Society for Mutual Relief quickly achieved a growth beyond anything known to black societies in the city's history, and Hamilton thought "this institution" would exist for members yet unborn.

The nationalism of William Hamilton in no way prevented him from expressing gratitude for the New York Manumission Society, founded in 1784, "a debt owed by Africans, and their descendants" in the state. He spoke of the men who founded that society in much the way Walker later spoke of friends of his people, rendering them "nought but unprofitable thanks." Though slavery's sources were "drying away" in the North and the condition of his people "fast ameliorating,"[26] Hamilton—like Walker, Garnet, and, later, Du Bois and Robeson—found no contradiction between the founding principles of the Republic and blacks' being responsible for themselves as a people. No black leader was more conscious of the need for black institutions after the winning of freedom than Hamilton. Celebrating the founding of the New York African Society for Mutual Relief, he addressed a central nationalist concern:

> Let us all be united, my Brethren, in rearing this edifice—steady to our several departments—and so on shall be raised a wide spreading dome that shall stand the admiration and praise of succeeding generations, and on its front shall be eternally engraven

MUTUAL INTEREST,
MUTUAL BENEFIT,
AND MUTUAL RELIEF.[27]

What is important about this affirmation is his refusal to abandon black institutions when the shadow of slavery was receding in the North. In a word, he formulated nationalist theory at a time when the status of his people was somewhat fluid and pressures had not built decisively for or against nationalism. Freedom for Hamilton was freedom for black people to be at home with themselves, working for their own interests after the end of racial proscription. For that reason he was later looked upon as a "father," at least by one important man who helped develop nationalist theory. To be sure, he was a pioneer among Northern blacks in his discovery of sufficient spiritual resonance in the values and heritage of his people for him to oppose absorption into the larger white world. At the same time, his thought contains no hint of fanaticism. For Hamilton, racial diversity did not have to encourage racial conflict. In that respect, as well, he was a model for nationalists to follow, and a number of them did indeed follow his example. But, colonizationists, who were men of influence, acted as if his strain of thought was nonexistent, and their activities would cause a major shift in how Northern blacks referred to themselves.

With the establishment of the Colonization Society, growing numbers of blacks avoided use of the term *African,* opting for a safer appellation, *colored,* because to continue to refer to oneself as African might encourage colonizationists to believe one wanted to be shipped *back* to Africa.[28] Perhaps a move was under way, dating from the formation of the society, for some blacks to cease thinking of themselves as African, and no doubt a heated debate over what they should call themselves took place when they heard that colonizationists were promoting the view that America was not the African's home. Owing to the fugitive nature of sources between 1816 and the appearance of *Freedom's Journal* roughly a decade later, one would have to rely almost exclusively on inferences to follow the names controversy for this period.

It is known, however, that by the late 1820s David Walker and other black leaders were making little if any distinction between the words *African, coloured,* and *black.* Walker used the terms interchangeably to designate people of African ancestry and, indeed, to identify them as Africans, not as cultural hybrids. He was doing what was becoming widespread among free blacks, attaching his own meaning to such terms as *black* and *colored* and investing them with the qualities, positive and negative, associated with being African, wherever people of African ancestry were found. Walker was certainly not alone in using more than one term to refer to his people. During the 1820s the contributors to *Freedom's Journal* used roughly the same ones with much the same intent.[29] It is reasonable to assume, however, considering the sharpness of the differences recorded in the late 1830s over what black people should call themselves, that by the time of Walker's *Appeal* growing numbers of Northern blacks had decided that they were merely descendants of Africa and that the relationship ended there.

I I I

One of the earliest drives to jettison the words *colored* and *African* took place at a meeting of the Negro convention movement in 1835, an effort spearheaded by the chief antagonist of racial designations, Mr. William Whipper, an integrationist and wealthy black lumberman from Pennsylvania. In the early 1830s, he had shown signs of advocating the dissolution of all organizations having an either all-black or all-white membership. But the complexities of thought and feeling that at times actuated Whipper warn against our labeling him or any other Afro-American leader of the time a pure integrationist or nationalist. The powerlessness of blacks in a land of contradictions—a society claiming to be free while sanctioning slavery, to be above racism while organized for white supremacy—caused even Whipper to combine nationalist and integrationist elements in his liberation strategy. The situation that confronted black leaders generally was in many ways so ambiguous, even anomalous, that their responses needed to be flexible, geared to changing racial realities. In Whipper's case, a certain ambivalence, despite his interest in a color-blind nation, manifested itself—a certain tension between wanting to involve white people in leadership roles in black organizations and, at times, acknowledging the peculiar interests of his people.[30]

As early as 1832, he revealed what was to become so characteristic of him as to be archetypal: a penchant for soliciting advice from whites on how the liberation of his people might best be effected. The minutes of the Second Annual Convention of the Free People of Color show that it was

Moved by Wm. Whipper, seconded by Abraham D. Shad, that a committee of three be appointed to invite such of our white brethren in the City of Philadelphia as may feel disposed to attend our deliberations, and that they be at liberty to make such communications, as in their opinion, will advance the objects of the Convention. Agreed.[31]

If whites never acquired an equal or dominant voice in the convention movement, it was through no fault of Whipper, who championed their right to participate freely. There was, nevertheless, that element of the nationalist about him that is recognizable in a declaration of sentiment which he signed in 1834 with William Hamilton. The same Whipper who championed a color-blind America and opposed complexional designations in organizations of all kinds was willing to sign his name to, and perhaps help draft, a nationalist declaration of an elevated nature. It was declared that the black population of America constituted something of a nation and that Africa was not a continent with many countries or nations but a country from which blacks in America came:

The separation of our fathers from the land of their birth, earthly ties and early affections, was not only sinful in its nature and tendency, but it led to a system of robbery, bribery and persecution, offensive to the laws of nature and of justice. . . . That we find ourselves, after the lapse of three centuries, on the American continent, the remnants of a nation amounting to three million people, whose country has been pillaged, parents stolen, nine generations of which have been wasted by the oppressive cruelty of this nation, standing in the presence of the Supreme Ruler of the Universe, and the civilized world, appealing to God of Nations for deliverance.[32]

But within a year Whipper began to move toward (if he had not been there all along) a position of calling for the dissolution of organizations with complexional features. At the 1835 meeting of the convention movement, a resolution was passed exhorting black people "as far as possible [to] abandon the use of the word 'colored,' when either speaking or writing concerning themselves; and especially to remove the title African from their institutions, the marbles of churches, etc." The minutes show that the resolution, put forth by Whipper, after "an animated and interesting discussion . . . was unanimously adopted."[33] A strong integrationist sentiment dominated free Negro leadership at that moment, sentiment that would build dramatically later in the decade.

Whipper's effort to have the word *African* removed from titles and from the marbles of churches and other institutions was a reflection of his desire to see black institutions disappear.[34] It is unlikely, however, that he made known the full intent of his resolution when it was discussed. That Whipper was cautious enough to ask that the term *colored* be abandoned "as far as possible" suggests an early willingness on his part to compromise. His reference to removing the word *African* from the marbles of institutions instead of openly urging that all-black structures be transformed into color-blind ones, as he would later, indicates he was reluctant in 1835 to mount a campaign for sweeping structural changes.[35] This raises several questions: Why did he make a measured response at that time? Was it that he continued to see some value in nationalism because of the oppression to which his people were being subjected? Or was he moving with some caution because he doubted that there was a strong enough feeling against black institutions to support an all-out attack on them? If one considers Whipper's subsequent strategy in the names controversy, the latter seems more likely. What appears clear, even during the 1835 meeting, is that in advocating the removal of the name *African* from the marble facades of churches and other black institutions he hoped to create fissures great enough to cause their eventual collapse.

Apparently some of the participants who supported the Whipper resolution felt the need to maintain control over their churches, lodges, and other institutions but hoped that one day there would be color-blind institutions for all.[36] Just as some blacks ceased referring to themselves as Africans following the establishment of the American Colonization Society, others thought involvement in all-black organizations might cause whites to regard them as even more alien. Such was Whipper's argument when the debate over names at a later date surfaced in the pages of the *Colored American*. By then he had put all caution aside, denouncing all complexional organizations, not just complexional titles.

For those overcome with shame at being of African ancestry, the opportunity to abandon the word *African* must have been welcome. In any case, the progressive loss of the word's popularity was accompanied, predictably, by a protracted campaign among numerous leaders to *prove* the right of their people to remain in America. And though some who thought their people should maintain their own institutions openly opposed the Colonization Society and proclaimed love of the African homeland, no doubt others, concentrating on being accepted by the larger society, kept their loyalty to Africa to themselves, the more easily to establish their *right* to remain in America. The fear evoked in numerous blacks by the prospect of expulsion from the only land they had known must have reached the proportions of terror, thus making it easier for them to turn their backs on institutions with the word *African* in their title. Another step was easy enough to take, the pursuit of freedom through interracial cooperation, and with it the hope of achieving some insulation from the hostility a self-propelled movement might invite. This appears to have been Whipper's line of reasoning.[37]

Though accused of abandoning all complexional designations, he denied that accusation in October 1838, arguing he had never been so fanatical as "to advocate the entire abolition of the word colored." He added,

We yet hope to use it to great advantage—and it will be well if some of those that now charge us with an attempt to "dodge it" will not be glad to take

shelter under the broad canopy of nondistinction. But we have too long witnessed the baneful effects of distinctions founded in hatred and prejudice, to
advocate the insertion of either the word "white" or "colored" . . . in
churches, schools, moral or benevolent institutions, for the promotion of religion, morality, or civil government.[38]

In response to Samuel Cornish's charge that not a dozen men in America shared Whipper's view, Whipper rejoined that he had a number of
supporters and that they opposed complexional designations because
they are unknown to the law of God and disowned by Him and by the
American government. In addition such distinctions violate principles of
right and justice "written on the hearts of all men . . . that all men are
created equal."[39] Those arguments were triggered by legislation introducing the word *white* into the new Pennsylvania constitution in a provi-
sion barring blacks from equal access to the franchise.

At no point did Whipper, a religious man, explain the coexistence of
men of different colors and the natural beauty of the racial spectrum, all of
which seemed seared from his consciousness by racism. Failing to appreciate the variety of humanity, he was not concerned about recognizing
what was distinctive in a positive way to his people and what should be
encouraged, irrespective of white attitudes. But negatives—and there
were mainly negatives—were to be rooted out. For blacks to argue the
vitality of aspects of their culture—indeed, to assert the existence of a
separate culture or institutions of their own—contained a certain horror
for him. He therefore attributed racism as readily to blacks as to whites,
whether he was considering institutions or words. His assertion that he
had not opposed the abolition of the word *colored* does not dispel the
impression that he considered such banishment, if not possible, certainly
desirable:

Our people will soon observe that the insertion of the words white and colored in institutions, is based upon the same principle, and supported by lack
of argument. The advocate of the former threatens the country with amalgamation, and the loss of the most distinguished offices of government, if
they do not disfranchise the blacks, while the latter, if you refuse to raise
your banner of distinction, asserts that your object is to spend all your means
and energies on those of an opposite complexion. The principle that activates
both is debasingly mean, and horribly contemptible.[40]

Whipper attempted to prove that, because Samuel Cornish had once
asserted that "separate schools, and separate churches, are the very
means most likely to perpetuate this wicked caste," Cornish should oppose the use of the word *colored* in the titles of institutions serving his
people. Even Cornish's contention that blacks "should never establish or
encourage separate institutions, when we can possibly do otherwise," did
not convince Whipper that there was no alternative, given white racism,

to black institutions and therefore to terms proper to them.[41] Moreover, Whipper was adept at sensing, among his opponents, any wavering of support for black institutions or complexional designations, and this led him to press his disdain to its limits. Not surprisingly, he sometimes made more of a phrase than circumstances warranted, as in the case of a fellow reformer and fine theorist of nationalism, William Watkins:

Our friend Watkins, while he is opposed to blotting out what he terms "the endearing epithet, *colored*," says that "I am unfriendly to a prodigal use, or unnecessary parallel of the word." We say, that we recommend its abandonment, as far as possible. What is the difference, except that, by pursuing our course, we are using the means necessary to procure the abolition of its prodigal use? In our advocacy of this subject we are maintaining principles that strike at the root of national prejudices. Our object is to denounce the . . . abettors of "the prejudicial caste" as "demons incarnate." . . . We are not among those that would excuse the *colored* man's guilt, on account of the *white* man's crime. To do so would degrade the former and elevate the latter.[42]

Watkins probed, Is there something objectionable in the term? Does it communicate degradation? Does it cast opprobrium upon those it identifies? He thought an affirmative response imprudent, and asked if Whipper feared that "the *use* of the word will *remind* the white people of this nation that one-sixth portion of their fellow countrymen may, by certain physical peculiarities, be distinguished from themselves?" He pronounced the term *colored* "philosophically correct," then raised the level of the debate:[43]

Permit us to say that words are used as the signs of our ideas, and whenever they perform this office, or are truly significant of the ideas for which they stand, they accomplish the object of their invention. In vain do we carp at some supposed inapplicability of a term as applied to a certain object, when impervious custom, or common consent, has so established the relation between the sign or word, and the thing signified, that as soon as the sign or word is presented to the eye, or its sound conveyed to the ear, the idea which it represents is immediately and distinctly brought to mind. This is the case with the word in question. Custom has fixed its meaning in reference to a particular people in this country, and from this decision, however arbitrary, there is, I am sure, no successful appeal.[44]

Watkins might have added that *black, Afro-American, Negro,* or other such designations reflected the ideas of Afro-Americans of his day. That he did not was, on the evidence available, probably not accidental. He found the word *African* not as "appropriate" as *colored*. Perhaps the word *African*—or the others, for that matter—did not suit him, because by 1838 most free black leaders in the North, as distinct from the mass of blacks, thought of themselves not as Africans but as Americans of African descent, and so by less frequent reference to the term they hoped to avoid some of the opprobrium attached to its use. Whether Watkins hoped for such a consequence or not, it accorded with a certain integrationist strain in his thought to shy away from using *African* as a name for his people. In any case, the term *colored* was by the late 1830s probably used more widely than any other in black leadership circles; it was used by integrationists and nationalists alike.

More essential than which term was preferred is what the names controversy, in its most serious light, reveals—a struggle between integrationists and advocates of nationalism over the ideological and institutional means by which Afro-American liberation might be accomplished. Watkins thought Whipper really was saying that exclusive activity on the part of blacks militated against their moral obligation "to do good to all men, agreeable to the principle of universal benevolence." While Watkins believed people of color "should do good to all, irrespective of color," he denied that an institution of exclusive caste "*necessarily* militates against those principles." On the contrary, exclusive action and the principle of doing good to all men were "perfectly reconcilable." That reconciliation was realized by helping people of color because they were despised and neglected for being colored.[45]

Therefore, activity solely for the benefit of black people presented no ethical difficulties. Moreover, there were decided advantages in such an organization if liberation were to be achieved. "Harmony in our deliberations is of the utmost consequence. Our honest differences should, if possible, be amicably adjusted."[46] The presence of whites, often arrogantly patronizing toward blacks, would not enhance the likelihood of that harmony and that adjustment. In a fine recognition of essentials, Watkins noted that "there is such a thing as propriety," that "for a people in our condition, just emerging from darkness and degradation, to assume the office of reforming the whole country, betrays, to say the least, a want of modesty." Some people of color—he had William Whipper in mind— promote "education" among those already educated and "promote the spread of universal liberty among a people thoroughly indoctrinated in those principles!"[47] Obviously, Watkins did not share the messianic vision, so characteristic of black leaders in the nineteenth century and later, that blacks should take the lead in saving mankind.

The *Colored American,* open to discussion on the question of an appropriate group name, carried an editorial by Samuel Cornish in its maiden issue in 1837 that explained the name of the paper. This indicates that pressure against complexional distinctions, building since Whipper's resolution of 1835, was an issue among educated blacks. Cornish's explanation for the title of the paper was that and more: he put forth a name and a definition of the position he thought people of color occupied in American life. Acknowledging that differences of opinion had been expressed over the name of the paper, and attempting to justify *Colored American* as an appropriate title, he raised a concern that had agitated sizable numbers of blacks since the founding of the Colonization Society: the black man's right to remain in America. As to the choice of the word *American,* the editor contended that the distinction was more proper to his people "than to five-sixths of this nation," and said that it was

one that we will never yield. In complexion, in blood, and in nationality, we are decidedly more exclusively "American" than our white brethren; hence the propriety of the name of our paper, *Colored American,* and of identifying the name with all our institutions, in spite of our enemies, who would rob us of our nationality.[48]

Cornish's statement that blacks were more American in complexion and in blood is puzzling. If he was referring to mixtures of Indian and white with black blood, then Afro-Americans were probably more American in the sense that in their biological makeup they represented a greater cross section of the people occupying the land. But esteem of that kind was not shared by those who took pride in their blackness.[49] In any event, Cornish's closeness to the word *American* was shared by free blacks in significant degree, though *colored* and *Negro* met with more success in ordinary usage and in organizational titles between 1816 and the Civil War years. Not until later did *American* enjoy popularity among black people as a way of referring to themselves, and then it was largely in the form of *Afro-American.*

It would be a mistake to interpret the *Colored American* editorial as an attempt to have people of color move away from group consciousness in order to win acceptance as individuals. As employed by Cornish and most blacks of the 1830s, the term *colored* reflected special interests of the group, just as *African* and *free African* conveyed a sense of mutuality among blacks. Without such a distinction, Cornish thought, it would be difficult for his people to "be known" or for their interests to be "presented in community." Thus the need for "some distinct specific name— and what appellation is so inoffensive, so acceptable as colored people— Colored Americans?":

We are written about, preached to, and prayed for, as Negroes, Africans, and blacks, all of which have been stereotyped, as names of reproach, and on that account, if no other, are unacceptable. Let us and our friends unite, in baptizing the term "Colored Americans," and henceforth let us be written of, preached of, and prayed for as such. It is the true term, and one which is above reproach.[50]

Why Cornish thought *colored* would not become offensive—in fact, was not *already* offensive to some whites and blacks—he did not explain. Perhaps he thought people of African ancestry would be more acceptable to whites if they began referring to themselves as colored Americans—a myth exploded in due course. In any event, Cornish's exhortation to blacks to call themselves colored Americans was not heeded by black contributors to his newspaper, in part because most blacks did not see a connection between one such name and the vital issues affecting their people.[51] On the other hand, Cornish's failure to evoke greater interest in the term *American* was in part due to the reality that most Northern blacks were being subjected to crushing political and economic oppression and therefore found it difficult to think of themselves as Americans, even as colored Americans. The belief in American citizenship was probably entertained by a tiny minority of Northern blacks.

The intensity of the debate over a group designation quickened when tied directly to strategies for securing the liberation of black people. Such a strategy was behind a Whipper attack in 1841 on the inclusion of a racial designation in the title the *Colored American*. Whipper by then was beyond question the chief antagonist of the use by people of color of terms that set them apart from white Americans. He was in fact Mr. Cosmopolite, the archetypal "integrationist" of antebellum America. As he called attention to "the incorporated feature of complexional distinction in our churches, schools, beneficial and literary societies," he asserted that those distinctions were always to be condemned, whether put forth by blacks or by whites. Scoring the convening of colored citizens at Albany, New York, in 1840 on the grounds of "complexional distinction," he broadened his assault to include the newspaper *Colored American*, charging that it had been "defaced" by the insertion of a complexional term.[52] In answering him, an editor, Charles B. Ray, struck through the surface debate to the heart of Whipper's argument—his opposition to separate black organizations and institutions—by explaining that those institutions came into existence as a result almost of "desperate necessity," not of a *spirit* of caste. Ray strongly objected to Whipper's desire to see the name of his paper "ground to powder." "How grind a name to powder? . . . Only by destroying the thing named."[53]

"As a people," Whipper fired back, "we are deeply afflicted with 'color-phobia' (and notwithstanding there may have been causes sufficient to implant it into our minds), it is arrayed against the spirit of Christianity, republican freedom, and our common happiness, and ought once now and forever to be abolished." Color phobia was an evil Whipper thought had to be met without delay, so he denounced the existence of black institutions more emphatically than in his first letter: "We must throw off the distinctive features in the charters of our churches and other institutions."[54] From his point of view, it was desirable that blacks have no institutions of their own, that they abandon them even if whites refuse to abandon their own—that is, if whites refuse freely to relate to blacks on a color-blind basis.

Though Whipper was a complex person whose views changed over time, it is difficult to avoid the conclusion, especially for the 1830s and

1840s, that he was ashamed of being of African ancestry. His urging his people to set aside color considerations in a society based on white supremacy was a doomed strategy, for it meant the surrender of blacks in America to prevailing standards and power relationships and thus the uncontested triumph of Anglo-Saxon values. This was the deeper significance of his call to remove the word *African* from the marbles of churches and other institutions. He might just as well have advocated the rejection of all things African in his people's culture, had he been aware of them, for he feared that any suggestion of difference between blacks and whites was undesirable not simply on political grounds but in and of itself.

I V

Whipper's letters on complexional distinctions provided the occasion for an extremely gifted theorist of black nationalism to express himself—almost certainly Garnet but one who simply signed his entries Sidney. The anonymous author's letters were apparently solicited by the editor Ray, who responded to Whipper's challenge that certain questions be answered by writing, "They will be attended to properly by us or some other members of the convention, though we confess we have, perhaps too great repugnance for such controversies. In the meantime, I hope AUGUSTINE will find in them something for him to do, to wake him up from his too long slumbers."[55] Had Ray himself answered Whipper, he would have done so in the editorial section or in a signed article elsewhere in his paper, so he was not the anonymous Sidney. Moreover, Ray, by his own admission, was disinclined to be further involved in the debate and, judging from indications of Sidney's youthfulness, was too old to have written the letters. Since Sidney described himself as young and "A Member of The Convention," and since Augustine (Lewis Woodson) was not at Albany, though present at the first of the Negro conventions a decade earlier, the latter must be excluded from consideration as the author of the letters.[56]

   The appearance of Sidney's letters, in 1841, reinforces the view that black nationalist thought had attained, through Walker, Sidney, and Garnet, a high degree of sophistication before Martin Delany established himself as a theoretician of nationalism.[57] The discovery of the identity of Sidney is therefore an important problem in Afro-American intellectual history—a problem that seems easily solved at first by turning to Thomas S. Sidney, a resident of New York State who had written a number of letters signed Thomas S. Sidney to the *Colored American* for at least two years before the appearance of the Sidney letters. Moreover, the call to the convention, issued roughly three months before the Albany deliberations, contained the name of Thomas S. Sidney, who was in fact a principal advocate of the convention's taking place. Then why was his name not mentioned in the proceedings—in the various reports and committee assignments to which names were attached? Given his reputation as a precocious thinker, and considering his influential circle of friends, one would think that Thomas Sidney would have been heard had he been at Albany.

A notice in the *Colored American* clarifies matters:

> We have this week to perform a very melancholy duty—to record the demise of another esteemed friend and associate, Thomas Sipkins Sidney, of this city, aged 23 years. His sickness was of short duration; a few weeks ago we mingled with him in the varied scenes of life. . . . Mr. Sidney was a young man of exceeding bright promise; he wore the care of years "upon the cheek of youth." . . . His enthusiasm and devotion to the cause in which we are engaged, was well known, it was with his counsel and by his advice that the meeting was held which issued the call for the convention of the 18th of August . . . and the last public act of his life was to attach his name to that call.[58]

The obituary appeared on June 20, 1840. The Albany convention convened on August 18, 1840, so the letters to the *Colored American* early in 1841 could not have been written by Thomas S. Sidney. Then who in attendance at Albany might have had reason to write the letters and to sign them in this manner? Three people there—Alexander Crummell, Henry Highland Garnet, and Patrick Reason—grew up with Thomas Sidney and attended school with him. Did one of them, seeking to immortalize him, write the seminal letters and sign them Sidney? Crummell would certainly have found nothing with which to take issue in the Sidney letters. He, like the other two and the Sidney who signed the letters, was the right age to have considered black leaders of an earlier period old enough to have been fathers to his generation. But there is something about the letters' emphasis on man, as opposed to religion, that does not comport with the positions associated with Crummell.[59] Reason can be quickly ruled out on the ground that he never developed anything like Sidney's intellectual sophistication.

A number of interesting clues point to Garnet, except for a report in the *Colored American* of December 12, 1840, that Garnet was seriously ill from having had a limb amputated, which seems to eliminate him from contention. It appears doubtful that he would have been in a state, physically or psychologically, to respond to Whipper's letter of January 3, 1841. The *Colored American* of December 19, 1840, however, noted, "We take this method with great pleasure to inform his [Garnet's] friends that a few days since, he was very comfortable, and rejoicing in hope that soon, should nothing unforeseen occur, he will be again at his post, laying himself out for the civil and religious welfare of our people."[60] Sidney's first letter was published on February 13, 1841, roughly two months following Garnet's operation. Since Garnet was recovering remarkably within weeks of his operation, he reenters the lists. For now, let us examine the contents of the series of letters by the extraordinary young man who called himself Sidney.

In the first of the four letters to the *Colored American,* Sidney probed beneath the surface of the names controversy and laid bare the fundamental ideologies and movements that were being contested. He perceived that Whipper's concern over what blacks should call themselves reflected a deeper problem, one involving both methodology and ultimate objective: Whipper wanted to see blacks and whites working in the same organizations with no concern for color distinctions, to help the country become free and color-blind. Sidney began his response by suggesting that Whipper's views were "by no means novel and unheard of," and indicated that, since the convention of 1835, Whipper had picked up new adherents:

> They represent the views of a respectable portion of our people. They are the sentiments which have characterized the controversy, which has been carried between many of our brethren . . . *carried on for the past three or four years with singular earnestness, and at times, with warm pertinacity.*[61]

Sidney propounded a fundamental nationalist precept, to which both those who believed in nationalism as a modus operandi and those who viewed nationalism as a possible end in itself subscribed: only blacks in the end can secure their freedom, no matter how great the support from their allies, for freedom is more than an end of physical oppression; it is a condition of mind and spirit, of being able to realize one's will without offending mankind. Abolitionists could redouble their efforts, and greatly "exert their means," but the conditions of blacks would remain essentially the same and their sufferings would go "unmitigated, unless we awaken to a consciousness of a momentous responsibility. . . . We occupy a position, and sustain relations which they cannot possibly assume. They are our allies—*Ours* is the battle."[62]

When documents demanding rights for blacks and claiming to represent their views have proved to be written by whites, Sidney held, the effort on behalf of blacks has fallen "powerless to the ground." This understanding of the need for people of color to do the basic work of liberation was not new, but the realization of the efforts of their elders, who had acted accordingly for years: "It was this conviction which led to the concentration of their energies in the annual conventions."[63] In other words, as Sidney correctly pointed out, the tradition of black leaders founding organizations and controlling them was an old one. What relationship did a "complexional distinction" have to the thrust of the movement and to alliances with others?

> In coming forth as colored Americans, and pleading for our rights, we neither preclude the necessity, nor forbid the action of our friends, no more than the Americans forbade the help of their French allies. We ask their sympathy,

and entreat their prayers and efforts. The American received the aid and the cooperation of their French allies; but they kept the idea of *American* resistance to oppression . . . distinct and prominent. As wise men, they knew much depended upon that. They knew not what evils—perhaps failure— might result from an admixture of extraneosities.[64]

To promote "the exertion of a people peculiarly interested in its objects" was the purpose of the Albany Convention of Colored Citizens to which Whipper had objected. Sidney believed blacks had a duty to carry out activities peculiarly their own, an obligation dictated by common sense, reason, "and the testimony of history." To answer any other theory or call would be to stray from the path of their fathers, who had come together along racial lines to attempt to solve their problems. For half a century they had striven to improve their lot through efforts "direct, harmonious, and effectual," which had "not been those of babes." Introducing a letter with a quote from William Hamilton—"Ought they not (the free people of color), to make one weak effort; nay, one strong, one mighty, moral effort to roll off the burden that crushes them?"—Sidney identified one of the leading architects of the tradition to which he alluded.[65] But divisions had recently occurred with the emergence of integrationists unimpressed with the fathers' adherence to the time-honored precept that the winning of freedom is the obligation of the oppressed.

Those fifty years of the fathers' effective leadership, to which Sidney referred, dated almost precisely from the founding of the Free African Society and other early mutual-aid societies among free blacks. There were then no unreconciled debates regarding appropriate principles and methods of organization. In the period from the 1780s to the 1830s, nationalists dominated the ranks of Afro-American leaders. It was that tradition, with its "harmonious accents of numerous men joining in a common effort, without discordant tones," that was being challenged by Whipper and others:

> The work is going on, but sympathy and uniformity have measurably departed. We now look in vain for that unity of purpose and operation, which once marked the carrying out of our convictions. We hear, now, in different places, strange and dissimilar sounds, one calling to this peculiar course, and another inviting to that, and no two alike in tone.[66]

If the fathers saw autonomous exertions as the principal means of securing the liberation of their people and did so for fifty years, then most of them were nationalists at roughly the time they were escaping from slavery in the South or emerging as free blacks in the North. Recall that as late as the 1820s it was natural for some black people in the North to think of themselves as Africans and to take pride in that identity. If they existed in the 1820s, though growing numbers of free Negroes were attempting to distance themselves from Africa, African links and loyalties must have been stronger for far more free Negroes in the earlier period, when blacks attached less shame to being African. It was then, in that fifty-year stretch, that Northern and Southern black leaders of opinion were in greater agreement on the question of autonomy than at any other time. That was the time, therefore, when free Negro leadership was perhaps best suited, if not to embrace, then to look with favor upon aspects of the culture of the African in slavery. But the problem even for a nationalist of Sidney's brilliance was the absence of the means, especially considering the anti-African propaganda of the larger society, to get a handle on that culture and this problem would persist for generations of nationalists thereafter. The best evidence, according to Sidney's logic, that there was much of inherent worth in slave culture was his argument regarding the fathers: that by relying on themselves essentially, they had provided enlightened leadership for their people. That slaves were at various times and in various ways fully capable of relying on themselves might have been inferred from the example of these fathers.[67]

Nothing in Sidney's view of Afro-American intellectual and political history suggests that whites contributed significantly to the decision of black leaders to assume primary responsibility for the liberation of their people. Indeed, the suggestion that whites were the inspirers of black autonomy would have been rejected by him. He did not argue that blacks were uninfluenced by the deeds of whites—he could and did recite instances of such influence—but insisted that the impulse to autonomous leadership was strong at the founding of the earliest national black organizations. Interesting questions follow from that position: To what extent, if any, as Pan-Africanization was occurring in the North, did examples of African ethnic loyalty and autonomy contribute to the development of black infrastructures? To what extent did the more inclusive conception of Africanity born of Pan-Africanization contribute to devotion to black institutional life in the North? Judging from what we know of the force of African cultural traditions in New England, Pennsylvania, New York, and elsewhere in the North, African influence in the founding and maintenance of black institutions generally was likely, especially if one bears in mind that the impact of Africa need not be consciously "felt" to shape values and to inform behavior.

Being of African ancestry and being treated accordingly formed a distinctive emotional bond for blacks everywhere in America, a condition given painful resonance by their status as outsiders. They were united emotionally and psychologically by the brand of proscription, by their status, universally acknowledged in America, of being outcasts because "tainted" by African ancestry. Only they knew the peculiar psychic tensions of racial oppression as they experienced them, and only they could give voice to them. Their impulse to create or maintain institutions, like their impulse to the creative act generally, sprang from that emotional context, and their institutions, like their forms of art, answered psychic as well as physical needs. Consciousness of their condition, in varying degrees and at varying moments, was an aspect of their experience of which Sidney was acutely aware, a consciousness that made them suited as no others to lead in their struggle. This shared "culture" was the irreducible and fundamental basis for their collective resentment of their oppression. On this showing, they were all Africans.

It is not likely that Sidney was preoccupied with African cultural influences on the institutions of his people. From what we know of him, and from what we know of black ideologists, including Garnet, of the nine-tenth century, it is likely that, in considering the question of autonomy, he was thinking primarily of political autonomy, though he believed strongly in the "spirit" of his people and gave more emphasis to it in discussing the struggle for liberty than did most leaders of his time. For him, therefore, the cultural was implied, not explicitly set forth, as when arguing that his people's development depended on their exerting whatever power they possessed, an exertion not made "by the employment of foreign aid." After citing the Irish—that "long-insulted and deeply injured people"— as an example of those who used exclusive effort to sweep away hindrances before them, he credited the reliance of colored men on themselves for their emancipation in the West Indies, in both cases implicitly raising the question of culture.[68] In using nations as analogues to the experiences of blacks in America, he implied that his people in the United States constituted a nation or possessed the potential to become one. In that regard, his approach recalls Walker's, as does his recounting of cruelties visited on his ancestors.

His review of the history of blacks in America was nearly as bleak as Walker's but reveals an interest in the processes of oppression that is indeed like Garnet's. His people were subjected to cruel wrongs and had been powerless to prevent their inheritance by succeeding generations— "every succeeding one receiving to itself the accumulated sufferings and indignities of all the preceding"—until there was so much oppression upon his generation "as to awaken a bitter sense and consciousness of degradation, and to reveal the alarming nature of that oppression which is destroying with fearful certainty and unerring precision." It was not failure to grasp the depths of their oppression and need for liberation that caused a split among black leaders; they knew that their oppression was real, that no chimeras were entertained regarding their *"actual condition"*: "we feel, that though not chattels, yet we are slaves."[69]

The *necessity* of effort to extricate ourselves from the deep pitfalls, and the loathsome cells of the dark prison-house of oppression, is a common conviction. And the determination, we think, is fully made, to hurl from us every vestige of proscription and degradation. In all this, we all agree. But there are differences among us. From whence do they proceed? Of what nature are they? They do not resolve themselves into *what* we shall do, neither *for whom* we shall do. The condition of our people . . . incites us to effort, and for the upraising of wronged, and pent up, and straitened humanity, as seen in the persons and condition of the colored people of this country. Do not the differences arise, then, let me respectfully ask, from the *mode of operation*— the *how* of the matter? This *we* think is the cause of the controversy.[70]

As the well-being of the individual depends on the judicious use of his various assets, the health of the group rests on the vigorous utilization of its own resources. Drawing on a biblical line also favored by Garnet, Sidney affirmed what he called "the great universal truth—whosoever hath to him shall be given.'" He therefore urged that self-exertion become "the great law of our being." An indisputable law of history is that the emancipated have through time based their struggles on their belief in themselves.[71] Such was the spirit of the leaders of the Exodus from Egypt, of the men at Bannockburn, Marathon, and Bunker Hill, of Washington, Tell, Bolívar, and L'Ouverture. One must look beyond the "changeful influence of temporary opinion" to historical truths. And there is no greater truth or law of history than this: "the history of the human race is but one continued struggle for rights." His sense of the historical process, of its fundamental dialectic, is close to the Hegelian conception that history is the coming into being of freedom. For Sidney the testimony on that point "is distinctly harmonious, univocal"—"as clear as the sun in heaven"[72]—which meant that struggle in the future was for him as fundamental an expectation as it was a fact of history.

The struggle for freedom could not possibly be anything but good and would bring good results for all. Through combined exertions, the oppressed bring out the best in themselves even to the benefit of the oppressor, for at the height of their surge toward freedom they "give indubitable evidence to the oppressor of a common nature in both." Then irresistible currents of revolt form, "sweeping away the strong barriers, and deep obstructions of time-sanctioned oppression and aged tyranny."[73] There should be no pleas for freedom, no simple prayers that everything can be accomplished without a rebelling mass. The deep intensities, inflexible purpose, and determined action of the oppressed must sweep away the rubbish of accumulated prejudice and penetrate "the dark meshes of error and sophistry" to reveal "the sympathies and affections of our common-brotherhood."[74] The struggle is not actuated by hatred but is aimed at furthering the recognition of the common humanity of blacks and whites—a position foreshadowed by Walker and supported by Garnet.

Sidney was convinced of the "peculiar ability" of the oppressed to liberate themselves, of "the necessary incapability of all others, even of the best of friends," to effect that purpose. The oppressed must suffer so that they know their condition is no longer bearable. They need such a consciousness in order to unify their divided ranks and to win the sympathy of those in power. Then, much like Garnet in his exhortation to the slaves to go to their masters and ask for wages, Sidney argued, perhaps influenced by the Declaration of Independence, that a statement of grievances should be presented to those in power to impress upon them the enormity of their crime, to make it clear "that their outrages have so proved the vital seat of suffering, as to arouse the deepest feelings and most inflexible determination of their insulted victims."[75]

> Now, from the nature of the case, this statement of grievance in all its fulness and power, can come from none other than those conscious of suffering. How is it possible, we ask, for men who know nothing of oppression, who have always enjoyed the blessedness of freedom, by any effort of imagination, by any strength of devotedness, by any depth of sympathy, so fully and adequately to express the sense of wrong and outrage, as the sorrowful presence and living desire of us who . . . drank the dregs of the embittered chalice?[76]

It is the question at the heart of the nationalists' opposition to allies directing the movement of their people toward freedom. And Sidney's position squares with the nationalist's desire to win allies, which explains his interest in having the oppressor hear the grievances from the mouth of the oppressed. Friends are free to offer advice, just as the oppressed must have the option of accepting or rejecting that advice, for the best representatives of the oppressed are the oppressed. Even an abrupt display of intense feeling from them is more effective than the most polished and refined eloquence from their allies. In the process of vindicating their character, which suffers from the stigma of inferiority projected onto them, the oppressed should not rely on "abstract disquisition from sympathizing friends" but must display "energy of character and elevation of soul."[77] In the spirit of David Walker, Sidney remarked,

> *This* is a radical assurance, a resistless evidence both of worth and manliness, and of earnest intention and deep determination. We maintain that these evidences—these feelings, desires and capacities, must stand out prominently, as coming from their proper source, to have their rightful influence . . . experience proves that they lose by retailment of admixture. Let an expression of our wants and feelings be produced by others, and should there be anything of character, intellect, or dignity connected with it, it is not predicated of our ability.[78]

No matter how propitious the circumstances and wise the counsel of friends, the elevation of the oppressed cannot occur until their inner disposition leads them to rise beyond their accustomed place. The appropriate qualities reside in the individual—"all the strength of personal character"—as well as in the group. In fact, the aid of friends can be potent:

> Yet vain that influence
> Vain their efforts, vain
> The sayings of the wise,
> In ancient and in modern books enrolled.
>
> . . . .
>
> Unless he feel within himself,
> Secret refreshings that repair their strength
> And fainting spirits uphold.[79]

This the fathers knew, and armed with this knowledge they dominated Afro-American leadership. In general, blacks were in agreement and following "in their wise and rational footsteps." But Whipper proposed a "great radical change," challenging the mode by which the oppressed, of all colors in recorded time, have risen to liberate themselves.[80] Whipper's position, which triumphed in the following century, had the baneful effect of warring against a consciousness, mass based, that would, in Sidney's formulation, assure the emergence of a people free in the best sense of the term, conscious of their rights with a knowledge of the means by which they might be safeguarded. With rising consciousness in each individual and in the group as a whole, "leaders" would be less important, large numbers of people being natural leaders in their own right, a position anticipating Paul Robeson by nearly a century.

Since Whipper cited no historical testimony to the wisdom of his theory, he speculated upon "heaven-born truth," despised specific means or actions, and therefore dealt "in nothing but generalities—universalities." Sidney and those he represented had no sympathy "with that cosmopoliting disposition which tramples upon all nationality" and, while encircling the universe, "theorises away the most needed blessings, and blights the dearest hopes of a people." In opposing the "cosmopoliting" spirit, he foreshadowed on a philosophical level a debate that occurred a century later on the aesthetic plane: To what extent should people of color be concerned with universals as defined by whites?[81]

Sidney ventured that, if one waters and preserves a plant that flourishes in one's room, it does not follow that one dislikes all other plants. He and those of like persuasion, he said, do "not believe that in loving our mother's sons, our brothers, that therefore we create a cord of caste, and exclude mankind from our rights." Whipper failed to understand that duties spring from relations: "Our responsibilities and obligations receive their hue and coloring from the situation we may maintain, and the connections we may have . . . we sustain relations to our people, so peculiar that white men cannot assume them, and according to these relations are our attending duties." Considering the nature of the problems of blacks, accumulating over generations, a "radical cure" was needed. In his final letter to the *Colored American*, he framed his thesis in a syllogism:

Our argument is this: Whenever a people are oppressed, peculiarly (not complexionally), distinctive organization or action, is required on the part of the oppressed, to destroy that oppression. The colored people of this country are oppressed; therefore the colored people are required to act in accordance with this fundamental principle.[82]

If autonomy was the linchpin of liberation for the fathers, basing their trust on the results of one historic struggle after another, then their offspring should not accept a "theory" unverifiable by either history or the experience of the day. Sidney's way of explaining the world, his people's place among men, and the means by which they might stand unencumbered was based on a clear analysis of history. In fact, most of his attention was devoted to historical evidence as he pursued his case against Whipper and others opposing the Albany convention. Not until that final letter did he address Whipper's main concern: "It will be seen that we have argued the matter thus far without any reference to *color*." In previous communications, it was his object to defend measures employed by his fathers in the past and by his brothers in the present in their "self-exertion to elevate themselves." While not avoiding the issue, he was disturbed by the emphasis given to color:

This endless clamoring about "color," is alike devoid of reason, as it is disreputable for us as a people. The people are perishing by oppression, and our leaders, one opposing the other, upon a *word* . . . when they should be using the resistless energy of principle, to vindicate their wronged and deeply injured brethren; and instead of giving living, productive action—proposing idle theories![83]

Wherever people are oppressed, distinctive action or organization is required of them. Color has been so disturbing to some blacks, he said, without naming anyone, that they "have written long articles to banish the designating term into oblivion." "The color God has given us," he asserted almost serenely, "we are satisfied with; and it is a matter of but little moment to us, who may be displeased with it." Aware that Whipper might attribute prejudice to any use of color, and therefore dissuade people from using the word *colored*, Sidney argued that, if prejudice "is the result of *color*, then it does not proceed from the word; and if the color is the cause, and Mr. W[hipper] desires to act upon the cause, then let him commence his operations upon the color."[84]

Prejudice proceeds more from the condition occupied by blacks and is therefore "a moral phenomenon, a wrong exercise of the sentiments and sympathies, and a disease of the will." White people simply have to get over their prejudices; blacks should not yield to them in this area. Since their color came from God, blacks should be pleased with it, "and so must they [whites] get to be. Surely the term colored is not disgusting to Mr. W. and his friends? They cannot be ashamed of their identity with the negro race!"[85] The term *colored* was acceptable to Sidney because, like all correct and proper definitions, it distinguishes its class or object from others. Since people from time immemorial have been so distinguished, there is nothing objectionable about applying the term to blacks in America. With red men, black men, white men, and others in mind, Sidney asked, "Do the *terms* create prejudice, or are they employed from prejudice?" He answered, "Neither one. There is, then, no such marvellous power in the word as to make it so repugnant to the tender sensibilities of Mr. W."[86]

One term was as good as the next, and most had come to mean the same thing, Sidney stated with quiet assurance:

> That we are colored, is a fact, an undeniable fact. That we are descendants of Africans, colored people—negroes if you will, is true. We affirm there is nothing in it that we need to be ashamed of; yea, rather much that we may be proud of. There is, then, on our part, as identified with the negro race, no reason why the term should be repudiated.[87]

Sidney encouraged originality, warning his people that it could not be realized in a vacuum, that much could be learned from a study of history. Since nationalism is predicated on self-reliance—the avenue to creativity—Sidney's affirmation of originality was logical enough. What was known to a conscious few needed to be known to far more: that the old takes on the appearance of the new, that originality consists of revealing new relations, not new aspects of reality. The way toward originality lies not in fashioning theories unrelated to human experience but in creating "new combinations of known truth."[88] His concern for originality, his testing of theory against the testimony of history, his understanding of the relationships and attending responsibilities growing out of oppression, his definition of history as one continual struggle for human rights—all expressed with clarity and analytical force, mark this "Member of the Convention" as a seminal thinker.

The available evidence suggests that Garnet, twenty-five at the time of Albany, was Sidney. He was close to Thomas S. Sidney and may have decided, in a final act of friendship, to honor his recently deceased friend with perhaps his most impressive theoretical effort. A letter appears over his signature on March 13, 1841, in the *Colored American,* a letter placed above another—entitled "William Whipper Letters"—signed by Sidney. He closed his letter (concerning the franchise for blacks in New York State) with words that contained, quite possibly, considerable irony: "Perhaps it is too much for one so young and humble as myself, to say that my remarks produced any effect upon the wise and learned . . . yet in humility, I think I may say, that God blessed the truth for its own sake."[89] It appears he was Sidney for numerous reasons: because Garnet loved verse and Sidney uses poetry on three occasions in his letters; because, as a learned Presbyterian divine, Garnet knew of the defeat of the

Presbyterians, referred to by Sidney, at Bothwell Bridge in the time of Charles II; because Garnet was a student of Latin, and there is a Latin phrase in one of Sidney's letters; because Garnet was catholic in intellectual reach, continually referring to history and other disciplines for verification of principles, as does Sidney; because Garnet, like Sidney, saw history as movement toward a gospel day of equality; because both men inveighed against "universals" and stressed the import of concrete conditions peculiar to their people; because Garnet's treatment of "cosmopolites" or integrationists is close enough to Sidney's to suggest the two were one—for these and other reasons, Garnet appears to have been Sidney. But it is possible that even he might be eliminated if a close textual analysis of style of writing—how they punctuated, for example—shows that the two were not the same.

V

Though not as original a theorist as Sidney, Frederick Douglass wrote brilliantly that people of color must direct their own liberation movement. That was by the time he had reached intellectual maturity and was not willing to see them dispense with the convention movement, newspapers, and other institutions (except the church) vital to their struggle for freedom. About the time when he was beginning to move away from William Lloyd Garrison and his abolitionist followers, he addressed the names controversy. An editorial by him in his *North Star* contains, in addition to the acknowledgment of continuing discord over approaches to freedom, the admission that different strategies of liberation were reflected in the debate over names. Douglass denied that black newspapers perpetuated repugnant distinctions between colored and white people and thereby worked against equality for many Americans: "We have, sometimes, heard persons reject the very mention of color and to counsel its abandonment." The *North Star* admitted of no such sentiment and denied being sensitive on this point: "Facts are facts; white is not black, and black is not white. There is neither good sense, nor common honesty, in trying to forget this distinction."[90] The basis of Douglass's position on the necessity for a group reference, therefore, was that color considerations could not be ignored, a position to which he consistently adhered in commenting on the condition of his people. As a leader of growing prominence, he could not have functioned differently and retained his following among blacks or whites. But he had reasons for his certitude on the question of the value of a color distinction that, while true of very large numbers of slaves and of scores of thousands of ex-slaves, would not be true of most nationally recognized black leaders: he rose to undisputed prominence as a leader after having experienced sharp and lasting tensions about a crisis of identity resulting from the circumstances in which he was born and those associated with the circumstances under which he was named. He wrote in *Narrative of the Life of Frederick Douglass,* "I do not remember to have ever met a slave who could tell his birthday. They seldom came nearer to it than planting-time, harvest-time, cherry-time, spring-time, or fall time. A want of information concerning my own was a source of unhappiness to me even during childhood."[91]

Such was the subjective stake he brought to the names controversy, because it was symbolic of a process that was more devastating for him than for most participants in the controversy. The controversy took on an immediacy for Douglass that few other leaders could possibly have known. He had been a slave until young manhood, had escaped by using the free papers and name of another black, and had, under the press of "life or death" circumstances, gone through a series of name changes, beginning with one right after the escape, one revealed in his marriage certificate, signed by J. W. Pennington, which read, "This may certify, that I joined together in holy matrimony Frederick Johnson and Anna Murray, as man and wife, in the presence of Mr. David Ruggles and Mrs. Michaels."[92] That started a rush of name changes, described against the backdrop of the name given him at the time of his birth:

> On the morning after our arrival at New Bedford, while at the breakfast-table, the question arose as to what name I should be called by. The name given me by my mother was, "Frederick Augustus Washington Bailey." I, however, had dispensed with the two middle names long before I left Maryland so that I was generally known by the name of "Frederick Bailey." I started from Baltimore bearing the name of "Stanley." When I got to New York I again changed my name to "Frederick Johnson," and thought that would be the last change. But when I got to New Bedford, I found it necessary again to change my name. The reason of this necessity was, that there were so many Johnsons in New Bedford, it was already quite difficult to distinguish between them. I gave Mr. Johnson [Mr. Nathan Johnson of New Bedford] the privilege of choosing me a name, but told him he must not take from me the name of "Frederick," I must hold on to that, to preserve a sense of identity. Mr. Johnson . . . at once suggested that my name be "Douglass."[93]

Such intensely personal and, at times, dangerous experiences help explain why, once he had recognized the necessity for a group name, a man like Douglass preferred to focus his energy and mind on changing the conditions that gave rise to the frustrating search for a group name rather than debate the names issue at great length.

Over most of the forties, Douglass was the chief spokesman for an integrationist approach to the race problem in America. That he lent his voice to the Garrisonians was a major advantage to those who felt blacks need not and could not provide the leadership in a movement directed at their liberation, which would mean they could not, as a people, lay claim to a role of leadership in the society to follow, since they had failed to lead in their own liberation. If the oppressed did not attempt to shape the values of a country in travail, then one could not reasonably expect them to assume that role in less demanding times. The logic of Douglass's argument, which led to his break with Garrison, ran powerfully in this direction because nationalism was for him, more than for most black nationalists, a means to liberation in America.[94]

Though he did not deny the role of color in antebellum America, Douglass's brilliance in applying to his people the principles upon which the nation was founded led him, when he was chairman of the "Committee on Declaration of Sentiments" of the national convention held in Rochester, New York, in 1853, to argue for the Americanness of his people:

> We are Americans, and as Americans, we would speak to Americans. We address you not as aliens nor as exiles, humbly asking to be permitted to dwell among you in peace; but we address you as American citizens asserting their rights on their own native soil. . . . We would not lay our burdens upon other men's shoulders; but we do ask, in the name of all that is just and magnanimous among men, to be freed from all unnatural burdens and impediments with which American customs and American legislation have hindered our progress and improvement. . . . We ask that, speaking the same language and being of the same religion, worshipping the same God, owing our redemption to the same Savior, and learning our duties from the same Bible, we shall not be treated as barbarians.[95]

Douglass's grounds for claiming that his people could call themselves Americans were primarily cultural—at least for the minority of blacks who met his criteria of Americanness. He was able to argue his case as persuasively as he did because the cultural attributes he described were indeed characteristically American and exhibited by a small minority of Northern blacks in particular. Douglass made that argument in July 1853, though he had earlier denied, when debating Garnet, that America was his home.

To say that he was American did not mean for him that he was not a colored American. He simply set aside the extended appellation to make his point that people of color had absorbed the cultural values of the larger society to a very significant measure. In that way, he could more easily get at the question of values beneath—or above—considerations of color. Douglass's was no integrationist argument, nothing so simple as that. He believed that blacks had to lead to gain respect, and respect themselves to lead—essentially a nationalist political stance. Nevertheless, by standing on the narrow ground of assimilated free blacks, his argument might have been turned against his intention to advance the interests of his people as a whole, for by no stretch of the imagination would he, given his two decades in the slave community, have argued that the slave shared the attributes he claimed constituted being American. This distinction between free blacks and the slave is made in the ambiguous context of Douglass's

linking of assimilated American blacks to nationhood in America. In a
letter to Harriet Beecher Stowe, he wrote,

> The black man (unlike the Indian) loves civilization. He does not make very
> great progress in civilization himself, but he likes to be in the midst of it, and
> prefers to share its most galling evils, to encountering barbarism. Then the
> love of country, the dread of isolation, the lack of adventurous spirit, and the
> thought of seeming to desert their "brethen in bonds," are a powerful check
> upon all schemes of colonization, which look to the removal of the colored
> people, without the slaves. The truth is, dear Madame, we are *here*, and here
> we are likely to remain. Individuals emigrate—nations never. We have grown
> up with this republic, and I see nothing in her character, or even in the char-
> acter of the American people, as yet, which compels the belief that we must
> leave the United States.[96]

Perhaps most important about Douglass's discussion of being American
is what it portended for the future. His affirmation of being American
represented a growing, but also strongly debated, trend in antebellum
America. The decade in which he claimed he was American was not the
most propitious for the propagation of that view, as evidenced by the
attention he gave to the feasibility of emigration at its close. One suspects
the optimism of even Voltaire's Dr. Pangloss, had he been black in America, would have been tried by the events of the day, and so was Douglass's: whatever might be said of him, he cannot be accused of having
been impractical for long. Preeminently a pragmatist, he agreed with
Walker, Garnet, and Sidney that one thing that really mattered was victory in the struggle for liberation, a position best stated by Garnet:

> How unprofitable it is for us to spend our golden moments in long and solemn
> debate upon the question whether we shall be called "African," "Colored
> Americans" or "Africo Americans," or "Blacks." The question should be,
> my friends, *shall we arise and act like men, and cast off this terrible yoke?*[97]

Douglass knew that the struggle could not be won unless blacks took
the lead in waging it. It is doubtful any black leaders, except for Walker
and Garnet, were more aware than he of the consequences of attempting
to fight for abolition while pursuing an independent course. Walker and
Garnet suffered more, but, when the break between Douglass and Garrison came, Douglass experienced a torrent of verbal abuse. Under intense fire from Garrison after moving to Rochester, New York, and
establishing the *North Star,* Douglass was in no mood to spend long hours
debating what his people should call themselves, but he revealed his preferences in the normal course of those turbulent times. He had no trouble
working within the context of the Negro convention movement, where
there was a place for nationalists and integrationists and neither was often
simply one or the other. To enhance effectiveness, to exploit the changing

nature of a cruel reality, some elements of the one ideology were combined in the other.

The convention movement was a movement of blacks relying mainly on themselves, the arena in which leading theorists of the race found a platform and following. In that spirit, Douglass and Martin Delany, a nationalist of rising importance, worked together on the *North Star*.[98] Unlike Douglass, who saw liberation coming through struggle in America, Delany thought that struggle in America alone could never achieve freedom for blacks in America. Though he agreed that free blacks should never accept racism, freedom was forever beyond their grasp in America unless those of talent emigrated to establish a nation for themselves, in the Americas or in Africa, that would generate such good that the lot of their people would be enhanced throughout the world.[99] Less optimistic than Douglass, he found an outlet for his tremendous energy by struggling on two fronts, which left him little time to waste on debating issues he felt would not lead, even if clarified, to significant change in the status of his people. Hence, he had no passion for a particular name for the group, though he was more concerned than most blacks of distinction about the uses of names to inspire his people. To this end, he took a Pan-African perspective, naming one of his sons Toussaint L'Ouverture, another Alexander Dumas, and a daughter Ethiopia—an instructive stance in its own right, since Delany was reputed to have been of Golah and Mandingo extraction.[100]

If there was anyone in America, outside the slave community, who might have known African names, it was he. However, rather than name his children after Africans, he chose instead, save in the case of his daughter, to name them after important blacks in the diaspora. But the lovely name given his daughter had a similar effect, *Ethiopia* standing for all of Africa and for all people of African descent. The names of his children, ideally, reflected a progression beyond ethnicity and reinforced a sense of oneness in their consciousness and in the consciousness of those blacks who called their names. Owing to the ordeal of people of African descent, the times demanded a perspective on names that carried beyond the insularity of ethnicity or, at the least, the choice of a name that in no way suggested ethnicity. Because Martin Delany knew so much about Africans in the modern world, his failure to choose ethnic names for his children and for his people in the United States is evidence that he might have regarded such choices, if acted on, counterproductive.

It was rare for black leaders to address the issue of African ethnicity in print, but Delany made as much of it as one would expect, given his exceptional grasp of African culture, linking the culture of Africans in New Orleans to that of Africans in Cuba without permitting ethnic considerations to obscure the larger cultural pattern in either location. Ethnicity came before him in an arresting context but did not cause him to break with nationalist tradition in naming his people. Just as Garnet saw a Pan-African mix in the African parade on Emancipation Day in New York, Delany read about one in "a popular American literary periodical" and found its analogue among the slaves in New Orleans, possibly among some of those observed by Bremer at the African Church in which the counterclockwise leap was witnessed. He commented on "El Dia de los Reyes," King's Day, in Cuba and related it to a ceremony in North America: "The demonstration consisted of a festival—physical, mental and religious—by the native Africans in Cuba, in honor of one of their monarchs; being identical, but more systematic, grand and imposing, with the 'Congo dance,' formerly observed every Sabbath among the slaves in New Orleans."[101]

He was referring to the parade of kings phenomenon that found an analogue in the Pinkster festival of New York State and had much in common with the parade of governors in New England and with John Kunering in North Carolina. Whether Delany was aware of the Pinkster and the parade of governor's festivals is not certain but likely. In a key passage quoted by him, one finds analogous patterns of African ceremony in the Americas that might have been considered in determining what it meant then and later to be African:

> [T]he Negroes pour out of the city gates [in Cuba] in crowds to assemble at the places where they are to dress . . . and the delicate ear is agonized by sounds proceeding from the musical instruments of Africa. They generally assemble according to their tribes. The Gazas, the Lucumis, the Congoes, and Mandingos, etc., in separate parties. One party ordinarily consists of from ten to twenty. There are about a half dozen of principal actors, and the rest hang around and are ready to do any extra dancing or shaking that may be required. . . . The king is dressed in a network of red cord, through the interstices of which glisten oddly enough square inches of the royal black skin. . . . Another has a hideous mask surmounted by horns. He is the prophet of the tribe, and is sometimes supposed to be gifted with magical powers—a full belief in charms being a part of the Negro's native creed. . . . The parties roam all over the city stopping in front of the principal houses, or before the windows in which they see ladies and children. They have also their favorite corners, and there they will go through with fifteen or twenty minutes violent agitation, during which the perspiration pours off their faces, and one unaccustomed to the sight is momentarily expecting to see them fall exhausted. . . . The only stoppage, however, is when that elaborately dressed personnage . . . so beruffled and beringed, hands round the box to the spectators for "pesetas" and "medios." He is the steward of the party, and after all is done, he produces the money which pays for the room in which they hold their balls at night—all night indeed, for they keep it up till morning.[102]

While the above passages recall John Kunering, the Pinkster celebration, and the parade of governors, the following does so as well and also recalls the scene in the Philadelphia graveyard:

The inside of the hall is extraordinary, but not pleasing. A piece of parchment stretched over a hollow log beaten with bones, or a box or gourd filled with beans or stone, rattled out of all time, comprise their instruments. . . . On this day they are allowed to use their own language and their own songs, a privilege denied them on other days.[103]

If Delany did not know that Mandingoes were in New Orleans, he knew that Congolese were there, as his reference to "Congo Dance" indicates. Yet for all the mention of African ethnicity in the piece and despite his reference to Congo influence in New Orleans, he makes no use of ethnicity. Significantly, however, his seeing New Orleans slave ceremonies as an extension of what Africans were doing in Cuba was a Pan-African cultural perception of some moment—one that, together with his understanding of African agricultural skills in the South, established him as a leading student of African culture. His knowledge of Africans leaves little doubt that, had he pursued the matter at some length, he might have provided a theory of culture, of the meaning of being African in America, and its significance for nationalism, to parallel his Pan-African political stance, but he did not.[104]

Years before he visited West Africa, Delany argued that black people had positive qualities that were peculiar to them, a view that was shared, among a handful of blacks of his era, by Alexander Crummell. Since he believed they would never be free in America, Delany urged the emigration of significant numbers to other parts of the hemisphere or to West Africa to let their example of state building win respect for their people everywhere. Devoted to no single designating term, he recognized the need for such terms in America because he thought most whites would not overcome racism.[105] Like Walker and Garnet in particular, he grouped his people with "colored" people generally, distinguishing between the traits of people of color and those of whites. The *colored races* was the term he most often used. Yet his reservations about the "white race" were not absolute. Once free, black people would, by extending certain of their values throughout the world, influence whites, but this view has been held by only a handful of black nationalists in history, because most have lacked an understanding of African culture and been unaware that there is anything African worth extending.[106] Delany drew attention to qualities peculiar to black people that, if developed, would enable them to exert tremendous influence in the world:

We have, then, inherent traits and attributes, so to speak, and native characteristics, peculiar to our race, whether pure or mixed blood; and all that is required of us is to cultivate these, and develop them in their purity, to make them desirable and emulated by the rest of the world.[107]

Though obviously unmindful of African sculpture, he wrote of Africans and other people of color, confident they had much to teach others:

That the colored races have the highest traits of civilization, will not be disputed. They are civil, peaceable, and religious to a fault. In mathematics, sculpture and architecture, as arts and sciences, commerce and internal improvements as enterprises, the white race may probably excel; but in language, oratory, metaphysics, theology, and legal jurisprudence—in plain language, in the true principles of morals, correctness of thought, religion, and law or civil government, there is no doubt but the black race will yet instruct the world.[108]

Within the "black race," Delany recognized shared cultural values irrespective of color, whether pure black or "mixed," and in doing so revealed his awareness of the power of culture, that light-skinned blacks, whether conscious of it or not, take on the culture to which they are mainly exposed. Although he spoke of "inherent" traits or "native characteristics," he obviously was not making a genetic argument, for he wanted to see the values of his people extended throughout the world—a form of universalism unimagined by Whipper. The nationalists' concern for values that go beyond race has largely been obscured by the rise of Marcus Garvey and other less sophisticated "nationalist" thinkers.

Being pioneers of civilization, black people were for Delany capable of carving a future for themselves and for whites as well. While Walker, among others, argued that they had a special role in lifting the moral sights of the world, through Christian messianism, Delany appears to have been alone in believing that blacks might influence people irrespective of color in a nonreligious sense. His ability to see examples of black genius in the contemporary world was a factor in his conviction that the genius of his people was a reality in ancient history and might again help shape the destiny of humanity.

Thus, he broke with the view of African barbarism in modern history by arguing for the existence of luminous aspects of Africanity from which Americans were already benefiting. In linking the values of blacks in North America to their kin in Africa, he provided the theoretical basis for raising the debate over names to a higher level and so came closer to developing a viable cultural nationalist position than any other nationalist of his day. This he did in identifying African agricultural contributions to America that included but went beyond the benefits of hard labor: "And from their knowledge of cultivation—an art acquired in their native Africa—the farming interests in the North and planting in the South were commenced with a prospect never dreamed of before the introduction on the continent of this most interesting, unexampled, hardy race of men."[109] In that passage, he suggests the continuing Africanity, the self-generative qualities, of those who built the foundations of the slave economy, a position paralleling the continuation of African religion in America recognized by Richard Allen, Daniel Payne, Walker, and Garnet. Nevertheless, the argument that *African-American* or *Afro-American* was an appropriate term because blacks in America were in important ways African in culture was not explicitly advanced, not even by Delany. Even so, in drawing attention to African cultivation of the soil and domestication of animals, he identified the means by which culture was first made possible, anticipating in one respect the historian Peter Wood:

> Hemp, cotton, tobacco, corn, rice, sugar, and many other important staple products, are all the result of African skill and labor in the southern states of this country. . . . Nor was their skill as herdsmen inferior to their other proficiencies, they being among the most accomplished trainers of horses in the world.[110]

Delany began the process among blacks in the antebellum North of calling attention to the African character not only of Southern black life but of Southern life generally. He draws attention, in the above passage, to slaves teaching others—proof of their ability, when free of white oppression, to work for themselves—proof, in short, of the autonomous nature of aspects of African culture in slavery. He might have argued, and undoubtedly understood, that an awareness of the strengths of one's culture—indeed, of its existence—is essential to ending that ambivalence about oneself that guarantees undue controversy. Had he held that African ways of doing things made blacks in America in important ways African, then terms like *Afro-American, African-American,* and *African* would have taken on a more substantial meaning, enough perhaps, on the merits of the argument, to have carried the day.

It should be said that Delany never spoke at length on the significance of an appropriate name for his people. Had he done so, it is possible, judging from his knowledge of African culture, that he might have done as much to resolve the continuing conflict as circumstances would have allowed—that is, in the absence of fundamental changes in the status of blacks in North America and in Africa. The wonder is that he knew as much as he did about Africa. A consideration of what he learned on his trip to Africa in relation to the names controversy would have illuminated the question immensely, for he had courage of mind and the habit, in the words of Daniel Payne, of traveling "with eyes and ears wide open,"[111] both essential to moving beyond stereotypes of Africa that prevented free blacks from getting beneath the names and revealing the values of which the names were, at best, emblematic. Perhaps he would have alienated his fellow leaders had he insisted that most blacks of his day were largely African in culture and for that reason should be called Africans. Judging from what Payne writes of Delany, the African cultural argument, at least as advanced by him, would have won few friends to his side:

> [H]e was too intensely African to be popular, and therefore multiplied enemies where he could have multiplied friends by the thousands. Had his love for humanity been as great as his love for his race, he might have rendered his

personal influence co-extensive with that of Samuel R. Ward in his palmiest days, or that of Frederick Douglass at the present time.[112]

At the time Delany was purging whites from the ranks of the African Civilization Society, of which he had become an important member, William Whipper joined the organization. This is a measure of the continuing strength of racism and perhaps the supreme example of how black leaders kept their options open, refusing to be frozen in ideological time when living in a world of shifting realities. Whipper's movement toward nationalism makes it clear that even his earlier stand for a color-blind America was not and could not have been a permanent one for a man of his intelligence and sincerity, which suggests precisely what occurred: his adjusting of strategies to meet perceived change or rigidity in oppressing structures, the jettisoning of a course pursued for years. Given American racial realities, change was at least as likely to occur in the attitudes of black leaders as in the objective conditions of the times.[113]

The cyclical pattern that saw integrationism and nationalism vying for ascendancy owes much, as the names controversy reveals, to a misreading or neglect of the past—a problem endemic to integrationist leaders in black America from 1830 onward. The period from 1830 to 1860, in which the forces of integrationism and nationalism first seriously contended for ascendancy, prefigured similar struggles among black Americans in the twentieth century. Those early years were years in which integrationists—spiritually rootless leaders with little sense of the relationship between their people's liberation and the historical process—were countered by nationalists, who marked out the material and to some extent the spiritual lines along which genuine liberation might be attained. The integrationist contribution to liberation theory in the slave era was almost nonexistent; its essential hollowness was its bequest to the post-emancipation era.

V I

"After the coming of freedom," wrote Booker T. Washington,

> there were two points upon which all the people were agreed, and I find that this was generally true throughout the South: that they must change their names, and that they must leave the old plantations for at least a few days or weeks in order that they might really feel sure they were free.[114]

Not wanting to carry the surnames of their former owners, a great many blacks immediately supplied themselves with last names. Though their new names were rarely African, theirs was an effort to recover at least a portion of the dignity they had lost with enslavement. Even so, the impact of American slavery on the African and his descendants is nowhere more evident than in the names blacks, once free, adopted for themselves. The new names, overwhelmingly indistinguishable from those of white Americans, refer one mostly to various parts of the British Isles and Europe rather than to sections of Africa. While the use of individual African names, surely available to those emerging from slavery, was a possibility in cultural terms, in political terms it would have seemed not very important, considering the exigencies of the day. The substance of freedom, as a life-and-death matter, overshadowed other issues for ex-slaves.

Emancipation did mean that blacks who had been free all along had their first real opportunity to get to know the black masses of the South, that those manumitted during slavery could relate to their people with a freedom previously unknown. Free blacks had an unprecedented opportunity to help bridge the cultural gap that separated them from their people as a result of law, prejudice, and the exigencies of nineteenth-century rural-urban life. It was an opportunity unrivaled short of the experience of having grown up among slaves, and the benefits would have been unrivaled, including those directly related to the contests between integrationists and nationalists over strategies of liberation, which continually emerged as the fundamental question of the dispute over names. The discovery of the enriching features of black culture, of its African sources, would have had all sorts of concrete implications for the spiritual life of black America and, as a natural by-product, would have enriched the debate over names even beyond what a reading of Delany would have revealed. Black leaders, in a word, had an opportunity to bring theory into line with reality, to begin bridging the divide between themselves and the masses, from whom the leaders, out of ignorance, held themselves aloof culturally.

The opportunity to know the masses culturally was there all along for Northern black leaders, but they did little to enlighten themselves on such matters. This did not augur well for future relations between leaders and those whom they purported to lead, in the North and the South. The cultural life of the mass of blacks as perceived by the black leadership and that of the black leadership itself appear to have moved on different planes as early as the last quarter of the eighteenth century and down to the time of emancipation. To be sure, the impact of the culture of the larger society was sharply felt by free black leaders, who were very conscious that they shared many cultural values with the members of the larger society. It is precisely the white influence on black leadership, through education and institutional life generally, that explains the absence of references in the names debate to black cultural forms that were recognized by white and black contemporaries as African.

With emancipation, even those black leaders most sensitive to the needs of the Southern masses gave a low priority to cultural questions, for economic and political questions loomed before them. As the opportunity to free their people from brutal oppression seemed within reach, black theorists gave primacy to political and economic emancipation. While not unmindful of the critical import of their people's spiritual needs in more conventional, Western terms, they knew that economic and political relief for the freedmen was by far the most important consideration. Besides, there was simply little opportunity or inclination to study the culture of blacks after the Black codes went into effect in 1865 and an effort was made, once again, to enslave them.[115] That terror gave such urgency to questions of the most elementary kind regarding the humanity of blacks that the priorities for the post-emancipation period appear to have been set without matters of African culture, however important to the masses—indeed, to the American nation—ever receiving a hearing.

Shortly after emancipation, a number of formerly free Negroes went south to work among the freedmen and, together with free Negroes from Southern cities, presented themselves as leaders, the assumption being that they were better prepared to lead than almost any ex-slave. There was tragedy in that assumption, for they assumed cultural superiority with little understanding of those to whom they were "superior." In fact, the artistic achievements of black people came exclusively from the slave population, as did the pioneering religious expression of which slave art was a vital part, but there is not a single reference in the sources on how the folktale, slave music, and dance relate to the naming of black people, and that no doubt was because of the absence of any awareness that positive African values, though influenced by Western values, remained a profound influence in slave culture. The great handicap of the slave community at the time of emancipation, then, was its lack of educated slaves, in the Western sense, to represent it in political assemblies. No matter how sincere the black political leadership in Reconstruction and later, that leadership did not understand the spiritual needs of the mass of emancipated slaves. That failure was of profound consequence, limiting the conception of freedom of integrationists and nationalists alike, and it established a pattern that has lasted over a century.

Though emancipation meant that black people looked forward to becoming citizens, it did not mean that most wanted to be known simply as Americans. Most ex-slaves knew only too well that whites with whom they had contact had no intention of treating them like human beings unless forced to do so, and that realization made them think of themselves as blacks in America.[116] Overwhelming in its intensity, their continuing African religiosity precluded a sense of being American, as did the brutality practiced against them in the days of the Black Codes and Reconstruction. While growing numbers of them probably began considering themselves as deserving American citizens, though black, there was interest in the motherland during Reconstruction and a continuing tendency for some to call themselves African. More important, African values, powerfully expressed in the ring shout and in folktales following slavery, were continually drawn on by the masses.

An 1870 editorial in the *Christian Recorder* on complexional designations in the West Indies and in North America reminded the reader that "freedom" had not brought an end to the Afro-American's sense of union with the past. The word *colored,* which enjoyed wide currency among blacks in America as an inclusive designation following as well as before emancipation, according to the editorial, was "used, throughout the whole of the West Indies, to denote persons of mixed race, that is, partly Caucasian and partly African whatever the shade of their complexion . . . but is never applied, as in America, to the full-blooded black." Furthermore, asserted the editorial, *Negro* was never "applied to any but the pure blacks in the West Indies."[117] In contrast, the designating term employed in the United States, whether *Negro, colored,* or another, encompassed all people of African descent, even those in Africa. Apart from isolated situations involving tiny fractions of Afro-Americans, the *gens de couleur,* and the few in the Brown Fellowship Society, the group name did not admit of color gradations among blacks anywhere, a consideration congenial to Pan-African political and cultural development.

Such was the understanding when the question was posed in 1870 in the *Christian Recorder:* "The Word African in Our Denominational Title: Should It Be Removed?" A. L. Stanford of Philadelphia noted "great victories" achieved "under the same old tricolored flag—'African'—'Methodist'—'Episcopal.' She glides swiftly on under a clear, blue sky of prosperity. . . But suddenly one of the watermen spies the old carcass rising from the deep." Stanford observed of the names controversy what Sidney had pointed to regarding the means by which black leadership proceeded toward freedom before Whipper struck a note of discord, confessing that, for a while at least, "the question had ceased to perplex our minds for we have as yet seen no disadvantages, accruing from our denominational title which are not common to all other titles of distinction."[118] At a time when some were calling for the A.M.E. Church to send missionaries to Africa, Stanford thought the removal of the word *African* from the A.M.E. title would be particularly dangerous since people of African ancestry in America might find it easier to forget their obligations to their people in Africa.

A few weeks later, a contributor to the debate, the Reverend A. Johnson of Cincinnati, Ohio, suggested that the initial *A* in the denominational title be retained, but that the word *African* be removed and the word *American* substituted. To those who wanted *African* retained out of respect for the accomplishments of the fathers, he answered,

   . . . I will say that the first fifty years and upward of our Zion, will be a lasting monument to their memory, and will be handed down to the remotest generations as a memorial of the sacrifices they endured, and the victories they achieved under God. . . . The first fifty years will tell what the fathers have done, under the old order of things, with the African title; the next fifty years will tell what their sons have done, under the new order of things, with the American title.[119]

Then, in a passage that strikes at the heart of the controversy and brings to the surface the deepest aspirations of integrationists and sets them beside the perceived disadvantages of the African inheritance, Johnson argued,

The former [*African*] reminds us of being slaves and chattel; the latter reminds us of freedom and true manhood. The former reminds us of being outcasts in American politics, the latter reminds us of being American citizens, incorporated in the body politic of this great republic.[120]

Even as Johnson's letter appeared in print, the forces of reaction were building, and Reconstruction governments were already under attack in various parts of the South; the light that shone so brightly on the horizon with the advent of Reconstruction was discolored, the Southern sky streaked with storm clouds. Yet blind to the lessons of the past, Johnson asserted, "While the bugle of 'Advance' is sounding, let us as a denomination take up the tramp with the onward march of progress. The command of the age is, 'Forward!' 'March!'"[121]

Richard Cain, a member of Garnet's African Civilization Society and later an impressive figure in South Carolina politics, took a different view. He argued that the greater the signs of progress for his people, the greater the likelihood of their acquiring the dignity that comes from being true to their origins—the children of their African ancestors. Prominent in South Carolina politics and a force in the A.M.E. Church, Cain rose in Congress to respond to a racist attack on his people:

The gentleman further states that the Negro race is the world's stage actor— the comic dancer all over the land; that he laughs and he dances. Sir, well he may; there are more reasons for his laughing and dancing now than ever before. There are more substantial reasons why he should be happy now than during all the two hundred years prior to this time. Now he dances as an African; then he crouched as a slave.[122]

The influence of the word *African* was such that not a few whites after emancipation, as in antebellum years, continued to refer to blacks as Africans. Others, as during the slave era, chose their designations according to what was respectable and fashionable among blacks themselves, or according to racist impulses. One of the many examples of white people unselfconsciously calling blacks Africans in the last half of the nineteenth century occurs in a description by John W. Forney of an encounter between the former vice-president of the Confederacy, Alexander Stephens, and Robert Brown Elliot, the black lawyer and legislator from South Carolina: "Mr. Stephens . . . spoke January 6, 1874, and Mr. Elliot, the colored champion of the liberated race, followed him the next day. I cannot describe the House when the two men addressed it, especially when the African answered the Caucasian."[123]

Much like Afro-American writing of history and the character of slave culture, the names controversy in the postslavery era reveals the workings of Pan-Africanization, a process more easily brought on since the "landlessness" of the Afro-American, his colonization, and his consequent weakness, strengthened his sense of belonging to a world community of blacks who recognized their differences in a way that Afro-Americans, because of their loss of ethnic differentiation, were scarcely able to. The logic of such a development for Afro-Americans—its momentum carrying over into the Reconstruction years—aimed at the achievement of an African family that had never existed before. It is precisely within this framework that the efforts of American blacks, for over a century and a half now, to promote black liberation elsewhere and at home is best understood. Nevertheless, the pull of Africa lost its hold on some as they became more accustomed to their new status following slavery.

But as the fires of Reconstruction were extinguished, the hopes of many blacks for citizenship expired among the embers. All but the very insensitive among them must have wondered if being American, in the sense of being as free as whites, would be possible for them. At that hour, the ambivalence of many toward their status in America was again reflected in formal debate over what they should call themselves, the controversy again involving the use of the word *African* by the African Methodist Episcopal Church. Once more the deeper conflict between the contending forces of integrationism and black nationalism were involved, as dissidents in the A.M.E. Church, who favored interracial churches at a time when black political power was but a shadow of what it had been, were vocal enough to cause a pivotal figure in the black church movement, Benjamin Tucker Tanner, to defend separate churches and the word *African* in African Methodist Episcopal Church:

> What then is the intended force of the title African? Is it doctrinal or national: it is first "doctrinal" and secondarily "national." The doctrinal goal to which the A.M.E. Church aspired was the humanity of the Negro . . . and means only that men of African descent are to be found there, and found as men, not slaves; as equals, not inferiors. The doctrine of the Negro's humanity is its primary significance.[124]

Near the end of the century, in 1888, the debate flared anew with the appearance in the *A.M.E. Church Review* of a piece by the Reverend H. C. C. Astwood advocating the substitution of *Allen*—after the church founder Richard Allen—for *African* in the title of the African Methodist

Episcopal Church because the mission of the word *African* ended "when the race became citizens of the United States, and accepted that citizenship."[125] As far as Astwood was concerned—and here he displayed more optimism than most blacks of the postslavery era—blacks had taken on the nationality of the larger society. It was a curious argument considering the insistence, backed by violence, that the South, the place of residence for the overwhelming majority of blacks, was the "white man's country" in the opinion of most whites in that section before, during, and after Reconstruction, a position supported by the federal government and white leaders of opinion in the North.

Astwood's argument was ahistorical in another, more fundamental sense, in as much as he was claiming American nationality for a people who were, in the main, African in religion and art. In a word, he ignored the cultural component of nationality, greatly simplifying the nature of the problem and obscuring richer possibilities of citizenship for all because of the presence of people of African descent in America. It was just a decade before Astwood made his argument that Bishop Payne, traveling through Philadelphia, where the *Church Review*'s office was located, discovered that African religion was the motive force in the "Christian" ceremony he witnessed. It was then that he asserted that African religion was a force so powerful in Philadelphia and in other Northern locales that he doubted whether a genuine regard for Christianity was likely among the mass of blacks anytime soon. Astwood, like his predecessors in the church and among free blacks in the North, was projecting his own hopes and ambitions upon his people, with little understanding of and much opposition to the African sources of their behavior.

With the defeat of Reconstruction, the Supreme Court's overthrow of the Civil Rights Act of 1875, and the dwindling number of black officeholders in the South as the immediate backdrop, Astwood pointed out that continued use of the word *African* would contribute to the maintenance of "the odious discrimination which we have battled so long and so faithfully to destroy." It was time for blacks to face their posterity bearing the proud name of citizens of America, throwing open the doors of their fathers' church and burying "within its sacred precincts the name of their past identity which served them so well." In place of the word *African*, he wanted to "raise a monument to Bishop Allen, the founder of this glorious institution, under which name all races and people and kindred and tongues can unite—'The Allen Methodist Episcopal Church.'"[126] Again the dispute over institutional designations led the antagonists of "complexional distinctions" to posit a more universal position. And once again it was advanced that, through the magic of a word, the elimination of all-black institutions could be effected and liberty won from whites. This was believed in some quarters, though the exertions of blacks for over a century had not secured freedom, and Radical Reconstruction had not brought about the hoped-for new order.

Yet there were blacks—no doubt concentrated mainly among more privileged elements—who agreed with or wanted to believe in Astwood's position, just as there had been a substantial number supporting Whipper. Astwood's assertion that the identity of blacks as Africans had been lost, absorbed by a nationality "which we have accepted and of which we feel justly proud," was made to order for those wanting to forget the pain of slavery.[127] That kind of argument from one in so high a position in the A.M.E. Church was more than an abstract argument; rather, it was a policy formulation and a warning to ex-slaves entering the church that African cultural practices were hardly to be condoned and that they must rid themselves of the cultural heritage of their fathers. Astwood was no more tolerant toward the mass of ex-slave churchgoers, no more perspicacious, than Bishop Payne.

That his position was excessive was demonstrated by the response to his call for the elimination of the word *African*. It came from the Reverend J. T. Jenifer, who presented an argument not easy for those of Astwood's persuasion to counter. Astwood and those of like mind, Jenifer said, were ashamed of their past, of their African ancestry, of their color, and that was why they exhorted their people to recoil from the word. "We are no 'Africans,'" Jenifer shrewdly accused Astwood and his followers of postulating, and he observed that Germans born in America were not ashamed of Germany and that the same was true of the Frenchmen, Irishmen, Englishmen, and other descendants of the various peoples making up the nation.

> Why, then, should the Negro of this country, with African blood and of African parentage, be ashamed of Africa? . . . Ashamed of Africa! The seat of the earliest civilization, the cradle of arts and sciences; the earliest nursery of the Church of God. Ashamed of the place where Abraham and Jesus went for refuge! Ashamed of the land of the Pyramids and the Ptolemies. . . . Ashamed of Africa![128]

The charge that the word *African* in the A.M.E. Church's title injected caste into the religion of that church was dismissed by Jenifer, who rejoined that prejudice was mainly responsible for the existence of African methodism: "To the proscribed and downtrodden colored people of this country this name was a symbol of hope; it was an *asylum and an inspiration*—a protest against religious oppression or proscription at the altar of God." An asylum from the degrading and blasphemous spirit of prejudice; a refuge where "free minds and space to rise" could be found, where black people could find "fields for usefulness or development," could exercise their individuality and rise on the basis of merit while helping advance their people in the United States and elsewhere.[129]

The A.M.E. Church, he argued, "has always felt that under God she had a special mission to the colored races, hence Africa has been a field of increasing interest." Having planted its first mission in Africa in 1821, the A.M.E. Church displayed Pan-African reach by following with missions in Haiti, San Domingo, and British Guiana.[130] Of signal importance to Jenifer was the fact that many leaders and members of that church had come from the depths of black life: "many of these cultured men and women were slaves, while others are the children of slave parents of one or two generations."[131] Not only were some black missionaries the cultured offspring of second-generation slave parents, but some were the offspring of Africans enslaved in North America. To ask them to abandon use of the term *African* was tantamount, Jenifer implied, to asking them to abandon their lineage and sense of communion with their ancestors.

That so many ministers of the church were ex-slaves or the children of slaves in part explains the strength of African religious practices within the A.M.E. Church, where the praying and singing bands flourished, despite virulent opposition, after emancipation. In addition to "ignorant" religious leaders who supported the ring shout and spirituals, some "intelligent" descendants of slave parents were among the large numbers of ministers condemned by Payne for stressing the importance of the ring to Christian conversion. As powerful as those singing and praying bands were in the 1870s in Philadelphia, they must have been more influential in the South, given the overwhelming numerical superiority of ex-slaves to blacks who were free in the slave era and considering the large concentrations of blacks in regions later to be referred to as the Black Belt.

The history of the A.M.E. Church after the 1880s is written in such broad outline that church ceremonies receive little attention and administrative issues dominate the detail that is there. What we do know about the subject suggests that the clash of forces was intense. The efforts of the church hierarchy to extirpate African influences continued as blacks stood powerless politically, increasingly questioning themselves, in the last decades of the century as violence against them reached a horrid intensity. Nevertheless, in the 1890s there was continuing support for a complexional designation, indeed for one linked to Africa. From the late 1880s down to the opening years of the new century, the term *Afro-American*, frequently used, easily competed with *Negro* as the most popular designation for black people. Especially then, *Afro-American* began appearing in the titles of black organizations.[132] In addition, the phrase was used with such regularity by blacks, especially in the North, that it was— together with *African* and *free African, colored* and *Negro*—one of the five most prominent designations used by them in the nineteenth century.

In 1892, J. C. Embry said he thought the term *Afro-American* superior to *Negro*, which he considered "an intruder—an outlaw in our literature—it is not the language of science, nor the voice of religion and fraternity." And though he had "the highest and most affectionate regard for 'the brother in black,'" believing him as "sure to be heard from in the years just before us as the government of God is sure and just," he considered *Negro,* when translated, "too narrow and exclusive to comprehend the race."[133] Embry could not understand why the name of the many millions of people of African descent should derive from color alone. The words *Indian, Mongol, Caucasian,* and *Arab* refer to the origins of the people in question, why shouldn't the designation for blacks? But he thought the term *Negro*—"an intended stigma which European and American slaveholders invented for us"—could not possibly do the job. *Colored American* was dismissed because it was too inclusive, covering people of color who were not of African descent as well as Africans and their descendants. Besides, *colored* represented no precise geographical division—an objection that received considerable support in the twentieth century.[134]

As the new century began, concern over titles again found its way into the pages of Afro-American newspapers and magazines. A debate early in the new century over names established a number of the main lines along which the controversy over names would proceed later in the century. Whether the word *Negro* should be capitalized was the question before a symposium of Afro-American leaders in 1904. The word had been employed with growing frequency among free blacks following the Colonization Society's formation in the second decade of the preceding century, and often was not capitalized, even by blacks submitting articles to various periodicals. In time, however, blacks came to regard the lowercase spelling as an insult to their people.[135] Even so, they were not in complete agreement regarding the wisdom of capitalizing the word *Negro.* A Negro newspaper, the *Independent,* broached the question of whether *Negro* should be capitalized, answering that since it qualified as an adjective—black—it should not. But the mere fact that there were blacks who wanted *Negro* capitalized reflected a growing regard for the word.

The *A.M.E. Church Review* thought the matter of sufficient import to sponsor a symposium entitled "A Minuscule," the question being, "In spelling the word Negro, would you always begin it with a small or a capital N?" Bishop Tanner raised the rather uncommon—for Afro-Americans—though interesting objection that, as applied to all nine million people of African ancestry, the word *Negro* was not appropriate. The government eschewed referring to black soldiers as Negro troops because "it would have deemed it an insult to her soldiers of all shades of color, but alike sharing African blood, to have called them negroes," for the prejudiced and ignorant rabble would quickly begin referring to "nigger" troops. He expressed concern that the term *nigger* was too close to *Negro* for the latter to be acceptable, and, just as the term *nigger* had an affinity to *Negro,* he thought *Negro* or *black* "full cousin to the term 'darkey,'" selected and insisted upon by enemies. Certainly one of his more curious objections to use of the word *Negro* was his belief that, if it were accepted, wives and daughters would be Negresses, "and God have mercy on the man of African blood that can stand it. If he can, he may rest assured that he can stand more than these wives and daughters are willing to stand."[136] Tanner insisted,

[A]ll of us are not black. . . . Far from it. It is questionable if it would not be a miserable misnomer to fully one-half of us. Taking us as a whole, it would be more nearly correct to describe us as a brown people, but a black, never. As little as many might be inclined to believe it, a genuinely black person among us is a rarity. . . . As a matter of fact, it is just as likely that you will discover quite as many who are genuinely white as you will find genuinely black. The vast majority will be brown and mixed.[137]

It is hard to avoid the conclusion that a dark complexion was objectionable to Tanner. His references to the use of the term *Negro* as "a miserable misnomer" for one-half of Afro-Americans, to being "a brown people, but a black, never"—these indicate that he conceived of black in the literal physical (as opposed to the psychological or sociological) sense and was repelled. One can infer that many Afro-American contemporaries shared Tanner's opposition to being called black, since those objecting to the term were legion generations later.[138] But, paradoxically, Tanner was not one to deny his African roots. On the contrary, he remarked that the word *Negro* had been thrust upon a people for whom *African* for centuries was "the one and only name recognized by us officially and by others as well." Moreover, "in common with a rule that is universal," his people had referred their name "to the continent whence we came. Who is the European but the man from Europe?" So too the Asiatic. "So we, being from Africa, regarded ourselves as Africans."[139]

Tanner focused on an important aspect of the names controversy with his argument that blacks were forced to stop calling themselves Africans when whites attempted to saddle them with the word *Negro*—a contention not inescapable from a consideration of the sources. Yet he is correct in arguing that blacks, meaning free blacks, "spurned the title, negro, and took that of Colored," as exemplified in the Colored Methodist Episcopal Church.[140] This assertion is in part borne out by an examination of the names people of color selected for their organizations: the term *Negro* almost never appears in titles. Nevertheless, it should be recalled, most leading blacks did not shrink from referring to themselves as Negroes, while giving priority, in organizational titles, to *colored* or some other term. The dichotomy between *colored* and *Negro,* then, was not as sharp for many as Tanner believed, the recoil from use of the word *Negro,* apart from organizational titles, not as rapid as he thought.

Tanner objected to capitalizing the word *Negro* on the grounds that, being primarily descriptive, it is exceptional and out of line with the manner by which other people are designated. Proceeding along lines established by Jenifer, he asked, "Why are the people of Europe, who are mainly white, not referred to as the Whites? And why are the peoples of Asia, who are mainly yellow, not referred to as the Yellows?" Indeed, if the designation is to be according to color, "why not take those with red hair, and have a class of Red Heads; and take all who have grey eyes and have a class of Grey Eyes, etc., etc." *Afro-American* was therefore more appropriate, just as *Anglo-American, German-American,* and *Franco-American* were for whites in America.[141]

Bishop Henry McNeil Turner, the African emigrationist and militant, took a different tack. With a feel for the practical, he argued that, since the term *Negro* "has been accepted by the Afro-American, or the colored race," it "should always begin with a capital letter." He granted that in its inception *Negro* was the white man's word for the African, "just as Buckra is the black man's appellation for whites, as applied in all parts of Africa."[142] Even though Turner was the most passionate of all advocates of back-to-Africa movements, he did not prefer the words *African* or *Afro-American* to *Negro*. Like outstanding leaders before him, he apparently considered the names controversy less important than other issues facing his people, another indication that the more serious the leadership, the less insistent its call for a single designating term.

Another participant in the "Minuscule" symposium, Dr. George W. Henderson, objected to use of the word *Negro* because it "is not national or geographical" and does not denote a nation. But after arguing, much as Tanner did, that *Negro* is inappropriate for those of mixed blood, he proceeded to suggest that perhaps the game was not worth the candle, and in the process he reduced the debate to absurdity:

> The term Afro-American possesses even less merit. . . . Some of us have English or French or Italian or Irish blood in our veins; some the blood of nearly all races; we are descendants of all continents. Hence, to be accurate, our proper designation would be English-Afro-, Franco-Afro-, Germanico-Afro-, Italico-Afro-, Spanish-Afro-, Dutch-Irish-Afro-, Russo-Afro-, or in some cases, English-Franco-Germanico-Spanico-Scotch-Irish-Afro-American![143]

In another culture, an argument similar to Henderson's would have made more sense, but in America, given the realities of racism, it amounted to sophistry, for admixtures of European blood did not change the status of Negroes. Moreover, his argument failed to take into account that the white peoples to whom he referred were not of unmixed heritage, and consequently, by his logic, should not have used such designations as *Irish-American* in referring to themselves. Henderson's position on a name for the group illustrated how ridiculous and what a waste of time the controversy over names could become when not treated seriously. His view, in short, failed to take into account, as had been observed a year earlier, that the consciousness of blacks, at most, was essentially double—American and Negro—not the product of greatly disparate and diffuse sources.[144]

VII

By 1904, nearly one hundred years of controversy over names had established beyond doubt that the major black figures of the nineteenth century, those involved in the fight for the liberation of their people, did not think it important to debate, unless forced to, the relative merits of various designating terms. But while they emphasized the necessity of decisive action and unrelenting effort on the part of their people if they were to be free, they did not countenance the view that nonracial appellations had magical properties that would exorcise the demon of racism. Nor did they maintain that one rather than another complexional designation would substantially affect the self-image of their people. They recognized that it would require more than a change in name to effect such a revolution in thought.

By the turn of the century, blacks who favored the term *Afro-American* appear on balance to have moved the argument to a higher level. *Afro-American* referred people of African ancestry in the Americas to the land, history, and culture of their forebears, while recognizing their presence as an unassimilated people in America. That Afro-Americans during most of the nineteenth century spent much time trying to agree on a single description for the group as a whole reflected, in sum, the transformation of their people from being Ibos, Akans, Angolans, and a score of additional African ethnics to a single people. Ethnic differences among blacks that were potentially counterproductive did not exist in easily recognizable form after slavery—and that has been a source of political and cultural strength, not weakness, for blacks. It is questionable whether that strength would be greater still if individual blacks knew the specific locations in Africa from which their ancestors came, especially when considering the retrogressive nature of much of ethnicity in Africa today. But what history has fashioned through Pan-African consciousness and, to an impressive degree, Pan-African culture, has important bearing not only on the status of the Afro-American but on the question of African liberation everywhere.

Though imperfectly understood, the pull of Africa profoundly influenced the thought and feelings of millions of blacks, whatever their political persuasion. Only under threat, real or imagined, had most ceased referring to themselves as Africans or as free Africans. In the nineteenth century, with the emergence of scientific racism, shame over Africa, though mixed with residual pride, was doubtless responsible for the eagerness with which many Afro-Americans rejected designations connecting them with that continent. The term *Afro-American*, even if its suggestion of symmetrical cultural development is overdone, has made it easier to force a confrontation with reality for those attempting to escape their African origins. Even a partial affirmation of Africa in a society in which Africa is regarded as a symbol of savagery by many is for blacks indispensable to securing a hold on themselves, to having some sane reference point. While the sense of shame of many was evident in the opening decade of the new century, almost no black leader, certainly none known, failed in the new century to defend some color designation for his or her people. The debate over names, which recurred again and again in the twentieth century, did not otherwise differ from the debates of the nineteenth century until the 1960s, when an impressive effort was made to resolve the controversy.[145]

The names controversy reveals important attitudes toward Africa, contending strategies of black liberation in America, and the place of black people and institutions in American life. Moreover, the record of this controversy might be read as an index to the continuing effects of the slave trade and slavery on Afro-American spiritual and psychological life and, as such, tells us how much of African culture was unknown even to the most loyal sons of Africa in the North. To be sure, the controversy illumines the bases on which the confusion over identity rests—the economic, political, and social structures oppressing black people in America. Long before the opening of the twentieth century, therefore, it was evident that only when the unjust treatment of blacks and the structural inequities perpetuating the crisis of identity end will the debate over names, too, have a chance of ending. The final resolution of the names controversy is not likely to come until African peoples as a whole have won freedom, a development inevitably linked to their status in America.

CHAPTER FIVE

W. E. B. Du Bois:
Black Cultural Reality
and the Meaning of Freedom

> This the American black man knows; his fight here is a
> fight to the finish. Either he dies or wins. If he wins it
> will be by no subterfuge or evasion of amalgamation.
> He will enter modern civilization here in America as a
> black man on terms of perfect and unlimited equality
> with any white man, or he will enter not at all. . . .
> There can be no compromise.
> —W. E. B. Du Bois, 1935

During a pilgrimage in West Africa in 1924, W. E. B. Du Bois "saw where
the ocean roars to the soul of Henry Highland Garnet." Perhaps first introduced to Garnet by reading Alexander Crummell, he had not felt the
impact of Garnet and other nationalists in any precise ways until he was
out of Harvard College. Before that time, largely on his own, he had arrived at an essentially nationalist stance, utilizing the Harvard environment as a kind of laboratory in which to conduct social experiments and
to deduce a strategy by which blacks might win freedom. In his college
years, apparently, he was not conversant with the activities of Walker,
Garnet, and other nationalists, and so thought himself "exceptional" in
his ideas on "voluntary race segregation." Whereas other blacks "saw
salvation only in integration at the earliest moment and on almost any
terms in white culture," he was "firm in [his] criticism of white folk,"
dreaming of "a Negro self-sufficent culture even in America."[1]

There was a world within but apart from that of white America that was
attractive to him, one of color with its own values and institutions. But
had he not gone to Fisk before attending Harvard and lived there among
Southern blacks, his feelings toward that world would undoubtedly have
been different. In particular, he might in such circumstances have recognized the need for Afro-American unity in order to attack racist controls,

but, without exposure to the richness of black culture, he would probably have been willing to see many of his people's values deemphasized in the interest of a new "harmony" between blacks and whites. Instead, his discovery and explorations of Southern black culture contributed profoundly to his conception of freedom for his people.

There was little tangible in the first sixteen years of his life to indicate that he might become a proponent of black autonomy, unless it was the brilliance with which he performed when competing against his classmates; unless, possibly, it was the racial insult he sustained when a classmate refused his greeting card, making him aware that there were differences in color between himself and the other students. But one doubts any depth of nationalism in his youth, especially since Du Bois was quite happy, compared with other black youths of his time.[2]

He was born in 1868 in Great Barrington, Massachusetts, into a lower-middle-class family of mixed ancestry, but he soon began to look out upon the world as a Negro, as a black person. Unlike Walker and Garnet, he had parents neither of whom was a slave. And unlike those men, he experienced no real hardship while young, whether through tragedy known to others close to him or through personal experience, except possibly for his mother's ordeal in having to raise him by herself. Her burden he did feel and her sacrifices on his behalf he was aware of; they figured in some way in the shaping of his interest in the liberation of women, an interest that in time led him to contribute to the dialogue on women's rights in the new century.[3]

Though he was short and rather slight of stature, it is as difficult, in hindsight, to think of Du Bois as being small in any way as it is to think of him as having been bald most of his life. His complexion was brown, his lips Negroid enough, his voice clear, strong, precise—even into his ninetieth year. And there was a romantic quality about him. He loved poetry, music, nature—especially the change of seasons. As he grew into his twenties, he wore spats, carried a cane, affected the European gentleman. Though a great believer in work, he cared little for money. In that regard, he was in the tradition of Walker, Garnet, and Robeson.[4]

There was a certain loftiness about him that some called arrogance, and that designation was probably accurate to some extent. However, he possessed refinement more than anything else. Frances J. Herskovits, who entertained Du Bois in her Evanston home, observed that, "except for Joyce, I had never seen anyone of his sensibility." His sense of self marked off a certain boundary that one could not cross except on invitation, and few were invited. Those who were invited tended to be men and women of learning with a sense of social obligation. To them he revealed a side one hardly imagines from a distance, and for them he often put aside his routine of going to bed at ten each night, a habit first cultivated in college. He has been described as "a well-disciplined and methodical

man. There were no loose moments, no unscheduled hours in his life."[5]
There was about him an undeniable aura of the aristocrat but no sense of
vulgar elitism. As he grew in age, he became increasingly radical even as
reaction crested. When Henry Miller saw him, Du Bois was over eighty
and the foremost intellectual and spiritual leader of his people, as he had
been for decades:

> It was quite a time before Du Bois appeared on the platform. When he did it
> was with the air of a sovereign mounting his throne. The very majesty of the
> man silenced any would-be demonstration. There was nothing of the rabble-
> rouser in this leonine figure—such tactics were beneath him. His words,
> however, were like cold dynamite. Had he wanted to, he could have set off an
> explosion that would rock the world. . . . As I listened to his speech I pictured
> him addressing a body of scientists in much this same way. I could imagine
> him unleashing the most devastating truths, but in a manner that one would
> be left stunned rather than moved to action. . . . Du Bois was no rabble-
> rouser. No, but to a man like myself it was all too obvious that what his words
> implied were—"Assume the spirit of liberty and you will be free."[6]

Miller thought Du Bois was really saying to blacks that the only education
worth having is that which makes you "assert and maintain your own
freedom. What other purpose could he have had, in citing all the marvellous examples of African culture, *before the white man's intrusion*,
than to indicate the Negroes' own self-sufficiency?"[7]

The examples of African achievement, as Miller perceived, made it
easier for Du Bois to establish the feasibility of self-sufficiency for his
people. Also important to him was the culture of the contemporary
Negro, for in his years at Fisk and at Harvard he knew little of Africa but
was nevertheless laying the foundation for his nationalist stance. His one
African possession—transmitted over time, from generation to generation, like fragments of the Ibo language preserved by the Robesons—was
a song.[8] And that had come to him naturally: his grandfather's grand-
mother, seized by a Dutch trader around 1700, was brought to New England as a slave and, despite the lapse of nearly two centuries, had
through music had a powerful influence on the youth. Her song was the
basis of his initial cultural bond with his ancestry, linking him, in matters
of spirit, to the mass of his people in America despite his birth in Great
Barrington. Others in his family had followed the unfortunate woman as
slaves to America, but it was she, little, black, and lithe, "who shivered
and shrank in the harsh north winds, looked longingly at the hills, and
often crooned a heathen melody to the child beneath her knees," a melody crooned to Du Bois at his mother's knee, thus:

> Do ba-na co-ba, ge-ne me, ge-ne me!
> Do ba-na co-ba, ge-ne me, ge-ne me!
> Ben d'nu-li, nu-li, nu-li, ben d'le.

He set the sad refrains to musical notation, and added, "The child sang it to his children and they to their children's children, and so for two hundred years it has travelled down to us and we sing it to our children, knowing as little as our fathers what its words may mean, but knowing well the meaning of its music." He called it "primitive African music" and compared it to a chanting song:

> You may bury me in the East,
> You may bury me in the West.
> But I'll hear the trumpet sound in that morning,

which he thought "the voice of exile."[9]

Sensitive to the vulnerability of his mother, and from an early age aware of the heritage of slavery in his family, he could easily identify with a black world larger than anything he imagined in Great Barrington. Growing up there, he began to know something of the exile's lot, which in part accounted for his being stirred anew by slave songs: "They came out of the South unknown to me, one by one, and yet at once I knew them as of me and of mine." When a Hampton choir sang these songs in the Congregational church, he "was thrilled and moved to tears and seemed to recognize something inherently and deeply [his] own."[10]

Fate played a role in his going south. Had it not been for Frank Hosmer, a graduate of Amherst and principal of Du Bois's high school, he might never have gone to Fisk and thus his insights into the culture of his people might not have been so searching. It seemed to him that Hosmer, unlike the high school principal who decades later directed racism at Robeson, thought his taking a college preparatory curriculum natural enough, so Du Bois studied algebra, geometry, Latin, and Greek. In a remark with tragic implications, he has written that, had Hosmer been a different sort of man and "recommended agriculture or domestc economy," he "would doubtless have followed his advice, had such 'courses' been available." But Hosmer was "quietly opening" doors to Northern white colleges, doors that in those days "were barred with ancient tongues."[11]

Despite the concerns of family and colored friends about his going south, a scholarship provided by white churchmen, very likely at Hosmer's urging, made it possible for Du Bois to attend Fisk, which had a reputation for excellent academic training. He later commented in regard to those who cautioned him against going south that "their Northern free Negro prejudice revolted at the idea" of his going into "the former land of slavery, either for education or for living." He added, "I am rather proud of myself that I did not agree with them." Yet one can appreciate why his family and friends feared even for his life:

No one but a Negro going into the South without previous experience of color caste can have any conception of its barbarism. . . . Lynching was a continuing and recurrent horror during my college days: from 1885 through 1894, 1,700 Negroes were lynched in America. Each death was a scar upon my soul, and led me to conceive the plight of other minority groups; for in my college days Italians were lynched in New Orleans, . . . and the anti-Chinese riots in the West culminated in the Chinese Exclusion Act of 1892. . . . Yet at this time the full force of legal caste in the South had not yet fallen on Negroes. Streetcars were not separate yet and there was still some Negro voting.[12]

Arriving at Fisk at seventeen, he saw Jubilee Hall. Erected with money raised by the Fisk Jubilee Singers in America and abroad, Jubilee Hall "seemed ever made of the songs themselves, and its bricks were red with the blood and dust of toil. Out of them rose for me morning, noon, and night, bursts of wonderful melody, full of the voices of my brothers and sisters, full of the voices of the past." Except for Robeson, no other nationalist in youth had such exposure to spirituals as Du Bois, and there was virtually no possibility that disrespect for them would be voiced by those connected with the institution. The spirituals were as vital a part of his education as his courses in the classics. In that sense, the two traditions, European and African, were brought together perhaps almost unconsciously when he was still in his teens.[13]

Fisk had a distinguished Northern white faculty, mostly graduates of Yale and Oberlin, dedicated to teaching the offspring of ex-slaves—a faculty itself the product of the spirit that actuated the Sea Islands experiment in which Higginson, Forten, and others attempted to prepare the slaves for freedom. There were thus reminders of slavery at Fisk other than slave music. The Fisk environment was stimulating intellectually and spiritually, and the young scholar could see it as a natural point of departure for further explorations. A child of the slave era, he was determined to know its ground:

> I was not content to take the South entirely by hearsay; and while I had no funds to travel widely, I did, somewhat to the consternation of both my teachers and fellow-students, determine to go out into the country and teach summer school. I was only 18 and knew nothing of the South at first hand, save what little I had seen in Nashville from the protected vantage ground of a college campus. I had not seen anything of the small Southern town and the countryside, which are the real South. . . . I was not compelled to do that, for my scholarship was sufficient to support me, but that was not the point. I had heard about the country in the South as the real seat of slavery. I wanted to know it. . . . Needless to say the experience was invaluable. I travelled not only in space but in time. I touched the very shadow of slavery.[14]

He considered the South the land of slaves and found at Fisk black students, most five to ten years older than he, who brought with them a rich and bitter experience of racial oppression since slavery. Most were from Alabama, Georgia, Mississippi, and Louisiana, whose slavery was of a more representative character than that of Tennessee, where Fisk was located. These students painted pictures of race relations in their various states, so the presence of racism loomed large and in vivid detail in the young Du Bois's mind. Some had seen mobs and lynching and "knew every phase of insult and repression; and too there were sons, daughters and clients of every class of white Southerner. A relative of a future president of the nation had his dark son driven to school each day."[15]

These were the students from whom the Fisk Jubilee singers were drawn. They were too young to have sung these songs during slavery, but they had heard slaves and ex-slaves sing them all their lives, for in the aftermath of slavery one was almost certain to have heard that music, whether born of slave or free Negro parentage. Where there was singing among Negroes there was dance; and dance, like song, was under African influence, both charged with the emotive force of black culture. That and more impressed Du Bois:

> Never before had I seen young men so self-assured and who gave themselves such airs, and colored men at that; and above all for the first time I saw beautiful girls. At my home among my white schoolmates there were a few pretty girls; but either they were not entrancing or because I had known them all my life, I did not notice them; but at Fisk the never-to-be-forgotten marvel of that first supper came with me opposite two of the most beautiful beings God ever revealed to the eyes of 17. I promptly lost my appetite, but I was deliriously happy![16]

It was in the countryside that he learned firsthand of the passionate eagerness of blacks for an education—there that he encountered poverty and sorrow. In two summers of teaching mainly the children of ex-slaves, he came to know people who lived in unpainted houses that appeared to spring from the very soil of hardship. There he met Josie, "a thin, homely girl of twenty, with a dark-brown face and thick, hard hair." She "had about her a certain fineness, the shadow of an unconscious moral heroism that would willingly give all of life to make life broader, deeper, and fuller for her and hers." One of his students, she wanted to go to Fisk and "studied doggedly." He loved his school, "and the fine faith the children had in the wisdom of their teacher was truly marvellous." But the condition of their immediate world and of the larger world militated against their making much progress. Almost all the adults around them and their older siblings had been slaves, and thus were heirs to the best and worst of their heritage—"swept on by the current of the nineteenth century while yet struggling in the eddies of the fifteenth century."[17]

It did not take the study of philosophy either at Fisk or at Harvard for Du Bois to recognize the anachronism of slavery in the modern world and the disadvantages dictated by such a heritage. When he entered Fisk, his own background gave him such an edge that he was placed in the second-year class. And his familiarity with the black peasantry kept him from being romantic about the place and power of slavery in the lives of his ancestors. In the countryside he found storytelling and wondrous song and a sense of earnestness—and a certain backwardness somehow appropriate to the "dull and humdrum" life many of the people led. Of the Burkes, he later wrote, "They used to have a certain magnificent barbarism about them that I liked. They were never vulgar, never immoral, but rather rough and primitive with an unconventionality that spent itself in loud guffaws, slaps on the back, and naps in the corner."[18] There was contact with others that provided his measure of pain and progress:

There were, however, some—such as Josie, Jim, and Ben—to whom War, Hell, and Slavery were but childhood tales, whose young appetites had been whetted to an edge by school and story and half-awakened thought. Ill could they be content, born beyond and without the World. And their weak wings beat against their barriers,—barriers of caste, of youth, of life. . . . [19]

The young Du Bois arranged a program to replace his "egocentric world by a world centering and whirling about [his] race in America." It was a transformation that one has reason to believe occurred naturally enough, considering the expectations for him, especially his mother's hopes and his need to fulfill them, and considering the nature of his involvement with his people in the South, especially those most in need of progress:

For this group I built my plan of study and accomplishment. Through the leadership of men like myself and my fellows, we were going to have these enslaved Israelites out of the still enduring bondage in short order. It was a battle which might conceivably call for force, but I could think of it mainly as a battle of wits; of knowledge and deed, which by sheer reason and desert, must eventually overwhelm the force of hate, ignorance and reaction.[20]

An unhappy experience helped him, perhaps unwittingly, arrive at a perspective regarding the value of dance, one that is tied to the music he heard but is not mentioned in that context:

In Great Barrington there was little chance to dance on the part of anyone but in the small group of colored folk there was always some dancing along with playing games at homes. When I came South and was among my own young folk who not only danced but danced beautifully and with effortless joy, I joined and learned eagerly.[21]

An effort by a black religious leader at Fisk to prevent dancing all but turned Du Bois against the church: "What kind of dancing he was acquainted with I do not know, but at any rate in his mind dancing figured as a particularly heinous form of sin." Du Bois resented the notion that dance is a sin because he danced "quite as naturally" as he ran and sang.

Since dancing was confined almost entirely to Great Barrington blacks, who had danced all their lives, their attitude toward it was probably a product of African influence, especially since African ceremony—the parade of governors followed by dinner and dancing through the night—was powerful in New England at least as late as the 1850s.[22] In any case, his reaction to attempts to curb dancing would have greatly disturbed Daniel Payne:

> The teachers intervened and tried to reconcile matters in a way which for years afterward made me resentful and led to my eventual refusal to join a religious organization. They admitted that my dancing might well be quite innocent, but said that my example might lead others astray. They quoted Paul: "If meat maketh my brother to offend, I will eat no meat while the world standeth." I tried to accept this for years, and for years I wrestled with this problem. Then I resented this kind of sophistry. I began again to dance and I have never since had much respect for Paul.[23]

Voices from the past were all around him at Fisk and in the surrounding city. Had he attended Nashville's First Baptist Church, he would have been exposed to the continuing impact of slave culture. In that "sophisticated" setting, when "a young man from Cincinnati was introduced by the pastor as the preacher for the time being," the young man took full advantage of the opportunity, thinking "to set the congregation to shouting, was the highest point to be attained, and he was equal to the occasion." In the ensuing ceremony there was swaying movement from the many ex-slaves in attendance: the church was filled, "and the minister had taken his text. As the speaker warmed up in his subject, the Sisters began to swing their heads and to reel to and fro, and eventually began a shout."[24]

A more fertile ground for exposure to the slave experience existed fifty miles to the east of Nashville. Du Bois ventured in that direction one night when "dimly across the fields a rhythmic cadence of song . . . died sorrowfully" as he approached a revival meeting. The excitement at the meeting was similar to what was noted about black religious services in New Orleans in the 1850s by Bremer and Olmsted and in Nashville by Wells Brown just five years before Du Bois arrived there. Brown had observed the ring shout in an "urban setting," in the Nashville church, but what Du Bois witnessed in the country was a form of that ceremony and more. On entering an unnamed village and "the little plain church perched aloft," he found the mass of blacks "possessed" with excitement. He could hardly have been closer to their religious experience:

> A sort of suppressed terror hung in the air and seemed to seize us,—a pythian madness, a demoniac possession, that lent terrible reality to song and word. The black and massive form of the preacher swayed and quivered as the words crowded to his lips in singular eloquence. The people moaned and

fluttered, and the gaunt-cheeked brown woman beside me suddenly leaped straight into the air and shrieked like a lost soul, while round about came wail and groan and outcry, and a scene of human passion such as I had never conceived before.[25]

The woman, an ex-slave, was doing some variant of the shout, though Du Bois makes no mention of the direction in which she leaped. And while the general state of possession was at least as much a part of communion with the ancestors as with Christ, he does not make the point, for he placed disproportionate emphasis instead on the Lord, though aware that the ceremony in important ways was African. To be sure, he described shouting as "the last essential of Negro religion and the one more devoutly believed in than all the rest." The participants embodied its manifestations, from low murmuring and moaning to silent-rapt attention "to the mad abandon of physical fervor,—the stamping, shrieking and shouting, the rushing to and fro and wild waving of arms, the weeping and laughing, the vision and the trance."[26]

What he observed as a teenager he did not then understand in theoretical terms. The language he later used to describe it, however, was informed by considerable study. The main components of the theory he later fashioned were developed from his black religious experiences Sunday mornings in the backwoods of the South. His analysis of the culture of the Negro to which he was exposed in his Fisk years, while influenced by, among others, Douglass, Higginson, and Lucy McKim, was nevertheless in most respects his own, and in some respects his contributions were original.[27] Ultimately, his analysis of the spiritual aspects of black culture was rooted in a more general concern for spirituality, to be addressed later, as a motor of history.

What made his discussion of black culture and the oppression of his people—indeed, of the problem of race in America—distinctively Du Boisean had to do with much more than just the formal scholarly training he received first at Fisk, then at Harvard, and later in postgraduate study in Berlin. His work was one of the earliest examples of a type of anthropological research of a high order, except that he was not doing research and had a relationship to his "field of study" that anthropologists have seldom had. By the mid-1880s, he had seen in the Tennessee countryside much of what Bremer and Olmsted saw in Louisiana and elsewhere, but as a participant-observer. The shout he first happened upon that evening he would be exposed to again and again.

In that period of apprenticeship, he discovered a passion that he later, with uncanny success, managed to get on paper, something that he might have been unable to do without his exposure to black religion in the countryside. When he wrote about it a decade later, he was able to capture and to interpret not only what he witnessed but also what he personally experienced. In fact, the whole range of the religious experience in the countryside was a primary source for his exploration of slave religious consciousness and behavior that he would write about in *The Souls of Black Folk* and in *Black Reconstruction*.

He had brought the Southern religious experience of his people with him to Harvard College. In fact, in the larger Southern context of the colored world, he had discovered a source of spiritual being that gave new form and meaning to his life. Those years in the South were important to him for what they suggested of the atmosphere of Reconstruction and for what they exemplified of its aftermath. They provided experiences that enriched his writings about black life—"the immediate flux of life which furnishes the material to our later reflection." That is how William James, one of his greatest professors, explained such a progression.[28]

Du Bois's thoughts of a Negro self-sufficient culture in America, which had developed in his Fisk years, were a sustaining force for him at Harvard. There he met and studied under James, perhaps the best student of religious experience, and so was able to place his observances of religion in Tennessee into a wider spatial and temporal framework. When he returned to the South in *The Souls of Black Folk*, he formulated his knowledge of the religious experiences of his people in terms of his training at Harvard and at Berlin, but did so without losing sight of what was distinctive and positive about black religion.

He explored the nature of communion in the shout "with the Invisible," and the formulation he worked out is impressive, despite its disporportionate emphasis on Christianity. He writes that "the Spirit of the Lord" seized devotees of the shout and made them "mad with supernatural joy," that many generations of slaves "firmly believed that without this visible manifestation of the God there could be no true communion with the Invisible." What he understood by then was that possession "was nothing new in the world, but old as religion, as Delphi and Endor."[29] What was perhaps less common than possession in the world was its relation, in the African religious faith, to the ancestors. For the slave convert to Christianity there was as much concern about relating to the ancestors as to a Christian God. Yet the slave's dramatization of devotion and his quest for union with invisible forces was an African ideal. Du Bois did not view such a religious attitude as negative, possibly because of James's influence but also because he brought a certain humility to his study of the religious ceremony of the descendants of slaves.

He was able to understand and come to terms with the heathenism from which a long line of earlier nationalists had recoiled, and so he realized that, in addition to frenzy, two other components characterized slave religion—music and the preacher.[30] The music with its rhythmic, chanting quality, especially "primitive" in the countryside, was beautiful and grand to his ears. It was transformed in the light of American experience:

"Sprung from the African forests where its counterpart can still be heard, it was adapted, changed, and intensified by the tragic soul-life of the slave, until, under the stress of law and whip, it became the one expression of a people's sorrow, despair and hope." The concept of "tragic soul-life" captures the pain of the experience and its transformation into art, and it calls to mind a neglected aspect of slave life: the intense nature of slave spirituality, which in some measure marks it off from religious experience in Africa and reflects its relationship to a new social reality.[31]

The argument that the counterpart of the Negro spiritual could be found in Africa, which Robeson later stated, was a contribution to the literature of the subject. How Du Bois was led to such a conclusion has not been considered. Of course, there are indications in the literature that some spirituals are more primitive than others, and there is his belief in the continuity of African culture in America, the two suggesting African sources for much of slave art including music. But the song heard at his mother's knee might have first suggested the African analogue, for he compared that song to the spiritual of exile. The songs were "the siftings of centuries," the music "more ancient than the words."[32]

His thesis that the slave preacher was a priest—a leap of intuition based mainly on concrete experiences—explains the prominence of black religious leaders on the plantations from the earliest moments of slavery and suggests a range of authority for the slave preacher that has yet to win a place in the scholarship on slavery. When Du Bois uses the term *preacher* in reference to slavery—a word he at times capitalizes—he means "priest," one able to relate, like the deacon with the staff-cross in Faulkner's "How the Slaves Worshipped," this world to the otherworld, to mediate between the living and the dead, in order to prevent or lessen hardship for the living. In days of youth, he had unusual contact with the Negro preacher. In fact, he made the "weekly sacrifice with frenzied priest at the altar of the 'old-time religion.'"[33]

Later, theory and practice are brought together as he provides the backdrop for his discussion of the variety of roles played by the preacher and sheds light on the process of Pan-Africanization: "the plantation organization replaced the clan and tribe and the white master replaced the chief with far greater and more despotic powers,"[34] a point of view that deserves full consideration in studies of Pan-Africanization. Du Bois was able to identify the institutional framework that replaced African institutions: the framework of power relations in which the movement toward ethnic unity was carried out. He looked at the process even more closely: "Forced and long-continued toil became the rule of life, the old ties of blood relationship and kinship disappeared, and instead of the family appeared a new polygamy and polyandry, which, in some cases, almost reached promiscuity."[35]

In such brief compass, he helps account for the movement of ethnic groups toward a composite of the whole as the pressures of the plantation system force the transformation of kinship relations from clan to more unpredictable and tenuous ones. Had he probed more deeply into the African background of the shout, he would have tempered his view of slavery's effect on the slaves' sense of family and clan. Yet he provides a sophisticated theoretical apparatus for understanding the controls of slavery and the means by which the African, with narrow access to African institutions, attempted to resist them. He is correct in arguing that a great social revolution occurred, which altered the group life of the African, but he underestimated the degree to which the African continued to practice a group life, despite the restraints of slavery; this leads him to conclude that some "traces were retained of the former group life." Still, he made an enormous breakthrough:

> . . . the chief remaining institution was the Priest or Medicine-man. He early appeared as the healer of the sick, the interpreter of the Unknown, the comforter of the sorrowing, the supernatural avenger of wrong, and the one who rudely but picturesquely expressed the longing, disappointment, and resentment of a stolen and oppressed people. Thus, as bard, physician, judge, and priest, within the narrow limits allowed by the slave system, rose the Negro preacher, and under him the first Afro-American institution, the Negro Church.[36]

At times, Du Bois refers to the priest as the only African institution to survive in America; at other times, he makes a similar claim for the church. In a word, the priest's presence in the church represented one African institution within another, which meant that the two reinforced each other in slavery. What is more intriguing than the failure of scholars to explore Du Bois's insights into African culture in slavery is how he arrived at them. Though this subject deserves sustained attention in its own right, and surely will receive it in due course, one finds growing support for a number of his conclusions regarding African culture in disciplines related to history, as when he argues the communal nature of some aspects of black life in America during slavery, a position that is supported in the folktale.

In the Reverend Faulkner's tales, the religious leader is personified by Brer Rabbit in one tale after another, especially in those in which Brer Rabbit is the defender of the interests of the weak and defenseless. While Faulkner does not present him without flaws, Brer Rabbit's overwhelming concerns are ethical, his principal function that of forwarding the struggle for communal freedom, attributes hardly at variance with those that Du Bois ascribed to the slave priest. If Faulkner provides the single richest source for Brer Rabbit as religious leader, the E. C. L. Adams collection, we should recall, contains a tale in which Brer Rabbit performs priestly functions in undiluted form.

The function of the priest with respect to forwarding the economic interests of the community continued during and beyond slavery:

> The Negro Church is the only institution of the Negroes which started in the African forest and survived slavery; under the leadership of the priest and medicine man, and afterward of the Christian pastor, the Church preserved in itself the remnants of African tribal life and became after emancipation the centre of Negro social life. The communism of the African forests with its political and religious leadership is a living, breathing reality on American soil to-day, even after 250 years of violent change.[37]

His contention that at first the slave church was African, "not by any means Christian," is corroborated by the findings in this volume. Before anyone else, he posited ethnic cross-fertilization in a process leading to fusion—"an adaptation and mingling of heathen rites among all the members of each plantation."[38] In other words, Africans of different backgrounds and religious practices made conscious efforts to find a common spiritual vision. Du Bois discusses this process in the context of his treatment of the three essentials of slave religion—the slave priest, the music, and the frenzy. His formulation leaves no doubt that the priest relied mainly on African values in seeking a solution to the problem of ethnicity, a conception of the Negro preacher or priest that may have led to James Weldon Johnson's thesis that the mediating influence of "the old Negro preacher" helped African ethnic groups find commonality. Through the work of Du Bois and Johnson, one better understands the means by which slaves from different ethnic backgrounds were fused into a single people in North America. What neither seemed to emphasize sufficiently, however, was that powerful African influences persisted throughout and beyond slavery.[39]

Du Bois was very likely correct in calling attention to the lack of organization in the African slave church, since organization along ethnic lines would have encouraged religious partisanship and exacerbated differences already difficult enough to bridge. The shadowy presence of the African church dictated a loose affiliation of ethnic peoples and practices at religious meetings, the ethnic aspects of which were necessarily secretive. It is such an important contribution that it bears repeating that Du Bois posited ethnic interaction in the religious realm "among all the members of each plantation across the South"; such recognition of African rituals is even today uncommon among historians of slavery and the acknowledgment that Africans consciously ordered them rarer still.

It is difficult to explain why Du Bois does not focus on the relationship of the spirituals to movement in the circle, all the more since he witnessed the relationship and as a graduate student encountered literature on the shout. His command of the Sea Islands experiment—his study of the Freedmen's Bureau grounded him in its literature of slave song—led him to encounter the circle with song in the writings of Higginson and others. Evidently he did not see the ring shout as an organizing principle in ethnic interaction or as essential to the music as art. The latter view would be understandable, since the spirituals were introduced to him without dance from early youth, which was how they were preserved by the Fisk Jubilee Singers, who "kept thrilling hearts, until a burst of applause in the Congregational Council at Oberlin revealed them to the world."[40]

The music caught his attention, and he considered it unrivaled in the New World. Moreover, he saw in the ability of the Jubilee Singers to sing "the slave songs so deeply into the world's heart that it can never wholly forget them again" a demonstration of the respect slave art could command.[41] The reputation of the singers was established some years before his arrival in Nashville, and his confidence in their music was supported almost half a century later with the advent of the singers Roland Hayes and Paul Robeson. What Du Bois sensed regarding the spirituals enabled him to proclaim them the national music:

> Little of beauty has America given the world save the rude grandeur God himself stamped on her bosom; the human spirit in this new world has expressed itself in vigor and ingenuity rather than in beauty. And so by fateful chance the Negro folk-song—the rhythmic cry of the slave—stands today not simply as the sole American music but as the most beautiful expression of human experience born this side the seas . . . it still remains as the singular spiritual heritage of the nation and the greatest gift of the Negro people.[42]

I I

Careful scholar that he was, Du Bois did not say the slaves became Christian, simply that the slave church was Christian, and he did not say precisely when it became so. Instead, he points to the forces behind the transformation: "Association with the masters, missionary effort and motives of expediency gave these African rites a thin veneer of Christianity" before the slave church became Christian.[43] But what we have seen following slavery, even on his evidence, is that blacks in the Christian church were much given not simply to African fervor but to placing the parameters of Africanity, via the shout, around Christianity, which meant it was Africanized. While it is impossible to know exactly how many slaves were Christian in 1865, Du Bois's figures are that well under half a million—probably closer to a quarter of a million—were Christian. What faith was practiced by those blacks who were neither Baptist nor Methodist? The evidence suggests, overwhelmingly, that large numbers of them at that time had little or no contact with Baptist and Methodist churches, that they preferred to affirm African religious values outside those denominations.[44]

It is surprising that Du Bois, who at Harvard wrote a pioneering dissertation on the slave trade, argues that there was a reduction in African cultural influence in the latter half of the eighteenth century, the peak period of the African slave trade into North America. This leads him to conclude that African spiritual influence had by 1750 failed to sustain a belief in African divinity, which made Africans ripe for the religion of resignation and patience that Christianity would foster. Had the slave trade not increased dramatically in the last half of the eighteenth century, the argument might be more understandable. But, considering the many thousands of Africans entering America in the decades following the American Revolution and the firm base of Africanity in their background, the mystery deepens, since no one in America had a surer grasp of the trade in all of its dimensions—cultural, economic, political, legal, and moral—than Du Bois at the time he made the argument in *The Souls of Black Folk*.[45]

There seems but one explanation; that he had underestimated the power of contemporary African cultures. This underestimation led him to conclude that New World blacks would lead the way to the redemption of Africa, a position from which he later backed away. In fact, scholarship on Africa at the time of the appearance of *Souls* was, except for that work, untouched by the complex and vital African influences on American slaves, the assumption being that nothing in the spiritual life of black Africa was worthy of study. It made little difference that the civilization of whites was represented in its lowest form in the South, for it was nonetheless deemed to be higher than that of the African. Du Bois realized that the African component made slave culture vastly superior to that of the slaveholder.[46]

Despite his underestimation of the continuing power of African culture in slavery, he had great faith in African potential, faith that gave him reason to believe that Afro-Americans, relying on themselves, might redeem Africa in the eyes of the world. He propounded this message after a two-year period of graduate study in Europe that profoundly influenced how he thought about the world. To be sure, it is remarkable that, steeped in European culture and history, he thought Africans would help determine the destiny of mankind. He held that view mainly because he believed that the currents of European civilization fed back into an ancient, original source, which gave him reason to conclude that black people had as much right as anyone to help fashion the future of the world.

The thesis that Africa had once been important in history was not encountered in class at Harvard. To be sure, professors there "continually stressed" in their classes "that there was a vast difference in the development of whites and the 'lower' races." At times, the generally cold atmosphere blacks endured during such discussions was more than matched by the books in which their people were discussed by some of their professors. George N. Shaler, who once ordered a white Southerner from class for objecting to the presence of a black student, thought blacks "by nature incapable of creating or maintaining societies of an order above barbarism." And Albert Bushnell Hart, who directed Du Bois's dissertation on the slave trade and encouraged him to do independent reading in Negro history, could write, "Race measured by race, the Negro is inferior, and his past history in Africa and in America leads to the belief that he will remain inferior in race stamina and race achievement."[47] There was no question in Cambridge that Europe had produced the highest form of civilization on earth.

With Africa and India at the center of her sphere of influence, it seemed England's reign in particular was unending, the status of people of color fixed forever as subordinate races. In fact, it appeared European civilization itself might last forever, a belief not easily shaken as Afro-Asia continued to sink beneath it as mudsill. The power of that civilization was ratified in the minds of men, reflected in magnificent museums and in cathedrals of grand design. Moreover, Du Bois observed that the development and the organization of European states for the past four centuries had been the norm and the pattern for the civilization of the world. While some nations had "stood apart, . . . in this century it can truly be said in Tokio and Hongkong—in Cairo and Cape Town—in Melbourne and Honolulu—in San Francisco and New York—as well as London, Paris and Berlin that the civilization of the 20th century is European."[48]

Harvard provided a key to that civilization but Berlin a greater one. It was, after all, one thing to study Europe from afar, another to study under its greatest professors at its best university. Du Bois elected to study at Berlin. His timing could hardly have been better. Not only was European political power cresting, but during his years there the German state had not been in existence long, which was especially important for one whose hero at Fisk was Bismarck: "He had made a nation out of a mass of bickering peoples," and this foreshadowed in Du Bois's mind "the kind of thing that American Negroes must do, marching forth with strength and determination under trained leadership."[49]

There was tangible evidence of European authority in German museums—ranked among the finest in the world—to which Du Bois devoted unusual attention, recording impressions in some detail in the course of explorations that took him to the great museums in the West, including one in which he saw a Rembrandt "in a burst of light at the end of the long hall in the gallery at Amsterdam." He thought *The Night Watch* masterly because of "its energy and action and wonderful play of light and shade." At Rome he saw Raphael's *Transfiguration*, in the galleries of Florence his picture of the Madonna and the Child and Saint John, and at Munich "others of his strangely beautiful conceptions of the Christ child." There was much more elsewhere and at Munich, where a great collection of

1,400 works of art in twelve salons and fourteen cabinets was "housed in a magnificent hall called the Alto [sic] Pinakothek."[50]

But the grandeur of the German polity was also evident; it was embodied in Wilhelm II, who "had utter faith in the future of Germany." Wilhelm envied the power of the British Empire, and "in his soul strove unceasingly the ambition of Bismarck and Prussia and the aristrocratic imperialism of his mother, a daughter of Queen Victoria." Du Bois saw him on the Unter den Linden when "time and again we students swung to the curb, and through the central arch of the Brandenburg Gate came the tossing of plumes and the prancing of horses, and splendid with shining armour and blare of trumpet there rode Wilhelm II, by the Grace of God, King of Prussia and German Emperor."[51]

The young scholar took each trip to a new European country and tied it to an interest in painting, sculpture, and architecture. Of the leading museums, he visited all but the one at Antwerp, studying the works of European masters. Not only was European political and economic power unquestioned, but European art was regarded as supreme. The evidence of European power even then towered toward the heavens, and was awe-inspiring, standing "as great monuments to European civilization." So it was when he sailed "along a blue rushing river, once, when suddenly rounding a bend, two dark and mighty towers seemed to shoot into the air, capping a wilderness of graceful fretwork and mighty buttress, standing there in that calm August day like twin giants. It was the Cathedral of Cologne."[52]

Du Bois saw a great deal of Europe and lectured about it on his travels on returning home to the black South. He saw the great green and yellow fields of Hungary that were "just fitted for sweeping and rolling winds" and, from Budapest east toward Poland, "wheeled across great fields glad with flocks and harvests, gliding sometimes for miles as straight as an arrow flies, then winding in great graceful curves." Among the peasants he "saw some faces as dark as mine own among men, with their wide flowing breeches, top boots and gaily ornamented jackets." And he saw and contemplated the history of Vienna:

> Here Marcus Aurelius, the Roman Caesar, died: here Charlemagne placed the bounds of his empire and here the great Rudolf of Hapsburg founded an empire that ruled the world five centuries. . . . Around Vienna the intrigues and victories of Napoleon centered . . . and here, after the downfall of the great Tyrant, sat the famous congress which parcelled out the world and declared the African slave trade a stench in the nostrils of humanity.[53]

Before an audience of Louisville blacks, he stressed the importance of European civilization and history: "How manifest it is, then, that the man or the nation that would know itself, must first know the vast organization of which it forms a part." Bearing in mind his experiences in Tennessee and possibly criticizing Booker Washington without mentioning him by name, he said that in a day

> when the battle of humanity is being fought with unprecedented fierceness and when the brunt of that battle is about to fall upon the shoulders of a black nation which though larger than the Greek State is half shrinking from its high mission to dabble in the mud of selfishness, it is well to pause in our perplexity and critically study the path before us, the hillsides round us—the dark heaths behind, where broods Sorrow. . . . [54]

At the Wilberforce Athletic Association in 1896, then later at Augusta, Georgia, before a less educated audience, he delivered his "The Art and Art Galleries of Modern Europe" lecture. Lofty in conception but altered in particulars, according to the audience, the lecture used the world of nature to ease the listener into art museums. In a passage clearly meant for humanity as a whole and blacks in particular, rather than for a privileged few, he said when addressing the athletic association,

> We who take interest in the training of men believe steadfastly and conscientiously in the full rounded development of man. We believe that there can be no sturdy moral growth without deep intellectual training; and we believe too that there can be no true lasting moral worth and mental development without healthy physical life. . . . [55]

He passed around a photo of the cathedral of Cologne and made reference, with commentary, to Praxiteles' *Venus of Milo,* which "stands today in the galleries of the Louvre at Paris." With a reference to the Arc de Triomphe, where the Parisian tour began, Du Bois and his audience swept down the Champs Elysées until at last they reached the Tuileries before passing marble statuary and clusters of gay Parisians, "until at last you approach great piles of buildings in the graceful renaissance architecture and passing by wings and through quadrangles you enter the famous galleries of the Louvre—without doubt the greatest art collection in the world." Again: "Here is a picture of the Cathedral of Cologne. Look at it and as you look let it grow larger: let the bold cruciform structure swell beyond the little confines of this room and of this building. . . . " And so on from one masterpiece to another.[56]

The lecture on art before the black audience in Georgia is an early indication of Du Bois's non-elitist approach to his people, of his belief in the capacity of the "ordinary," even small-town Southern blacks to appreciate the luminous world he brought before them. He thus distributed black-and-white photos of art objects while providing commentary as if he and his auditors were actually walking through a gallery. One wonders what Booker Washington, who thought few things as absurd as a Negro boy reading a French grammar in a country shack, would have thought of sizable numbers of relatively uneducated blacks in the Black Belt listening to a lecture entitled "The Art and Art Galleries of Modern Europe."

Wearing his spats and gloves and sporting his cane, Du Bois seemed to want to be European. But there is no better proof of the falsity of that impression than his interest in the uses to which nationalism might be put by his people. Self-respect and an awareness of what it had achieved in the past dictated that interest, for "the dawn of the twentieth century found white Europe master of the world and the white peoples almost universally recognized as the rulers for whose benefit the rest of the world existed." Indeed, there was every indication that Europeans thought people of color inferior and themselves superior. Recalling that period, Du Bois remarked,

Never before in the history of civilization had self-worship of a people's accomplishments attained the heights that worship of white Europe by Europeans reached. . . . The white race was pictured as "pure and superior; the black race as dirty, stupid, and inevitably inferior; the yellow race as sharing, in deception and cowardice, much of this color inferiority; while mixture of races was considered the prime cause of degradation and failure in civilization. Everything great, everything fine, everything really successful in human culture, was white.[57]

At that moment in history, Du Bois returned to Fisk to linger "in the joy and pain of meeting old school-friends." Ten years had gone by and there came over him a sudden longing to pass beyond the hills and "see the homes and the school of other days, and to learn how life had gone with [his] school-children; and [he] went." Josie had died, her mother saying simply, "We've had a heap of trouble since you've been away." Another student, with sufficient promise to have entered West Point, was in jail instead, and yet another, thoughtless and bold and "flushed with the passion of youth, bestowed herself on the tempter, and brought home a nameless child." His schoolhouse was gone, and in its place stood a certain ugly progress. He peered through the window and found that some things were familiar. Though the blackboard was not the same, "the seats were still without backs." His journey done, he wondered, "How shall man measure Progress there where the dark-faced Josie lies? How many heartfuls of sorrow shall balance a bushel of wheat?"[58]

The 1890s was the decade in which Du Bois discovered the tradition of black nationalism, to which he was especially susceptible following his years in the South. But his preference for a self-sufficient Negro culture might not have existed had he not known the richness of the folk heritage. At Harvard his studies of American Negro history, encouraged by Hart, were encompassing and deep. Through antebellum black writers, he first discovered that Africans played a decisive role in the construction of civilization, which was a main source of his faith in his people. Moreover, he became aware that self-assertion was central to the thought and activity of many antebellum black leaders, and he came to believe that nationalism alone would make possible an effective struggle by blacks. Because of his earlier and creative contact with his people and his intense study of them at Harvard, he was not overwhelmed by European civilization.

Nevertheless, the German example of nation building was one from which lessons might be learned by blacks fragmented on the African continent and wherever concentrated in the world. Yet Du Bois's reflections on his people were so rooted in artistic and spiritual concerns, so opposed to their absorption into the larger white culture, that the German model was far from adequate as a guide. He realized this and proceeded to develop his own views, which in time were highly critical of Western civilization generally. But he was under its influence then and, inevitably, throughout his life; much from that civilization would continue to strike him as valuable.

Like other intellectuals of his day, he first read history as the record of what the great world races, as opposed to nations, had achieved. Just as the English represented "constitutional liberty and commercial freedom," the Germans "science and philosophy," and the Romance peoples "art and literature," so other groups sought to bring to fruition their peculiar traits and ideals. The view that various races have special attributes, widely held by intellectuals of his time, dovetailed neatly with his own views, but he did not believe that one race had the right to abuse or to subjugate another or that there were superior and inferior people. He was, moreover, quite willing to set aside racial categories: "Three, five, twenty races were differentiated, until at last it was evident that mankind would not fit accurately into any scientific delimitation of racial categories; no matter what criteria were used, most men fell into intermediate classes or had individual peculiarities."[59]

In the tradition of nineteenth-century leaders of Afro-American thought, and in accordance with the terminology of his day, he considered people of color in America members of the "Negro race," and he hoped they would follow the logic of their largely unrecognized but natural tendencies of development. Before the American Negro Academy, of which Alexander Crummell was president, he asserted in 1897,

> If the Negro is ever to be a factor in the world's history—if among the gaily-colored banners that deck the broad ramparts of civilization is to hang one uncompromisingly black, then it must be placed there by black hands . . . hallowed by the travail of 200,000,000 black hearts beating in one glad song of jubilee. . . . The advance guard of the Negro people—the 8,000,000 people of Negro blood in the United States of America—must soon come to realize that if they are to take their just place in the van of Pan-negroism, then their destiny is *not* absorption with the white Americans.[60]

The contention that Afro-Americans constitute a progressive element among people of African ancestry with abilities that placed them in "the van of Pan-negroism" was in fact made by numerous nineteenth-century blacks, including Garnet and Crummell. This conception was pivotal to Du Bois's theory of Pan-African *leadership* that he developed for half a century following the address before the academy. His belief in racial gifts as the motive force of history, strongly held at the turn of the century, later yielded to the view that economic and psychological factors are more important shapers of man's past, present, and future. Nonetheless, he thought black people a permanent and distinct group in America with certain nonnegotiable values. They constituted "a *nation* stored with wonderful possibilities of culture," the destiny of which was "not a servile imitation of Anglo-Saxon culture, but a stalwart originality which shall unswervingly follow Negro ideals."[61]

The position that his people should unfailingly follow their own ideals meant that, though they should be aware of, they should not follow the ideals of others, certainly not unthinkingly. Thus, he rejected integration, unless it meant an exchange of values between blacks and whites. Otherwise, the struggle of blacks to overcome oppression would be absurd, especially considering his reservations in regard to American culture, later spelled out in some detail in *Souls*. He could not countenance Afro-American integration into a culture that he considered in many respects nonexistent, for he believed that white America had produced no art of value, no religion that it believed in, no human relations that gave it authority to counsel others.

In mentioning "Negro ideals," he was referring to African peoples as a whole. He thought *Africans* had a contribution to make to humanity and civilization that only they could make; it followed logically, from this premise, that people of African ancestry in America should maintain their racial identity until the fulfillment of their mission. Integration in its usual meaning of blacks entering a racist-free America would simply be an affirmation of continued white dominance, a new form of racism. Only when color no longer favored whites in this and other ways should blacks cease to organize around it.[62]

What is arresting in Du Bois's black nationalist projections before the American Negro Academy—in addition to his emphasis on the importance of originality—is his recognition of the need for "a Negro School of literature and art."[63] It is likely that he wanted to work out an autonomous aesthetic, one independent of European values and enabling black writers and artists to contribute to the liberation of their people. He was closer to the capability of his people than even he knew at the time, for the folklore of the slaves and their descendants offers an aesthetic that is peculiarly suited to interpreting the American reality. It is the natural base on which such a school of literature might be constructed, just as upon its foundations jazz—a Negro form of music—would soon be erected.

Du Bois's thought was marked by an emphasis on self-help. He urged

Negro intellectuals to impress upon their people "that they must not expect to have things done for them—THEY MUST DO FOR THEMSELVES"—must understand that "a little more dogged work and manly striving would do us more credit and benefit than a thousand force or Civil Rights bills." He thought no other "race more capable in muscle, in intellect, in morals, than the American Negro."[64] It is an intriguing formulation, which depended partly on his own authority and partly on the intellectual and moral record of a line of antebellum black leadership with which he had established contact by 1897. That line, passing through Alexander Crummell and Frederick Douglass, helped inspire, through Du Bois, a new generation of black leaders.

I I I

Du Bois saw Crummell at a Wilberforce commencement—"Tall, frail, and black . . . with simple dignity and an unmistakable air of good breeding." The young scholar displayed an uncharacteristic eagerness to talk and came to know the fineness of character of the older man, who for "fourscore years had . . . wandered in this same world of mine within the Veil." That commencement must have been a year or so before Du Bois's American Negro Academy address, and it is doubtful if anyone in his young manhood made a greater imprint on him than Crummell, before whom he bowed instinctively, "as one bows before the prophets of this world." There was irony in that act since Du Bois, in some respects, would prove himself to be greatly prophetic.[65]

Du Bois discovered that what Crummell experienced at Oneida had amounted to a revelation of desire and thought that resulted in a commitment to his people that would not be broken. He put the experience in terms especially appealing to Du Bois, who by that time personally knew the hardships of ex-slaves and had himself reached out in their direction. There came to Crummell at Oneida a

> vision . . . mystic, wonderful. . . . Yonder, behind the forest, he heard strange sounds; then glinting through the trees he saw, far, far away, the bronzed hosts of a nation, calling—calling faintly, calling loudly. He heard the hateful clank of their chains; he felt them cringe and grovel, and there rose within him a protest and a prophecy. And he girded himself to walk down the world.[66]

As the "host of a nation," whirling "like mad waters," turned toward him, Crummell "stretched forth his hands eagerly" and

> brought within his wide influence all that was best of those who walk within the Veil. They who live without knew not nor dreamed of that full power within, that mighty inspiration which the dull gauze of caste decreed that most men should not know. And now that he is gone, I sweep the Veil away

and cry, Lo! the soul to whose dear memory I bring this little tribute. I can see his face still, dark and heavy-lined beneath his snowy hair. . . . The more I met Alexander Crummell, the more I felt how much that world was losing which knew so little of him. In another age he might have sat among the elders of the land in purple-bordered toga. . . . [67]

A few years after his death, Crummell's name brought forth, "no incense of memory or emulation." His fate in the end was not unlike Garnet's, and he remained poor until death. What Du Bois said of him might easily have been said of Garnet: "And herein lies the tragedy of the age: not that men are poor,—all men know something of poverty; not that men are wicked,—who is good? Not that men are ignorant,—what is Truth? Nay, but that men know so little of men." The passage of Crummell's soul in death, in Du Bois's mind, recalled a primary source of inspiration of earlier times: "He sat one morning gazing toward the sea. He smiled and said, 'The gate is rusty on the hinges.' That night at star-rise a wind came moaning out of the West to blow the gate ajar, and then the soul I loved fled like a flame across the seas. . . . "[68]

Du Bois declared in 1900 that the history of the world, "both ancient and modern, has given many instances of no despicable ability and capacity among the blackest races of men": a handful of free blacks in the North, Crummell among them, had sought mastery of principles of European civilization and represented for Du Bois the qualities of leadership needed by the race. More especially, the intellectual-activist types who joined the antislavery movement constituted the principal model for the leadership theory that he was developing at the close of the century. Thus, knowledge of Negro history enabled him to master the essentials of Afro-American leadership of the past, to grasp and disentangle its main lines, and to select one he considered particularly relevant to his people's needs in the twentieth century.

There was the advocacy of violence of Gabriel and Vesey and Turner, which represented one line of leadership; the attempt to adjust to the will of the larger society another, represented by Purvis and Forten, before, failing in that direction, they turned to abolitionism "as a final refuge"; and, "finally, a determined effort at self-realization and self-development despite environing opinion," represented first by the formation of the African Methodist Episcopal Church, later by Remond, William Wells Brown, Nell, and Douglass, who ushered in "a new period of self-assertion and self-development":

To be sure, ultimate freedom and assimilation was the ideal before the leaders, but the assertion of the manhood rights of the Negro by himself was the main reliance, and John Brown's raid was the extreme of its logic. After the war and emancipation, the great form of Frederick Douglass, the greatest of American Negro leaders, still led the host. Self-assertion, especially in political lines, was the main programme, and behind Douglass came Elliot, Bruce,

and Langston, and the Reconstruction politicians, and less conspicuous
but of greater social-significance, Alexander Crummell and Bishop Daniel
Payne.[69]

Just as David Walker's "appeal against the trend of the times showed
how the world was changing after the coming of the cotton-gin," and just
as slavery by 1830 "seemed hopelessly fastened on the South," the defeat
of Reconstruction and the investments of the dominant North in the
South, with black political and civil rights no longer of concern to the
nation, meant that a new current would overwhelm any movement of
black people to assert their collective will. The time was not ripe for a
surge from below by a black minority in America, with colonialism growing in strength in Africa, Asia, and elsewhere in the colored world.
Hence, Du Bois's thesis, asserted almost as a challenge and growing out
of white domination of people of color: "THE problem of the twentieth
century is the problem of the color-line, the relation of the darker to the
lighter races of men in Asia and Africa, in America and the islands of the
sea."[70]

By the time of the appearance, in 1903, of his "The Talented Tenth"
essay, segregation by law was the rule in the South, and blacks, systematically removed from officeholding, were almost completely disfranchised.
Given the widespread and brutal suppression of black rights and the low
level of their education, one can understand why Du Bois did not think
them prepared to play a collective role in their liberation. With politics
and economics closed to them as a way out of oppression, he thought that
the exceptional among them would be their salvation, that blacks like all
other people would be saved by their men and women of genius: "The
problem of education, then, among Negroes must first of all deal with the
Talented Tenth; it is the problem of developing the Best of this race that
they may guide the Mass away from the contamination and death of the
Worst, in their own and other races."[71]

This position derived in part from the succesful educational experience
of a minority of blacks but in larger part from his recognition of the disadvantages that slavery had imposed. Whatever the limitations of his application of middle-class values to the mass of his people, his approach
showed an awareness of the degradation of slavery. He recognized that
middle-class values might in some respects serve a cleansing purpose for
blacks. But he failed to understand that educated blacks in most cases
would not devote themselves totally to their people's liberation, which
was what he intended.

Even a cursory reading of Du Bois makes clear his belief in the capacity
of the masses, so his Talented Tenth represented in some measure those
among his people who had benefited from opportunity as well as from
native endowment. Perhaps the most serious weakness of his theory,

however, was what he thought educated blacks had achieved in the past and how he assessed the traditions and customs of the black masses. His view that "from the very first it has been the educated and intelligent of the Negro people that have led and elevated the masses" seems to apply almost exclusively to the North, and even there it is not clear that this actually occurred. He is more persuasive when he argues for the importance of being aware of one's world and how it works. In that regard, it is true that free blacks had certain advantages in securing and acting on information of that kind and indeed did so. Without such an awareness, one could hardly function effectively when in competition with powerful men who benefited from the advantage of being white as well.

Du Bois underestimated the culture of the mass of his people during slavery and consequently to some extent thereafter; this led him to rely too strongly on the educated Negro, especially in the realm of values. Unfortunately, his treatment of the relationship of the "college-bred Negro" to the Negro cultural past lacks the integration of Negro culture and Negro leadership implicit in *The Souls of the Black Folk:* "It need hardly be argued that the Negro people need social leadership more than most groups; that they have no traditions to fall back upon, no long established customs. . . . All these things must be slowly and painfully evolved."[72]

For all his insight into slave culture, even Du Bois was unaware that that culture was affected by continuing African influences that were powerful and grounded in traditions going back a thousand years. His failure to see the ring shout in its wholeness was a factor in his not fully appreciating the power of African tradition in America. And yet that was not, as we have seen, entirely true, which leads one to wonder why he has nothing to say, in "The Talented Tenth" essay, about the artistic riches of the mass of blacks, of which he was the leading authority of his day. Could it be that, sensing the recoil from slave culture of most educated blacks, he thought it politic to stress the values of Western civilization? But it would have been out of character for him to set aside deeply held beliefs for the sake of currying favor with his contemporaries. Besides, all who were familiar with his writings by then knew that he was a champion of the culture of his people. We are left, then, with the explanation that the overwhelming concern of his essay—that blacks master the white man's world in order to have a chance of liberation—completely took the place of what normally would surely have found some expression.

Yet, one must also bear in mind that at the turn of the century Du Bois thought Africans uncivilized, and this at bottom is responsible for his notion that their descendants need the guidance, at least for a while, of an educated and dedicated few. He argued that blacks might be taught trades:

but that alone will not civilize a race of ex-slaves; we might simply increase their knowledge of the world, but this would not necessarily make them wish to use this knowledge honestly; we might seek to strengthen character and purpose, but what end if this people have nothing to eat or to wear? . . . our system of training must set before itself two great aims—the one dealing with knowledge and character, the other part seeking to give the child the technical knowledge necessary for him to earn a living under the present circumstances. These objects are accomplished in part by the opening of the common schools on the one, and of the industrial schools on the other. But only in part, for there must also be trained those who are to teach in these schools—men and women of knowledge and culture and technical skill who understand modern civilization, and have training and aptitude to impart it to the children under them.[73]

He had focused on a problem of compelling importance: How might the mass of black people earn a living and eventually live as knowledgeable beings on terms of relative equality with the majority of whites? That was the question confronting his people as the new century opened, when they were at one of the lowest points in their history and Booker Washington's leadership was still in the ascendancy.

One reason that Du Bois's criticism of Washington was relatively slow in coming, however, was that the two men shared the perception that "economic power must underlie all efforts of the American Negro to establish himself," and Washington had come forth with "the first clear and coherent plan to this end," enunciated in his celebrated speech at the Cotton States Exposition in Atlanta, in 1895. In addition, Du Bois believed that Washington, despite a certain opportunism, was genuinely interested in the liberation of his people, describing him as a man of "high ideals."[74]

But there was an irony in Du Bois's support of Washington in the 1890s because, as he was to demonstrate later, black workers immediately following slavery had the command of skilled jobs in the South that Washington, a generation later, urged them to achieve. In fact, most of the trades taught at Tuskegee were possessed by blacks in slavery, for how else might the plantations have been autonomous units? Not only did blacks cultivate the rice, tobacco, cotton, and other principal crops, but it has yet to be demonstrated that whites taught them the skills of that cultivation. While it is not certain that Du Bois, like Delany, knew whether Africans brought such knowledgte to America, there is no doubt that he knew their labor was the source of the South's wealth and of much of the nation's.[75]

Whatever the achievement of the masses of blacks, leadership was still required, and in this context Du Bois saw clearly the continuing need for the formally trained black to protect and build on the gains of the Reconstruction era. Of all who had helped them during Reconstruction, only their teachers were not driven away by the overthrow of Reconstruction. It was, in fact, through the private colleges, the public schools, and the organization of the Negro church that the Negro "acquired enough leadership and knowledge to thwart the worst designs of the new slave drivers." What Du Bois observed of his people in Tennessee he later described: "They bent to the storm of beating, lynching and murder, and kept their souls in spite of public and private insult of every description; they built an inner culture which the world recognizes in spite of the fact that it is still half-strangled and inarticulate."[76] Du Bois wanted to tap that cultural potential without delay: He was the custodian of the unencumbered spirit of his people. On the other hand, Washington wanted black people to be indispensable to whites, considering this their chief means of freeing themselves—when they had already been indispensable to whites during slavery.

Probably no one was as conversant as Du Bois with the terror the emancipated slaves experienced as the white South, through the Black Codes, attempted to reenslave them. Having studied the slave era and Reconstructon on his own at Harvard, he knew Washington was misguided in thinking that blacks started at the top rather than at the bottom following slavery. It was, therefore, not just the violence that swept over blacks in the last quarter of the century that caused Du Bois to question Washington's position. Nor was it merely Washington's lack of depth on economic issues. It was also the white South's lack of respect for and hatred of slaves, no matter how they behaved, that was behind Du Bois's growing dissatisfaction with Washington.

Moreover, Du Bois had stormed the heights of European civilization. What he never said about that civilization in relation to Washington is perhaps as important as what he stated: that one had to have command of its theoretical postulates, of the sources of its strength, in order to protect oneself from—in order to oppose—its power. In a sense, therefore, Washington's deemphasis on higher education struck Du Bois as absurd. There was, in a word, a qualitative difference in the conceptions of freedom the two men envisioned for their people. Almost with each essay, as the new century opened, Du Bois was building the case against Washington, which became overwhelming with the appearance of *The Souls of Black Folk*.

In fact, the foundation of his assault on Washington was laid as early as 1897 with the publication of "Strivings of the Negro People," in which he exhibits a faith in the potential of the mass of his people that Washington never had. Symbolic of that faith was the lecture entitled "The Art Galleries of Europe" before an ordinary assemblage of Negroes. And just as "Strivings of the Negro People" became "Of Our Spiritual Strivings" in *Souls*—and conceptually one of the most important statements on race relations in this century—"The Freedmen's Bureau," published in 1901, became "Of the Dawn of Freedom." Moreover, in 1901, his direct response to Washington, in firm but carefully honed language, was published as "The Evolution of Negro Leadership" before appearing as "Of Mr. Booker T. Washington and Others."[77]

It was simply a matter of timing, of deciding when Washington's program had been given adequate opportunity to show its worth that was decisive for Du Bois, not whether he shared in any fundamental way Washington's vision of the future of black people. Du Bois's whole orientation, his intellectual references and historical models were far removed from those of Washington, who admired capitalists and hated unions. As he would make increasingly clear with time, Du Bois was struck by the essential vulgarity of the Andrew Carnegies and was opposed to any alliance of black workers with a system responsible for the enslavement of their fathers.

There is a dimension of Du Bois's thought, also related to Washington, that merits additional attention, namely, his belief in the importance of refinement of character as an object of leadership. On this matter, his training in philosophy served to deepen his interest in a subject natural to one of his ethical concerns. But another influence was every bit as decisive in determining his attitude toward character formation. Its source can be traced back to Walker in Du Bois's writings, an interesting development since his earliest written reference is to Walker's "wild *Appeal*," a view that later, for reasons not altogether clear, underwent drastic revision.[78]

It is fortunate that it did, for who in the nineteenth century had a greater interest in character building than Walker? In his *Appeal* one finds perhaps the most compelling moral case against American slavery on record, a curious mixture of moral suasion and the utility, if men do not change their ways, of violence. The moral component in his thought is what attracted Garnet to him and what Du Bois was eventually aware of in calling the *Appeal* "that tremendous indictment of slavery." Du Bois saw it call to resistance "coming down through the work of the Niagara Movement and the National Association for the Advancement of Colored People in our day." In fact, he hailed the *Appeal* as the harbinger of the abolitionist movement and saw in it a "program of organized opposition" to the racism of whites that included "ceaseless agitation and insistent demand for equality. . . . It involves the use of force of every sort: moral suasion, propaganda and where possible even physical resistance." Walker's almost desperate exhortation to unity is echoed in Du Bois's acknowledgment that the success of such a program presupposes "a large degree of inner union and agreement among Negroes." The tradition fostered by Walker was as important in Du Bois's spiritual maturation, through Crummell in particular, as anything out of Europe.[79]

It is noteworthy that he linked Walker's *Appeal* to the program of the

Niagara movement, because the worsening condition of blacks made it necessary to protest vigorously against the rising tide of reaction after 1900. A new organization of leadership was needed. Thus, in the Niagara movement, whose very composition and symbolism gave substance to the theory behind Du Bois's leadership concept, men of the caliber of Monroe Trotter, Carter G. Woodson, and John Hope joined forces at places like Harpers Ferry, "the scene of John Brown's martyrdom"; Oberlin, Ohio, the center of western abolitionism; and Niagara Falls, where runaway slaves sought refuge on the Canadian side. The spirit of militancy was thereby evoked almost poetically in the selection of meeting places. A certain deceptive serenity among those gathered at Niagara in 1905 was captured as Du Bois sat for a photo wearing a bow tie and the broad brimmed hat of the day, flanked by half a dozen others with bow ties, a number of them wearing derbies.[80]

Within a few years the Niagara movement gave way to the NAACP, which Du Bois helped found, and that organization continued in a more sustained and specialized form the legal, educational, and other concerns of Niagara. Du Bois became director of research and publications and created one of the most important little magazines of the century, the *Crisis,* which supported itself for many years and largely made possible Du Bois's autonomy of voice within the NAACP. As he did for Niagara, so he did for the NAACP: he defined the nature of the struggle for racial justice and set forth the objectives toward which the civil rights movement would exert itself in the twentieth century. Tremendous self-discipline and confidence were required, for Du Bois, in a series of books and in countless journal pieces, often went against authority. His scholarship proved to be as important in the long run as his civil rights work, and he insisted on having at hand in his NAACP office in New York a sizable library on which to draw in developing his thoughts on how to vindicate people of African ancestry.

I V

Despite his respect for European civilization, Du Bois early set himself the task of exploring and writing the history of his people, relating it at critical points to the history of Europe and to the history of the world, with the result that his published work as a whole constitutes the most impressive argument to date against the theory and practice of racism. Indeed, much of his thought lends itself to what has become known as Negritude theory, especially the belief that people of African ancestry have spiritual, artistic, and psychological qualities that distinguish them from Europeans. That belief and the defense of the race against attempts to traduce it in history are indeed essential ingredients of the Negritude thought developed by him. In this regard, his formulations prefigured much of the theorizing of Aimé Césaire, Leopold Sedar Senghor, and, before them, Paul Robeson. Yet one must keep in mind that Martin Delany laid a portion of the foundation of Negritude thought.

Du Bois was almost certainly influenced by Delany in developing his position on spiritual and other values peculiar to his people, for Delany offers the classic antebellum statement on the subject and provides a point of departure for those developing the Negritude tradition since his time. His observations regarding the artistic and moral/spiritual attributes of African people ushered in a nascent form of Negritude. His urging that the positive values of his people be universalized was far-seeing and remains an important point of illumination in an era in which parochialism characterizes a "black nationalist" mode of thought that has little in common with the best of nineteenth-century black nationalism.[81]

Du Bois's thought shows the influence of the typical Social Darwinist statement of spiritual and psychic racial differences, but his modifications are significant. Moreover, since he subscribed to the view that Africa strongly influenced Afro-American culture and that this influence was worth preserving, he revealed an appreciation for the contemporary cultures of Africa, whatever his reservations, that was almost completely absent from the thought of previous nationalists, except for Delany. In so doing, he effected a revolution in the development of black nationalist thought. But his formulations on the distinguishing features of people of African ancestry did not develop suddenly; they were in fact elaborated throughout much of his life, as were his ideas about how African liberation might be achieved.

Du Bois's Pan-Africanism and the Negritude theory that he brought to fruition were of a piece in his thought and activity, for he developed various components of each over his entire adult life. Both concepts were integral to his vision of his people as free and whole. In fact, he brought an unusual grasp of the spiritual life of African people to his Pan-African concerns, and he used black folklore as an important index to their spiritual condition. In addition, he held high the ideal of autonomy that had been preserved by generations of free blacks, extending from Walker's generation to that of Garnet and beyond. The idea of African autonomy in the arts was perceived in its fullness by Du Bois as early as the American Negro Academy address and had a prominent place in his concept of nationalism, not least because art was for Du Bois a means of providing his people with a better sense of what they could become, which Negritude theory took into account.

That theory sprang in part from a duality—from being "an American, a Negro; two souls, two thoughts, two unreconciled strivings; two warring ideals in one dark body whose dogged strength alone keeps it from being torn asunder." His insistence that such a crisis should be identified and treated was an important advance, positing, as he did, a black identity in addition to being American and asserting, as was true, that his people as a whole were struggling to preserve their identity as blacks. In so doing, he highlighted the central need of his people—to be themselves. This recognition, together with his insights into the culture of slavery, enabled him to go a long way toward distinguishing between that which is African and that which is American in the black ethos. He was therefore able to begin to offer an extended explanation of why Afro-Americans behave as they do. With this knowledge he was in a position to strengthen the African side of their consciousness. It was important work, for the tension in the souls of black folk was often quite destructive.

> This waste of double aims, this seeking to satisfy two unreconciled ideals, has wrought sad havoc with the courage and faith and deeds of ten thousand thousand people,—has sent them often wooing false gods and invoking false means of salvation, and at times has even seemed about to make them ashamed of themselves.[82]

He believed that white people should not attempt to resolve the problems of race by having people of African descent turn their backs on their heritage. The nature of the gifts of black people was such that they should appropriate only certain features of the larger society. Each race could learn from the other; the goal of human brotherhood could be achieved through a unifying conception of race, with the two "world-races" (the black and the white) giving "each to each characteristics both so sadly lack":

> We the darker ones come not altogether empty-handed . . . there is no true American music but the wild sweet melodies of the Negro slave; the American fairy tales and folk-lore are Indian and African; and, all in all, we black men seem the sole oasis of simple faith and reverence in a dusty desert of dollars and smartness.[83]

Freedom, then, would mean reciprocity. Blacks would be prepared at the very least to negotiate an arrangement by which their artistic and spiritual values would be protected in any new order. If the Americans were wise, they would embrace those values themselves, just as Afro-Americans should take advantage of certain features of the larger society, especially technology. That would not mean approval of capitalism, however, for this would conflict with his view that his people provided a gift of the spirit, which is not acquisitive.[84] His opposition to capitalism was not pronounced in his university days or shortly thereafter, but one senses it in his American Negro Academy address as well as in the statement above.

For all their gifts to America, blacks suffered from being black in a world controlled by whites who insisted that black was ugly and dirty and white beautiful and pure; as a result, many blacks believed what they

were taught about themselves. A corrective was needed, and Du Bois
sought in part to supply it, in 1899, in poetic form:

> I am the smoke king
> I am black
> I am darkening with song;
> I am hearkening to wrong;
> I will be black as blackness can
> The blacker the mantle the mightier the man
>
> . . . .
>
> The blacker the mantle the mightier the man
>
> I am carving God in night,
> I am painting hell in white,
> I am the smoke king
> I am black.[85]

In this poem we find a distinctive characteristic of Negritude poetry.
Specifically, Du Bois transforms blackness into a desirable characteristic,
inverts the qualities usually associated with whiteness, suggesting the
blackness of God and the whiteness of hell. Here surely he was attempting to strengthen the Afro-American's acceptance of being black, of being
Negro. In addition, Du Bois felt that blackness must somehow be accepted by whites if mutual respect was to be achieved. His interest in a
cultural synthesis implied as much, and that interest was repeated by
poets and philosophers of Negritude following him.[86]

Du Bois thought the attributes of being Negro developed "deep in the
forest fastness and by the banks of low, vast rivers, in the deep tense quiet
of the jungle," where "the human soul whispered its folk tales, carved its
pictures, sang its rhythmic songs, and danced and danced and danced."
The emphasis on rhythm is often repeated in his descriptions of African
ceremony and in some ways anticipated Robeson on the subject. But his
references to the human soul also include one that recalls the tragic soul-
life conception, his hearing in the spirituals "the sorrow of riven souls
suddenly articulate . . . the defiance of deathless hope"—the uncon-
querableness of the human spirit.[87]

In "Star of Ethiopia," a pageant that played before thousands of his
people during World War I, Du Bois attempted to use the past, in
Negritude style, to erase self-hatred among his people, to inspire in the
present and ennoble in the future. Against the European canon of black
inferiority, he placed a contribution, alleged to have been African, to
man's emergence into the industrial era—the smelting of iron. He proclaimed a "Dark inspiration of iron times," implying that Africans were
the first to smelt iron, a position later contradicted by the view that iron
smelting began somewhere in the vicinity of Turkey.[88]

The anthropologist Franz Boas had introduced Du Bois to the thesis that Africans were the first to smelt iron, as he had introduced him to the history of kingdoms of the Sudan while visiting at Atlanta University in 1906, and both perspectives made a powerful impact on Du Bois. As important as they were, and despite Du Bois's use of them in attempting to establish, before the incredulous American intellectual community, some record of respectable human history—of humanity—for his people, there was a need to address their history at an earlier time in the Nile Valley, for nineteenth-century scholars presented blacks in the most unfavorable light possible. The argument went that blacks had not improved upon their condition for thousands of years, because their native endowment hardly allowed for progress.

The assault led to a black response, almost as an act of self-defense. Of the long line of Afro-American writers who did respond, it was Du Bois who answered the traducers of African peoples in the most impressive way. In a series of histories over the span of thirty years, he responded to the most important argument of the detractors; that Egypt was a white civilization and Ethiopia "a far-off frontier and slave mart." Scholarship on Egypt was so consequential because "it was in the valley of the Nile that the most significant continuous human culture arose, significant not necessarily because it was absolutely the oldest or the best, but because it led to that European civilization of which the world boasts today and regards in many ways as the greatest and last word in human culture.[89]

So strong was racist thought that whites who disagreed with the thesis that ancient Egypt was white kept silent. Others, more common, denied the evidence of their eyes while looking at the achievements of black humanity. Though the comte de Volney, the noted French scholar, called the Nile Valley civilization Negro after visiting there, such was the "barrage of denial from later men that he withdrew his earlier conclusions, not because of further investigation, but because of scientific public opinion in the nineteenth-century." The American Egyptologist George Andrew Reisner unearthed a black civilization in Ethiopia but quickly said it was not a Negro civilization. To this Du Bois countered that the whole effort "to delimit" races might be given up, "but we cannot if we are sane, divide the world into whites, yellows and blacks, and then call blacks white."[90]

No argument concerning the place of the Negro in Egyptian civilization could be more persuasive than the manner in which Egyptians depicted themselves and those contending for power with them going back thousands of years. Slaves with full lips and kinky hair are on the walls of ancient buildings in such numbers as to indicate their impact in the culture if their kind had never helped to form the royal line. As Du Bois wrote, moreover, "The Egyptians painted themselves usually a brown, sometimes dark brown, sometimes reddish brown. Other folk, both Egyptians and non-Egytians, were painted as yellow."[91] Other kinds of evidence, too, support Du Bois's thesis that blacks were an integral component of Egyptian civilization.

A walk through the British Museum reveals, so routinely as to be shocking, a black presence in the features of those depicted in statues that line the corridors of the Egyptian section. But that presence is found in splendor in artifacts in the Cairo Museum, where a single reign, that of Tutankhamen, revealed the truth of Du Bois's argument not only that Egypt is on the continent of Africa but also that black men and women are prominent in its royal history. In addition to blacks being represented on the throne of the pharaoh and as a part of royalty generally, their significant influence on Egytian leadership and society can be established in other ways: a stool in the Cairo Museum, on which the pharaoh places his feet in mockery, contains the carved faces of dangerous foes—and the faces are black.[92]

The validity of Du Bois's thesis that Egyptians have long been a mulatto population is suggested by contemporary Egyptians, who in general range from brown to light in complexion, with those of unmistakable blackness often represented as well. In fact, there seems no basis whatever for the argument, developed in the slave era, that Egyptians are white and that blacks enter that civilization, when they enter at all, as slaves or as menials. That argument was vital to the slaveholding thesis that blacks are inherently inferior, the natural subjects of white men. If they were—and leading theorists like Harvard's Louis Agassiz implied as much—then blacks were simply ciphers in human memory. One's place in history, consequently, has been an important concern of proponents of Negritude theory, and Du Bois led in countering advocates of black inferiority:

> There can be but one adequate explanation of this vagary of nineteenth-century science: it was due to the fact that the rise and support of capitalism called for rationalization based upon degrading and discrediting the Negroid peoples. It is especially significant that the science of Egyptology arose and flourished at the very time that the cotton kingdom reached its greatest power on the foundation of American Negro Slavery. We may then without further ado ignore the verdict of history.[93]

He argued that the earliest Egyptians were Negroid, that at a later time the mulatto population of Egypt, according to tradition, "believed themselves descended not from the whites or the yellows, but from the black peoples of the South. Thence they traced their origin, and toward the South in earlier days they turned the faces of their buried corpses."[94] This would seem to be consistent with the theory that human civilization was carried north from black Africa, a view that has gained new adherents with recent archaeological discoveries in Kenya that suggest that the dim light of civilization glowed there, surrounded by a sea of darkness, for thousands of years before being extended elsewhere. The anthropologist Charles M. Nelson of the University of Massachusetts is inclined to believe that civilization began and underwent significant development in the area of present-day Kenya 18,000–15,000 years before the birth of Christ with the discovery of the cultivation of grain and the domestication of cattle.

In a report in the *New York Times,* in 1980, Nelson commented, "From our earliest school days we are taught that civilization first developed in the Middle East and then spread to India, Central Asia, Europe and North Africa." But the new discoveries have caused him to doubt that thesis. The presence of nonindigenous cattle in the area of the discovery 15,000 years ago figured in the pre–Iron Age economy of the people, leading him to reason that "a relatively sophisticated society existed at the time." That society "could have spread its mores, living modes and philosophy, eventually reaching the fertile crescent of the Euphrates River Valley, where the present-day regions of Iraq, Syria, Lebanon, Jordan and Israel are often referred to as the cradle of civilization." But Nelson remarked that the findings of his team of anthropologists "and recent discoveries by other scientists of 18,000-year-old domesticated grain crops in Africa raised doubts about that position."[95]

Du Bois's affirmation of a thesis advanced by Joseph P. Widney, long before the findings of Nelson and other scholars working in Kenya were known, seems far more perceptive today than when Du Bois was first intrigued by it, seventy years ago:

> Back in the centuries which are scarcely historic, where history gives only vague hintings, are traces of a widespread, primitive civilization, crude, imperfect, garish, barbaric, yet ruling the world from its seats of power in the valley of the Ganges, the Euphrates, and the Nile, and it was of the Black races. The first Babylon seems to have been of a Negroid Race. The earlier Egyptian civilization seems to have been Negroid. It was in the days before the Semite was known in either land. The Black seems to have built up a great empire, such as it was, by the waters of the Ganges before Mongol or Aryan. Way down under the mud and slime of the beginnings . . . is the Negroid contribution to the fair superstructure of modern civilization.[96]

It was, therefore, no integrationist impulse that led Du Bois to seek mastery of European culture and to urge other blacks to do so. His efforts here represent a new dimension of Negritude thought, since he was convinced that black Africa more than fertilized the field of European culture. Thus he wrote,

> I sit with Shakespeare and he winces not. Across the color line I move arm in arm with Balzac and Dumas, where smiling men and welcoming women glide in gilded halls. From out of the caves of evening that swing between the strong-limbed earth and the tracery of the stars, I summon Aristotle and Au-

relius and what soul I will, and they all come graciously with no scorn nor condescension. So, wed with Truth, I dwell above the Veil.[97]

Precisely because the expectations of European civilization had been so continuous and high and its power seemingly limitless, the decline of that civilization was doubly traumatizing. World War I was the first portent of the eventual collapse of the European order, an event that shook the faith of even formerly sanguine admirers. It was under the circumstances, easier than ever for one with Du Bois's understanding of Europeans and their history to question certain European standards, including those of physical beauty. He rejected "the blue-eyed, white-skinned types" encountered in literature and school, as "old standards of beauty" beckoned once more—"rich, brown and black men and women with glowing dark eyes and crinkling hair." And he was convinced that "the plantation song of the slave is more in unison with the 'harmony of the spheres' than Wagner's greatest triumph."[98] But Du Bois sensed a watershed in the history of Africa with the clash of opposing forces in Europe and saw in the war the hope of a growing unity among Africans, despite their suppressed status everywhere. Still, the cost to Africa was real and lasting as thousands died in battle. Senegalese troops faced the German guns and "raised the war cry in a dozen different Sudanese tongues" until their cries "became fainter and fainter and dropped into silence as not a single black man was left living on that field." They had not faltered when the artillery was fired but, poorly armed and untrained, had marched "straight into death." To Blaise Diagne, a Senegalese deputy in the French parliament who had sent a hundred thousand African soldiers to France at a critical moment, Du Bois went "to ask the privilege of calling a Pan-African Congress in Paris during the Versailles Peace Conference."[99]

Diagne was the "ace" Du Bois had up his sleeve after failing to get a conference with Woodrow Wilson, who he had hoped might help arrange a Pan-African Congress. Apparently Diagne was actuated by a questionable amount of African nationalism, for Du Bois wrote, "He was a tall, thin Negro, nervous with energy, more patriotic in his devotion to France than many of the French." Nevertheless, Du Bois convinced him of the importance of having a Pan-African Congress. Diagne used his influence with Clemenceau, and after a delay of two months permission was given for the congress to convene in Paris in the winter of 1919. "Of the fifty-seven delegates," from fifteen countries, recorded Du Bois, "nine were African countries with twelve delegates. Of the remaining delegates, sixteen were from the United States and twenty-one from the West Indies." But most of the delegates were already residing in France. Many more would have been in attendance, representing the black world, had the colonial powers and America not "refused to issue special visas."[100]

Even so, the congress was one of the more sizable gatherings of *leaders* from various parts of the African diaspora. The mere fact that the meeting, as modest as it was, took place indicates that an important change was taking place in the modern world, that the unity of black leaders from various parts of the world was beginning to grow.

Though imperialism and colonialism were strong in Africa in 1919 and though the Paris meeting "had no deep roots in Africa itself," Du Bois hoped that self-determination for Africans in increments would lead eventually to African repossession of the continent, which might bring enormous consequences: "We can, if we will, inaugurate on the dark continent a last great crusade for humanity. With Africa redeemed, Asia would be safe and Europe indeed triumphant."[101] That and other news of the congress was picked up by the American press, and some of the media sought additional information. Walter Lippmann, the young editor of the *New Republic,* wrote to Du Bois "in his crabbed hand," on February 20, 1919, "I am very much interested in your organization of the Pan-African Conference, and glad that Clemenceau has made it possible. Will you send me whatever reports you may have on the work?"[102]

What were Du Bois's deepest reflections on the Pan-African past and its relationship to the future as the congress occurred? His ideas on the sources of Pan-Africanism led him to consider ethnic interaction as its basis. He saw in that a reflection in microcosm of the Pan-African ideal "of one Africa to unite the thought and ideals of all native peoples of the dark continent." That ideal, he thought, belongs "to the twentieth century and stems naturally from the West Indies and the United States."[103]

His ability to relate the New World black experience to the problems of the ancestral home, to grasp the most important aspect of that experience and place it at the center of the Pan-African vision, was revolutionary: in the Americas, "various groups of Africans quite separate in origin, became so united in experience and so exposed to the impact of new cultures that they began to think of Africa as one idea and one land."[104] In a word, he placed Pan-Africanism on its foundation and saw the connection between pan-Africanization and the free black's concern for the whole of Africa. "Thus late in the eighteenth century when a separate Negro church was formed in Philadelphia it called itself 'African'; and there were various 'African' societies in many parts of the United States."[105] He put his finger on the vital nexus and was, therefore, the father of pan-Africanism in that very special way.

Du Bois integrated relevant documentation on Africans into his thinking on Pan-Africanization and associated that evidence with Negritude as well; and he associated the roots of Negritude in America with ethnic interaction in slavery. A section of a book by the German traveler Georg August Schweinfurth especially caught his eye, one in which underlying

African unities are discussed with richly suggestive implications for blacks in New World slavery:

> If we could at once grasp and set before our minds facts that are known (whether as regards language, race, culture, history, or development) of that vast region of the world which is comprehended in the name of Africa, we should have before us the witness of an intermingling of races which is beyond all precedent. And yet, bewildering as the prospect would appear, it remains a fact not to be gainsaid, that it is impossible for any one to survey the country as a whole without perceiving that high above the multitude of individual differences there is throned a principle of unity which embraces well-nigh all the population.[106]

The suppression of black rights in the United States never led Du Bois to deemphasize the importance of Pan-Africanism. Indeed, the summer of 1919, when white mobs turned on blacks with murderous fury, was a time when the need for African unity was self-evident. Thus, he promoted the rights of all Africans from his NAACP office in New York as naturally as he fought for the rights of Afro-Americans because, in his mind, theirs was the same struggle. Consequently, within months of the Pan-African Congress, in September 1919, in the afterglow of the "red summer," he raised "the terrible weapon of Self-Defense," declaring in a *Crisis* special number on labor that no people had ever given submission and passive resistance "to Evil longer, more piteous trial." But patience should have run its course as the number of lynchings of Afro-Americans reached well over two thousand in the period following Reconstruction to the summer of 1919.

> When the murderer comes, he shall not longer strike us in the back. When the armed lynchers gather, we too must gather armed. When the mob moves, we propose to meet it with bricks and clubs and guns . . . but we must carefully and scrupulously avoid on our own part bitter and unjustifiable aggression against anybody. Honor, endless, and undying Honor to every man, black or white, who in Houston, East St. Louis, Washington and Chicago gave his life for Civilization and Order.[107]

A few years later, Du Bois made his first trip to Africa. He visited the Palm Grove cemetary where Garnet is buried, and he went into the "bush" of several West African countries—Liberia, Sierra Leone, and Senegal among them—to mingle with ethnic Africans. In Liberia, standing before a thatched hut and flanked by an African man and woman, Du Bois, shading his eyes from the sun, in bow tie and carrying an umbrella, posed for a picture that later appeared in the *Crisis*. In the picture, he appears entirely at home. In fact, his spirit was refreshed at the fount of African culture in ways that recall aspects of slave culture: in two months in West Africa, he met "no impudent children or smart and overbearing young folk." Not only did he encounter only politeness in personal contact with Africans but, what seemed to him more relevant: he also saw "the natives uniformly polite to each other-to old and young." Considering "the awkward and ignorant missionaries sometimes sent to teach the heathen," he thought it would be a fine thing "if a few natives could be sent here to America to teach manners to black and white."[108]

On Christmas Eve he found African men, women, and children—Krus and Fanti—singing and marching through the night into the dawn. They had felt the impact of Christianity, absorbed it, and sung back revival hymms in words "hidden in an unknown tongue-liquid and sonorous." Du Bois found the music "tricked and expounded with cadence and turn . . . that same trick . . . heard first in Tennessee 38 years ago." The song was "raised and carried by the men's strong voices, while floating above in obbligato" could be heard "the high, mellow voices of women—it is the ancient African art of part singing so curiously and insistently different." As they sang and marched, the dark warm heat of night steamed "up to meet the moon. And the night is song."[109]

In "little Portraits of Africa," he sang of Africa's spell:

The spell of Africa is upon me. The ancient witchery of her medicine is burning my drowsy, dreamy blood. This is not a country, it is a world—a universe of itself and for itself, a thing. . . . Different, Immense, Menacing, Alluring. It is so burning, so fire encircled that one bursts with terrible soul inflaming life. One longs to leap against the sun and then calls, like some great hand of fate, the slow, silent, crushing power of almighty sleep—of Silence, of immovable Power beyond, within, around. Then comes the calm. The dreamless beat of midday stillness at dusk, at dawn, at noon. . . . Life slows down and as it slows it deepens; it rises and descends to immense and secret places. Unknown evil appears and unknown good. Africa is the Spiritual Frontier of human kind.[110]

He apparently missed the irony of his posture: "I am riding on the singing heads of black boys swinging in a hammock. The smooth black bodies swing and sing, the neck set square, the hips sway. O lovely voices and sweet young souls of Africa."[111] His perceptions seem the more remarkable when it is borne in mind that he was describing indigenous Africans, not Americo-Liberians.

By no means consistent in references to his African contemporaries, he was more impressed after contact with them than he had been from afar. Yet it should be said that his knowledge of contemporary Africans grew dramatically after contact with Boas and was unusual for an American of his time. The best of his thought on the subject appeared in the *Crisis* together with mention of the most advanced activity and thought of Afro-Americans. In the same issue of the *Crisis* that contains his most entrancing prose on Africa—a prose that seems equal in eloquence to any poetry—there is, for example, a photo of Paul Robeson and an announcement that Robeson will play the lead in "Eugene O'Neill's 'All God's Chillun Got Wings,' with the Provincetown players in April."[112]

Du Bois thought that Africa, standing at the spiritual frontier of the world, presented "the wild and beautiful adventures of its taming! But oh the cost thereof—the endless, endless cost!"[113] It was no naive boast, considering the bursts of creativity with which slave artists met oppression, their potential not half-realized under such circumstances. Besides, African values were among the most ancient in the world, and it was Africa that was destined to give birth, painful as it would be, to a new humanity that would utilize the material and the spiritual in new ways. Du Bois sketched a dazzling picture of mankind's perfection, of humanity's mastery of what Robeson later called the art of living:

> Then will come a day—an old and ever, ever young day when there will spring in Africa a civilization without coal, without noise, where machinery will sing and never rush and roar, and where men will think and sleep and dance and lie prone before the rising suns, and women will be happy. *The objects of life will be revolutionized.* Our duty will not consist in getting up at seven, working furiously for six, ten and twelve hours, eating in sullen ravenousness or extraordinary reflection. No—we shall dream the day away and in cool dawns, in little swift hours, do all our work.[114]

The word from which *Negritude* is derived did not disturb Du Bois. He had written books—*The Philadelphia Negro* and *The Negro*—with that appellation in the title. It is true that he seemed to prefer *black* in naming his books—*The Souls of Black Folk, The Gifts of Black Folk, Black Reconstruction, Black Folk Then and Now, The Black Flame,* and so on. Still, as a 1928 exchange revealed, he was not offended by references to his people as Negroes. Sounding much like Sidney, he conjured his critic not to mistake names for things. If a thing is not respected, whatever the reason, "you will not alter matters by changing its name." He added,

> Without the word that means Us, where are all those spiritual ideals, those inner bonds, those group ideals and forward strivings of this mighty army of 12 millions? Should we abolish these with the abolition of a name? Do we want to abolish them? Of course we do not. They are our most precious heritage.[115]

V

In contrast to the African optic on the external world, the external world for the European, Du Bois thought, is mere matter to be controlled—manipulated by man, but not necessarily for the well-being of all or even the few. He began thinking seriously about this position while a graduate student and developed it for at least fifty years thereafter, concluding that the European has dangerously generalized his attitude toward the external world to include other human beings; that externality for the European is not limited by the unconscious material world but is everything that is not oneself. Thus, science developed in the West as a "Frankenstein" monster, and freedom became the "freedom to destroy freedom"—a thesis Du Bois put forward in the 1930s, a few years following the presentation of essentially the same argument by Paul Robeson, who was writing from London.[116] While it was not an original argument, both men in their own terms, working independently, placed it in a context that made it so—the need to counter such a threat to human civilization through the affirmation of African values that oppose the primacy of the individual over mankind and nature.

Before an all-black audience in Louisville, Kentucky, earlier in the century, Du Bois had set forth a position related to the European attitude toward nature, and he greatly elaborated on it in subsequent years. In his "Spirit of Modern Europe" address, he noted that in the eighteenth century Europeans began "to center almost exclusively upon the individual: individual freedom, individual development, individual responsibility all led inevitably to a doctrine which interpreted the whole universe in the terms of single men and induced even souls of exceptional capacity to regard their own personal salvation as the chief end of existence." In this regard, it is a peculiar irony that the Renaissance in Europe was largely made possible by the "new light with which Asia and Africa illumined the Dark Ages of Europe," for "with this new world came fatally the African slave trade and Negro slavery in the Americas." There was a new degradation of labor, new forms of cruelty, new hostility toward men. "The temptation to degrade human labor was made vaster and deeper by the incredible accumulation of wealth based on slave labor, by the boundless growth of greed, and by world-wide trade." Because labor was degraded, humanity was more easily despised and "the theory of 'race' arose."[117]

That was "the collective purpose" that European men of power assigned to existence. In Du Bois's view, the African communal conception was at odds with capitalism just as the socialism espoused by European rebels was in opposition to unrestrained individualism. He rejected the individualism at the heart of capitalism for more than economic reasons alone: he saw history as the struggle between different value systems, of which the patterns of human life are expressions. Thus, for him the substance of history is spiritual history—not pure, cold intellectual history but the passionate spirit of sermon and song, storytelling and dance, thought and action, aimed always at the elevation of man.

The external world for European man is mere matter to be used, controlled, manipulated—for the pleasure of certain men. Therefore, the European denial of the sacred in that world ends up being the denial of the sacredness of human life:

With professed reverence for female chastity, white folk have brought paid prostitution to its highest development; their lauding of motherhood has accompanied a lessening of births . . . and this has stopped the growth of population in France and threatened it in all Europe. Indeed, along with the present rate of divorce, the future of the whole white race is problematical.[118]

Despite his admiration for Marxism and the Soviet Union, his philosophical inclinations seem to fit more appropriately into Hegelianism than into dialectical materialism, since he seems to lean toward the idea of the autonomous human spirit. But he is not explicitly Hegelian and does not take a clear dogmatic position on the question. He was very different from Hegel in not accepting the view that modern man had arrived at some sort of "end" of history.[119] Like Marx, he was acutely aware of the contradictions shattering modern society and longed for the externalization of the harmonious world of the spirit. He saw in Marxism an intellectual means—and a political means of organization—by which this could be realized (and so he joined, decades later, the Communist Party, U.S.A.)

He was no more dogmatic about Marxism than about Hegelianism and read Marx on his own, since at Harvard "Marx was mentioned but only incidentally and as one whose doubtful theories had long since been refuted." But Marx and the Bolshevik Revolution were of great interest to him, and he managed several months away from his NAACP work in 1926 to visit the Soviet Union, mostly moving about on his own with an interpreter. What he saw greatly impressed him, and even then he allowed for the possibility of excesses in that country. Yet he knew the depths of corruption of the czarist past and the ignorance, poverty, and suffering that persisted as a consequence. He saw much of this himself: "Alone and unaccompanied I have walked miles of streets in Leningrad, Moscow, Nijni Novgorod and Kiev at morning, noon and night . . . and sat still and gazed at this Russia, that the spirit of its life and people might enter my veins." After over two thousand miles of travel and months among the Russian people, Du Bois concluded,

"I stand in astonishment and wonder at the revelation of Russia that has come to me. I may be partially deceived and half-informed. But if what I have seen with my eyes and heard with my ears . . . is Bolshevism, I am a Bolshevik."[120]

He associated himself with socialism and the Communist movement in order to build a rational world without necessarily having espoused all the philosophical underpinnings of Marxism. He genuinely wanted a Communist society, and, for decades before his death, he considered Marxism the most adequate intellectual tool with which to organize people to construct such a society at this juncture in human experience. But he wanted to give to human consciousness a degree of autonomy more extensive than Marx would allow from the point of view of both material and social reality, and he was intent on applying Marxism to the specific conditions faced by people of African ancestry in America, conditions rooted in slavery and influenced by their heritage in Africa.

Du Bois thought that the conflict between the African and the European points of view took concrete form in late-nineteenth- and early-twentieth-century imperialism, as it had before in the slave trade and slavery, and he considered slavery and imperialism expressions of the European will to dominate the world, that will being the motor of their civilization. He knew that what rendered American slavery so traumatizing was the fact that the principles of free and slave communities in North America were so different from those of both slave and free societies in Africa. And he understood that the American slave, driven almost entirely by the desire of whites to optimize investments, was punished not because what he did was wrong but because it was costly—a vision of the world as new to the African as the racism that denied his humanity.

"Beneath this educational and social propaganda," Du Bois wrote in *Black Reconstruction,* "lay the undoubted evidence of the planter's own expenses. . . . All observers spoke of the fact that the slaves were slow and churlish; that they wasted material and malingered at their work. Of course, they did. This was not racial but economic. It was the answer of any group of laborers forced down to the last ditch. They might be made to work continuously but no power could make them work well."[121] The fleshing out of the humanity of the slave in the face of the least-merited attempts to deny it is the particular strength of that formulation.

In fact, Du Bois pioneered in making credible the full humanity of the American worker. This he accomplished by defending the worker considered least human. In the process, Du Bois did something that had not been done before. He integrated the slave into the history of the American working class and, with unparalleled skill, showed the pitfalls of both race and class in the struggle of the American worker for liberation, which for him was the key to democracy. But the greatest tragedy of the American working class, he was certain, was its lack of interest in a workers' democracy, a subject on which he wrote with great insight.

Black Reconstruction, the most important work in which he takes up that subject, was recognized at the start by a number of critics as a work of rare quality, and then was virtually ignored for decades. Harry Hansen, an influential reviewer in the thirties, wrote in the *New York World-Telegram,* on June 13, 1935, that it was comparable to the Beards' *Rise of American Civilization* and said the book "crowns the long, unselfish, studious and brilliant career of Dr. Du Bois and will carry his name down to other generations of American historians." The reviewer of the work for the *New York Herald Tribune,* the Wellesley College history professor Henry Raymond Mussey, captured its dimensions, calling it "solid history . . . an economic treatise, a philosophical discussion, a poem, a work of art all rolled into one." Mussey's description of the book must have pleased Du Bois, who wanted *Black Reconstruction* "to be an interpretation of the human soul." [122]

Thus far, Du Bois is the only scholar who has enabled us to feel the psychic and spiritual pain of the slave, to know what it was like to be under a "master." That he managed such an act of empathy is a tribute to his learning and to his own humanity. In this respect, he has done for the academic community through scholarship what Robeson does when we hear him sing spirituals. Almost of necessity such a feat presupposes respect for the human personality wherever found. That both men were nationalists again attests to the catholicity of their concern for humanity and indirectly relates to their forefathers—to Douglass and Garnet and Crummell and Walker. On the one hand, Du Bois could write,

> . . . African history became the tale of degraded animals and subhuman savages, where no vestige of human culture found foothold. . . . The hurt to the Negro in this era was not only his treatment in slavery; it was the wound dealt to his reputation as a human being. Nothing was left; nothing was sacred. . . . If they fought for freedom, they were beasts; if they did not fight, they were born slaves. If they cowered on the plantations, they loved slavery; if they ran away, they were lazy loafers. . . . Nothing—nothing that black folk did or said or thought was sacred.[123]

On the other hand, he could also link the struggles of his people to the struggles of the oppressed everywhere with uncommon conviction:

> The attempt to make black men American citizens was in a certain sense all a failure, but a splendid failure. It did not fail where it was expected to fail. It was Athanasius contra mundum, with back to wall, outnumbered ten to one, with all the wealth and all the opportunity, and all the world against him. And only in his hands and heart the consciousness of a great and just cause; fighting the battle of all the oppressed and despised humanity of every race and color, against the massed hirelings of Religion, Science, Education, Law, and brute force.[124]

The overthrow of Reconstruction and the forcing of blacks back toward slavery at the close of the century were blows to the spiritual life of black people, who rebounded by creating an art that transmutes pain into beauty and gives back to the people what would be taken away—confidence in themselves and the willingness to go on. If Du Bois did not capture the blues in full bloom, he understood the growing self-awareness of the newly emancipated. And he was not surprised that, given the effects of the slave trade and slavery on the white world, an attempt would be made to extinguish the light of that awareness. The tragedy of that development was that it occurred when, "in the sombre forests of his striving," the ex-slave's "own soul rose before him, and he saw in himself some faint revelation of his power, of his mission." It was when, with slavery finally behind him, the ex-slave "began to have a dim feeling that, to attain his place in the world, he must be himself, not another," that the carnage of lynching was unleashed.[125]

To be "heavy-laden" and confronted by Garnet's "up-hill course" was the context for the spiritual descent that occurred in the lives of large numbers of blacks with the overthrow of Reconstruction and the violence visited upon them in the last two decades of the century. To know the trajectory of their spirit from emancipation to that low point, one must understand what emancipation meant to them, and Du Bois goes back in time to reveal this. With the spiritual insight of the prophet, and in powerful, eloquent prose, he illumines the consciousness of blacks at the moment of freedom:

> There was joy in the South. It rose like perfume—like a prayer. Men stood quivering. Slim dark girls, wild and beautiful with wrinkled hair, wept silently; young women, black, tawny, white and golden, lifted shivering hands, and old and broken mothers, black and grey, raised great voices and shouted to God across the fields, and up to the mountains.[126]

At the same time, Du Bois offers a new perspective, at least in printed sources, on the meaning of emancipation to white workers. For them the magic of freedom suddenly coming to four million people meant little; they saw in it no phase of the emancipation of labor and recognized in it no measure of self-emancipation. There was not only the degradation of labor that slavery effected but also the disturbing racial component that weighed heavily in the scales of capitalist exploitation of people of color in America and elsewhere. As for America:

> Of all that most Americans wanted, this freeing of slaves was the last. Everything black was hideous. Everything Negroes did was wrong. If they sang, they were silly; if they scowled, they were impudent. . . . They caused the war—they, its victims. They were guilty of all the thefts of those who stole. They were the cause of wasted property and small crops. They had impoverished the South, and plunged the North into endless debt. And they were funny, funny—ridiculous baboons, aping man.[127]

Considering such rabid racism, the fate of blacks for generations to come seemed sealed. It is small wonder that Du Bois, reviewing the history of blacks, thought what they experienced as a result of slavery "represented in every real sense the ultimate degradation of man." This was doubly sad, for we must remember, as he notes insightfully, that the black worker, "the ultimate exploited," "formed the mass of labor which had neither wish nor power to escape from the labor status, in order to directly exploit other laborers, or indirectly, by alliance with capital, to share in their exploitation," an attitude hardly reciprocated by white workers following emancipation. Whites "were not willing to regard themselves as a permanent laboring class," and this had long been true of immigrants. The more thrifty and energetic among them "caught the prevalent American ideal that here labor could become emancipated from the necessity of continuous toil and that an increasing proportion could join the class of exploiters, that is of those who made their income chiefly by profit derived from the hiring of labor."[128]

The black slave, or worker, as Du Bois calls him was "the founding stone of a new economic system in the nineteenth century and for the modern world," and as such was indispensable to the rise of capitalism in so short a time span. This thesis was implicit in the work of Walker and Garnet and hardly new in European and American intellectual circles generally. But Du Bois draws on accumulated scholarship, then goes beyond it, making that thesis the leitmotif of his work, bringing the sensibility of an artist to the subject. He treats the impact of such oppression on the interior life of the victim and reveals all sorts of ironies: as the "giant forces of water and steam were harnessed to do the world's work" and as the black worker "bent at the bottom of a growing pyramid of commerce and industry," they were the cause of new alignments and political demands, "of new dreams of power and visions of empire."[129] While he thought the slave trade and slavery laid the basis for the rise of capitalist industry, there is another context in which he places the black worker, one in which, with the rise of world colonialism, no earlier nationalist had put him—that of colored people on a global scale doing the work and supplying the mineral resources for Europe—jointly making possible the wealth of the white world while being discriminated against on grounds of color:

> That dark and vast sea of human labor in China and India, the South Seas and all Africa; in the West Indies and Central America and in the United States— that great majority of mankind, on whose bent and broken backs rest today the founding stones of modern industry—shares a common destiny; it is despised and rejected by race and color; paid a wage below the level of decent living; driven, beaten, prisoned and enslaved in all but name; spawning the world's raw material and luxury—cotton, wool, coffee, tea, cocoa, palm oil, fibers, spices, rubber, silks, lumber, copper, gold, diamonds, leather—how shall we end the list and where?[130]

Du Bois was not concerned with salaries—he once asked the NAACP for equal pay when he discovered that a white secretary was being paid more than he—and, like Garnet, he never accumulated any money. While he may have liked his spats and cane, one knows that he was prepared to throw them away at any moment.

VI

Some things Du Bois saw more certainly with the advent of the Great Depression, not the least among them being the continued status of blacks as the most oppressed group in the land. Not only had their economic condition worsened more than that of whites, but they continued to be disfranchised by the millions in the South, and there were few if any signs that segregation was abating. In addition, the lynching of Negroes went on, the case of the Scottsboro boys the representative one of the decade. Though the condition of blacks was compounded by the Depression, only the Communist party, of all American political parties, seemed genuinely interested in ridding the country of racism. There was a painful irony for the party members in having obliterated "thoroughly and completely the color bar within their own ranks, but by so doing, absolutely blocked any chance they might have had to attract any considerable number of white workers to their ranks." This situation for the party was aggravated in the eyes of Du Bois by the insistence of Communists that their black members "put themselves blindly under the dictatorship of the Communist Party."[131] It was an analysis marked by independence of thought from one whose sympathies with communism, if anything, deepened in the years of the Great Depression. In some respects, the analysis was brilliantly innovative. Speaking of Marxism, Du Bois wrote,

> This philosophy did not envisage a situation where instead of a horizontal division of classes, their was a vertical fissure, a complete separation of classes by race, cutting square across economic layers. Even if on one side this color line, the dark masses were overwhelmingly workers, with but an embryonic capitalist class, nevertheless the split between white and black workers was greater than that between white workers and capitalists; and this split depended not simply on economic exploitation but on a racial folk-lore grounded on centuries of instinct, habit and thought and implemented by the conditioned reflex of visible color. This flat and incontrovertible fact, imported Russian Communism ignored, would not discuss.[132]

This analysis did not reinforce his doubts about the limitations of his thesis that the color line is the problem of the century. In fact it was that assessment that led Du Bois to seek a path toward economic justice for blacks that would not too greatly enrage the capitalist oppressor or the white working class. While a black state on the margins of white America might draw an all-out attack from its powerful, hostile neighbor, he thought separate Negro sections might increase racial antagonisms but would make organized self-defense possible, heighten self-confidence, and increase opportunities for economic cooperation. He was convinced that racism would prevent America's leaders from planning for the survival of blacks or for their future, if such planning meant self-assertive manhood for blacks.

Despite a curious disclaimer that he was advocating black nationalism, Du Bois drafted a prospectus for a self-contained black community in America in which blacks would control numerous aspects of their lives. Various features of his plan, developed in the 1930s, were revealed then and in the 1940s, as he considered the feasibility of black nationalism in America on a programmatic basis. He thought precolonial West African societies might be drawn upon for values by which Afro-Americans might order their lives in cooperative communities. Rather than accept the capitalist ethic, Du Bois proposed that his people occupy cooperative islands in a vast sea of capitalism. His faith was predicated on the ability of blacks to transcend American materialism—"on an inner Negro cultural ideal." This ideal was spawned by "ancient African communism, supported and developed by memory of slavery and experience of caste," and would eventually "drive the Negro group into a spiritual unity precluding the development of economic classes and inner class struggle."[133]

Here was as direct a linkage of African culture and Afro-American nationalism as one might conceive with the African communal spirit still *present* and informing, though in attenuated form, black communities in America, and inspiring them to greater group effort. But Du Bois's optimism, at least in the short run, proved excessive, as class differences and class antagonisms developed among many blacks in the United States, especially in the period following World War II.

Before those class lines and preferences became obvious, however, he thought the few were to take as their task the raising of the cultural and intellectual sights of the many in "a new trial of democratic development without force among some of the worst victims of force":

> How can it be done? It can be done through consumers' groups and the mutual interests that these members have in the success of the groups. It can bring the cultured face to face with the untrained and it can accomplish by determined effort and planned foresight the acculturation of the many through the few, rather than the opposite possibility of pulling the better classes down through ignorance, carelessness, and crime.[134]

The cooperative black societies he envisioned were to be the chief vehicles of the transformation of the masses, through trained leadership, into leaders in such numbers that the fullest democracy in intellectual as well as economic terms might be realized. It was a vision of democracy that would unlock the creative potential of the masses within a context best suited to nurture that potential and direct it toward the common good— provided, of course, the surrounding capitalist system would permit it.

Du Bois thought self-assertion alone promised meaningful results. He came to understand that in opposing race prejudice black people "were facing age-long complexes sunk now largely to unconscious habit and irrational urge" that demanded they have not only the patience to wait but also the power to entrench themselves "for a long siege against the strongholds of color caste." Economic structures of their own were required for such a struggle to enable blacks to begin a genuine process of social uplift, "so far as this was neglected by the state and nation, and at the same time carry out even more systematically and with greater and better-planned determination, the fight that the NAACP had inaugurated in 1910."[135]

There were those among his people who thought the rulers of America would not permit that sort of autonomy in blacks or their existence in America on terms even approaching justice. It was they, black emigrationists, who advocated an exodus of a good number of their people from America, most often to Africa, and Du Bois felt it necessary to treat their position within the context of his effort to attack the problem of black oppression during the Great Depression.

One reason he could not favor emigration was that white people had "annexed the earth and held it by transient but real power." By emigrating—he used the phrase "running away"—the black man would fail to escape white control. At best, emigrants would be successful in hiding "in out of the way places where they [white people] can work their deviltry" and do so "without photograph, telegraph, or mail service." Yet he allowed that "back to Africa" movements commended themselves not simply to demagogues "but to the prouder and more independent type of Negro," to those black people who were tired of begging for justice from people who appear "to have no intention of being just and do not propose to recognize Negroes as men."[136] Nevertheless, Du Bois admitted that his plan

> would not decline frankly to face the possibility of eventual emigration from America of some considerable part of the Negro population, in case they could find a chance for free and favorable development unmolested and unthreatened, and in case the race prejudice in America persisted to such an extent that it would not permit the full development of the capacities and aspirations of the Negro race.[137]

Du Bois thought those capacities vast, even when espousing his Talented Tenth ideal of leadership. Admitting that he once advocated "flight of class from mass"—educated blacks working on behalf of and in some respects apart from the masses—he expected, nonetheless, that "the power of this aristocracy of talent was to lie in its knowledge and character and not in its wealth." Vital was the relationship between "leadership and authority within the group, which by implication left controls to wealth"—a contingency of which Du Bois said he "never dreamed"—but, with the changes in "the white economic trends of the world," mass and class must unite for the salvation of the world. He advanced a thesis related to his African cultural ideal of cooperation: "We who have had least class differentiation in wealth can follow in the new trend and indeed lead it."[138]

Yet it should not be forgotten that, since emancipation, the advance of the group has been due largely to "the extraordinary success in education, technique and character among a small number of Negroes and that the emergence of these exceptional men has been largely a matter of chance." This formulation regarding talent anticipated Robeson's statement that "the problem of talent is the problem of opportunity." And therein lay the ground on which Du Bois launched a major assault on elitism: the triumph of the Talented Tenth "proves that down among the mass, ten times their number with equal ability could be discovered and developed, if sustained effort and sacrifice and intelligence were put to the task."[139]

Looking back some forty years, Du Bois thought educated blacks "too often forgetful" of their responsibility "to increase and increase rapidly and widely among the masses of people within our group . . . the ability, physical strength and spiritual wealth, of which they are possessed." That, in fact, would constitute the very process of democracy: "Democracy is tapping the great possibilities of mankind from unused and unsuspected reservoirs of human greatness." In his reflections on the Talented Tenth in the 1930s and later, he did not ignore the creative potential of the masses. He made clear his position on the intellectual's responsibility to oppressed humanity wherever found. In an address to Haitian intellectuals, for example, he remarked, "Instead of envying and seeking desperately outer and foreign sources of civilization, you may find in these magnificent mountains a genius and variety of human culture, which once released from poverty, ignorance and disease, will help guide the world."[140]

With that perspective on the inherent worth of humanity—and Du Bois appears to have had it from his days at Fisk—he not surprisingly considered his own people capable not only of shaping their own destiny but also of helping shape the destiny of man. Such a reading alone accounts for his being so convinced of their capacity that he regarded the "loosening of outer racial discriminatory pressures" an opportunity for them "to become a group cemented into a new cultural unity, capable of absorbing socialism, tolerance, and democracy, and helping to lead America into a new heaven and new earth."[141]

Du Bois wrote that he "was going too fast for the NAACP" with his "vaster conception of the role of black men in the future of civilization." Of the top leadership, he charged, "The board was not interested in Africa. Following postwar reaction it shrank back into its narrowest program: to make Negroes American citizens." The Depression, which eroded the financial autonomy of the *Crisis*, undercut the independent stance of Du Bois, making the magazine dependent for support on the main office of the NAACP. Du Bois thought that, had this financial difficulty not arisen, he could have developed his program of a greater role for African peoples in the future of the world to such a level that it would have been "on the way to adoption by American Negroes."[142] But the NAACP was not built for such purposes.

Never one to resist modifying his ideas in the face of changing realities, he changed his initial strategy of having black people as a group successfully assail the bars of racism to a more complex and radical one: that of emphasizing the relationship of the worldwide struggle of people of color to the Afro-American fight for freedom. This strategy grew to maturity in the 1930s and was an additional cause of the split between him and the NAACP. The NAACP, he remarked with considerable understatement, was not disposed to support a strategy that called for Afro-Americans to put behind their demands "not simply American Negroes, but West Indians and Africans, and all the colored races of the world." [143]

But his differences with NAACP were fundamental in another, related sense. He deemed it unthinkable that the Negro exchange his birthright for white approval, that he abandon his self-respect in search of "freedom." In a formulation that would have satisfied the most exacting nineteenth-century nationalist, he wrote in the middle of the Depression,

This the American black man knows; his fight here is a fight to the finish. Either he dies or wins. If he wins it will be by no subterfuge or evasion of amalgamation. He will enter modern civilization here in America as a black man on terms of perfect and unlimited equality with any white man, or he will enter not at all. Either extermination root and branch, or absolute equality. There can be no compromise. This is the last great battle of the West. [144]

A black movement that recognized that for some time American racial barriers would be insurmountable incurred the disapproval of conservative NAACP Negroes; a movement to create consumer cooperatives that would preclude the profit motive displeased them even more, as did acknowledging that individual blacks should be prepared to sacrifice for the sake of the whole. When an effort by Du Bois to secure support for such a plan through a change in board members failed, his resignation from the organization was assured. He left in the spring of 1934. [145]

An offer quietly put to him five years earlier by John Hope was accepted—to return to Atlanta University. There were no doubt better places for him, but he rather welcomed the return to academic life there. He was by then nearing seventy and, besides, white universities were not open to blacks even of his talent and achievement. He understood perfectly well and did not complain: "No matter what his ability, no Colored scholar has more than one chance in a hundred for appointment on a white college faculty in the United States." Writing to Atlanta University, regarding a black economist, "a Harvard head professor said, 'Frankly, we gladly would appoint this man here if he were not colored.'" [146]

After additional work at Atlanta, Du Bois completed *Black Reconstruction,* which he had begun while still with the NAACP: "Next I naturally turned my thought toward putting into permanent form that economic program of the Negro which I believed would succeed, and implement the long fight for political and civil rights and social equality which it was my privilege for a quarter of a century to champion." The permanent form was his "The Negro and Social Reconstruction," a treatise, solicited by the Howard University professor Alain Locke, that was to appear under the auspices of the American Association for Adult Education. But Locke, frightened off by the radical thrust of the volume—"If the leading Negro classes cannot assume and bear the uplift of their own proletariat, they are doomed for time and eternity"—rejected it in a letter to Du Bois in 1936 that he knew would reach Du Bois while he was on a world tour.[147]

Working in conjuncton with a group of young black intellectuals, Du Bois set forth a credo that bears his stamp. The credo affirmed "unity of racial effort, so far as this is necessary for self-defense and self-expression," and endorsed "the goal of a united humanity and the abolition of all racial distinctions"; it repudiated not only the "deification of race separation as such" but also "an ennervating philosophy of Negro escape into an artificially privileged white race"; it expressed its faith "in the ultimate triumph of some form of Socialism the world over; that is, common ownership and control of the means of production and equality of income"; and it urged Negroes to join labor unions and form workers councils that would promote interracial understanding and "fight race prejudice in the working class."[148]

In 1939, when group solidarity was very much on his mind, Du Bois revealed in *Black Folk Then and Now* that for some time he had known of the existence of an African institution in slavery that possessed some characteristics not unrelated to those still deficient in his people: "internal development and growth of self-consciousness among the Negroes: for instance, in New England towns during colonial times, Negro 'governors' were elected." Even more interesting is what he makes of that development,—that it "was partly the African chieftainship transplanted"—which is relevant here because of the close similarities of the Negro governor and the Pinkster king. Du Bois was therefore aware by 1939 that an African institution in addition to the priest and the church had survived, at least in part, in North America—that of the chieftainship represented by the governor.[149]

By 1942, if not before, he was aware of yet another African institution which, together with the others, may have substantially altered his conception of the persistence of African cultural values and forms in the slave era. Across his desk when editor of *Phylon* had come a piece entitled "The John Canoe Festival," based mainly on its manifestations in North Carolina. Written by Ira De A. Reid, it described the central character's introduction to the accompaniment of "rhythmic chant and amid a cacophony of motley noises—bell ringing, horn tooting, beating of pots and pans, yells, peals of laughter and musical shouting." Then it added,

In the van of the assembly pranced a costuming king, bedecked in an outfit
. . . of tatters and rags, a grass skirt, a jacket fringed with diamond-like glass,
arms covered with playing cards, striped trouser legs, a white boot encasing
one foot, a shapeless black shoe the other. Atop this outfit was a head-piece
house-like in form . . . below which glared a most hideous and grotesque
white masked face. . . . This was John Canoe, Negro "king." . . .[150]

VII

Du Bois attended the Fifth Pan-African Congress, at Manchester, England, in 1945, at which Africans from the continent regarded the fate of
American Negroes and those from the islands inextricably tied to their
own, and informed them that their aspirations were "bound up with the
emancipation of all African peoples." The congress went further and recognized the links of African people with "dependent people and the working class everywhere," a position that recalled "the coming unities"
thesis espoused by Du Bois in *The Negro* a generation earlier.[151] The
congress's resolution on the struggle of the people of India reflected an
interest in Indian nationalism held by Du Bois and others as well, and the
congress's fraternal greetings to the peoples of Vietnam "in their struggle
against French imperialism" expressed a concern that Robeson restated
nearly a decade later.

It was fitting that Du Bois, by the time of the Manchester conference,
no longer thought New World blacks would lead a movement for African
liberation. His revision of previous ideas on the subject represented a
culminating point in fifty years as a Pan-Africanist in which he had consol-
idated and gone beyond much of earlier nationalist thought. One of his
greatest achievements was to buttress earlier efforts by blacks to write the
history of people of African ancestry. While impressive work, in the nationalist tradition, was done by Garnet in particular, nothing nearly as
erudite or as creative as Du Bois's work was a part of the tradition. He
brought to his work a global focus in which he treated, as scholar, the
movement of his people over time—especially in relation to the rise of
industry and imperialism in the West.

Du Bois finely balanced passion and scientific detachment, though detachment won out, his armor being a control under fire that would have
fatally seared most men. He mastered language and expressed, with effortless ease, great power on the printed page—power harnessed and set to
music by the sheer lyricism of his prose. That control was evident in his
appearance, comportment, and thought when speaking, and that is what
led Henry Miller to imagine him addressing an assemblage of scientists.

His writing on slave culture at the turn of the century has for eighty
years proved to be the most original on the subject by a historian. Not
only was he able to enter the interior world of the slave and take us there,

he also used his intuitive genius to go beyond available sources to locate the institutions of the African priest and church on the plantations of the South and to raise the question of the role of the priest in melding various African ethnic groups into a single people. His ability to penetrate to the foundations of black culture and to relate his Pan-African and Negritude theory to them amounted to a tremendous breakthrough. Though he never integrated into a theory of slave culture African institutions other than those of the church and priest, his scholarship ultimately did not allow two additional ones to elude him; they were a part of his consciousness on the subject.

Du Bois was able to accept slave culture on its own terms more easily than any previous nationalist, and this necessary step toward fuller understanding was enchanced by his living among ex-slaves soon after slavery, when he was at a particularly impressionable age. Despite the oppression of Africans everywhere at that time, he brought a humility to the experiences of the black masses that was rare for that day or any other. Moreover, he moved with ease among his people and participated in their most sacred ceremonies, and this, too, marked a new development in the nationalist tradition.

He was thus able to pioneer in determining what is African and what is European in the Afro-American experience and thereby to direct attention to problems of consciousness and behavior that needed to be addressed. His greatly neglected prescription for partially resolving the problem of double consciousness is part of the literature of black nationalism that should by now win attention: the idea that Europe owes much of its civilization to Africa—a creative application of a nationalist thesis on which he brought to bear much of the accumulated scholarship of his day. His treatment of integration should henceforth be seen in a different light, as should his treatment of the Talented Tenth.

While Walker and Garnet provided a protosocialist tradition for black intellectuals, Du Bois explicitly espoused socialism and, like them, lived a life largely free of material concerns. He revealed a deep antagonism to monopoly in capital, and he considered socialism, with roots in ancient African communal societies, altogether preferable to capitalism. There was for him no conflict between socialism and black nationalism.

No other American intellectual has approached the extent to which Du Bois related the theoretical to the practical in matters of race relations— that is, combined a deep grounding in the literature of race relations, much of which he created, with more than sixty years of activity "in the field." A realist with the gift of intuition, he was able to anticipate the shape of governing preferences, a fact not unrelated to his pioneering scholarship. He offered the best comment on his role as a social theorist:

> I think I may say without boasting that in the period from 1910 to 1930 I was a main factor in revolutionizing the attitude of the American Negro toward

caste. My stinging hammer blows made Negroes aware of themselves, confident in their possibilities and determined in self-assertion. So much so that
today common slogans among the Negro people are taken bodily from the
words of my mouth.[152]

He was called back to the NAACP in 1944 to assume the post of director of special projects and to represent the organization at the founding of
the United Nations in San Francisco. Once again, he displayed independence of mind in promoting an appeal to the Commission on Human
Rights of the United Nations, submitted on behalf of the NAACP; he
asserted that a "nation" has descended from "the Africans brought to
America during the sixteenth, seventeenth, eighteenth and nineteenth
centuries and reduced to slave labor." He argued, in fact, that blacks in
America were "in size one of the considerable nations of the world."
That position was guaranteed to cause problems before long—at least it
would alienate influential Negroes in the organization—because, as Du
Bois explained a few years before returning to the NAACP, "the upper
class Negro has almost never been nationalistic. He has never planned or
thought of a Negro state. . . . This solution has always been a thought up-
surging from the mass, because of pressure which they could not with-
stand and which compelled a racial institution or chaos."[153]
Meanwhile, he remarked at the end of World War II, "We are face to
face with the greatest tragedy that has ever overtaken the world." He
recalled "the boundless faith" European man reposed in himself. There
were centuries during which it was believed "without argument or reflection that the cultural status of Europe and of North America represented
not only the best civilization which the world had ever known, but also a
goal of human effort destined to go on from triumph to triumph until the
perfect accomplishment was reached." "But the war signaled fear, nervous breakdown, and despair born of "the sudden facing of this faith with
calamity." Under such circumstances, what was needed above all was
"calm common sense"—an inquiry into the nature of the past that produced the horror of World War II. And there was no doubt in his mind
that the vast colonial empire of colored people, at the base of which were
the cornerstones of slavery and the slave trade, was the cause of the split
of interest in the white world that led to war.[154]
Such concerns were as foreign to the leadership of the NAACP as was
Du Bois's conception of the meaning of freedom. He had returned to the
organization at a time when it would soon be at its lowest point in history
with respect to intellectual and spiritual leadership, a condition exacerbated during the Cold War. But by then he was gone, for persisting problems of jealousy and ideological differences had been sufficient to force
his departure. Trouble came especially from Walter White, whose intellectual and spiritual qualities, by comparison, were deeply deficient. Roy

Wilkins, less gifted than White, probably never dreamed of acting to bol-
ster Du Bois's position, and never fully understood it. In sum, Du Bois
was surrounded by men to whom he might speak intelligibly in the narrowest of terms, and they knew it. They wanted an end to the black race
in America if possible, and he knew it. The historian Joel Williamson has
struck at the heart of their differences: "The NAACP would have a very
successful life. . . . Ultimately, however, it would find that it could go only
so far in making white people out of black people. . . ."[155]

A letter to Du Bois at the moment of his final break with the NAACP
contained the essence of his meaning to young blacks of an earlier generation and forms an ironic backdrop to how coming generations of blacks,
those of the 1950s and later, would view him. The break had come when
White, having decided to represent the NAACP on the colonial question
at a meeting of the United Nations in Paris in 1948, asked Du Bois to write
a speech that he might deliver, when Du Bois was the logical person to
represent the NAACP on that occasion. "Not a single Negro in America
had done as much as you have to focus the attention of the white world on
the oppression and exploitation of Negroes in Africa and other parts of
the world," wrote the journalist Thomas L. Dabney to Du Bois, after
hearing of the ensuing dispute. He considered Du Bois his "spiritual father—the man who with others helped to keep me from giving up in utter
despair when I was in my teens. . . . *The Crisis* under your editorship
saved hundred of thousands of young Negroes from spiritual death."[156]

Du Bois's refusal to write White's speech and his attack on White's,
and by implication the NAACP's, support of U.S. imperialism in the
Afro-Asian world were immediate causes of his dismissal from the organization. Over eighty at the time, without funds and without a job, he accepted an invitation from Paul Robeson and joined the Council on African
Affairs at no salary but with free office space and secretarial assistance.
That arrangement brought the two men closer together, when others were
already beginning to distance themselves from them in a time of growing
reaction and of increasing hostility between the United States and the
Soviet Union.

Before long Du Bois was barred from college campuses and denied access to the media. The national office of the NAACP used its influence to
prevent him from speaking on the University of California campus and
before local NAACP chapters. When the federal government accused Du
Bois of being "an an agent of a foreign power," White visited Washington
and was told by the government that Du Bois was guilty, and there was no
support for him from the NAACP. When a dinner was planned to honor
him on his eighty-third birthday, those associated with the affair were
persecuted so much that it was held with great difficulty:

> I can stand a good deal, and have done so during my life; but this experience
> was rather more than I felt like bearing, especially as the blows continued to

fall: my colored graduate fraternity voted down a birthday greeting to me, and accompanied the action by bitter criticism in its private debate on the matter. In Washington, I had been finger-printed, handcuffed, bailed and remanded for trial. I was more than ready to drop all thought of the birthday dinner.[157]

The dinner was held—in a Negro nightclub, because white hotels in New York refused to rent facilities for that purpose. Paul Robeson "spoke courageously and feelingly," but Du Bois's name was already one not often spoken by middle-class blacks, certainly not in public. From being a man whom every black person in America had known by name, "and hastened always to entertain or praise," he had become anathema in most black as well as in white liberal circles.[158]

Though he remained active in his years of exile at 31 Grace Court in Brooklyn, his schedule continued to provide much time for study and reflection. Visitors knew in advance how much time was available to them, and, after their time was up, Shirley Graham Du Bois graciously directed some upstairs to see a portrait of the young Frederick Douglass, at the same time leaving Du Bois with his books in his vast library, which reached from the floor to the ceiling around his study.

In Columbia, South Carolina, in 1946, he had proclaimed,

The future of the American Negro is in the South. . . . This is the firing line not simply for the emancipation of the American Negro but for the emancipation of the African Negro and the Negroes of the West Indies; for the emancipation of the colored races; and for the emancipation of the white slaves of modern capitalistic monopoly.

Then, to youths gathered to hear him, he addressed the subject of how change might be brought about in the South:

Nevertheless reason can and will prevail; but of course it can only prevail with publicity—pitiless, blatant publicity. You have got to make the people of the United States and of the world know what is going on in the South. You have got to make it impossible for any human being to live in the South and not realize the barbarities that prevail here.[159]

Black youths were acting on such a prescription for change when Du Bois took up citizenship in Ghana, in West Africa, where he lies buried. Still, he had no illusions about the continuing force of racism in America. His prediction in the early 1940s that generations of racial segregation, despite advances, awaited Americans is as impressive as his anticipation of the weapon of publicity to be drawn in opposing such segregation. In years of increasing isolation before and after his trial, his feelings about his fate were to some extent like those Garnet experienced in his last years.

But despite the problems confronting his people at the time he left America—by that time his prophecy of rebellion in America had come true—he was convinced the struggle for freedom would assume more impressive dimensions, that a broader upsurge from below could not be averted. Sooner or later black workers would find a way of expressing their collective will and help in an effort "to guide and rule the state for the best welfare of the masses." While that prospect seems as remote now as it did then, the assumption on which it was based—"that out of the downtrodden mass of people, ability and character, sufficient to do this task effectively, could and would be found"—was for him the only basis for genuine democracy, industrial and political. Unless one understands that about his thought—that democracy is a sham without full participation of the masses in the decisions affecting them—then one does not understand him. For he has written, "I believed this dictum passionately. It was, in fact, the foundation stone of my fight for black folks; it explained me."[160]

CHAPTER SIX

On Being African:
Paul Robeson and the Ends of
Nationalist Theory and Practice

> Meanwhile, in my music, my plays, my films, I want
> to carry always this central idea—to be African.
> Multitudes of men have died for less worthy ideals;
> it is even more eminently worth living for.
> —PAUL ROBESON, 1934

More than a generation following his college days, when he had referred to Dr. Du Bois as "the Doctor," Paul Robeson, himself beleaguered and seated beside a piano in Chicago in the 1950s, looked up from *Black Reconstruction* and quietly remarked, "We must support Dr. Du Bois, for he is the wisest one among us." He so admired Du Bois that, after letting him and Shirley Graham Du Bois use his London flat for a couple of weeks in 1958, he returned from a trip to the Continent and hung a sign on his door that read "Dr. Du Bois slept here."[1] Though he respected Du Bois more than any other American intellectual and activist, the greatest single influence on Robeson was his father, whose ideals were not unlike those of Du Bois, and there came a time very early on when the values and example of the one reinforced those of the other in Robeson's life.

After running away from slavery in North Carolina at fifteen, Robeson's father educated himself and eventually took a pastorate in Princeton, New Jersey, where Paul was born in 1898. Fifteen at the time of his escape, Paul's father continued to live for a while the experience of slavery through his enslaved mother, whom he secretly visited on at least one occasion after freeing himself. Like David Walker, who drew strength from the pain of knowing that his father was a slave and his mother defenseless, the Reverend Robeson grew in spiritual strength as he contemplated his mother's condition in slavery. And the generational bond in slavery, as with the Garnets, strengthened the opposition of the Robesons to slavery. Indeed, much like Garnet, Paul Robeson later focused with telling insight on the history of slavery not only in his family but over the generations in black America.[2]

Through his father, Robeson had the most direct contact with slavery possible short of having been a slave. Though his father did not discuss slavery with him, his example as a runaway at so early an age was the best indication to Robeson of how he felt about having been enslaved. But by the time he left slavery, William Drew Robeson already embodied aspects of slave culture that were African and later understood to be so by his son, who pointed to them in demonstrating his links to Africa.[3] Robeson had advantages in relation to black culture—derived directly from his family—not consciously shared by nationalists before him, advantages on which he would build, as artist and theorist of culture, in the future. In this regard, it is worth noting that the depth of African culture in New Jersey communities of blacks, especially in Princeton, strongly resembled Africa's impact on the New York communities in which Garnet grew to maturity.

Still, life in Princeton gave Robeson a sense of the South not easily duplicated elsewhere in the North in the early part of this century. There was in fact little relief for those ex-slaves, including relatives of the Robesons, who moved north to Princeton, in which Robeson spent the first ten years of his life. Not only was there segregation, but the intellectual elite, based at the university, held a conception of the place of blacks in the life of the country hardly softened by emancipation and Reconstruction. Not only was the mind of Princeton, like the mind of the South, controlled by Wall Street, but Bourbon and banker were one in that town, where "the decaying smell of the plantation Big House was blended with the crisper smell of the countinghouse." That was Robeson's way of looking at it, and he added that the theology was Calvin and the religion cash. "Princeton of my boyhood (and I don't think it has changed much since then) was for all the world like any small town in the deep South. Less than fifty minutes from New York, and even closer to Philadelphia, Princeton was spiritually located in Dixie."[4]

Southern black culture moved north with those blacks who migrated to Princeton, merging with the culture of the black North, that which was African and common to blacks in the North and the South easing the process. The migration north of members of the Robeson family and of other North Carolina blacks following emancipation meant that some blacks to whom John Kunering and other African cultural practices were familiar, including the performance of the spirituals, helped form the culture on which the Robeson's drew, particularly in Princeton, for spiritual sustenance. Young Robeson was at the center of that culture, though unaware in any theoretical sense of its meaning. But being there gave him a sense of how the culture of his people was used in isolated regions of the South where spiritual renewal was especially needed, and it laid the basis for what became a lifelong interest in the fate of his people in the Deep South, no doubt because so much around him called to mind their slave past:

> Traditionally the great university—which is practically all there is in the town—has drawn a large part of its student body and faculty from below the Mason-Dixon Line, and along with these sons of the Bourbons came the most rigid social and economic patterns of White Supremacy. . . . Rich Princeton was white: the Negroes were there to do the work. An aristocracy must have its retainers, and so the people of our small Negro community were, for the most part, a servant class. . . . Under the caste system in Princeton, the Negro, restricted to menial jobs at low pay and lacking any semblance of political rights or bargaining power could hope not for justice but for charity. The stern hearts and tight purses of the master class could on occasion be opened by appeals from the "deserving poor."[5]

Robeson's relationship to his father in youth was in some respects similar to the one Garnet had with his. For both fathers, there had been long periods of crisis in slavery not simply for themselves but for their families, a pattern to some extent repeated after each escaped from slavery. Neither appears to have been diminished spiritually by the difficulties before them, but, following slavery, William Robeson, perhaps even more than George Garnet, continued to confront white people who reminded him in various ways of the slaveowning class. If that was not trying enough, there was a period of conflict between him and others in his church that led to poverty for his family, a blow that might have been too powerful for most men to rise from. Robeson recalled that development, noting,

> That a so-called lowly station in life was no bar to man's assertion of his full human dignity was heroically demonstrated by my father. . . . After more than two decades of honored leadership in his church, a factional dispute among the members removed him as pastor. Adding to the pain was the fact that some of his closest kin were part of the ousting faction. . . .[M]y father, then past middle age, with an invalid wife and dependent children at home, was forced to begin life anew. He got a horse and wagon, and began to earn his living hauling ashes for the townsfolk. This was his work at the time I first remember him and I recall the growing mound of dusty ashes dumped into our backyard at 13 Green Street.

Despite his work, Robeson was convinced that "no man carried himself with greater pride" than his father.[6]

Robeson thought the ex-slaves and their descendants in Princeton generally hardworking and "filled with the goodness of humanity" and a strength of spirit—here he had his father uppermost in mind—that seemed forged like steel. Apparently there was little complaining over the poverty and misfortune of those years, an attitude toward hardship found in black art and related to a love of life among his people that greatly impressed him. He noted that quality in relatives who worked menial jobs that brought them into daily contact with whites without their spirits being dimmed, or so it seemed to him. In fact, he had "the closest of ties" with victims of poverty. That some were relatives contributed to his sense of solidarity with them; the generosity of others contributed to a sense of solidarity with the larger black community—that is, with black people in America as a whole: "Hard-working people, and poor, most of them, in worldly goods—but how rich in compassion!"[7]

Robeson's identification with black people began at an early age. When he was six, his mother, born a free Negro in Pennsylvania and a woman of brilliance, died tragically in a fire. Those around Paul, especially his father, helped him overcome those times when he felt "the sorrows of a motherless child." For years following the death of his mother, he was the only child at home, and his father's care bound them together. And across the street and down each block were aunts, uncles, and cousins— "including some who were not actual relatives at all"—who established warm relations with the youth.

> In a way, I was adopted by all these good people, and there was always a place at their tables and a place in a bed (often with two or three other young ones) for Reverend Robeson's boy when my father was away on one of his trips to the seashore or attending a church conference. . . . There was the honest joy of laughter in these homes, folk-wit and story, hearty appetites for life as for the nourishing greens and black-eyed peas and cornmeal bread they shared with me.[8]

In this setting with continued segregation of Southern Negroes in Princeton, it is not surprising that Robeson in later years "immediately found" in West African languages "a kinship of rhythm and intonation with the Negro—English dialect" which he heard spoken around him as a child. It was to him "like a home-coming."[9] This is significant because his linguistic ties to Southern Negro speech—through his relatives and through other Negroes in New Jersey—constituted a means of direct and continuing contact with the speech patterns of the slaves. He acquired a sense of how they sang by listening to the singing of those who had once been slaves and to those, like himself, who were their immediate off-spring. Indeed, his family together with other blacks who migrated to New Jersey provided Robeson with unusual exposure to Southern culture, which was America's most direct path to Africa:

> William Robeson . . . was of pure black stock, probably very close to the African. The people of the North Carolina community from which he came are said to have been of the Bantu tribe. In any case, his simple relatives on the paternal side, who followed the minister from North Carolina to Princeton, became in a sort Paul's female guardians after the death of his mother. . . . This southern clan might still, so far as culture went, have been living in a primitive rural community, and it was much the same with his father's congregation in Somerville, New Jersey.

That background was mainly responsible for cultivating the Reverend Robeson's voice, which Paul described as "the greatest speaking voice" he had ever heard. "It was a deep, sonorous basso, richly melodic and refined, vibrant with the love and compassion which filled him."[10]

It was a unique conjunction when he took his father's hand and "walked at his side, . . . as he moved among the people." His father was of "very broad shoulder," his physical bearing reflecting "the rock-like strength and dignity of his character," on which Robeson appears to have drawn heavily. He found it "utterly impossible" as a child to understand how one so noble could have been a slave—"to be bought and sold, used and abused at will."[11] As Crummell noted of George Garnet, there was about William Drew Robeson a spirit that seemed unsullied by his years in slavery, a quality passed on from his generation of slaves eventually to inhere in his son, which together with Paul's intellectual prowess caused the black community and his father to expect greatness from him:

> I early became conscious—I don't quite know how—of a special feeling of the Negro community for me. . . . Like my father, the people claimed to see something special about me. Whatever it was, and no one really said, they felt I was fated for great things to come. Somehow they were sure of it, and because of that belief they added an extra measure to the affection they lavished on their preacher's motherless child. . . . I wondered at times about their notion that I was some kind of child of destiny and that my future would be linked with the longed-for better days to come.[12]

Such generosity from relatives and neighbors later helped keep Robeson from losing his sense of values when wealth was available to him, and their expectation that he would contribute to their liberation figured in his commitment to socialism. Indeed, it was the generosity of poor blacks toward him that had fertilized his spirit for the seeds of socialism that would later fall upon it.

Their spirit of cooperation informed much of their art—an art close to them and deeply felt, which contributed to its freshness despite sources of origin that reached back more than a century in America and many more in Africa. A sense of their people as a whole was reflected in their art, and Robeson was a participant in their ceremonies, which from an early age reinforced the bonds of community:

> Yes, I heard my people singing!—in the glow of parlor coal stove and on summer porches sweet with lilac air, from choir loft and Sunday morning pews—and my soul was filled with their harmonies. Then, too, I heard these songs in the very sermons of my father, for in the Negro's speech there is much of the phrasing and rhythms of folk-song. The great, soaring gospels we love are merely sermons that are sung; and as we thrill to such gifted gospel singers as Mahalia Jackson, we hear the rhythmic eloquence of our preachers, so many of whom, like my father, are masters of poetic speech.[13]

The African trait of one cultural form expressing the essentials of another was heard in his father's sermons and in the "richly melodic" quality of his speaking voice. The phrasing and rhythms of Negro speech help explain the ease with which his father's sermons became song.

Robeson was exposed from early youth to currents of Africanity flowing from many directions toward him, and he absorbed them, which laid the foundation for his understanding of blacks in the Deep South and in the nation. In fact, there could hardly have been a better field for exploring African culture in America than his early New Jersey environment. Not surprisingly, given the richness of that culture in his family, he saw a variant of the ring shout—possibly the shout itself—during the sermons of his father. "When he felt very happy," Robeson said of him, "he'd start what you call moving about," a form of sacred dance, as we have seen, often associated with ceremonies in which the ring shout occurs. Since the Reverend Robeson at times danced during religious services, it follows that members of his congregation rose to dance on such occasions.

Small wonder another aspect of the culture of his youth was African in inspiration—the ready acceptance, among most of the blacks in the communities in which he lived, of major forms of black secular music, with few if any objections on religious grounds. Certainly the absence of a thriving black middle class must have been a factor in the black community's affirmation of its music, a music in which patterns of sound that characterize one form are heard in others, most with roots in the sacred. That jazz and blues were being created in the first decade of Robeson's life contributed to reciprocity of forms and was a source of enormous inspiration and instruction to musicians and singers living in black communities. A lot of music was heard in the everyday process of living, the songs sung in natural settings:

Here in this little hemmed-in world where home must be theatre and concert hall and social center, there was a warmth of song. Songs of love and longing, songs of trials and triumph, [of] deep-flowing rivers and rollicking brooks, hymn-song and ragtime ballad, gospels and blues, and the healing comfort to be found in the illimitable sorrow of the Spirituals.[14]

An incident occurred that helped Robeson discipline himself. His father was sixty-three when Robeson, ten at the time, disobeyed, running away when he was called. His father ran after him, fell, and knocked out a tooth. The horrified youngster rushed back and helped him to his feet. He never forgot the emotions that overwhelmed him—"the sense of horror, shame, ingratitude, selfishness." He said that he adored his father, would have given his life for him "in a flash—and here [he] had hurt him, disobeyed him!" That incident with his father is a metaphor for what Robeson's relationship to his people would eventually be. In any case, his father never had to admonish him again, and the experience "became a tremendous source of discipline which has lasted through the years."[15]

Robeson attended a segregated elementary school in Princeton and mixed schools in Westfield and Somerville, New Jersey. His contacts with white youngsters and their parents were positive. He called them "friendly connections" and thought that was so in some cases because the parents hoped he might favorably influence their children. In the integrated school in Westfield, he was a leader among his peers, which enhanced his confidence in himself—a process heightened in his Somerville, New Jersey, years in high school. There the press of racism was largely absent, and once again he found himself in competition with and a leader of white youngsters. He was encouraged to sing in the glee club and was befriended by several of his white teachers. Except for those with the principal, who hated Robeson because of his intelligence, relations with whites were warm and open for him in high school. No doubt such positive relationships, rare for a Negro youth at the time, were responsible for his seeing whites as individuals, not as a monolith.[16]

His studies were supervised by his father and, on occasion, by an older brother who attended the University of Pennsylvania Medical School. His father's education, though late in life, was "along the classic pattern," for he learned to read Greek and Latin, which required, in addition to intelligence, a tremendous desire for self-improvement. He supervised his young son's study of the classics in high school and in college. According to Robeson, his father was with him "page by page through Virgil and Homer and other classics in which he was well grounded." Robeson added, "A love of learning, a ceaseless quest for truth in all its fullness—this my father taught."[17]

That the Reverend Robeson, despite his classical training, was so deeply and unashamedly African was an indication of how one might be African in spiritual outlook and behavior while also embracing aspects of the Christian faith. It is therefore not unlikely that George Garnet, while in Maryland and in New York, remained African while practicing the Christian faith as well. But the Reverend Robeson's grasp of the Western intellectual tradition meant that there was no great gap in the degree of education he attained in relation to that of his son, which helps explain the favor with which the son viewed the African religion of his father, since one as "educated" as the Reverend Robeson did not look down on the religion of his people. Indeed, he respectfully practiced their religion and had faith in their ability, which led him to demand of them all of which they were capable.[18]

The Reverend Robeson eschewed industrial education as the principal focus of educational endeavor for himself and other blacks. While it is unclear how he viewed the debate between Du Bois and Washington, in a practical sense he came down on the side of Du Bois, "flatly rejecting

Washington's concept that Negro education be limited essentially to manual training. He firmly believed that the heights of knowledge must be scaled. . . . Latin, Greek, philosophy, history, literature—all the treasures of learning must be the Negro's heritage as well." Moreover, thanks to some of his high school teachers, Robeson was referred "to standard reference works on sociology, race relations, Africa and world affairs" and felt "great pride when the books and articles proved to be by our Dr. Du Bois and often loaned these to . . . fellow-students, who were properly impressed by his . . . acknowledged authority."[19]

Attendance at Princeton was not possible for him and had not been for an older brother, Bill, who was not admitted despite superb academic credentials. (So strong was racism in the town that Bill, not permitted to attend the white high school, had to travel eleven miles to Trenton to attend high school.) When the Reverend Robeson spoke to Woodrow Wilson about opening the doors of the university to Bill, he was told it was out of the question, as it was when Paul came along, so Paul went to Rutgers.[20] Before he enrolled, just two black students had been there since the college was founded in 1766. The only Negro in his class of 1915, Robeson suffered all manner of abuse. When word went out that he planned to join the football team, the reaction of the players on the team was "Send him out—we'll kill him," and they tried. On his first day out for the team, they broke his nose—an injury that troubled him as a singer from then on—and dislocated a shoulder. Returning after confinement to bed, he made a tackle and, while down, was cleated on the right hand. It "took every single one of the fingernails off my right hand," he recalled. "That's when I knew rage!"

> The next play came around my end, the whole first string backfield came at me. I swept out my arms . . . and then three men running interference went down. The ball carrier was a first-class back named Kelly. I wanted to kill him, and I mean't to kill him. . . . I got Kelly in my two hands and I heaved him up over my head. . . . I was going to smash him so hard to the ground that I'd break him right in two, and I could have done it, but just then the coach yelled . . . "Robey, you're on the varsity!"

Whereupon Robeson, who was six feet three and 215 pounds, lowered Kelly to the ground.[21]

After that first attempt to make the team, Robeson admitted that he didn't know how much more he could take. "But my father . . . had impressed upon me," he said, "that when I was out on a football field or in a classroom or anywhere else . . . I had to show that I could take whatever they handed out. . . . This was part of our struggle." A great deal had to be handled by the seventeen-year-old who entered that freshman Rutgers class and made the team: he lived in segregated housing facilities on road trips, often had to take his meals on the team bus, and faced racial violence in game after game. Against West Virginia, he returned blow for blow. At halftime, the West Virginia coach told his players that Robeson had given "as good as he's gotten and without squealing," that he should therefore be given a break. But after the game he remarked, "Why, that colored boy's legs were so gashed and bruised that the skin peeled off when he removed his stockings."[22] His football career was oddly symbolic of the level of political resistance he would later encounter when racist forces of the society ganged up against him. Yet Robeson won All-American football honors in 1917 and 1918 and was hailed by Walter Camp as the greatest end ever to play the game. He won a total of thirteen varsity letters in athletics and was elected to Phi Beta Kappa in his junior year.[23]

At a family reunion in 1918, he presented an address entitled "Loyalty to Convictions." His choice of that topic was not accidental, for that was the text of his father's life—loyalty to one's convictions:

> Unbending. Despite anything. From my youngest days I was imbued with that concept. This bedrock idea of integrity was taught by Reverend Robeson to his children not so much by preachment . . . but, rather, by the daily example of his life and work. . . . So I marvel that there was no hint of servility in my father's make up. Just as in youth he refused to remain a slave, so in all the years of his manhood he disdained to be an Uncle Tom. From him we learned, and never doubted it, that the Negro was in every way the equal of the white man. And we fiercely resolved to prove it.[24]

An important dimension of the theory set forth in Robeson's commencement address grew directly out of the example of his family and out of experiences with the black communities of Princeton, Westfield, and Somerville—but especially out of that early Princeton environment. One must remember that by the time of his graduation he had acquired a classical education and had read widely. And while he was influenced by the American libertarian tradition, through his early admiration of Abraham Lincoln, and by American radicalism, through his reading of Wendell Phillips, the address seemed inspired chiefly by his contact over the years with the black community. In it he considered the resources that must be drawn on for the liberation of black America, and he concluded that blacks must rely primarily on themselves. Blacks of talent—more precisely, those fortunate enough to receive an education—must seek, as a natural obligation, the liberation of their people, must acknowledge "a sacred call to that which lies before us."[25] Here the influence of his father and that of Du Bois came together in his consciousness and were reinforced, for Du Bois's example and his charge to black intellectuals were known to Robeson at the time. There was in Robeson's affirmation of the call Du Bois's conception of intellectual obligation and, in addition, an emphasis on the role of those further down the social ladder reminiscent of Sidney:

> I go out to do my part in helping my untutored brother. We of this less favored race realize that our future lies chiefly in our own hands. On ourselves alone will depend the preservation of our liberties and the transmission of them in their integrity to those who will come after us. And we are struggling on to show that knowledge can be obtained under difficulties; that poverty may give place to affluence; that obscurity is not an absolute bar to distinction, and that a way is open to welfare and happiness to all who will follow the way with resolution and wisdom; that neither the old-time slavery nor continued prejudice need extinguish self-respect or paralyze effort; that no power outside himself can prevent man from sustaining an honorable character and a useful relation to his day and generation. We know that neither institutions nor friends can make a race stand unless it has strength in its own foundations; that races like individuals must stand or fall by their own merit; that to fully succeed they must practice their virtues of self-reliance, self-respect, industry, perseverance and economy.[26]

Robeson's family—his father, two of his brothers and a sister—exemplified the above qualities. His sister became an educator, one of the brothers a minister and the other a doctor. But another brother, Reed, took a different path, one that led his father to ask him to leave because he might have a bad influence on the younger Paul. Paul, who loved Reed, has provided the best description of him:

> He won no honors in classroom, pulpit or platform. Yet I remember him with love. Restless, rebellious, scoffing at conventions, defiant of the white man's law—I've known many Negroes like Reed. I see them every day. Blindly, in their own reckless manner, they seek a way out for themselves; alone, they pound with their fists . . . against walls that only the shoulders of the many can topple. "Don't ever take low," was the lesson Reed taught me. "Stand up to them and hit back harder than they hit you!" When the many have learned that lesson, everything will be different and then the fiery ones like Reed will be able to live out their lives in peace and no one will have cause to frown on them.[27]

Robeson also envisioned his people as a whole moving toward liberation by relying on their spiritual and intellectual resources. Spiritual resources were found in abundance through black religion and black art in his father's church and elsewhere. And though such resources were present, the intellectual resources of his people, as Du Bois had noted, had to find more effective means of expression, given the crisis of oppression before them. Moreover, Robeson realized that blacks, considering their status as a minority, could not achieve their liberation without a greater spirit of community among Americans as a whole. Still, his faith in the educated black's loyalty to his people, as in the case of Du Bois, was largely misplaced because, like Du Bois, he did not adequately consider the role of class in black America.

The summer of 1919 was a terrible one in many parts of the country as blacks, including some in U.S. Army uniforms, were beaten and lynched. Though fear of competition from blacks in the labor market was a factor in many of the disturbances, the racial attitudes prevalant in the nation caused whites to feel virtual immunity from prosecution in carrying out acts of racial violence, a feeling not unrelated to the Wilson administration's promotion of segregation in the nation's capital, which helps explain Robeson's call for broader racial cooperation. He expressed the hope that the war effort would generate the necessary spirit of brotherhood—a new idealism—that would lead to racial harmony. An editorial in the Rutgers University newspaper, *Targrum,* written by Robeson's former classmates, gave little indication that they shared his perception of the state of race relations in America:

> But one fact which deserves consideration, is too frequently neglected, is that equality does exist . . . for those colored men and women who struggle for success. Look at Paul Robeson, former All-American football player and one of four men tapped for the Senior honor society. . . . What other nation has a record of encouraging Negro achievement even remotely comparable to that of the United States?[28]

I

Following graduation from Rutgers, Robeson entered Columbia Law School. What he learned about discipline at Rutgers carried over into his years of law school, as he balanced an extraordinarily diverse extracurricular life with serious attention to his studies. At Columbia, his acting and singing careers began, and on weekends he played professional football. Described by classmates as very sociable, he graduated with honors and, shortly thereafter, was hailed as a superb bass-baritone and as an actor of uncommon ability. The reach of his brilliance in his teens was the foundation for later activities no less various that won international acclaim for him, as first one then another career, as if by magic, shimmered before him, and he seemed an instrument of a special destiny.

Such was Robeson's success in Eugene O'Neill's *The Emperor Jones* that O'Neill, in inscribing a volume of his plays to him, wrote that he had found in the young actor's interpretation of Brutus Jones "the most complete satisfaction an author can get—that of seeing his creation born into flesh and blood." And George Jean Nathan, a stern and influential critic, assessed Robeson's acting in *All God's Chillun Got Wings* and *The Emperor Jones* in very encouraging terms. Though Robeson had relatively little training and experience, he thought him "one of the most thoroughly eloquent, impressive, and convincing actors" he had listened to and looked at "in almost twenty years of theatre-going."[29]

Robeson had even less training, in a formal sense, as a singer. In fact, his career on the concert stage began almost by accident. There was a chance meeting with Lawrence Brown, the musical scholar and accompanist of Roland Hayes, to whose playing Robeson sang one day. And there was encouragement, after hearing him sing, from James Light of the Provincetown Players, with whom Robeson achieved success in doing the O'Neill plays. At Light's urging, Robeson agreed to give a concert at the Greenwich Village Theater with Brown as accompanist—a concert, Robeson decided, that would consist entirely of Negro spirituals. Such a repertoire was an unprecedented conception, and the prospect of a career on the stage triggered in Robeson memories of countless occasions in youth when he sang and heard spirituals. As he prepared for the concert, as selections were made and the program took shape, he reflected on the meaning of the music as never before, which was inevitable, since he would be the only singer on stage. His task was to convince not merely his own people that their music was worthy of such emphasis but sophisticated white music lovers as well. On April 19, 1925, a little over a week following his twenty-seventh birthday, the concert was given. The music critic of the *New York World* wrote;

> All those who listened last night to the first concert in this country made entirely of Negro music . . . may have been present at a turning point, one of those thin points of time in which a star is born and not yet visible. . . . Paul Robeson's voice is difficult to describe. It is a voice in which deep bells ring.[30]

Though Robeson's success with spirituals seemed sudden, he had gone through a long period of preparation, without planning to sing professionally. He had been to music school in the black church, and that training prepared him for a concert career before audiences, no matter how sophisticated. His performance of spirituals on the concert stage was a radical departure from the context in which they were traditionally sung. Since their world value as art depended on the song rather than on their broader relationship to the culture of black people, through the shout, Robeson won a lasting place for that music on the stage, a development in which there was no small irony. His emergence brought an incomparable rendering of the music in the tradition of the African slaves, and by then that tradition could claim in Du Bois a major interpreter of the spirituals.

In contrast to Roland Hayes, the greatest interpreter of the spirituals after Robeson, Robeson wanted to preserve the beauty of the "black voice," which could not be done by employing the techniques of another tradition. James Weldon Johnson referred to "the sheer simplicity" with which he sang spirituals, to his singing "without any conscious attempt at artistic effort and by devoted adherence to the primitive traditions."[31] Thus, the very music of slaves—created within the circle of culture—was the music he sang, in time consciously tracing its linguistic and other features back to African sources. That the voice was of a tradition that placed the highest premium on natural delivery meant that, at its best, its qualities were the source of an appeal of universal reach. When he sang, the slave community expressing itself in song was as much in evidence as its expression in the folktale or in dance. The critic of the *New York Times* wrote after that first Robeson concert,

> His Negro Spirituals have the ring of the revivalist; they hold in them a world of religious experience. It's their cry from the depths, this universal humanism, that touches the heart. . . . Mr. Robeson's gift is to make them tell in every line, and that not by any outward stress, but by an overwhelming inward conviction. Sung by one man, they voiced the sorrow and hopes of a people.[32]

Robeson's success as a singer owed much to the time and circumstances of his birth and early development. Time and context were relevant, for he became the preeminent interpreter on the concert stage of the culture of the Southern Negro, and through him the culture of the African, despite the fact that, like Du Bois, he was born in the North. Since so much of his personal life, through his father and relatives, was tied to the experiences of his people before emancipation and the essentials of their experience distilled in the folklore he heard as a child, Robeson was well situated to interpret slave culture through song. Knowing slave music from the inside for over two decades, he had few barriers of technique and feeling to overcome when singing that music professionally. The time of his birth, a few years after slavery, was important because ex-slaves at that time dominated black culture through their own efforts and those of their offspring. Paul's was the ultimate example of that domination on the concert stage.

In his early years of concertizing, he sang only the songs of his people, some of which he heard in youth and others of which were brought to his attention by Lawrence Brown. Songs that were personal in the most private sense were shared with his audiences but none more naturally as when he sang to "re-create for an audience the great sadness of the Negro slave in 'Sometimes I Feel Like a Motherless Child,'" his upper register rendering of "True believer" among the most inspired voicings of faith and sorrow:

> Sometimes I feel like a motherless child,
> Sometimes I feel like a motherless child,
> Sometimes I feel like a motherless child,
> A long ways from home;
> A long ways from home;
> True believer
> A long ways from home
> A long ways from home

The strain of living as slaves in an alien land, at the heart of the song, gains in resonance with repetition:

> Sometimes I feel like I'm almost gone,
> Sometimes I feel like I'm almost gone,
> Sometimes I feel like I'm almost gone,
> A long ways from home;
> A long ways from home;
> True believer
> A long ways from home
> A long ways from home[33]

Robeson's belief that religion is the foundation of black culture is convincing evidence of his understanding of African culture. Though it is not certain when he came to that awareness, he very likely did so early in his career, even before he recognized the extent of African influence in that culture. He found in "I Gotta Home in Dat Rock" an ideal vehicle for that view, one constructed from a sense of the value of communal being, a fundamental feature of the Christian faith that won easy affirmation from the African, who came from cultures in which the community held primacy over the individual. "I Gotta Home in dat Rock," a signature piece for Paul as artist and man, was recorded before his voice took on all the power of its later years. Yet one senses his potential vocal power as one senses the strength to come in the tree that has begun a regal climb. Robeson's strength radiated outward in a quietly lyrical expression of faith:

> I got a home in dat rock,
> Don't you see?
> I got a home in dat rock,
> Don't you see?
> Between the earth an' sky,
> Thought I heard my savior cry,
> You got a home in dat rock,
> Don't you see?

Considering his experiences in youth with poor but generous people, there is a sentiment expressed in the song with which he could readily identify:

> Poor man Laz'rus, poor as I
> Don't you see?
> Poor man Laz'rus, poor as I
> Don't you see?
> Poor man Laz'rus, poor as I,
> When he died he found a home on high,
> He had a home in dat rock,
> Don't you see?

It was easy for him to identify with a stanza of the song that is critical of
the rich:

> Rich man Dives, he lived so well,
> Don't you see?
> Rich man Dives, he lived so well,
> Don't you see?
> Rich man Dives, he lived so well,
> When he died he found a home in Hell,
> He had no home in dat rock,
> Don't you see?

And he sang the closing stanza with a lyricism as serene as that with
which he began the song, a central concern—the oppression of the poor
by the rich—resolved in a prophecy of doom:

> God gave Noah the rainbow sign,
> Don't you see?
> God gave Noah the rainbow sign,
> Don't you see?
> God gave Noah the rainbow sign,
> No more water but the fire next time,
> Better get a home in dat rock.[34]

Robeson wanted his listeners to know "the strong, gallant convict of
the chain gang, to make [them] feel his thirst, understand his naive boast-
ing about his strength in 'Water Boy,'" a song whose rhythms determine
the rise of the hammer, the arc of its descent, and the grunt of the singer at
the point of impact. Thus, he brought the work song, with its peculiar
requirements of rhythm, to the concert stage and with it the awful plight
of chain gang workers, so prominent a feature of the Southern landscape
following Reconstruction and in the opening decades of the twentieth century. The song, a declaration of pride amid horror, is about the black
worker creating while working after slavery as before:

> Der aint no hamma
> Dats on a dis mountain
> Dat a rings a like mine, boys
> Dat a rings a like mine
> Done bust dis rock, boys
> From here to Macon
> All de way to de jail, boys
> Yes, a back to de jail[35]

Robeson's career on the concert stage got off on so high a level of
critical acclaim and public acceptance that his singing, together with his
acting, made him a highly visible talent of the "Harlem Renaissance"
years. Moreover, he was a more authentic Harlemite than most of the
black artists associated with Harlem, though he spent the last years of the

twenties abroad.[36] Although his Harlem years were years of great activity
for him in the arts, the period 1925-27 was also one of study and reflection,
a period during which he began to know more of the African sources of his
art. But his role as an artist at this time was not necessarily more nationalistic than his earlier efforts as a scholar, for each endeavor was directed at helping his people achieve self-confidence and autonomy. His
sense of obligation to them enabled him to view his endeavors as indis-
solubly linked to their destiny. His very early demonstration of the unity
of mind and body was the grounding for his assurance, later given theoretical expression, that nature did not intend their separation. Thus, his
own wholeness of being was the basis for his emergence as one of the few
genuinely renaissance men of our time.

In him the dichotomy between art and politics probably never existed,
despite his contention that he was not political prior to the thirties. In any
case, the effects of his concertizing were political and of consequence to
nationalist theory.[37] Moreover, his sense of responsibility to his people
made possible the fulfillment of nationalist promise in such unlikely areas
as sports. To act on that sense of responsibility was not so much a challenge to others as a way of measuring oneself against an ideal that is self-
generated, and that later guided his thought on the question of nationalism, individually and collectively. Before Robeson the possibilities
for nationalist expression had not been so broadly conceived and practiced within the Afro-American experience. Even so, nothing advanced
by him was outside the boundaries of nationalism established by those
whose thought on the subject he, together with Du Bois, came to represent so well. As we have seen, such early black leaders as Walker,
Garnet, and the nationalists of the nineteenth century generally may have
failed to understand the culture of their people, but they affirmed autonomy for them, thereby creating boundaries broad enough to encompass
black cultural expression, from acting to the ring shout.[38]

While Robeson observed aspects of the ring shout in youth, by the time
he left for London in 1927 he was familiar with some of the literature on
the subject. That is known because there appeared in 1926 James Weldon
Johnson's *American Negro Spirituals,* a work that would have attracted
his attention because its commentaries on the subject are among the most
learned and elegant. It should also be noted that the volume contains a
masterly collection of spirituals, one that Robeson, as their most authentic interpreter, would have known. And in that volume Johnson acknowl-
edges Robeson's success in singing spirituals along the lines of their
creation, and he discusses the spirituals and the ring shout. It is likely,
therefore, that Robeson was among the first to read *American Negro Spirituals.* In addition, we know from other sources that he respected Johnson's views on cultural matters, and that the two men had more than a
passing acquaintance.[39]

They in fact saw each other at important social events before Robeson's departure for England. On one occasion, Clarence Darrow and he read at a party given by Johnson. As Darrow sat "under a lighted lamp, the only one in the room left lighted, reading in measured tones from his book *Farmington*," those assembled heard "the rising and falling melody of his voice . . . the words falling, falling . . . through their minds" to lodge "in their hearts with strange stirrings." Robeson followed, reading from Johnson's *God's Trombones*, which drew from Darrow "the words of Agrippa to Saint Paul, 'Almost thou persuadest me to be a Christian.'" The year was 1927, and *God's Trombones* had appeared then with its brief but brilliant reference to the slave preacher mediating differences and melding various African ethnic groups into a single people. So once again, after having read Du Bois's *Souls*, Robeson encountered in the Johnson volume the African priest who mingled heathen rites. By that time, then, African ethnic interaction in slavery was a consideration that Robeson was at least occasionally taking into account when reflecting on slave culture.[40]

For understandable reasons, Robeson rejected Johnson's conclusion, so reminiscent of nineteenth-century observers, that the shout was "quasi-religious," "semi-barbaric music." He made this rejection in print in the 1930s and later on the concert stage, as he demonstrated that perhaps the most important source of the religious chant of American blacks was the African religious festival. While not "strictly" classifying the spirituals with the shout, seeing them as allied, Johnson allows that a form of the spirituals is found—though "not true Spirituals'—within the circle.[41] In addition, he reversed what appears to have been the natural order of things, arguing that the shout was a kind of appendage to Christianity:

The "ring shout," in truth, is nothing more or less than the survival of a primitive African dance, which in a quite understandable way attached itself in the early days to the Negro's Christian worship. I can remember seeing this dance many times when I was a boy. . . . The music, starting perhaps, with a spiritual becomes a wild monotonous chant. The same musical phrase is repeated over and over one, two, three, four, five hours . . . the very monotony of sound and motion produces an ecstatic state.[42]

But recognizing dance when he saw it, he knew too much of black culture to be taken in by the argument that because there was no crossing of one's legs dance did not occur in the shout, a perception available to Robeson by the time he left for England and had begun investigating the African background on numerous levels, including the relationship of African dance to religious ceremonies in black America.

I I

Paul Robeson moved to London in 1927, and his studies at the London School of Oriental Languages sparked the beginning of a momentous development: he became the only artist of the "Harlem Renaissance" to cultivate scholarship on Africa and to have wide and continual contact with Africans from around the world. During this time, he began putting theories, arrived at after much reflection, into practice as an actor and singer attempting to become more and more attuned to his heritage. There is no doubt that, despite an impressive effort as an actor, Robeson's performances on the concert stage represented a far better realization of that objective than his best efforts on stage and in film, for on the concert stage he had near total control over what and how he would sing, and there he gave unprecedented emphasis to the songs of his people. Commenting on his suitability for singing the spirituals, he remarked in the opening years of his career that the artist should confine himself to the art for which he is qualified, and that one can be qualified only by an understanding that was born in one, not cultivated.[43]

In what can only be described as a nationalist stance, the young artist could not see how a Negro could really feel the sentiments of a German, or an Italian, or a Frenchman. Nor could he see where the achievement lay in singing an opera in the languages of European peoples. Of course, if a black man were to write a great opera on an African theme it would be "just as insignificant for a white opera singer to give a creditable performance of it." Robeson believed that if one did not understand the philosophy or psychology of the Italian, German, or Frenchman, then one could not sing their songs. Since their history had nothing in common with that of his slave ancestors, he decided that he would not sing their music, or the songs of their ancestors—a position he altered by 1930.[44]

When Robeson expanded his repertoire to include the music of other people, he displayed a decided preference for the body of world folk music, which he thought closer to the music of his people than most European "classical music." Though he had warned that it was no "achievement to sing in the white man's Opera House," his exhaustive studies of the languages and music of many lands led him to choose Bach over Schubert because the German Romantic spirit was "foreign" to him and Bach's spirituality and religious quality closer to his soul. Furthermore, he found Russian music more satisfying than that produced by Germans because it often reflected an experience closer to that in Negro music, for the serfs of Russia had lived under an oppression not far removed from that of Negro slaves:

What was wrong with our despised music if it was akin to the great Russian? Had we a value that had been passed by? Were the outcast Negroes, who were studying to assimilate fragments of the unsympathetic culture of the

West, really akin to the great cultures of the East? It was a fascinating thought. I began to make experiments, I found that I—a Negro—could sing Russian songs like a native. I, who had to make the greatest effort to master French and German, spoke Russian in six months with a perfect accent, and am now finding it almost as easy to master Chinese.[45]

Robeson pointed to specific African inflections of voice and approaches to song that were analogous to the song style of American Negro religious leaders and their followers. In demonstrating this view, he sang sacred music from Africa and Afro-America, in the process showing the Negro spiritual's indebtedness to Africa apart from the context of its creation— the ring shout. It is probable that he was one of the few scholars of music in the Western world—perhaps the only one—to have demonstrated such analogues, drawing on family history in doing so.[46] In that demonstration, he offered an example of the type of cultural common denominators that might provide the basis for a greater degree of Pan-African cultural consciousness. Here was the sort of nationalist theoretical work that only Du Bois before him had engaged in: Robeson's work in this area recalls Du Bois's conclusions regarding his having heard the counterpart of the spiritual in Liberia. Ironically, the scene for Robeson's most formal presentation of such findings was Carnegie Hall in a concert in 1958, a time of frenzy over integration that threatened the Negro's sense of himself.

In that concert, Robeson illustrated the similarities between a Negro religious chant from America, an African chant, a Czech chant, and a Hassidic chant. He commented, before introducing the African music, that in searching for the source of Negro religious music he had gone back to Africa "and found the same forms that were in the African religious festivals." He found in East African music "melodies and a *form* which were very close to . . . forms of the early church of the middle ages." He told his audience that this was true "because the Abyssinian Church and the Church of the Sudan were a part of the eastern churches of Byzantium, and so they too had a music quite comparable to the music of the Near East. . . ." In that concert, before reciting an excerpt from Shakespeare's *Othello,* he informed his audience that Desdemona had not been killed "from savage passion," that Othello had come from "a culture as great as that of ancient Venice, from an Africa of equal stature."[47]

Robeson had earlier expanded on some of the results of his explorations of other cultures:

. . . I know the wail of the Hebrew and the plaint of the Russian. I understand both, as I do the philosophy of the Chinese, and I feel that both have much in common with the traditions of my race. And because I have been frequently asked to present something other than Negro art I may succeed in finding either a great Russian opera or play, or some great Hebrew or Chinese work, which I feel I shall be able to render [with the] necessary degree of understanding.[48]

Loth to comment on matters whose essentials he had not grasped, he did not bring out his first essay on Africa until he knew several African languages and many works on African peoples. While studying linguistics and African languages at the School of Oriental Languages, he tested his ability as an Africanist, honing his knowledge by "seeking out all kinds of people with whom to argue the colonial question," debating that issue with Rebecca West and with a few liberals in the British Foreign Office, who generally defended the view that Africans should ascend to the level of civilization.[49] More important than conversations with West and others about Africa—there is some question regarding the extent of their knowledge of the interior life of the African—was Robeson's wide reading on Africa, his study of African languages, and his contact with Africans. Still, whatever the source of his information on Africa, England introduced him to Africa in a way that America could not have done. There were many Africans in England, and Robeson and Eslanda, his wife, sought them out:

> Paul and I [would] seek out all the Africans we could find, everywhere we went: In England, Scotland, Ireland, France; in universities, on the docks, in slums. The more we talked with them, the more we came to know them, the more convinced we were that we are the same people: They know us, and we know them; we understand their spoken and unspoken word, we have the same kind of ideas, the same ambitions, the same kind of humor, many of the same values.[50]

Most of what Robeson learned about Africa he learned in London. His wife assessed the state of African studies in England during the period they were there:

> In England, on the other hand [in contrast to America], there is news of Africa everywhere: In the press, in the schools, in the films, in conversation. . . . There are courses on Africa in every good university in England; African languages are taught, missionaries are trained, and administrators are prepared for work "in the field." Everywhere there is information about Africa.[51]

The friendship between Robeson and Jomo Kenyatta provides a clue to one aspect of Robeson's reflections on African societies, for it is likely that the two men discussed Bronislaw Malinowski, under whom Kenyatta and Eslanda Robeson studied at London University. The leading anthropologist in England, Malinowski, thought by some to be the anthropologist of imperialism, saw little of intrinsic value in "savage" African societies. If Robeson did not discuss the influential teacher's functionalist theories with Kenyatta, surely he discussed them with his wife, for Malinowski was sometimes invoked by those who opposed Robeson's defenses of Africans and their cultures.[52]

Whatever the opposition in England to African liberation, and despite those who thought African cultures savage, the English offered opportunities to study Africa that were unsurpassed outside Africa, and Robeson benefited greatly from the state of scholarship on Africa there. Consequently, England afforded useful vantage points from which to determine what was African and what was American in Afro-American culture. So there was a substantial advantage to one studying Africa in being in the metropolis of a colonial power at a time when experts of various kinds were accumulating documentation on Africa and when debates on the nature of African societies were often intense.[53]

Robeson's interest in African nationalism was in part a reflection of the growing strength of nationalist currents in the thirties. Numerous colonial subjects moved in London circles at that time and were nationalists, mostly with socialist leanings. Such men helped to create an atmosphere congenial to the further development of that nationalism to which Robeson gave precocious expression in his commencement address in college. Beyond that, nationalism and Marxism were lodestars for the world's leading revolutionaries, almost all of whom had had some experience with colonialism. Revolutionaries in China were making impressive theoretical assaults on problems inherent in adapting Marxism to the imperatives of that ancient, sprawling land; others sought a Communist resolution of the problems of Vietnam, one that would, above all, guarantee the independence of their country. Still other nationalists, though not revolutionaries, among them Jawaharlal Nehru and V. K. Krishna Menon, sought freedom for their people short of sweeping structural changes, though it is true that Menon, like Nehru a friend of Robeson in his London years, was moving in the direction of Marxism in his quest for a solution to the problems confronting his people. More than most Afro-Asian nationalists then realized, more than most nationalists in the Americas then perceived, the twentieth century was destined to be the century of nationalist revolutions, under the guidance of socialists, in numerous parts of the world.[54]

Considering the intellectual, political, and social atmosphere in London and Robeson's wide contact with Afro-Asian nationalists there, it is small wonder that his nationalism flowered during his years abroad. From that vantage ground, he was better able to understand the strengths and weaknesses of his people, to relate them to how they might come into their own. A less committed man would no doubt have yielded to the allure of European culture, especially given such access to it. But Robeson was able to take its measure and not be dispirited by its claims to superiority. Hardly insecure in the presence of Americans abroad, he nevertheless was not often pleased to be among them, particularly since they were likely to remind him of the most unpleasant aspects of American life. Referring to her Paris years in the late twenties, Gertrude Stein writes,

Carl Van Vechten . . . sent us Paul Robeson. Paul Robeson interested Gertrude Stein. He knew american values and american life as only one in it but not of it could know them. And yet as soon as any other person came into the room he became definitely a negro. Gertrude Stein did not like hearing him sing spirituals. They do not belong to you any more than anything else, so why claim them, she said. He did not answer. Once a southern woman, a very charming southern woman, was there, and she said to him, where were you born, and he answered, in New Jersey and she said, not in the south, what a pity and he said, not for me. Gertrude Stein concluded that negroes were not suffering from persecution, they were suffering from nothingness. She always contends that the african is not primitive, he has a very ancient but a very narrow culture and there it remains. Consequently nothing does or can happen.[55]

A year or so later, Robeson identified important elements of character of Afro-Americans, "a people upon whom nature has bestowed, and in whom circumstances have developed, great emotional depth and spiritual intuition."[56] Their value system, especially as reflected in their art and spirituality, gave rise to the only significant *American* culture since the inception of the country. However, a deep sense of inferiority, more than any other factor, prevented black people from being aware of the richness of their heritage. In the tradition of nationalists before him, he focused on that feeling of inadequacy, observing that sufferings undergone had "left an indelible mark" on the soul of the race and had caused the Negro to become the victim of an inferiority complex that led him to imitate white people. "It has been drummed into him that the white man is the Salt of the Earth and the Lord of Creation, and as a perfectly natural result his ambition is to become as nearly like a white man as possible." Robeson was convinced that movement in that direction could never bring peace to the Negro.[57]

Robeson found a particular eagerness among young and "intelligent" Negroes "to dismiss the Spiritual as something beneath their new pride in their race . . . as if they wanted to put it behind them as something to be ashamed of—something that tied them to a past in which their forefathers were slaves." Those blacks who turned their backs on their folk music were contributing to their own destruction, for the spirituals were "the soul of the race made manifest"—a profound statement, considering the ancestral context of their formation. Moreover, his respect for the spirituals was linked to his concern that the black artist might give emphasis to the art "of other people in our Negro programs, magnificent and masterly though they may be." He felt that concessions to European music would lead to the "eventual obliteration of our own folk music, the musical idioms of our race . . . the finest expression and the loftiest we have to offer."[58]

To prevent such obliteration, he was not opposed to the emigration of portions of his people to Africa, for he argued that if black musical groups did not "arise all over the land [America] to cherish and develop our old

Spirituals" some of his people would have to leave the country and "go to Africa, where we can develop independently and bring forth a new music based on our roots." His concept of emigration was new in the sense that he was making a provisional case for emigration on cultural grounds, which was radically different from previous arguments for returning to Africa. The latter stressed the benefits New World blacks would make available to Africans; Robeson stressed what the American Negro might gain in a spiritual and artistic sense from Africans, a process that would make them more African than they could otherwise be. But he did not explain how such an enterprise might flourish, indeed be permitted, under colonialism. Nonetheless, his interest in re-creating new forms from on-the-spot African inspiration has hardly been common in the history of blacks in America.[59]

Whether he returned to Africa or not, it was essential that the black man "set his own standards," all the more because American whites, closer to Europeans in life-styles, were dangerously, perhaps fatally, entrapped by European dependence upon abstractions and hostility to emotive and intuitive values.[60] Not to set one's own standards in the midst of white Americans would constitute an egregious error, since blacks, more than any other people on American soil, were cultural protagonists. Their most important role in American life was identified by Robeson in a formulation that linked the sources of their creativity to, among other factors, the tragic circumstances of their history. Thus, he rejected the naive assumption that there is opposition between creativity and tragedy, realizing that a degree of human pain is inevitable, though forms of oppression are not:

> Now, as to the most important part which . . . the Negro is qualified to play in the American scene. I would define it as "cultural" with emphasis upon the spiritual aspect of that culture. With the passing of the Indians, the Negroes are the most truly indigenous stock in North America. They have grown up with that country, becoming part of the soil itself. They have had a better chance than any other of the races which have come to America to identify themselves with the atmosphere of the place, if only because they have been there much longer. They have been unhappy and badly treated, but they have retained (though they have not been allowed fully to express) their best and most characteristic qualities: a deep simplicity, a sense of mystery, a capacity for religious feeling, a spontaneous and entirely individual cheerfulness; and these have found expression in the only culture which Americans can point to as truly belonging to their country.[61]

In fact, the whole of American culture might secure from black culture "those qualities which appeal most directly to the intelligent European who values a depth of native tradition in art." Despite the long period of repression that the black man's "cultural actualities" have survived, "they can develop only with great difficulty in a hostile environment."

Here Robeson raised an issue that had long concerned Du Bois: how oppression prevented blacks from developing their genius more fully. But both Du Bois and Robeson believed that blacks could interpret their condition, despite the limitations imposed on them, in ways that might be revealing to much of mankind. The American scene, uncongenial to full creativity, Robeson called the "new Egypt," out of which he wanted to lead his people.[62] Nevertheless, the new promised land did not have to be Africa if blacks decided to build upon the founding stones of their culture, upon the folk amalgam of essentially African elements.

Robeson rejected nationalism as the ultimate goal of man, for he pointed out that the "family of nations" ideal must become the reality if mankind is to survive, a point of view that Walker and Garnet before him and certainly Du Bois shared. He wanted finally to see a world striving for deep spiritual and cultural values that transcend "narrow national, racial, or religious boundaries." With the right encouragement, the transforming impulse could come from blacks in America but, as he observed some years later, not unless they were prepared to participate in the New World culture as Africans—a goal to study and work for, not to will. Robeson was convinced, therefore, that if the Negro artist denies his heritage, his potential cannot be realized: "Let us take a concrete example. What would have become of the genius of Marie Lloyd if she had been ashamed of being Cockney? Would Robert Burns have been as great a poet if he had denied his ploughman speech and aped the gentlemen of his day?" He warned of the dangers of the impulse that causes those born to inequality to cloak their true value "under a false foreign culture, applied from outside, when, instead, natural growth [comes] from within," an argument, in broad outline, brilliantly made by Garnet in his Sidney letters.[63] While Garnet came at the question more directly than most black intellectuals, eschewing "universals," nationalists generally supported the sort of self-exertion urged by Robeson, but their problem was in distinguishing what was foreign from what was their own.

In the late twenties and throughout the thirties, Robeson observed trends in Western art and met the leading artists of his day—including Picasso, Milhaud, Stravinsky, Brancusi, and Jacob Epstein, all of whom were interested in African art. Critical of blacks in the plastic arts, he again pointed to the root cause of their failings: "While Negro artists attempt pale copies of Western art, Epstein derives inspiration from ancient Negro sculpture. No Negro will leave a permanent mark on the world till he learns to be true to himself." He reasoned that one cannot expect a Negro given to self-hatred to value the positive features of his people until "something has happened to restore his respect for them." "Why was it," he asked, "a white man who wrote Green Pastures and made a fortune from it?" Here again a portion of his criticism misfires, since racism prevented black playwrights from having much access to the legitimate theater. But surely concern over the failure of blacks to write plays that tap the rich veins of their heritage was a legitimate matter for the young artist to air. An actor knowledgeable about the plight of blacks around the world, he was conscious of his people's need for gifted writers, for only then was the Negro actor likely to reveal to his people the greatness of their heritage and the tragic dimensions and consequences of their dependency on white values.[64]

To assist others in understanding the psychology of the oppressed, Robeson compared the psychological experiences of the Negro with those of exploited workers, women, and European Jews: "All those people will understand what it is that makes most Negroes desire nothing so much as to prove their equality with the white man—on the white man's own ground." Though such groups might "feel for the Negro," not many would realize that the same impulse "which drives them to copy those with the desired status is killing what is of most value—the personality which makes them unique."[65] When treating the psychology of the oppressed and reflecting on music, sculpture, and poetry in relation to the oppressed, Robeson was drawing on experience that encouraged comparative thought. It was not that his basic conclusion regarding the baneful effects of imitation and self- hatred was original, for it was known to those in the nationalist tradition at least as early as Walker. What was fresh and original was the wide, comparative context in which he chose to carry on the discussion.

Robeson came to understand that the split of interest among blacks was not only economic but also cultural and that it was manifested in a variety of ways. In his opinion, the privileged among the Negro people, especially those in the North, suffered more than others from the promise and effects of assimilation. While certain Negro intellectuals try "to suppress in the Negro papers every element of our own culture in favor of the so-called higher values of white culture," still others among the educated and wealthy do their utmost to achieve assimilation on numerous levels, all too badly on most.[66] Robeson drew attention to the seeming paradox of well-to-do Negroes set against themselves, victims of the blandishments and the whiplash of America. The effectiveness of his analysis of the condition of his people, however, rested on his ability to locate the ultimate sources of the vigor and torpor of spirit of African peoples here and abroad.

I I I

In "I Want to be African," which appeared in *What I Want from Life* in 1934, Robeson described the American Negro as that "tragic creature, a man without a nationality." Though you might claim to be American, to be French, to be British, "you cannot assume a nationality as you would a

new suit of clothes." With notable courage and insight, he remarked that
the assumption of African nationality is "an extremely complicated matter, fraught with the greatest importance to me and some millions of coloured folk."[67] Prior to that time, no nationalist theoretician had noted the
extent of the difficulty of assuming African nationality. Nor had any focused on the objective of getting his people actually to ground themselves
in African values, which were constantly in a state of some flux, for that
purpose. He thereby introduced a consideration not easily ignored, that
consciousness of the attributes proper to black people was required before a genuine sense of nationality could be achieved. But more than consciousness of kind was needed to realize nationalism in a meaningful
sense. Afro-Americans must open themselves to African influences and
create self-propelled movements rooted in part in their African heritage.
His description of Afro-America as a "kind of nation" was an indication
of the work to be done if they were to know genuine nationhood.[68]

Relating his knowledge of the self-hatred of blacks to their achieving a
nationalist consciousness, Robeson noted that the inferiority complex of
large numbers of them militated against their developing a sense of nationality. Such self-abnegation was buttressed by their belief that they
"had nothing whatever in common with the inhabitants of Africa"—a
view reinforced by American educators, who, with rare exception, carried in their heads comforting stereotypes of African peoples and their
history.[69] Though American blacks are surely a people in whom self-
doubt is present, as Du Bois above all others demonstrated, this condition
need not be permanent. But more than viewing Africa from afar is required if the Negro is to secure the benefits of a nation in the absence of
nationhood in the literal sense:

> In illustration of this take the parallel case of the Jews. They, like a vast
> proportion of Negroes, are a race without a nation; but, far from Palestine,
> they are indissolubly bound by their ancient religious practices—which they
> recognize as such. I emphasize this in contradistinction to the religious prac-
> tices of the American Negro, which, from the snake-worship practiced in the
> deep South to the Christianity of the revival meeting, are patently survivals of
> the earliest African religions; and he does not recognize them as such. Their
> acknowledgement of their common origin, species, interest, and attitudes
> binds Jew to Jew; a similar acknowledgement will bind Negro to Negro.[70]

Upset that blacks from the West Indies and from various sections of
Africa joined the American Negro in aping European values, Robeson
went before the League of Colored People and urged its members to avoid
becoming "cardboard Europeans." In their respective homes, this process continued, with the French Negro imitating the French, the English
Negro the English, and the American Negro American whites. This was
tragic, since "the Negro is really an Eastern product and builds something
false by imitating occidental culture."[71] Certainly for the American

Negro and possibly for blacks everywhere, he thought that those most assimilated to European culture were victims of a double consciousness reflecting the values of their people as well as those of Europeans. What he had learned earlier from Du Bois on that question and his later experiences abroad prepared him to consider the question of double consciousness in relation to his people across much of the spectrum of colonial Africa. He and Du Bois anticipated much that was to follow in the work of Frantz Fanon.

But Robeson and Du Bois knew that the mass of blacks were far less likely to be European in culture in critical ways than their educated brethren, largely because their numbers insulated them in ways less available to more assimilated Negroes. Nevertheless, so deep were the psychological problems of blacks as a whole that Robeson set himself the task of seeking, through "patient inquiry," to lay the foundations on which a new awareness of black culture and tradition could be based, a project Du Bois had begun in his own way decades earlier. The two men were using related but different means to achieve the same goal, Robeson having decided to rely mainly on linguistic studies and his work as artist. He determined to investigate a great many questions regarding Africa and America and hoped, before the decade ended, to reach the peak of a campaign "to educate the Negro to a consciousness of the greatness of his own heritage." His "patient inquiry" actually had begun some years earlier, for he reported during the same year (1934) that he had already "penetrated to the core of African culture when [he] began to study the legendary traditions, folk-songs and folklore of the West African Negro."[72]

Americans, in the years before the wars, were often as dreadfully uninformed about African languages as about other aspects of African culture. Robeson's findings in this regard were for that reason of special interest to American Negroes, many of whom thought Africans communicated their ideas solely through gestures and sign language. "As a first step" in dispelling the "regrettable and abysmal ignorance of the value of its own heritage in the Negro race itself," he decided to launch a comparative study of the main language groups—Indo-European, African, and Asian—"choosing two or three principal languages out of each, and [to] indicate their comparative richness at a comparable stage of development." He estimated it would take him five years to complete his project, and he hoped the results would be sufficient to form a solid foundation "for a movement to inspire confidence in the Negro in the value of his own past and future."[73]

His study of West African cultures since he left the United States in 1927 had been no academic exercise. Writing in the *Spectator* some eight years later that it had been like a return home, he wanted to interpret the "unpolluted" African folk song and do for it what he had done for the spiritual, to make it respected throughout the world; all of which, he hoped, would make it easier for blacks in America not only to appreciate this aspect of their heritage but to play a role in exploring the "uncharted musical material in that source."[74] Black artists would have an opportunity, relying on their interpretive gifts, to use some portion of the new material, as they used the materials of music generally, to interpret the new world into which their people had been plunged. Only one with special expertise in African languages, however, could do the required job of pioneering. Robeson's researches into the folklore of west Africa and his proficiency in languages of the area equipped him for the task at hand.[75]

Robeson argued that the dances, songs, and religion of the black man in America were derived from those of his "cousins centuries removed in the depths of Africa, whom he has never seen, of whose very existence he is only dimly aware," an argument similar to Du Bois's discussions of the African qualities of being Negro. Moreover, that discussion of the African sense of rhythm is similar to Du Bois's discussion of dance when considering the sources of being Negro: the American Negro's "peculiar sense of rhythm," he writes, his "rhythm-consciousness," stamped him "indelibly as African."[76] The identification of rhythm consciousness as a common denominator of African peoples reinforces Du Bois's contention that qualities of being Negro developed in the forest fastnesses of Africa. It was a remarkable stance in Robeson's precise formulation, in part because rhythm consciousness was demonstrated in America in extremely complex forms with the development of jazz, the rhythms of which owe much to those of the African continent, to those of the ring shout.

Indeed, the pulsing rhythms of the shout, accelerating with time, was the one sacred source that may have been indispensable to the creation of jazz, as is suggested by the forms of dance developed around burial mounds and in other sacred precincts where the ancestral ceremony was performed.[77] It is not known whether Robeson held that view, though we do know that for him there was no bifurcation of the sacred and the secular in black music. In fact, no concert artist produced in black America has been as receptive to jazz and blues. Being favorably disposed toward those forms, which are related to the shout, is a step in the direction of affirming that ceremony, of a possible willingness to accept it on its own terms. And while Johnson was Robeson's principal intellectual influence with respect to the shout in the middle to late thirties, Robeson had opened himself to numerous African influences bearing on that ceremony that went beyond anything experienced or studied by American students of the subject prior to that time, a quest furthered by the appearance of Johnson's important autobiography in 1933.

In *Along This Way*, Johnson describes his reaction to the shout in the late 1870s and early 1880s in Jacksonville, Florida. His descriptions of elderly blacks in his neighborhood recall Sister Dicey of Virginia in antebellum times. He tells us that one Aunt Elsie was "a very old and benign woman with a noble, black face that took on a positive beauty under the red bandanna . . . she wore over the white cotton on her head." Behind her house, in the same yard, was Aunt Venie's house. Aunt Venie, though younger than Aunt Elsie, "had reached a certain age" and was therefore also addressed as Aunt. Because she had "fits," the children were afraid of her, and it was thought the fits resulted from religious "excesses." The performance of the shouters, "the weird music and the sound of thudding feet set the silences of the night vibrating and throbbing with vague terror." As Robeson continued to read, his eyes fell on the following passage:

> Many a time, I woke suddenly and lay a long while strangely troubled by these sounds, the like of which my great-grandmother Sarah had heard as a child. The shouters formed in a ring, men and women alternating, their bodies close together, moved round and round on shuffling feet that never left the floor. With the heel of the right foot they pounded out the fundamental beat of the dance and with their hands clapped out the varying rhythmical accents of the chant; for the music was, in fact, an African chant and the shout an African dance, the whole pagan rite transplanted and adapted to Christian worship. Round and round the ring would go: one, two, three, four, five hours, the very monotony and sound and motion inducing an ecstatic frenzy. Aunt Venie, it seems, never, even after the hardest day of washing and ironing, missed a "ring shout:"[78]

The "ecstatic frenzy" that Johnson observed was not foreign to Robeson's experiences among his people in New Jersey, nor was the "African chant" that helped induce it. The religious ceremony described by Johnson could hardly have been closer to the one Robeson referred to—and illustrated—in the Carnegie Hall performance mentioned earlier. The chant illustrated on that occasion was, in his view as in Johnson's, a manifestation of the spiritual.

Robeson thought that the spirituals had reached their highest stage of development in slavery, that they would not be improved by a more conscious concern for making them "artistic." Rather, in his view, that approach runs the risk of vitiating music that is already great. But his attitude did not rule out a Roland Hayes bringing to spirituals all the refinement that Western training, together with his own special genius provided. Nor did it rule out "the superstructure of conscious art that might be reared upon them," in James Weldon Johnson's phrase. It is simply that, unlike Johnson, Robeson did not think such a structure would enhance spirituals: he believed that the greatness of slave music would enrich the classical tradition, if applied to it, and that was as much his reason as any other for urging Negro classical composers to introduce such themes as "Go Down Moses" and "Deep River" into classical compositions. It was precisely that angle of vision that enabled him to sight the irreducible integrity of the form, that led him to declare that Count Basie "is as important a pianist as any in the world."[79]

Sometime before the appearance of *Along This Way*, Robeson sang James and J. Rosamond Johnson's "Lift Every Voice and Sing," which is considered the black national anthem, a designation that meant rather more for him than for Negro Americans generally, although while singing this song American blacks feel a bond of oneness perhaps stronger than at any other time. Robeson's singing the song provided a rare opportunity for him to bring his nationalist impulses fully into play, an experience most closely paralleled when he sang African songs in African languages. Unfortunately, he never recorded "Lift Every Voice and Sing," or, if he did, the recording, among the rarest, is not available. He sang the song informally and together with others, as was especially common in the pre-World War II period, at Negro churches. By the time of the appearance of Johnson's autobiography, which discusses the evolution of the lyrics, no one was better suited than Robeson to do justice to such lines as "Sing a song full of the faith that the dark past has taught us. Sing a song full of the hope that the present has brought us."[80]

In a breakthrough of enormous significance, the African ancestral ring is related, though imperfectly, to the ring shout at the outset of the screen version of *The Emperor Jones*, which appeared in 1933 and starred Robeson. The film opens with Africans chanting and dancing in a circle and then fades to a Negro church in America where the ring shout is being performed. It could well be that those scenes mark the first time so suggestive an association of African and black American culture was actually depicted. Only one aware of the culture of the African and the American Negro could make the precise association, and only Robeson among scholars at the time appears to have had the requisite knowledge of black culture on both sides of the Atlantic to urge the comparison. But whether he was responsible for those scenes or someone else, in the ring ceremonies he found the chief means by which to explore the foundations of American Negro culture, and that might account for his certitude thereafter that the American Negro's spiritual home is Africa.[81]

He tested that thesis in London, and on his return trips to the United States he discovered that many African and American Negro dances were "the same." Evidence that might have resulted from "field work" for most scholars was routinely gathered by him as a participant in African social functions and at functions of American Negroes. Just as certainly he came to know African analogues to the culture of blacks in America from observing scenes from *Sanders of the River*, one of his least successful films by most standards, including his own. But his excitement about African culture in the film had most to do with what it revealed of the diffusion of that culture in the New World and is best explained by an observation of Lydia Parrish, writing of the Georgia Sea Islands:

There is another exotic performance on St. Simon's Island, called by the incongruous railroad term "Ball the Jack." A few years ago I saw it demonstrated by an old resident of Eleuthera, in the Bahamas, and its protrayal in the film *Sanders of the River*—for which "background shots" were made in villages along the Congo—indicates the region from which it originally came.[82]

It is important to note that Marshall and Jean Stearns's classic *Jazz Dance,* which explores the relationship between African and Afro-American dance, was published in 1968, more than thirty years following Robeson's observations about that relationship. The findings of the Stearns's support and reinforce Robeson's thesis regarding the enormous influence African dance continued to have on Afro-American dance following slavery:

A few years ago, watching films of West African dancing taken by Professor Lorenzo Turner of Roosevelt University, the present writers saw the Ibibio of Nigeria performing a shimmy to end all shimmies, the Sherbro of Sierra Leone executing an unreasonably fine facsimile of the Snake Hips, and a group of Hausa girls near Kano moving in a fashion closely resembling the Lindy, or Jitterbug. . . . Again, in her analysis of African dance films, the director of the Philadelphia Dance Academy, Nadia Chilkovsky, found close parallels to American dances such as the Shimmy, Charleston, Pecking, Trucking, Hucklebuck, and Snake Hips, among others.[83]

There are important additional clues to the source of Robeson's thesis that the various cultures of black people, despite their many differences, had sufficient similarities to provide the basis for a common, united culture among them in the New World and in Africa. A single passage from thoughts set down in 1936 reflects the extent to which he was aware of underlying unities among those cultures and means by which cultural values are transmitted from generation to generation:

I am a singer and an actor. I am primarily an *artist*. Had I been born in Africa, I would have belonged, I hope, to that family which sings and chants the glories and legends of the tribe. I would have liked in my mature years to have been a wise elder, for I worship wisdom and knowledge of the ways of man.[84]

Respect for age is the basis of much of black African culture and the principal inspiration for its art. That respect was deeply held by blacks of Robeson's generation and later, particularly in the South, where it gained a powerful foothold. What Robeson found in the communities of his youth was discoverable among Africans in London and in works of scholarship on Africa to which he was exposed during his stay abroad. It is highly relevant that he solved the chief cultural problem of the American Negro and understood the means by which his people might distinguish the African from the European in their culture: he knew the ground of their being, the sacred domain of the ancestors and those soon to be ancestors. It is possible, in this context, to understand why Robeson believed he had penetrated to the core of African culture in studying the traditions of West Africa, for that tradition above all is based on respect for the ancestors and the elders, the African's art being a living, evolving monument to that respect. Robeson could hardly have failed to be reminded, as he worshiped wisdom, that he was guided along that path by his father, an elder by the time of Paul's birth.[85]

The achievement of Robeson's scholarship on African culture in the thirties is evident when one takes into account the extreme backwardness of America's colleges and universities vis-à- vis Africa and her descendants in that period. Even progressive and advanced scholars like Franz Boas, Ruth Benedict, and Melville Herskovits—the latter into the 1930s—had not recognized the role Africa played in helping to fashion the black ethos in America. Advocates of the "culturally stripped" thesis, Boas and Benedict were joined by the Chicago school of sociology, which failed to perceive the creative, African dimension of black culture in America. But unlike Boas and his students, most white intellectuals were unaware of the role of Africa in world history. Apart from Herskovits, few even came close to understanding the continuing impact of African culture on blacks in this country, just as there were few who believed Africa had a history worthy of respectful attention.[86]

Robeson made a serious effort to respond to that state of mind. His uncanny perception of the Africanness of the American Negro resulted from growing up in the culture of his people, from associating with Africans in England, and from studying African anthropology, folklore, and linguistics, all of which qualified him as few have been to compare African and Afro-American cultures—to see African influence on the American Negro as an expression of a continuing process. What frequently appear as findings in succinct essays and interviews are distillations resting on a foundation of research and learning in areas few scholars possess the preparation to enter. Thus, the contention that central features of the spiritual life of the American Negro consist mainly of African-derived elements, which he made in the early thirties, may to some still seem ridiculous, considering the state of knowledge of Afro-American culture among most American scholars and intellectuals today. Even the less radical view that African elements account for that which is distinctive in American Negro culture remains somewhat unorthodox.

Admittedly more concerned about similarities among Africans than differences, Robeson was painfully aware of their differences. Even so, his speeches, interviews, and published writings of the period do not give much emphasis to ethnic differences as such. As far as the public record is concerned, he made ethnic distinctions when appropriate but did not stress them. For example, he simply sang a song in a particular African language, the song representative of an African cultural complex, as he did in Carnegie Hall and elsewhere years after returning from England. For him, as for Du Bois and earlier nationalists, consciousness of African ethnicity meant consciousness of its potential divisiveness. More often, Robeson put ethnicity in a neutral perspective, using a particular one at times as a metaphor for the whole of black Africa.[87]

Robeson's belief that his family was of the Ibo people was reinforced one day on a movie set in London at which large numbers of Africans were employed, speaking many languages. He overheard a number of them use words he instantly understood, though he had not studied their language. He approached them and began conversing with them in Ibo, a language not greatly removed from other Nigerian languages that he spoke and one from which members of his family had apparently passed on words and phrases from one generation to another. It was in this unusual incident that he also experienced his "homecoming." If his awareness of the ethnic group from which his family stemmed, on his father's side, caused him to think more of his ancestry than before—and there is no indication that he did—his not saying so resulted from historical forces that had rendered such distinctions counterproductive long before his birth.

Since the rehabilitation of Africa was central to his campaign to heighten the consciousness of American Negroes, he had to confront the fundamental issue of the nature of black African history while continuing his investigation into various aspects of contemporary African cultures. The schools of the West, especially in the United States, stressing African backwardness, made these concerns inescapable for him. He asserted, in fact, that the younger generation of Negroes look toward Africa and want to know what there is to interest them; they want to know what Africa has to offer that the West cannot provide:

At first glance, the question seems unanswerable. He sees only the savagery, devil-worship, witch doctors, voodoo, ignorance, squalor, and darkness taught in American schools. Where these exist, he is looking at the broken remnants of what was in its day a mighty thing; something which perhaps has not been destroyed but only driven underground, leaving ugly scars upon the earth's surface to mark the place of its ultimate reapppearance.[88]

Still, much that was impressive was not hidden. "Africa," he remarked in 1936, "has a culture—a distinctive culture—which is ancient, but not barbarous." He thought it a fabrication to assert that the black man's past in Africa "is a record of mere strife between paltry tyrants." Like Du Bois, Robeson was impressed by certain qualities of culture of precolonial Africans, especially by their manner of organizing societies in such a way that material as well as spiritual needs were met. Life in Africa has been, he thought, balanced and simplified to a degree scarcely understood in the

white world, and the satisfaction of material needs has not called for prolonged or strenuous exertions on the part of the people. He believed that
African communities, developing in their own way and along their own
lines, once reached "a point of order and stability which may well be the
envy of the world today."[89]

His artistic sensibility contributed to his penetrating observations on
the place of oral tradition in African societies. To be sure, his reflections
on this dimension of African life revealed as much about him at the time as
they did about Africa—more and more he was regarding himself as African. Described by a *New York Times* reporter as "a champion talker,"
he correctly observed that his ancestors in Africa considered sound to be
of particular importance and that they thus produced "great talkers, great
orators, and, where writing was unknown, folktales and oral tradition
kept the ears rather than the eyes sharpened." He added, "I am the same.
. . . I hear my way through the world." Such emphasis on hearing, especially in a culture in which song is as important as it is in Negro-African
culture, was indeed a factor in his achievement of great singing, for it was
Robeson who reported having "heard my people singing!"[90]

Remarkably, he did not hesitate to affirm without a trace of shame some
of the very qualities that whites thought stamped blacks as inferior: with
pleasure he referred to the African's rich emotional heritage, his genius
for music, his religiosity—traits from which many black intellectuals recoiled. So passionate was his celebration of specifically Negroid or "Eastern" traits that at times he seemed to be forming stereotypes of his own.
This conclusion is difficult to avoid when assessing his reflection "I, as an
African, feel things rather than comprehend them. . . ."As Descartes
demonstrated, there is no necessary contradiction between feeling and
reason, but Robeson seems to be suggesting—despite a seeming contradiction between the two—understanding through flashes of insight. Perhaps it is debatable whether his insistence that Africans possess an "inner
logic" that "for want of a better title is often called mysticism" enabled
him, in the final analysis, to stop short of stereotyping. Leopold Sedar
Senghor, whose approach to African perceptions is almost exactly like
Robeson's, discusses this problem of epistemology in his essay "The
Problematics of Negritude."[91]

I V

While acquiring knowledge of Africa that he hoped would inspire pride in
millions of Negroes in the Americas, Robeson was waging a more immediate and directly political-cultural struggle with colonial powers by proclaiming that much of black Africa had a respectable level of culture. This
eventually brought a visit by British intelligence, which he has described
together with the circumstances leading up to that encounter:

As an artist, it was natural that my first interest in Africa was cultural. Culture? The foreign rulers of that continent insisted that there was no culture worthy of the name in Africa. . . . As I plunged with excited interest into my studies of Africa at the London School of Oriental Languages, I came to see most African culture was indeed a treasure-store for the world. . . . Now there was a logic to this cultural struggle I was making. . . . The British Intelligence came one day to caution me about the political meaning of my activities. For the question loomed of itself: *If African culture was what I insisted it was, what happens to the claim that it would take 1,000 years for Africans to be capable of self-rule?*[92]

His inquiry was comprehensive and painstaking, covering major sections of the continent. He learned Swahili, Zulu, Mende, Ashanti, Ibo, Efik, Edo, and Yoruba. And he argued that some of these languages were exceedingly flexible and sophisticated.[93] However, convincing some black Americans that what they had been taught about Africa was false would very likely continue to be difficult. This was, as Robeson had indicated earlier, certainly true of the more privileged, the "better-educated," young blacks, who were generally not favorably disposed to revising their prejudices about their cultural heritage. But if large numbers of blacks in America had difficulty grasping the ultimate significance of Robeson's cultural explorations, colonial and racist leaders abroad and in the United States did not.

Meanwhile, his decision to sing the folk music of cultures in addition to his own—those of the Chinese, the Hebrews, Russians, and others—was in phase with his deepening and expanding political involvement, with his ability to identify with oppressed humanity irrespective of color. In this context he described a critical problem of the West, one with dire implications for the whole of mankind—"the cost of developing the kind of mind by which the discoveries of science were made has been one which now threatens the discoverer's very life." In fact, he argued, Western man appears to have gained greater powers of abstraction "at the expense of his creative faculties,"[94] a position that would be fully aired in American philosophical circles in the following decade, and later in some artistic circles as well. In "Primitives," Robeson wrote,

But because one does not want to follow Western thought into this dilemma, one nonetheless recognizes the value of its achievements. One would not have the world discount them and retrogress in terror to a primitive state. It is simply that one recoils from the Western intellectual's idea that, having got himself on to this peak overhanging an abyss, he should want to drag all other people—on pain of being dubbed inferior if they refuse—up after him into the same precarious position.

He added, "That, in a sentence, is my case against Western values."[95] So it was not simply that America was uncongenial to meaningful, creative living; the Western world as a whole seemed, short of drastic changes, an unlikely place in which new forms of freedom, a new humanity, could develop. The West had gone astray as far back as the time of the Renaissance, probably much earlier:

> A blind groping after Rationality resulted in an incalculable loss in pure Spirituality. Mankind placed a sudden dependence on the part of his mind that was brain, intellect, to the discountenance of that part that was sheer evolved instinct and intuition; we grasped at the shadow and lost the substance . . . and now we are not altogether clear what the substance was.[96]

He believed that before the Renaissance the art, music, and literature of Europe were closer to the cultures of Asia, apparently because European man during the medieval period held spiritual values in greater regard than in the following epoch. During the Renaissance, Europeans began to give reason and intellect primacy over intuition and feeling, a process that resulted in great strides not only toward the conquest of nature but also toward the utilization of technological advantages to conquer the human world. Robeson held that a man who embraced Western values completely would, in time, find his creative faculties stunted and warped and would become almost wholly dependent on external gratification. As frustration in this direction grew and neurotic symptoms developed; the victim would see that life is not worth living, and in chronic cases he might seek to take his life: "This is a severe price to pay even for such achievements as those of Western science."[97]

A reading of Robeson's brief against Western values makes evident that he had little hope that Western man, left to his own devices, would be able to halt his momentum and pull back from the precipice. The depth of the European disorder seemed to him obvious in the fact that as abstract intellectualism became enthroned in Europe the artistic achievements of that section of the world became less impressive: He found in European art "an output of self-conscious, uninspired productions" that discriminating people recognize as dead imitations rather than "the living pulsing thing."[98] "To what end does the West rule the world," he asked, "if all art dies?" He proceeded to pose a question that, as later developments demonstrated, was the most important of all questions for him: "What shall it profit a man if he gain the whole world and lose his own soul?" This he thought the West had "come very near to doing, and the catastrophe may yet come. The price of science's conquest of the world has been the loss of that emotional capacity that alone produces great art. Where are the Westerners now who could paint an Old Master, compose a Gregorian Chant, or build a Gothic cathedral?"[99]

What is manifest among artists "is only a symptom of a sickness that to some extent is affecting almost every stratum of the Western world." To the question "Is there no one to bring art back to its former level?" Robeson responded that this is where people of African ancestry and the

Eastern peoples come in. Now that nature has been virtually conquered by the West, "visionaries dream of a world run by scientists who would live like artists." But in Robeson's opinion Westerners no longer know how to live like artists, having "brought misery with their machines."[100] This concern—the introduction of a certain malady with the machine—was pivotal to some of the more thoughtful and sophisticated men and women of the Afro-Asian world, and it is possible that Robeson and Jawaharlal Nehru, who met and became close friends during the 1930s, discussed this problem. At that time one of the few Americans to give substantial attention to such a concern, Robeson believed that the people who first learn to hold in balance the emotional and the intellectual, to couple the use of the machine with a life of true intuition and feeling, will produce the superman.[101]

But no one people are likely, relying solely on their own values, to produce the new man. Such a creation involves "a mingling of new values," some of which reside in Africa, "this new and mystic world." He noted, in one of his rare references to leadership of African peoples coming from transplanted Africans, that "the lead in culture is with the American Negro, the direct descendant of the African ancestors. . . . Yet the Negroes are the most self-conscious of all . . . if the real great man of the Negro race will be born, he will spring from North America." In an adjustment of his oft-stated precept that people of African ancestry throughout the world are radically different from whites, he acknowledged that European influences on the North American blacks are so great that the latter differ more "from his South American brother than from a white man." It is likely that Robeson was referring to broader cultural influences, that is, to those that go beyond the arts and religiosity.[102]

An aspect of the problem that concerned him globally was taken up with respect to the American scene by F. S. C. Northrop in *The Meeting of East and West:*

> The mere reflection upon the nature of this culture [American] suffices to indicate that it has a predominantly political, economic, technological and practical emphasis. In it a religion of the emotions and cultivation of the aesthetic intuition for its own sake have been neglected. Its Negro members have these values as Paul Robeson shows in superlative degree. By the white people, they must be slowly and painfully acquired. The Negroes, similarly, must with equal patience, through education and training, acquire the political understanding and the scientific knowledge and skills necessary for any man to live in the contemporary world.[103]

Blacks in America would have a better chance of fashioning the new humanity if they cultivated those qualities in their culture that tie them to Africa and the East. In the context of a discussion of African and Asian ties, Robeson said that "Negro students who wrestle vainly with Plato would find a spiritual father in Confucius or Lao-tsze. . . ." While the

Negro "must take his technology from the West, instead of coming to the Sorbonne or Oxford," he noted, "I would like to see Negro students go to Palestine and Peking." He added that he "would like to watch the flowering of their inherent qualities under sympathetic influences there."[104] Nevertheless, he remarked that it has been a boon to the American Negro that he has managed, despite his presence in the white man's uncongenial spiritual world, and despite centuries of oppression, to retain a worldview that is still largely non-Western, predicated on sensibilities similar to those of his African ancestors and to those of people who live in cultures that place a higher priority on concrete symbols than on abstractions:

> For it is not only the African Negro, and so-called primitive peoples, who think in concrete symbols—all the great civilizations of the east (with possibly the exception of India) have been built up by people with this type of mind. It is a mentality that has given us giants like Confucius, and Mencius, and Lao-Tze. More than likely it was this kind of thinking that gave us the understanding and wisdom of a person like Jesus Christ. It has given us the wonders of Central American architecture and Chinese art. It has, in fact, given us the full flower of all the highest possibilities in man—with the single exception of applied science. That was left to a section of Western man to achieve and on that he bases his assertion of superiority.[105]

There is an epistemological problem here. Scientists are quick to point out that there is not, in their work, so sharp a contrast between reason and intuition. In fact, some of the most distinguished deny a dichotomy altogether, insisting that they rely on intuition as well as reason.[106] Yet Robeson's treatment of the effects of Western science, of the celebration of reason and the essential lack of sufficient regard for emotive, intuitive, and aesthetic values in the lives of the people is impressive. He is, moreover, quite correct in arguing that the people of Africa and Asia generally have far greater regard for intuition and spirituality than does modern man in the West. It should be remarked, however, that problems associated with too heavy a dependence on those attributes, while they have not threatened the existence of man, have been substantial in man's history in the Afro-Asian world—which doubtless accounts for Robeson's insistence on the importance of Afro-Asian man's mastering Western technology.[107]

That Robeson refers to impressive strides made by the West in *applied* science suggests that he was aware of the role of Egyptian and other ancient civilizations in spawning and developing fundamental principles of science. His one specific published reference to Egyptian civilization appears to confirm the suggestion: "We have an amazingly vivid reconstruction of the culture of ancient Egypt, but the roots of almost the whole of the remainder of Africa are buried in antiquity." It would be especially rewarding to know his views on science in the ancient Afro-Asian world, but it is likely that he never put them into writing. In any event, Alfred

Kroeber speaks of "the sciences of Egypt, Mesopotamia, India, China, and Japan, which are less known [than Occidental] science and in part poorly datable." Though Kroeber does not seem to appreciate the fact that Egypt is on the continent of Africa, and is therefore African, he does note that "whatever is pre-Greek, whatever the Greeks and their heirs built on, originated there" and in Mesopotamia, which he refers to as the Near East.[108]

Robeson warned American blacks against the perils of isolation and pointed out that it was necessary from a social and economic standpoint for them to understand Western science: "Now I am not going to try to belittle the achievements of science. Only a fool would deny that the man who holds the secrets of those holds the key position in the world." But he added,

I am simply going to ask, having found the key, has Western man—Western bourgeois man . . . sufficient strength left to turn it in the lock? Or is he going to find that in the search he has so exhausted his vitality that he will have to call in the cooperation of his more virile "inferiors"—Eastern or Western— before he can open the door and enter into his heritage?[109]

It was a position in the best tradition of nationalism, one with which Walker and Du Bois would hardly have taken issue. If anything, nationalist intellectuals tended to be less insular than others in the black community, Robeson's father's love of learning and grounding in the classics illustrating something of the sweep of their intellectual concerns.

Robeson ultimately rejected the view that cultural traits are inherited in the genes, conceding that many blacks in America had become "pure intellectuals." Even his reference to "pure intellectuals"—he certainly did not want to be associated with them—was ironic because he was indisputably intellectual. But that was all the more reason for him to question whether black intellectuals should proceed all the way down "this dangerous by-way when, without sacrificing the sound base in which they have their roots, they can avail themselves of the now-materialized triumphs of science and proceed to use them while retaining the vital creative side."[110] This creative dimension, which he championed while championing intellectual pursuits, had made possible the Afro-American's artistic and spiritual achievements, the invigorating influence of which was unmistakable in America.

Since the objective of cultural revolution is man's mastering of the emotional and intellectual dimensions of his personality, when he learns "to be true to himself the Negro as much as any man" will contribute to the new cultural order. But Robeson cautioned, "Unless the African Negro (including his far-flung collaterals) bestirs himself and comes to a realization of his potentialities and obligations there will be no culture for him to contribute."[111] In his view, potentialities had to be developed into actualities that would tighten the bonds among blacks, especially in America. Without moving closer to nationality, to making more effective use of the attributes of a nation, they could not effect the needed cultural transformation. And nations contributing to the new cultural dispensation would be answering the demands of a world necessity that would lead in time, Robeson hoped, "to the family of nations' ideal."[112]   The posture of the artist toward society would be decisive in determining the success or failure of the cultural movement. This relationship was of major concern to Robeson, and the position he took is but one more illustration of his special angle of vision: "The whole problem of living can never be understood until the world recognizes that artists are not a race apart." Artists, Robeson added, do not have potentialities unknown to large numbers of other human beings, for creativity means more than the ability to make music, to paint, or to write. Each man has something of the artist in him; if this is uprooted, "he becomes suicidal and dies." Robeson believed that, given the opportunities for creative development, many people could contribute to the sum of the artistic and spiritual achievements of a given society. Positing an organic tie between artist and society—a reciprocity of interests—he took an aesthetic stance that was clearly more African than Western, more congenial to socialist than to capitalist theory.[113]

When he turned to America, he saw the worst qualities of Europe in magnified form. Having applied research and reflection to the identifying and interpreting of life-styles peculiar to people on the major continents of the world, he placed white America in this broad cultural setting and found her wanting. He believed there was little of value there apart from technology, and, as a socialist, he thought capitalism militated against the humane application of scientific innovations, which severely handicapped American culture and presaged increasing difficulties. From London, the great artist offered withering criticism:

> The modern white American is a member of the lowest form of civilization in the world today. My problem is not to counteract his prejudice against the Negro . . . that does not matter. What I have set myself to do is to educate my brother the Negro to believe in himself. . . . We are a great race, greater in tradition and culture than the American race. Why should we copy something that is inferior.[114]

Black liberation in such a country could not be achieved through the NAACP's emphasis on racial cooperation. Many Afro-Americans, Robeson said during a visit to the Soviet Union in 1935, will have to fight and die for their freedom. "Our freedom is going to cost so many lives," he remarked, "that we mustn't talk about the Scottsboro case as one of sacrifice." He continued, "When we talk of freedom we don't discuss lives." The recognition that black people, given objective conditions, would have to make greater use of violence before achieving their freedom was by no means the only, or even the most significant, example of Robeson's prophetic insight. With awesome precision, he predicted that if Negroes persist in efforts "to be like the white man, within the next generation they will destroy themselves."[115] Rather than follow that path, Robeson argued, "the Negro must be conscious of himself and yet international, linked with the nations which are culturally akin to him." To those in England who labeled his interest in Africa "jingoistic," he said he was "not trying to 'escape' race oppression in America and Europe by taking a nationalist attitude":

> I came here [to the Soviet Union] because the Soviet Union is the only place where ethnology is seriously considered and applied. . . . Africa does not realize that it has something to contribute. The Africans . . . go European as soon as they can. The African and American Negro problem is not purely racial. These cultures must be freed, formulated, and developed, and this cannot be done without a change in the present system. The Negro cannot develop his culture until he is free. . . . Stalin speaks of the culture of the different nationalities of the Soviet Union as socialist in content and national in form.[116]

While in the Soviet Union, he witnessed the potential of "backward races" being realized. Within twenty-five years the peoples east of the Urals, the Yakuts, the Uzbeks, and others, under the influence of socialism, had compressed time. They were running their own factories and directing their own theaters and universities; their ancient cultures were "blooming in new and greater richness." "That showed me," Robeson remarked, "that the problem of 'backward' peoples' was only an academic one." He noted that, "if provided the opportunity, one segment of humanity would perform on the same level of culture as any other,"[117] and that socialism provided that opportunity. But he had not come to socialism through the Soviets. His socialist views initially owed more to the influence of the British Labour party than to Russia, and perhaps even more to the manner in which blacks around him related to him in his youth. But his formal apprenticeship in socialism began when he followed developments on the labor front in England. Even so, he was profoundly influenced by what he saw in the Soviet Union and received a reception from the Soviet people that went beyond anything he had known in the West. For the first time in his life, he said he breathed freely, unencumbered by the problems of race. In the Soviet Union he was convinced the Afro-Asian world, then submerged in colonialism, had a great friend, one that was pointing the direction into the future: "In Russia you feel the vitality of a people who are building a new world; in comparison, other countries are dead."[118]

As he advanced his obligations as an artist and acted upon his convictions, Robeson demonstrated, in theory and practice, that there is no necessary tension between being a black nationalist and a socialist. In addition, his conscious selection of songs from the world's store of folk music, his uses of and commentaries on the music of his own people, the essential simplicity of the life he chose to lead—all this and more, as we shall see, indicates that explicitly socialist and black nationalist aspirations were, for him as for Du Bois, easily joined. And like Du Bois, balancing the related and complementary concerns of classical black nationalism and socialism, he resisted the allure of power and the seductions of ease. C. L. R. James, the Trinidadian writer and theoretician, has remarked that Robeson remained, throughout his long stay in England, unmoved by fame, the rich, and the powerful. Lawrence Brown noted this quality: "I don't know what to call him but a genius—though a unique genius. It seemed to me that if he strove in any direction, it was towards knowledge for its own sake. After the greatest ovations, Paul would go home and read or study languages—an African dialect or Russian." [119]

V

In due course, his interest in the folk music of other countries, together with widening contacts with ordinary people of many lands, weakened feelings of rootlessness and helped him live away from the United States, but the problem of being abroad was not and would not be solved for him. At one point, on the question of a permanent home, he noted that where he lived was not important: "But I am going back to my people in the sense that for the rest of my life I am going to think and feel as an African—not as a white man. Perhaps that does not sound a very important decision. To me, it seems the most momentous thing in my life." [120] It was indeed because by then Robeson considered himself African in thought and sensibility and was able, thanks to experience, study, and reflection, to know a great deal about what being African means.

At times he longed for environs more congenial to his own personality, which seemed devoid of that concern for "manners" and "culture" that kept people apart rather than together. In an address before the League of Colored People, he expressed his intention of removing himself from living "under the sword of Damocles" all his life. Regarding himself as a "Negro wandering through the world," he found opportunities for naturalness and self-expression, which he considered important, limited in England and wanted to be where he could "be African and not be Mr. Paul Robeson everyday." [121] Such moods contributed to his effectiveness at identifying with Africa in song and in his career as an actor on screen. Indeed, a vehicle that expressed, implicitly, his restlessness of spirit and, explicitly, his longing for a home elsewhere came along in *Song of Freedom*, a movie produced in 1936.

In *Song of Freedom*, he portrays a descendant of Africa living in London who, with glowing conviction, expresses a desire to go to Africa.

Though he does not know the particular ethnic group from which he is descended, his return is what is of primary importance. To the question, "Will you come with me?" his wife responds favorably and accompanies him to Africa. Thereafter, negative features of the film are painfully evident as it directly confronts the issue of African culture. Burning with the intention of helping his people, he urges upon them the values of the West. In a word, he chose to compromise, electing the lesser of what appeared to be two evils, either taking the best role available to him in film or none at all. But the role was of such limited value that one can question the wisdom of his choice.[122]

Such problems with the movie industry would not be easily overcome, for that industry was an apologist for racism and the subordination of blacks around the world. *Song of Freedom*, in fact, was additional proof to Robeson that he could not look to the film industry to assist him in his grand design of promoting a sense of pride in his people. How Africa was presented in that film was so unrelated to what he had come to know, through study, of that continent that he must have had doubts about the value of a career in the movies.

Since his people were trapped in oppression in the Americas and the West was responsible for their colonized status in Africa, he thought cultural unity for them essential. Awareness of their strengths would enable them to overcome feelings of inadequacy and make the most of their potential. His conception of the role of black culture in the lives of black people was analogous to but more far-reaching than the politics of Pan-Africanism: he envisioned a unified, systematically developed black culture extending across geographical barriers and directed toward a global, messianic objective: "The world today is full of barbarism, and I feel that the united Negro culture could bring into the world a fresh spiritual, humanitarian principle, a principle of human friendship and service to the community."[123]

As we have indicated, Robeson rarely singled out American Negro culture for exclusive attention; rather, he wanted to see the unified development of black cultural communities throughout the world, a vision of the future of his people that was original and grounded in a knowledge of those communities. To be sure, his thesis regarding the possibility of a united black culture—a thesis supported by the findings in this volume—flowed logically from his understanding that black cultures were generally impelled by roughly similar sensibilities and values. Although he thought Negroes in America would play a special role in the liberation of their people elsewhere, he emphasized the vital roles to be played by blacks in the Caribbean, South America, and especially Africa in forwarding the liberation of their peoples. In short, there could be no substitute for united political and cultural action across geographical boundaries, action growing out of an awareness, ultimately, of the need to be African in the modern world, and he stressed the difficulties that this entailed, including the growing importance of class as a factor in the lives of the oppressed.

Indeed, the struggle of African peoples the world over was a difficult one, and Robeson was not optimistic about their being liberated in the immediate future. In fact, he said, it is "impossible to be optimistic. For a long time Africa will still be under the control of Europeans," and there will be no alternative to protracted struggle if Africans are to win genuine freedom. Meanwhile, considering black people everywhere of the African family, he contended that wherever found they must "stand in one camp, fighting for freedom and social justice." In addition to North America, they were found in a number of "centers of Negro population"—the Caribbean, Brazil, the whole of South America, and Africa. "In these various regions Negroes speak different languages, but in spite of that, even the American Negroes feel instinctively in sympathy with their own blood, the black men of the whole world." But he made it clear that he was not opposing one people against another: "We have not the slightest idea of Africa, as a united continent of Negroes, ever standing against the other races."[124]

Robeson went beyond the boundaries of Pan-Africanism to establish an Afro-Asian political perspective, ground skillfully worked by Walker and Delany in earlier times and by Du Bois before Robeson. The logic of African oppression and the imperatives of liberation dictated his stance, as did his contacts with Asian nationalists. Noting that it was understandable that he should be interested in 13 million Negroes in America, 150 million in Africa, and 40 million in the Caribbean, Robeson said that he had come to feel that India constituted one of the most decisive cases for racial freedom. If colored people there and elsewhere gain their freedom, "it will surely have a strong bearing on the case of the American Negro."[125]

Robeson abhorred "rabid nationalism" and rejected the suggestion that the emergence of black nationalism would constitute a menace to white people; he thought African nationalism would threaten only those who wanted continued white overlordship. Nevertheless, at times he underplayed the role of racism in imperialist policy in Asia and Africa, remarking in an interview in 1936 that it was "not a race problem at all," that race did not enter into it. But later in the same discussion he stated that it was not a matter of race not entering into it; rather, it was a question of emphasis, of the relative importance of race and economics. Economic considerations were, he believed, more important in the understanding of imperialism than was race.[126] Clearly by then his position on the issue had been influenced by socialist thought. His awareness of class differences among people of color was for him suggestive of the primacy of class over race in human oppression generally, a position that harked back to Garnet and Du Bois.

Distressed by the Italian invasion of Ethiopia, Robeson opposed what he called the "civilizing influence of European nations that go out to do their civilizing with bombs and machine guns." There was no reason to believe that Italy could work out Ethiopia's problems. He urged that close attention be given to the behavior of the victims of colonial oppression: "Look at the war in Africa now. What is this Italian army fighting Ethiopia? Three fourths of them are black fellows. And what goes on in Manchuria—yellow Japanese making war on yellow Chinese. The race question isn't of primary importance." [127] Yet his own reflections suggest that racism, if not a force of its own, has been a vital factor in European aggression against the peoples of Asia and Africa. Moreover, it is not likely that racists in a particular area, say, in cultural matters, can avoid allowing racism to influence their thought in other important areas. This was true of racists in Garnet's time as well. Whatever the weaknesses in Robeson's conception of racism—weaknesses less evident in Du Bois's—his belief in the need for black autonomy was a compensating factor, as that belief was for Garnet.

As he came to know the vast landscape of humanity, Robeson realized that, just as the oppression of people of color was a direct outgrowth of European aggression, the liberation of Afro-America was ineluctably tied to the disenthrallment of Afro-Asia: in this context, African ethnic allegiance, a tragedy in the world of colonialism, would be a tragedy after independence, undermining the unity without which there could be no genuine freedom for Africa as a whole. The more he was exposed to people of color from various parts of the world, the more convinced he became of this. The success of colored people in one section of the world would remain in doubt as long as people of color elsewhere suffered on grounds of race and economics.

In a personal sense, Robeson followed the logic of that argument, asserting that his individual success was as nothing—"did not matter in the least"—compared with the plight of his people. His own father, his own brother, could not go where he went, could not come in behind him, and that displeased him, causing him to believe more than ever that the only meaningful freedom is that which a whole people win for themselves: "It is no use telling me that I am going to depend on the English, the French, or the Russians. I must depend on myself." He was speaking generically—all people of African descent must depend on themselves, not on others. [128] It should go without saying that he was not arguing against support from one's international friends, from those opposing colonialism and racism. He meant merely that a people should attempt to be as self-respecting, therefore as self-reliant, as possible. For all the reasons cited by Sidney approximately a century before Robeson committed such thoughts to paper, any other position would have been unmanly and intolerable for a leader of an oppressed people.

Though Robeson's increasing concern for the oppressed of all lands was causing him to feel his isolation less sharply, the tension created by his presence in a foreign, white culture, as attractive as it was in many ways, was eventually, after considerable restlessness of spirit, reduced to manageable proportions. So great was his ability to empathize with others—characteristic of the nationalists in this study—that for years before returning to America he had become a champion of all the oppressed. One incident, in particular, typified his concern for the downtrodden: he heard an English aristocrat talk to his chauffeur as if to a dog. "I said to myself, Paul, that is how the Southerner in the United States would speak to you.' . . . That incident made me very sad for a year," he later remarked.[129]

The unhappy occurrence was fateful, reminding him of the treatment of blacks in Princeton and reinforcing in his mind the unity of the struggle of the oppressed throughout the world—in fact, contributing to his belief "that the fight of the oppressed workers everywhere was the same struggle."[130] Thus, his appearance in Spain to sing songs of freedom during the Spanish civil war was a logical expression of his broadening interests, which included the political and cultural conditions of the oppressed regardless of color. Just as moving from the art of others to concern for them as people had the appearance of virtual inevitability for Robeson, interest in their political and social condition usually led him to their music. Because theory and practice so often seemed to him to merge, when he caught the vision of the unity of mankind, he committed himself to the alleviation of oppression, irrespective of the race of the aggrieved.

Robeson demonstrated, through darkly beautiful renderings of the inner joy and pain of many peoples, that music is the language of the human spirit. The naturalness of his voice was perhaps its most marvelous achievement, a quality as elemental, it seems, as the movement of wind on an open plain. Such qualities were admired by Pablo Neruda:

> It would be small praise
> if I crowned you king
> only of the Negro voice,
> great only among your race,
> among your beautiful flock
> of music and ivory,
> as though you only sang for the dark children
> shackled by cruel masters.
> No,
> Paul Robeson,
> you sang with Lincoln,
> covering the sky with your holy voice,
> Not only for Negroes,
> but for the poor,
> whites,
> Indians,
> for all peoples.[131]

At Royal Albert Hall, at a rally of the National Joint Committee for Spanish Relief of the Basque Refugee Children on June 24, 1937, Robeson remarked, "Again I say, the true artist cannot hold himself aloof. The legacy of culture from our predecessors is in danger. It is the foundation upon which we build a still more lofty edifice. It belongs not only to us, not only to the present generation—it belongs to our posterity—and must be defended to the death." [132]

Nicolás Guillén, the Cuban poet, saw Robeson in Spain at the Hotel Majestic after Robeson had been to the front singing to the troops opposing fascism. At the time, "blockaded by a crowd of people hanging on his most insignificant gestures" and towering above those around him, Robeson "pays attention to everyone, smiling. He poses repeatedly for photographers, answers the most diverse questions without tiring." In a description of him that recalls the Bakongo, Guillén writes that the singer "talks passionately, his enormous hands contracted and turned palms up, an invariable gesture of his when talking." He adds that Robeson, dressed "with great simplicity," when asked why he was in Spain, said that artists owe their formation and well-being to ordinary people, that it would be "dishonorable to put (oneself) on a plane above the masses, without marching at their side," without knowing their sorrows and anxieties. He noted that black people "could not live if fascism triumphed in the world." [133]

At a time when it appeared his star could not have risen higher in Europe, Robeson seemed to become increasingly radical, proclaiming solidarity with the peasants and workers and ethnic minorities of the world. From 1937 to the outbreak of World War II, he gave up his career in conventional terms. He resented performing primarily before the well-to-do and instructed his agent to see to it that ticket prices for his engagements were scaled down so that working-class people could have good seats. Furthermore, he turned his back for good on Hollywood, so often had that industry presented blacks in a negative light. His decision to carry his art to the people was perhaps unique in the modern history of great performing artists in the West. It was a prelude to the free concerts he later gave in the United States and in the West Indies. His dream of a Negro theater may not have come to fruition, but he brought to a fine consistency his roles of performing artist and philosopher of culture. [134]

The strength of reaction in Europe caused Robeson to devote less time to academic studies. As Hitler and Mussolini made their malevolence increasingly vivid, the singer-actor-scholar identified more and more with the movement against nazism and fascism. As he did, he said he found a new faith in life, a faith that generated new enthusiasm and energy, causing him virtually to "live around the piano." At the time when his commitment to the well-being of oppressed non-Africans the world over was greatest, he revealed that his dedication to the liberation of people of African ancestry had, if anything, deepened. For him, there was no contradiction. He explained, "Everything I have done is an extension of my feelings about my own people. I feel some way I've become tied up with this whole problem of human freedom. I have no end to my artistic horizon."[135]

A year before leaving England, in 1938, an interviewer asked him why he was so interested in his people. Robeson rejoined, "My father was a slave. Can I forget that? Hell, I can't forget that! My own father a slave!" He added, "There can be no greater tragedy than to forget one's origin and finish despised and hated by the people among whom one grew up. To have that happen would be the sort of thing to make me rise from my grave." He also noted, "Sure, I got a better deal, but not the people I came from. For them things got worse, in fact. They are prevented from joining trade unions, and are shot down, as in Jamaica and Trinidad. There is no extension of democracy for them; things, on the contrary, are being tightened up. My personal success as an artist has not helped them."[136]

As his more than ten years' stay abroad approached an end, Robeson said that contact with the cultures of the world—with oppressed peasants and workers—had made his loneliness vanish, had helped prepare him to "come home" and to sing his songs "so that we will see that our democracy does not vanish." Having observed a Europe increasingly under the menace of Hitler's Germany, he remarked that he felt closer to America than ever, that he felt peace rather than, as before, lonesome isolation. "I return," he said, "without fearing prejudice that once bothered me," for "people practice cruel bigotry in their ignorance, not maliciously."[137]

By 1939 the goal he had earlier set for himself, that of making black people aware of their greatness, had not been attained. But no one man could possibly have reached this objective. Only a mass movement based on the kinds of values set forth by Robeson could have had a chance of bringing a genuine sense of greatness to people subjected to brutal oppression for nearly four centuries. It should be noted, however, that Afro-American newspapers gave extraordinary coverage to his activities abroad, usually in the form of reprints from foreign newspapers. And when interviewed, he seldom missed an opportunity to communicate with his people, almost invariably addressing African concerns, speaking through European media to Africans around the world. Considering the volume of news stories on Robeson and what he symbolized, it is reasonable to conclude that not a few people of African ancestry began to rethink negative attitudes toward themselves and their people generally. Only Marcus Garvey affected the sense of African consciousness of more black people in Africa, the West Indies, and the United States over the first forty years of the century than did Robeson. In sum, his influence on African peoples on the continent and in the diaspora was substantial materially and spiritually.[138]

To be sure, he gave a number of benefit performances for African liberation movements during the 1930s and 1940s. In addition, he provided financial aid for West Indian causes: one of his first concerts on returning to London in the late fifties was for the benefit of West Indian students. The extent to which he was esteemed by significant numbers of Africans can be determined in part from an incident attending the filming of a movie in which he was cast. As he prepared to make the film, a film unit connected with the project went to Africa to shoot background material: "According to a reporter in the *Sunday Graphic,* September 20, 1936 'the entire population [of Sierra Leone] crowded to the landing stage, hoping to see Robeson.' His picture, framed or unframed, according to the financial standing of its possessor, was in every shack."[139]

Among Robeson's most lasting contributions may be one we have, ironically, for a long time known the least about: after years of study and reflection, he succeeded in bringing together most of the salient strands of black nationalism while extending meanings in a variety of ways. And while he was influenced by other nationalists, especially by Du Bois, what is decisive here is that he carried to new heights of clarity and power a number of important points of ideology shared by nineteenth-century nationalists. Moreover, he saw Africa in America in that ubiquitous but strangely elusive region of the ring shout where one finds the springs of the Afro-American ethos. This was a great contribution to nationalist theory and the basis for his belief in the possibility of the unity of black cultures across geographical boundaries. And he attempted with some success, through his scholarship, art, and uses of experience, to become less Western, to move closer to being African—all the while developing a new, more spacious conception of what being African could mean.

Original with him were his views on the uses to which his people should put African languages—he held that languages were "unnecessary barriers" to unity—in attempting to realize their potential for cultural and political growth. And there is his striking formulation that African peoples should seek out and build upon, as he was doing, their common traits with an eye to developing a more expansive and unified black culture. In addition to his interest in the sensibilities that inform Afro-American and African cultural forms, there is the sophistication with which he related African to world cultural patterns, seeking the grand synthesis that would, ultimately, preclude conflict among people without vitiating that which is creative and positive in various cultures. Robeson's recognition that no such new order could be achieved within a capitalist industrial system was fundamental to his cultural philosophy. With its deep roots in the African heritage and its receptivity to the cultures of the East, his philosophy was on balance, for all his admiration for European socialism, vastly more non-Western than were the theoretical formulations of any black thinker of note to emerge in the New World in this and in previous centuries.

In his thought, there is such a close link between cultural and political nationalisms that the two are virtually indistinguishable. In fact, he came to perceive art as an instrument of revolutionary change. Any dichotomy between the cultural and political was, in the end, meaningless in his thought. Not dissimilarly, his vaulting conception of Negritude—his suffusing of the cultural with the political and of the political with the cultural—eliminates any need to label his form of Negritude merely cultural. By the time he departed from England, he was no more a believer in art for art's sake than the slave bard or storyteller. In that sense, he was African, and with his emergence the African art of the slave was for the first time central to the repertoire of a great concert artist. In that regard, he was a major theorist of the relation of slave art not only to African art but to world art as well. His most daring intellectual achievement, however, was in positing the fundamental Africanity of black culture in America well into this century, a thesis that will find increasing support as the subject is pursued.

The least culture bound of Western men, Robeson called attention to the supreme artistry of West African sculpture, which inspired leading European artists; recognized the intricacies of African musical rhythms, which were more complex than anything attained by Western composers; stressed the flexibility and sophistication of African languages, which could convey subtleties of thought beyond what was suspected by those unacquainted with African linguistics; and emphasized the rich cultural heritage of Africa, which was related to the great civilizations of the East. While a long line of New World blacks stressed the need for "more advanced" Western blacks to play the vanguard role in the liberation of African peoples, Robeson considered Africans best suited to determine the imperatives of their freedom and the terms of their new lives.[140]

His commitment to the oppressed of the world and his growing radicalism in the face of new and fiercer barbarisms from Europe—these traits, backed by the singular compass of his gifts, were destined to make him a marked man in America. The acute provincialism of most Negro intellectuals and civil rights leaders in the United States made them, when he later incurred the hatred of American rulers, ill-suited to understand the values he was defending. Nevertheless, there is little doubt that he meant it when he said he was returning to America without bitterness. The very qualities that led him to take that position, however, soon caused him to lash out against continued American oppression of people of African ancestry. In time, forces of repression plunged him into an isolation in the land of his birth far more painful and protracted than anything he had encountered abroad. Still, he experienced, on his return in 1939, years of continued acclaim before various ruling elites attempted to silence him completely.

V I

Not surprisingly, Robeson was concerned about the disposition of colonies following the war, and preoccupied with the overall reorganization of the war-ravaged world. In a speech at Hamilton College in 1940, he expressed continuing interest in the cultures of the world, stating that, when the war was over and realignments of power effected, "not only Western culture, but also that of Hindus, Africans and Chinese would each contribute to the realization of a true and lasting human culture."[141] There was need for an international culture based on sets of perceptions and sensibilities that would enlarge man's chances for utilizing the creative elements of human character. The president of Hamilton College remarked,

> In honoring you today, we do not, however, press our enthusiasm for your histrionic and musical achievements alone, we honor you chiefly as a man—a man of tremendous stature, energy, and physical dexterity; a man of brilliant mind, a man whose sensitive spirit makes possible your penetrating interpretations; a man who, above all else, travels across the world as an example of the humanity and the greatness of our democratic heritage.[142]

Robeson's performances brought forth such throngs that room had to be made on concert stages for some of the people in his audiences. In June 1941, he sang before 23,000 people in Newark and provided encore after encore. Three weeks later on a chilly evening, 14,000 people turned out to hear him sing in New York, and two weeks later, when he sang with the Philadelphia Orchestra, the season's attendance record was broken.[143]

In July 1943, backed by the New York Philharmonic, Robeson sang before thousands. The *New York Times* music critic Howard Taubman wrote,

> [B]y the end of the evening it was unmistakable that Mr. Robeson was the principal attraction. He was not, however, the whole show. The 20,000 in the field and concrete seats shared that distinction with the baritone. For when Mr. Robeson completed the listed group of songs at the end of the concert, the audience virtually took over. Roars arose from every section of the amphitheatre. Men and women shouted their favorite encores. Mr. Robeson smiled and said, "I'll get to 'em I hope." He got to a good many. When the reviewer left, Mr. Robeson had been singing encores for half an hour. . . . Some in the far reaches of the stadium took to chanting their requests in unison. Mr. Robeson kept assuring the crowd, "O.K., I heard it." The encores were virtually a concert in themselves.[144]

Robeson's greatest triumph on the stage occurred on Broadway in Shakespeare's *Othello*. The Old Vic had offered him the role of Othello in 1937, opposite Laurence Olivier's Iago. At the time, he did not consider himself "ready" for the role, but then he studied *Othello* in German,

French, Yiddish, and Elizabethan English to determine nuances of meaning in the play.[145] Moreover, he steeped himself in the history of Morocco and Spain and, before leaving England, had occasion to apply his reflections on the Moor in Renaissance Europe to the racism of his time and found in the play a cathartic value that gave him a deeper understanding of the limits of racism.

Just as he brought the meaning of *Othello* to the experiences of his life, he was able, with much effort, to reverse the process when acting the role, and the naturalness that distinguished him as singer and man marked his characterization of Othello. Before going on the stage to perform the role, he often recalled the rage he had felt when his football teammates injured him, which made it easier for him to express Othello's resentment that his color was an important factor in his being betrayed. But that was one of many instances of racial wrongs that gave the play resonance. Indeed, he found it "deeply fascinating to watch how strikingly contemporary American audiences from coast to coast found Shakespeare's *Othello*—painfully immediate in its unfolding of evil, innocence, passion, dignity and nobility, and contemporary in its overtones of a clash of cultures, of the partial acceptance of and consequent effect upon one of a minority group." The protagonist's jealousy against that background "becomes more credible, the blows to his pride more understandable, the final collapse of his personal, individual world more inevitable."[146]

One doubts that the human voice has ever been presented to greater advantage in the theater than was Robeson's in *Othello*. There were times when it not only filled the theater but also dominated one's consciousness. Representing the character of Othello while taking on qualities of transcendence, his voice ranged from thunder tones as natural as in a sea of rain to whispers so tender they became a song: "Soft you! a word or two before you go. I have done the state some service, and they know't. No more of that . . . I kissed thee ere I killed thee. No way but this, Killing myself, to die upon a kiss."[147]

‚Played over the 1943–44 theater season, *Othello* set a record for Shakespearean plays on Broadway, running for 296 performances. Robeson received the gold medal of the American Academy of Arts and Sciences for the best diction in the American theater and, in 1944, the Donaldson award for best actor in the American theater that year.[148] But acclaim was not new to him, and success had not caused him in the past to forget his convictions. New American successes did not alter that pattern.

Near the close of the war, he returned to the theme that the great white powers had to be prepared to accept the humanity of Africans and other colonial peoples. Remarking that Americans in the past had not known much about Africa "beyond the caricatures occasionally represented in American movies," he added that large numbers of them had begun to realize that the welfare of Africans and other dependent people was linked to their own, a truth brought home by the significant role played by colonies and colonial peoples in the waging of the war.[149] In fact, World War II marked a great watershed in American attitudes toward Africa. Already certain Americans looked to Africa as "the last great continental frontier of the world for the white man to cross . . . the jackpot of World War II." Other Americans were contending that, while there had been "some mistakes and shortcomings in colonial rule," Africans were too backward to be granted immediate freedom—an argument that Robeson had heard in England from more sophisticated, if limited, white intellectuals and that, if insisted on, would threaten a peace won at unprecedented human cost.[150]

For over a decade a supporter of radical causes around the world, Robeson was not reluctant to associate with the left in America. Besides, the Democrats and Republicans were offering little that was of interest to him. The Democratic party continued to be the home of Southern racists, who held significant power in Congress, and the Republican party continued to oppose the freedom of blacks, as it had since betraying black rights with the overthrow of Reconstruction in 1876. It is not surprising, therefore, that Robeson, considering his respect for the Soviet Union and his identification with the oppressed of the world, was a participant at a Madison Square Garden meeting sponsored by the National Council of Soviet-American Friendship. Dean Acheson, who represented the State Department at the meeting, has provided an intriguing description of the atmosphere of the occasion and of Robeson's singing:

The vast place was packed and vociferous. In its center an elevated boxing ring had been erected with a runway going up to it from a curtained enclosure in which I met my fellow performers: Corliss Lamont, president of the Council, a son of Thomas W. Lamont, Chairman of the Board of J.P. Morgan & Company; Joseph E. Davies, who had been Ambassador to Moscow and written an enthusiastic account entitled *Mission to Moscow;* Paul Robeson, the great Negro bass; . . . and, to top the list, the Very Reverend Hewlett Johnson, the "Red" Dean of Canterbury Cathedral. On the floor below the prize ring an orchestra played incendiary music. . . . Paul Robeson and Dean Johnson were clearly the favorites. Indeed, the "Red" Dean received a tumultuous ovation, as he sashayed around the ring like a skater, in the long black coat and gaiters of an English prelate, his hands clasped above his head in a prize fighter's salute. Corliss Lamont opened with a brief welcome. Then Paul Robeson's magnificent voice began the low rumble of "Ole Man River," that moving song of the oppressed and hopeless. It did not end in hopelessness and resignation as the river just kept on rolling along, however, but in a swelling protest, ending on that magnificent high note of defiance produced by a great voice magnified by all the power of science. The crowd went wild.[151]

Throughout the period following his return from London, Robeson devoted time to directing the Council on African Affairs. He had been instrumental in founding the council not long before leaving London. That organization, which was founded in London and existed for nearly two decades, was the most important one in America working for African liberation during the 1940s and 1950s. W. Alphaeus Hunton, who for years served as its secretary, did not exaggerate in contending, "The Council on African Affairs for many years stood alone as the one organization in the United States devoting fulltime attention to the problems of the peoples of Africa." In addition to being a clearinghouse for information on Africa, that organization rendered under Robeson's direction a multiplicity of services to Africa. Dr. Z. K. Mathews, a leader of the African National Congress in South Africa, has written that, when a severe drought struck the Eastern Cape Province of the Union of South Africa, "hundreds of Africans . . . had cause to be thankful that such a body as the Council on African Affairs was in existence. . . . The Council made available financial aid and food supplies of various kinds. . . . Many African children, women and older people in the area concerned owed their lives to the assistance given by the Council." The council, through its African Aid Committee, which Du Bois headed, also aided "the families of 26 miners shot down during a strike in the coal pits of Enugu, Nigeria."[152]

Robeson remarked that the "Council on African Affairs was very fortunate and proud when Dr. Du Bois joined our organization as Chairman in 1949." He thought Du Bois made a meaningful contribution to the struggle of African people, especially in South Africa, an area of Africa that for Du Bois, as for him, was of long-standing interest, and one they often discussed. But the two men, as one might imagine, shared views on many subjects, including the black folk heritage, particularly black folk music, which both found to be under African influence and which Du Bois "loved and found deeply moving. He often stressed the importance of this special contribution to American culture. We had interesting discussions about the likeness of our Negro folk music to many other folk musics throughout the world."[153]

Robeson repeatedly linked the oppression of Africans to that of American Negroes and called on Afro-Americans, as beleaguered as they were, to come to the aid of their brothers and sisters in Africa because they faced a common enemy. In particular, he attacked "the vicious system of racial exploitation and oppression practiced in the Union of South Africa." Referring to South Africa as a part of "President Truman's free world," he observed that dozens of the largest American oil, auto, mining, and other trusts "have highly profitable holdings in that country," that U.S. laws were used to accelerate the exploitation of South African resources: "Hence it is clear that in raising our voices against the Malan regime we simultaneously strike a blow at the reactionary forces in our own land who seek to preserve here, in South Africa, and everywhere else the super-profits they harvest from racial and national oppression."[154]

Of course, Du Bois shared Robeson's vision of African liberation and its link to New World blacks. In fact, Robeson found that vision brilliantly formed throughout Du Bois's writings and recognized him as the father of Pan-Africanism. That they shared a commitment to the socialist world, a world that greatly expanded after World War II, best explains why the two men, uncompromising on African freedom and the indispensability of socialism to that freedom, were persecuted during the Cold War. An Africa working toward socialism was what both had in mind. Considering the history of the continent and the history of blacks in America—and both men were profoundly cognizant of that history—formal independence, they hoped, would be the initial step in a movement leading to a socialist Africa.

Robeson and Du Bois celebrated special moments despite the scrutiny of a federal government concerned about them and their associates. Robeson remembered "a wonderful Thanksgiving dinner" at the Du Bois home at 31 Grace Court in Brooklyn:

> He had invited some guests from the United Nations, because he knew they had heard and read about Thanksgiving, but had no personal experience and understanding of this special American holiday. So this was as typical a Thanksgiving dinner and evening as he and his wife Shirley could make it, with the good Doctor a gay and witty host, explaining everything step by step—from turkey and cranberry sauce to pumpkin pie and early American history.[155]

Though subjected to harassment, Robeson intensified his support of the liberation causes of Afro-Asia, about which he thought the American people had much to learn. For some time he had believed that Americans who opposed Afro-Asian liberation did not understand the nature of the times, did not realize that revolutionary change was occurring in the world. In "Reflections on Othello and the Nature of Our Times," he wrote that "we stand at the end of one period in human history and before the entrance of a new." It was his opinion that "all our tenets and tried beliefs were [being] challenged." Since the challenge was at home as well, the liberal intellectuals, members of the professions, scientists, artists, and scholars had a special responsibility:

> They have an unparalleled opportunity to lead and to serve. But to fulfill our deep obligations to society we must have faith in the whole people, the emergence into full bloom of the last estate, the vision of no high and no low, no superior and no inferior—but equals, assigned to different tasks in the building of a new and richer human society.[156]

Not one to respect the chasm between the ideal and the reality of freedom, Robeson wanted to bridge, to unify, to meld those realms. His perspective on the world and his willingness to support it with everything he possessed meant that conflict between him and white America had been inevitable—more especially because the rulers of America realized, probably as early as 1945 and certainly thereafter, that if ever there was a New World black prepared to risk all in defense of Africa it was Robeson. His nationalist base was irreducible in that fundamental sense.

The multifaceted genius compared the postwar era with the breakdown of medievalism that preceded the Renaissance, and he foresaw a similar "shattering of a universe" because entrapped, pent-up forces of color, for centuries subjected to European suzerainty, were beginning to break loose, threatening to make the European vision of itself sadly unrealizable, the European focus of world power soon irretrievable.[157] The day was not too distant when the most incandescent dreams of nationalists from Walker to Robeson would achieve, however uncertain the workings of the human will, the tangibility of freedom.

Notes

CHAPTER ONE
Introduction: Slavery and the Circle of Culture

1. Peter Wood, who makes interesting use of African ethnicity in relation to work and resistance, notes of the colonists, "Most white colonists would have marvelled at the ignorance of their descendants, who asserted blindly that all Africans looked the same." Peter Wood, *Black Majority: Negroes in Colonial South Carolina from 1670 through the Stono Rebellion* (New York: Knopf, 1974), 179. Also see chap. 2, 9, and 11. In general, slave masters in the nineteenth century paid little attention to African ethnicity, which was of immense value in the process of Pan-Africanization—of Africans, despite ethnic differences, becoming a single people—since masters did not attempt to maintain ethnic barriers. The most extended treatment of the slave masters' perceptions of ethnicity in the colonial period is found in Daniel C. Littlefield's *Rice and Slaves* (Baton Rouge: Louisiana State U. Press, 1981), chap. 1. For the most thorough treatment of ethnicity and the Atlantic slave trade, see Phillip Curtin, *The Atlantic Slave Trade* (Madison: U. of Wisconsin Press, 1969).

2. E. C. L. Adams, *Nigger to Nigger* (New York: Scribner's, 1928), introd., vii and viii.

3. Adams, "The King Buzzard", in *Nigger to Nigger*, 13–14.

4. Ibid., 14–15.

5. Concern for the spirit is tied to concern for a proper burial, for without a proper burial the spirit is certain to be restless, and that restlessness can lead to problems for those responsible for the burial. Talbot states it well:

> So much significance, indeed, is attached to funeral rites that it is not unknown for aged people, especially women, to commit suicide after they have accumulated enough wealth for the ceremonies—particularly so among the Ibo and Semi-Bantu, or when the person in question has only one son, so that if he died first there would be none left to carry out the burial. This is not surprising when it is remembered that the dead are in most places regarded as more powerful than the living and more able to affect one for good or ill; their goodwill is essential for prosperity and success in life.

See P. Amaury Talbot, *The Peoples of Southern Nigeria* (London: Oxford U. Press, 1926), 3:469.

6. Arthur Glyn Leonard, *The Lower Niger and Its Tribes* (New York: Macmillan, 1906), 142.

7. Ibid. See C. K. Meek, *Law and Authority in a Nigerian Tribe* (London: Oxford U. Press, 1937), 309. Also see George Thomas Basden, *Among the Ibos of Nigeria* (Philadelphia: Lippincott; London: Seeley, Service, 1931), 115–16.

8. It is likely that ethnicity was greatly depreciated by slaves well before the close of slavery, that new arrivals from Africa quickly learned its limitations in the new environment. But it is equally likely that the process of Pan-Africanization had not completely run its course by the end of slavery, that the consciousness of being of a particular ethnic background, and even the continuing ability to speak a particular African language, was maintained by elderly African-born blacks.

9. Adams, "Gullah Joe," in *Nigger to Nigger,* 227.

10. Ibid., 227–28. Consciousness of the "whiteness" of their captors is clearly established in the tale by the time the Africans are tricked at sea. More commonly, however, Africans were under white control before boarding ships, and those moments taught them, since only blacks were chained and whites lorded it over them, that "race" was a decisive factor in their new lives, one intensified during the Atlantic voyage with no prospect of attenuation. Under such circumstances, consciousness of white claims to superior humanity was impressd upon them—a force with which they would have to deal for the rest of their lives. Very early on in captivity color became for Africans, for the first time, a source of unity across ethnic lines. That link between color and their fetters was an irreducible foundation of Pan-Africanism, a basis on which their melding of cultural traits would in time rest.

11. Adams, "Gullah Joe," 228.

12. Ibid.

13. See Lorenzo Turner, *Africanisms in the Gullah Dialect* (Chicago: U. of Chicago Press, 1949), 193. Turner writes that approximately two dozen African ethnic groups were enslaved in South Carolina with representation along the west coast from Senegal to Angola: "The important areas involved were Senegal, Gambia, Sierra Leone, Liberia, the Gold Coast, Togo, Dahomey, Nigeria, and Angola." He adds that "the vocabulary of Gullah contains words found in the following languages, most of which are spoken in the above-mentioned areas: Wolof, Malinke, Mandinka, Bambara, Fula, Mende, Vai, Twi, Fante, Ga, Eue, Fon, Yoruba, Bini, Hausa, Ibo, Ibibio, Efik, Kongo, Umbundu, Kimbunda, and a few others." Ibid., 1–2. The author thanks the linguist John Rickford of Stanford for bringing the Kikongo word mfinda, after having seen the tale, to his attention. Interview with Rickford, Spring 1981.

14. Adams, "The Slave Barn," in *Nigger to Nigger,* 234–35.

15. Ibid., 235.

16. Ibid., 236.

17. E. C. L. Adams, "Ole Man Rogan," in *Congaree Sketches* (Chapel Hill: U. of North Carolina Press, 1927), 51–55.

18. Ibid., 51.

19. The presence of such a rich body of slave folklore implies that much exists that has not yet been recorded, that much has been lost with the passage of time, and that, considering the African character of slave folklore, much of what is known is not understood.

20. Robert F. Thompson estimates that 30 percent of the Africans brought to North America during the slave trade were brought from the Congo-Angola region

of Africa. Phillip Curtin, on whom Thompson relied for the estimate, notes in some detail the complexities involved in determining Congo-Angolan influences in the New World. For example, regarding the nineteenth century, Curtin writes, "The 'Angola' of earlier tables can now be divided into two—'Congo North' taking in coastal points from Cape Lopez southward to and including the mouth of the Congo River, and 'Angola' now taken as Angola proper, the region from Ambriz southward to Benguela." Thompson argues that what apparently happened in the New World was that "a mixture of Kongo and Kongo-related cultures were brought together" to strengthen the more important and salient "shared general Bakongo cultural traits, a fusion in which the memory and the grandeur and the name of Kongo itself was maintained." The estimate by Thompson of the percentage of Bakongo brought to North America is based on a lecture by Phillip Curtin. Conversation with Robert F. Thompson, July 24, 1986. James Rawley writes that 25 percent of the Africans brought into slavery in North America were from Congo-Angola and almost as many from Nigeria-Dahomey-Togo-Ghana: "Scrutiny of the African origins of American slaves in general reveals that about one-quarter of the whole came from Angola [Congo-Angola] and a lesser portion from the Bight of Biafra. Of the remainder, in descending order, the Gold Coast, Senegambia, the Windward Coast, and Sierra Leone, the Bight of Benin, and Mozambique-Madagascar supplied the rest." See Curtin, *Atlantic Slave Trade*, 241; Robert F. Thompson, *The Four Moments of the Sun* (Washington, D.C.: National Gallery of Art, 1981), 148; and James H. Rawley, *The Transatlantic Slave Trade* (New York: Norton, 1981), 335. A minimum of 50 percent of the Africans brought to North America—to the colonies and states discussed in this volume—were from Congo-Angola and from Nigeria, Dahomey, Togo, the Gold Coast, and Sierra Leone.

21. Talbot, *Southern Nigeria,* 804. Talbot writes, "The vast majority of dances in Southern Nigeria may be said to have to do with fertility in one or other of its aspects. It is interesting to think that it was out of similar dances, from the dithyrambs at the spring festival of Dionysus, of which the main object was the magical promotion of the food supply, that the drama of ancient Greece arose."Ibid.

22. Ibid., 803.

23. Thompson, *Four Moments,* 54,28.

24. Parrish's observation that "the solo ring performance is apparently the only form in use" in North Carolina and Virginia and that "the ring shout seems to be unknown" is probably wide of the mark, as we shall see. Lydia Parrish, *Slave Songs of the Georgia Sea Islands* (New York: Creative Age Press, 1942), 54; Melville J. Herskovits, *Dahomey,* (New York: Augustin, 1938), 1:216.

25. Herskovits, *Dahomey,* 67–68.

26. Thompson, *Four Moments,* 28.

27. Ibid. .

28. Suzzane Blier, "The Dance of Death," *Res* 2 (Autumn 1981) :117.

29. Interview with Earl Conteh-Morgan, Spring 1984. Conteh-Morgan's description of the storyteller encircled by his listeners closely resembles Higginson's description of a storytelling scene in the Sea Islands, one that he rightly regarded as a major source of the means by which education occurred in the slave community:

Strolling in the cool moonlight, I was attracted by a brilliant light beneath the trees, and cautiously approached it. A circle of thirty or forty soldiers sat around a roaring fire, while the old uncle, Cato by name, was narrating an interminable tale, to the insatiable delight of his audience. . . . It was a narrative, dramatized to the last degree . . . and even I . . . never witnessed such a piece of acting. . . . And all this . . . with the brilliant fire lighting up their red trousers and gleaming from their shining black faces,—eyes and teeth all white . . . This is their university; every young Sambo before me, as he turned over the sweet potatoes and peanuts which were roasting in the ashes, listened with reverence to the wiles of the ancient Ulysses, and meditated the same.

Thomas Wentworth Higginson, *Army Life in a Black Regiment* (New York: W. W. Norton, 1984), 36–38 (originally published in 1869).

30. Interview with Conteh-Morgan, Spring 1984.

31. Ibid.

32. Melville J. Herskovits, *The Myth of the Negro Past* (Boston: Beacon Press, 1941), 106–7.

33. The Arabic scholar and professor of African history John Hunwick disputes Turner's rendering of the pronunciation of the word *saut*. *Saut*, according to Hunwick, simply means "voice" or "sound." Interview with Hunwick, Spring 1984.

34. Melville J. Herskovits, *Rebel Destiny* (New York and London: Whittlesey House, McGraw-Hill, 1934), x, and chap. 1.

35. Ibid., 8, 9; R. S. Rattray, *Ashanti* (London: Oxford U. Press, 1923), 209–10.

36. Herskovits, *Rebel Destiny*, 8.

37. Marshall Stearns, *The Story of Jazz* (New York: Oxford U. Press, 1956), 12–13. The Lomaxes saw "shouts" in Texas, Louisiana, and Georgia as well as in the Bahamas, and they saw "voodou rites in Haiti":

All share basic similarities: (1) the song is "danced" with the whole body, with hands, feet, belly, and hips; (2) the worship is, basically, a dancing-singing phenomenon; (3) the dancers always move counter-clockwise around the ring; (4) the song has the leader-chorus form, with much repetition, with a focus on rhythm rather than on melody, that is, with a form that invites and ultimately enforces cooperative group activity; (5) the song . . . steadily increasing in intensity and gradually accelerating, until a sort of mass hypnosis ensues. . . .

The Lomaxes added, "This shout pattern is demonstrably West African." See John A. Lomax and Alan Lomax, *Folk Song U.S.A.* (New York: Duell, Sloan and Pearce, 1947), 335. Courlander notes that as the tempo of the shout builds, singing is interspersed with exclamations peculiar to some Negro church ceremonies, until the tempo reaches "a tense peak close to an ecstatic breaking point of excitement," at which time "such exclamations as 'Oh, Lord!' and 'Yes, Lord!' turn into nonsense syllables and cries. . . ." See Harold Courlander, *Negro Folk Music, U.S.A.* (New York: Columbia U. Press, 1963), 194.

38. For Brer Rabbit and headless horseman, see "The Dance of the Little Animals," in Adams, *Nigger to Nigger*, 178; also see "Bur Rabbit in Red Hill Churchyard," Ibid., 171.

39. Adams, "Churchyard," 171.

40. Ibid.

41. Ibid., 172.

42. Ibid.

43. Ibid.

44. Melville and Frances Herskovits, *Suriname Folklore* (New York: Columbia U. Press, 1936), 520.

45. Adams, "Churchyard," 172–73.

46. Ibid., 173.

47. Herskovits, *Suriname Folklore*, 521. As "Churchyard" demonstrates, the absence of explicit references to an African God or to African gods in slave folklore, especially in the tale, should not be taken to mean that slaves, in embracing Christianity, did so without a continuing consciousness of the African Godhead. Moreover, the African God, in conception, is close to the Judaic God as presented in Christianity, that is, the conception of God as Spirit. It should also be noted that the exposure to Islam of sizable numbers of blacks in Africa made it easier, because of the Judaic influence in Islam, for some enslaved Africans to accept Christianity. A note of caution must be sounded with respect to slave references to God: for slaves to refer openly to an African God would have invited brutal repression from slave overlords. Mbiti writes of the African God, "It is commonly believed that God is Spirit, even if in thinking and talking about Him African peoples may often use anthropomorphic images. As far as is known, there are no images or physical representations of God by African peoples . . . one clear indication that they consider Him to be a Spiritual Being." African concepts of God are strongly influenced by the geographical, historical, social, and cultural environment and background of each people, which

> explains the similarities and differences which we find when we consider the beliefs about God from all over the continent. It is this which partly accounts also for the beliefs parallel to those held by peoples of other continents and lands, where the background may be similar to that of African peoples. This does not rule out the fact that through contact with the outside world, some influence of ideas and culture has reached our continent. But such influence is minimal and must have operated in both directions. There are cardinal teachings, doctrines and beliefs of Christianity, Judaism and Islam which cannot be traced in traditional religions. These major religious traditions, therefore, cannot have been responsible for disseminating those concepts of God in traditional religions which resemble some biblical and semite ideas about God. . . .

John S. Mbiti, *African Religions and Philosophy* (New York: Doubleday, 1969), 38, 44.

48. David Dalby, "Jazz, Jitter and Jam," *New York Times,* Nov. 10, 1970, op-ed page.

49. I wish to thank the anthropologist Paul Riesman for bringing Songhai burial ceremonies, and the place of the violin in them, to my attention. Interview with Riesman, Spring 1982.

50. Adams, "Bur Jonah's Goat," *Nigger to Nigger,* 174. Dalby's thesis regarding Malian influences on slaves in America is supported by linguistic studies of Lorenzo Turner, who notes the prominence of Malian linguistic influences among Gullah-speaking blacks in the Sea Islands of South Carolina and Georgia, where Wolof, Malinke, Mandinka, and Bambara ethnic groups were represented in antebellum America.

51. Sir Charles Lyell, *A Second Visit to the United States of America* (New York: Harper, 1849), 262–69.

52. On the Hopeton plantation, moreover, there was a distinct preference among slaves, during Christian baptism, for "total immersion," a widespread practice in

Central and West Africa. On such occasions, the "principal charm" for slave women was "decking themselves out in white robes." Since in Georgia the Episcopal bishop, one Dr. Elliott, "found that the negroes in general had no faith in the efficacy of baptism except by complete immersion, he performed the ceremony as they desired." Lyell, *Second Visit*, 269.

53. John Fanning Watson, *Annals of Philadelphia* (Philadelphia, 1850), 2:265. It is almost certain that slaves in the Philadelphia graveyard were doing the ring shout, for as late as the 1870s the shout was pervasive and powerful among blacks in that city. Blassingame makes mention of the ring shout in treating slave culture, and Raboteau gives more than passing attention to that ritual. Genovese perceptively notes that the dance of the shout is the foundation of jazz dance, and Levine presents the shout over several pages in his work. While these scholars, all important contributors to scholarship on slave culture, were by no means unmindful of the importance of the shout, they did not probe its significance in African ancestral terms. See John W. Blassingame, *The Slave Community* (New York: Oxford U. Press, 1972), 65–66; Albert J. Raboteau, *Slave Religion* (New York: Oxford U. Press, 1978), 66–73, 339–40; Eugene D. Genovese, *Roll, Jordan, Roll* (New York; Pantheon Books, 1974), 233–34; Lawrence W. Levine, *Black Culture and Black Consciousness* (New York: Oxford U. Press, 1977), 37–38; 165–66. Some attention is given to the ring shout in an unpublished essay by Robert L. Hall, "Africanisms in Florida: Some Aspects of Afro-American Religion." Also see Charles Joyner, *Down by the Riverside* (Urbana: U. of Illinois Press, 1984), 160–61.

54. Watson, *Philadelphia*, 265. Although the ring shout was vigorously employed by countless thousands of slaves, some African religious practices either did not survive the slave experience in any significant degree—which is suggested by their relative absence from slave oral literature—or survived in greatly reduced form: African superstitions, such as the belief that death or sickness resulted from "medicine" used against one and could be prevented by the right "medicine," could not compete with the power of the master class, which was great enough to hold the African in slavery. The overwhelming majority of slaves, consequently, refused to rely on obviously ineffective African means in opposing their white overlord. The classic case of a slave recognizing the limitations of superstition in opposing slavery involved Frederick Douglass and Sandy, "a genuine African" who "had inherited some of the so-called magical powers said to be possessed by the eastern nations." "He told me," Douglass said, "that if I would take that root and wear it on my right side it would be impossible for Covey an overseer to strike me a blow." But when wearing the root and attacked by Covey, "I forgot all about my root, and remembered my pledge to stand up in my own defense. The brute was skillfully endeavoring to get a slipknot on my legs. . . . " See Douglass, *The Life and Times of Frederick Douglass* (New York: Collier Books, 1962), 137, 139, quoted from the rev. ed., 1882. W. E. B. Du Bois captured the essence of the problem for the slave: "Slavery . . . was to him the dark triumph of Evil over him." Since the master was the avatar of that evil, slaves were far too clever to think magic would solve the problem of their oppression. See Du Bois, *The Souls of Black Folk* (Grennwich, Conn.: Fawcett Books, 1953), 146 (originally published in 1903).

55. Watson, *Philadelphia*, 265.

56. Until recently, the existence of African ritual forms in slavery was denied, and areas of heavy concentrations of slaves were not even thought to provide a source of African values. That a handful of persons were able to maintain African explanatory values—values that illumine vital aspects of the culture of their people—was not seriously considered, the focus being on African values in relation to more dominant, it was assumed, Christian values. Now we know that African values not only existed in significant degree but were, as in the case of Pennsylvania slaves, thought of and discussed in African languages on American soil. That this occurred in the North strongly argues that it often occurred when Africans of similar linguistic backgrounds were together—and alone—in Southern slavery.

57. No matter how "contemplative" the African may have appeared, it is doubtful that his religion would have been respected by Christians, who were in a dominating, superior frame of mind. But vigorous movement from the pelvic region while dancing to handclapping and song—dancing until overcome by almost complete exhaustion as the perspiration dampened one's clothing and the ground—was too foreign to white religious sensibility to merit much of a response, short of pity and a certain revulsion.

58. Parrish, *Slaves Songs*, 20.

59. Talbot, *Southern Nigeria*, 802. Dancing affords the African

the one means of representing, as perfectly as possible, their otherwise inarticulate sense of the mystery of existence, the power of the supernatural influences which enfold them, the ecstasy of joy in life—of youth and strength and love—all the deeper and more poignant feelings so far beyond expression by mere words . . . and, whether the occasion be one of rejoicing or grief, of victory in war or funeral obsequies, of thanksgiving to the gods for their blessings of crops and children or of mere social amusement, it is by far the chief, and almost the only way of picturing and depicting their affections and sensibilities.

Ibid. Of course, dance as a means of expressing victory in warfare ceased to exist in North America. So, too, did dance to urge on those engaged in war at home or away—a practice especially common among Ashanti women, who were found in sizable numbers in the North and the South. For a discussion of the uses of dance and song in urging African men to acts of valor in battle, see Joshua Leslie and Sterling Stuckey, "The Death of Benito Cereno: A Reading of Herman Melville on Slavery," *Journal of Negro History* 67 (Winter 1982): 290; also see Frederick Augustus Ramsayer and Johannes Kuhne, *Four Years in Ashantee*, English trans. (Chicago: U. of Chicago photoduplication, 1967), 52, 209–10.

60. "In the Euro-Christian tradition," writes Courlander, "dancing in church is generally regarded as a profane act." He argues mistakenly, however, that the ring shout reconciled this objection, in that shouters avoided crossing their legs and thereby stopped short of dance—and hence the compromise. For one thing, neither Courlander nor anyone else has demonstrated that the crossing of legs was ever a part, essential or otherwise, of the shout. See Courlander, *Negro Folk Music*, 195.

61. Georgia Writers' Project, *Drums and Shadows* (Westport, Conn.: Greenwood Press, 1973), 107 (originally published in 1940).

62. Parrish, *Slave Songs*, 71. At Possum Point in the Sea Islands, blacks "alluz

[always] does [one] dance. We calls it 'Come Down tuh duh Myuh.' We dance roun and shake duh han an fiddle duh foot. One ub us kneel down in duh middle uh duh succle. Den we all call out an rise an shout roun, and we all fling duh foot agen." Georgia Writers' Project, *Drums and Shadows*, 141.

63. Jean and Marshall Stearns, *Jazz Dance* (New York: Shirmer Books, 1964), 31, 32.

64. Higginson, *Black Regiment*, 188.

65. Ibid., 187–88.

66. Ibid., 188.

67. Ibid., 189–90.

68. Ibid., 190.

69. Dena Epstein, *Sinful Tunes and Spirituals* (Urbana: U. of Illinois Press, 1977), 281.

70. Higginson, *Black Regiment*, 199.

71. Stearns, *Story of Jazz*, 130.

72. Genovese, *Roll, Jordan, Roll*, 278.

73. Rawley, *Slave Trade*, 402. As will be evident in the discussion of slave culture that immediately follows, too much attention can be given to whether slaves were African born in considering the continuing African spiritual and artistic influences in American slavery. In Virginia, as in North Carolina, generations passed without large importations of slaves directly from Africa. By 1778, in fact, the trade was effectively outlawed in Virginia, the large slave population even then growing by natural process. Yet almost three-quarters of a century later, extremely esoteric African cultural forms were in evidence there. Thus, the heavy involvement of Virginia slaves in the domestic slave trade as the glutted market was reduced was a development fraught with cultural significance, for by the late-eighteenth-century Virginia slaves, with their largely African spiritual values, were being sold to the lower South and the Southwest, where they had cultural contact with other slaves. For additional data on the Atlantic trade to Virginia, see ibid., 401–4.

74. Ibid., 407. The cultural impact of the trade in Africans to North Carolina from Virginia was considerable. Slaves entering from Virginia were likely, at the least, to want to continue the cultural practices to which they were accustomed. When they were not permitted to do so, the desire to do so must certainly have been there, influencing their thought and, in some degree, regulating their behavior, making it more tentative until new ways became accustomed ways, easing the process of setting aside old ones.

75. William John Faulkner, *The Days When the Animals Talked* (Chicago: Follette Publishers, 1977), 38; Rawley, *Slave Trade*, 407.

76. Faulkner, *The Animals Talked*, 52–59.

77. Ibid., 54.

78. Ibid., 56–57.

79. Ibid., 57.

80. Thompson, *Four Moments*, 35.

81. Ibid., 34, 46.

82. Ibid., 43.

83. Ibid. 43.

84. Faulkner, *The Animals Talked*, 58. See Laurie Abraham, "The Dead Live"

(Research paper for History CO1-2, Fall 1985, on Bakongo influences in Virginia during slavery, Reserve Room, Northwestern U. Library). Abraham's analysis of slave song during the conversion ceremony is pathfinding.

85. Thompson, *Four Moments,* 43.

86. Ibid., 43–44. The Kalunga line was represented horizontally on the cross-staff carried by the deacon.

87. Faulkner, *The Animals Talked,* 58.

88. This thesis is borne out by the fact that, as demonstrated here, conversion to Christianity characteristically occurred within the ancestral circle. Moreover, the evidence is overwhelming that slave converts to Christianity preferred to worship alone, often in forests or in praise houses, with no whites in view. It follows that the more African the ceremony, the more likely its occurrence when outsiders were not present.

89. Charles Colcock Jones, *The Religious Instructions of the Negroes in the United States* (Savannah, Ga., 1842), 176; William W. Freehling, *Prelude to Civil War* (New York: Harper & Row, 1965), 73, 337. Raboteau provides insight into the degree of Christian influence in the slave community near the end of slavery, quoting Du Bois's figure of "468,000 black church members in the South in 1859." Raboteau adds a statement that deserves attention: "Within forty years after emancipation, however, a black population of 8.3 million contained 2.7 million church members. This astounding figure sheds some light on the extent to which slaves had adopted Christianity in the antebellum South." Though Raboteau, in his valuable study of slave religion, has carefully set forth the extent to which white Christians converted slaves, one might differ with the conclusion he draws, namely, that much progress was made in this regard during and following slavery. Rather, what is surprising is that so few blacks were members of the Christian faith. Raboteau, *Slave Religion,* 209.

90. James Weldon Johnson, *God's Trombones* (New York: Penguin Books, 1976), 3.

91. Ibid., 2.

92. Faulkner, *The Animals Talked,* 35.

93. Ibid., 37.

94. Ibid., 36; Stearns, *Story of Jazz,* 57–63.

95. Faulkner, *The Animals Talked,* 39.

96. Ibid.

97. Quoted from Georgia Writers' Project, *Drums and Shadows,* by Robert Farris Thompson, "African Influences on the Art of the United States," in Armstead Robinson, ed., *Black Studies in the University* (New Haven: Yale U. Press, 1969), 151. For a fine treatment of slave burial rites, see David Roediger, "And Die in Dixie," *The Massachusetts Review* 22 (Spring 1981), no. 1.

98. Thompson, "African Influences," 150-51.

99. Ibid., 150. A superb student of African and Afro-American cultures, Thompson argues in this essay that "the main outlines" of the West African burial "tradition appear in parts of Mississippi, Georgia, and South Carolina as an almost classic demonstration of the nature of a generic survival." Ibid. Actually, those outlines are also found in Virginia, as we have seen, and in North Carolina and Arkansas. In West Memphis, Arkansas, the burial mounds of two ex-slaves support their essence. Saucers and cups rest on each mound, as do spoons with

handles in the mounds and a pipe the stem of which extends into one of the mounds. The husband had been a mulatto who married a dark-skinned slave—a mulatto who shared the values of the slave community, as did mulattoes generally on plantations. Hazel Todd, the daughter, visited the grave with family members from Detroit, Chicago, and Memphis in the 1950s and observed those objects and broken glass on the mounds. Interview with Todd, Spring 1984.

100. Arna Bontemps, *Black Thunder* (Bostson: Beacon Press, 1968), 52 (originally published in 1936). In a close reading of the scene, Anne Spurgeon noted Bontemps's reference to "the place where the two worlds meet," which indicates an uncommon grasp of Bakongo religion on the part of Bontemps and, like his treatment of the burial mound, an unusual understanding of the Bakongo faith. See Anne Spurgeon, "The African Religious Culture of the Afro-Americans" (Seminar paper for History C92, Spring 1985, Reserve Room, Northwestern U. Library).

101. Curtin found that from 1733 to 1807 some 40 percent of the African imports into South Carolina were from Congo-Angola, which helps explain the foundation of Bakongo and Bakongo-related cultural traits in that colony and state. The cultural effects of such imports were of lasting value. See Curtin, *Atlantic Slave Trade*, 157.

102. See Gerald W. Mullin, *Flight and Rebellion* (New York: Oxford U. Press, 1972), chap. 5; Freehling, *Prelude*, 56.

103. Robert S. Starobin, *Denmark Vesey: The Slave Conspiracy of 1822* (Englewood Cliffs, N.J.: Prentice-Hall), 30–31.

104. For a fine study of the role of language and slavery in the New World, see David Dalby, *Black through White* (Bloomington: Program of African Studies, Indiana U., 1971).

105. Quoted in Starobin, *Vesey*, 38, 30–31.

106. Quoted ibid., 31–32.

107. Quoted ibid., 64–65.

108. Quoted ibid., 51–53.

109. Quoted ibid., 25.

110. Freehling, *Prelude*, 58.

111. See Amasa Delano, *Voyages and Travels* (Boston, 1817), chap. 18; John Barbour, *The History of The Amistad Captives* (New Haven, 1841). Also see Leslie and Stuckey, "Death of Benito Cereno," 287–301; and Joshua Leslie and Sterling Stuckey, "Avoiding the Tragedy of Benito Cereno: The Official Response to Babo's Revolt," *Criminal Justice History* 3 (Winter 1982): 125–31.

112. Starobin, *Vesey*, 4. Peter Wood has written of Angolan influences in slave resistance in South Carolina. In particular, he has pioneered on Angolan resistance in relation to slave runaways. And there is, of course, his major finding regarding Africans from Sierra Leone and the cultivation of rice in South Carolina, a finding prefigured by Martin Delany in the 1850s. See Wood, *Black Majority*, esp. chaps. 2, 9, and 11.

113. Starobin, *Vesey*, 4.

114. Quoted ibid., 2; Freehling, *Prelude*, 55.

115. Quoted in Sterling Stuckey, "Through the Prism of Folklore: The Black Ethos in Slavery," *Massachusetts Review* 9 (Spring 1968): 427.

116. Starobin, *Vesey*, 5; quoted ibid., 21.

117. Quoted ibid., 41.

118. Quoted ibid., 43.

119. Quoted ibid., 46.

120. Quoted ibid., 45.

121. Ibid., 3.

122. Ibid., 5.

123. Quoted ibid., 34.

124. Quoted ibid., 60.

125. Freehling, *Prelude*, 60; Starobin, *Vesey*, 131.

126. Freehling, *Prelude*, 73.

127. Fredrika Bremer, *America of the Fifties: Letters of Fredrika Bremer*, ed. Adolph B. Benson (New York: Oxford U. Press, 1924), 275.

128. Ibid., 275–76.

129. Ibid., 276–77; Stearns, *Story of Jazz*, 13.

130. Bremer, *America*, 277–78.

131. James Baldwin, *The Fire Next Time* (New York: Dell, 1962), 49–50.

132. W. E. B. Du Bois, *The Souls of Black Folk*, in John Hope Franklin, ed., *Three Negro Classics* (New York: Avon Books, 1965), 339 (originally published in 1903).

133. Drawing on Douglas, Burns writes, "It is in the interests of authority to control people, and frenzied convulsions are a threat to any attempt at control. . . . Once a people do not subscribe to the authority which aims to control them, convulsions are likely to occur. . . . Mary Douglas added that convulsions can be a form of protest by the 'inferior' members of society. Women are thus more inclined to engage in convulsions." Greg Burns, "Comparisons of Spirit Possession in African and African-American Cultures" (Seminar paper for History C92, Spring 1985, Reserve Room, Northwestern U. Library).

134. Ibid.

135. Thomas A. Blair, *Weather Elements* (New York: Prentice-Hall, 1931), 210.

136. The ring ceremony in Ashanti appears to be one source of the jumping of shouters in North America, the Ashanti priests, dancing in a great circle, leaping and "pirouetting like Russian dancers." Rattray, *Ashanti*, 158. See Daniel Alexander Payne, *Recollections of Seventy Years* (New York: Arno Press, 1968), 92–94 (originally published in 1888).

137. In churches in which the benches were not nailed down, much of the latitude taken under the sky at night or the sun at dawn could be taken. Still, the architecture of the church worked its own, subtle influence even in such circumstances. One should not, however, overemphasize the effects of that architecture, whether benches were nailed down or not, for a great deal of the naturalness—of emotional release and joyous affirmation of the faith—occurred despite the surroundings, an authentic African ceremonial atmosphere being created to remarkable degree. One can make this argument with confidence, because the quality of being able to achieve an authentic emotional experience in an environment far removed from what the celebrants are accustomed to is an impressive feature of black culture today in America. At the Smithsonian Institution, Southern Negroes repeatedly demonstrated the principle, as was noted by one participant, Jamila, who remarked of those present, "They turned the whole thing into a church. You knew when you saw people walking up there that that's what they were doing. I do

believe I was among them in doing that.'' Quoted in Sterling Stuckey, ''Tragic Voice: The Great Singing Movements of the Sixties'' (Evaluation of the Civil Rights Movement Conference, Smithsonian Institution, Jan, 30–Feb. 3, 1980).

138. Bremer, *America*, 105. There is little or no evidence supporting the view that slaves gave up dancing on becoming Christian; it is a view, in fact, that has little basis in slave action when slaves were alone or in the company of that rare white who seemed nonthreatening.

139. Bremer, *America*, 279; Higginson, *Black Regiment*, 41.

140. Bremer, *America*, 280.

141. Thompson, *Four Moments*, 149.

142. Frederick Law Olmsted, *A Journey in the Back Country* (New York: Schocken Books, 1970), 90 (originally published in 1860).

143. Frederick Law Olmsted, *The Cotton Kingdom* (New York: Knopf, 1953), 240-41 (originally published in 1861).

144. Ibid., 242.

145. Ibid., 243.

146. Ibid., 244–45.

147. Ibid., 245–46.

148. Ibid., 246.

149. Ibid.

150. William Wells Brown, *My Southern Home* (Upper Saddle River, N.J.: Gregg Press, 1968), 191 (originally published in 1880).

151. Ibid., 192.

152. Ibid., 193.

153. Ibid., 194.

154. Ibid.

155. Georgia Writers' Project, *Drums and Shadows*, 127–28, 131, 186–87.

156. Ibid., 159.

157. Herskovits, *Myth*, 133; Georgia Writers' Project, *Drums and Shadows*, 174.

158. Roscoe Lewis, *The Negro in Virginia* (New York: Arno Press, 1969), 89.

159. Ibid., 90. When slave fiddlers called figures, slaves most commonly responded with African figures, mainly dances in which animal movements were emulated. Fiddlers who called for whites in the big house certainly elicited different responses from blacks, who usually responded with African dance when not mocking white dance movements. Such a fiddler was Louis Cave: ''Chile, he sho' could strung dat fiddle. Never did do much work . . . he used to play and' call de figgers 'long as dere was anyone on de floor. Chile, when I was a girl guese I'd ruther dance dan eat.'' When a slave danced ''on de spot,'' someone might take ''a charred corn-cob an' draw a circle on de flo', den call one arter de odder up an' dance in de circle. Effen yo' feet tetch de edge you is out.'' This dance, more than most, may have called for extra effort, since the circle was drawn on the floor, its sacred significance inspirational. Ibid., 91.

160. Ibid., 93.

161. Ibid.

162. Ibid. The balancing of objects on the head, a skill not peculiar to Africans but as characteristic of them as of any people—widespread in black Africa but not in Europe—persisted throughout slavery and carried over into the postslavery era. That skill, which seemed particularly characteristic of women but was by no

means confined to them, was manifested in scenes of everyday life three-quarters of a century after slavery: an enormous basket of flowers on the head of a hat-wearing, middle-aged woman, her eyes shaded from the sun; an elderly woman carrying, in pyramid fashion, two large metal containers on her head while holding a third in her right hand—she also carries a purse that hangs from her right fore-arm—as she looks out from the page unperturbed; and a large woman, her left hand on her hip, her hair braided, stands before a wooden fence, an enormous straw basket on her head. See Doris Ulmann, *The Darkness and the Light* (Miller-ton, N.Y.: Aperture, 1974), 21, 42, 46. Not surprisingly, in the same masterly photographic essay, one finds a tombstone with the inscription "Hackless Jenkins, June 15, 1878 to June 23, 1926" and a mound on which there are jars, cups, glasses, a water pitcher, and other intimate objects of the deceased. Ibid., 60.

163. Dougald MacMillan, "John Kuners," *Journal of American Folk-Lore* 39 (Jan.–March 1926): 54–55.

164. Ibid., 54.

165. Talbot, *Southern Nigeria*, 760–61.

166. Ibid., 761.

167. Joshua Leslie, "Among the Yoruba" (unpublished MS). Leslie's observa-tions are supported by Herskovits's; this is a measure of the continuing force of the Egun masquerade in West Africa today. "In Nigeria, the Egungun go masked about the streets; there are no attendants for the masked figures, who themselves carry whips, chastise those . . . who do not show them the proper respect." Herskovits, *Dahomey*, 2:246.

168. Herskovits, *Dahomey*, 1:246–47. "The importance of women as singers of songs is a Dahomean innovation . . . On the other hand, the costuming, and, it is said, many of the songs, are Nigerian. Certainly the concept of the Egu as a power emanating from the spirits of the dead has been taken over directly from Nigeria." Ibid., 247.

169. Talbot, *Southern Nigeria*, 763. Although John Kunering was mainy associ-ated with Christmas in North America, some scholars contend the ceremony was performed at other times as well. "This in no manner detracts from the fact that it originally was confined to a period which marked the close of the year, but opens an avenue of study relative to trait culture dissemination and change in social significance." Ira De A. Reid, "The John Canoe Festival: A New World Af-ricanism," *Phylon* 3 (1942): 351.

170. Edward Warren, *A Doctor's Experiences on Three Continents* (Baltimore: Cushings and Baily, 1885), 201.

171. Ibid., 200.

172. Ibid., 201.

173. Ibid.

174. Ibid., 201–2.

175. Ibid., 202.

176. Douglass, *Life and Times*, 54–55.

177. Warren, *A Doctor's Experiences*, 203.

178. Ibid., 200.

179. The music historian Eileen Southern, who has deeply researched black cul-ture, is an exception to the rule in her findings regarding slave ceremony in the

North during the colonial period and in her conclusions regarding the African character of much of that ceremony then and later. See Southern, *The Music of Black Americans* (New York: Norton, 1971), chaps. 1 and 2.

180. Hubert H. S. Aimes, "African Institutions in America," *Jounal of American Folk-Lore* 18 (Jan.–March 1905): 15.

181. Orville H. Platt, "Negro Governors," *Papers of the New Haven Colony Historical Society* 6 (1900): 319; Aimes, "African Institutions," 98; Lorenzo Greene, *The Negro in Colonial New England* (New York: Atheneum, 1968), 36 (originally published in 1942).

182. Aimes, "African Institutions," 15. Lorenzo Greene is one of the few historians to write about the "Negro Governor." In fact, he does so in some detail. See Greene, *Negro in Colonial New England,* 249–55. For a more recent treatment of this ritual, see Joseph P. Reidy, "Negro Election Day and Black Community Life in New England, 1750–1860," *Marxist Persectives* 1 (Fall 1978): 102–17.

183. Quoted in Platt, "Negro Governors," 324.

184. Jane De Forest Shelton, "The New England Negro: A Remnant," *Harper's Monthly Magazine,* March 1894, 537.

185. Platt, "Negro Governors," 324.

186. Quoted ibid., 331. Rhode Island masters "foresaw that a sort of police managed wholly by the slaves would be more effectual in keeping them within the bounds of morality and honesty, than if the same authority were exercised by the whites." Quoted ibid. Thus, a compromise in some respects mutually beneficial was effected between slave and master as a result of the Negro governor practice. The relative mildness of slavery in New England provided crevices that were exploited by blacks in the interest of values proper to them in certain areas—in ceremonies and in personal contact.

187. Ibid., 322–23.

188. Aimes, "African Institutions," 20.

189. Quoted ibid.

190. Quoted in Platt, "Negro Governors," 326.

191. Aimes, "African Institutions," 20.

192. Dr. James Eights, "Pinkster Festivities in Albany Sixty Years Ago," *Collections on the History of Albany,* vol. 2 (Albany, 1867), 323.

193. Ibid., 324.

194. Ibid., 325.

195. Ibid.

196. Ibid., 325–26.

197. Ibid., 326.

198. Higginson, *Black Regiment,* p. 41.

199. Ibid.

200. Ibid., 47; Melville writes of the cook in *Redburn,* one Mr. Thompson, that he "sat over his boiling pots, reading out of a book which was very much soiled and covered with grease spots. . . . I could hardly believe my eyes when I found this book was the Bible." Herman Melville, *Redburn* (New York: Penguin Books, 1976), 137 (originally published in 1849).

201. Higginson, *Black Regiment,* 46–47.

202. Ibid., 45, 55.

203. Ibid., 44–45. "Give these people their tongues, their feet, and their leisure,

and they are happy," observed Higginson. "At every twilight the air is full of singing, talking and clapping of hands in unison. . . ." Since he did not grasp the substance of their religious belief, it is not surprising that Higginson, whose intelligence and sensitivity on matters of black culture were superior to that of most of his contemporaries, believed the memories of the blacks around him "a vast bewildered chaos of Jewish history and biography; and most of the great events of the past, down to the period of the American Revolution, they instinctively attribute to Moses." As principled and faithful a friend of blacks as he could comment, "They seem the world's perpetual children, docile, gay, and lovable, in the midst of this war for freedom on which they have intelligently entered." Ibid., 36–38, 44, 45, 49, 51. Little did he realize that their tales of greatest depth—he had heard only those in a humorous vein—contained attacks on oppression sharper than anything managed by the keenest and most sympathetic intellectuals in the North. Melville, *Redburn*, 137–38.

204. Edward Channing Gannett, "The Freedmen at Port Royal," *North American Review* 101 (1865): 10.

205. Ibid., 9. The protracted praying and self-examination resembles, in the context referred to by Gannett, the praying of the Egungun mentioned by Talbot in his discussion of the Nigerian ceremony to which John Kunering may well have been related. See Talbot, *Southern Nigeria*, 761.

206. Gannett, "Freedmen," 9–10.

207. Charlotte Forten, *The Journal Charlotte L. Forten* (New York: Dryden Press, 1953), 149, 151.

208. Forten, "Life on the Sea Islands," *Atlantic Monthly*, May 1864, 593.

209. Ibid., 594.

210. Ibid., 592; Gannett, "Freedmen," 7.

211. Forten, "Sea Islands," 593; Leslie and Stuckey, "Death of Benito Cereno," 290.

212. Forten, "Sea Islands," 593–94.

213. Higginson, *Black Regiment*, 136. Higginson noted, "The habit of carrying bundles on the head gives them erectness of figure, even where physically disabled. I have seen a woman, with a brimming water-pail balanced on her head, or perhaps a cup, saucer, and spoon, stop suddenly, turn round, stoop to pick up the missile, rise again, fling it, light a pipe, and go through many evolutions with either hand or both, without spilling a drop." Ibid., 52. The dignified demeanor of the laundress is not unrelated to the manner in which Negro "kings" and "governors" conducted themselves in parades in New England and New York State and in the West Indies.

214. Bremer, *America*, 114–15.

215. Ibid., 119; Herskovits, *Dahomey*, 214. Had Bremer been unobserved in the tent in which the slaves were beating their breasts, she undoubtedly would at some point have witnessed the ring ceremony, so prevalent was the ceremony in Georgia during the slave era. And while sacrifices of animals were not unknown in American slavery, that practice was severely curtailed in the new environment because the master did not tolerate the killing of animals for such purposes. For abundant evidence of the ring ceremony in Georgia during slavery see Georgia Writers' Project, *Drums and Shadows*. Human sacrifice, associated with the ring ceremony in Dahomey and elsewhere in Africa, came to an abrupt end in North

American slavery, for the lives of Africans were no longer spared or taken according to traditional practices, since the basis for such practices was shattered by property relations.

216. Bremer, *America*, 119.

217. Lyell, *Second Visit*, 270.

218. Ibid.

219. John Michael Vlach, *The Afro-American Tradition in Decorative Arts* (Cleveland: Cleveland Museum of Art, 1978), 47.

220. Ibid.

221. Ibid.

222. Ibid. Anne Spurgeon further illumines Bakongo dimensions of the quilt, noting of its upper left corner that it is "of a darkened diamond shape, with sun-like figures glowing at the four corners of the diamond. There are two cross shapes above this image, and below it are the figures of four humans in a semi-circle, and another sun-image with some sort of ray extending out of it. Both the crosses and the diamond signify the life cycle, and are a comment on the human figures below." Regarding the lower right-hand corner of the quilt, Spurgeon writes that it "is a scene from the crucifixion of Jesus Christ, with the two thieves hanging from crosses on either side and below him. Above the Christ figure, there is a line which connects a bright sun at the left to a dark one at the right—the path from day to night, or from life to death. This is a complex religious symbol, which is a very clear physical example of the mixture of newly acquired and long retained spiritual understanding." See Spurgeon, "African Religious Culture,"[6].

223. Vlach, *Decorative Arts*, 47.

224. Payne, *Recollections*, 253–54.

225. Ibid., 92–94.

226. Payne further notes that the ring practices "vary somewhat in different localities," which helps explain differences reflected in the New Orleans African Church, where jumping was the cardinal feature and the more common form of expression of that ceremony. That improvisation was a feature of the shout guaranteed some variation from locale to locale. Ibid., 254–55.

227. Ibid., 256.

228. Ibid., 254.

229. Ibid., 255–56. It is especially ironic that Payne, believing that the ceremony that so offended him "far from being in harmony with the religion of the Lord Jesus Christ . . . antagonizes his holy religion," failed to realize that the faith of Africans helped them, in the spirituals, give expression to Christianity on a level that has yet to be surpassed over the past two centuries. See W. E. B. Du Bois, *Black Reconstruction* (New York: Russell and Russell, 1935), chap. 5.

230. Stearns, *Story of Jazz*, 13.

231. Ibid., 59–60.

232. Ibid., 14.

233. The author saw Monk dance at the Five Spot in New York in the 1960s.

234. Clifton Joseph Furness, "Communal Music among Arabians and Negroes," *Musical Quarterly* 16 (1930): 47–48.

235. Anne M. Spurgeon, "From the Wellspring of Africa: African Spirituality in Afro-American Culture" (Senior thesis, Northwestern U., 1986), 22.

236. Furness, "Communal Music," 47–51. Spurgeon writes,

Maum Hester was quite sure that the sun would carry word of her actions that day to the world of the dead and of the ancestors, where Jesus waited to sit in judgment over her behavior. She achieved this communication with the other world by dancing the circle dance and chanting her phrase until it became almost a song. It is very significant that it was the sun which served as the portal between two worlds, through which was passed the record of her deeds. She refers to the apparent motion of the sun over the earth as "shoutin," showing that she sees a parallel between the circle of the ring shout and the daily cycle of the sun—the four moments of the sun.
Spurgeon, "African Spirituality," 23.

237. Zora Neale Hurston, *The Sanctified Church* (Berkeley: Turtle Island, 1981), 103. This volume was published posthumously.

238. James Baldwin, *Go Tell It on the Mountain* (New York: Dell, 1952), 14–15.

CHAPTER TWO
David Walker: In Defense of African Rights and Liberty

1. John Hope Franklin, *The Free Negro in North Carolina* (Chapel Hill: U. of North Carolina Press, 1943), 60.

2. Henry Highland Garnet, *Walker's Appeal, with a Brief Sketch of His Life* (New York: J. H. Tobitt, 1848), vi.

3. Charles Wiltse, ed., *David Walker's Appeal* (New York: Hill and Wang, 1965), 4, 5 (hereafter referred to as Walker, *Appeal*; originally published in 1829).

4. Guion Johnson, *Ante-Bellum North Carolina: A Social History* (Chapel Hill: U. of North Carolina Press, 1937), 599.

5. Manumission of slaves, which had almost doubled the free Negro population by that time, was also a factor, considering the troublesome nature of a free Negro population in proximity of slaves. See Johnson, *North Carolina*, 593–94.

6. Franklin, *Free Negro*, 58.

7. More precisely, Walker found unity of interest among blacks everywhere. It is simply that the Haitian example was such an inspirational one, one in which he saw hope for the eventual liberation of all Africans. See Walker, *Appeal*, 59.

8. Johnson, *North Carolina*, 584.

9. Ibid., 585.

10. Franklin, *Free Negro*, 62.

11. There were, nevertheless, stern laws—at times enforced—against kidnapping. At least one North Carolina white was "given the death sentence for selling a free Negro. In 1806 a certain Micajah Jackson was sentenced to be hanged in Fayetteville for selling a free Negro boy in Virginia." See Johnson, *North Carolina*, 461, 597

12. The negative thrust of restrictive legislation "drove some free Negroes out of the state," which no doubt contributed to the movement of some from North Carolina to the North. See Johnson, *North Carolina*, 583–84.

13. Johnson, *North Carolina*, 461.

14. Franklin, *Free Negro*, 165. Garnet contends that Walker, on arriving in the North, was not able to read or write, but this is hard to accept, considering the range and depth of Walker's knowledge of history. Moreover, given Walker's thirst for knowledge, which was great, it is likely that he found a means of learning to read and write in Wilmington and was largely responsible for educating himself while still in the South. See Garnet, *Sketch*, vi; Walker, *Appeal*, 31.

15. Franklin, *Free Negro*, 166.

16. Ibid., 169.

17. Johnson, *North Carolina*, 600.

18. Franklin, *Free Negro*, 63.

19. Robert Russell, *North America: Its Agriculture and Climate* (Edinburgh: Adam and Charles, 1857), 158.

20. Edward Warren, *A Doctor's Experiences on Three Continents* (Baltimore: Cushings and Baily, 1885), 203

21. Russell, *North America*, 160.

22. Ibid., 158–59.

23. Ibid., 550–52.

24. Dougald MacMillan, "John Kuners," *Journal of American Folk-Lore* 39 (Jan.–March 1926): 53.

25. Ibid., 53–54.

26. Ibid., 54.

27. Ibid.

28. Ira De A. Reid, "The John Canoe Festival," *Phylon* 3 (1942): 350–51.

29. MacMillan, "Kuners," 54.

30. Warren, *A Doctor's Experiences*, 201–2.

31. Ibid., 202.

32. Ibid., 202–3.

33. Ibid., 200–201; Reid, "John Canoe Festival," 349–51.

34. Quoted in Johnson, *North Carolina*, 558.

35. Quoted ibid., 553.

36. But geography apparently had little or nothing to do with the protracted nature of slave recreation. Rather, a release from oppression together with the centrality of music and dance in the life of the African determined the attention slaves devoted to such pursuits. For Virginia and South Carolina supplying slaves to North Carolina, see James A. Rawley, *The Transatlantic Slave Trade* (New York: Norton, 1981), 409–10.

37. Johnson, *North Carolina*, 554.

38. Ibid.

39. Quoted ibid., 555.

40. Rev. James Jenkins, *Experience, Labours, and Sufferings of James Jenkins of the South Carolina Conference* (n.p., 1842), 32.

41. Of course, the broken glass was mainly for those not following the deceased into the other world. See Robert Farris Thompson, "African Influences on the Art of the United States," in Armstead Robinson, ed., *Black Studies in the University* (New Haven: Yale U. Press, 1969), 151.

42. Jenkins, *Experience*, 32.

43. Johnson, *North Carolina*, 556.

44. Ibid.

45. Ibid., 555.

46. Jane De Forest Shelton, "The New England Negro," *Harper's Monthly Magazine*, March 1894, 537; Johnson, *North Carolina*, 86.

47. Franklin reports, "In 1860, the mixed group mulattoes constituted more than 70 percent of the free Negro population in North Carolina." See Franklin, *Free Negro*, 35.

48. But when one takes into account the determination of some free Negroes to fraternize with slaves despite laws against such contact, it is hard to avoid the conclusion that the secular aspects of slave culture were fully appreciated by some free Negroes, though their sacred sources may not have been. After all, secular aspects of black culture are prominent in Afro-American and American life today—for example, jazz dance—but relatively few who are influenced by that culture understand its sacred sources.

49. We will do well to note, in this connection, that Paul Robeson, a student of African linguistics whose family migrated to New Jersey from North Carolina after the Civil War, was conscious of African influences in the speech of those around him in the opening decades of the twentieth century. See the discussion of this matter in chap. 6, below.

50. The domestic slave trade and its movements through the South must be considered a principal means by which African culture in its varied ethnic manifestations was spread from one community of blacks to another, a process that of its very nature contributed to underlying unities. Here is a subject of great import for future investigation.

51. And since the religion of the quarters—the Africanized Christianity, to say nothing of African religion unaffected by Christianity—was not threatened by the religion of the master class, it follows that African dance could hardly have been challenged by European dance. As a result, just as Walker saw Kuners dancing African dance on the streets of Wilmington, if he attended social events at which slaves were present, he was far more likely to witness African rather than European dance. Harold Courlander, a distiguished student of black culture, argues unconvincingly that European dance took over in the slave quarters, that "African-style dances" became "obsolete." See Courlander, *Negro Folk Music, U.S.A.* (New York: Columbia U. Press, 1963), 194–202.

52. Walker treated the role of Christian hypocrisy in relation to blacks: "The Christians, ...seeing the ignorance and consequent degradation of our fathers, instead of trying to enlighten them, by teaching them that religion and light with which God had blessed them, they have plunged them into wretchedness ten thousand times more intolerable, than if they had left them entirely to the Lord, and to add to their miseries, deep down into which they have plunged them tell them, that they are an *inferior* and *distinct race* of beings. ..."Walker, *Appeal,* 19.

53. Johnson, *North Carolina,* 401–6.

54. Walker, *Appeal,* 37.

55. Ibid., 39.

56. G. W. Feathersonhaugh, *Excursion through the Slave States* (New York: Harper, 1844), 1:119–21.

57. On the other hand, there is hardly more reason to believe that free blacks were more given than whites to distiguishing between one African ethnic group and another in nineteenth-century America. Moreover, such distinctions, when made by free blacks, seemed of little consequence culturally because, however different Africans were ethnically, Africans of different ethnicity evidently appeared to be essentially the same to free blacks and whites alike. If such was not the case, there is little in the record to indicate as much. See, for example, the treatment of the subject by blacks in Dorothy Porter, *Early Negro Writing* (Boston: Beacon Press, 1971), pts. 1–7.

58. Johnson, *North Carolina,* 140–45.

59. Ibid., 142.

60. Ibid., 128.

61. Walker, *Appeal,* 14.

62. Wiltse writes, "We know nothing of [Walker's] early life, except that some-how he acquired an education. We have his own testimony that he traveled widely throughout the United States, and particularly the South, where he saw slavery in all its aspects....Sometime in the 1820's Walker, so repelled by what he had seen of Negro life in the South that he could no longer passively endure its proximity, settled in Boston. By 1827 he had a shop on Brattle Street . . . where he dealt in old clothes." Wiltse, ed., *Appeal,* vii–viii.

63. Russell, *North America,* 157.

64. Franklin, *Free Negro,* 185,225.

65. A reference to Cornish that Walker later made indicates he must have known him personally. It is likely that his admiration for Allen stemmed in part from personal contact as well. These two men are the only ones among national black leaders of the time to whom Walker refers by name. Moreover, as we shall see, his intimate knowledge of black youth in Philadelphia and New York indicates he spent some time in both locations.

66. *Freedom's Journal* (New York), March 16, 1827.

67. Ibid.

68. *Freedom's Journal,* March 16, 1827.

69. For the best treatment of Northern racial attitudes and practices, see Leon Litwack, *North of Slavery* (Chicago: U. of chicago Press, 1961).

70. Garnet, *Sketch,* vi.

71. Litwack, *North of Slavery,* chap. 5.

72. Garnet, *Sketch,* 2; *Freedom's Journal,* March 16, 1827.

73. Garnet, *Sketch,* 2.

74. *Freedom's Journal,* Oct. 24, 1828.

75. Ibid.

76. Ibid.

77. Johnson, *North Carolina,* 142.

78. *Freedom's Journal,* Dec. 20, 1828.

79. Ibid.

80. The phrase is used somewhat out of context. It is Scruggs's way of describing the freedom with which John Hope Franklin writes in *Racial Equality in America* (Chicago: of Chicago Press, 1976).

81. Black nationalist theory in its truest, richest form is found, of course, in slave folklore, the foundation of which, as we saw in Chap. 1, is African. In his time, then, Walker was the leading advocate of nationalism among free blacks.

82. Walker, *Appeal,* 7.

83. Ibid., 16–17.

84. Ibid., 2, 3, 4, 64, 67.

85. Ibid., 33.

86. Ibid., 17.

87. Ibid., 8–9.

88. Ibid., 9.

89. Ibid., 10, 15.

90. For a detailed discussion of black intellectuals and African culture, see Sterling Stuckey, "The Spell of Africa: Afro-American Thought on Africa, 1829–1945" (Ph. D. diss., Northwestern U., 1971). See esp. the chapter on Alexander Crummell.

91. Walker, *Appeal*, 11; *Freedom's Journal*, Dec. 20, 1828.

92. Walker, *Appeal*, 22.

93. Ibid., 20-21.

94. Ibid., 22.

95. Ibid., 21.

96. Ibid., 64.

97. Ibid., 62–63.

98. Ibid., 63.

99. Ibid., 28.

100. Ibid.

101. Ibid., 19.

102. Johnson, *North Carolina*, 461–62, 569–72.

103. Walker, *Appeal*, 46, 50.

104. Ibid., 43, 47, 69.

105. While some consideration has been given to the extent to which the West has benefited from slavery and the slave trade, little or no attention has been given by historians to the comfort and ease enjoyed by whites as a result of slavery. Perhaps the best treatment of the subject is that of the poet Sterling A. Brown. See "Strong Men" and "Bitter Fruit of the Tree" in Sterling A. Brown, *The Collected Poems of Sterling A. Brown* (New York: Harper & Row, 1980), 56–58, 200.

106. Walker, *Appeal*, 41.

107. Johnson, *North Carolina*, 462.

108. Walker, *Appeal*, 65.

109. Ibid., 47.

110. Ibid., 14–15.

111. Ibid., 58.

112. See Benjamin Banneker's letter to Thomas Jefferson, in Herbert Aptheker, ed., *A Documentary History of the Negro People in the United States* (New York: Citadel Press, 1951), 1:24; *Walker, Appeal*, 12.

113. Walker, *Appeal*, 71,

114. Ibid., 15 (italics added).

115. Ibid.

116. Ibid., 66, 70.

117. Ibid., 70.

118. Ibid., 60–61.

119. Ibid., 68.

120. Ibid., 61.

121. Quoted ibid., 76.

122. Ibid., 18.

123. Ibid., 58.

124. "No trifling portion of them will beat us nearly to death, if they find us on our knees praying to God,—They hinder us from going to hear the word of God—they keep us sunk in ignorance, and will not let us learn to read the word of God. . . . /

They will not suffer us to meet together to worship the God who made us." Ibid., 37, 65.

125. Ibid., 57.

126. Ibid., 29–30.

127. Ibid., *Appeal*, 50.

128. E. C. L. Adams, *Nigger to Nigger* (New York: Scribner's, 1928), 236.

129. Franklin, *Free Negro*, 66–67.

130. Ibid., 68. Johnson reports that, when Walker's *Appeal* was found in North Carolina, "a great many people, otherwise conservative and slow to take alarm, were seized with panic. They felt, especially in Eastern North Carolina, that an insurrection was imminent." The patrol system was overhauled and the patrol could visit plantations to inspect slave quarters at will, thereby, it was hoped, preventing a possible uprising. Johnson, *North Carolina*, 515, 517.

131. Walker, *Appeal*, 71–72.

132. Maria W. Stewart, "An Address Delivered at the African Masonic Hall" (Boston, Feb. 27, 1833), in Porter, *Early Negro Writing*, 130, 135.

CHAPTER THREE
Henry Highland Garnet: Nationalism, Class Analysis, and Revolutions

1. Garnet, a great disciple of Walker, was born in New Market, Kent County, Md., on Dec. 23, 1815. See Alexander Crummell, *Africa and America* (Springfield, Mass.: Wiley, 1891), 272–73.

2. See Daniel Alexander Payne, *Recollections of Seventy Years* (New York: Arno Press, 1968), 92–94 (Originally published in 1888).

3. James A. Rawley, *The Transatlantic Slave Trade* (New York: Norton, 1981), 407.

4. James McCune Smith, *Introduction to a Memorial Discourse; by Rev. Henry Highland Garnet* (Philadephia: Joseph M. Wilson, 1865), 17–18.

5. Ibid., 18.

6. Ibid., 19.

7. Garnet made this point on at least two levels, by stressing the example of the ancestors as one of self-assertiveness and manliness and by noting that black leaders of the past believed it their responsibility to win freedom for their people. He makes the latter argument with some elaboration in his "Sidney" letters, which are discussed in the following chapter.

8. Crummell, *Africa*, 274.

9. Ibid.

10. Dr. James Eights, "Pinkster Festivities in Albany," *Collections on the History of Albany*, vol. 2 (Albany, 1867), 326.

11. Thomas F. DeVoe, *The Market Book: A Historical Account of the Public Markets in the Cities of New York, Boston, Philadelphia, and Brooklyn* (New York, 1862), 344.

12. Ibid.

13. "For this market they must be young, the younger the better if not quite children." From a merchant quoted in Rawley, *Slave Trade*, 390. That the New York market favored both sexes reinforces our view that ancestral and other Af-

rican values were entertained, the presence of girl slaves making it easier for slave communal activity to occur.

14. Smith, *Discourse*, 21.

15. Ibid.

16. Ibid., 20.

17. Ibid., 24.

18. Ibid.

19. Ibid.

20. Ibid., 24–25.

21. Ibid., 22, 23; also see Crummell, *Africa*, 275.

22. There appears to have been a difference in religious outlook between Henry and his father, beginning perhaps with Henry's apprenticeship to Wright, a process intensified as the youth pursued a formal education under teachers who were Christian as well. Yet, given his regard for his father, and his father's affirmation of certain aspects of Christianity, differences between them may not have appeared pronounced at the time. What is almost certain is that, considering what we know of African Methodism of the era, Henry's conception of slave religion as heathen came not from his father but from his educational and religious mentors—a view universal among them at the time. In this regard, it is worth noting that Henry "attached himself to the Sunday—school of the First Presbyterian church, under the care of the celebrated Rev. Theodore S. Wright," not to African Methodism, the denomination of his father. See Crummell, *Africa*, 277. Smith notes that Wright, who later officiated at Garnet's wedding,

> encouraged him to prepare himself for the holy ministry, and towards that end rendered him every assistance in his power. As David loved Jonathan, so this father in Israel knit to his son in the Lord Jesus. In Garnet's youth, now budding into manhood, and in the maturer years that followed, they were...one in spirit, one in effort, one in all their noble resistances to caste and slavery...asserting together their native, noble manhood, in the teeth of all comers.

Smith, *Discourse*, 29.

23. Frederick Douglass, *Narrative of the Life of Frederick Douglass* (Cambridge: Harvard U. Press, 1960), 146 (originally published in 1845).

24. Crummell, *Africa*, 276; Smith, *Discourse*, 25, 26.

25. Crummell, *Africa*, 277.

26. Smith, *Discourse*, 26.

27. Ibid.

28. Charles C. Andrews, *The History of the New York African Free-Schools* (New York: Negro Universities Press, 1969), 10 (originally published in 1830). Considering his background as a slave and the attempts of numerous whites in Northern cities, including New York, to kidnap blacks and sell them into slavery in the South, Henry found it easy to look upon the New York Manumission Society with much favor. Andrews mentions one reason for the coming into being of the society: "It appears that, in the years 1785–6, the disgraceful business of kidnapping persons of color, and selling them at the South, was carried on in this city and its vicinity, to an alarming extent, and that the measures pursued by the man-stealers were too bold and daring, either to be mistaken, or pass without a corrective." Ibid., 8, 9.

29. At fifteen, Isaiah DeGrasse, addressing the American Convention for Promoting the Abolition of Slavery, spoke for Garnet and most of his classmates at the New York African Free School:

> I feel myself highly honored by addressing you in behalf of myself and the African race. I am but a poor descendant of that injured people. When I reflect on the enormities which continue to be practiced in many parts of our otherwise favored country, on the ill-fated Africans, and their descendants...I ought to return thanks to Almighty God, for having put it into the hearts of such distinguished men as you, to udertake the cause of the Abolition of slavery. . . .

Andrews, *Free Schools*, 67.

30. Ibid.

31. Crummell, *Africa*, 279.

32. Ibid., 279–80.

33. Dwight L. Dumond, *Antislavery Origins of the Civil War* (Ann Arbor: U. of Michigan Press, 1939),55.

34. Crummell, *Africa*, 281.

35. Ibid.

36. Ibid., 282–83. Indeed, as Crummell has written, "he had within him all the elements of a hero; great consciousness of power, and that love of authority which made him in all conditions and at every period of his life a leader of men." Ibid., 299.

37. Ibid.; Dwight L. Dumond, ed., *Letters of James Gillespie Birney, 1831–1857* (New York: Appleton-Century, 1938), 1:577.

38. Crummell, *Africa*, 301.

39. Ibid., 287–88.

40. Quoted Ibid., 289.

41. *Colored American* (New York), June 11, 1840.

42. Dumond, *Antislavery Origins*, chap. 5. Here one finds the basis of Garnet's faith in the founders, in his respect for the Declaration of Independence, for "the generation which launched the new nation expected slavery to be speedily abolished. . . ." Ibid., 73.

43. *Colored American*, June 11, 1840.

44. *Emancipator and Free American*, March 3, 1842.

45. Ibid.

46. Ibid.

47. Ibid.

48. Henry Highland Garnet, *An Address to the Slaves of the United States of America*, in Herbert Aptheker, ed., *A Documentary History of the Negro People in the United States* (New York: Citadel Press, 151), 1:227–22.

49. Garnet, *Address,*232.

50. See the treatment of Hamilton in the following chapter.

51. Garnet, *Address,*232–33.

52. That would be logical, considering the religiosity of his grandfather and father. Being an adult when captured, and an African chief, his grandfather was deeply grounded in African religious values—that is, he communed with the ancestors, a process that Chrisitanity could not have brought to an end, especially since this dimension of the African's faith was hardly comprehended by Chris-

tians. And since Garnet's father was also a man of religion, close to his father even in slavery and living in a Maryland environment under powerful African ancestral influences, regard for the ancestors almost certainly was a legacy passed down from one generation of Garnets to another, enabling young Henry to embrace it as well.

53. Garnet, *Address*, 283.

54. Ibid., 227–28.

55. Ibid., 232.

56. John W. Barber, *A History of the Amistad Captives* (New Haven: E. L. and J. W. Barber, 1840), 27. A reading of this volume would have revealed much to Garnet and his contemporaries in leadership about West African customs and values, enabling them to understand better African peoples and practices. Nevertless, it is extremely doubtful if such knowledge would have made a differene in their overall attitudes toward Africans and their cultures.

57. Garnet, *Address*, 231–32.

58. Ibid., 230.

59. Ibid., 230–31.

60. Abolitionist scholarship, in treating moral suasion and slavery, has overlooked the operation of moral suasion within hearing of the slave master. Slave folklore was the most powerful expression of the moral argument for ending slavery and Frederick Douglass the best student of that subject. Douglass notes that slave songs

> breathed the prayer and complaint of souls boiling over with the bitterest anguish. Every tone was a testimony against slavery, and a prayer to God for deliverance from chains. The hearing of those wild notes always depressed my spirit, and filled me with ineffable sadness. If any one wishes to be impressed with the soul-killing effects of slavery, let him go to Colonel Lloyd's plantation, and, on allowance-day, place himself in the deep pine woods, and there let him, in silence, analyze the sounds that shall pass through the chambers of his soul—and if he is not thus impressed it will only be because there is no flesh in his obdurate heart.

Douglass, *Narrative*, 37–38.

61. Howard H. Bell, *Proceedings of the National Negro Conventions* (New York: Arno Press, 1969), p. 13 of the Buffalo proceedings. Douglass thought remarks such as Garnet's would "lead to an insurrection," but "wanted emancipation in a better way, as he expected to have it." Ibid.

62. Douglass, *Narrative*, 107; Bell, *Proceedings* (Buffalo), 13. Douglass added, "From what I know of the effect of these holidays upon the slave, I believe them among the most effective means in the hands of the slaveholder in keeping down the spirit of insurrection. Were the slaveholders at once to abandon this practice, I have not the slightest doubt it would lead to an immediate insurrection among the slaves." Douglass, *Narrative*, 106–7.

63. *Liberator*, Dec. 3, 1843.

64. Garnet, *Address*, 226–27.

65. The behavior of the grand marshal and that of his attendants on Emancipation Day in New York is an example of how "cultural process" reflects continuing practices in different contexts. Apparently, aspects of the demeanor of Africans on that occasion were common to them in several ceremonies, including Pinkster: methods of "marching," of playing instruments, and of dancing usually cut across

ceremonies in sufficient measure to be common to a larger African cultural complex, and thereby remained accessible to large numbers of blacks in America.

66. In those early days in Troy, while studying theology under Amos Beamon, Garnet taught at a local colored school. He was, by training and temperament, a superb teacher with a marvelous capacity to relate to young people, which enabled him to attract them to the various churches at which he pastored. "Naturally amiable, with large affluence of kindness and love, he was exceedingly popular. The young of both sexes delighted to come to his house and spent long hours in the joyous converse which he would pour out sparkingly, hour after hour, amid his friends." See Crummell, *Africa*, 300–301.

67. Commenting on Garnet's selflessness, Crummell writes, "Every stranger, minister, foreigner, fugitive, refugee, was welcome to his board, and could command his purse. The great fault in his character was in that direction. . . . There was a princeliness in his largeness which not seldom landed him into poverty." Ibid., 298–99.

68. Joel Schor, *Henry Highland Garnet* (Westport, Conn.: Greenwood Press, 1977) 28, 29.

69. Crummell, *Africa*, 183–84.

70. Ibid., 292.

71. Schor, *Garnet*, 29.

72. Dumond, *Antislavery Origins*, 63–64.

73. According to Garnet's logic and conception of spirituality, the continuation of slavery, whatever the changes in the world, meant suffering compounded with the passage of time, linking growing millions of the departed to millions of the living in bondage.

74. For the context of Garnet's discussion of progress, see his speech "At an Enthusiastic Meeting of the Colored Citizens of Boston," *Weekly Anglo-African* (New York), Aug. 6, 1859.

75. He was not alone in this respect. Other nationalists also fought for the franchise as a matter of principle and necessity: the more free they were in the North, the more effectively they could struggle against slavery. For opposition of nationalists to racism, see Sterling Stuckey, ed., *The Ideological Origins of Black Nationalism* (Boston: Beacon Press, 1972).

76. Anti-Slavery Standard, Sept. 11, 1845.

77. Ibid.

78. Ibid.

79. Ibid.

80. Garnet offered assistance to hundreds of "flying fugitives" during his fight against slavery. See his Boston speech, in *Anglo-African*, Aug. 6, 1859.

81. Douglass is quoted in John W. Blassingame, ed., *The Frederick Douglass Papers* (New Haven: Yale U. Press, 1979), 69.

82. Bell, *Proceedings* (Syracuse), 31; Crummell reflected on Garnet's youthful vision of slave insurrection, finding it "a most fortunate circumstance that his parents brought him . . . out of slavery; equally providential that he was crippled in his early teens." He added, "I have no idea that he could ever have been made a submissive slave." Crummell, *Africa*, 300.

83. Crummell, *Africa*, 300. Crummell writes of those days,

You will be interested to hear that he was one of a company of our school-mates in New York who at from thirteen to sixteen years resolved, that while slavery existed we would not celebrate the Fourth of July; and we did not. For years our society met on that day, and the time was devoted to planning schemes for the freeing and upbuilding or our race. The other resolve which was made was, that when we had educated ourselves we would go South, start an insurrection and free our brethren in bondage. Garnet was a leader in those . . . resolves.

Ibid.

84. Frederick Douglass, *The Life and Times of Frederick Douglass* (New York: Collier Books, 1962), 271 (reprinted from the revised edition of 1892).

85. See the chapter on Du Bois for a discussion of Du Bois's lectures, particularly in the South, before black audiences, on the art galleries of Europe.

86. Henry Highland Garnet, *The Past and present Condition, and the Destiny of the Colored Races: A Discourse* (Troy, N.Y.: Kreeland, 1848), 6, 7.

87. Garnet, *Address,* 229.

88. Garnet, *Past and Present,* 28–29. Interest in the sciences was not new for nationalists. Certainly Walker before Garnet had such an interest, as did Du Bois and Robeson after him.

89. Garnet, *Past and Present,* 27.

90. See the discussion that follows of his relationship to slave song during a visit abroad.

91. The African significance of such values has best been expressed by Du Bois, who writes of an inner African cultural ideal that is essentially socialistic. See W. E. B. Du Bois, *Dusk of Dawn* (New York: Schocken, Books, 1968), 219 (originally published in 1940). For Robeson's development with respect to antimaterialism in his youth, see the final chapter of this volume.

92. *North Star,* Jan.19, 1848.

93. Ibid.

94. *Anglo-African,* Aug. 6, 1859.

95. *North Star,* Sept. 15, 1848.

96. Ibid.

97. Ibid. Karl Marx, *Capital* (Moscow: Progress Publishers), 1:284 (originally published in 1887).

98. *North Star,* Sept. 15, 1848.

99. Ibid.

100. Ibid.

101. *Liberator,* Jan. 7, 1832. American communitarianism or communalism, beginning in the seventeenth and continuing into the nineteenth century, emphasized the importance of the individual struggle in isolated communities apart from the "sinful" world, a view Garnet could no more affirm than he could accept the blindness of such people to class considerations. But the utopian ideal of universal Christian brotherhood was one to which he subscribed. See Arthur E. Bestor, Jr., *Backwoods Utopias* (Philadelphia: U. of Pennsylvania Press, 1950), esp. chap 1.

102. *North Star,* Sept. 15, 1848.

103. Ibid., Jan. 19, 1848.

104. Ibid.

105. Ibid., March 2, 1849. Garnet said that his mind "of late, has greatly changed

in regard to the American Colonization Society scheme. So far as it benefits the land of my fathers, I bid it Godspeed, but so far as it denies the possibility of our elevation here, I oppose it. I would rather see a man free in Liberia than a slave in the United States." Ibid., Jan. 26, 1849. In a statement that seems less visionary with the passing of time, Garnet serenely contended that "this republic, and this continent, are to be the theater in which the grand drama of our triumphant Destiny is to be enacted," that the West *"is destined to be filled with a mixed race."* The possibility of Mexico's being subjected to the corrosions of slavery did not disturb him; on the contrary, he would bring those "dark-browed and liberty-living brethren to [his] embrace. Aye! let them come with the population of seven and a half millions." He thought one-fifth of the people of Mexico were white, two-fifths Indians, and two-fifths "black and mixed races." Joyful at the prospect of millions more of people of color—red, black, and brown—being added to the American population, he conceived a mixed racial makeup as the ideal for the country, which would mean it would no longer be a haven for whites. Therein lay a nationalism that had many cultural implications, and therein lay, deep in the current of his thought, yet another anchor for his emigration policy. Garnet, *Past and Present*, 22–23.

106. *North Star*, July 27, 1849.

107. Ibid., Aug. 17, 1849. See Stuckey, ed., *Ideological Origins*, Introd.

108. *North Star*, July 27, 1849; Smith, *Discourse*, 54.

109. *Anti-Slavery Reporter*, Oct. 1, 1850, 160.

110. Ibid., June 2, 1851, 87.

111. Ibid., 54, 86.

112. Ibid., 86.

113. Ibid., Oct. 1, 1850, 161.

114. Ibid.

115. Smith, *Discourse*, 55; Schor, *Garnet*, 128, 129.

116. See Leon Litwack, *North of Slavery* (Chicago: U. of Chicago Press, 1961), chap. 8.

117. *Frederick Douglass's Monthly* (Rochester), Feb. 1859.

118. Ibid.

119. *Anglo-African*, Aug. 6, 1859.

120. Ibid.

121. Ibid.

122. Ibid.

123. Ibid., Sept. 17, 1859.

124. Ibid.

125. A master in the techniques of debate, Garnet related a story that helped him make his point with maximum effectiveness. He asserted that those who refused to go to Africa reminded him

of a crooked old deacon...who always opposed everything that he did not originate. The spirit of God was about being poured out on the Church and the community, and it was resolved to have a protracted meeting. He arose, after several had spoken, and said, as usual, "Brethren, I cannot give my assent to that; I think it is not exactly the time; I don't think we'd better go at it now." Another good deacon got down on his knees and prayed to God after this manner: "Oh Lord! here is this dear brother who has been bothering and pestering us for many years; we've tried to cure him, convert him. We have failed; and now Lord, if thou canst, convert him and sanctify his soul, and take him up into the kingdom of glory, and let him no more come out forever." (laughter). The old deacon jumped up and said, "*I won't go.* (Great merriment.)

Anglo-African, Sept. 17, 1859.

126. Ibid. Also see below, n. 138.

127. Though Garnet's basic stance in relation to the Colonization Society remained the same, he was not above securing funding from that organization for his emigration plan. Schor, *Garnet,* 157.

128. *Anglo-African,* Sept. 17, 1859. He had been consistent in arguing that America was his home, stating on an earlier occasion,

> The upright man will love his native country. A country every man has. For everyone there is some tract of land to which he can point with more than ordinary pleasure, and say, there is my country. He may call himself a citizen of the world, and such he may be as far as possible, but still there is one land, which his mind and memory favor above all others. Fame may mask it, and the sword may devour, nevertheless the magnate of his soul will point to it. Brothers may prove to be monsters and the archers may shoot at him, and hate him, but nothing can take away the magic from the words, the land of my fathers.

North Star (Rochester), May 12, 1848. In light of that position, it is small wonder that he reacted with indignation when accused of not believing that America was the home of people of color. His reaction was as justified as the incredulity of some who heard his position and were troubled by it: what meaning America as homeland could have for millions of slaves in the South, how such a conception comported with the deaths in slavery of millions more, he did not say, nor was he able to see the relationship between his position on that question and the strength of African values everywhere in evidence in the South and in numerous places in the North.

129. *Anglo-African,* Sept. 17, 1859.

130. Ibid.

131. Ibid.

132. Ibid.

133. Ibid.

134. Smith, *Discourse,* 61, 63.

135. Ibid., 64.

136. Bell, *Proceedings* (Syracuse, 1864), 19–20.

137. Ibid., 27.

138. Ibid., 27–28. Garnet added, "Mr. Downing made the objection that the African Civilization Society takes money from white men. . . . If Jeff. Davis would send an amount to educate the colored children, I would gladly receive it; and I would say to him, 'That is one good act you have done, if you have done no other." Ibid.

139. Joel Schor helps explain Downing's attitude toward Garnet: "Downing and Garnet were of opposite temperaments. Downing, a wealthy, light-skinned businessman and Garnet, a poor black minister with strong ancestral memories, had very different approaches to...black advancement." Schor, *Henry Highland Garnet* (Westport, Conn.: Greenwood Press, 1977), 204.

140. Smith, *Discourse,* 65.
141. Ibid., 86.
142. Ibid., 87.
143. Ibid., 80.
144. Ibid., 87.
145. Earl Ofari, *Let Your Motto Be Resistance* (Boston: Beacon Press, 1972), 119.
146. Quoted Ibid., 120.
147. Ibid., 121.
148. *Christian Recorder* (Philadelphia, Feb. 26, March 6, 13, 27, 1869).
149. Crummell, *Africa,* 302.
150. Ibid., 303.

CHAPTER FOUR
Identity and Ideology: The Names Controversy

1. Alexander Crummell, *Africa and America* (Springfield, Mass.: Wiley, 1891), 304–305.
2. African attitudes toward naming are found in Lorenzo Turner, *Africanisms in the Gullah Dialect* (Chicago: U. of Chicago Press, 1949), 31–43. Turner's discussion of the subject shows that the Gullah people of the United States "have used the same methods as their African ancestors in naming their children." Though our discussion is focused on the attitudes toward the naming of literate blacks, mostly those in positions of leadership, Turner's summation of the continuing influence of African attitudes toward naming on blacks in America suggests an intricacy of retention in this sphere that parallels the less well-known African influences discussed in the opening section of this book.
3. James McCune Smith, *Introduction to a Memorial Discourse*; by Rev. Henry Highland Garnet (Philadelphia: Joseph M. Wilson, 1865), 20.
4. Sojourner's precise words are important here: "Afterward I told the Lord I wanted another name [other than Sojourner], cause everybody else had two names." Sojourner Truth, *Narrative and Book of Life* (Chicago: Johnson, 1970), 126–127.
5. A fine treatment of naming ceremonies in one part of Africa, Yorubaland, can be found in Samuel Johnson, *A History of the Yorubas* (Lagos: C.M.S. [Nigeria] Bookshops, 1921), chap. 5.
6. Turner, *Gullah Dialect*, 5–11.
7. See ibid., 11–14, for a discussion of the caution exercised by the Gullah people in the presence of whites and of all strangers.
8. See ibid.; David Dalby, *Black through White: Patterns of Communication* (Bloomington: African Studies Program, Indiana U., 1970), 20.
9. Turner, *Gullah Dialect*, 38–39.
10. "Slips of the Tongue," in *The Standard Edition of the Complete Psychological Works of Sigmund Freud*, ed. James Strachey, vol. 6 (London: Hogarth Press/Institute of Psycho-Analysis, 1960), 83–84.
11. Of course, an association easily made with the branding of Africans is that of branding cattle; the victims in both cases were placed on roughly the same level.

Branding, which occurred on both sides of the Atlantic, was used as a form of punishment as well as identification in America. See Kenneth M. Stampp, *The Peculiar Institution* (New York: Random House, 1956), 188–210.

12. For discussions of naming in slave communities, see Peter Wood, *Black Majority: Negroes in Colonial South Carolina from 1670 through the Stono Rebellion* (New York: Knopf, 1974), 181–185, and Herbert Gutman, *The Black Family in Slavery and Freedom* (New York: Vintage Books, 1977), 185–201.

13. Sterling Stuckey, "Through the Prism of Folklore: The Black Ethos in Slavery," *Massachusetts Review* 3 (Summer 1968): 426–427. An example of *Negro* being used as a synonym for *slave* is found in an oration by William Hamilton in commemoration of the abolition of slavery in New York in 1827 when Hamilton declares, " 'the last agony is o'er,' the africans are restored! No more shall the accursed name of slave be attached to us—no more shall *negro* and *slave* be synonymous." See Dorothy Porter, *Early Negro Writing* (Boston: Beacon Press, 1971), 97; W. E. B. Du Bois, *Black Reconstruction* (New York: Russell and Russell, 1962), 39.

14. Harold Isaacs, *The New World of Negro Americans* (New York: John Day, 1963), 65.

15. E. Franklin Frazier, *The Negro in the United States*, 2d ed., rev. (New York: Macmillan, 1957), 77–78.

16. Ibid.

17. Ibid., 78.

18. St. Clair Drake, "The American Negro's Relation to Africa," *Africa Today* 14, no. 6 (Dec. 1967): 12.

19. Among the organizations in the titles of which black people placed the word *African* were Abyssinia Baptist Church, New York City (1800), Free African Presbyterian Church, Philadelphia (1807), and African Methodist Episcopal Church, Philadelphia (1816). These are but a few of the hundreds of organizations with the word *African* in their title. In addition to churches, the Africans in America designated halls, schools, and societies by that name. The first national "society" was the Free African Society of Philadelphia, Penn., 1787. An examination of the constitutions of the African societies enables one to see just how Western and American in consciousness a number of educated Africans were becoming— that is, apart from the strong mutual-aid or communal aspects of the societies, which could well have reflected more African than American influence. Moreover, there was a proliferation of African organizations dating especially from the period of American independence. It is not unreasonable to assume that a significant number of the African societies were spawned as expressions of a desire for independence on the part of numerous black people. Drake, "Negro's Relation to Africa," offers a list of early organizations with the word *African* in their title.

20. Porter, *Early Negro Writing*, 43–44.

21. Ibid.

22. Smith, *Discourse*, 20–21; Porter, *Early Negro Writing*, 33.

23. Porter. *Early Negro Writing*, 37.

24. Ibid., 35.

25. Ibid., 39.

26. Ibid.

27. Ibid., 41.

28. St. Clair Drake offers this thesis, which is persuasive, in "The Meaning of Negritude: The Negro's Stake in Africa," *Negro Digest* 13, no. 8 (June 1964): 39.

29. In almost exactly the same way W. E. B. Du Bois and Paul Robeson used the terms *Negro*, *colored*, and *black*. Neither man attached much importance to the relative merits of the words. See chaps. 5 and 6. Any issue of *Freedom's Journal* chosen at random should support this conclusion. Note those of April 20 and Aug. 17, 1827, for examples of more than one appellation being used.

30. For a discussion of this essential duality in Negro thinkers, shared by large numbers of blacks in America for well over a century, see James Weldon Johnson, *Negro Americans, What Next?* (New York: Viking Press, 1935), 12–18.

31. Howard H. Bell, *Proceedings of the National Negro Conventions* (New York: Arno Press, 1969), 9.

32. Ibid., p. 28 of the Fourth Annual Convention.

33. Ibid., pp. 14–15 of the Fifth Annual Convention.

34. As we shall see in the post-emancipation period as well, when an effort was made to remove *African* from the title of the A.M.E. Church, eventual absorption into the larger society was strongly implied when not openly affirmed. See the discussion of the names controversy during and following Reconstruction.

35. The crossing of swords with Sidney some years later marked that moment when Whipper abandoned what caution he may have had, and advocated the disppearance of black institutions. See his letters in the *Colored American* (New York), Jan. 3, 12, 17, 1841.

36. That some of the men who supported all-black organizations may well have favored the destruction of racial organizations as quickly as possible is supported by the testimony, to be discussed later, in which Garnet contends that large numbers of black peole in the antebellum North were desirous of discarding all racial distinctions and focusing entirely on "universals."

37. Though the term was not used in the antebellum period, integrationism achieved classic expression in the thought of Whipper. That is, Whipper was probably the first black figure to develop fully those central ideas later associated with integration: that there should be no all-black institutions, because such arrangements reinforce prejudice against blacks and militate against racial justice; that black people must depend primarily on the goodwill or power of someone else, not themselves, for their liberation; and that black people should not be concerned about the preservation of their values, because they have no values worth maintaining.

38. *National Reformer* (Philadelphia), Oct. 1938.

39. William Whipper estimated that in Pennsylvania alone, blacks "were nurturing and sustaining in [their] midst near one hundred institutions with 'Colored and African' charters." *Colored American*, Feb. 6, 1841.

40. *National Reformer*, Oct. 1838.

41. Ibid.

42. Ibid.

43. Ibid.

44. Ibid.

45. Ibid.

46. Ibid.

47. Ibid.

48. *Colored American*, March 4, 1837.

49. During his stay in England, Garnet remarked that every drop of blood in his veins was African. *Anti-Slavery Reporter*, Oct. 1, 1850, 161. According to Frederick Douglass, who thanked God for having made him a man, Delany thanked God for having made him a black man. Martin Delany, *The Condition, Elevation, Emigration and Destiny of the Colored People of the United States* (New York: Arno Press, 1969), introd. The concept of double consciousness, later formulated by W. E. B. Du Bois, was not what Cornish had in mind, for he did not understand, or at least did not articulate, the radically different ways in which black and white people perceived America.

50. Cornish believed in nationalist methods—black institutions, etc.—but ascribed American nationality to black people; he accused those who would deny them freedom of trying to "rob us of our nationality." *Colored American*, March 4, 1837.

51. Surely this was the pattern throughout the nineteenth century, and in the first half of the succeeding one - that is, no one appellation absolutely dominated. Two or three were usually more popular than the others, and often were used interchangeably. See ibid., March 11, 1837, for examples of the unwillingness of blacks to adhere to a single designation.

52. Ibid., Jan. 3, 1841.

53. Ibid., Jan. 30, 1841.

54. Ibid., Jan. 12, 1841.

55. Ibid. Jan. 30, 1841.

56. For Sidney's description of his youthfulness, see ibid., Feb. 13, 1841.

57. Delany is perhaps most often referred to as the father of black nationalism. Floyd Miller is correct in his contention that Lewis Woodson (Augustine) was an earlier proponent of the nationalist ideology. Miller's detective work in uncovering the identity of Augustine is found in his "The Father of Black Nationalism: Another Contender," *Civil War History* 17 (Dec. 1971): 310–319.

58. *Colored American*, June 20, 1840.

59. For a discussion of Crummell and his possible relationship to Sidney, see Stuckey, ed., *The Ideological Origins of Black Nationalism* (Boston: Beacon Press, 1971), 15–17.

60. *Colored American*, Dec. 19, 1840.

61. Ibid., Feb. 13, 1940 (italics added).

62. Ibid., March 6, 1841.

63. Ibid.

64. Ibid.

65. Ibid., March 6, Feb. 13, 1841.

66. Ibid., Feb. 13, 1841.

67. This Garnet knew beyond doubt, having seen not only his father but his uncles as well rely on themselves in escaping from slavery. For his views on this subject, see the discussion in chap. 3, above.

68. *Colored American*, Feb. 20, 1841.

69. Ibid., Feb. 13, 1841.

70. Ibid.

71. Ibid., Feb. 20, 1841.

72. Ibid.
73. Ibid.
74. Ibid.
75. Ibid., March 6, 1841.
76. Ibid.
77. Ibid.
78. Ibid.
79. Ibid.
80. Ibid.
81. Ibid.
82. Ibid., March 13, 1841.
83. Ibid.
84. Ibid.
85. Ibid.
86. Ibid.
87. Ibid.
88. Ibid.
89. Ibid.
90. *North Star*, Jan. 7, 1848.
91. Frederick Douglass, *Narrative of the Life of Frederick Douglass* (Cambridge: Harvard U. Press, 1960), 23 (originally published in 1845).
92. Ibid., 146.
93. Ibid., 147–48.
94. Douglass and Garrison clashed over the feasibility of establishing a Negro press under Douglass's direction. Garrison argued that since the *Liberator* existed there was no need for Douglass's projected paper. Douglass went ahead and established the *North Star*. He believed that black people would have to plan their own strategies and do their own philosophizing on the nature of the peculiar institution, on their status in America, and proceeded to act upon those principles. Moreover, as he proclaimed time and time again, his people would have to take primary responsibility for their own liberation. The Douglass of antebellum America, then, was more nationalist than integrationist in formulating a strategy of liberation.
95. Bell, *Proceedings* (Rochester), 8–9.
96. Ibid., 36.
97. Henry Highland Garnet, *The Past and Present Condition, and the Destiny of the Colored Races: A Discourse* (Troy, N.Y.: Kreeland, 1848), 19.
98. At the point at which nationalists and integrationists inevitably meet—in opposition to racism—they possess most in common, and as long as they remain in America opposition to racism is the foundation of their common struggle for freedom.
99. This assumption underlay the classic emigrationist position. See Howard H. Bell, ed., *Search for a Place* (Ann Arbor: U. of Michigan Press, 1969), introd.
100. Daniel Alexander Payne, *Recollections of Seventy Years* (New York: Arno Press, 1968), 160 (originally published in 1988). Jessie Fauset, "Rank Imposes Obligations," *Crisis* 33 (Nov. 1926): 9.
101. Martin Delany, *Blake: The Huts of America* (Boston: Beacon Press, 1970), 299 (originally published in 1888).

102. Delany, *Blake*, 299–300.

103. Ibid., 301.

104. A theory of black culture in America presupposes paying attention to precise and decisive ways in which black values are to be distinguished from those of white Americans and taking into account black oppression in America. As we shall see, Delany grasped some essentials of the culture common to Africans generally but did not apply them, at least not systematically, to his people in America. See Delany, *Condition*, p. 588., into which Delany fails to integrate his important insights into African culture in America.

105. See Martin Delany, "The Political Destiny of the Colored Race," in Stuckey, ed., *Ideological Origins*, 195–98.

106. Ibid., 203.

107. Ibid.

108. The power of humanism conveyed by Delany is related to his urging the universalizing of the subjectivity of his people: "We admit the existence of great and good people in America, England, France, and the rest of Europe, who desire a unity of interests among the whole human family, of whatever origin or race . . . . But it is neither the moralist, Christian, nor philanthropist whom we now have to meet and combat but the politician, the civil engineer, and skillful economist, who direct and control the machinery which moves forward, with mighty impulse, the nations and powers of the earth." Delany, "Political Destiny," 204.

109. Ibid., 216.

110. Ibid., 216–17.

111. Payne, *Seventy Years*, 160.

112. Ibid.

113. For a discussion of the flexibility of nationalists in particular, see the introductory essay in Stuckey, ed., *Ideological Origins*.

114. Booker T. Washington, *Up from Slavery*, in John Hope Franklin, ed., *Three Negro Classics* (New York: Avon Books, 1901), 41.

115. For a discussion of the Black Codes in relation to the suppression of economic and other rights of blacks, see John Hope Franklin, *Reconstruction after the Civil War* (Chicago: U. of Chicago Press, 1961), 48–50.

116. While it is true that blacks, more than ever following emancipation, began to think of themselves as Americans, it is doubtful if many did so with a sense of psychological security. The violence visited upon them across the South through the application of the Black Codes immediately following the war was an effective reminder to millions that they were still not far removed from slavery. Moreover, the terror of Reconstruction, begun quite early in some states, contained its own grisly message. Real freedom, real citizenship, blacks knew all too well before the close of Reconstruction, was not to be enjoyed by them. Under such circumstances, it was difficult, at best, for almost any black person to regard himself as American and to believe, in actuality, he was American. The most powerful argument yet that whites did not regard blacks as Americans is found in W. E. B. Du Bois, *Black Reconstruction* (New York: Russell and Russell, 1935), esp. chaps. 1–5.

117. *Christian Recorder* (Philadelphia), Sept. 24, 1870.

118. Ibid., July 23, 1870.

119. Ibid., Aug. 20, 1870.

120. Ibid.

121. Ibid.

122. Quoted in Beatrice Carpenter Young, "The Speeches of South Carolina Legislators to the National Congress" (M.A. thesis, U. of Chicago, M.A.T. Program, Dec. 1964), 28.

123. Young, "Speeches," 28.

124. Quoted in Archie Epps, "A Negro Separatist Movement of the 19th Century," *Harvard Review* 4 (Summer–Fall 1966):79.

125. Rev. H. C. C. Astwood, "Shall the Name of the African Methodist Episcopal Church be Changed to That of the Allen Methodist Episcopal Church?" *A.M.E. Church Review* 4 (Jan. 1888): 319.

126. Ibid.

127. Ibid., 320.

128. Rev. J. T. Jenifer, "Why I Am an African Methodist," *A.M.E. Church Review* 7 (Jan. 1891): 287.

129. Ibid.

130. Ibid.

131. Ibid., 289; As for the less distinguished members of the black churches, the great mass of black people, according to Jenifer, "*feel freer and better satisfied in them.*" Jenifer added that black churches should be retained because "they are their own creatures and their own possessions, and they exhibit an effort at self-help." Jenifer, "African Methodist," 291 (italics added).

132. Perhaps the most prominent organization bearing that title was the Afro-American League, founded by T. Thomas Fortune at Chicago in 1890. Herbert Aptheker, ed., *A Documentary History of the Negro People in the United States* (New York: Citadel Press, 1964), 2:679 (originally published in 1951).

133. Embry's attack on the word *Negro* was one of the harshest in the name controversy prior to the emergence of the nation of Islam movement of the 1930s. Embry thought the term *Negro* deserved "banishment from our literature." Rev. J. C. Embry, "The Afro-American Christian Scholar," *A. M. E. Review* 9 (Oct. 1892): 180–182.

134. Ibid., 180. Embry's statement that slaveholders invented the word *Negro* especially for black people is one of the few such references uncovered in nineteenth-century Afro-American literature, though such references abound in Nation of Islam literature of the 1960s. Embry prefigured Richard B. Moore, the Afro–West Indian who waged the longest and most intense battle against the word *Negro* in the twentieth century. See Moore, *The Name "Negro": Its Origin and Its Evil Use* (New York: Afro-American Publishing, 1960).

135. Apparently this insult was intended since white publishers and reporters continued, despite protests from black people, to use the lowercase well into the new century. It took the *New York Times* until March 15, 1930, to begin using the uppercase.

136. Tanner raised a profoundly moral concern in insisting, quite correctly, that the term *Negro* had been forced upon Afro-Americans, and *that* was a reason for opposing it. But he erred in contending that "whenever we as a people have spoken the appellation has been discarded." He was much closer to the mark in a passage worth quoting in full: "In the early days of the century just passed, and the last days of the century that immediately preceded it, the one and only name

recognized by us officially, and by others as well, was the name African." "A Minuscule," *A.M.E. Church Review* 21 (Oct. 1904): 128–29.

137. Ibid., 127 (see pp. 3–40).

138. Considering the fantastic meanings that Englishmen, who pioneered in racist thought, for centuries attached to blackness, it is perfectly understandable that very large numbers of black people, bombarded with negative impressions respecting their color, would be somewhat ashamed of being black. Clearly the degree of shame varied from person to person. Winthrop Jordan, in *White over Black* (Chapel Hill: U. of North Carolina Press, 1968), chap. 1, has provided detailed information on the meaning of blackness.

139. "A Minuscule," 128.

140. Ibid.

141. Ibid., 130–131.

142. Ibid., 132.

143. Ibid., 135.

144. W. E. B. Du Bois, *The Souls of Black Folk*, in Franklin, ed., *Three Negro Classics*, chap. 1 (originally published in 1903).

145. The 1960s marked the first significant effort on the part of the blacks in America to give themselves African names, a movement that carried over into the following decades, as blacks, ranging from intellectuals to athletes, took African names. Interestingly, most took Moslem names, perhaps in protest against their Christian oppressors.

CHAPTER FIVE
W. E. B. Du Bois: Black Cultural Reality and the Meaning of Freedom

1. W. E. B. Du Bois, *Dusk of Dawn* (New York: Schocken Books, 1968), 34–35 (originally published in 1940). Also see *The Autobiography of W. E. B. Du Bois* (New York: International Publishers, 1968), 136.

2. Du Bois, *Dusk,* 13–14.

3. "Of the Damnation of Women" appears in W. E. B. Du Bois, *Darkwater* (New York: Schocken Books, 1969), first published in 1920. One has to go to Herman Melville's "The Paradise of Bachelors" and "The Tartarus of Maids" to find comparable insight into the oppression of women. See *Selected Writings of Herman Melville* (New York: Modern Library, 1952), 185–211.

4. In an interview in Cairo, Egypt, in Spring 1972, Shirley Graham Du Bois talked about Du Bois, while living in West Africa, "missing the change of seasons."

5. Andrew Paschal quoted in W. E. B. Du Bois Memorial Issue, *Freedomways* 5 (Winter 1965): 36.

6. Henry Miller, *Plexus* (London: Weidenfeld and Nicolson, 1963), 501–2.

7. Ibid., 502–3.

8. W. E. B. Du Bois, *The Souls of Black Folk,* in John Hope Franklin, ed., *Three Negro Classics* (New York: Avon Books, 1963), 380 (originally published in 1903). For a discussion of the Ibo language and the Robeson family, see chap. 6, below.

9. Ibid., 380–81.

10. Du Bois, *Autobiography,* 106.

11. Ibid., 101.

12. Ibid., 121–22.

13. Du Bois, *Souls,* 378.

14. Du Bois, *Autobiography,* 114.

15. Ibid., 108.

16. Ibid., 107.

17. Du Bois, *Souls,* 253–55.

18. Du Bois, *Souls,* 266.

19. Ibid., 258.

20. Du Bois, *Autobiography,* 112–13.

21. Ibid., 110.

22. Ibid., 110–11.

23. Ibid., 111.

24. William Wells Brown, *My Southern Home* (Upper Saddle River, N.J.: Gregg Press, 1968), 191 (originally published in 1880).

25. Undoubtedly Du Bois was right in asserting, "Those who have thus not witnessed the frenzy of a Negro revival in the untouched backwoods of the South can but dimly realize the religious feeling of the slave. As described, such scenes appear grotesque and funny, but as seen they are awful." *Souls,* 338.

26. Ibid., 339.

27. From Douglass's "The songs of the slaves represent the sorrows of his heart," Du Bois conceived "Of the Sorrow Songs." See Frederick Douglass, *Narrative of the Life of Frederick Douglass* (Cambridge: Harvard U. Press, 1960), 38 (originally published in 1845). Of Higginson and McKim, Du Bois has written, "Thomas Wentworth Higginson hastened to tell of these songs. Miss McKim and others urged upon the world their rare beauty." Du Bois, *Souls,* 379.

28. Quoted in Bertrand Russell, *A History of Western Philosophy* (New York: Simon and Schuster, 1945), 813.

29. Du Bois, *Souls,* 339.

30. Ibid., 338.

31. Ibid., 338–39.

32. Ibid., 380.

33. Du Bois, *Autobiography,* 119.

34. In a formulation related to the role of the slave priest, Du Bois wrote,

> First, we must realize that no such institution as the Negro church could rear itself
> without definite historical foundations. These foundations we can find if we remember
> that the social history of the Negro did not start in America. He was brought from a
> definite social environment,—the polygamous clan life under the headship of the chief
> and the potent influence of the priest. His religion was nature-worship, with profound
> belief in invisible surrounding influences, good and bad, and his worship was through
> incantation and sacrifice. The first rude change in this life was the slave ship. . . .

Du Bois, *Souls,* 341.

35. Ibid., 341–42.

36. Ibid., 342.

37. Brer Rabbit tales in which the communal ethic is affirmed are, in addition to "How the Slaves Helped Each Other," "Brer Tiger and the Big Wind," "How the Cow Went Underground," "Brer Rabbit Rescues His Children," and "Who Got Brer Gilyard's Treasure." See William John Faulkner, *The Days When the*

Animals Talked (Chicago: Follette Publishers, 1977), pt. 2. See W. E. B. Du Bois, "Some Efforts of the Negroes for Their Own Betterment," *Atlanta University Studies* (Atlanta, 1898).

38. Du Bois, *Souls,* 342.

39. Johnson's discussion of the slave preacher within the context of Pan-Africanization is also discussed in the following chapter, on Paul Robeson.

40. Du Bois, *Souls,* 379.

41. Ibid.

42. Ibid., 378.

43. Ibid., 342.

44. This is indicated by the special vigor of the shout for generations in sanctified churches, such as the one in which James Baldwin preached in Harlem and about which he writes in *Go Tell It on the Mountain.* The most fruitful research on culture in America awaits the scholar in the sanctified churches of the urban North and South.

45. Du Bois, *Souls,* 344. His pioneering dissertation on the slave trade appeared in 1896, as the first volume of the Harvard Historical Studies. See W. E. B. Du Bois, *The Suppression of the African Slave Trade* (Baton Rouge: Louisiana State U. Press, 1969).

46. Du Bois, *Souls,* 220.

47. Du Bois, *Dusk,* 38. Du Bois added,

> I remember once in a museum, coming face to face with a demonstration: a series of skeletons arranged from a little monkey to a tall well-developed white man, with a Negro barely outranking a chimpanzee. Eventually in my classes stress was quietly transferred to brain weight and brain capacity, and at last to the "cephalic index." . . . In the graduate school at Harvard and again in Germany, the emphasis again altered, and race became a matter of culture and cultural history. The history of the world was paraded before the observation of students. Which was the superior race? Manifestly that which had a history, the white race; there was some mention of Asiatic culture, but no course in Chinese or Indian history or culture was offered at Harvard, and quite unanimously in America and Germany, Africa was left without culture and without history.

Ibid., 98. See George Nathaniel Shaler, *The Neighbor* (Boston: Houghton Mifflin, 1904), 153; Albert Bushnell Hart, *The Southern South* (New York: Negro Universities Press, 1969), 105 (originally published in 1910).

48. W. E. B. Du Bois, "The Spirit of Modern Europe," in Herbert Aptheker, ed., *Against Racism* (Amherst: U. of Massachusetts Press, 1985), 51.

49. Du Bois, *Autobiography,* 126.

50. W. E. B. Du Bois, "The Art and Art Galleries of Modern Europe," in Aptheker, ed., *Against Racism,* 34–41. The speech was delivered in 1897.

51. W. E. B. Du Bois, *The World and Africa* (New York: International Publishers, 1965), 6 (originally published in 1946).

52. Du Bois, "Art Galleries," 35, 37.

53. Du Bois, "Spirit of Europe," 52–54.

54. Ibid., 52.

55. Du Bois, "Art Galleries," 33.

56. Ibid., 38, 39.

57. Du Bois, *Africa,* 20, 26. Du Bois added, "In order to prove this, even black

people in India and Africa were labeled as 'white' if they showed any trace of progress; and, on the other hand, any progress by colored people was attributed to some intermixture, ancient or modern, of white blood or some influence of white civilization." Ibid., 20.

58. Du Bois, *Souls*, 258–59, 261.

59. W. E. B. Du Bois, *The Conservation of Races* (Washington, D.C.: American Negro Academy, 1897), 9; Du Bois, *Africa*, 115–16.

60. Du Bois, *Conservation*, 10.

61. Ibid. Du Bois considered originality the highest nationalist objective intellectually and spiritually—thus, the point on which he broke most decisively from integrationists. Not since Sidney/Garnet had there been such emphasis on originality. In fact, he pressed self-reliance to its ultimate state in calling for his people to be themselves and to bring that which is new and creative into being.

62. Du Bois, *Conservation*, 15.

63. Du Bois also called for Negro colleges, newspapers, and business organizations—for those infrastructures on which any "nation" must base itself. In this regard, he noted that the very segregation or "isolation" of the American Negro meant a start in the direction of nationality. But only a start: "I have called my community a world, and so its isolation made it. There was among us but a half-awakened common consciousness, sprung from common joy and grief, at burial, birth or wedding; from a common hardship in poverty, poor land and low wages; and, above all, from the sight of the Veil that hung between us and Opportunity." Du Bois *Conservation*, 10; Du Bois, *Autobiography*, 120.

64. Du Bois, *Conservation*, 13, 18.

65. Du Bois, *Souls*, 234.

66. Ibid., 357.

67. Ibid., 362. There is no doubt that Du Bois, who read Crummell and thought Garnet a strong writer, had a more than passing familiarity with Garnet as man and activist. Yet there appears to be little of Garnet's influence on him in a direct sense, perhaps because Garnet firmly believed in the uses of violence by the oppressed—as perhaps the only means by which liberation will come—whereas Du Bois was never at ease with such a position, the role of reason ever occupying primacy in his mind. Blacks in the Western abolitionist tradition, with their greater attraction to rebellion, appear therefore to have been less appealing to him than those who followed William Lloyd Garrison and moral suasion.

68. Du Bois, *Souls*, 362.

69. Ibid., 244–5. For a treatment of black abolitionists, see Benjamin Quarles, *Black Abolitionists* (New York: Oxford U. Press, 1970). Note that Du Bois leans toward eastern abolitionists and moral suasion. But his assertion that they took the lead in self-assertion among black leaders and maintained such a tradition is open to question because Charles L. Remond, Wells Brown, and James C. Nell, like Douglass, were long essentially under Garrison's tutelage. Robert Brown Elliot, Blanche K. Bruce, and John M. Langston were all prominent black politicians in the South during Reconstruction.

70. Du Bois, *Souls*, 244, 239. While Du Bois later had reservations about this prophecy, the history of the twentieth century bears out the importance of race as well as economics in human oppression. For a discussion of the matter, see John

Hope Franklin's foreword to *The Suppression of the African Slave Trade* (Baton Rouge: Louisiana State U. Press, 1969, x–xi.

71. Du Bois, "The Talented Tenth," in August Meier, Elliott Rudwick, and Francis L. Broderick, eds., *Black Protest Thought in the Twentieth Century* (Indianapolis: Bobbs-Merrill, 1965), 48 (originally published in 1903).

72. Du Bois, "Talented Tenth," 50–51.

73. Ibid., 51–52.

74. Du Bois, "The Negro and Social Reconstruction," in Aptheker, ed., *Against Racism*, 113, 114.

75. Mungo Park's travels in West Africa are helpful here. The Scottish physician was the subject of a song created extemporaneously, sparked by the humanity of African women:

> The winds roared, and the rains fell
> The poor white man, faint and weary
> Came and sat under our tree
> He has no mother to bring him milk
> No wife to grind his corn.

> CHORUS
> Let us pity the white man
> No mother has he. . . .

At another point, Park writes, "The rites of hospitality thus being performed towards a stranger in distress; my worthy benefactress . . . called to the female part of her family, who had stood gazing on me the while in fixed astonishment, to resume their task of spinning cotton; in which they continued to employ themselves [the] great part of the night." See Mungo Park, *Travels in the Interior Districts of Africa* (New York: Arno Press, 1971), 197–98 (originally published in 1799). In an important study of a South Carolina slave community, Charles Joyner comments beneath illustrations of slave laborers: "The use of the hoe as an all-purpose implement continued an African practice"; "Slaves dropped seed rice into trenches and covered them with the foot in the African manner"; "Pouring 'fanned' rice into mortar, threshed rice was winnowed by being 'fanned' in the wind in hand-coiled fanner baskets. Both the baskets and the method of winnowing represent continuity with African traditions"; and "Unhusked rice is gently ground in this hollow-log mortar with a wooden pestle in a manner identical to that of West African rice producers." Charles Joyner, *Down by the Riverside* (Urbana: U. of Illinois Press, 1984), between pp. 48 and 49.

76. Du Bois, *Black Reconstruction* (Millwood, N.Y.: Kraus-Thomson, 1973), 667.

77. Herbert Aptheker, introd. to Du Bois, *The Souls of Black Folk* (Millwood, N.Y.: Kraus-Thomson, 1973), 10–11.

78. *Du Bois, Souls*, 244.

79. Du Bois, *Dusk*, 193.

80. As though he had a different vision, as surely he did, Du Bois is the only one who does not look into the camera. The photo is found on the back of the Du Bois Memorial Issue of *Freedomways*.

81. For Martin Delany's cultural nationalist views, see his "The Political Destiny of the Colored Race," in Stuckey, ed., *Ideological Origins*, 195–236.

82. Du Bois, *Souls*, 215, 216.

83. Ibid., 220, 378.

84. In 1907, two years after he founded the Niagara movement, Du Bois declared his sympathy for socialism, displaying, as in all matters, independence of mind. Opposing the "entire abolition of private property," he asserted that he believed "that most of the human business called private is no more private than God's blue sky." He added, "In the socialistic trend lies the one great hope of the Negro American . . . Not in a renaissance among ourselves in Get and Grab—Not in private hoarding, squeezing and cheating, lies our salvation, but rather in that larger ideal of human brotherhood, equality of opportunity, and work not for wealth but for Weal—here lies our shining goal." W. E. B. Du Bois, "Socialist of the Path" and "Negro and Socialism," in *Horizon* 1 and 2 (Feb. 1907); 7, 8. *Horizon* was the publication of the Niagara movement.

85. "The Song of the Smoke," in W. E. B. Du Bois, *Selected Poems* (Accra: Ghana U. Press, 1964), 12. The poem originally appeared in *Horizon* in 1899.

86. For a general consideration of Negritude theory, see Sterling Stuckey, "Du Bois, Woodson and the Spell of Africa," *Negro Digest* 16 (Feb. 1967): 20–24, 60–74.

87. W. E. B. Du Bois, "What is Civilization? Africa's Answer," *Forum* 73 (Feb. 1924): 185–86.

88. Boas wrote in the Atlanta University Leaflet, no. 19,

> It seems likely that at times when the European was still satisfied with rude stone tools, the African had invented and adopted the art of smelting iron . . . It seems not unlikely that the people who made the marvellous discovery of reducing iron ores by smelting were African Negroes . . . At the time of the great African discoveries toward the end of the past century, blacksmiths were found all over Africa from north to south and from east to west.

89. Du Bois, *Africa*, 98–99, 117.

90. Ibid., 118–119.

91. Ibid., 105. Immanuel Wallerstein has addressed the problem as follows:

> It perhaps would not matter who the Egyptians were, had such an issue not been made of it during the period of European colonization . . . [t]he nonexistence of Negro achievements was fundamental to colonial ideology, which attempted to attribute all signs of human accomplishment to Egyptians, or Hittites, or Phoenicians, or Arabs, or Hamites, and never to Negroes. It was assumed, or implied, or indeed on occasion boldly asserted that Egyptians or Hittites or Phoenicians or Arabs or Hamites were white men; or at least whiter men than the Negroes. Suffice it to say now for purposes of discussing the African past, that the best evidence of today seems to indicate a very great racial intermingling in Africa as elsewhere over the past five thousand years, and that the "Egyptians" or "Hamites" of yesteryear might well find themselves classified as Negroes today, in precisely those countries where such classifications matter. Suffice it further to note that many of the archaelogical remains . . . at first credited to "Arabs" or "Hamites," have on closer, or less biased, inspection, turned out to be unmistakably Negro-African in origin.

Wallerstein, *Africa: The Politics of Independence* (New York: Vintage Books, 1961), 12–13.

92. The writer in the spring of 1972 visited the British and Cairo museums and found, to his amazement, an enormous black presence in Egyptian civilization at widely different times in history. Du Bois bases his conclusions regarding black influence in Egypt on scholars ranging from Herodotus to Randall-MacIver and Flinders Petrie in the twentieth century. He quotes Randall-MacIver:

> The more we learn of Nubia and the Sudan, the more evident does it appear that what was most characteristic in the predynastic culture of Egypt is due to intercourse with the interior of Africa and the immediate influence of that permanent Negro element which has been present in the population of southern Egypt from remotest times to our own day.

Du Bois, *Africa*, 106–7. "According to Dr. F. L. Griffith of Oxford," writes Du Bois, "more than one Nubian, dark-colored or Negroid, can be traced as holding a high position in Egypt or even in the royal court at Memphis during the Fifth Dynasty." Ibid., 108. Du Bois's observations regarding those threatening Egypt takes on special significance after the viewing of the stool referred to: "One king of the Twelfth Dynasty, Usertesen III, was especially triumphant over the Negroes who were threatening Egypt from the South, and this Pharoah set up a boundary across which the Nubians must not come." Ibid., 112.

93. Ibid., 99.

94. Ibid., 106.

95. Bayard Webster, "Finding of Ancient Cattle Bones in Africa Stirs Scientific Debate," *New York Times*, Aug. 27, 1980.

96. Quoted in Joseph P. Widney, *Race Life of the Aryan Peoples* (New York: Funk & Wagnalls, 1907), 2: 238–39.

97. Du Bois, *Souls*, 284.

98. Du Bois, *Africa*, 7.

99. Ibid. Du Bois saw his old colleague John Hope in Paris at the time, and they discussed, as they usually did, the "reformation of the world." Du Bois, *Dusk of Dawn*, 315.

100. Du Bois, *Africa*, 6, 10.

101. Ibid., 8–9.

102. Ibid., 10.

103. Ibid., 7.

104. Ibid.

105. Ibid.

106. Quoted from George A. Schweinfurth, *Heart of Africa* (London: Sampson, Low, Marston Low and Searle, 1873), 1:313.

107. W. E. B. Du Bois, "Opinion," *Crisis* 18 (Sept. 1919): 231.

108. W. E. B. Du Bois, "African Manners," *Crisis* 28 (June 1924): 58. For Du Bois's itinerary in Africa, see *Crisis* 28(May 1924): 31.

109. W. E. B. Du Bois, "Africa," *Crisis* 27 (April 1924): 249.

110. W. E. B. Du Bois, "Little Portraits of Africa," *Crisis* 27 (April 1924): 274.

111. Ibid., 273.

112. He says of Boas,

> Franz Boas came to Atlanta University where I was teaching history in 1906 and said to the graduating class: You need not be ashamed of your African past; and then he recounted the history of the black kingdoms South of the Sahara for a thousand years. I

was too astonished to speak. All of this I had never heard and came then and afterwards to realize how the silence and neglect of science can let truth utterly disappear or even be unconsciously distorted.

Du Bois, *Black Folk*, vii. For the announcement of Robeson's appearance in *All God's Chillun*, see *Crisis* 27 (April 1924): 268.

113. Du Bois, "Little Portraits," 217, 274.

114. Ibid., 274.

115. W. E. B. Du Bois, "The Name 'Negro,'" *Crisis*, 35 (March 1928): 96.

116. Du Bois, *Black Folk*, 126, 128.

117. Du Bois was not the first critic of slavery to note its negative impact on white workers, on "free"labor. The abolitionists were keenly perceptive on this matter, and it hardly escaped Karl Marx's attention. See *Black Folk,* 128–129.

118. Du Bois, *Africa,* 24.

119. For the influence of Hegel on Du Bois, see Joel Williamson, *The Crucible of Race* (New York: Oxford U. Press, 1984), chap. 13. However advanced Hegel may have thought the Europe of his time, Du Bois did not think the finest flowering of the human spirit had occurred:

> And then reaching back to my archives, I whisper to the great Majority: To the Almighty Dead. . . . In every name of God, bend out and down, you who are the infinite majority of all mankind and with your thoughts, deeds, dreams and memories, overwhelm, outvote, and coerce this remnant of human life which lingers on, imagining themselves wisest of all who have lived just because they still survive. . . . Our dreams seek Heaven, our deeds plumb Hell. Hell lies about us in our Age: blithely we push into its stench and flame. Suffer us not, Eternal Dead to stew in this Evil—the Evil of South Africa, the Evil of Mississippi. . . . Reveal, Ancient of Days, the Present in the Past and prophesy the End in the Beginning.

Du Bois, *Autobiography*, 422. His lack of dogmatism is especially relevant with respect to violent revolution as the only means of bringing about socialism that will lead, finally, to communism. In 1936, in an unpublished essay, he wrote,

> Most American communists have become dogmatic exponents of the inspired word of Karl Marx as they read it. They believe, apparently, in immediate, violent and bloody revolution and make it one of their main objectives. This is a silly program even for white men. For American colored men, it is suicidal. . . . In the first place, its logical basis is by no means sound. The great and fundamental change in the organization of industry which Marx foresaw must, to be sure, be brought about by revolution; but whether in all times and places and under all circumstances that revolution is going to involve violence, war and bloodshed, is a question which every sincere follower of Marx has a right to doubt.

Du Bois, "Negro and Social Reconstruction," 142.

120. W. E. B. Du Bois, "Russia, 1926," *Crisis* 32 (Oct. 1926): 8.

121. Du Bois, *Black Reconstruction*, 40.

122. Herbert Aptheker, introd. to Du Bois, *Black Reconstruction* (Millwood, N.Y.: Kraus-Thomson, 1975), 11, 23.

123. Du Bois, *Black Reconstruction*, 39, 125.

124. Ibid., 708.

125. Du Bois, *Souls*, 219.

126. Du Bois, *Black Reconstruction*, 124.

127. Ibid., 125.

128. Ibid., 17.

129. Ibid., 5.

130. Ibid., 15.

131. Du Bois, *Dusk*, 205.

132. Ibid.

133. Du Bois, *Autobiography*, 392.

134. Du Bois, *Dusk*,218-19.

135. Ibid., 291-97.

136. Ibid., 195.

137. Ibid., 199.

138. Ibid., 217. Du Bois was not unmindful of the difficulties posed by his plan.
Indeed, he found it necessary to state explicitly that cooperation with the authorities might be essential. The Negro people, under the new dispensation, could see
to it that "no action of this inner group is opposed to the real interests of the
nation. . . . Within its own group it can, in the last analysis, expel the anti-social
and hand him over to the police force of the nation. On the other hand, it can avoid
all appearance of conspiracy. . . ." Even more formidable was the task of convincing blacks that they could raise among themselves infrastructures of their own. He
would have Negroes

> take over the whole of their retail distribution, to raise, cut, mine and manufacture a
> considerable proportion of the basic raw materials, to man their own manufacturing
> plants, to process foods, to import necessary raw materials, to invent and build ma-
> chines. . . . Large numbers of other Negroes working as miners, laborers in industry and
> transportation, could without difficulty be transferred to productive industries designed
> to cater to Negro consumers.

Ibid., 211, 216.

139. Ibid., 218.

140. W. E. B. Du Bois, "Colonialism, Democracy, and Peace after the War," in
Aptheker, ed., *Against Racism*, 235, 242–43.

141. Du Bois, *Autobiography*, 393.

142. Ibid., 291–92. Apparently he believed that his Pan-African program, with its
economic dimension in the United States, might have been successful in spite of
the influence of moderate blacks in the NAACP had the *Crisis* remained financially solvent. Such was his appeal to significant numbers of his readers, moreover, that he seems to have thought he might win the masses to the banner of Pan-
Africa in spite of white NAACP leadership that was conservative on economic
issues. Regarding the former, he wrote, "I realized that too much in later years
the Association had attracted the higher income group of colored people, who
regarded it as a weapon to attack the sort of social discrimination which especially
irked them; rather than as an organization to improve the status and power of the
whole Negro group." Of NAACP whites, he wrote, "They wanted to help the
Negroes, as they wanted to help the weak and disadvantaged of all classes in
America . . . but most of them still believed in the basic rightness of industry as at
present organized. . . ." This meant that the NAACP leadership, white and black
alike, would not have looked with favor on African nationalism directed at establishing socialism in the black world. Du Bois, *Dusk*, 290, 297.

143. Du Bois, *Dusk*, 304.

144. Du Bois, *Black Reconstruction*, 703.

145. Du Bois was clear on the subject of the relation of self-aggrandizement within the ranks of blacks and his plan for economic renewal: "This will call for self-control. It will eliminate the millionaire and even the rich Negro; it will put the Negro leader upon a salary which will be modest as American salaries go and yet sufficient for a life under modern standards of decency and enjoyment." Du Bois, *Dusk*, 215.

146. W. E. B. Du Bois, "On the Scientific Objectivity of the Proposed Encyclopedia of the Negro and on Safeguards against the Intrusion of Propaganda," in Aptheker, ed., *Against Racism*, 166.

147. Du Bois, *Dusk*, 319; "The Negro and Social Reconstruction" in Aptheker, ed., *Against Racism*, 149.

148. Du Bois, *Dusk*, 320–21.

149. Du Bois, *Black Folk*, 200.

150. Ira De A. Reid, "The John Canoe Festival," *Phylon* 3 (1942): 349.

151. George Padmore, ed., *History of the Pan-African Congress* (Manchester, Eng.: Susan Tully, 1947), 67. In *The Negro*, the first comprehensive treatment of the history of the kingdoms of the Sudan, Du Bois left no doubt of his commitment to the working classes of all nations, of his belief that the movement of freedom by African people, when it gains in strength, must be accompanied by a movement of working people generally: "Already the more far-seeing Negroes sense the coming unities: a unity of the working classes everywhere, a unity of the colored races, a new unity of man." In a very real sense, the attitudes of white workers were crucial, he thought, to the solution to the problem of oppressed masses everywhere, a view that is less persuasive in some respects today, as intriguing as it remains: "The proposed economic solution of the Negro problem in Africa and America has turned the thoughts of Negroes toward a realization of the fact that the modern white laborer of Europe and America has the key to the serfdom of black folk, in his support of militarism and colonial expansion." But Du Bois, echoing Marx and Garnet, was indisputably on the mark in contending that "so long as black laborers are slaves, white laborers cannot be free." W. E. B. Du Bois, *The Negro* (Millwood, N.Y.: Kraus-Thomson, 1975), 241–42 (originally published in 1915).

152. Du Bois, *Dusk*, 303.

153. Ibid., 305.

154. Du Bois, *Africa* 1.

155. Williamson, *Crucible of Race*, 78.

156. Quoted in Herbert Aptheker, ed., *The Correspondence of W. E. B. Du Bois*, vol. 3 (Amherst: U. of Massachusetts Press, 1978), 247.

157. W. E. B. Du Bois, *In Battle for Peace* (New York: Masses and Mainstream, 1952), 64.

158. Ibid., 394–95.

159. W. E. B. Du Bois, "Behold the Land," *Freedomways* 4, no. 1 (Winter 1964): 12.

160. Du Bois, *Dusk*, 284–86.

CHAPTER SIX

On Being African: Paul Robeson and the Ends of Nationalist Theory and Practice

1. Robeson made the remark regarding the wisdom of Du Bois at the home of Alan Booth, then his accompanist, in Chicago in the summer of 1952. Shirley Graham Du Bois related the incident concerning the sign and travel to the Continent in an interview in her Cairo apartment, overlooking the Nile, in the spring of 1972.

2. A statement of his position delivered in 1949 in Detroit recalls Garnet's approach to the ancestors: "I don't get scared when Fascism gets near. . . . The spirit of Harriet Tubman, Sojourner Truth, Frederick Douglass fills me with courage and determination." *Daily Worker*, Oct. 12, 1949.

3. "Patterns of Folk Song," from Robeson, *Ballad for Americans* (Carnegie Hall Concert, May 9 and 23, 1958) vol. 2. VSD-79193.

4. Paul Robeson, *Here I Stand* (New York: Othello Associates, 1957), 18.

5. Ibid., 10.

6. Ibid., 19–20.

7. Ibid., 23.

8. Ibid., 15.

9. Paul Robeson, "The Culture of the Negro," *Spectator* (London), June 15, 1934, 916.

10. Elizabeth Shepley Sergeant's "Appreciation" of Robeson in the *New Republic* is quoted in the *Crisis* 32 (May 1926): 39–39. Robeson, *Here I Stand*, 17.

11. Robeson, *Here I Stand*, 17, 20, 21.

12. Ibid., 24.

13. Ibid., 23.

14. Ibid.

15. Ibid., 17.

16. IBid., 25, 27, 28.

17. Ibid., 26.

18. George Garnet, the evidence indicates, was no less committed to the education of Henry. In fact, there is no indication that he was not as committed as Paul's father to his people fufilling their potential as a people. See James McCune Smith, *Introduction to a Memorial Discourse; by Rev. Henry Highland Garnet* (Philadelphia: Joseph M. Wilson, 1865), 21.

19. Robeson, *Here I Stand*, 26; Paul Robeson, "The Legacy of W. E. B. Du Bois," Du Bois Memorial Issue, *Freedomways* 5, no. 1 (Winter 1965): 36.

20. Robeson, *Here I Stand*, 19.

21. Quoted in Marie Seton, *Paul Robeson* (London: Dennis Dobson, 1958), 21.

22. Harry Edwards, "Paul Robeson: His Political Legacy to the Twentieth-Century Gladiator," in *Paul Robeson: The Great Forerunner* (New York: Dodd, Mead, 1971), 20.

23. Paul Robeson, Jr., "Paul Robeson: Black Warrior, *Freedomways* 2, no. 1 (1971): 22.

24. Robeson, *Here I Stand*, 8, 9, 11.

25. Paul Leroy Robeson, "The New Idealism," *Targum* 50 (June 1919): 570.

26. Ibid., 570–71.

27. Robeson, *Here I Stand*, 21.

28. Edwards, "Paul Robeson," 21.

29. O'Neill is quoted in Paul Robeson, Jr., "Paul Robeson: Black Warrior," 25; Nathan is quoted in Seton, *Paul Robeson*, 34.

30. Quoted in Seton, *Robeson*, 36–37.

31. James Weldon Johnson, *American Negro Spirituals* (New York: Viking Press, 1925), 29. Though the Fisk Jubilee Singers had done superb work in promoting Negro spirituals on concert stages, they sang as a choral group. Roland Hayes's singing of spirituals was of lasting value but he had not relied nearly so heavily on slave song as Robeson. See Roland Hayes, *Angel Mo' and Her Son* (Boston: Little, Brown, 1942). This enormously important but neglected work reveals deep currents of nationalism in Hayes despite his attempt, for a long time, to sound "white." See esp. chaps. 4–7.

32. Quoted in Seton, *Robeson*, 37.

33. Paul Robeson, *Songs of My People*, RCA Victor (recorded on Jan. 7, 1926). LM-3292.

34. Ibid. (recorded on May 9, 1927).

35. Ibid. (recorded on Jan. 7, 1926).

36. For a trenchant attack on the thesis that there was a "Harlem Renaissance," see Sterling A. Brown, "The New Negro in Literature, 1925–1955," in Rayford Logan, ed., *The New Negro Thirty Years Afterwards* (Washington: Howard U. Press, 1955). What we know of the circle of culture in America suggests that the renaissance of African genius on American soil began in slavery.

37. Remarkably, nationalist theoreticians, except for Du Bois, over a period of decades saw no apparent connection between Robeson's singing and nationalism, but that could have resulted from a general weakness of nationalists as well as integrationists on matters of black culture. Du Bois's assertion that Robeson had "spread the pure Negro folk song over the civilized world" has become the classic statement of nationalist influence through folk song. A major theoretician of the spirituals and of black folk culture generally was Roland Hayes, who has been ignored in this respect. See W. E. B. Du Bois, *Autobiography* (New York: International Publishers, 1968), 397. Also see Hayes, *Angel Mo'*, which throughout reflects Hayes's nationalism.

38. In addition, such theorists of nationalism, through an emphasis on autonomy, favor the search for autonomous forms. By contrast, integrationists have tended to recoil from even the suggestion of autonomy in black life.

39. Robeson refers to Johnson in the "Patterns of Folk Song" selection—from his Carnegie Hall concert of 1958—in relation to Negro art generally. And well he might have, for Johnson, in 1925, wrote,

> Now, the Negro in America had his native musical endowment to begin with; and the Spirituals possess the fundamental characteristics of African music. They have a striking rhythmic quality, and show a marked similarity to African songs in form and intervallic structure. But the Spirituals, upon the base of the primitive rhythms, go a step in advance of African music through a higher melodic and an added harmonic development. . . . One has never experienced the full effect of these songs until he has heard their harmonies in the part singing of a large number of Negro voices.

Paul Robeson, *Ballad for Americans* (Carnegie Hall Concert), vol. 2, VSD-79193. Also see Johnson, *Negro Spirituals*, 17.

40. James Weldon Johnson, *Along This Way* (New York: Viking Press, 1933), 124.

41. Johnson argues that "shout songs" are not "even truly religious," a position for which he is not able to produce evidence. "This term 'shout songs' has no reference to the loud, jubilant Spirituals, which are often so termed by writers on Negro music; it has reference to the songs or, better, the chants used to accompany the 'ring shout.'" But Johnson himself, more effectively than anyone else, has demonstrated that such chants form the basis for the spirituals: "Thus it was by sheer spiritual force that African chants were metamorphosed into the Spirituals; that upon the fundamental throb of African rhythms were reared those reaches of melody that rise above earth and soar into the ethereal blue. And this is the miracle of the creation of the Spirituals." One should recall that Higginson heard numerous spirituals sung as Africans moved in counterclockwise direction, as did Bishop Payne. While many sirituals sung in the circle were more than chants, most rested on African foundations: "A study of the Spirituals leads to the belief that the earlier ones were built upon the form so common to African songs, leading lines and responses. It would be safe, I think, to say that the bulk of the Spirituals are cast in this simple form." Our knowledge of both the degree to which the ring shout was practiced by blacks and its defining power in relation to Christianity makes it hard to imagine slave Christians singing spirituals, except in the presence of whites, without the ring shout being everywhere evident. Besides, Johnson remarked, "The music is supplemented by the clapping of hands. As the ring goes around it begins to take on signs of frenzy. The music, starting, perhaps, with a Spiritual, becomes a wild, monotonous chant. . . . The words become a repetition of an incoherent cry." Johnson, *Negro Spirituals* 21, 25–28, 33.

42. Ibid., 33.

43. Robeson, "Culture of the Negro," 916.

44. Ibid. Robeson's global approach to music was analogous to the broad range of intellectual activity that characterized nationalists such as Walker, Garnet, and Du Bois and was, therefore, in the nationalist tradition of catholicity of reach.

45. There is doubt as to whether Robeson's accent in speaking Russian was "perfect." Alexander I. Ovcharenko, a leading scholar in the Soviet Union who met Robeson, described his Russian as "grammatical" but said he "spoke slowly, enunciating each syllable." Jao-Yao Zeng, a Chinese scholar visiting the United States, on hearing Robeson's Chinese, described it as "clear and grammatical." Interview with Ovcharenko, Fall 1982; Interview with Zeng, Spring 1984.

46. In "Patterns of Folk Song" Robeson describes his father "moving about" while preaching and invokes the name of Johnson. In such a context, one thinks immediately of the old-time slave preacher and his relationship to the ring shout. Robeson, *Ballad for Americans*, vol. 2.

47. Robeson, *Ballad for Americans* (Carnegie Hall Concert, May 9 and 23, 1958), vol. 2, VSD-79193.

48. *New York World-Telegram*, Aug. 30, 1933.

49. Interview with Paul Robeson, Jr., Summer 1975.

50. Eslanda Robeson, *African Journey* (New York: John Day, 1945) 15.

51. Ibid., 13.

52. Robeson, *Here I Stand*, 33–35.

53. Not only was London perhaps the best place outside of Africa in which to study Africans and their culture, but, in the thirties, London, according to Frances Herskovits, was generally "very exciting intellectually." Interview with Frances Herskovits, Autumn 1972.

54. Seton, *Robeson*, 77.

55. Gertrude Stein, *The Autobiography of Alice B. Toklas* (New York: Random House, 1933), 237–38, 211.

56. Robeson, "Thoughts on the Colour Bar," *Spectator*, Aug. 8, 1931, 178.

57. Paul Robeson, "I Want to be African," in E. G. Cousins, ed., *What I Want from Life* (London: George Allen & Unwin, 1934), 72; and Robeson, "Culture of the Negro," 916.

58. *New York Times*, April 5, 1931.

59. Ibid. The prospect of emigrating from America, even when a young man, did not disturb Robeson. Still, he considered the suggestion that whites had more right to be in America than blacks an absurd view. See Robesin, *Here I Stand*, 11.

60. Robeson, "To Be African," 76.

61. Robeson, "Colour Bar," 178. "Sidney," the brilliant theoretician of the nineteenth century, as far as we know, never wrote a word on art, but he was probably Garnet, who was, more than any other antebellum leader, Robeson's philosophical and spiritual ancestor. The philosophical and political precepts found in the Sidney letters square perfectly with Robeson's reasons for wanting to rid his people of a sense of inferiority, for wanting to build unity within their ranks. The writing in the letters—reflective, succinct, hermetic in tightness of argumentation—is similar to Robeson's writings of the thirties.

62. Robeson, "Colour Bar," 178.

63. *Chicago Defender*, Jan. 26, 1935.

64. Ibid.

65. Ibid.

66. *London Daily Herald*, Jan. 26, 1935; *Jamaican Daily Gleaner*, July 17, 1935. Certainly Robeson's views were not being suppressed in the Negro press. In fact, no black in America in the thirties received more attention in the Negro press than he, even though he was not in the country. Contrary to his emphasis, then, some Negro publishers were not against publishing black nationalist thought.

67. Robeson, "To Be African," 71.

68. Paul Robeson, "The Negro Artist Looks Ahead," *Masses and Mainstream*, Jan. 1952, 7.

69. Robeson, "To Be African," 72.

70. Ibid., 76–77.

71. *Louisiana Weekly*, Sept. 9, 1933.

72. Robeson, "Culture of the Negro," 916.

73. Ibid., 917.

74. Ibid., 916; Robeson, "To Be African," 77.

75. Robeson, "To Be African," 75.

76. Ibid. Robeson added that a slight variation of the Negro's sense of rhythm "is to be found among the Tartars and Chinese, to whom he is much more nearly akin than he is to the Arab, for example." Ibid. Alvin Ailey, the distinguished choreographer, supports Robeson's observation on comparative dance styles,

contending that Afro-American (and black African dance) is closer to Chinese dance than to the dances of the Arabs. Interview with Alvin Ailey, Winter 1971.

77. Marshall Stearns, *The Story of Jazz* (New York: Oxford U. Press, 1956), chap. 1.

78. Johnson, *Along This Way*, 22.

79. Ibid., 152. Robeson made the remark about Basie on arrival at the airport in Trinidad in 1948. See Sterling Stuckey, "Paul Robeson in the Caribbean" (forthcoming essay).

80. Johnson, *Along This Way*, 154–55.

81. But one notes a peculiarity in the depiction of the African dancers—they are presented moving in a clockwise direction, a vital detail that hardly corresponds to the pervasiveness of counterclockwise dance in black Africa, irrespective of the purpose of the dance. James Weldon Johnson is said to have had a hand in putting together cultural aspects of the film. Of course, Johnson knew that the ring shout derived from African ritual, but how much he knew of African ring dance is another matter. Robeson's readings in African anthropology make it doubtful that he was unaware of the counterclockwise direction of most African ring dance. What is likely is that Robeson, playing the lead in *Emperor*, had little to do with the actual mechanics of the ring shout scene—a scene that may well have been grafted on to the rest of the film.

82. Lydia Parrish, *Slave Songs of the Georgia Sea Islands* (New York: Creative Age Press, 1942), 13–14. Referring to blacks on St. Simon's Island, Parrish writes, "Several of our Negroes 'Ball the Jack,' as well as the African performer who did a similar serpentine wriggle at a wedding ceremony in the motion picture. . . . Some day, if I ask enough questions, I may discover the original name of the dance—if it had one." Ibid., 117. "Ball the Jack" was not the only dance, apart from the ring shout and the buzzard lope, that Parrish recognized as belonging to Africa and countries in the Americas, including the United States. While in South Carolina and Georgia, she saw another dance—"clearly an African survival"— that, "from its description, seems similar to one she saw performed by primitive Negroes North of Haiti." Ibid., 13.

83. Marshall and Jean Stearns, *Jazz Dance* (New York: Schirmer Books, 1964), 13.

84. Paul Robeson, "From Handwritten Notes," in *Selected Writings* (New York: Paul Robeson Archives, 1976), 54.

85. In this connection, George Garnet comes to mind, as do other aged blacks of his era, especially those in slavery. Douglass noted the importance of elders on the plantations: "Strange, and even ridiculous as it may seem, among a people so uncultivated, and with so many stern trials to look in the face, there is not found, among any people, a more rigid enforcement of the law of respect for elders, than they maintain." Frederick Douglass, *My Bondage and My Freedom* (New York: Arno Press, 1968), 69 (originally published in 1855).

86. Herskovits himself was somewhat late in coming to a recognition of African influences on Afro-American lifestyles. He moved beyond his position advanced in 1925 in Alain Locke's *The New Negro* (New York: Albert and Charles Boni, 1925) to an advocacy of African survivals in the 1930s. Herskovits, then, came to the African survival position somewhat later than Robeson and decades after Du Bois. Nevertheless, Robeson was influenced by Herskovits's later researches into

African and Afro-American cultural ties. Paul Robeson, Jr., reports that his father had a number of Herskovits's works in his enormous library—together with the works of Du Bois, Carter Woodson, and scores of other writers on African and other cultures. Interview with Paul Robeson, Jr., Summer 1971.

87. To be sure, Robeson did not bother even to identify the ethnicity of the African song he sang, for example, in "Patterns of Folk Song" in Carnegie Hall in 1958.

88. Robeson, "To Be African," 73.

89. J. C. O'Flaherty, A.M., "An Exclusive Interview with Paul Robeson," *West African Review* 7, no. 107 (Aug. 1936): 16.

90. *New York Times*, April19, 1942.

91. *Black World* 20, no. 10 (Aug. 1971): 4–24.

92. Robeson, *Here I Stand*, 42–43. Robeson added, "My pride in Africa, and it grew with the learning, impelled me to speak out against the scorners. . . . Those who scorned the African languages as so many 'barbarous dialects' could never know, of course, the richness of those languages and of the great philosophy and epics of poetry that have come down through the ages in those ancient tongues." Ibid.

93. Ibid., 42. In discussing languages, Robeson remarked, "It is astonishing and, to me, fascinating to find a flexibility and subtlety in a language like Swahili, sufficient to convey the teachings of Confucius, for example. . . ." In the same context, he offered an observation that could scarcely have been more consonant with qualities proper to his people. He said it was his "ambition to guide the Negro race by means of its own peculiar qualities to a higher degree of perfection along the lines of its natural development." Ibid.

94. Paul Robeson, "Primitives," *New Statesman and Nation*,Aug. 8, 1936, 191.

95. Ibid.

96. Ibid.

97. Ibid.

98. Ibid.

99. *Chicago Defender*, Jan. 26, 1935. Robeson acknowledged that Europe's "entire peasantry, large masses of its proletariat, and even a certain percentage of its middle class have never been really touched by attempts of others to reduce life to a mechanical formula," "to kill this creative emotional side." "Of such persons," he added, "one can mention Blake and D. H. Lawrence. In fact one could say that all the live art which Europe has produced since the Renaissance has been in spite of, and not because of, the new trends of Western thought." Ibid.

100. Ibid.

101. Ibid.

102. *Daily Gleaner*, March 10, 1934.

103. F. S. C. Northrop, *The Meeting of East and West* (New York: Macmillan, 1952), 160.

104. *Chicago Defender*, Jan. 26, 1935.

105. Robeson, "Primitives," 190.

106. Interview with Armand Borel, Mathematics Section of the Institute for Advanced Study, Princeton, N.J., Spring 1971.

107. See Herbert J. Muller, *The Uses of the Past* (New York: Oxford U. Press, 1952), for a sensitive study of the ironies inherent in the cultures of East and West.

108. Robeson, "To Be African," 71; Alfred L. Kroeber, *Configerations of Culture Growth* (Berkeley and Los Angeles: U. of California Press, 1944), 98, 174.

109. Robeson, "Primitives," 189–90.

110. Ibid., 190.

111. Robeson, "To Be African," 73.

112. Ibid.

113. Robeson, "Primitives," 191.

114. *Daily Gleaner*, Aug. 21, 1933.

115. Paul Robeson, "I Breathe Freely," Interview in Moscow by Julia Dorn, *New Theater*, July 1935, 5.

116. Ibid.

117. Robeson, *Here I Stand, 35–36; New York Times*, April 19, 1942. To a surprising degree, a recent report in the *New York Times* from Serge Schmemann supports a number of Robeson's findings, especially his assertion of the degree to which time has been compressed and certain Asiatic republics brought into the twentieth century with much of their ancient cultures, including their languages, intact. Though in attenuated form, Islam remains alive in Soviet Central Asia:

> Sarmarkand, in Uzbekistan, is arguably the most breathtaking of Central Asia's ancient towns, with its profusion of blue-domed, mosaic-encrusted mosques and mausoleums. The architectural ensemble at Registan Square, with the soaring arches of three grand madrasahs, framed by tall minarets and surmounted by gleaming, sky-blue domes, faces on a vast plaza. It is arguably an emsemble without parallel in the Moslem world.

Schmemann, "In Central Asia, Age-Old Islam Meets Soviet Rule," *New York Times*, July 8, 1985.

118. *New York Herald-Tribune*, Oct. 27, 1935.

119. James, A Troskyite by the time he and Robeson met, said of Robeson, "That was an unusual man. I've met a lot of people you know, a lot of people in many parts of the world and he remains, in my life, the most distinguished and remarkable of them all. That I will say and that I am going to write." Interview with C. L. R. James, Summer 1970. Lawrence Brown is quoted in Seton, *Robeson*, 59.

120. *Journal and Guide*, Jan. 5. 1935.

121. *London Daily Herald*, Jan. 26, 1936.

122. Whatever the response of African independence leaders on seeing *Song of Freedom*, and no matter how superior the film was to Negro films of the thirties, it fell so far short of Robeson's conceptualization of African culture as to almost caricature it. For an earlier, different interpretation, see the discussion of *Song of Freedom* in Stuckey, "I Want to Be African," 131.

123. *Daily Gleaner*, March 10, 1934.

124. Ibid., July 17, 1935.

125. Ibid., *New York Post*, Dec. 10, 1943.

126. Ibid., Jan. 11, 1936.

127. *New York World-Telegram*, Jan. 11, 1936; *New York Herald-Tribune*, Jan. 12, 1936.

128. *Journal and Guide*, Jan. 5, 1935.

129. Seton, *Robeson*, 59.

130. Ibid.

131. From Pablo Neruda, "Ode to Paul Robeson," in *Salute to Paul Robeson* (75th Anniversary Booklet, Carnegie Hall, April 15, 1973).

132. *Daily Worker*, Nov. 4, 1937.

133. Interview of Paul Robeson by Nicolás Guillén, *Daily World*, July 25, 1976 (originally published in *Mediodiá*, Havana, Cuba, 1938).

134. See Loften Mitchell, "Time to Break the Silence Surrounding Paul Robeson," *New York Times*, Aug. 6, 1972.

135. *New York Times*, April 19, 1942.

136. Harvey, "Paul Robeson," 710.

137. Julia Dorn, "Paul Robeson Told Me," *Tac* 1, no. 12 (July–Aug. 1939): 23.

138. See Sterling Stuckey, "I Want to be African: Paul Robeson and the Ends of Nationalist Theory and Practice," *Massachusetts Review* 17 (Spring 1976): 131.

139. Interview with Paul Robeson, Jr., Summer 1971; Seton, *Robeson*, 106–7.

140. Robeson, "Culture of the Negro," 916; Robeson, "Primitives," 191–92. Only Robeson, of that long line, appears to have avoided the pitfall that New World blacks should take the lead in "uplifting," in "redeeming" Africa. Though he thought transplanted Africans in the Americas should be prepared, if necessary, to die for Africa, he generally held that men born on the continent were themselves best suited to decide what was good for Africa: "A continent of almost 200,000,000 people [a substantially higher figure than his previously quoted 150,000,000], with virility and intelligence, will eventually work out its own destiny." Robeson's intimate knowledge of various aspects of African cultures, in combination with his belief that Western civilization was dying, no doubt contributed to his position that Africans must do their own leading. *New York Post*, Jan. 11, 1936.

141. Quoted in Seton, *Robeson*, 126–28.

142. *New York Times*, Jan. 22, 1940.

143. Ibid., Jan. 22, 1940, June 24, July 10, 1941.

144. Ibid., July 2, 1943.

145. Interview with Paul Robeson, Jr., Summer 1971.

146. Paul Robeson, "Reflections on Othello and the Nature of Our Times," *American Scholar* 14 (Autumn 1945): 390.

147. *Othello*, act 5, sc. 2, lines 339–41, 359–60.

148. Paul Robeson, Jr., "Paul Robeson: Black Warrior," *Freedomways* 2, no. 1 (1971): 24–25.

149. Paul Robeson, "Opening Statement," *For a New Africa: Proceeding of the Conference on Africa, New York, April 14, 1944* (New York: Council on African Affairs, 1944), 10.

150. Ibid.

151. Dean Acheson, *Present at the Creation* (New York: Norton, 1969), 130.

152. Alpheus Hunton, "A Note on the Council on African Affairs," appendix E in Robeson, *Here I Stand*, 126-28.

153. Paul Robeson, "Legacy of Du Bois," 37–38.

154. "An Important Message from Paul Robeson," *Spotlight on Africa* (News Letter, Council on African Affairs), Feb. 25, 1952. Robeson wrote in *Freedom* newspaper,

American Negroes have a real duty to our African brothers and sisters, a sacred duty. . . . Negroes who have not lost pride and dignity know that if we are at all serious about our full freedom here in America we must understand what the future of Africa means. . . . Can we fail to bring pressure upon the corporations involved, not to sabotage the African struggle? Can we fail to point the finger at Malan? Should we not do all in our power to help people there. . . . Should we not arouse the youth in the universities? Should we not swing our churches, fraternal bodies, professional groups, women's organizations and civic clubs into action. . . . Not only is this a struggle in the interests of African people. Their freedom and dignity will be of immeasurable assistance in our final break-through here in these United States. New Africa in the end will mean . . . new Mississippi.

Freedom, May 1953.

155. In Robeson's view, whatever other Americans came to believe, the government never made a secret of the sources of its fear and hatred of him. In a brief intended to support the denial of his right to travel abroad, the government disclosed that Robeson's fight for the freedom of black people was a fundamental reason for its attempt to silence him:

Furthermore, even if the complaint had alleged, which it does not, that the passport was cancelled solely because of the applicant's recognized status as spokesman for large sections of Negro Americans, we submit that this would not amount to an abuse of discretion in view of appellant's frank admission that he has been for years extremely active politically in behalf of independence of the colonial people of Africa.

Quoted in Robeson, *Here I Stand*, 72. As the government broadened its attack to include Du Bois as well as Robeson, many black people, lacking leadership from the NAACP, were willing to answer a thrusting question from Du Bois—applicable to himself and to Robeson—in the affirmative.

It was a dilemma for the mass of Negroes; either they joined the current beliefs and actions of most whites or they could not make a living or hope for preferment. Preferment was possible. The color line was beginning to break. Negroes were getting recognition as never before. Was not the sacrifice of one man, small payment for this?

For accounts of the persecution of Du Bois and Robeson, see Du Bois, *Autobiography*, chaps. 21–23, and Robeson, *Here I Stand*, chap. 3.

156. Robeson, "Reflections on Othello," 391.

157. Ibid., 390–91.

Index

415